ENDING
THE CIVIL WAR

ENDING THE CIVIL WAR

*The Bloody Year
from Grant's Promotion
to Lincoln's Assassination*

Benton Rain Patterson

McFarland & Company, Inc., Publishers
Jefferson, North Carolina, and London

Photograph research by Victoria Harlow

LIBRARY OF CONGRESS CATALOGUING-IN-PUBLICATION DATA

Patterson, Benton Rain, 1929–
Ending the Civil War : the bloody year from Grant's promotion
to Lincoln's assassination / Benton Rain Patterson.
p.   cm.
Includes bibliographical references and index.

ISBN 978-0-7864-6964-2
softcover : acid free paper ∞

1. United States — History — Civil War, 1861–1865 — Campaigns.
2. United States — History — Civil War, 1861–1865 — Peace.   I. Title.
E470.P37 2012   973.7'3 — dc23   2012005932

BRITISH LIBRARY CATALOGUING DATA ARE AVAILABLE

Front cover images: General Ulysses S. Grant; President Abraham Lincoln;
the grand review at Washington, May 23, 1865 (Library of Congress)

Manufactured in the United States of America

*McFarland & Company, Inc., Publishers
Box 611, Jefferson, North Carolina 28640
www.mcfarlandpub.com*

To my beloved historian brothers,
E. Palmer Patterson and
W. Morgan Patterson

Table of Contents

Introduction

What follows is the story of the Civil War's most critical period, the war's last year, from March 1864 to April 1865.

At the start of that year, President Abraham Lincoln appointed a new general in chief of the United States Army, his latest and last choice to wrest victory from the armed forces of the eleven seceded states. In that last year a new course for the conflict was charted, a massive, monstrously bloody campaign of coordinated warfare on all fronts. In that last year new heroes gained lasting fame, others shame. In that last year new names were added to the nation's list of hallowed shrines and historic places. In that last year President Lincoln, chief guardian of the Union, was re-elected, his leadership affirmed. In that last year the abolition of slavery was confirmed, the promise of freedom for all was made. In that last year an assassin took the life of the nation's most revered president and altered the course of history. In that last year the United States won the final battle for peace. In that last year the sundered nation was reunited.

With dramatic accounts, narrated by eyewitnesses where possible, the following pages describe those last-year events, the events that decided whether the nation that was so nobly conceived and dedicated could long endure.

The Change of Command,
March 1864

The man in the soiled, wrinkled linen duster that covered most of his Army uniform walked up to the registration desk at Willard's Hotel, two blocks down Pennsylvania Avenue from the White House, and asked for a room for him and his young son, standing beside him. The hotel clerk answered that there might be a room available on the top floor. That was fine, the man replied and then took up a pen from the counter and scratched his name on the guest register. When the clerk swiveled the register around to read the name and put a room number beside it, he saw scrawled in wet ink: "U.S. Grant and son, Galena, Ill."

Suddenly all animation and helpfulness, the clerk scurried out from behind the counter, grabbed up the general's bag to carry it upstairs for him and led the distinguished guest and his fourteen-year-old son, Fred, to the suite that had been reserved for him on the second floor.

Few in Washington were unaware that the country's most renowned general, the newest hope of the fractured nation, was coming to the capital and that he was coming for an especially auspicious occasion. But true to his modest style, Grant had arrived at the hotel without escort or advance party. Two members of his staff, Lieutenant Colonel John Rawlins, his chief of staff, and Lieutenant Colonel Cyrus Comstock, an aide-de-camp, had traveled by train with Grant from Nashville, but upon their arrival at the Washington railroad station they immediately had left for the War Department to report to Major General Henry Halleck, the Army's general in chief.

In his suite the general and Fred took their time to wash and spruce up, then descended the stairs back down to the lobby and entered the dining room for dinner. When they walked into the dining room, heads turned at nearby tables, and they could hear whispers of "There's Grant!" At one table a man stood and started rapping loudly on the tabletop with his knife until he had the attention of the other diners and he told them he had the honor of announcing that General Grant was present in the dining room. At his announcement, many of the diners rose from their chairs and began chanting, "Grant! Grant! Grant!" One diner called for three cheers from the crowd, which answered in roaring response.

By then Grant and Fred had taken seats at a table, and as the cheering sounded, Grant got up and, seeming embarrassed, bowed to the crowd, then returned to his chair. Throughout his meal he was repeatedly interrupted by well-wishers who stopped by his table to shake hands with the newly famous general, until finally he and Fred cut their dinner short and took refuge back in their suite of rooms.

They were not there long before there was a knock on the door by an emissary bringing an invitation to the public reception being held at the White House that evening. Unable to refuse, Grant made his way through the blustery March night to the White House. With him were Colonel Rawlins and Colonel Comstock, who had finally caught up with Grant after failing to find General Halleck.

The turnout at the president's reception was huge, one account claiming that the crowd was the closest thing to a mob ever seen in the White House. The report that General Grant might be there apparently had encouraged attendance despite the bad weather. It was about nine-thirty when Grant arrived and upon his entrance, the crowd inside parted to allow him a clear path to where President Lincoln stood greeting his guests in the Blue Room, shaking hands with everyone who passed before him in the long line of visitors. Mrs. Lincoln had been standing to his right, but at last had grown weary of the greetings and had stepped back to be among a cluster of women she knew. Near the president were arrayed the members of his cabinet, their wives engaged in conversation with Mrs. Lincoln.

Soon after he entered the Blue Room, Grant was spotted by the president, who, never having seen Grant face to face, like the others, recognized him from photographs. "Why, here is General Grant!" Lincoln exclaimed, instantly striding toward Grant as he approached. "Well, this is a great pleasure, I assure you," the president told him, grabbing Grant's hand and pumping it in a long, hearty handshake.[1] Grant stood with his head bent slightly forward, his eyes turned upward to look into the beaming face of the president, who towered some eight inches over the five-foot-eight-inch general. The two held a brief conversation, then the president introduced him to Secretary of State William Seward, who gave Grant another warm greeting and led him to Mrs. Lincoln, who after being introduced, chatted with him for several minutes while the crowd grew more demonstrably eager to share in the introductions to the general.

Seward, taking notice of the crowd's restiveness, piloted Grant through the throng and into the East Room, a larger chamber that could better contain the press of the crowd, which now, like the diners at Willard's Hotel, began chanting, "Grant! Grant! Grant!" and set off rounds of cheers. Seward managed to persuade Grant to step up onto a sofa and stand there for what turned out to be nearly an hour of greetings, handshaking and public viewing. Meanwhile President Lincoln and the secretary of war, Edwin Stanton, waited for him in a drawing room nearby. At last the excitement and commotion abated somewhat, and Grant was escorted to where the president and Stanton sat biding their time.[2]

Now was when Lincoln got around to the matter that had brought Grant to Washington, his first visit since he passed through it after his graduation from West Point. The White House reception was merely a preliminary. The main event was scheduled for the next day, March 9, 1864. It, too, was to be held at the White House, with President Lincoln presiding. A week and a half earlier, on February 26, Lincoln had signed into law a bill passed by Congress that re-created the Army rank of lieutenant general. Until then, the highest rank was major general. The purpose behind the action by Congress was to confer that superior rank on Major General Grant and thus make him the country's No. 1 general, outranking everybody else in the Army, including Henry Halleck, the general in chief, who was on his way out. The Senate had later confirmed the rank for Grant.

Sharing a trait of many successful men whose superior abilities in one area lead them to believe their abilities in all areas are superior, Lincoln was guilty of sometimes over-managing his generals and the war. He had appointed as generals men without military experience or training, political figures appointed for political reasons — Benjamin Butler, Nathaniel Banks, John McClernand and Stephen Hurlbut, for example — and had them placed in important commands. Some whom he appointed did have military experience, but proved themselves incompetent for the jobs he gave them. The over-all results of his military management were not all that good. Despite the successes in the West, including the opening of the Mississippi River, the public perception was that the war was not going well. The Virginia campaign, vital to the capture of Richmond, the capital, heart and symbol of the Confederacy, was stalled. The Union's Army of the Potomac, commanded by Major General George G. Meade, had shown itself unable to cope with General Robert E. Lee and his Army of Northern Virginia.

Now just a month away from entering its fourth year, the war was far from over. Much of the public and the press were sick of it and so eager to end it that they were ready to cut a deal with the Confederacy, a sentiment being exploited by Lincoln's political rivals in this year of a new presidential election. Lincoln, too, of course was eager to settle the conflict, but even more than quick peace, he wanted the Union preserved. A deal with the Confederacy was likely to preserve the Confederacy. The United States must *win* the war, Lincoln insisted, not merely end it. What he and the country urgently needed, he was convinced, was a man of superior military ability who could win the war *and* end it. After three years, he realized he was not that man.

And so he was turning to someone who looked like *he* might be the man: forty-two-year-old Major General Ulysses S. Grant, who had risen from oblivion as a clerk in his father's leather-goods store at the beginning of the war to become commander of the mighty Army of the Tennessee and hero of the outstanding victories at Vicksburg and Chattanooga. His military career had started in June 1843, when he graduated from West Point, which he had attended only because his father wanted him to get the free education the government provided cadets. He served as a lieutenant in the Mexican War, mostly as a quartermaster, and later as an infantry captain at a remote post in northern California. Unhappy with that assignment, he had resigned his commission and quit the Army. He had tried farming near St. Louis on land his father-in-law had given his wife, Julia, and failed at that. He had tried selling real estate and failed at that. At age thirty-eight, with a wife and three children to support, a pile of debts and no other job prospects, he had gone to work for his father in Galena, Illinois, clerking at the leather-goods store. Then came Fort Sumter in April 1861. Two months later he was appointed by the governor of Illinois to command the Twenty-first Regiment of the Illinois militia. When the regiment was federalized shortly thereafter, he became a colonel and a regimental commander in the U.S. Army. His way to destiny had been opened.

On March 3, 1864, at his headquarters in Nashville, Grant had received a telegram from General Halleck, telling him, "The Secretary of War directs that you report in person to the War Department as early as practicable...." Immediately after receiving that message, he had got another one from Halleck: "The Secretary of War directs me to say to you that your commission as lieutenant general is signed and will be delivered to you on your arrival at the War Department. I sincerely congratulate you on this recognition of your distinguished and meritorious services."[3] The next day, March 4, he had boarded a train for Washington.

Now, in private with the president and Stanton, Grant was briefed on the ceremony to be held the next day, March 9, the day after his arrival in Washington. It was to be a formal presentation of his commission as lieutenant general. Lincoln would say a few words, and Grant was to offer a brief response. Lincoln, his tendency to manage generals re-emerging, then told Grant what he should say in his response. "There are two points that I would like to have you make in your answer," Lincoln instructed. "First, to say something which shall prevent or obviate any jealousy of you from any of the other generals in the service. And second, something which shall put you on as good terms as possible with the Army of the Potomac."[4]

About one o'clock the next afternoon Grant showed up at the White House for the ceremony, accompanied by Fred and Rawlins and Comstock. Before an audience of cabinet members and members of the president's staff, Grant and Lincoln stood facing each other while Lincoln read his little speech. "The nation's appreciation of what you have done," he said to Grant, "and its reliance upon you for what remains to do, in the existing great struggle, are now presented with this commission, constituting you lieutenant general in the Army of the United States. With this high honor devolves upon you also a corresponding responsibility. As the country herein trusts you, so, under God, it will sustain you. I scarcely need to add that with what I here speak for the nation goes my own hearty personal concurrence."[5]

Then it was time for Grant to make the speech requested by the president. "Mister President," he began reading from the note he had penciled earlier, "I accept this commission with gratitude for the high honor conferred. With the aid of the noble armies that have fought on so many fields for our common country, it will be my earnest endeavor not to disappoint your expectations. I feel the full weight of the responsibilities now devolving upon me and know that if they are met, it will be due to those armies, and above all to the favor of that Providence which leads both nations and men."[6]

That was it. There was no mention of either of the two points Lincoln wanted him to make. They were simply ignored, an act that showed, perhaps, how different a general the president could expect Ulysses Grant to be.

Grant had already heard Lincoln profess to want a commanding general who would think and act independently. "In my first interview with Mr. Lincoln alone," Grant wrote in his memoirs, "he stated to me that he had never professed to be a military man or to know how campaigns should be conducted, and never wanted to interfere in them; but that procrastination on the part of commanders, and the pressure from the people at the North and Congress, which was always with him, forced him into issuing his series of 'Military Orders'—one, two, three, etc. He did not know but they were all wrong, and did know that some of them were. All he wanted or had ever wanted [he said] was some one who would take the responsibility and act, and call on him for all the assistance needed, pledging himself to use all the power of the government in rendering such assistance."[7] Grant was taking the president at his word.

Lieutenant General Grant lost no time in acquainting himself with the army that would be his foremost responsibility. On March 10, the day after the commissioning ceremony, he took a train to Brandy Station, Virginia, about seventy miles from Washington, and visited the headquarters of the Army of the Potomac, conferring with its balding, gray-bearded, doleful-eyed, forty-nine-year-old commander, General Meade. Meade had become a controversial figure. Although generally hailed for his masterful direction of the Army of the Potomac at the Battle of Gettysburg in July 1863, where he stopped Lee's advance into Pennsylvania, he had been roundly criticized for failing to aggressively pursue Lee's army as it fled southward to safety and for being unable to defeat Lee or even bring him to a decisive battle in Virginia. Charles A. Dana, the assistant secretary of war, had already told Grant that the feeling in the War Department was that "from that army [the Army of the Potomac] nothing is to be hoped under its present commander."[8] Many now expected Grant to relieve Meade of his command.

Grant had known Meade slightly during the Mexican War and had had no contact with him since then, but when he met him again at Brandy Station, he quickly took a liking to him, finding him frank and straightforward. In talking about a possible change of command in the Army of the Potomac, Grant related in his memoirs, "He said to me that I might want an officer who had served with me in the West, mentioning Sherman specially, to take his place. If so, he begged me not to hesitate about making the change. He urged that the work before us was of such vast importance to the whole nation that the feeling or wishes of no one person should stand in the way of selecting the right men for all positions.

"For himself," Grant wrote, "he would serve to the best of his ability wherever placed. I assured him that I had no thought of substituting any one for him. This incident gave me even a more favorable opinion of Meade than did his great victory at Gettysburg the July before."[9]

Grant's meeting with Meade lasted through the evening, the two generals discussing past and future campaigns of the Army of the Potomac, and Grant taking the occasion to meet Meade's chief of staff, Brigadier General Andrew Humphreys, and other general officers of the Army of the Potomac, some of whom he already knew. When the meeting was over, Meade felt good about it. He wrote to his wife that, "He is so much more active than his predecessor [Halleck], and agrees so with me in his views, I cannot but be rejoiced at his arrival, because I believe success to be the more probable from the above facts."[10] Grant spent the night at Brandy Station and returned to Washington the next day, March 11.

By now he had grown weary of Washington. He had become, as his aide, Colonel Horace Porter, reported, "so much an object of curiosity, and had been so continually surrounded by admiring crowds when he appeared in the streets, and even in his hotel, that it had become very irksome to him."[11] Grant could not understand why he should attract so much public attention and he now began to avoid it. President Lincoln had issued him an invitation to come to the White House for a special state dinner that evening, but Grant begged off, claiming it would cost him a whole day if he stayed for the dinner and that the urgency of the things that required his attention in Nashville demanded his prompt return. "Besides," he told the president, "I have become very tired of this show business."[12]

Following his own schedule, Grant left late that day, March 11, by train for Nashville. While he was en route on the three-day journey, the War Department on March 12 issued the formal orders confirming the change of command of the nation's armies. General Grant was the new commander. General Halleck, the orders stated, had been relieved of command at his own request and now was assigned as chief of staff under the direction of the secretary of war and of "the lieutenant general commanding." Halleck's possible reaction to the change of command had been fretted over by some in the Army and in Washington, but according to Adam Badeau, a member of Grant's staff and semi-official historian of Grant's command, Halleck "indeed seemed glad to be relieved from the cares and responsibilities of supreme command."[13] Halleck would man a desk in Washington, handling administrative affairs from the offices of the War Department, while Grant's own chief of staff, Colonel Rawlins, would be with him in the field, Grant having no intention of being bound to the wearisome confines of Washington.

Grant arrived in Nashville on March 14 and three days later, on March 17, he met, as arranged, with the man he most wanted to see, his friend and comrade in arms, Major General William T. Sherman, who had come over from his headquarters in Memphis for the meeting. In greeting Grant, Sherman told him, "I cannot congratulate you on your promotion. The responsibility is too great."[14] Evidently afraid that Grant's new lofty position might somehow change him, Sherman had already written Grant a letter of caution and advice, telling him, "You are now [George] Washington's legitimate successor, and occupy a position of almost dangerous elevation; but if you can continue, as heretofore, to be yourself—simple, honest and unpretending—you will enjoy through life the respect and love of friends and homage of millions of human beings that will award you a large share, in securing to them and their descendants a government of law and stability."[15] Sherman then issued a terse directive to his commander: "Don't stay in Washington." Halleck, Sherman told Grant, "is better qualified than you to stand the buffets of intrigue and policy."[16]

Badeau, who had suffered a wound in his foot at the battle for Port Hudson, the last Confederate stronghold on the Mississippi River to fall to Union forces, was present on crutches when Grant and Sherman met and in recounting the event, he took the opportunity to describe both men:

> The contrast between the two was striking. One [Sherman] was tall, angular, and spare, as if his superabundant energy had consumed his flesh; sandy-haired, sharp-featured; his nose prominent, his lips thin, his grey eyes flashing fire as fast as lightning on a summer's night; his whole face mobile as an actor's, and revealing every shade of thought or emotion that flitted across his active mind; his manner pronounced; his speech quick, decided, loud....
>
> The chief was smaller, but stouter in form, younger in looks and years; calmer in manner a hundredfold. His hair and beard were brown, and both heavier than Sherman's; his features marked, but not prominent; while his eye, clear but not piercing nor penetrating, seemed formed rather to resist than aid the interpretation of his thought, and never betrayed that it was sounding the depths of another nature than his own. A heavy jaw; a sharply-cut mouth, which had a singular power of expressing sweetness and strength combined, and at times became set with a rigidity like that of Fate itself.... The habitual expression of his face was so quiet as to be almost incomprehensible; strong, but its strength concealed by the manner of wearing hair and beard. His figure was compact and of medium height, but though well-made, he stooped slightly in the shoulders. His manner plain, placid, almost meek.... In utterance he was slow and sometimes embarrassed, but the words were well-chosen, never leaving the remotest doubt of what he intended to convey, and now and then fluent and forcible, when the speaker became aroused. The whole man was a marvel of simplicity, a powerful nature veiled in the plainest possible exterior.... Not a sign about him suggested rank, or reputation, or power....[17]

Far from taking offense at Sherman's remarks, Grant let him make his case, which urged Grant to command from a headquarters in the West. "Here you are at home," Sherman argued. "You are acquainted with your ground. You have tested your subordinates. You know us, and we know you. Here you are sure of success. Here, too, you will be untrammeled. At the East you must begin new campaigns in an unfamiliar field, with troops and officers whom you have not tried, whom you have never led to victory. They cannot feel towards you as we do.

"Near Washington, besides, you will be beset and, it may be, fettered by scheming politicians. Stay here," Sherman urged, "where you have made your fame, and use the same means to consolidate it."[18] Sherman had clearly grasped the situation in which the new general in chief now found himself. He had laid out in worrying detail the very thoughts that likely were coursing through Grant's own deliberating mind. Grant, however, had already trudged through those considerations and had reached the conclusion that he should make his base where the most crucial action was likely, and expected, to occur. He must be near Washington, he had decided, to control all the operations of all the armies without interruption so that he could implement the plans he had drawn for winning and ending the war.

In Nashville he took time for a conference with generals James McPherson, Grenville Dodge, John Logan and Philip Sheridan, along with Rawlins, all of whom were comfortable old friends to him. He led them on a visit to the Tennessee capitol to meet the governor, Andrew Johnson, then to the theater to see a production of "Hamlet," and then to dinner at a restaurant where they stayed so long, enjoying themselves around the table, that the owner, not knowing who her lingering customers were, had to ask them to leave, explaining that the curfew ordered by General Grant required her to close at midnight.

The next day Grant again met with his generals, reporting on his visits to Washington and to the Army of the Potomac, which he called the finest he had ever seen, "far superior to any of ours in equipment, supplies and transportation."[19] He also announced to them that he would be making his headquarters with the Army of the Potomac and that he was placing Sherman in command of the armies in the West. He also sketched out for them the plans he had formed for the campaign that would soon commence.

His business in Nashville at last finished, Grant boarded a train on March 19 and headed back to Washington. He had asked Sherman to accompany him as far as Cincinnati, "so that we could talk over the matters about which I wanted to see him," Grant related, especially including the co-ordination of Sherman's command with the Army of the Potomac when the spring campaign got under way. Grant explained, Badeau reported, the "plan he had devised for the entire campaign and defined the particular part he expected Sherman to perform.... The principal ideas were fully developed by one general, and as fully comprehended by the other."[20]

On March 23 Grant arrived again in Washington, one step nearer to commencing the campaign by which he intended to settle the awful conflict.

The Plan for Victory,
March 23 to May 3, 1864

With General Grant on the train to Washington were his wife — the former Julia Dent of St. Louis, the sister of his West Point roommate, Fred Dent — as well as the Grants' youngest son, six-year-old Jess, the other children having been left in St. Louis with family friends. The Grants arrived in the capital on March 23. Julia and Jess took rooms in a boarding house, and Grant, after seeing them comfortably settled, on March 26 boarded a train for Culpeper, Virginia, about ten miles below Brandy Station and about twelve miles north of the Rapidan River. There he would set up his headquarters in a brick house near the Culpeper train station. To provide additional space for his staff several tents would be erected in the yard of the house.

General Meade, who had selected the house for Grant, was waiting for him when he arrived and rode with him to the house, which was about six miles from Meade's headquarters near Brandy Station. Adam Badeau, the biographer who was a member of Grant's staff, was with the general as he surveyed his new base of operations. Badeau described the setting:

> The ground was historic all around. Bull Run, the first important battle of the war, was fought not thirty miles in rear of Culpeper; Cedar mountain, the scene of one of Banks's fights, was in full view on the western front; and McDowell, Pope, Hooker, Burnside, Meade, and Lee, by turns, had led their armies up and down these very fields, and made the landscape desolate. Outside the town, not a house nor a fence, not a tree was to be seen for miles, where once all had been cultivated farm-land, or richly wooded country. Here and there, a stack of chimneys or a broken cistern marked the site of a former homestead, but every other landmark had been destroyed. The very hills were stripped of their forest panoply, and a man could hardly recognize the haunts familiar to him from his childhood.
>
> This desert extended almost from Washington to the Rapidan. At rare intervals it was broken by groups of buildings near a railway station, or where a hamlet had been left for military purposes, to serve as the head-quarters of a command or for a depot of ordnance or supplies. Culpeper was at one of these stations, and, during the war, had changed masters several times. From this spot, Grant issued his orders to all the soldiers of the republic.[1]

Before those orders began flowing from his Culpeper headquarters, though, Grant took time on the day after his arrival to write to Julia, telling her, "I arrived here yesterday well but as on my former trip brought wet and bad weather. I have not been out of the house today and from appearances shall not be able to go out for several days. At present however I shall find enough to be indoors. From indications I would judge the best of feelings animate all the troops here toward the changes that have been made."[2]

Grant had already assayed the task that lay before him and his troops. There were two main rebel armies that must be defeated. One was the Army of Northern Virginia, commanded by General Robert E. Lee, which occupied a position on the south side of the Rapidan River. The other, commanded by General Joseph E. Johnston, was at Dalton, in northwest Georgia, near the Tennessee border and facing Sherman's army in and around Chattanooga, some twenty-five miles to the northwest of Johnston's force. There were also Confederate troops guarding the Shenandoah River valley, from which the rebel armies drew much of their food supply, and other rebel troops were protecting the Confederate line of communication from Richmond to Tennessee. In addition, there was the large, highly mobile and dangerous cavalry force commanded by Lieutenant General Nathan Bedford Forrest, which presented a threat to Union positions in middle and west Tennessee.

The area held by Union forces was defined by Grant: "The Mississippi River was guarded from St. Louis to its mouth; the line of the Arkansas [River] was held, thus giving us all [of] the North-west north of that river. A few points in Louisiana not remote from the [Mississippi] river were held by the Federal troops, as was also the mouth of the Rio Grande.

"East of the Mississippi we held substantially all north of the Memphis and Charleston Railroad as far east as Chattanooga, thence along the line of the Tennessee and Holston rivers, taking in nearly all of the State of Tennessee. West Virginia was in our hands; and that part of old Virginia north of the Rapidan and east of the Blue Ridge we also held. On the sea-coast we had Fortress Monroe and Norfolk in Virginia; Plymouth, Washington and New Berne [*sic*] in North Carolina; Beaufort, Folly and Morris islands, Hilton Head, Port Royal and Fort Pulaski in South Carolina and Georgia; Fernandina, St. Augustine, Key West and Pensacola in Florida. The balance of the Southern territory, an empire in extent, was still in the hands of the enemy."[3]

It was in the East that the war's stalemated status was most evident, particularly to government leaders in Washington and the nation's clamorous press. "The opposing forces," Grant pointed out, "stood in substantially the same relations towards each other as three years before, or when the war began; they were both between the Federal and Confederate capitals.... Battles had been fought of as great severity as had never been known in war, over ground from the James River and Chickahominy, near Richmond, to Gettysburg and Chambersburg, in Pennsylvania, with indecisive results, sometimes favorable to the National army, sometimes to the Confederate army...."[4]

Grant intended to break the stalemate. "My general plan now," he explained in his memoirs, "was to concentrate all the force possible against the Confederate armies in the field."[5] The Army of the Potomac would become the center of the front opposing the Army of Northern Virginia. To the west, north of the line held by Union forces, as far as Memphis, would be Grant's right wing, commanded by Sherman; and to the east would be the Army of the James, a unit being created from elements of the Department of Virginia and North Carolina and the Department of the South. It would be commanded by Major General Benjamin Franklin Butler, now commanding the Department of Virginia and North Carolina, and it would form Grant's left wing. Grant's idea was to have every army of the total Union force move against the enemy simultaneously, so that neither Lee nor Johnston could shift detachments of one army to reinforce the other.

President Abraham Lincoln. After three years of managing the war, he admitted that he and Secretary of War Stanton had done a poor job of "trying to boss this job." In March 1864 he appointed Ulysses Grant general in chief and gave him authority to conduct the war as Grant saw fit. (NATIONAL ARCHIVES AND RECORDS ADMINISTRATION)

To effect his plan Grant was counting on overwhelming numbers. He promised Sherman that if Lee sent any force to Johnston, "I will send you two men where he sends one."[6] On the north side of the Rapidan the Army of the Potomac, which consisted of the Second, Fifth and Sixth infantry corps plus a cavalry corps, and also the Ninth Corps, which was under a separate command, and altogether Grant's force numbered some 116,000 troops, "present for duty, equipped."[7] Lee's Army of Northern Virginia — three infantry corps and one cavalry corps — was estimated at between 60,000 and 65,000 men.

The total strength of Grant's command, in twenty-one Army corps spread across the country, numbered some 533,000 troops present for duty, equipped.[8] His challenge was to marshal them to the battlefield from distant posts and irrelevant assignments. For example, some 40,000 troops were stationed in nine northern states where the threat of a rebel attack was nonexistent. Another 40,000 troops, skilled veterans of the war in the West, under the command of Major General Nathaniel Banks, were heading up the Red River to capture Shreveport, an expedition endorsed by the War Department and Lincoln, but of no help to Grant in the task now before him.

Where possible, Grant began shifting men out of unnecessary or less vital assignments and into areas of the fight that awaited him. His shifts were not without challenges from commanders and others who preferred to keep things as they were. When a high-ranking commissary officer balked at following one of Grant's orders, on the grounds that it had not come from the commissary department, Grant told him that although he could not force him to obey the orders, he could relieve him and replace him with a line officer who would obey orders of the general in chief. That case ended up in the president's office. The president backed Grant, telling him, "There is no one but myself that can interfere with your orders, and you can rest assured that I will not."[9]

In another case, Secretary Stanton objected to Grant's transferring men from the defenses around the city of Washington and when he called in Grant to protest, Grant told him, "I think I rank you in this matter, Mister Secretary."

"We shall have to see Mister Lincoln about that," Stanton shot back.

The two of them trotted off to the White House, where Stanton pressed his case to the president.

"You and I, Mister Stanton," Lincoln replied, "have been trying to boss this job and we have not succeeded very well with it. We have sent across the mountains for Mister Grant, as Mrs. Grant calls him, to relieve us, and I think we had better leave him alone to do as he pleases."[10] That settled the matter.

Grant kept the president, and Stanton as well, in the dark about his campaign plans. He had been warned by Stanton and Halleck that he should not tell Lincoln what he planned to do, that the president could not resist passing along such information to friends. Grant wrote in his memoirs that, according to Stanton, the president was "so kind-hearted, so averse to refusing anything asked of him, that some friend would be sure to get from him all he knew."[11] Lincoln himself, recognizing his inability to keep a secret, had told Grant that he didn't want to know what Grant proposed to do.

But despite his disclaimers about further interfering in military matters, Lincoln could not keep his ideas to himself. At one meeting, according to Grant, Lincoln "brought out a map of Virginia on which he had evidently marked every position occupied by the Federal and Confederate armies up to that time. He pointed out on the map two streams which empty into the Potomac, and suggested that the army might be moved on boats and landed between the mouths of these streams. We would then have the Potomac to bring our supplies [he said], and the tributaries would protect our flanks while we moved out.

"I listened respectfully," Grant related, "but did not suggest that the same streams would protect Lee's flanks while he was shutting us up."[12]

On April 1 Grant went to see General Butler at his headquarters at Fort (or Fortress) Monroe, which stood on the New Point Comfort tip of the Virginia peninsula, guarding the entrance to Chesapeake Bay. Despite Virginia's entry into the Confederacy, the U.S. Army had managed to keep its grip on the old fort. This visit was Grant's first meeting with Butler, whose previous assignments included command of the troops that occupied New

Orleans after its capture by Admiral David Farragut in 1862. Butler had become a controversial, even notorious, figure during his tough military rule over the defiant city. Husky, jowly and balding, he looked tough.

Before getting into the specifics of his plan, which called for Butler to advance his troops toward Richmond, Grant tactfully solicited Butler's opinion on how a drive on the rebel capital should be conducted.

There were only two feasible routes that Butler's army could take. One was on the north side of the James, the other on the south side. The one on the north side ran up the peninsula formed by the York and the James rivers. It was the road taken by McClellan in the failed campaign of 1862. That route could enable Butler to communicate more easily with Meade, but it offered no other major advantage. The road on the south side, on the other hand, would allow Butler to threaten Lee's and Richmond's communications with rebel-held territory to the south and west. Grant favored the south side, since he intended to have Meade's army cross the James and operate against Lee from the south side.

Butler told Grant he preferred the route on the south side. Grant was delighted with Butler's choice and later wrote to him to let him know. "I went to Fortress Monroe for the express purpose of seeing you," he wrote, "and telling you it was my plan to have the force under you act directly in concert with the army of the Potomac, and as far as possible towards the same point. My mind was entirely made up what instructions to give, and I was very much pleased to find your previously conceived views exactly coincided."[13]

Before leaving Fort Monroe Grant spelled out his instructions for Butler in a note. Two weeks later, on April 16, he wrote to him again from Culpeper, telling him, "All the forces that can be taken from the coast have been ordered to report to you at Fort Monroe by the 18th, or as soon thereafter as possible. What I ask is, that with them, and all you can concentrate from your own command, you seize upon City Point [Hopewell, Virginia, southeast of Richmond], and act from there, looking upon Richmond as your objective point...."[14]

Two days later he wrote to Butler again: "I will, as you understand, expect you to move from Fortress Monroe the same day General Meade starts from here. I will telegraph you as soon as it can be fixed.... You also understand that, with the forces here, I shall aim to fight Lee between here and Richmond, if he will stand. Should Lee, however, fall back into Richmond, I will follow up and make a junction with your army on the James river.... I would say, therefore, use every exertion to secure a footing as far up the south side of the river as you can, and as soon as possible."[15]

Grant wrote to Sherman on April 4, giving him his instructions, apprising him of the instructions issued to other corps commanders and outlining the planned offensive:

> *General:*— It is my design, if the enemy keep quiet and allow me to take the initiative in the spring campaign, to work all parts of the army together, and somewhat towards a common centre. For your information I now write you my programme, as at present determined upon.
>
> I have sent orders to Banks, by private messenger, to finish up his present expedition against Shreveport with all dispatch; to turn over the defence of Red River to General Steele and the navy, and to return your troops [ten thousand of Sherman's troops that had been lent to support Banks's force] and his own to New Orleans; to abandon all of Texas, except the Rio Grande, and to hold that with not to exceed four thousand men; to reduce the number of troops on the Mississippi to the lowest number necessary to hold it, and to collect from his command not less than twenty-five thousand men. To this I will add five thousand men from Missouri. With this force he is to commence operations against Mobile as soon as he can. It will be impossible for him to commence too early.
>
> [Major General Quincy A.] Gillmore joins Butler with ten thousand men, and the two

operate against Richmond from the south side of the James River. This will give Butler thirty-three thousand men to operate with, [Major General] W.F. Smith commanding the right wing of his forces and Gillmore the left wing. I will stay with the Army of the Potomac, increased by [Major General Ambrose E.] Burnside's corps of not less than twenty-five thousand effective men, and operate directly against Lee's army, wherever it may be found.

[Major General Franz] Sigel collects all his available force in two columns, one, under [Major General Edward O.C.] Ord and [Major General William W.] Averell, to start from Beverly, Virginia, and the other, under [Major General George] Crook, to start from Charleston on the Kanawha, to move against the Virginia and Tennessee Railroad.

Crook will have all cavalry, and will endeavor to get in about Saltville, and move east from there to join Ord. His force will be all cavalry, while Ord will have from ten to twelve thousand men of all arms.

You I propose to move against Johnston's army, to break it up and to get into the interior of the enemy's country as far as you can, inflicting all the damage you can against their war resources.

I do not propose to lay down for you a plan of campaign, but simply lay down the work it is desirable to have done and leave you free to execute it in your own way. Submit to me, however, as early as you can, your plan of operation.

As stated, Banks is ordered to commence operations as soon as he can. Gillmore is ordered to report at Fortress Monroe by the 18th inst. [April], or as soon thereafter as practicable. Sigel is concentrating now. None will move from their places of rendezvous until I direct, except Banks. I want to be ready to move by the 25th inst. [April], if possible. I know you will have difficulties to encounter in getting through the mountains to where supplies are abundant, but I believe you will accomplish it.

From the expedition from the Department of West Virginia I do not calculate on very great results; but it is the only way I can take troops from there. With the long line Sigel has to protect, he can spare no troops except to move directly to his front. In this way he must get through to inflict great damage on the enemy, or the enemy must detach from one of his armies a large force to prevent it. In other words, if Sigel can't skin himself he can hold a leg while some one else skins.

I am, general, very respectfully, your obedient servant,

U. S. GRANT,

Lieutenant-General[16]

To General Meade Grant on April 9 wrote a similar letter informing him of who would do what and giving him detailed instructions as well as a single guiding directive. "Lee's army will be your objective point," he told Meade. "Wherever Lee goes, there you will go also."[17]

Grant's plan by then was nearly completely formed. Still undecided, though, was whether it would be better for Meade's troops, in their attempt to flank the Army of Northern Virginia, to cross the Rapidan River upstream of Lee's position or downstream of it. The problem in deciding was supply. "By crossing above," Grant told Meade, "Lee is cut off from all chance of ignoring Richmond and going north on a raid [which Lee was wont to do]. But if we take this route, all we do must be done whilst the rations we start with hold out. We separate from Butler so that he cannot be directed how to co-operate. By the other route Brandy Station can be used as a base of supplies until another is secured on the York or James rivers."[18] Grant told Meade the two of them would talk it over and then decide.

His announcement of his decision came at a meeting with senior members of his staff. Held in the front room of the house that was his headquarters, the meeting began in the evening of May 3 and lasted till well past midnight. He described the considerations for both routes, then said he had decided to cross below Lee's position, to the right flank of the Army of Northern Virginia. "I shall not give my attention so much to Richmond as to

Lee's army," he elaborated to his staff, "and I want all commanders to feel that hostile armies, and not cities, are to be their objective points."[19]

Grant also spelled out to the staff members what he expected of them in transmitting his orders and his wishes to commanders. "I want you to discuss with me freely from time to time the details of the orders given for the conduct of a battle, and learn my views as fully as possible as to what course should be pursued in all the contingencies which may arise."[20] He said he would send them to critical points in the lines so that they could keep him informed of what was taking place. When emergencies arose and there was not time for them to report to headquarters, he said, he wanted them to explain his views to commanders and urge them to take immediate action, without waiting for specific orders. He said he would position his headquarters near Meade's and that his orders would be issued through Meade's headquarters or, in the case of General Burnside's corps, which was not part of Meade's command, through Burnside's headquarters.

By the time he met with his staff that night, on the eve of the commencement of his armies' coordinated drive against the Confederates, Grant already knew that General Banks had taken himself— and his troops — out of the picture. Determined to pursue his campaign against Shreveport, he had ignored Grant's orders, had suffered a major defeat at the hands of a rebel army near Pleasant Hill, Louisiana, about forty-five miles south of Shreveport, on April 8 and had lost nineteen pieces of artillery and an immense quantity of wagons and supplies.[21] On April 9 Banks's army had had another fight with the pursuing Confederates, and although the rebels were repulsed that day, Banks fell back farther, eventually retreating to Alexandria, which he had reached on April 27, his army bereft of supplies and in disarray.

Grant had received that news with chagrin. He reacted to it in a telegram to General Halleck: "I have been satisfied for the past nine months that to keep Banks in command was to neutralize a large force and to support it most expensively. Although I do not insist on it, I think the best interests of the service demand that [Major] General [Joseph J.]Reynolds [commander of the forces in New Orleans] should be placed in command at once, and that he should name his own successor to the command of New Orleans."[22]

Halleck responded with an explanation of the political facts of life. "General Banks is the personal friend of the President, and has strong political supporters in and out of Congress. There will undoubtedly be a very strong opposition to his being removed or superseded. And I think the President will hesitate to act unless he has a definite request from you to do so, as a military necessity, and you designate his successor or superior in command.... Do not understand me as advocating his retention in command. On the contrary, I expressed to the President some months ago, my own opinion of General Banks's want of military capacity...."[23]

Without having yet taken the field, Grant had already suffered a significant defeat. Banks kept his job, and the fruitless drive against Shreveport was continued.

The campaign to win the war, however, continued to develop. To Sherman on May 2 Grant wrote, "Move at the time indicated in my instructions. All will strike together." To Butler on May 2 he wrote: "Start on the date given in my letter. There will be no delay with this army." To Meade on May 3 he wrote: "You will move according to the orders issued. Burnside knows the fact, and has certainly made arrangements for guarding his stores." To Burnside: "All of General Meade's troops will be away from Brandy Station tomorrow morning."[24]

And to General Halleck in Washington, at 12:30 P.M. on Tuesday, May 3, went the last of the telegrams from the general in chief: "This army moves to-morrow morning."[25]

3

The Massacre,
March 25 to April 13, 1864

In June 1861, shortly after the citizens of Tennessee voted two-to-one to secede from the Union, Nathan Bedford Forrest, a former Memphis alderman who had made a small fortune as a slave trader, land speculator and cotton planter, signed on as a soldier in the Confederate cause, enlisting, along with his fifteen-year-old son, William, and his brother Jeffrey, as a private in the Tennessee Mounted Rifles.

Days after his enlistment, and just before his fortieth birthday, he was commissioned a lieutenant colonel, thanks to his connection with Tennessee Governor Isham Harris and to his political supporters and the editorials of his friends at the Memphis *Avalanche*. In his new rank he was directed by the governor to raise a battalion of cavalry to command, which he promptly did, advertising for volunteers in the *Avalanche* and Memphis *Appeal* and traveling from Tennessee into the small towns of western Kentucky seeking enough recruits to form a regiment. The ad he ran in the August 26, 1861, edition of the *Avalanche* read as follows:

> FOR ACTIVE SERVICE!
> A few more companies are needed to complete a mounted regiment, now being formed here for active service. There is also room for a few more recruits in a company of independent rangers not to be attached to any regiment unless on the option of the members. Applicants for membership in the Rangers to furnish their own arms and horses. To those desiring to engage in the cavalry service an excellent opportunity is offered. Now, freemen! rally to the defense of your liberties, your homes and your firesides!
> N.B. Forrest[1]

His energetic recruitment efforts soon attracted not only individuals but entire cavalry units that had already formed in Alabama, Texas, Kentucky and Tennessee. Whole companies joined at once. At summer's end Forrest commanded some 650 troopers comprising a battalion of eight companies, four from Alabama, two from Kentucky, one from Texas and one from Memphis.

In October, within six months of the start of the war, Forrest and his troopers were ordered to duty around Fort Donelson, a hastily constructed rebel fortification built to guard the Cumberland River, about thirty miles west of Clarksville, Tennessee, and Fort Henry, a similar fortification situated just west of Fort Donelson and intended to block

Union passage up the Tennessee River. The swampy area around the fortifications, however, made cavalry action impracticable, and Forrest requested a change of orders to allow him to operate in cavalry-friendly western Kentucky instead. Three days after Christmas 1861 he went into battle for the first time, executing a successful charge against a Union position near Sacramento, Kentucky, where, according to Forrest's report, "the best mounted men of my companies coming up, there commenced a promiscuous saber slaughter of their rear, which was continued at almost full speed for two miles beyond the village, leaving their bleeding and wounded strewn along the whole route."[2]

After an assignment to serve as a rear guard for Confederate troops retreating from Hopkinsville, Kentucky toward Nashville, Forrest and his men were sent back to Fort Donelson to aid its defense. Both forts, Henry and Donelson, ultimately fell to Union forces, but Forrest distinguished himself by waging a vigorous defense before the capitulation and by boldly forcing his way through the Union lines to avoid having five hundred or more of his cavalrymen be among the some seventeen thousand Confederate troops surrendered to Brigadier General Grant on February 16, 1862.

From his just-in-time escape at Fort Donelson Forrest went on to Nashville and then to the battle at Shiloh Church, where his troopers waged another ferocious assault and where, protecting the rebels' hurried withdrawal toward Corinth, Mississippi, Forrest on April 8 led a fierce attack on General Sherman's pursuing troops, stopping their pursuit, and although wounded, he managed to narrowly escape capture in the furious melee.

After those combat experiences, Forrest's wording in his recruiting ads became a bit more spirited:

200 Recruits Wanted

I will receive 200 able-bodied men if they will present themselves at my headquarters by the first of June with good horse and gun. I wish none but those who desire to be actively engaged. My headquarters for the present is at Corinth, Miss. Come on, boys, if you want a heap of fun and to kill some Yankees.

N.B. Forrest
Colonel, Commanding
Forrest's Regiment[3]

Those familiar with his background and personality, having known him for years, might have believed Forrest actually did consider killing Yankees a heap of fun. The eldest of eleven children of a blacksmith who died when Forrest was fifteen years old, he became the chief breadwinner and defender of his hard-pressed family, which then was living on a rented farm in Tippah County, Mississippi, not far from the Tennessee state line. He and his brothers laboriously cleared more and more land, spending long days expanding the area under cultivation, gradually making the farm prosper, sacrificing formal schooling in the process. By his late teens he had grown to be six-foot-one, taller than most, and 180 pounds, lean and muscular, tough and combative.

One of his earliest scrapes was with a neighbor who had a farm adjacent to the Forrests'. The neighbor's ox kept breaking down the separating fence and then feeding on the Forrests' crops. Forrest let the neighbor know that the next time the ox came through the fence, it would be shot. The neighbor responded with a warning that he would shoot anybody who shot his ox. When the ox again came onto the Forrests' land, Forrest shot and killed it, whereupon the neighbor, gun in hand, climbed the fence to come onto the Forrests' property. At that, Forrest opened fire on him, riddling his clothes with shot holes. The neighbor tumbled off the fence, got up and ran away.

In March 1845, when he was twenty-three years old and in the horse-trading business with his uncle, Jonathan Forrest, in Hernando, Mississippi, he and his uncle were involved in a heated dispute with three brothers named Matlock and an overseer who worked for the Matlocks. The dispute turned into a shootout when one of the Matlocks drew a pistol and, intending to shoot young Forrest, instead hit and killed his uncle, causing young Forrest to pull out his pistol and with only two shots in its chamber fire on two of the Matlocks, hitting them both. He took a knife to the others. The reports vary on the results of the fight, some saying two of the Matlocks were killed or mortally wounded, others that two were merely hit, one having to have an arm amputated. Forrest was also struck by a bullet, suffering a slight wound on his arm.

About six months later Forrest impressively rescued a widow and her eighteen-year-old daughter, strangers to him, who were stranded in their carriage in a muddy creekbed near Hernando. He then turned to the two young gentlemen, acquaintances of the women, who had sat idly by on their horses while the women's black carriage driver vainly tried to free the carriage from the mud. He berated them for not helping the driver free the carriage and ordered them to leave the scene immediately, threatening them if they didn't. The threats drove them off, and Forrest then introduced himself to the widow and her daughter, who had apparently instantly attracted his interest.

With permission from the widow, Elizabeth Montgomery, to come calling at her home, intending to see more of the daughter, Mary Ann, Forrest days later went to visit her. On the Montgomerys' porch when he arrived he found the two young men who had proved helpless beside the creek. They also were calling on Mary Ann. Forrest bullied them into making a quick departure.

Bullying, threatening and fighting became standard procedure for Forrest, but did not deprive him of charm, which he could turn on when needed. He managed to win the affection, or at least the admiration, of Mary Ann, and she agreed to marry him. First, though, he needed the consent of her uncle and guardian, a Presbyterian minister, and he refused to give it, telling Forrest his objections. "You cuss and gamble, and Mary Ann is a Christian girl."

"I know it," Forrest answered, "and that's just why I want her."[4] The uncle relented and performed the wedding ceremony weeks later.

By then Forrest had become constable of the town of Hernando and had been elected county coroner. He also ran a livery stable and farm-supply store in Hernando and traded in horses and other livestock. From trading in horseflesh he moved to a commodity considerably more valuable, black humans. He moved from Hernando to Memphis, where the slave market offered more opportunity, and entered a partnership with a veteran slave trader, Byrd Hill, running ads in Memphis newspapers to seek new business:

FIVE HUNDRED NEGROES WANTED

We will pay the highest cash price for all good Negroes offered. We invite all those having Negroes for sale, to call on us, at our Mart, opposite Hill's old stand, on Adams Street. We will have a lot of Virginia Negroes on hand, for sale, in the fall. Negroes bought and sold on commission.

HILL & FORREST

With his dealing in slaves, keeping them passive in a pen as they waited to be sold, came all the practices associated with suppressing and disciplining them as necessary, especially including whippings with a bullwhip. Reports of Forrest's handling of his slaves seem contradictory, some saying he treated them kindly, others that the slaves greatly feared him, evidently with reason. By 1855 he had become the senior partner in a new firm and had expanded his operations, employing his brothers to help him. Now his ads read:

> Forrest & Maples
> SLAVE DEALERS
> 87 Adams Street
> between Second and Third,
> Memphis, Tennessee,
>
> Have constantly on hand the best selected assortment of FIELD HANDS, HOUSE SERVANTS & MECHANICS, at their Negro Mart, to be found in the city. They are daily receiving from Virginia, Kentucky and Missouri, fresh supplies of likely young Negroes. Negroes Sold On Commission and the highest market price is always paid for good stock.
>
> Their jail is capable of containing Three Hundred, and for comfort, neatness and safety, is the best arrayed of any in the Union. Persons wishing to purchase are invited to examine their stock before purchasing elsewhere. They have on hand at present, Fifty likely young Negroes, Comprising Field Hands, Mechanics, Home and body Servants, &c.[5]

By 1858, while he was buying land with his slave-trading profits, Forrest was making his presence felt in Memphis. He was elected alderman and with his membership on the sixteen-man board of aldermen, he introduced a reformist and common-sense approach to the city's governance. When a long-time alderman, Thomas Finnie, criticized his fellow aldermen for a controversial decision, calling their action "coward-like," Forrest told a Memphis *Appeal* reporter that "he did not think Alderman Finnie meant him in his attack, for he [Finnie] knew he was a fighting man."[6] In 1860 Forrest ended his career in elective office, resigning his seat ostensibly to spend more time tending his cotton plantations but apparently aggravated by the board of aldermen's prolonged quarrel over the city's sale of some railroad bonds, $50,000 of which Forrest had purchased and sold at a $10,000 profit.

Ten months after his resignation as an alderman he joined the rebel army. The army didn't change him much. He still did things his way, sometimes disobeying orders, sometimes insisting on new orders, sometimes initiating confrontations with his superiors. In one outrageously insubordinate confrontation he dressed down and threatened Lieutenant General Braxton Bragg, the Confederates' over-all commander in the West, catching him alone in his tent outside Chattanooga in the autumn of 1863. Forrest's tirade was recounted by J.B. Cowan, the chief surgeon of Forrest's command and his wife's cousin, who accompanied Forrest on his visit to Bragg.

Refusing Bragg's hand as Forrest entered his tent, Forrest told Bragg, "I'm not here to pass civilities or compliments with you, but on other business. You commenced your cowardly and contemptible persecution of me soon after the battle of Shiloh, and you have kept it up ever since. You did it because I reported to Richmond facts, while you reported damned lies. You robbed me of my command in Kentucky and gave it to one of your favorites — men that I armed and equipped from the enemies of our country.

"In a spirit of revenge and spite, because I would not fawn upon you as others did, you drove me into west Tennessee in the winter of 1862 with a second brigade I had organized, with improper arms and without sufficient ammunition, although I had made repeated applications for the same. You did it to ruin me and my career. When in spite of all this I returned with my command well equipped by captures, you began again your work of spite and persecution ... and now this second brigade, organized and equipped without thanks to you or the government, a brigade which has won a reputation for successful fighting second to none in the army, taking advantage of your position as the commanding general in order to humiliate me, you have taken these brave men from me.

"I have stood your meanness as long as I intend to. You have played the part of a damned scoundrel, and are a coward, and if you were any part of a man, I would slap your jaws and force you to resent it. You may as well not issue any more orders to me, for I will not obey them, and I will hold you personally responsible for any further indignities you endeavor to inflict upon me.

"You have threatened to arrest me for not obeying your orders promptly. I dare you to do it, and I say to you that if you ever again try to interfere with me or cross my path, it will be at the peril of your life."[7]

Forrest then turned and stormed out, followed by Cowan. Both men mounted their horses, and as they rode off, Cowan told Forrest, "Well, you are in for it now."

"He'll never say a word about it," Forrest replied. "He'll be the last man to mention it. And mark my word, he'll take no action in the matter. I will ask to be relieved and transferred to a different field, and he will not oppose it."[8]

Forrest did indeed request a transfer, and Bragg approved the request, and that was all that came of the insubordination.

From Bragg's command Forrest was moved farther west. He made his headquarters at Okolona, Mississippi and was promoted to major general about that same time. He would now be serving under Lieutenant General Leonidas Polk and would command Confederate cavalry forces in north Mississippi and west Tennessee. In late February 1864 Polk added to Forrest's command three cavalry regiments from Kentucky that were short of horses, and Forrest determined to get the needed horses by executing raids into Kentucky. By March 25, he was standing with two thousand of his troops on the outskirts of Paducah. There he hoped to capture some of the horses and supplies that he needed.

And there, to his surprise, he encountered an enemy force he had never before engaged — black soldiers of the United States Army, many of them runaway slaves or slaves liberated by U.S. forces in Union-occupied sections of the upper South. The Union Army had been accepting blacks into its ranks for two years or more, arousing fierce anger and resentment among many rebel soldiers, officers as well as enlisted men. The mere idea of arming slaves was repugnant to white Southerners generally; using them to oppose the forces of their former masters was outrageous. More than a third of the 665 defenders of the Paducah fortification were black, members of the U.S. First Kentucky Heavy Artillery (Colored).

After taking over most of the town of Paducah and capturing several hundred horses and large quantities of medical supplies, Forrest's Confederates forced the outnumbered Union defenders into their earthworks fortification near the Ohio River. The rebels' assault on the fortification was repulsed, however, and when it failed, Forrest fell back on one of his old tricks. He sent a note to the Union commander, Colonel Stephen Hicks, demanding his surrender, telling him that if he surrendered the fortification and its troops, the troops would be treated as prisoners of war, including by implication the black soldiers. But if the Confederates had to storm the works, Forrest warned, "you may expect no quarter."[9]

It was a stratagem Forrest had used before with success, most recently on March 24, 1864 at Union City, in northwestern Tennessee, when Forrest's forces bluffed Union Colonel Isaac Hawkins into surrendering a 475-man garrison to a smaller rebel force. That was the second time Hawkins had been intimidated into yielding to Forrest's troops.

This time, however, the Union commander, Colonel Hicks, rejected Forrest's surrender-or-else ultimatum. In a move not unusual for Forrest, while under a flag of truce he shifted some of his troops and an artillery battery into a more advantageous position. Once the truce had ended, he launched a new assault on the Union works. It, too, was repulsed. Two other attacks followed it, and they, too were repulsed. Repeatedly beaten back, Forrest's troops for hours kept up a steady fire on the works from nearby buildings. Finally, around eleven-thirty that evening, Forrest gave up the fight and pulled his men out of Paducah, later claiming that he had held the town for ten hours and could have held it longer, but evacuated it after learning there was a smallpox epidemic in the town.

Forrest and his troopers made their way back to Jackson, Tennessee, where Forrest had established his base of operations. On April 4 he sent General Polk a note saying that he was headed for Fort Pillow, on the east bank of the Mississippi River about forty miles above Memphis, where more horses and supplies might be captured from its Union garrison. The fort was an earthworks fortification the Confederates had begun building in June 1861 and was named for Confederate Brigadier General Gideon Pillow. It was built to block the passage of Union vessels coming down the Mississippi, its big guns bristling from its formidable face on a bluff along a half-mile of the river. Its east side and the approaches above and below it were not so well armed or defended. The works had been abandoned by the Confederates in the spring of 1862 following their loss of forts Henry and Donelson and the defeat at the Battle of Pittsburg Landing (Shiloh). Once the right flank of the Confederates defensive line had been turned, the rebel high command considered Fort Pillow untenable. Union forces had then occupied it, using it mostly as a base to recruit Union-sympathizing citizens of west Tennessee and to protect west Tennessee Unionists from marauding rebel guerrillas.

In January of 1864 General Sherman, commanding the U.S. Army's Department of the Tennessee, had ordered Major General Stephen Hurlbut, commander of the Army corps that operated in western Kentucky and western Tennessee, to shut down Fort Pillow, believing it to be no longer worth holding. Hurlbut complied with that order, but on February 8, a month later, the fort was re-occupied by Union troops, the first unit arriving being the Thirteenth Tennessee Cavalry, commanded by Major William F. Bradford. Two weeks later, on February 21, a unit of the Second U.S. Colored Light Artillery arrived, commanded by Lieutenant Alexander Hunter. On March 28 the First Battalion of the Sixth U.S. Colored Heavy Artillery arrived, commanded by Major Lionel F. Booth. With those infusions of troops and the addition of new recruits drawn from the area, by early April the Fort Pillow garrison totaled nineteen officers and 538 men, 262 of whom were blacks.[10] In command was Major Booth, whose commission predated Bradford's. Booth had enlisted in the regular Army in 1858 and had served in a Missouri regiment earlier in the war. As had become customary for white officers serving in black units (there were no black officers), Booth had had a rapid ascent in grade, going from sergeant in a white unit to major in a black unit in less than a year.

Alongside the fort was a thriving community of camp followers of various sorts—Union sympathizers escaping the harassment of their Tennessee neighbors, runaway slaves (called "contrabands"), merchants and tradesmen from the North—all of them dependent on the fort for safety, their fate tied to that of the fort's garrison.

On April 10 Forrest ordered Brigadier General James R. Chalmers to lead the attack force that would move against Fort Pillow. Sharing his commander's penchant for artifice, Chalmers sent a brigade and two other units toward Memphis with instructions to leak out reports that they were on their way to assault the city of Memphis, hoping thereby to have General Hurlbut take his eyes off Fort Pillow and prepare to defend Memphis. The feint on Memphis went so far as to have Forrest's rebel forces build pontoon bridges on the Wolf

River on the northeast side of town and to drive in Union pickets on the south side of Memphis. Hurlbut took the bait. He ordered four regiments to hurry up from Union-occupied Vicksburg to aid in Memphis's defense.

On April 11 rebel General Chalmers sent units from two other brigades to Brownsville, Tennessee, east of Fort Pillow, and then ordered them on a non-stop, forty-mile, rain-soaked, all-night march to Fort Pillow. Guiding the rebel troops was a civilian, W.J. Shaw, who had been arrested and held inside Fort Pillow, but had escaped on the 11th and was eager to give Forrest's men the benefit of the knowledge he had so recently gained about the fort and its defenses, as well as voluntarily leading the Confederates to the fort through the dark of night.

Troops of Colonel Robert McCulloch's brigade reached the southern end of the fort's outer perimeter just as the rising sun was beginning to lighten the sky on April 12. McCulloch ordered the Confederate Second Missouri Cavalry regiment to swarm across the Union picket line, drive the pickets back and force their way into position opposite the fortification. Forrest's instructions to Chalmers were to have his troopers invest the Union works, preventing any of the garrison from escaping, and hold their positions until Forrest arrived.

McCulloch's men dismounted and moved toward the outer works from the south and southeast while units of Colonel Tyree Bell's brigade approached the fortification from the east and the north. As troopers of McCulloch's lead column advanced, they came upon the camp of the fugitive contrabands and set it on fire, the panicked contrabands dashing for the landing at the base of the bluff in an effort to find safety. Black soldiers

Confederate Lt. Gen. Nathan Bedford Forrest. In reporting his capture of Fort Pillow and the casualties inflicted on the fort's defenders, many of whom were black, Forrest wrote that "It is hoped that these facts will demonstrate to the Northern people that negro soldiers cannot cope with Southerners." (LIBRARY OF CONGRESS)

in the post infirmary near the contraband camp fled to the inner fort as sounds of musket fire set off a general Confederate assault on the outer perimeter.

The garrison's black artillery units then opened fire on the advancing rebels, their shells whistling over the heads of the fort's defenders to land among the attackers. On the river the guns of the Union gunboat *New Era*, posted offshore of the fort, also opened fire, directed by signals from within Fort Pillow.

The Confederates kept up a blistering musket fire on the defenders, forcing them to fall back from the outer line and retreat into the fort. An eyewitness, one of the Union combatants, reported, "The firing continued without cessation, principally from behind logs, stumps and under cover of thick underbrush.... We suffered pretty severely in the loss of commissioned officers by the unerring aim of the rebel sharp shooters...."[11] Among the earliest casualties was Fort Pillow's commandant, Major Booth, the former sergeant, slain by a musket ball that struck him in the chest.

General Forrest gave his own account of the action: "By the time I reached the field, at 10 A.M., [General Chalmers] had forced the enemy to their main fortifications, situated on the bluff or bank of the Mississippi River at the mouth of Coal Creek.... Assuming command, I ordered General Chalmers to advance his line and gain position on the slope, where our men would be perfectly protected from the heavy fire of artillery and musketry, as the enemy could not depress their pieces so as to rake the slopes, nor could they fire on them with small-arms except by mounting the breastworks and exposing themselves to the fire of our sharp-shooters, who, under cover of stumps and logs, forced them to keep down inside the works. After several hours' hard fighting the desired position was gained, not, however, without considerable loss. Our main line was now within an average distance of one hundred yards from the fort, and extended from Coal Creek on the right to the bluff or bank of the Mississippi River on the left."[12]

Forrest then tried his standard ploy. Around three o'clock in the afternoon he instructed General Chalmers to display a white flag of truce atop a hillock and when the firing had stopped, he sent Captain Walter Goodman, one of Chalmers' staff officers, to the fortification with the usual note, addressed to Major Booth, not knowing that Booth had been killed. The note read:

HEADQUARTERS FORREST'S CAVALRY
Before Fort Pillow, April 12, 1864

Major Booth, Commanding United States Forces, Port Pillow:

Major — The conduct of the officers and men garrisoning Fort Pillow has been such as to entitle them to being treated as prisoners of war. I demand the unconditional surrender of this garrison, promising you that you shall be treated as prisoners of war. My men have received a fresh supply of ammunition, and from their present position can easily assault and capture the fort. Should my demand be refused, I cannot be responsible for the fate of your command. Respectfully,

N.B. FORREST
Major-General Commanding[13]

While the ceasefire was in effect, two steamboats were spotted steaming up the Mississippi toward the fort. From the eminence on which Forrest had been watching the assault he could see that one of the vessels, the *Olive Branch*, was loaded with blue-jacketed Union troops, and he immediately concluded that they were reinforcements headed for Fort Pillow. He quickly ordered his acting adjutant general, Captain Charles W. Anderson, to take three companies of McCulloch's troops and rush down to the landing and take a position at the foot of the bluff on the south end of the fortification to prevent the Union troops from coming ashore. He also ordered a detachment occupying a position on the north side of the fortification to advance toward the river, a further move to prevent the Union troops from landing. Forrest's swift reaction, taken while the truce was in effect and therefore constituting an apparent breach of protocol, proved needless, however, for the *Olive Branch*'s captain, evidently unaware of the fort's distress and believing the musket shots fired at the boat were from guerrillas, steamed on by the fort, continuing his voyage to Cairo, Illinois.

The white soldiers in the fort took the opportunity of the truce to stand at the parapets and exchange banter with the Confederates, now close enough to hear them clearly. The black soldiers also shouted out to the attackers, some of them, according to one report, indulging in "provoking, impudent jeers."[14]

The response to Forrest's demand for surrender was issued by Major Bradford, who asked for an hour to consult with his officers and who signed Booth's name to the note he sent to Forrest, not wanting Forrest to discover that Booth was no longer in command. Forrest refused to grant an hour, sending a note back to Bradford saying he had but twenty minutes to comply. Bradford replied with a note saying, "Your demand does not produce the desired effect," and signed it with Booth's name. Unsure of what that message meant, Forrest responded with a note saying he must have an answer in plain English. Back came Bradford's answer in plain English:

> General: I will not surrender.
> Very respectfully, your obedient servant,
> L.F. BOOTH,
> Commanding U.S. Forces, Fort Pillow[15]

Forrest's hand had again been called, as at Paducah. Now, if he was going to protect the fearsomeness of his threats, he would have to make a decisive assault on Fort Pillow. "We must take them," one of his sergeants heard him say.[16] About 3:15 P.M. rebel bugles blared out the charge, and Forrest's troopers burst out of the ravines and the six-foot-deep trench in which they had sought cover, then rushed toward the beleaguered fort and its outnumbered defenders, screaming their rebel yell. The rebel soldiers arose "from out the very earth on the center and north side, within twenty yards of our works," Lieutenant Mack Leaming of the U.S. Thirteenth Tennessee Cavalry Battalion recounted. Hit by the defenders' first volley, the attackers "wavered, rallied again and finally succeeded in breaking our lines."[17] Union soldiers had to stand at the parapet to fire on the attackers and when they did, were picked off by Confederate sharpshooters, who also prevented the Union artillerymen from manning their pieces, scattering gun crews with musket fire whenever they stood to service their guns.

Soon the rebel troopers were pouring across the fort's parapet, overwhelming the defenders. "Our boys," according to one Union eyewitness, "when they saw that they were overpowered, threw down their arms and held up their handkerchiefs and some their hands in token of surrender."[18] It was then that rage seemed to take over Forrest's rebels, and the horror implicit in his ultimatum began.

The rebels, officers and men alike, were "exasperated by the Yankees' threats," Sergeant Achilles Clark of the Confederate Twentieth Tennessee Cavalry recounted, and many refused to accept prisoners.[19] "The slaughter was awful," Clark wrote in a letter to his sisters. "Words cannot describe the scene. The poor deluded negroes would run up to our men, fall upon their knees and with uplifted hands scream for mercy but they were ordered to their feet and then shot down. The whitte [sic] men fared but little better. Their fort turned out to be a great slaughter pen. Blood, human blood stood about in pools and brains could have been gathered up in any quantity. I with several others tried to stop the butchery and at one time had partially succeeded but Gen. Forrest ordered them shot down like dogs, and the carnage continued."[20]

Daniel Stamps, a sharpshooter with the U.S. Thirteenth Tennessee Cavalry who was posted at the base of the river bluff, saw black soldiers running out of the fort and down the bluff near his position. "Then I saw the white [U.S.] soldiers coming down after them, saying the rebels were showing no quarter. I then threw down my gun and ran down with them, closely pursued by the enemy shooting down every man black and white. They said they had orders from Forrest to 'kill the last God damn one of them.' While I was standing at the bottom of the hill I heard a rebel officer shout out an order of some kind to the men who had taken us, and saw a rebel soldiers standing by me. I asked him what the officer had said. He repeated it to me again. It was, 'kill the last damn one of them.' The soldier replied to his officer that we had surrendered; that we were prisoners.... The officer replied, seeming crazy with rage that he had not been obeyed, 'I tell you to kill the last God damned one of them.' He then turned and galloped off....

"I saw 2 [apparently white] men shot down while I was under the bluff. They had their hands up; had surrendered, and were begging for mercy. I also ... saw at least 25 negroes shot down, within 10 or 20 paces from the place where I stood. They had also surrendered, and were begging for mercy."[21]

Desperate to escape, many of the garrison's troops hurried to the Mississippi River and dived into it, then swam toward a number of barges moored in the stream or run aground on the riverbank. By then the *New Era*, seeing the Stars and Stripes gone from the fort's flagpole, had abandoned the fight and steamed away. Several hundred of the fleeing troops, according to a Confederate newspaper reporter on the scene, were shot on the barge or in the river, their heads above the water presenting easy targets. None of the swimmers survived.

Doctor Charles Fitch, Fort Pillow's post surgeon, despite suffering a wound in his leg, quickly set up an aid station on the river bank and began receiving wounded defenders. When Forrest's troopers overran the position, Fitch, surrendering, sought out Forrest himself for protection against the atrocities he had seen being committed by the rebel soldiers. He found Forrest atop the bluff and identified himself to Forrest as the post surgeon. "You are a surgeon of a damn nigger regiment," Forrest replied, according to Fitch's account. Fitch said he was not, and Forrest told him, "You are a damn Tennessee Yankee then." Fitch said he wasn't a Tennessean, that he was from Iowa. "What in hell are you down here for?" Forrest demanded. "I have a great mind to have you killed for being down here." On second thought, however, his passion swiftly waning, Forrest turned Fitch over to one of his troopers, ordering that he be kept safe.[22]

The slaughter involved far more heinous acts than merely shooting to death prisoners and others after the fort's surrender. A white officer of the U.S. Thirteenth Tennessee Cavalry, Second Lieutenant John C. Akerstrom, was reported to have had his wrists and feet nailed to the side of a house, which was then set on fire. Some of the black soldiers were reported to have had their hands nailed to logs that were then set afire. One witness, a master's mate from the *New Era* who went ashore the next day to gather the wounded under a flag of truce, reported that he saw the body of one black man on his back on a tent floor, nails having been driven through his clothes to pin him down. Parts of his outstretched arms were burned off, and his legs were burned nearly to a crisp. "His face was not burned," the witness reported, "but was very much distorted, as if he had died in great pain."[23]

On the morning after the battle the armed Union steamer *Silver Cloud* opened fire on rebel pickets to drive them away from the fort's landing and then rescued about twenty Union soldiers who were hiding between the bluff and the water's edge. Later, under a flag of truce, the Confederates asked the steamer's captain, U.S. Navy acting master William Ferguson, to send a party ashore to remove the Union wounded and help bury the dead. Ferguson was with the party that went ashore and reported that they found "about 70 wounded men in the fort and around it, and buried, I should think, 150 bodies." He went on to describe the scene:

The Fort Pillow Massacre. Six weeks after the massacre the Confederate congress passed a resolution thanking Forrest and his troopers for the "brilliant campaign" that left the Mississippi River, according to Forrest, "dyed with the blood of the slaughtered." (LIBRARY OF CONGRESS)

All the buildings around the fort and the tents and huts in the fort had been burned by the rebels and among the embers the charred remains of numbers of our soldiers ... could be seen.... Bodies with gaping wounds, some bayoneted through the eyes, some with skulls beaten through, others with hideous wounds as if their bowels had been ripped open with bowie-knives, plainly told that but little quarter was shown to our troops. Strewn from the fort to the river bank, in the ravines and hollows, behind logs and under the brush where they had crept for protection from the assassins who pursued them, we found bodies bayoneted, beaten, and shot to death, showing how cold-blooded and persistent was the slaughter....[24]

The Union dead, including the thirty-one who died from their wounds following the battle, totaled between 277 and 295 — or up to 53 percent of the garrison. Sixty-one of the wounded survived their wounds. Two hundred and thirteen were taken prisoner. Thirty-four managed to escape both death and Confederate prisons.[25] In an anomaly of warfare, more than twice as many men were killed as were wounded. Among white Union soldiers the number killed was between 29 and 33 percent of the whites' total. Among black soldiers, however, it was 65 percent of their total.[26]

Confederate losses amounted to between thirteen and twenty killed and eighty-three to eighty-six wounded,[27] figures more in keeping with the expectable ratio of killed to wounded.

Before daylight faded from the horrific scene of carnage, General Forrest headed back toward Brownsville with part of his force, leaving General Chalmers in charge of the grim tasks still to be performed before the remainder of Forrest's troopers would abandon the ruined fort. Those tasks included gathering up the Confederate wounded, burying the dead of both sides and, under a flag of truce, escorting a group of Union officers, newly arrived by steamer, through the fort and its environs the next day.

One of those Union officers was Captain John G. Woodruff of the 113th Illinois Infantry Regiment, who reported that the group

> saw the dead bodies of 15 negroes, most of them having been shot through the head. Some of them were burned as if by powder around the holes in their heads, which led me to conclude that they were shot at very close range. One of the gun-boat officers who accompanied us asked General Chalmers if most of the negroes were not killed after they [the Confederates] had taken possession. Chalmers replied that he thought they had been, and that the men of General Forrest's command had such a hatred for the armed negro that they could not be restrained from killing the negroes after they had captured them. He said they were not killed by General Forrest's or his orders, ... that both Forrest and he stopped the massacre as soon as they were able to do so. He said it was nothing better than we could expect as long as we persisted in arming the negro.[28]

Three days after the fall of Fort Pillow General Forrest wrote to his commander, General Polk, reporting his success:

> ... The victory was complete, and the loss of the enemy will never be known, from the fact that large numbers ran into the river and were shot and drowned. The force was composed of about five hundred negroes and two hundred white soldiers. The river was dyed with the blood of the slaughtered for two hundred yards. There was in the fort a large number of citizens who had fled there to escape the conscript law. Most of these ran into the river and were drowned. The approximate loss was upward of five hundred killed, but few of the officers escaping. It is hoped that these facts will demonstrate to the Northern people that negro soldiers cannot cope with Southerners....[29]

Six weeks later the Confederate congress in Richmond, ignoring the reports of the brutal massacre — or contemptuous of them — in a joint resolution expressed its gratitude to Forrest and his troopers "for their late brilliant and successful campaign in Mississippi, West Tennessee and Kentucky — a campaign which has conferred upon its authors fame as enduring as the records of the struggle which they have so brilliantly illustrated."[30]

Lee, April 1864

On the south side of the Rapidan General Robert E. Lee's Army of Northern Virginia waited along a long line of entrenchments, the watchful eyes of the troops gazing northward across the two-hundred-foot-wide river, its banks steep, its fords difficult to cross. From across it the threat of attack grew with each passing spring day. The trenches stretched some twenty miles and were manned by several brigades of infantry, with the main body of Lee's army—the corps of Lieutenant General Richard S. Ewell and of Major General Ambrose P. Hill—encamped to the rear of the trenches, in position to move forward or to either flank of the attenuated rebel force, now the chief defender not only of Richmond, the vital Confederate capital, but of the Confederate cause itself.

Crossings above and below the stretch of river guarded by the entrenchments were patrolled by details of Lee's cavalry, the main body of which was posted along the Rappahannock near Fredericksburg, to the east, where remaining forage in the ravaged land could still be found for the troopers' mounts. To Gordonsville, southwest of Lee's position, was being rushed the Army of Northern Virginia's third corps, commanded by General James Longstreet, marching from Tennessee to reinforce Lee's line.

On his retreat from the bloodied slopes of Cemetery Ridge at Gettysburg the previous summer Lee had fallen back as far as the Rapidan, then had moved forward against General Meade's pursuing Army of the Potomac and had waged a fruitless campaign that concluded with the Army of Northern Virginia entrenched on the south side of the Rappahannock, the southeastward-flowing river that springs from the Blue Ridge Mountains and sweeps across the breadth of northern Virginia, joined by the east-flowing Rapidan just west of Fredericksburg. Lee had intended to make a stand at the Rappahannock if attacked by Meade, but in early November 1863, threatened by a massive Union buildup, he had promptly withdrawn southward, and on November 10 the Army of Northern Virginia was back at its former defensive line on the south bank of the Rapidan.

Meade had shown some signs that he would attempt to force a crossing of the Rapidan, but the signs turned out to presage no new offensive, and the opposing armies had then settled down to endure the hard, cold winter until spring should bring a renewed vigor for battle.

Lee had a lot to occupy his thoughts while he waited. He was bedeviled by shortages of clothing and shoes and blankets that were causing severe hardships in the ranks of his army. Worse, the short supply of food had become critical. To stretch out the available provisions, the troops' daily rations were reduced to four ounces of bacon or salt pork and one pint of corn meal per man. Lee allowed himself no more than his men received. Shortages of food for the army's workhorses were even more severe. The horses were slowly starving for want of hay and corn. Artillery horses, needed to pull field pieces and caissons, were particularly hard hit, their deaths from hunger depriving fighting units of artillery. In desperation Lee had written to President Davis on April 12, 1864, telling him,

> My anxiety on the subject of provisions for the army is so great that I cannot refrain from expressing it to Your excellency. I cannot see how we can operate with our present supplies. Any derangement in their arrival or disaster to the railroad would render it impossible for me to keep the army together, and might force a retreat into North Carolina. There is nothing to be had in this section for men or animals. We have rations for the troops to-day and to-morrow. I hope a new supply arrived last night, but I have not yet had a report....[1]

A big part of the problem was the inadequacy of rail transportation in the South. Provisions and supplies were not getting to the army when they were needed. In his April 12 letter to Davis, Lee wrote that "Every exertion should be made to supply the depots at Richmond and at other points. All pleasure travel should cease, and everything be devoted to necessary wants."[2] He wrote those words a month after his new quartermaster-general, General A.R. Lawton, had reported that the Confederacy's rail lines were then hauling more goods for the army than at almost any other period of the war.[3]

Lee was also beset by a manpower shortage. When Longstreet's troops were in place, Lee would have some sixty thousand to sixty-five thousand men to oppose the more than one hundred thousand of Grant. The expedition into Pennsylvania that had ended with the disaster at Gettysburg had cost Lee about twenty-three thousand men, and the recent vain attempt to drive Meade back across the Potomac had cost another twelve hundred casualties. Replacements for those losses were hard to find. The enormous disparity in population between North and South (twenty-two million in the Union versus nine million, three and a half million of whom were slaves, in the eleven seceded states) had become starkly evident. President Lincoln in March had issued a call for 700,000 new troops to be enlisted and marched into the fray. Such a number, or anything approaching it, was unthinkable in the Confederacy. According to one estimate, in the seceded states there were but 126,000 white men between the ages of eighteen and fifty-five who were still available for service.[4]

To make sure the Confederate army was getting as many men as the South's population could yield, Lee pushed for a tougher conscription law that would extend age limits and would close loopholes that allowed many otherwise eligible draftees to dodge service. He wrote to President Davis urging changes in the conscription law, telling him, "The law should not be open to the charge of partiality, and I do not know how this can be accomplished, without embracing the whole population capable of bearing arms, with the most limited exemptions, avoiding anything that would look like a distinction of classes."[5] Lee refused special consideration for families who needed sons or husbands at home to care for the family's farm or business, or for those families who had several brothers serving. "It is impossible to equalize the burdens of this war," he said. "Some must suffer more than others."[6]

He did eventually get some help from the Confederate congress, which in February and March 1864 had enacted legislation lowering the conscription age limit to seventeen and raising it to fifty — on condition that the youngest and oldest conscripts be used only for state defense — and establishing stricter exemption and disability regulations.

Then there were Lee's personal concerns that sometimes filled his busy mind as the winter had worn on. The health of his invalid wife, Mary, had worsened when he last saw her in December. She was practically helpless. His daughter-in-law, Charlotte, wife of his second son, William Henry Fitzhugh Lee, known as Rooney, had died of an illness in late December. Hers was the second death in Lee's immediate family, his daughter Annie having died in 1862. Rooney, a Confederate major general of cavalry, had spent much of the '63-'64 winter as a prisoner of war, but in February he had been exchanged for a captured Union general, Neal S. Dow. Two other sons were also serving in the Confederate army, Custis, Lee's oldest son, and Robert Jr. (Rob), his youngest.

The war had an imposed a further burden on the family by depriving the Lees of Arlington, the family home and estate, which had been confiscated by the United States through an 1862 tax law designed to punish citizens of the seceded states. The new Lee residence, where Lee's ailing wife now lived, was a rented house in Richmond, considerably less grand than Arlington.

Lee had observed his fifty-seventh birthday in January and was beginning to look older than his years, his beard and the hair at his temples having turned gray since the war began. Formerly indefatigable, he had lost much of his robustness to wounds and wartime injuries, to the cares and worries of his responsibilities, to the general wear and tear inflicted on his body by life in the field and to intermittent bouts of rheumatism, which sometimes were so severe he was unable to mount his horse, the handsome gray gelding, Traveller. During those times he traveled by ambulance.

Lee was aware that he now faced the North's most successful general, U.S. Grant, newly promoted to lieutenant general and elevated to the command of the entire United States Army. He doubtless realized it would be Grant, not Meade, who would be masterminding what Lee assumed would be the next campaign to capture Richmond. Lee was hardly awed. Instead, he felt inspired by the challenge of clashing with Grant. "We have got to whip them," he told his aide, Colonel Walter H. Taylor. "We must whip them, and it has already made me better to think of it."[7]

Days of early April rain were reducing the imminence of the impending assault on Lee's line, the roads becoming too miry for the movement of masses of men and the machines of war, and through the gloomy days everything was on hold, waiting for the roads to dry for the movement of the Army of the Potomac and in the meantime preparing for countermoves by the Army of Northern Virginia, Lee always thinking of offense, forever planning to seize the initiative.

(In Richmond on the last day of April there occurred a misfortune that showed tragedy needed none of the terrors of war to strike heart-rending sorrow in the life of a Civil War family. Five-year-old Joe Davis, the second son and the third of President and Mrs. Davis's four children, the apple of his father's eye, was killed in a thirty-foot fall from a balcony at the family's home.)

Through all the desperate shortages and handicaps, despite facing an overwhelmingly superior force, Lee's hope of victory seemed never to fade. By now his fervor for the Confederacy's cause — having developed beyond his original feelings of mere Virginia patriotism — had become entwined with his religious sentiments. In orders issued to his troops on August 13, 1863, he wrote as if he now believed that God, too, favored the Confederate cause and would bless its defenders if they would repent of their errant ways and let God work His wondrous ways to bring victory:

... Soldiers! we have sinned against Almighty God. We have forgotten His signal mercies, and have cultivated a revengeful, haughty, and boastful spirit. We have not remembered that the defenders of a just cause should be pure in His eyes; that "our times are in His hands," and have relied too much on our own arms for the achievement of our independence. God is our only refuge and our strength. Let us humble ourselves before Him. Let us confess our many sins, and beseech Him to give us a higher courage, a purer patriotism, and more determined will; that He will convert the hearts of our enemies; that He will hasten the time when war, with its sorrows and sufferings, shall cease, and that He will give us a name and place among the nations of the earth.[8]

As the day of battle drew much closer, on April 28, 1864 he wrote to a favorite cousin, Margaret Stuart, telling her:

... I dislike to send letters within reach of the enemy, as they might serve, if captured, to bring distress on others. But you must sometimes cast your thoughts on the Army of Northern Virginia, and never forget it in your prayers. It is preparing for a great struggle, but I pray and trust that the great God, mighty to deliver, will spread over it His almighty arms, and drive its enemies before it....[9]

His apparent lack of familiarity with Grant permitted Lee further hope for ultimate success. Lee had already blunted the careers of three commanders of the Army of the Potomac, McClellan, Burnside and Hooker, the three of them defeated by Lee in succession. Without knowledge of the character of the commander they now faced, Lee and his staff, their morale high despite Gettysburg, saw no reason they could not handle Grant. A big defeat, some heavy losses, and Grant, the North's present idol, as Colonel Taylor called him, would pull back, as the others had done. Taylor, perhaps reflecting Lee's confidence, in January had written, "I believe if we whip the Yankees good again this year, they will quit in disgust."[10] And on April 18, a month after Grant had assumed command of the U.S. Army, Taylor wrote, "We are in better condition and more hopeful than ever."[11]

Lee himself wrote that if the Army of the Potomac's flanking movement against Richmond could be stopped by his planned assault on it at the Rappahannock, "I have no uneasiness as to the result of the campaign in Virginia."[12]

To his son, however, he expressed more fatalistic thoughts as the climactic clash of forces approached: "To resist the powerful combination now forming against us will require every man in his place. If victorious, we have everything to hope for in the future. If defeated, nothing will be left for us to live for.... My whole trust is in God, and I am ready for whatever He may ordain."[13]

As he trusted in God so did the men of his army trust in Lee. "We firmly believed," his son Rob wrote, "that 'Marse Robert,' as his soldiers lovingly called him, would bring us out of this trouble all right."[14]

The "trouble" was Grant's menacing army. On Wednesday, May 4, 1864 the expected trouble came, and Lee came out to meet it.

The Grant Offensive Begins,
May 2 to May 7, 1864

General Lee had asked his three corps commanders and several of his division commanders to meet with him on Clark's Mountain, which rises six hundred or so feet on the south side of the Rapidan, north of Orange, where from the Confederate signal station atop the eminence they could get a clear and sweeping view of the Virginia countryside and the streaming waters of the river that separated the Army of Northern Virginia from the threatening forces of General Grant. Some ten miles to the north of Clark's Mountain was Culpeper, where nearby in rows of white tents was encamped Grant's army. To the east, downriver, were the two fords where Grant was most likely to make a crossing — Germanna Ford and, six miles farther downstream, Ely's Ford.

On May 2 the Confederate generals stood and studied what Lee wanted them to see, the vast battlefield that was to be. Grant's forces, if they intended to cross at Germanna, would come down the Germanna Ford road from the northwest, marching southeastward, and once across the river, would continue to the southeast for about five miles, to where the Germanna Ford road intersected the Orange Turnpike, also called the Old Stone Road. At that crossroads, distinguished by a deserted tavern that stood near it, Grant's intentions would become evident. He would either turn westward and strike the Confederate line on its right flank or he would continue southeastward toward Richmond, passing through a forbiddingly dense and rugged woods, known for good reason as the Wilderness, in an attempt to flank Lee's defenses and place his army between Lee's force and the Confederate capital that it must defend. If Grant crossed the Rapidan at Ely's Ford, his options would be the same.

Lee was ready to oppose either of Grant's most likely moves and, leaving no stone unturned, prepared for a third possibility, that of Grant's coming across the Rapidan upstream of the rebel entrenchments and attempting a flanking movement from the west. To protect against that possibility Lee ordered General Ewell to have a brigade of his corps keep watch over the upper Rapidan's crossing points.

By the time the Confederate commanders descended Clark's Mountain, they had a good idea of what they were facing.

The seemingly endless train of slow-moving wagons, burdened with all that Grant's army needed to pursue his offensive, had begun its journey to the Rapidan, with a cavalry escort, on the afternoon of May 3, even before Grant had briefed his senior staff in his Culpeper headquarters during the evening of May 3. Then, around midnight, on the morning of Wednesday, May 4, the fighting troops of Grant's army began moving out from their bivouac around Culpeper and Brandy Station, forming up on the road to Stevensburg, the place where the marchers would divide into two long columns, one headed for the Germanna crossing, the other for Ely's. Galloping past the infantry and artillery were cavalry units assigned to chase off rebel pickets posted at the two river crossings. Behind the cavalry came the engineers who would lay pontoon bridges across the Rapidan as soon as the rebel troops were driven away.

By 5 A.M. on the 4th General Meade and his staff were moving out with the troops, and about 8 A.M. Grant and his staff left his headquarters at Culpeper and also fell into the line of march. Grant was mounted on his big bay, Cincinnati. He was clad, as an eyewitness[1] recorded, in an unbuttoned uniform frock coat with a waistcoat beneath it. Yellowish-brown gloves were on his hands, and on his feet and lower legs were knee-high boots, with spurs at his heels. On his head was a black felt slouch hat with a gold-colored cord that circled the crown. At his waist were a sash and sword. He was headed for the Germanna crossing.

The sun was well up now, warming the columns of marchers and casting rays of light through the trees along the road, their branches having recently come alive with the yellowish-green and pale green leaves of early spring. Unthinking soldiers, sweating in the bright sun and from the exertion of the march, by the scores shed their overcoats and dropped them beside the dusty road. General Grant's overcoat, the same as those issued to his enlisted men, was rolled up and strapped to the back of the saddle of Grant's orderly.

The cavalry division of Brigadier General James H. Wilson, riding ahead of the column that was headed for Germanna Ford, had reached the bluff overlooking the ford about 2 A.M., and when it did, a unit of the Third Indiana Cavalry Regiment promptly dashed into the river and, crossing it, scattered a detail of the First North Carolina Cavalry Regiment that was posted on the south bank. The bridge builders then had swiftly gone to work. At 5:50 A.M. General Wilson had sent a message to Major General Gouverneur K. Warren, commanding the U.S. Fifth Corps, saying that Wilson's rearmost cavalry regiment was then fording the river, getting out of the way of Warren's advancing column, and reporting that the canvas pontoon bridge was all but complete. A parallel, wooden pontoon bridge was also laid, and at 7 A.M. the leading units of General Warren's infantry and artillerymen had started streaming across the Rapidan on the two bridges. Before the morning was gone, army engineers would lay five bridges across the Rapidan, including the two at Germanna, two similar ones at Ely's and one wooden pontoon bridge at Culpeper Mine Ford, about midway between Germanna and Ely's.

As Warren's troops trod across the Germanna bridges, Wilson's cavalry, taking the infantry's crossing as their signal, started moving toward the Wilderness Tavern, some five miles away, their reconnaissance patrols cautiously scouting out each trail that led up to Brock Road, on which they were now advancing southeastward into Confederate-held territory, into the Wilderness. By noon they had reached the tavern and there they halted, then sent patrols westward along the Orange Turnpike, establishing a line of pickets, warily feeling out the rebel defenses.

Behind Warren's Fifth Corps in the long, blue column of march came the U.S. Sixth Corps, commanded by Major General John Sedgwick, which crossed the river, posted a division at the bridges to guard them and encamped along the Germanna road on the south side of the Rapidan. Down the river, at Ely's Ford, the U.S. Second Corps, commanded by Major General Winfield Scott Hancock, by the middle of the day had also crossed the river and had halted near Chancellorsville, to the east, at the intersection of the Ely's Ford road and the Orange Turnpike, about four miles south of the ford.

Despite the desirability of a quick passage through the Wilderness, Grant's troops had, according to plan, stopped their advance by mid-afternoon, while hours of daylight remained. Grant worried that the fast-moving fighting units would get too far ahead of the slow-moving wagon trains, which were plodding across the bridges at Ely's Ford and at Culpeper Mine Ford, allowing a broad space into which Lee's highly maneuverable force might drive and separate Grant's army from its supplies. "The troops might have easily continued their march five miles further," the Army of the Potomac's chief of staff, Major General Andrew A. Humphreys, explained, but "that would have left the right too open during the forenoon of the 5th, and it was more judicious to let the troops remain for the night where they had halted, as it made the passage of the [wagon] trains secure, and the troops would be fresher when meeting the enemy next day, of which there was much probability."[2]

General Grant rode across one of the bridges at Germanna shortly before noon, then urged Cincinnati to carry him to the top of the bluff that overlooked the Rapidan on the south side, where a dilapidated and deserted old farmhouse stood. Across the front of the house was a porch, and inside, the house had been stripped of furniture except for a table and two chairs. Grant decided to make his headquarters there, which, it turned out, was not far from where General Meade had made his headquarters. After inspecting the house, Grant took a seat on the front steps, lighted a cigar and sat watching the troops of General Sedgwick's Sixth Corps pour across the bridges. After minutes of silence, he pronounced his satisfaction with his army's progress. "Well, the movement so far has been as satisfactory as could be desired," he remarked. "We have succeeded in seizing the fords and crossing the river without loss or delay. Lee must by this time know upon what roads we are advancing, but he may not yet realize the full extent of the movement. We shall probably soon get some indications as to what he intends to do."[3]

When a newspaper reporter traveling with him then asked Grant how long it would take to get to Richmond, Grant replied, "I will agree to be there in about four days — that is, if General Lee becomes a party to the agreement. But if he objects, the trip will undoubtedly be prolonged."[4]

Grant ate a cold lunch at the table that had been left behind in the house's dining room, then waited for his headquarters tents to arrive, which they did later that afternoon. The tents were set up in the yard, near the house, and shortly before dark Grant and the officers of his staff had dinner beneath the fly of a large tent, where the dining room table had been moved. Grant ate less and talked less than the staff officers, who came and went as their duties allowed, some lingering to chat as long as possible.

After dinner General Meade came to confer with Grant, and the two of them sat on camp chairs beside a fire of fence rails while smoking Grant's cigars and discussing plans for the next day. During their discussion telegrams from Washington were delivered to Grant reporting that General Sherman was advancing in Georgia, General Butler was moving up the James River, and General Sigel's forces were moving up the valley of Virginia, all according to Grant's grand plan.

Following Meade's departure Grant retired to his tent around midnight and turned in for the night. His bed was a folding cot of canvas stretched over a wooden frame. His only other furniture was two folding camp chairs, a plain pine table, an iron tripod that held a tin wash basin, and his camp trunk, containing a suit of clothes, an extra pair of boots, underwear and some toilet articles. It would be another short night for him, his sleep ending at daylight, when he and his staff would rise to meet a new day, May 5, feeling that, as one staff member expressed it, "in all probability they would witness before [the next] night either a fight or a foot-race — a fight if the armies encountered each other, a foot-race to secure good positions if the armies remained apart."[5]

General Lee's lookouts at the signal station atop Clark's Mountain had spotted the advancing Union force moving like a long, blue cascade down the roads to the crossings at Germanna and Ely's fords, and around nine o'clock on the morning of May 4 the lookouts had displayed to Lee and his waiting army the signal flags of warning. Lee had taken swift action. Anticipating an assault on his right flank, he had ordered both General Ewell and General Hill to move eastward, Ewell's corps by way of the straight-line Orange Turnpike, Hill's corps taking the meandering Plank Road, which roughly paralleled the turnpike farther south, and he had ordered General Longstreet to come up from around Gordonsville to support them. Lee rode with Hill's corps.

Lee then still didn't know in which direction Grant would move after crossing the Rapidan, whether to the southwest, where, after the repositioning of the rebel army, Grant would face Lee's forces head on, or whether he would continue southeastward, which would mean passing through the Wilderness. The latter course was what Lee was expecting — and hoping for. Lee would be able to attack the moving column on its flank, reducing the advantage that Grant had in superior numbers. And in the dense woods and thickets of the Wilderness, Grant's artillery, much superior to the rebels' in numbers and power, would be virtually useless. Exactly a year earlier, in early May of 1863, Lee had won an important battle against the considerably larger Union force he attacked in the Wilderness, defeating General Hooker at Chancellorsville and turning back the Army of the Potomac. He felt confident that if Grant chose the Wilderness course, the Army of Northern Virginia could do to Grant what it had done to Hooker.

If, on the other hand, Grant moved westward, Lee figured that with a part of his army he would a make a stand behind Mine Run, a stream that ran perpendicular to the Rapidan and flowed into it about two miles west of Germanna Ford, and with the remainder of his force he would maneuver against Grant, a tactic familiar to the wily Lee. In the meantime, he would wait to see what Grant would do once his army had crossed the Rapidan, unopposed. In any case, Lee intended to launch an assault against the Union force as soon as General Longstreet's corps arrived. That evening, May 4, General Hill's troops, with Lee among them, bivouacked in the woods at Verdiersville.

While there, Lee received messages from couriers bringing to him some of the same news that was telegraphed to Grant. A Union force commanded by General Sigel was advancing up the Shenandoah valley, another Union army had landed at Bermuda Hundred on the James River, threatening the rail line that linked Richmond and Petersburg, and still another Union force was reported as threatening the Virginia and Tennessee Railroad. Lee could now see the scope of the new Union offensive. He had already guessed that the new offensive would have several fronts, but had concluded that the most critical campaigns would be waged in Georgia and Virginia.

One of the other messages he received that evening was from General Longstreet, reporting that he hoped to reach the location called Richard's Shop, six miles south of Lee's present position at Verdiersville, by noon on May 5, the next day. Now, on the strength of Longstreet's report, Lee decided the time had come to strike.

Later that night General Jeb Stuart told Lee that his cavalry had discovered that the Union force was still in the Wilderness, and when morning came, Thursday, May 5, with no sign that Grant's army was turning westward, Lee concluded that Grant intended to continue his southeastward march through the Wilderness — exactly what Lee had been hoping he would do. General Hill's corps soon formed up on the Plank Road and resumed its eastward advance, General Lee riding at the head of the column with Hill, aiming for a collision with the Army of the Potomac on its flank as it moved through the Wilderness. On the Orange Turnpike, to Hill's left, was General Ewell's corps, also advancing eastward, a few miles ahead of Hill's column, and Lee sent word to Ewell to adjust his rate of march so that the two columns would hit the Union flank at about the same time. Within a matter of minutes now the two rebel columns would enter the Wilderness on the two east-west roads, approaching steadily from the west, headed for an anticipated crash against a southward-moving enemy.

Grant's army had begun moving at 5 A.M. on the 5th. Hancock was to move from around Chancellorsville to Shady Grove Church on the Catharpin Road, which intersected Brock Road about eight miles south of the Wilderness Tavern. The church was about three miles southwest of the intersection. Warren's Fifth Corps was to proceed from the Wilderness Tavern along Brock Road to its intersection with the Plank Road and position the head of its column at Parker's Store on the Plank Road, about three miles west of Brock Road. Sedgwick was to move his Sixth Corps westward from the Wilderness Tavern along the Orange Turnpike and see what developed.

At his headquarters camp overlooking the Rapidan at Germanna Ford Grant lingered after breakfast in hopes of seeing General Burnside when his troops would begin arriving at the crossing. At 7:30 A.M. he received a message from General Meade, who was at Wilderness Tavern:

> The enemy have appeared in force on the Orange Pike, and are now reported forming line of battle in front of Griffin's division, Fifth Corps. I have directed General Warren to attack them at once with his whole force. Until this movement of the enemy is developed, the march of the corps must be suspended. I have, therefore, sent word to Hancock not to advance beyond Todd's Tavern for the present. I think the enemy is trying to delay our movement, and will not give battle, but of this we shall soon see. For the present I will stop here, and have stopped our trains.[6]

Grant wrote back to Meade. "If an opportunity presents itself for pitching into a part of Lee's army," Grant instructed with a touch of nineteenth-century vernacular, "do so without giving time for disposition."[7]

Around 8:40 A.M., his eagerness to get to the front overcoming his patience, Grant decided not to wait any longer for Burnside, whose troops by then were crossing the Germanna bridges. Instead of delivering instructions to Burnside in person, he wrote him a note directing him to move up behind Sedgwick's corps as soon as possible. Grant then ordered his staff to mount up and ride with him southward on the Germanna road. They had gone about a mile when a colonel from Sedgwick's staff came galloping up to them and, reining up in front of Grant, told him, "General Meade directed me to ride back and meet you, and say that the enemy is still advancing along the turnpike, and that Warren's and Sedgwick's troops are being put in position to meet him."[8]

Soon after Hill's corps entered the Wilderness, moving eastward on the Plank Road, Lee, riding with Hill behind Stuart and units of Stuart's cavalry, was approached by a member of General Ewell's staff, who reported that Ewell's corps was continuing to advance along the turnpike and that Ewell wanted to know if Lee had any instructions for him. Lee replied that General Ewell should adjust his rate of march so that his column would not get far ahead of Hill's and that Lee wished Ewell would not engage the enemy before Longstreet's corps arrived.

After crossing Mine Run, Hill's column encountered a detachment of U.S. cavalry, which was soon turned back by a brigade of Hill's infantry. Then about eleven o'clock Lee received a message from Ewell saying that U.S. troops could be seen moving in a column across the turnpike on the Germanna Ford road, about two miles east of his position, heading toward the Plank Road. Lee now was sure that Grant intended to attempt a flanking movement against Lee's right.

About an hour later sounds of fierce gunfire erupted from the direction of the turnpike. The distance between the turnpike and Plank Road now had become much greater as Plank Road curved farther southward and the two rebel columns had lost easy contact with each other. Around three o'clock Lee drew up in an elevated field that gave him a view of the land ahead. While there, with Hill and Stuart, a skirmish line of blue-coated infantry emerged from the woods to the left, at some distance, but within musket range. Lee quickly called for Colonel Walter Taylor, his adjutant general, to order troops up to his position to drive back the Union skirmishers. Without firing a shot, the Union skirmishers quickly withdrew, apparently alarmed that they had stumbled onto a sizeable rebel force, but their presence had confirmed Lee's fear that Grant's forces would find the gap between Ewell's right on the turnpike and Hill's left on the Plank Road. Lee then ordered Major General Cadmus Wilcox to have his division peel off from the column on the left side of Plank Road and force its way through the thickets and scrub forest to make contact with Ewell's corps and thereby close the gap between the two Confederate corps. At the same time, the division of Major General Henry Heth, leading Hill's column, was ordered to deploy across the Plank Road in a line of battle, ready to face an attack coming from the east.

Some two miles away to the north, across the band of wilderness that separated the two rebel columns, Ewell had run into the division of Brigadier General Charles Griffin, of Warren's U.S. Fifth Corps. Halted by Meade's order to discontinue the advance, Griffin had had his troops hurriedly dig a line of breastworks across the turnpike and then had sent out skirmishers a half mile or so to locate the rebel column that was moving toward him.

Guided by Lee's instructions to avoid a general engagement until Longstreet's corps arrived, Ewell sat waiting. And Griffin, though Grant desired immediate engagement, had not received Meade's instructions given to General Warren, from whom Griffin took his orders. Warren had been told by Meade, "If there is to be any fighting this side of Mine Run, let's do it right off."[9]

While Griffin's division was stalled behind its newly built breastworks on the turnpike, the three other divisions of Warren's corps were stretched out for three miles along a narrow, rough road that led off the turnpike to the southwest, passing through the woods, past Chewning's farm, and ending at Parker's Store on the Plank Road, which had been Warren's original objective in Grant's battle plan. The leading units of that hemmed-in column, with which Warren was riding, constituted the left flank of Warren's corps, while the breastworks astride the turnpike formed his right.

When the order finally did reach Griffin, he was reluctant to obey it, being persuaded that the Confederates were about to launch an attack themselves and advising Warren that the Union attack should be delayed. Warren passed that advice to Meade, who, true to his reputation for a quick temper, shot a scalding rebuke at Warren. Warren then had ridden to the front on the turnpike and hand-delivered to Griffin the order to attack. Griffin's troops finally started moving out around one o'clock, advancing down both sides of the turnpike some six hours after the attack had first been ordered.

Griffin's troops hit Ewell's advance brigade, shattering it and driving it back in a rout, killing the brigade commander, and chasing the fleeing rebels through the brush and woods alongside the road for nearly a mile. Meade attempted to press the attack against Ewell's corps, ordering one of Sedgwick's divisions to advance on Griffin's right while Warren's other divisions tried to advance on Griffin's left. Neither effort succeeded. The divisions called in to support the drive never found the front. The area became blanketed with a heavy haze of gunsmoke and smoke from dry, burning leaves that covered the ground, set ablaze by sparks from the massive gunfire. Soldiers of both sides became practically invisible to one another in the thickening smoke, and at last Griffin's attacking units found themselves cut off, their flanks unprotected, and were forced back when Ewell sent in reinforcements, withdrawing all the way back to their line of breastworks, nothing having been gained. The entire Union effort on the turnpike became a disaster, costing hundreds of casualties as units tried to force their way through the woods and underbrush and were repeatedly thwarted by the Wilderness terrain, the smoke and the determined Confederate infantry.

On the Plank Road Hill's corps continued to advance, brushing off minor attacks by Union cavalry as they proceeded toward Brock Road. Around mid-morning Grant and Meade saw the danger in allowing Hill to get much farther. If Hill's force should reach Brock Road and command its intersection with the Plank Road, the Confederates would split the Union forces in two, separating Hancock's corps south of Plank Road from the other corps now clustered along the turnpike. About 10 A.M. Brigadier General George W. Getty, commanding a division of Sedgwick's corps that was positioned near the Wilderness Tavern, was given orders to send a brigade to reinforce Brigadier General Horatio Wright's division, which was struggling against Ewell's troops in the woods near the turnpike, and take the rest of his division, about six thousand men, to the Plank Road, about two miles from his position, turn west and stop Hill's advancing column. Hancock, having reached the vicinity of Todd's Tavern on Brock Road, about four miles south of the Plank Road, was instructed to march his corps northward on Brock Road to the Plank Road, turn west and support Getty.

Immediately responding to orders, Getty marched his division southward on Brock Road to its intersection with Plank Road. Turning westward on Plank Road, Getty could see patrols of Hill's corps moving slowly toward him in the distance. He ordered a line of skirmishers to move out and turn back the rebel patrols, then formed two battle lines across Plank Road, a few hundred yards west of the intersection. He intended to have the lines stretch through the woods and make contact with the left flank of General Warren's line. His skirmishers were able to drive back Hill's patrols, but the troops on the right of Getty's lines, moving through the woods, soon encountered a considerable force of Confederates where Warren's left had been. Getty then decided to hold his lines and wait for the arrival of Hancock's corps.

For two hours he waited while opposing skirmishers swapped musket fire, sending wounded casualties back into their lines for aid, but neither side attempted a big push toward the other. In mid-afternoon, with Grant's patience reaching its limit, Meade dispatched a staff officer to order Getty to launch an attack forthwith and not wait for Hancock. Getty had no sooner received that order than the lead units of Hancock's column were seen coming up Brock Road from the south.

Getty and Hancock held a quick conference, Getty urging an immediate assault, in compliance with the orders he had just received, and Hancock preferring to wait until he could get his troops off narrow, confining Brock Road and into a favorable position. Finally, about four o'clock, Getty sent his men forward, with two of Hancock's divisions joining in the attack, which quickly developed into a furious battle between infantrymen, the artillery rendered nearly unmanageable and virtually useless in the overgrown sapling forest. Riflemen dropped to the ground and lay prone to fire, or took scant cover behind tree trunks, stumps or fallen trees, shooting through curtains of smoke at an unseen but evident enemy, their constant, blind fire taking a toll on both sides. Anyone so foolish as to stand up was almost bound to be hit by the storm of lead tearing through the tree branches and brush.

Colonel Theodore Lyman, one of Meade's staff officers, had been ordered by Meade to go to the intersection of Brock Road and the Plank Road, find Hancock and report back to Meade on the action. Lyman gave his eyewitness account, as seen from the intersection:

> At the dotted cross-road with the plank sat Hancock, on his fine horse — the *preux chevalier* of this campaign — a glorious soldier, indeed! The musketry was crashing in the woods in our front, and stray balls — too many to be pleasant — were coming about. It's all very well for novels, but I don't like such places and go there only when ordered.
>
> "Report to General Meade," said Hancock, "that it is very hard to bring up troops in this wood, and that only a part of my Corps is up, but I will do as well as I can." Up rides an officer: "Sir, General Getty is hard pressed and nearly out of ammunition!" Another officer: "General Mott's division has broken, sir, and is coming back."
>
> "Tell him to stop them, sir!" roared Hancock in a voice of a trumpet. As he spoke, a crowd of troops came from the woods and fell back into the Brock road. Hancock dashed among them. "Halt here! Halt here! Form behind this rifle-pit. Major Mitchell, go to Gibbon and tell him to come up on the double-quick!"
>
> It was a welcome sight to see Carroll's brigade coming along the Brock road, he riding at their head as calm as a May morning. "Left face — prime — forward," and the line disappeared in the woods to waken the musketry with double violence. Carroll was brought back wounded.
>
> Up came Hays's brigade, disappeared in the woods, and, in a few minutes, General Hays was carried past me, covered with blood, shot through the head.[10]

The superior numbers of the Union force gradually worked effects on the rebels, slowly forcing them back, though at heavy cost, the Vermont brigade of Getty's division losing some one thousand men alone. As the afternoon slipped into dusk, the Union line continued to present a formidable front to Hill's Confederate corps. Getty's division and two divisions of Hancock's corps, Major General David Birney's on the right and Brigadier General Gershom Mott's on the left of Getty's, were now joined by the division of Brigadier General James S. Wadsworth, from Warren's corps, which had forced its way through the jungle of Wilderness growth to reach the right side of the Union line and extend it deeper into the woods. Hancock's orders to his division commanders were to drive the rebels back as far as Parker's Store, keeping the Brock Road-Plank Road intersection clear and safe for the passage of Grant's army.

Valiantly persevering, the Confederates were fighting with but two of Hill's divisions, his third division, commanded by Major General Richard H. Anderson, being still on the march from Orange and not expected to arrive at the front until morning. By day's end, the two divisions were steadily losing ground, their line in disarray. The enveloping darkness then suddenly became a timely ally. With nightfall, the noise of gunfire diminished, but was replaced by the sound of axes crashing against trees as troops on both sides cut down saplings to fashion hasty breastworks of logs.

While the troops labored, braving sporadic musket fire, a new menace appeared. Flames from burning leaves were spreading across the forest floor, and from the woods there erupted piteous cries from the wounded who still lay where they had fallen, helpless and a mortal danger to comrades who had to face enemy gunfire in trying to save them from the flames. In one case, the wounded soldier, apparently a member of the Fifth Maine Regiment, called out for help as the flames neared him, and when two comrades ran out to get him, they were struck down by rebel gunfire. Risking no more men, a Union sergeant, by the light of the blaze, lifted his musket and from a distance shot the wounded soldier to death to save him from the agony of being burned alive. In another case, a wounded and helpless Confederate soldier, facing death, repeatedly cried out Jesus's desperate words of despair on the cross, "My God, my God, why hast thou forsaken me!" According to one estimate, at least two hundred Union soldiers died in flames during the night.[11]

Grant's troops nevertheless had come within hours of a breakthrough that could have shattered Lee's army and hastened an end to the entire conflict. But darkness had intervened. At his headquarters in the field Grant now determined to resume the fight as soon as possible, at first light on the new day, Friday, May 6. Grant was aware that Longstreet's corps was on the move, hurrying to Lee's aid, and Grant was eager to strike Lee's front again before Longstreet's additional twenty thousand troops arrived. Grant told Meade to have Hancock's divisions resume the attack at 4:30 A.M. Meade pleaded for more time to give the men rest, urging that the attack begin at six. Grant relented only slightly, moving the resumption to five o'clock.

The plan, as related by Brigadier General Horace Porter, then a lieutenant colonel on Grant's staff, was for Hancock and Wadsworth to make an attack on Hill, beginning at five o'clock, "so as to strike him if possible before Longstreet could arrive to reinforce him. Burnside, who would arrive early in the morning with three divisions, was to send one division ([Brigadier General Thomas G.] Stevenson's) to Hancock, and to put the other two divisions between Wadsworth and Warren's other divisions, and attack Hill's flank, or at least obliquely, while Warren and Sedgwick were to attack along their fronts, inflict all the damage they could, and keep the troops opposed to them from reinforcing Hill and Longstreet. Burnside's fourth division was to guard the wagon trains."[12]

Always trying to think the thoughts of his foe, General Lee anticipated Grant's new move against Hill's embattled troops and, attempting to draw Grant's attention away from Plank Road and relieve the pressure on Hill, at least till Longstreet could enter the fight, he ordered Ewell to commence a heavy fire on Warren's forces on the turnpike first thing in the morning. The attempt failed. Ewell's assault began moments after Hancock's first wave of skirmishers moved forward and set off an intense exchange of musket fire up and down the advancing Union line. Warren's forces at the same time remained steadfastly in position.

Hancock's force, along with Wadsworth's division, which had lost 60 percent of its troops the day before, swung toward Lee's right flank, and under the immense pressure, the Confederate right began to yield. "We are driving them!" Hancock excitedly told a colonel from Meade's staff who came to get a report on the action. "Tell General Meade we are driving them most beautifully!" When the colonel informed Hancock that the lead divisions of Burnside's corps were about to enter the fray, Hancock all but leaped for joy, exclaiming, "If he could attack now, we would smash A.P. Hill all to pieces!"[13]

Within an hour of the launching of the assault, Hancock's men had advanced more than a mile on the Plank Road, so far westward that Lee's supply train was threatened. Lee himself rode up to the front to rally his rebels and seeing the danger they faced, ordered the wagon train be made ready to roll for a speedy escape. Riding along the Plank Road, through the smoke and noise and confusion, troops streaming past him as they headed for the rear, he became surrounded by the retreating South Carolina brigade commanded by Brigadier General Samuel McGowan, a brigade with a reputation for fighting hard. When he spied McGowan among the troops, he shouted to him from atop Traveler, "My God, General McGowan! Is this splendid brigade of yours running like a flock of geese!"

"General, this men are not whipped," McGowan answered. "They only want a place to form and they will fight as well as they ever did."[14]

In desperation, four batteries of Lee's artillery commanded by Lieutenant Colonel William Poague had planted a line of metal on the west side of a clearing, one of the very few in the Wilderness, the guns' menacing muzzles pointing toward the fleeing Confederates and the advancing Union infantry behind them, the cannoneers waiting for the area to clear of rebels before opening on the bluecoats with grape and canister in a last-ditch effort to halt their advance. Then Hill, fearful that the guns would be captured during the delay and anxious to do something to stop the advance, gave the order to commence firing into the woods, firing just over the heads of the retreating rebel infantrymen. After several rounds, the firing stopped, and into the area slashed by rebel artillery dashed about twenty counterattacking Confederate infantrymen, quickly followed by a host of their comrades. Lee watched them and shouted out, "Who are you, my boys?"

"Texas boys!" they shouted back. They were from the lead brigade of Major General Charles W. Field's division, from Longstreet's corps. Just in the nick of time, Longstreet had finally arrived.

"Hurrah for Texas!" Lee yelled and waved his hat in a rare display of exuberance. "Hurrah for Texas!"[15] He became so carried away by the Texans' timely arrival and their immediate, fearless plunge into action, that he had to be restrained from joining them in the charge against the oncoming Union troops. A sergeant grabbed Traveler's bridle and halted both horse and rider. Lee's attention was then diverted to Longstreet himself, who urged him to move farther to the rear.

Two divisions of Longstreet's corps deployed into a line across the Plank Road, Brigadier General Joseph Kershaw's division on the right side of the road and General Field's on the left. They opened a gap to allow the retreating troops of Heth's division to pass through their line, jeering them as they did, then moved forward to meet the oncoming bluecoats. After minutes spent regrouping, the battered divisions of Heth and Wilcox were positioned on the left of the new line. Lee, realizing his lapse of composure, turned over to Longstreet, his senior general, the direction of the counterattack and withdrew to oversee the further deployment of his artillery.

The ten thousand fresh troops of Longstreet's corps now became the driving force of a renewed Confederate movement. At the same time, the Union troops became so disarranged that their forward movement stalled. Wadsworth's diminished division had arrived at the Plank Road, driving the Confederates back, but had come onto the road obliquely, shoving the troops of Birney's division off to the left, breaking their formations, creating alternating gaps and crowding along a now confused line. Longstreet's men hit the Union line just then, striking Birney's left first, and the Union troops now struggled to avoid being turned back. Around 7 A.M. Hancock sent Meade a message saying, "They are pressing us on the road a good deal. If more force were here now I could use it, but I don't know whether I can get it in time or not."[16] Meade promised help, but for some reason still unknown, none came. Colonel Lyman, Meade's aide, described the scene on the road:

> Birney's and Getty's men held fast and fought with fury, a couple of guns were put in the plank road and began to fire solid shot over the heads of our men, adding their roar to the other din. The streams of wounded came faster and faster back; here a field officer, reeling in the saddle; and there another, hastily carried past on a stretcher. I stood at the crossing and assisted in turning back stragglers or those who sought to go back, under pretext of helping the wounded. To some who were in great pain I gave some opium, as they were carried past me....[17]

A Confederate eyewitness described the scene in the woods: "These bullets all seemed to go through [the trees at] about the height of a man's waist. In tumbling down, [the trees] made almost an impassable barrier. Together with this obstacle the dead and the dying were so thick that we could not help stepping on them."[18] The Texans whom Lee had cheered so enthusiastically lost nearly two-thirds of their men. Other rebel brigades also suffered heavy casualties. A reporter for the New York *Tribune* wrote: "No room in that jungle for maneuvering; no possibility of a bayonet charge; no help from cavalry, nothing but close, square, face-to-face volleys of fatal musketry. The wounded stream out, and fresh troops pour in. Stretchers pass out with ghastly burdens and go back reeking with blood for more."[19]

Nevertheless, by ten o'clock the Confederate reinforcements had not only stopped the Union advance against Hill's corps, but had forced Grant's troops back to the positions from which they had started at daybreak. Lee now was thinking, as he had been since the evening before, of a way to turn Grant's left flank south of the Plank Road, then hitting him on the flank and front simultaneously. He sent the Army of Northern Virginia's chief engineer, Major General Martin L. Smith, over to Longstreet to confer about the possibilities, and Longstreet directed Smith to reconnoiter the area south of the Plank Road to see if there might be a way to cut through the woods and slip past the Union left. Smith returned with the news that he had discovered an unfinished and abandoned railroad that led, evidently, from Orange to Fredericksburg, not far south of the Plank Road. It did not appear on the maps the Confederates were using. The line passed through a long cut that would allow Longstreet's troops to march around the Union left flank.

About 11 A.M. the sounds of battle burst through the woods from the direction of the cut. Three brigades of Longstreet's corps, commanded by Longstreet's adjutant general, Lieutenant Colonel Moxley Sorrel, had made their way through the cut and fallen on the Army of the Potomac's left flank and were driving the bluecoats northward back toward the Plank Road. A few units of the pursuing brigades had already crossed the road. The rebel army was attacking from both the west and the south. Victory over Grant, as over his predecessors, was now for Lee a shining promise.

General Longstreet, eager to be among his wildly cheering, eagerly pursuing troops, rode off to the northward-moving front, dangerously alive with heated action. A Confederate artillery major, Robert Stiles, was also riding to the front, seeking a position where his field pieces might be placed to good effect. He described the events that followed his approach to the scene of the furious action:

> I had been sent forward, perhaps to look for some place where we might get into the fight, when I observed an excited gathering some distance back of the lines, and pressing toward it I heard that General Longstreet had just been shot down and was being put into an ambulance. I could not learn anything definite as to the character of his wound, but only that it was serious — some said he was dead. I followed it a little way, being anxious for trustworthy news of the General. The members of his staff surrounded the vehicle, some riding in front, some

on one side and some on the other, and some behind. One, I remember, stood upon the rear step of the ambulance, seeming to desire to be as near him as possible. I never on any occasion during the four years of the war saw a group of officers and gentlemen more deeply distressed. They were literally bowed down with grief. All of them were in tears. One, by whose side I rode for some distance, was himself severely hurt, but he made no allusion to his wound, and I do not believe he felt it. It was not alone the general they admired who had been shot down — it was, rather, the man they loved.

I rode up to ambulance and looked in. They had taken off Longstreet's hat and coat and boots. The blood had paled out of his face and its somewhat gross aspect was gone. I noticed how white and dome-like his great forehead looked and, with scarcely less reverent admiration, how spotless white his socks and his fine gauze undervest, save where the black red gore from his breast and shoulder had stained it. While I gazed at his massive frame, lying so still, except when it rocked inertly with the lurch of the vehicle, his eyelids frayed apart till I could see a delicate line of blue between them, and then he very quietly moved his unwounded arm and, with his thumb and two fingers, carefully lifted the saturated undershirt from his chest, holding it up a moment, and heaved a deep sigh. "He is not dead," I said to myself, "and he is calm and entirely master of the situation — he is both greater and more attractive than I have heretofore thought him."[20]

Longstreet, the old warhorse, as Lee affectionately called him, had been hit in the throat and shoulder, accidentally shot by his own men in the confusion of a battle occurring just four miles from the site near Chancellorsville where Stonewall Jackson was shot by his men a year earlier. Longstreet would survive his wounds, but his services to Lee and the Confederate cause would be lost for months.

The loss of Longstreet stunned his troops, who by now had encountered a problem similar to the one that had earlier snagged the Union forces. General Field, who took command when Longstreet was wounded, explained it: "My division and some others probably were perpendicular to the [Plank] road and in line of battle, whilst all those which had acted as a turning force were in line parallel to the road, and the two were somewhat mixed up. No advance could possibly be made till the troops parallel to the road were placed perpendicular to it."[21] While the rebel troops halted to regroup, Hancock was given time to regroup also and to position his men behind the entrenchments they had earlier constructed, facing the Confederates several hundred yards to the west. By 3 P.M. the slowed fury had let the battle degenerate into little more than an exchange of sporadic volleys of musket fire.

Grant now called for a new assault. He sent orders to Hancock and Burnside to have them resume the offensive at 6 P.M.

Lee had the same idea. About 4:15 P.M. a new Confederate assault commenced. When the left side of the Union line could not be budged, Lee rode over to the Union's right side about five-thirty and found Ewell and Lieutenant General Jubal Early and thirty-one-year-old Brigadier General John B. Gordon, one of Early's brigade commanders, conferring together. Lee asked them what they could do to take some of the pressure off the Confederate right side. "Cannot something be done on this flank?" he wanted to know. The left side of Lee's line had been stalemated all day, and Ewell and Early could think of nothing more they could do. Gordon then entered the discussion and said he had discovered that the extreme right of the Union line was exposed. He had earlier reported the same thing to Ewell and asked permission to attack, but Ewell insisted the Union right flank was supported by Hooker's Ninth Corps and had denied permission. Lee, apparently knowing Gordon's observation was correct, now ordered Gordon to make the attack.

Gordon quickly answered the order and met with some success as his brigade, supported by twenty-seven-year-old Brigadier General Robert D. Johnston's brigade, advanced across a mile of Sedgwick's Union line and took some six hundred prisoners, but by then darkness had crept over the armies' positions, and the attack had to be called off. Frustrated, Lee rode back to his headquarters at the Tapp house, the growing night revealing the countless fires burning in the woods, smoke everywhere in the air, frantic cries for help sounding from the flaming thickets.

As the second day of the Battle of the Wilderness drew to an indecisive close, the casualty lists grew longer. The estimates of the total casualties vary, from fourteen thousand to more than eighteen thousand on the Union side, counting more than twenty-two hundred killed — a fairly consistent estimate among the sources — nine thousand to twelve thousand wounded, and more than three thousand captured or missing. On the Confederate side the estimates of total casualties range from seventy-five hundred to more than eleven thousand. The higher estimates count about fifteen hundred killed, about eight thousand wounded and about seventeen hundred captured or missing.

At the end of the second day Lee was left wondering what Grant would do next. Would he, like Hooker a year earlier, recross the Rapidan and retreat northward, or would he break off and turn eastward along the Rappahannock, or would he fight another day before doing anything different, or what? Lee's feelings told him that Grant would fight at least one more day. And so during the night of May 6 and the dark early morning of May 7 the troops on the right side of Lee's line worked at constructing formidable entrenchments, preparing for a renewal of the Union assault on their section of the line, where a new assault seemed most likely.

Grant was not wondering. He had already decided what he was going to do and after a refreshing night's sleep he was up at daybreak. At six-thirty that foggy, smoky morning he wrote instructions for Meade, issued some other orders, then sat down to a relaxed breakfast with some of his staff officers.

The officers and men of Lee's infantry in their strengthened entrenchments stood ready to face the enemy's new assault at dawn on the 7th. None came. The morning wore on, without a sign of a movement against their position. While hours passed, the sole sounds of combat were from pickets exchanging a few shots now and then. Then Lee received intelligence that Grant's cavalry had withdrawn from the area, and from the far left of the Confederate line came a report from General Early that the Union position in front of his division had been abandoned. The Union troops had picked up and left.

To Lee that news meant that Grant was no longer concerned with protecting his line of communication across the Rapidan at Germanna Ford. And *that* meant Grant was not retreating. He was not planning to recross the Rapidan, at least not at Germanna. He and his army were on the move to somewhere. But where exactly?

The Red River Debacle,
March 2 to May 21, 1864

General Sherman felt it was important to have a face-to-face meeting with Nathaniel Banks — and for good reason. Banks was one of the politicians whom President Lincoln had appointed generals despite their having had no military training or experience, and he was about to lead an expedition up the Red River in Louisiana, taking ten thousand of Sherman's troops with him.

Banks had risen from childhood poverty to become, by age forty-eight, a lawyer, a congressman from Massachusetts, speaker of the U.S. House of Representatives, governor of Massachusetts and, since May 1861, a major general in the U.S. Army. His service in the field, mostly in Virginia, was a history of failures and had made him the butt of Confederate jokes. He lost such large quantities of Union supplies to the rebels that Jeb Stuart called him "the best commissary or quartermaster general that Stonewall Jackson ever had."[1] But Lincoln stuck by him, and in November 1862 he was sent to New Orleans, which had been captured from the Confederacy the previous April, to replace General Butler, another politician general, as commander of the U.S. Army's Department of the Gulf, which embraced southeastern Louisiana and the coastal parts of Texas, Mississippi and Florida.

Always a charming politician, he had, with the aid of his wife, made his presence felt in New Orleans society as well as in the affairs of the city. "The Bankses," according to one account, "with their fashionable clothes, bodyguards, servants, and stylish airs, were comparable to royalty. Mrs. Banks had her weekly receptions at the St. Charles [Hotel] and all the 'best ladies appear there in lace and diamonds.'"[2] Somewhat of a dandy, trim and dashing in his tailored uniforms, Banks became known in New Orleans as "the dancing master."

On March 2, having traveled from Vicksburg by steamer, Sherman arrived in New Orleans and, as he wrote in his memoir, "found General Banks, with his wife and daughter, living in a good house, and he explained to me fully the position and strength of his troops, and his plans of action for the approaching campaign."[3]

The plans, ordered from Washington, involved a whole set of ambitious objectives. One was to show a military presence that would quash any plot against Texas or the United States that might be in the mind of the emperor of France, Napoleon the Third, who had put French troops in Mexico two years earlier and was, in March 1864, a month away from

46

installing the Austrian archduke Maximilian as emperor of Mexico. Another objective assigned to Banks was to secure areas of Texas and provide encouragement to Union loyalists in Texas, in hopes that Confederate control could be vanquished and the state promptly returned to the Union.

The president's political considerations were a big part of the plans. A national election was coming up in November, and its outcome was far from certain. Restoring Texas to the Union would allow Texas to cast votes in the Electoral College, and those votes could be expected to go to President Lincoln. Louisiana was being groomed for a similar role. Banks was not only an army commander but was also Louisiana's military governor and had been instructed by Lincoln to replace Louisiana's secessionist government with a new one loyal to the United States, an action that could bring the state back into the Union fold. Banks had arranged an election, and on February 22 Michael Hahn, the loyalist candidate, a Bavarian immigrant, lawyer and newspaper publisher, had been elected Louisiana's governor.

Once a new state government, including the new governor, a new legislature and a new state constitution, was completely formed and Louisiana was back in the Union, the state's electoral votes in November were expected to go to Lincoln. Banks's expedition into Louisiana's heartland was intended to hasten the state's return to the Union.

And then there was cotton, probably the most important objective in the planned Red River campaign that Banks would lead. Called "King Cotton," it was America's leading export, a commodity vital not only to the economy of the United States but to the economy of much of Europe. The enormous textile industry of Great Britain alone processed some four hundred thousand tons of cotton annually, and 77 percent of that cotton came from the American South. The wartime blockade that had virtually shut off shipments of cotton from the South had idled a third of Britain's cotton mills, throwing a half million people out of work. Cotton-mill operators everywhere were hard pressed to keep their businesses going. Many mills in the American Northeast had closed. The government in Washington was feeling intense pressure to do something to relieve the painful shortage, while cotton prices had shot up from around ten cents a pound before the war to as much as $1.89 a pound by 1864.

For those who could get their hands on it — and ship it out to the open market — the potential profits were dizzying. The entire Mississippi River valley, according to one account, "seethed with cotton speculation."[4] Civilians and members of the military alike tried ways legal and illegal to obtain and sell whatever cotton they could find. Some army and navy officials, on both sides of the conflict, confiscated all the cotton they could discover, for their own enrichment. Characterizing cotton speculators, Rear Admiral David Dixon Porter, commander of U.S. naval forces on the Mississippi River and soon to become part of the Red River expedition, claimed that "a greater pack of villains never went unhung"— although he was not one to pass up an opportunity to acquire cotton himself.

Banks had received reports — perhaps merely rumors — that tens of thousands of bales of cotton were stockpiled in the western parts of Louisiana and that they could be seized or purchased cheap. That information was helping Banks change his mind about taking an expedition up the Red River, a mission he had once steadfastly opposed.

At the time he was first sent to New Orleans, Banks was told by General Halleck, then the Army's general in chief, that President Lincoln considered the opening of the Mississippi River "the first and most important of all our military and naval operations,"[5] and so Banks's primary objective had been to free the lower Mississippi from Confederate control. After a two-year struggle, the Mississippi was at last opened following Grant's victory at Vicksburg on July 4, 1863 and the surrender of Port Hudson, Louisiana four days later. Now, in March 1864, spurred by Lincoln to get on with the task of returning Louisiana to the Union and lured by the seductive call from those reported huge stockpiles of cotton, Banks had agreed to launch the Red River expedition.

Also won over was Sherman, who four weeks before going to New Orleans to meet with Banks, wrote to him and told him, "I will be most happy to take part in the proposed expedition, and hope, before you have made your final dispositions, that I will have the necessary permission."[6] Sherman never received the necessary permission and by the time he left for New Orleans he knew he would not take part in the expedition. At that time General Grant commanded the Military Division of the Mississippi, which included Sherman's command, the Department of the Tennessee, but it did not include Banks's jurisdiction. "General Banks," Sherman remarked, "was acting on his own powers, or under the instructions of General Halleck in Washington, and our [Sherman's] assistance to him was designed as a loan of ten thousand men for a period of thirty days...."[7]

Grant had opposed the Red River expedition, but, he said, had "acquiesced because it was the order of my superior at the time."[8] His acquiescence meant the loan of those ten thousand men from Sherman's corps, troops he expected to get back within thirty days, on successful completion of the Red River mission, so that they — and Banks — could be used in Grant's overall plan, which included the capture of Mobile, turning it from a Confederate base of supply into a Union base for Deep South operations.

Propelled by the president's desires, by Halleck's orders and by Banks's newfound enthusiasm, the Red River expedition got under way. The expedition's plan called for the convergence in Shreveport, in the northwest corner of Louisiana, of four different forces: 17,000 troops from Banks's command, who would move up along Bayou Teche, headed first for Alexandria; 15,000 men from Major General Frederick Steele's Department of Arkansas, who would march from Little Rock down into Louisiana, headed first for Monroe, then for Shreveport; the 10,000 men from Sherman's command, headed for a rendezvous with Banks's force in Alexandria; and a Navy fleet composed of thirteen ironclads and seven lightly armored, shallow-draft gunboats, called tinclads, including the *Black Hawk*, then the flagship of Admiral Porter, commanding the naval part of the operation.

Banks's units started from Berwick Bay, near Morgan City (then known as Brashear City), on March 7, running days behind schedule for the planned March 17 rendezvous in Alexandria, and they soon ran into more delays, caused by heavy rains that turned muddy roads into quagmires. On March 9 Banks, still in New Orleans working on forming a new state government, sent word that he would be further delayed in joining his troops, who were under the command of Major General William B. Franklin.

On March 10 Sherman's troops, commanded by Brigadier General Andrew Jackson (A.J.) Smith, boarded transports that carried them down the Mississippi from Vicksburg and on March 12 turned up the Red River to take them as far as Simmesport, where they disembarked under the protection of the fleet's guns and began their overland march to Alexandria, pressing back whatever Confederate troops they encountered as they moved northward. By then Smith had received a wire from Banks informing him that because of the delays, Banks's troops would not be able to reach Alexandria before March 21.

In Arkansas General Steele, for his own reasons, was not moving at all, but he sent word to Sherman that when he got around to participating in the expedition he could send only seven thousand troops, not the 15,000 Banks was expecting. The combined armies of

Banks and A.J. Smith alone, Steele told Sherman, would be enough to drive the Confederates into the Gulf of Mexico.[9]

While four of the gunboats proceeded up the Red River to clear away obstructions known to have been planted in the river, Smith's troops marched up beside the river without significant opposition, scattering rebel defenders as they went. Their first objective was the rebels' Fort DeRussy, a formidable earthworks fortification that stood beside the river about thirty miles northwest of Simmesport and about twenty-five miles below Alexandria, presenting a threat to Union vessels moving up the river. Reaching the fort on the morning of March 14 and drawing the fire of its guns, Smith instructed Brigadier General Joseph Mower to have his division assault it while the remainder of Smith's force fended off a possible rebel attack on its left flank. A valiant leader who had served in the Mexican War as a private, who had been commissioned and had risen rapidly in grade by virtue of his fighting ability, Mower ordered his men to charge the works. Two brigades dashed forward under covering fire from Mower's skirmishers that forced the rebel defenders to keep their heads down. The Union troops swiftly swarmed over the fort's parapets, confronted the heavily outnumbered 350-man Confederate garrison and forced its surrender. Mower's casualties were three killed and thirty-five wounded. Confederate casualties totaled five killed, four wounded and most of the rest of the garrison taken prisoner. Captured, too, were the fort's ten guns. The battle had lasted about twenty minutes.

The way to Alexandria, by river and by land, was now clear. Once the obstructions were removed from the river below Fort DeRussy, Admiral Porter's vessels steamed up to the fort, where the transports on the evening of March 15 took most of A.J. Smith's troops aboard to carry them to Alexandria, leaving behind the command of Brigadier General Thomas Kilby Smith to destroy the fort. Mower's troops entered Alexandria and relieved the 180 U.S. sailors who under the command of Lieutenant Commander [later Captain] Thomas O. Selfridge, captain of the ironclad *Osage*, on the morning of March 16 had moved into the town, recently abandoned by the Confederates, and occupied it, awaiting the arrival of the Army.

Banks's troops, originally scheduled to rendezvous with A.J. Smith's force at Alexandria on March 17, did not start arriving until March 19, when Banks's cavalry showed up. It was not until March 26 that Banks's entire force assembled in Alexandria. Banks himself had arrived by the 24th and had set up a headquarters in Alexandria. On March 27, when General Grant's orders dated March 15 caught up with him, Banks learned the intentions that Grant, now lieutenant general and the Army's general in chief, had for Banks's army and the Red River expedition. A.J. Smith's troops were to rejoin Sherman's army for the campaign against Atlanta, and Banks's army was to take Mobile. The Red River expedition was to complete its tasks as soon as possible and was not to hinder the planned campaigns against Atlanta and Mobile. If Shreveport was not taken by April 25, A.J. Smith and his men were to pull out of the expedition and return to Vicksburg—even, Grant's orders stated, if doing so "should lead to the abandonment of the expedition."[10] Grant also instructed Banks to turn over the defense of the Red River to General Steele and the Navy. He was to abandon all of Texas except the Rio Grande, which he was to hold with not more than four thousand men.[11]

With those orders in his hands, Banks faced a big decision. He had less than a month to capture Shreveport before his army would be split apart and even if he took Shreveport by then, its use as a base for operations in Texas, a large part of the rationale for going to the trouble of taking Shreveport, had been foreclosed by Grant's order. Except for the cotton, what was the point of continuing the expedition? Why not abort the expedition now? The cotton, however, mattered a great deal, and Banks decided to continue on toward Shreveport.

Lieutenant Commander Selfridge's gunboat, the *Osage*, was one of the vessels that were ordered to proceed up the Red River above Alexandria to support the movement of the troops on their march to Shreveport. Selfridge described that action:

> On March 29th fourteen of the squadron left Alexandria for the upper river, the *Eastport* and *Osage* being in the advance; thus fourteen days of precious time had been lost [from the time the gunboats and transports had first reached Alexandria], allowing the Confederates to concentrate their forces for the defense of Shreveport, our objective point. As we advanced [,] the enemy's scouts set fire to all the cotton within ten miles of the river-bank. Millions of dollars worth of it were destroyed, and so dense was the smoke that the sun was obscured, and appeared as though seen through a smoked glass. One Sunday morning a man was seen waving a white handkerchief in front of a handsome dwelling. Captain Phelps and myself stopped and went ashore to inquire the reason. He told us his name was Colhoun; that he was a brother of Captain Colhoun of the United States navy; that, being over age, he had taken no part in the conflict, but had remained at home cultivating his plantation. With tears in his eyes he told us that that night his cotton pile, of 5000 bales, had been set on fire, and his gin-house, costing $30,000, destroyed. He was a rich man the night before, and the morning found him penniless. A bale of cotton was worth at that time $400 in New Orleans, so that he had lost at a single blow $2,000,000. He was but one of many innocent persons who suffered the loss of all their property through this indiscriminate destruction.
>
> Our supply of coals having given out, we were dependent upon fence rails for fuel. Two hours before sunset the fleet and transports would tie up to the bank, and whole crews and companies of soldiers would range over the country, each man loading himself with two rails, and in an incredibly short time the country would be denuded of fences as far as the eye could see. So dependent were we upon these rails for fuel that it was a saying among the Confederates that they should have destroyed the fences and not the cotton. Had they done so, our progress would have been much slower. As it was, it proved a laborious task for the crews of the gun-boats to cut up these cotton-wood rails in lengths to fit the furnaces, which were much shorter than those of the transports.[12]

On April 7 Admiral Porter left Grand Ecore, about halfway between Alexandria and Shreveport, on the tinclad *Cricket*, bound for Shreveport. Along with one other tinclad and four ironclads, he was convoying the twenty transports bearing the seventeen hundred troops of Kilby Smith's division to Springfield Landing, where they were to rendezvous with the troops moving toward Shreveport by land. The river then, Selfridge reported, was "at a lower stage than usual at this season, and there was barely water to float the gun-boats."[13]

On April 10 the fleet of gunboats and transports arrived at Springfield Landing, "about 30 miles, as the crow flies, from its destination [Shreveport], meeting with no obstructions beyond the usual bushwhacking," Selfridge reported. At Springfield Landing, though, "the channel was found obstructed by the sinking of a large steamboat, the *New Falls City*, across the channel, both ends resting upon the banks."[14] There the convoy was forced to halt, stymied by the scuttled Confederate steamboat blocking its way.

There also Admiral Porter, having received a message by courier from General Banks, summoned the fleet's commanders to a meeting aboard his flagship, *Cricket*, to be told the disastrously bad news he had just received. Banks and his army had turned around and were headed back toward Alexandria.

The Confederates who had repeatedly fallen back before the advance of Banks's troops moving up the west side of the Red River had been reinforced and under the command of

Major General Richard Taylor (son of former U.S. President Zachary Taylor) had formed a battle line at Sabine Crossroads, just below Mansfield, some thirty miles from Shreveport, and there, eleven thousand strong, they had awaited the approach of Banks's forces. The Union troops had arrived at mid-morning on Friday, April 8 and had begun forming a line of battle. About four o'clock in the afternoon, after a series of exchanges between skirmishers of both sides, Taylor, although outnumbered, had launched an attack on both flanks of the Union front. Two Union divisions were rolled up, and the whole Union line was driven back.

By nightfall that attack had been beaten off, but at 2 A.M. the next day, Saturday, April 9, strengthened by newly arrived reinforcements, Taylor had put his troops in motion to catch Banks's hastily retreating army, in hopes of demolishing it. Late that afternoon the Confederates caught up with it at Pleasant Hill, where A.J. Smith's troops had been left. About 5 P.M. the rebels attacked, Brigadier General Thomas J. Churchill's troops hitting the Union left flank, the weakest part of the line, scattering it and threatening to set off a chain reaction along the extent of the Union position. Smith promptly ordered his veteran warriors to charge the entire Confederate line, Mower's division leading the way. Under that onslaught the Confederates gave way and began falling back in confusion, their formation broken, their retreat taking them back as far as six miles from the front, a lone brigade of cavalry covering their speedy withdrawal.

The Battle of Pleasant Hill was over. In the two days of fighting, Union casualties totaled some four thousand; Confederate losses totaled about thirty-five hundred.

Maj. Gen. Nathaniel Banks. One of President Lincoln's political generals, Banks led the failed Red River campaign, which Navy Capt. Thomas Selfridge called "one of the most humiliating and disastrous [expeditions] that had to be recorded during the war." (LIBRARY OF CONGRESS)

Banks then thought of resuming the advance toward Shreveport, but during the night he decided to continue the retreat to Grand Ecore, and his army was reunited there on April 11. Banks entrenched at Grand Ecore, laid a pontoon bridge across the river, placed a strong detachment on the north side of the river and asked for reinforcements from New Orleans and Texas.

Meanwhile, Porter's fleet was facing danger of its own. Lieutenant Commander Selfridge described the situation:

It was announced [at the commanders' meeting with Admiral Porter on April 10] that it would be necessary for the fleet to go back. The gun-boats were distributed through the transports, and my vessel, the *Osage*, was directed to bring up the rear.

The return of the fleet was fraught with peril: The Confederates, being relieved by the falling back of the army, were now free to attack us at any point of the river. There were but half-a-dozen gun-boats to defend the long line, two of which were light-draughts, known as "tinclads," from the lightness of their armor, which was only bullet-proof. The river was falling; its narrowness and its high banks afforded the best possible opportunities for harassing attacks, and the bends of the river were so short that it was with the greatest difficulty they were rounded by vessels of the *Osage* type. Steaming with the current, the *Osage* was almost unmanageable, and on the morning of April 12th the transport *Black Hawk* was lashed to her starboard quarter, and thus the descent was successfully made till about 2 P.M., when the *Osage* ran hard aground opposite Blair's Plantation, or Pleasant Hill Landing, the bows down stream and the starboard broadside bearing on the right bank. While endeavoring to float her, the pilot of the *Black Hawk* reported a large force gathering in the woods some three miles off dressed in Federal uniforms. I ascended to the pilot-house, and scanning them carefully made sure they were Confederates, and at the same time directed Lieutenant Bache of the *Lexington* to go below and open an enfilading fire upon them.... The [Confederate] battery unlimbered near the *Lexington*, but a caisson being blown up they quickly withdrew. The enemy came up in column of regiments, and, protected by the high and almost perpendicular banks, opened a terrific musketry fire, and at a distance not exceeding one hundred yards. Shell-firing under the circumstances was almost useless. The great guns of the *Osage* were loaded with grape and canister, and, when these were exhausted, with shrapnel having fuses cut to one second. Our fire was reserved till the heads of the enemy were seen just above the bank, when both guns were fired.... This unequal contest could not continue long, and after an hour and half the enemy retreated with a loss of over four hundred killed and wounded, as afterward ascertained.... The *Osage* sustained a loss of seven wounded....[15]

By April 15 the gunboats and transports were back at Grand Ecore. The worst was yet to come. On the way from Grand Ecore to Alexandria the ironclad *Eastport* struck a torpedo (or mine) eight miles below Grand Ecore and sank. With a lot of difficult work and the help of two steam-pump boats, the *Eastport* was repaired and refloated, but twice grounded when its voyage was resumed, and under the threat of rebels along the river bank was ordered blown up to avoid capture. The tinclads *Cricket*, *Juliet* and *Fort Hindman* had gone about twenty miles below Grand Ecore when the rebels opened on them with twenty pieces of artillery. "Nineteen shells went crashing through the *Cricket*," Selfridge reported, "and during the five minutes she was under fire she was struck thirty-eight times and lost twelve killed and nineteen wounded out of a crew of fifty, one third of whom were negroes. The escape of the *Cricket* [the flagship] was almost miraculous, and was largely owing to the coolness and skill of the admiral. The remainder of the squadron turned up stream [to escape the artillery fire], except the two pump-boats, *Champion No. 3* and *No. 5*, which being unarmed [unarmored] were destroyed."[16] The next day the boats got up a head of steam and ran past the Confederate guns despite their heavy fire. The *Juliet* suffered the loss of fifteen killed and wounded, and the *Fort Hindman* seven.

Bailey's dam. Lt. Col. Joseph Bailey designed this dam to raise the level of the Red River in Louisiana and allow the U.S. Navy's retreating gunboats to pass through the river's shallow water to escape the Confederates and what threatened to become a huge naval disaster. (JOHN CLARK RIDPATH)

By April 27 the fleet had reassembled at Alexandria — except for twelve of the gunboats. They were stalled by the low water at the rocky falls just above Alexandria. Colonel Richard B. Irwin, Banks's assistant adjutant general, explained the problem: "In the month that had elapsed since the fleet had, even then with some difficulty, ascended the rapids, the river had fallen more than six feet; for a mile and a quarter the rocks were now bare; there were but three feet four inches of water, the gunboats needing at least seven feet; and in some places the channel, shallow as it was, was narrowed to a mere thread."[17] An unthinkable disaster loomed.

Then someone proposed a possible solution. "From this danger the navy," Colonel Irwin related, "from this reproach the army, from this irreparable disaster the country was saved by the genius and skill of Lieutenant Colonel Joseph Bailey, of the 4th Wisconsin regiment, then serving on General Franklin's staff as chief engineer."[18] Bailey's plan was to build a dam to increase the river's depth enough to allow the boats to slip over the rocks and the falls and into the deeper water below the falls. The dam would be constructed with a gap, or gate, through which the boats could shoot when the water was deep enough.

"It seemed almost an impossibility to accomplish what had before been attempted without success in more peaceful times," Selfridge remarked, "but it was only necessary to propose the plan for both army and navy to enter into the scheme with characteristic American energy."[19]

Irwin described the project and the results: "From the north bank a wing dam was constructed of large trees, the butts tied by cross-logs, the tops toward the current, and kept in place by weighting with stone, brick, and brush. From the cultivated south bank, where large trees were scarce, a crib was made of logs and timbers, filled in with stone and with bricks and heavy pieces of machinery taken from the neighboring sugar-houses and cotton-gins."[20]

The current was rushing through the gap in the dam at a rate of nine miles an hour, while another foot of water was needed to float the larger boats. To close the 150-foot-wide gap, two of the Navy's loaded coal-barges were shipped into it, secured by lines from the river banks.

"The work was begun on the 30th of April and finished on the 8th of May," Irwin related. "The water having been thus raised five feet four and half inches, three of the light-draught boats passed the upper fall on that day. On the morning of the 9th the tremendous pressure of the pent-up waters drove out … the barges, making a gap sixty-six feet wide, and swung them against the rocks below. Through the gap the river rushed in a torrent. The admiral [Porter] at once galloped round to the upper fall and ordered the *Lexington* to run the rapids. With a full head of steam she made the plunge, watched in breathless silence of suspense by the army and the fleet, and greeted with a mighty cheer as she rode in safety below. The three gun-boats (*Osage, Neosho,* and *Fort Hindman*) that were waiting just above the dam followed her down the chute; but six gun-boats and two tugs were still imprisoned by the falling waters."[21]

The problem had only been half solved. Now Colonel Bailey — and the troops of Banks's army — sought the solution's other half. Below the upper falls Bailey built two more wing dams, stretching out from either bank. Those dams raised the river another few inches. "Hawsers were run out from the gun-boats to the shore," Selfridge related, "and these manned by a brigade, and the united force of three thousand men, enlivened with a band of music, dragged them over the bottom till they floated in the deeper water below, and both army and navy breathed more freely in this rescue of the squadron upon seeing them anchored in the stream below Alexandria."[22]

By May 13 all the surviving vessels of the fleet were back at Alexandria. Lost were the gunboat *Eastport*, the two pump boats, *Champion No. 3* and *No. 5*, and two small gunboats, *Covington* and *Signal*. Also lost were the more than two hundred men who had been aboard the two pump boats, and an estimated one hundred and twenty other Navy casualties, including killed, wounded and missing.[23]

Banks's defeated army marched out of Alexandria and reached Simmesport on May 16. On the way, its rear guard came under attack near Yellow Bayou, and in the fight the Union troops suffered 267 casualties. The Confederates lost an estimated 452 killed and wounded.

Colonel Bailey, the engineering genius of the ill-fated expedition, fashioned a bridge out of steamboats for Banks's army to cross the Atchafalaya River, and by May 19 the entire surviving force had safely crossed over. General A.J. Smith's troops, those men borrowed from Sherman's army, embarked on transports bound for Vicksburg shortly thereafter.

When the expedition's cost in men was added up, U.S. Army casualties in the debacle amounted to 454 killed, 2,191 wounded and 2,600 captured or missing. Confederate losses totaled 3,976 killed, wounded, captured or missing.

"On the 21st of May, the squadron and transports reached the Mississippi," Captain Selfridge wrote, concluding his account. "And thus ended the Red River expedition, one of the most humiliating and disastrous that had to be recorded during the war."

All of the expedition's strategic missions having failed, only the acquisition of cotton remained as an accomplished objective. According to one account, Admiral Porter and General Banks competed with each other in securing that objective. While the fleet waited in Alexandria for Banks's arrival Porter had sent his sailors out into the countryside in search of cotton, and they had seized whatever they found. An estimated three thousand bales had been seized by the time Banks arrived. Unable to stop Porter, Banks responded by ordering his troops to take wagons into the countryside and grab whatever cotton they could before Porter's sailors found it. Thousands of bales were reportedly seized by the Army. Without wagons of their own, Navy personnel allegedly stole Army wagons and mules, painted over the wagons' Army designations, rebranded the mules and expanded their quest, roving deeper into the Louisiana countryside.

Rumors inevitably arose that both Porter and Banks had connections to cotton traders and were allowing speculators to join the expedition. Colonel Irwin vigorously defended Banks from such rumors and charges of corruption and rebutted similar charges against the Navy. "I feel it a duty," he responded, "to express my entire disbelief in all the many tales that seek to cast upon the army or its commander the shadow of a great cotton speculation. These stories, as ample in insinuation as they are weak in specification, are false. The speculators who certainly went with the army as far as Alexandria, had for the most part passes from Washington; the policy under which they were permitted to go was avowedly encouraged by the Government, for reasons of state. When General Banks sent them all back from Alexandria, without their sheaves, they returned to New Orleans furious against him and mouthing calumnies.

"All the cotton gathered by the army was turned over first to the chief quartermaster, and by him to the special agent of the Treasury Department designated to receive it. All the cotton seized by the navy was sent to Cairo, was adjudged 'lawful prize of war,' and its proceeds distributed as prescribed by the statute."[24]

When all was said and done, the Red River expedition's one signal success was the dispossession of Louisiana's cotton from its growers and owners. Among the men in the ranks cotton was believed to be the whole reason the expedition was conducted. "Whatever its merits," a soldier in the Forty-seventh Illinois Regiment wrote, "the Red River campaign was viewed ... as a veritable cotton raid for the enrichment of speculators, and was, therefore, extremely repugnant and entered upon ... with ill grace."[25]

For the Union's cause the expedition did have one salutary effect. As a result of the outstanding failure to take Shreveport and secure Louisiana, General Banks, on whom the blame fell like a collapsed building, was swiftly superseded. President Lincoln had at last seen the light: Banks was no military leader, no help in the increasingly vigorous effort to win the war. On May 7 Major General Edward Canby, a West Pointer and veteran of the Mexican War, was appointed commander of a new Military Division of West Mississippi, which included the Department of the Gulf and Arkansas, Banks's command.

The new table of organization having made Canby Banks's superior, on May 18 at Simmesport Canby took over from Banks the command in the field, and Banks returned to New Orleans, still in nominal command of his department but relegated to administrative duties. That was another victory for Grant.

Death at Spotsylvania,
May 7 to May 19, 1864

Before sunrise on May 7 General Grant was up and on his way to breakfast, which he ate seated at a table beside his headquarters campfire as the sun's early rays, seeping through fog and the lingering smoke of the woods fires, brightened the eastern sky. He looked fit and eager after an undisturbed night of rest. Breakfast finished, at six-thirty he issued orders to General Meade, to be relayed to the corps commanders. The entire army was moving out, and Grant specified to Meade how he wanted the move to be made:

> Make all preparations during the day for a night march to take position at Spottsylvania [sic] C. H. [Court House] with one army corps, at Todd's Tavern with one, and another near the intersection of the Piney Branch and Spottsylvania road with the road from Alsop's to Old Court House. If this move is made the [wagon] trains should be thrown forward in the morning to the Ny [sic] River.
>
> I think it would be advisable in making the change to leave Hancock where he is until Warren passes him. He could then follow and become the right of the new line. Burnside will move to Piney Branch Church. Sedgwick can move along the pike to Chancellorsville and on to his destination. Burnside will move on the plank road to the intersection of it with the Orange and Fredericksburg plank road and then follow Sedgwick to his place of destination.
>
> All vehicles should be got out of hearing of the enemy before the troops move, and then move off quietly.[1]

For a while after leaving the breakfast table and issuing his orders, Grant, cigar in hand, sat on a camp stool in front of his tent and talked with his staff, reflecting on the two days of fighting just past. He seemed satisfied with the way it had gone. He realized his losses were severe, but believed the Confederates' losses were worse, although they weren't. He may not have won the Battle of the Wilderness, he conceded, but neither had the Confederates. The rebel forces had gained no advantage despite their repeated attacks. "We remain in possession of the field," he said, pointing out that Lee's army had withdrawn some distance from the front and had gone into a defensive position. He viewed his army's having crossed the Rapidan as a victory in itself, an important achievement in his plan to maneuver around the Confederates' right flank and force them to do battle in open country, outside their prepared positions.

During the day, as his troops made ready for the resumption of their southward march,

Grant received messages informing him that both Sherman and Butler were moving on their parts of the over-all plan, Butler having reached City Point and captured it on May 5 and Sherman having attacked Joe Johnston on that day, the 7th. He also was notified that General Sheridan, already moving southward from Grant's present position, had run into rebel cavalry at Todd's Tavern and had routed them, clearing the way for the Union troops who would be taking the road to Todd's Tavern that night.

A major task to be completed during the day was removing the bridge at the Germanna crossing and erecting it at Ely's Ford so that the wounded of the fighting that lay ahead could be evacuated as speedily as possible. The wagon trains were scheduled to begin rolling at four o'clock that afternoon, to get a head start on the infantry, which would move out at 8:30 P.M. Once the infantrymen had begun their march, the wagons were to move off the road and stop, allowing the infantrymen to pass them.

Shortly after dark General Warren withdrew his Ninth Corps from the front to have it form up in a long column on Brock Road. Grant himself, astride Cincinnati, took to the road not long after nightfall. He described an event at the beginning of the march:

> Warren's march carried him immediately behind the works where Hancock's command lay on the Brock Road. With my staff and a small escort of cavalry I preceded the troops. Meade with his staff accompanied me. The greatest enthusiasm was manifested by Hancock's men as we passed by. No doubt it was inspired by the fact that the movement was south. It indicated to them that they had passed through the "beginning of the end" in the battle just fought. The cheering was so lusty that the enemy must have taken it for a night attack. At all events it drew from him a furious fusillade of artillery and musketry, plainly heard but not felt by us.[2]

Spotsylvania Courthouse, the Union army's destination, comprised the courthouse itself and a village, about ten miles southeast of Grant's Wilderness position. It sat on a three-and-a-half-mile-wide spot on the ridge between the Po and Ni rivers, two small streams with high, wooded banks that made them difficult to cross. As General Humphreys, the Army of the Potomac's chief of staff, pointed out, Spotsylvania Court House had "nothing in its site ... that gave it special military strength. Its military importance was derived from its proximity to the Richmond and Fredericksburg Railroad and the stage and telegraph roads between those towns. Roads also radiated from it in all directions, including a good wagon road to Richmond."[3] Grant wanted to get there because, as he wrote in his memoir, "I did not want Lee to get back to Richmond in time to attempt to crush Butler before I could get there," and because "I wanted to get between his army and Richmond if possible; and if not, to draw him into the open field."[4]

By now General Lee, though, from intelligence he had received and from his instincts had surmised that the destination of Grant's army was Spotsylvania Courthouse, some six miles beyond Todd's Tavern as the Brock Road dived southeastward toward Richmond. Since it seemed obvious that Grant was not retreating, it was toward Richmond that the Union army was headed, Lee assumed, and the Brock Road's path via Spotsylvania Courthouse to Richmond was but half the distance of a route to Richmond through Fredericksburg, which was due east of Grant's Wilderness position and a logical destination only if establishing a new supply line were now Grant's first concern. On that assumption, Lee began to move. He ordered Brigadier General William Pendleton, a onetime Episcopal priest who was now Lee's chief of artillery, to hack out a roadway southward through the smoldering Wilderness woods, roughly paralleling Brock Road and intersecting Catharpin Road at Shady Grove Church, west of Todd's Tavern. The tavern stood at the intersection of Catharpin and Brock roads. On that newly hacked-out roadway, in the dark of night,

Lee would send his troops to Spotsylvania Courthouse in a race to get there ahead of Grant.

The race was not going speedily for either force, but particularly for Grant's army. Around 11 P.M. Grant and Meade were informed that the slow-moving wagons and escort units of their headquarters entourages, positioned at the head of the column of march, were delaying Warren's troops, marching behind them. Grant decided to get out of the way by taking a lesser road, an alternate route, to Todd's Tavern. In attempting to do so, the headquarters party, following a guide, took a wrong turn, moving off to the right and placing themselves in danger of running into Lee's troops advancing on the hacked-out parallel road. In the dark the guide had become confused, and the headquarters party had to backtrack and return to Brock Road. When they reached it, they stationed an orderly at the juncture to give directions to Warren's column when it got that far, to avoid having Warren's men make the same wrong turn. Grant and Meade and the rest of the headquarters party then proceeded on to Todd's Tavern, which they reached about midnight and where they bedded down on the ground in the darkness and awoke the next morning, Sunday, May 8, to find they had been sleeping beside a pig pen.

General Jeb Stuart was doing his best to further slow the Union advance by blocking Brock Road with Confederate cavalry, which could not be dislodged by Grant's cavalrymen. It took the superior numbers of Warren's infantry to move Stuart's troopers out of the way, causing more delay. As the day came on, the Union troops found they had to confront other impediments to their advance. The rebels had felled trees across the road, forcing repeated stops to clear away the obstacles.

The race went to the Confederates. Longstreet's corps, now commanded by Lieutenant General Richard H. Anderson, having marched through the stubble and stumps of the hacked-out roadway, pushed their way to the Catharpin Road during the night, then turned east and arrived at Spotsylvania Courthouse about eight o'clock Sunday morning. They had forgone the break they were intended to take en route, the still burning woods offering no suitable place to bivouac, and had continued to march. General Anderson quickly had his men start digging — or improving on works that had been previously dug — what was to become a jagged, semi-circular, four-mile-long trench on the north and east sides of Spotsylvania Courthouse.

As the leading units of the Union army approached, Grant related, "Warren was not aware of his [Anderson's] presence, but probably supposed it was the cavalry which [Brigadier General Wesley] Merritt [commanding a Union cavalry squadron] had engaged earlier in the day. He [Warren] assaulted at once, but was repulsed. He soon organized his men, as they were not pursued by the enemy, and made a second attack, this time with his whole corps. This time he succeeded in gaining a position immediately in the enemy's front, where he intrenched."[5]

Grant explained the Army of the Potomac's standard operating procedure for entrenching: "…in every change of position or halt for the night, whether confronting the enemy or not, the moment arms were stacked the men intrenched themselves. For this purpose they would build up piles of logs or rails [,] if they could be found [,] in their front, and dig a ditch, throwing the dirt forward on the timber. Thus the digging they did counted in making a depression to stand in, and increased the elevation in front of them. It was wonderful how quickly they could in this way construct defences of considerable strength. When a halt was made with the view of assaulting the enemy, or in his presence, these would be strengthened or their positions changed under the direction of engineer officers."[6]

Battle of Spotsylvania Courthouse. Having moved through the Wilderness, Grant pushed his army southward and to the right of General Lee's defending force, confronting the rebel army at Spotsylvania Courthouse. Among the battle's casualties was Maj. Gen. John Sedgwick, one of Grant's most beloved commanders. (JOHN CLARK RIDPATH)

Sedgwick's Sixth Corps, which had followed Warren's corps, reached Spotsylvania about 5 P.M. Sunday and immediately took a position to the left of Warren's troops and began digging in. A West Point graduate who had been a schoolteacher before the war began, the affable, 50-year-old Sedgwick, known to his men as Uncle John, spent that night sleeping on the ground some distance behind the line of rifle pits his troops were digging. The next morning, Monday, May 9, he was up early to inspect the line and make adjustments to it. While he was doing so, sporadic musket fire erupted from the Confederate line. The Sixth Corps' chief of staff, Major General Martin McMahon, who was with General Sedgwick on the line, recounted what happened then:

> As the bullets whistled by, some of the men dodged. The general said laughingly, "What! What! Men, dodging this way for single bullets! What will you do when they open fire along the whole line? I am ashamed of you. They couldn't hit an elephant at this distance." A few seconds after, a man who had been separated from his regiment passed directly in front of the general, and at the same moment a sharp-shooter's bullet passed with a long shrill whistle very close, and the soldier, who was then just in front of the general, dodged to the ground. The general touched him gently with his foot, and said, "Why, my man, I am ashamed of you, dodging that way," and repeated the remark, "They couldn't hit an elephant at this distance." The man rose and saluted, and said good-naturedly, "General, I dodged a shell once, and if I hadn't, it would have taken my head off. I believe in dodging." The general laughed and replied, "All right, my man; go to your place."

For a third time the same shrill whistle, closing with a dull, heavy stroke, interrupted our talk, when, as I was about to resume, the general's face turned slowly to me, the blood spurting from his left cheek under the eye in a steady stream. He fell in my direction; I was so close to him that my effort to support him failed, and I fell with him.

Colonel Charles H. Tompkins, chief of the artillery, standing a few feet away, heard my exclamation as the general fell, and, turning, shouted to his brigade-surgeon, Dr. Ohlen-schlager. Major Charles A. Whittier, Major T.W. Hyde, and Lieutenant-Colonel Kent, who had been grouped near by, surrounded the general as he lay. A smile remained upon his lips but he did not speak. The doctor poured water from a canteen over the general's face. The blood still poured upward in a little fountain. The men in the long line of rifle-pits, retaining their places from force of discipline, were all kneeling with heads raised and faces turned toward the scene; for the news had already passed along the line....

Returning [from having informed General Meade] I met the ambulance bringing the dead general's body, followed by his sorrowing staff. The body was taken back to General Meade's headquarters, and not into any house. A bower was built for it of evergreens, where, upon a rustic bier, it lay until nightfall, mourned over by officers and soldiers....[7]

While General Sedgwick's body was being transported to his home in Connecticut for burial, death was coming to thousands in days of slaughter at Spotsylvania.

Monday was occupied with the two sides improving their breastworks, and Grant waited until Tuesday, May 10, to make his first major move against the rebel position. Hancock's corps had moved opposite Lee's left flank, but was separated from it—and from the rest of the Army of the Potomac—by the Po River. Seeing the strength opposing his left flank, Lee had shifted troops of Early's command from the right of the rebel line to the left during the night of the 9th, and when Hancock prepared to cross the Po on the morning of May 10, he found the strengthened left side of the Confederate line firmly entrenched on high ground that overlooked the river, with artillery commanding the crossing. After an attack by Early drove back the division at the rear of Hancock's formation, inflicting severe casualties, Hancock gave up his attempt to cross the Po then.

Advised of the reinforcement on the rebel left, Grant realized that Lee had weakened some other part of his line to strengthen the left. He planned to find the weakened spot and exploit it. He ordered attacks by Warren's Fifth Corps and by the Sixth Corps, now commanded by Major General Horatio Wright. Both onslaughts were repulsed with heavy losses, and in the assaults Union Brigadier General T.G. Stevenson was, like Sedgwick the day before, shot dead by a rebel sniper. In the lull that followed the second attack, rebel soldiers left their trenches to scurry out onto the battlefield, where scores of dead and dying Union soldiers lay, and gathered up the muskets and cartridge boxes of the dead and wounded and took them back into their lines to be distributed among their comrades, extra muskets, loaded and ready to fire, being almost as good as repeating rifles. The rebel scavengers also ransacked the haversacks of the Union fallen, seizing whatever coffee, sugar or food they found, sometimes braving Union fire to do so.

Near sundown another Union attack was launched. It, too, was repulsed, and the day's fighting came to an end as night spread over the bloodied field. The next day, Wednesday, May 11, dawned rainy, cold and miserable. No attacks came from Grant's army, but the Confederates noticed some movement on the Union line during the day. From that movement Lee guessed that Grant was again maneuvering toward his left, attempting to flank Lee's right, and anticipating that move, Lee moved most of his artillery from the left and center of his line and ordered his troops to be ready for a quick withdrawal that night.

At the center of the Confederate line, at the spot where the breastworks turned abruptly from facing mostly northward to facing eastward, was a salient that was created when the Confederates found they had to run their line around a hill that dominated their position, lest the Union forces occupy the hill and threaten the entire rebel line. That salient, which was at first called "the Mule Shoe" and would come to be known as "the Bloody Angle," was about 1,200 yards wide at its base and about a mile deep, from its point facing the Union line to its base within the Confederate line. "Such projections on a defensive line," Confederate Major General Evander Law commented, "are always dangerous if held by infantry alone, as an attack upon the point of the angle can only be met by a diverging fire; or if attacked on either face, the troops holding the other face … are more exposed than those on the side attacked. But with sufficient artillery, so posted as to sweep the sides of the angle, such a position may be very strong."[8]

Now, though, Lee had removed from it all but two batteries of his artillery. Major General Edward Johnson, commanding the rebel division defending the salient, on the night of the 11th discovered that a Union force was concentrating on his front and he urgently called for the return of the artillery, expecting a Union assault to come the next morning. At 4 A.M. on the 12th a battalion of Confederate artillery was ordered to return to the salient, but it arrived too late. At dawn a mass of blue-coated infantry emerged from the pines half a mile in front of the salient and rushed to the attack. They came on, General Johnson wrote, 'in great disorder, with a narrow front, but extending back as far as I could see.'"[9]

The artillery that Johnson had urged to be returned reached the salient in time to be seized by the swarming attackers from Hancock's corps, who leaped over the rebel breastworks, struck the defenders in hand-to-hand combat, using their muskets as clubs, overran the salient and captured General Johnson and twenty-eight hundred of his men, practically his whole division. "The whole thing happened so quickly," Law remarked, "that the extent of the disaster could not be realized at once."[10]

Lee, for once, had guessed wrong. But his determined troops would not let his mistake mean defeat. The defenders fell back to a secondary line at the base of the salient, and there they began to rally. Norton Galloway of the Ninety-fifth Pennsylvania Volunteers, a twenty-two-year-old participant, gave his account of the battle:

Upon reaching the second line of Lee's works, held by Wilcox's division, who by this time had become apprised of the disaster to their comrades, Hancock met with stern resistance, as Lee in the meantime had been hurrying troops to Ewell from Hill on the right and Anderson on the left, and these were sprung upon our victorious lines with such an impetus as to drive them hastily back toward the left of the salient.

As soon as the news of Hancock's good and ill success reached army headquarters, the Sixth Corps — Upton's brigade being in advance — was ordered to move with all possible haste to his support. At a brisk pace we crossed a line of intrenchments a short distance in our front, and, passing through a strip of timber, at once began to realize our nearness to the foe. It was now about 6 o'clock, and the enemy, reenforced, were making desperate efforts to regain what they had lost. Our forces were hastily retiring at this point before the concentrated attack of the enemy, and these with our wounded lined the road. We pressed forward and soon cleared the woods and reached an insidious fen, covered with dense marsh grass, where we lay down for a few moments awaiting orders. I cannot imagine how any of us survived the sharp fire that swept over us at this point — a fire so keen that it split the blades of grass all about us, the minies moaning in a furious concert as they picked out victims by the score….

Under cover of the smoke-laden rain the enemy was pushing large bodies of troops forward, determined at all hazards to regain the lost ground…. [T]hey were crawling forward … until, reaching a certain point, and raising their usual yell, they charged gallantly up to the very muzzles of our pieces and reoccupied the Angle….

At this moment, and while the open ground in rear of the Confederate works was choked with troops, a section of Battery C, 5th United States Artillery, under Lieutenant Richard Metcalf, was brought into action and increased the carnage by opening at short range with double charges of canister. This staggered the apparently exultant enemy.... The dead and wounded were torn to pieces by the canister as it swept the ground where they had fallen. The mud was half-way to our knees, and by our constant movement we were almost buried at our feet....

Toward dusk preparations were made to relieve us. By this time we were nearly exhausted, and had fired three to four hundred rounds of ammunition per man. Our lips were incrusted with powder from "biting cartridges." Our shoulders and hands were coated with mud that had adhered to the butts of our rifles.

The troops of the Second Corps, who were to relieve us, now moved up, took our position, and opened fire as we fell back a short distance to re-arrange our shattered ranks and get something to eat, which we were sadly in need of. When darkness came on we dropped from exhaustion.

About midnight, after twenty hours of constant fighting, Lee withdrew from the contest at this point, leaving the Angle in our possession. Thus closed the battle of the 12th of May....

On the 13th, early in the day, volunteers were called for to bury the dead. The writer volunteered to assist....

A momentary gleam of sunshine through the gloom of the sky seemed to add a new horror to the scene [at the Angle]. Hundreds of Confederates, dead or dying, lay piled over one another in those [rifle] pits. The fallen lay three or four feet deep in some places, and, with but few exceptions, they were shot in and about the head. Arms, accouterments, ammunition, cannon, shot and shell, and broken foliage were strewn about. With much labor a detail of Union soldiers buried the dead by simply turning the captured breastworks upon them. Thus had these unfortunate victims unwittingly dug their own graves. The trenches were nearly full of muddy water. It was the most horrible sight I had ever witnessed.[11]

Another Union soldier provided another view of the carnage: "From dawn to dusk the roar of the guns was ceaseless; a tempest of shell shrieked through the forest and plowed the field. When night came, the angle of those works where the fire had been hottest, and from which the enemy had finally been driven, had a spectacle for whoever cared to look that would never have enticed his gaze again. Men in hundreds, killed and wounded together, were piled in hideous heaps — some bodies, that had lain for hours under the concentric fire of the battle, being perforated with wounds. The writhing of wounded beneath the dead moved these masses at times; at times a lifted arm or a quivering limb told of an agony not quenched by the Lethe of death around. Bitter fruit this; a dear price it seemed to pay for the capture of a salient angle of an enemy's intrenched work, even though the enemy's loss was terrible."[12]

Meanwhile, a cavalry battle raged nearby. Sheridan, with twelve thousand troopers, had moved across the North Anna River, about twenty miles below Spotsylvania, on a mission to sever the Confederates' supply line and destroy as much of Lee's supplies as could be found. When he had proposed the mission, during an argument with Meade, Sheridan boasted that he would take on Jeb Stuart and whip him if given a chance. Meade reported Sheridan's remarks to Grant, who responded by asking, "Did Sheridan say that? Well, he generally knows what he is talking about. Let him start right out and do it."[13] Sheridan had set out early the next morning, Monday, May 9.

On May 10 Stuart learned of Sheridan's menace. One of Stuart's brigades rode into Beaver Dam Station and discovered the smoldering ruins of the Confederate supply depot where a million and a half rations of meat and bread had been destroyed, as well as a large quantity of the rebel army's medical supplies. The Beaver Dam raid, conducted by the cavalry brigade of Brigadier General George Armstrong Custer, also included the destruction of several railroad locomotives and rail cars and ten miles of track and the release of 375 Union soldiers who had been captured in the Wilderness and were being taken to Richmond. With as much passion as courage Stuart determined to chase after Sheridan's corps with his five thousand Confederate troopers, intending to strike Sheridan in the flank as he moved toward Richmond. The attack on Sheridan's troopers was to be made at Yellow Tavern, an abandoned roadhouse situated at a crossroads about six miles north of Richmond. By pausing only a few hours for rest during the night, Stuart had managed to reach Yellow Tavern around ten o'clock the next morning, May 11, ahead of Sheridan.

Stuart's plan went awry when the leading units of Sheridan's thirteen-mile-long column of horsemen reached Yellow Tavern about noon and, having learned that Stuart was lying in wait, made no further move toward Richmond but instead turned toward Stuart's line on the left side of the road. In the clash that followed, fought valiantly by the outnumbered Confederates, rebel Brigadier General James B. Gordon was killed and Stuart was shot in the stomach by a dismounted Union trooper at close range. The thirty-one-year-old Stuart, a dashing figure in his gray cape with its red lining, a bright yellow sash about his waist, slumped in his saddle, his hat, adorned with a peacock feather, tumbling to the ground. "Are you wounded badly?" an officer near him asked.

"I am afraid I am," he answered. He was taken by ambulance to the home of a relative in nearby Richmond, where he sent for his wife, Flora. She arrived too late. He died at 7:38 P.M. on May 12, the day after being shot. He was survived by Flora and a son and daughter. His last words came in a final whisper: "I am resigned. God's will be done."

The stormy weather, with constant rain, brought a temporary halt to the hard-fought Battle of Spotsylvania. During a five-day recess in the fighting, from May 13 to May 17, the Confederates gradually shifted eastward to match the eastward creep of the Union force. On Wednesday the 18th Grant launched another assault on the rebel line, sending Hancock's corps and Wright's corps again to the Bloody Angle, but the heavy fire of thirty Confederate artillery pieces, firing solid shot first, then case shot and finally canister as the blue-coated infantrymen drew nearer, stopped the Union charge and turned it back before the troops even came into range of rebel muskets.

On the 19th, having given up on taking the Confederate entrenchment — despite his having told General Halleck that he would "fight it out on this line if it takes all summer"[14] — Grant issued orders for his army, now strengthened by newly arrived replacements from Washington, to move out at midnight. This time they were headed for the North Anna River, twenty miles closer to Richmond.

The fighting at Spotsylvania had cost both sides dearly. Union losses were estimated to exceed eighteen thousand men, including more than two thousand killed, more than thirteen thousand wounded and more than two thousand captured or missing. On the Confederate side total losses were estimated to be between twelve thousand and thirteen thousand, including some fourteen hundred killed, more than six thousand wounded and more than five thousand captured or missing.

Repulse at Cold Harbor,
May 21 to June 12, 1864

Grant's departure for the North Anna, scheduled to start at midnight on Thursday, May 19, was delayed by an attack from General Ewell's corps, which the Confederates launched by leaving their breastworks to strike units of Hancock's corps on Grant's extreme right flank late in the afternoon on May 19. The assault was apparently unplanned, Ewell's move being intended only as an armed reconnaissance to discover Grant's movements. It was repulsed, but it caused Grant to postpone his shift to the North Anna to the night of May 21.

Having become aware of the impending move by Grant, Lee put his army in motion, too, and having a more direct route and shorter distance to travel, he reached the North Anna first. The leading units of the rebel army arrived at the river about noon on the 22nd, and by nightfall Lee's entire army was in position on the river's south bank. The Confederates gained a night of undisturbed sleep and were well rested when Grant's troops appeared on the river's north bank around mid-day on the 23rd.

The subsequent clash of the two armies at the North Anna was summarized by nineteenth-century Civil War historian John William Draper:

> When Grant arrived at the railroad crossing over the stream on the 23d, he ordered Warren, whose corps was on the right, to cross at Jericho. This was done, and the enemy driven back nearly to the Virginia Central Railroad. Lee now attacked Warren very violently, and for a short time with success; eventually, however, he was repulsed, leaving 1000 prisoners in Warren's hands.
>
> Hancock reached the river at the county bridge, a mile west of the railroad crossing, and found it covered by a strong line of intrenchments. He, however, succeeded in forcing a passage. On the next morning his corps had moved over the bridge and made good its position on the south side of the river.
>
> The 6th Corps crossed at Jericho. Grant's forces had, therefore, thus passed the river at two points, about four miles apart. It was soon found, however, that they could not communicate with each other, on account of a strong salient in Lee's lines resting on the bank of the river between two points of passage. Lee had so posted his troops that his right wing was thrown back at an obtuse angle to his left; he was intervening between the two points at which the passage had been made. In spite of Grant's attempts, Lee succeeded in maintaining his centre in its salient position, and in keeping the Army of the Potomac divided so as to render it incapable of

advancing without imminent risk. Burnside had vainly tried to make a crossing at a middle point, but was repulsed with heavy loss, and a division which attempted a demonstration from Warren's front toward this middle point was forced back upon the river, and narrowly escaped disaster. Finding his antagonist's position impregnable, Grant gave orders to withdraw the army to the north side, and commenced another turning movement.[1]

By the time Grant gave those orders, his army had suffered an estimated 2,623 casualties in the battle at the North Anna. The Confederates had lost an estimated 2,517 men.[2]

Grant's latest turning movement would take his army southeastward around Lee's right flank again. Repeatedly skirting Lee's right, rather than his left, which lay to the west, was dictated by Grant's logistics. His army was now being supplied by water routes, not rail, with transport steamers coming up Virginia's rivers from Chesapeake Bay. Grant could not afford to risk Lee's maneuvering his troops into a position between the Union army and its lines of supply.

Sheridan's cavalry corps, having rejoined the main body of Grant's army, led the Union advance, leaving the area of the North Anna in the afternoon of the 26th, feeling out the positions and strength of the Confederates as it went. Grant's infantry and artillery — stealthily and apparently without Lee's noticing — began moving out shortly after dark that same day, and by 3 A.M. on the 27th they were on the north side of the North Anna, their pontoon bridges removed and the fixed bridges destroyed. As the main body moved out, the cavalry division of Brigadier General James H. Wilson rode behind the column of infantry, guarding its rear.

At 9 A.M. on the 27th Sheridan reported that his troopers had occupied Hanovertown, on the south side of the Pamunkey River, about seventeen miles north of Richmond. That was where Grant's army was now headed. From Hanovertown there was a direct road to Richmond, and an elaborate network of roads that served the communities between Hanovertown and Richmond was accessible from Hanovertown.

When dawn had come on the 27th, the Confederates saw that Grant's army had disappeared during the night. It had, as Confederate General Law put it, "folded its tents like the Arab and quietly stolen away." By the time its absence was discovered, Law related, "The Army of the Potomac was already on its march for the Pamunkey River at Hanovertown." Quickly reacting to the dangerous new situation, Law reported, "Lee moved at once to head off his adversary, whose advance column was now eight miles nearer Richmond than he was."[3]

Two of Sheridan's cavalry divisions, one commanded by Brigadier General David Gregg and the other by Brigadier General Alfred Torbert, had been assigned to cover the advance units of the Army of the Potomac as they crossed the Pamunkey. On May 28, finding the cavalry units of Major General Wade Hampton and Major General Fitz Lee dismounted and lying in wait behind a breastworks along a line of woods near Enon Church, Gregg and Torbert dismounted their Union troopers and attacked the line of rebel cavalrymen about a mile west of an important crossroads, at which stood a blacksmith shop called Haw's Shop. The intense rifle fire of the rebels halted the Union charge, and after a failed Confederate counterattack, the fight became an hours-long exchange of rifle and carbine fire. Sheridan then ordered Custer, who had arrived with his band blaring *Yankee Doodle*, to throw his brigade into the battle, telling him, "I want you to go in and give those fellows hell!" Staying mounted while his troopers charged the Confederate line on foot, Custer, waving his hat, led his men into the rebels' works, forcing Hampton's and Fitz Lee's cavalrymen to withdraw, thereby securing the Haw's Shop intersection for the Army of the

General Grant at his command post at Cold Harbor. Having suffered heavy losses in repeated assaults on the Confederate position, Grant years later remarked that "Cold Harbor is, I think, the only battle I ever fought that I would not fight over again under the circumstances." (LIBRARY OF CONGRESS)

Potomac's infantry, allowing it to continue its advance. In the battle the Union forces suffered an estimated 544 casualties, counting killed, wounded and missing; the Confederates lost an estimated four hundred men, including eighty-five taken prisoner. Among the killed was Custer's horse.

On May 29 Grant sent three of his four corps to move to the right in three different directions to discover the location of the main body of Lee's army. Hancock's Second Corps, after probing some three miles southwestward from the Hanovertown road, on May 30 encountered the Confederates, ten divisions of them, strung out in a strongly fortified position along the south bank of eastward streaming Totopotomoy Creek. Attempts were made to ford the creek and storm the rebel entrenchments, but failing at that, Grant ordered Hooker's Ninth Corps — which now had been incorporated into the Army of the Potomac — and Warren's Fifth Corps to move eastward along the creek to flank Lee's right. By noon, the two Union corps had crossed to the south side of the creek. Lee, who was then recovering from a serious attack of dysentery, responded by having General Early's corps attempt to turn Grant's left. That attempt failed, and Early withdrew his troops to the west, effectively ending the fight, temporarily. In the engagement along Totopotomoy Creek the Confederates suffered an estimated 1,159 casualties, the Union forces 751.

"The night of the 30th," Grant recorded, "Lee's position was substantially from Atlee's Station on the Virginia Central Railroad south and east to the vicinity of Cold Harbor. Ours was: The left of Warren's corps was on the Shady Grove Road, extending to the Mechanicsville Road and about three miles south of the Totopotomoy. Burnside to his right, then Hancock, and Wright on the extreme right, extending toward Hanover Court House, six miles south-east of it. Sheridan with two divisions of cavalry was watching our left front towards Cold Harbor.... The enemy attacked Sheridan's pickets, but reinforcements were sent up and the attack was speedily repulsed and the enemy followed some distance towards Cold Harbor.

"On the 31st," Grant continued, "Sheridan advanced to near Old Cold Harbor. He found it intrenched and occupied by cavalry and infantry. A hard fight ensued but the place was carried. The enemy well knew the importance of Cold Harbor to us, and seemed determined that we should not hold it. He returned with such a large force that Sheridan was about withdrawing without any effort to hold it against such odds; but about the time he commenced the evacuation he received orders to hold the place at all hazards, until reinforcements could be sent to him. He speedily turned the rebel works to face against them and placed his men in position for defence. Night came on before the enemy was ready for assault."[4]

Cold Harbor, or more precisely, Old Cold Harbor, to be differentiated from New Cold Harbor, was a crossroads about twelve miles east and slightly north of Richmond, at which was situated Cold Harbor Tavern, the tavern/inn for which the site was named and which apparently had taken its name from places in England where inns provided travelers with shelter and rest but no hot meals. Grant considered Old Cold Harbor important because from it ran roads by which he could threaten both the rebel army and the rebel capital, Richmond, and by which he could protect his supply depot at White House, where he was receiving shipments via the Pamunkey River. To do battle in the vicinity of Old Cold Harbor he had some 108,000 men, including the newly arrived troops of Major General William F. "Baldy" Smith's Eighteenth Corps, rushed from Bermuda Hundred to reinforce him. Lee's army, also recently reinforced — by the seven thousand troops of Major General Robert F. Hoke's division, reluctantly sent by General Beauregard from their defensive position at Bermuda Hundred — totaled some 59,000 men.

General McMahon, the Union Sixth Corps' chief of staff, who wrote of the death of his beloved commander, General Sedgwick, (and who rose through the ranks from private to brevet major general and after the war was awarded the Congressional Medal of Honor for meritorious service under enemy fire at White Oak Swamp, Virginia in June 1862) was with the Sixth Corps, now commanded by General Wright, as it hurried toward the showdown at Old Cold Harbor. In an article written for *The Century* magazine McMahon recorded his view of the action:

... To this point [Old Cold Harbor], during the night, marched the vanguard of the Army of the Potomac, the Sixth Corps, under Wright, over roads that were many inches deep in dust. The night was sultry and oppressive. Many of our horses and mules were dying of thirst, yet they had to be forced through streams without halting to drink. Frequent messengers from Sheridan came during the night, urging the importance of rapid movement. About 9 the next day (June 1st) the head of the column reached Sheridan's position, and the cavalry was withdrawn. The enemy, who had been seriously threatening Sheridan, withdrew from our immediate front to within their lines and awaited us, occupying a strong outer line of intrenchments in front of our center, somewhat in advance of their main position, which included that on which the battle of Gaines's Mill had been fought two years before. It covered the approaches to the Chickahominy, which was the last formidable obstacle we had to meet before standing in front of the permanent works of Richmond. A large detachment, composed of the Eighteenth Corps and other troops from the Army of the James, under General W.F. Smith, had disembarked at White House on the Pamunkey, and was expected to connect that morning with the Sixth Corps at Cold Harbor. A mistake in orders caused an unnecessary march and long delay. In the afternoon, however, Smith was in position on the right of the Sixth Corps. Late in the afternoon both corps assaulted.

The attack was made vigorously, and with no reserves. The outer line in front of the right of the Sixth and the left of the Eighteenth was carried brilliantly, and the enemy was forced back, leaving several hundred prisoners in our hands. On the left, where [Brigadier General David] Russell advanced, our losses were severe. The men went forward under a terrible fire from front and flank, until they were ordered to lie down under such shelter as was afforded by the ground and the enemy's impenetrable slashing, to which they had advanced. Russell was wounded, but remained upon the field all day. This left the well and the old tavern at Cold Harbor in our rear, and brought us in front of the most formidable position yet held by the enemy. In front of him was a wooded country, interspersed with clearings here and there, sparsely populated, and full of swamps....[5]

That was the first attempt at the Confederate line at Old Cold Harbor. The second attempt occurred on the morning of Friday, June 3. It had been planned for the afternoon of June 2, but despite all preparations for it having been made, new orders came to the corps commanders, postponing the attack until 4:30 A.M. on the 3rd. McMahon described the situation and the engagement:

The enemy's general line, although refused [set back] at certain points and with salients elsewhere, because of the character of the country, was that of an arc of a circle, the concave side toward us, overlapping on both flanks the three corps intending to attack. The line of advance of Wright's command holding the center was therefore perpendicular to that of the enemy. Hancock's line, connecting with Wright's left, extended obliquely to the left and rear. A movement upon his part to the front must necessarily take him off obliquely from the line of advance of the center. The same was true of Smith's command upon the right. What resulted from this formation on the 3d of June developed. No reconnaissance had been made other than the bloody one of the evening before [June 1]....

Promptly at the hour named on the 3d of June the men moved from the slight cover of the rifle-pits, thrown up during the night, with steady, determined advance, and there rang out suddenly on the summer air such a crash of artillery and musketry as is seldom heard in war. No great portion of the advance could be seen from any particular point, but those of the three corps that passed through the clearings were feeling the fire terribly. Not much return was made at first from our infantry, although the fire of our batteries was incessant. The time of actual advance was not over eight minutes. In that little period more men fell bleeding as they advanced than in any other like period of time throughout the war. A strange and terrible feature of this battle was that as the three gallant corps moved on, each was enfiladed while receiving the full force of the enemy's direct fire in front. The enemy's shot and shell were plunging through Hancock's battalions from his right. From the left a similarly destructive fire was poured in upon Smith, and from both flanks on the Sixth Corps in the center. At some points the slashings and obstructions in the enemy's front were reached. [Brigadier General Francis] Barlow, of Hancock's corps, drove the enemy from an advanced position, but was himself driven out by the fire of their second line. [Brigadier General] R.O. Tyler's brigade (the Corcoran Legion) of the same corps swept over an advance work, capturing several hundred prisoners. One officer alone, the colonel of the 164th New York [James P. McMahon, General McMahon's brother], seizing the colors of his regiment from the dying color-bearer as he fell, succeeded in reaching the parapet of the enemy's main works, where he planted the colors and fell dead near the ditch, bleeding from many wounds. Seven other colonels of Hancock's command died within those few minutes. No troops could stand against such a fire, and the order to lie down was given all along the line. At points where no shelter was afforded, the men were withdrawn to such cover as could be found, and the battle of Cold Harbor, as to its result at least, was over.[6]

Going into the fight, Grant felt sure that he had the rebels on the ropes. In a message dated May 26 he told General Halleck, "Lee's army is really whipped. The prisoners we now take show it, and the action of his army shows it unmistakably. A battle with them outside of intrenchments cannot be had. Our men feel that they have gained the *morale* over the enemy, and attack him with confidence. I may be mistaken, but I feel that our success over Lee's army is already assured."[7] Believing that to be the case, Grant would not forgo what he saw as a chance to penetrate the rebel defenses, shatter Lee's army, take Richmond and end the war quickly. Lives would be lost now, but in the long run, he reasoned, many more lives would be spared. The possible rewards, he decided, were worth the gamble.

Grant's plan for the attack employed the same logic he was applying in his total effort against the Confederate forces: Press the enemy everywhere simultaneously to prevent units in one sector from being reinforced by units from other sectors. An all-out attack along the length of the rebel line at Old Cold Harbor would compel all of Lee's units to stay in place and defend their own ground. It would also, Grant was thinking, reveal whatever weakness there might be in the Confederate line so that Union troops could be concentrated to exploit the weakness and break through the rebel defense.

Although a failure, the battle at least brought some satisfaction to Meade. He boasted that he had masterminded the operation — one that had cost the Union some seven thousand casualties and the Confederates no more than fifteen hundred. "I had immediate and entire command on the field all day," he wrote to his wife in a spite-tinged letter the next day, "the Lieutenant General honoring the field with his presence only about one hour in the middle of the day."[8] Meade actually had nothing to be proud of while he possessed "entire command." According to historian Gordon C. Rhea, Meade "did virtually nothing to reconnoiter the ground, coordinate the assault columns, or bring up reserves. His abdication of responsibility reflected the underlying tension between him and Grant. Meade disagreed with Grant's penchant for army-wide offensives but lacked the backbone to air his dissatisfaction forcefully. Although his corps commanders made it clear by 7:00 A.M. [on June 3] that the assault could not succeed, Meade was loath to cancel the offensive and risk Grant's disapproval."[9]

Grant, moreover, in an order issued at 7 A.M. on the 3rd had told Meade, "The moment it becomes certain that an assault cannot succeed, suspend the offensive; but when one does succeed, push it vigorously and if necessary pile in troops at the successful point from wherever they can be taken."[10]

An exchange of fire continued throughout the morning, but Union commanders, seeing the futility, were making less than half-hearted attempts at a new assault, Union troops merely firing from where they lay. About eleven o'clock Grant conferred with the corps commanders and accepted reality. At half past noon he instructed Meade to call off the frontal attack and have the men begin digging siege works. "The opinion of corps commanders not being sanguine of success in case an assault is ordered," Grant told Meade, "you may direct a suspension of farther advance for the present. Hold our most advanced positions and strengthen them. Whilst on the defensive our line may be contracted from the right if practicable. Reconnoissances should be made in front of every corps and advances made to advantageous positions by regular approaches."[11]

The digging proved to be one more deadly hazard, as General McMahon reported:

> The work of intrenching could only be done at night. The fire of sharp-shooters was incessant, and no man upon all that line could stand erect and live an instant. This condition of things continued for twelve days and nights: Sharp-shooters' fire from both sides went on all day; all night the zigzags and parallels nearer the enemy's works were being constructed.... Rations and ammunition were brought forward from parallel to parallel through the zigzag trenches, and in some instances where regiments whose term of service had expired were ordered home, they had to leave the field crawling on hands and knees through the trenches to the rear. At 9 o'clock every night the enemy opened fire with artillery and musketry along his whole line. This was undoubtedly done under the suspicion that the Army of the Potomac had seen the hopelessness of the task before it and would withdraw in the night-time for another movement by the flank, and, if engaged in such a movement, would be thrown into confusion by this threat of a night attack. However, no advance was made by the enemy.[12]

The field in front of the Union forces, who remained vigilant by day and labored at night, presented a grim and heart-rending scene. The dead and wounded lay on the ground unattended in the no-man's-land between the opposing lines, corpses rotting, the wounded dying hideously in the heat of the summer sun. Some of them McMahon recognized. "The 2d Connecticut Heavy Artillery," he recorded, "a new regiment eighteen hundred strong, had joined us but a few days before the battle. Its uniform was bright and fresh; therefore its dead were easily distinguished where they lay. They marked in a dotted line an obtuse angle, covering a wide front, with its apex toward the enemy, and there upon his face, still in death, with his head to the works, lay the colonel, the brave and genial Colonel Elisha S. Kellogg."[13]

A few brave souls, responding to the piteous moans and cries of the wounded, crept out from their entrenchments at night to drag wounded comrades back into the Union lines, despite orders and the risk of almost certain death. Grant attempted to gain a ceasefire that would halt hostilities long enough to recover the wounded and bury the dead, but Lee insisted that Grant ask permission to recover the wounded and dead under a flag of truce, which Grant was reluctant to do because sending a flag of truce, according to tradition, indicated the field of battle had been lost to the side to which the flag of truce was sent.

Belatedly responding to the need, while wounded men lay dying, Grant on June 5 wrote to Lee:

It is reported to me that there are wounded men, probably of both armies, now lying exposed and suffering between the lines occupied respectively by the two armies. Humanity would dictate that some provision should be made to provide against such hardships. I would propose, therefore, that hereafter, when no battle is raging, either party be authorized to send to any point between the pickets or skirmish lines, unarmed men bearing litters to pick up their dead or wounded, without being fired upon by the other party. Any other method, equally fair to both parties, you may propose for meeting the end desired will be accepted by me.[14]

Neither the dictate of humanity nor of his professed Christianity could move Lee to agree to Grant's proposal, which, Lee said, would lead to "misunderstanding and difficulty."[15] Lee insisted that Grant send a flag of truce, the admission of defeat. "It will always afford me pleasure," Lee replied, "to comply with such a request as far as circumstances will permit."[16]

Grant wrote back on June 6:

Your communication of yesterday's date is received. I will send immediately, as you propose, to collect the dead and wounded between the lines of the two armies, and will also instruct that you be allowed to do the same. I propose that the time for doing this be between the hours of 12 m. [sic] and 3 P.M. to-day. I will direct all parties going out to bear a white flag, and not to attempt to go beyond where we have dead or wounded, and not beyond or on ground occupied by your troops.[17]

Lee could not agree to that proposal either. He replied to Grant saying that "when either party desired such permission it should be asked for by flag of truce," and according to Grant, Lee "had directed that any parties I may have sent out, as mentioned in my letter, to be turned back."[18] Grant then wrote to Lee again:

The knowledge that wounded men are now suffering from want of attention, between the two armies, compels me to ask a suspension of hostilities for sufficient time to collect them in, say two hours. Permit me to say that the hours you may fix upon for this will be agreeable to me, and the same privilege will be extended to such parties as you may wish to send out on the same duty without further application.[19]

Lee at last agreed. Delays in transmitting his latest response, however, prevented the rescue and retrieval efforts from beginning before the evening of June 7, some forty-eight hours after Grant had first proposed the truce. By then all but two of the wounded had died.

The Confederates' outstandingly successful stand at Old Cold Harbor was made all the more remarkable by the condition of Lee's troops. Grant had appraised the rebels' morale as low and had decided Lee's army therefore could be vulnerable to a powerful Union assault that might prove decisive in ending the conflict. That appraisal was evidently based on the reports of discouraged deserters and did not reflect the feelings of the great mass of the Army of Northern Virginia. Sergeant Major George Cary Eggleston, a Virginia artilleryman, was evidently more representative of the men of Lee's army than were any deserters whose dissatisfactions were reported to Grant. The trying circumstances under which the Confederates were then living and the resilience of the rebel soldiers despite those circumstances were poignantly described in an account written by Sergeant Eggleston after the Battle of Cold Harbor:

We had absolute faith in Lee's ability to meet and repel any assault that might be made, and to devise some means of destroying Grant. There was, therefore, no fear in the Confederate ranks of any thing that General Grant might do; but there was an appalling and well-founded fear of starvation, which indeed some of us were already suffering. From the beginning of that campaign our food supply had been barely sufficient to maintain life, and on the march from

Spotsylvania to Cold Harbor it would have been a gross exaggeration to describe it that way. In my own battery three hard biscuits and one very meager slice of fat pork were issued to each man on our arrival, and that was the first food that any of us had seen since our departure from Spotsylvania, two days before. The next supply did not come till two days later, and it consisted of a single cracker per man, with no meat at all.

We practiced a very rigid economy with this food, of course. We ate the pork raw, partly because there was no convenient means of cooking it, but more because cooking would have involved some waste. We hoarded what we had, allowing ourselves only a nibble at any one time, and that only when the pangs of hunger became unbearable.

But what is the use of writing about the pangs of hunger? The words are utterly meaningless to persons who have never known actual starvation and cannot be made otherwise than meaningless. Hunger to starving men is wholly unrelated to the desire for food as that is commonly understood and felt. It is a great agony of the whole body and of the soul as well. It is unimaginable, all-pervading pain inflicted when the strength to endure pain is utterly gone. It is a great despairing cry of a wasting body — a cry of flesh and blood, marrow, nerves, bones, and faculties for strength with which to exist and endure existence. It is a horror which, once suffered, leaves an impression that is never erased from the memory, and to this day the old agony of that campaign comes back upon me at the mere thought of any living creature lacking the food it desires....

With mercenary troops or regulars the resistance that Lee was able to offer to Grant's tremendous pressure would have been impossible in such circumstances. The starvation and the excessive marching would have destroyed the *morale* of troops held together only by discipline. No historical criticism of our civil war can be otherwise than misleading if it omits to give a prominent place, as a factor, to the character of the volunteers on both sides, who in acquiring the steadiness and order of regulars, never lost their personal interest in the contest or their personal pride of manhood as a sustaining force under trying conditions. If either side had lacked this element of personal heroism on the part of its men it would have been driven from the field long before the spring of 1865.[20]

Reflecting on the battle, Lee was pleased with the way things had gone for the Confederates. On the evening of the 3rd, the major fighting having ended, he wrote to President Davis and reported, "Our loss today has been small, and our success, under the blessing of God, all that we could expect."[21]

Grant, too, reflected on the battle — and expressed regrets. "I have always regretted that the last assault at Cold Harbor was ever made," he confessed in his memoirs years later. "No advantage whatever was gained to compensate for the heavy loss we sustained."[22] On another occasion he remarked that "Cold Harbor is, I think, the only battle I ever fought that I would not fight over again under the circumstances."[23]

On the evening of Sunday, June 12 he put Cold Harbor behind him and had his troops begin moving out from their positions after dark, headed for the Chickahominy River crossings. This time their objective was Petersburg, the rebels' vital communications center, their jugular, on the far side of the James River, just below the Confederate capital.

The Georgia Invasion,
May 4 to July 17, 1864

Joseph Eggleston Johnston in the spring of 1864 was fifty-seven years old, still trim, with a straight-back military bearing that made him seem taller than he was (five foot seven). Smartly appareled in his tailored, pearl-gray Confederate general's uniform, with a graying mustache and van Dyke beard and a bald spot that rose from his brow to the crown of his head, he didn't look like someone who would be called "Joe." He seemed too reserved, too dignified, too formal. One infantryman, a member of the First Tennessee Regiment, observed him while Johnston was on an inspection tour and remarked that "In his dress he was a perfect dandy.... His hat was decorated with a star and feather, his coat with every star and embellishment, and he wore a bright new sash, big gauntlets, and silver spurs. He was the very picture of a general."[1] Even so, to those who knew him best, including General Robert E. Lee, his fellow Virginian and fellow member of the West Point class of 1829, he was Joe. The men of his army, who learned to love him, called him Ol' Joe.[2]

As the U.S. Army's quartermaster general in 1861, holding the rank of brigadier general, he was the most senior officer to quit the U.S. service and join the Confederacy's cause, which he did ten days after Fort Sumter was assaulted

Confederate Gen. Joseph E. Johnston. He was a West Point graduate who gained a reputation as a skillful defensive general as he tried to check Sherman's advance on Atlanta, but his lack of aggressiveness angered Confederate President Jefferson Davis, who replaced him with Gen. John B. Hood. (LIBRARY OF CONGRESS)

and five days after the secession of Virginia. Although he had never commanded a force larger than four companies in the field — which in fact was considerably more experience than many generals on both sides could claim — Johnston, appointed a brigadier general in the Confederate army, was given command of some six thousand men and sent by President Jefferson Davis to defend Harpers Ferry, in western Virginia, site of the U.S. armory and armament factory that had been seized by the Confederates and that Johnston later abandoned because he deemed Harpers Ferry indefensible. His first combat in the war came in July 1861 at Manassas, where he shared command — and credit for the rebel victory — with Beauregard. Five weeks after that, he, along with Lee and Beauregard and two others (Samuel Cooper and Albert Sidney Johnston, no relation to Joe), was named a full general. He later was given command of the rebel army whose mission it was to oppose the advance of a Union force led by General McClellan that had landed on the Virginia peninsula in May 1862. In the course of that action, at the Battle of Seven Pines, Johnston was so severely wounded he had to relinquish his command.

Following his recovery he was assigned as commander of the Confederates' Department of the West, a job that included overseeing the defense of Vicksburg, the vital fortress city on the Mississippi. Seeing the inevitability of the city's fall, Johnston, from his headquarters in Jackson, Mississippi, urged that Vicksburg be abandoned so that its army of defenders could be saved instead. His urging went unheeded by the defenders' commander in Vicksburg, Lieutenant General John Pemberton, and when the city was surrendered to Grant on July 4, 1863, the Confederacy lost not only Vicksburg but its twenty-six thousand troops, who became prisoners of war.

On November 28, 1863 General Bragg, bedeviled by his failures at Chattanooga, at Lookout Mountain and Missionary Ridge and beset with hostility from his general officers, resigned his command of the Army of Tennessee, which was then encamped at Dalton, Georgia, an important railroad junction through which ran the East Tennessee & Georgia and the Western & Atlantic rail lines. Bragg and his army had fled to Dalton after being driven from the outskirts of Chattanooga by the Union army Bragg supposedly had been besieging. To replace Bragg President Davis, as a last resort, appointed Johnston, although it grieved him to do so, Johnston being an object of Davis's intense dislike and viewed by him as a political enemy in league with other political enemies of Davis. Those personal considerations aside, Davis also found significant fault with Johnston's fighting style, which had given him a Fabian reputation for resorting to defensive reactions to the enemy's offensives instead of taking the initiative with persistent attacks. But generals Hardee and Polk had declined the job, and Davis had no one else to turn to. The notification of Johnston's appointment came to him in a telegram he received on December 18,1863, and on December 27 he arrived in Dalton to take over the defeated, demoralized rebel Army of Tennessee. Mounted on his well-groomed bright bay horse, he rode through the rows of tents in the camps on an informal inspection of his new command, the men turning out to stand and greet him with cheers. Johnston acknowledged their welcome by doffing his hat and gracefully sweeping it down to his stirrups. The troops' show of enthusiasm, as one of Johnston's biographers noted, may have been owing as much to their relief over Bragg's no longer being their commander as to their elation over Johnston's being their new chief.[3] Johnston, though, had gained a reputation as a general who took care of his troops, and the hearty welcome was doubtless a sincere expression of approval.

On January 1, 1864, five days after his arrival, Johnston received an irksome letter from President Davis dated December 23. "In it," Johnston complained, "he, in Richmond, informed me of the encouraging condition of the army, which 'induced him to hope that I would soon be able to commence active operations against the enemy,' — the men being 'tolerably' well clothed, with a large reserve of small-arms, the morning reports exhibiting an effective total that exceeded in number 'that actually engaged on the Confederate side in any battle of the war.'"[4]

Johnston's inspections, however, made soon after assuming command, revealed, as he said, that "the army was very far from being [a] 'matter of much congratulation.' Instead of a reserve of muskets there was a deficiency of six thousand and as great a one of blankets, while the number of bare feet was painful to see. The artillery horses were too feeble to draw the guns in the fields, or on a march, and the mules were in similar condition; the supplies of forage were then very irregular, and did not include hay…. The last return of the army was of December 20th, and exhibited an effective total of less than 36,000, of whom 6000 were without arms and as many without shoes."[5] Johnston's remedies came quickly, and he soon showed how the hearts of his men were won. Almost immediately he ordered two days' rations issued to each of the men, with bacon, a scarce commodity, to replace the rancid beef that they had been eating. He promised the troops that tobacco and whiskey would be issued twice a week. He ordered new uniforms for the men, especially including shoes for the unshod. He also ordered more tents to shelter them. To make all those orders and promises possible he also promptly reorganized the army's supply system to assure a steady flow of supplies. For the disenchanted who had gone AWOL he ordered pardons, and as a reward for those who had doggedly toughed out the long days of defeat and demoralization he granted furloughs. One third of his army at a time was permitted to go home, the individuals chosen by lot, and those who chose not to go were allowed to give or sell their places to comrades. The horses and mules got a break, too. "It was necessary," Johnston wrote, "to send all of these animals not needed for camp service to the valley of the Etowah, where long forage could be found, to restore their health and strength."[6]

His troops responded to the new treatment. "A new era had dawned," one of the soldiers remarked in a survey. "He was loved, respected, admired; yea, even worshipped by the troops. I do not believe there was a soldier in his army but would gladly have died for him."[7] Another commented, "We knew we had a general that would take care of his men."[8]

Taking care of the men, however, was not President Davis's prime concern. His major interest was initiating an offensive against the Union force threatening to sweep down through northwest Georgia from Chattanooga, endangering Atlanta and the rest of the state. Knowing Davis's eagerness to take the offensive, Johnston wrote a letter to him on February 27, spelling out the preparations necessary for a rebel offensive: "large additions to the number of troops, an ample supply of field transportation, subsistence stores, and forage, a bridge equipage, and fresh artillery horses."[9] The letter drew a written reply from Bragg, who as a continuing Davis favorite, had been taken onto Davis's staff as a sort of executive officer "charged with the conduct of military operations in the armies of the Confederacy."[10] Hand delivered by Bragg's secretary, Colonel John Sale, on March 18, the reply described a plan to have the Army of Tennessee move up from Dalton and invade Tennessee with a force of seventy-five thousand men, including Longstreet's corps, then encamped near Morristown, in east Tennessee, as well as other units. According to the plan, Longstreet would march to a rendezvous with Johnston at Kingston, Tennessee and join the offensive thrust there.

Johnston didn't think much of the plan. Asked for his views, he pointed out that the enemy could strike either his force or Longstreet's while on the march, before the two forces could be combined, or could attack Johnston's force at Dalton before it was ready to begin the offensive. "I proposed therefore," Johnston recounted, "that the additional troops should be sent to Dalton in time to give us the means to beat the Federal army there [at Dalton], and then pursue it into Tennessee, which would be a more favorable mode of invasion than the other."[11]

Bragg dismissed Johnston's proposal, telling him in a telegram on March 21: "Your dispatch of 19th does not indicate an acceptance of the plan proposed. The troops can only be drawn from other points for an advance. Upon your decision of that point further action must depend."[12] When Johnston tried to explain to Bragg that he accepted the idea of an offensive but disagreed on some of the details of the plan Bragg offered, he received no response.

"In the mean time," Johnston related, "our scouts were furnishing evidence of almost daily arrivals of Federal reenforcements, which was punctually communicated to the Administration through General Bragg. From these indications it was clear that the military authorities of the United States were assembling in our front a much greater force than that which had driven us from Missionary Ridge a few months before.... It was as plain that these Federal preparations were made not for the purpose of holding the ground won from us in the previous campaign, but for the resumption of offensive operations."[13]

Apparently ignoring Johnston's warnings of the Union troop build-up at the front of Johnston's position, the administration sent Lieutenant Colonel A.H. Cole of the Quartermaster's Department to Johnston. Cole arrived in Dalton on April 3 and informed Johnston that he, Cole, was there "to superintend the procuring [of] the number of artillery-horses and the amount of field-transportation required by the army for an offensive campaign."[14] So much for President Davis's concern over the menacing Union troop build-up. His concern, or lack of it, underwent no change despite subsequent warnings from Johnston that the Army of Tennessee lacked sufficient strength and resources to defend successfully against an apparently impending massive Union assault.

"In the morning of the 2d May," Johnston recounted, "a close reconnaissance of our outpost at Tunnel Hill [about eight miles northwest of Dalton on the way to Chattanooga] was made under the protection of a strong body of infantry, cavalry, and artillery. The reports received on the 1st, 2d, and 4th, indicated that the beginning of an active campaign was imminent. They showed that the enemy was approaching our position, and repairing the railroad from Chattanooga to Ringgold [about fifteen miles northwest of Dalton]. The intelligence received on each day was immediately transmitted to General Bragg. That officer suggested to me, on the 2d, that I was deceived, probably, by *mere demonstrations*, made for the purpose."[15] So much for Bragg's military perspicacity.

Pursuant to General Grant's instructions, General Sherman had put his troops in motion throughout the first week of May. His command, the Military Division of the Mississippi, was composed of the Army of the Ohio, commanded by Major General John M. Schofield, the Army of the Tennessee, commanded by Major General James B. McPherson, and the Army of the Cumberland, commanded by Major General George H. Thomas. The Army of the Ohio had fourteen thousand men and 28 artillery pieces. The Army of the Tennessee had twenty-five thousand men and 96 artillery pieces. The Army of the Cumberland had sixty thousand men and 130 artillery pieces. Altogether Sherman's force amounted to ninety-nine thousand troops, with 254 pieces of artillery.[16]

In early March units of the Army of the Cumberland had moved from Chattanooga as far south as Ringgold, Georgia, where a base was established, and on Wednesday, May 4 the remainder of the Army of the Cumberland took a position near Ringgold while the Army of the Ohio marched out of east Tennessee through Cleveland, northwest of Chattanooga, and turned due south to cross the state line into Georgia and take a position on Thomas's left around Catoosa Springs. McPherson's Army of the Tennessee advanced to a position on Thomas's right, around Lee & Gordon's Mills, west of Dalton. The line of Sherman's united front then, from McPherson's right to Schofield's left, covered a distance of some sixteen miles. Sherman placed himself at Ringgold, in the center of the line, joining General Thomas, who was Sherman's classmate at West Point and a long-time friend.

Johnston held a strong position above Dalton. Since taking over from Bragg he had had his troops strengthen the line of fortifications to the point that it was, in the words of one Union commander, "practically impregnable." The fortifications, including a line of entrenchments, took advantage of a series of rocky ridges than ran northeast to southwest and a creek that Johnston had ordered dammed to deepen it across part of his front. "In front, therefore, and on either flank for miles to the rear," Jacob Cox, then a brigadier general in the U.S. Army of the Ohio, reported, "Dalton was so strong as to be safe from a *coup de main*; too strong, indeed, to make it probable that the Federal commander would seriously attack the works, if caution counted for anything in his character."[17]

Sherman had been advised by Thomas, who was familiar with the area, that there was a way around Johnston's flank, a route that passed through Snake Creek Gap, about ten miles south and slightly west of Dalton. About ten miles southeast of the gap was the town of Resaca, and about eight miles due east of the gap was the village of Tilton, both communities situated on the East Tennessee & Georgia Railroad. Thomas volunteered to send his troops through the gap to turn the left end of Johnston's line and attack Johnston from the rear. Sherman accepted the idea of the flanking movement, but turned down Thomas's offer to lead it. He wanted to keep the superior numbers of Thomas's army in front of the rebel line to withstand a possible attack by Johnston. Instead of Thomas's troops, Sherman chose to use the two corps of McPherson's army for the turning movement. In a note he wrote to McPherson on May 5 Sherman set forth his plan, which called for Thomas and Schofield to make a feint on Johnston's front while McPherson slipped around to his rear. "I want you to move," he told McPherson, "...to Snake Gap [*sic*], secure it and from it make a bold attack on the enemy's flank or his railroad at any point between Tilton and Resaca.... I hope the enemy will fight at Dalton, in which case he can have no force there that can interfere with you. But, should his policy be to fall back along his railroad, you will hit him in the flank. Do not fail in that event to make the most of the opportunity by the most vigorous attack possible, as it may save us what we have most reason to apprehend — a slow pursuit, in which he gains strength as we lose it. In either event you may be sure the forces north of you will prevent his turning on you alone."[18]

Meanwhile, Johnston, at work in the two-story, wood-frame house in Dalton that was his headquarters, knowing the blue-coated armies stood a scant dozen miles away from the north and west faces of his fortifications, was pondering the possibilities of Sherman's next move and how he would counter it. He was attempting to make the best of his situation, which required him to oppose Sherman's ninety-nine-thousand-man force with a rebel army of no more than sixty thousand.[19] That rebel army, though, had the advantage of being entrenched and defending from behind fortifications, where, in the words of General Cox, "one man in the [defending] line was, by all sound military rules, equal to three or four in the attack."[20] Even so, seeing the numbers before him, Johnston wired Richmond urgent appeals for reinforcements, which this time were answered.

Although aware that Sherman might try to turn his left flank, Johnston apparently believed Snake Creek Gap presented little danger to him. He therefore had left it unguarded and, as Cox deduced, "rested securely in the belief that his position could only be turned by a much longer detour, and one involving many more contingencies for his opponent."[21]

On May 2, having decided that Sherman was ready to move on him, Johnston notified the wives of his staff officers that they would have to leave Dalton immediately. Leaving with them was his own wife, Lydia, who boarded a train bound for Atlanta.

Five days later, on Saturday, May 7, following Sherman's instructions, General Thomas directed his three corps to start the advance toward the rebel line. The Fourteenth Corps, commanded by Major General John M. Palmer, moved out from Ringgold toward Tunnel Hill. The Fourth Corps, commanded by Major General Oliver O. Howard, marched from Catoosa Springs westward toward a designated house (Doctor Lee's) on the road to Tunnel Hill, there to take a position in support of Palmer. The Twentieth Corps, commanded by Major General Joe Hooker, moved out from Lee & Gordon's Mills southeastward toward Trickum, where it was to take a position about three miles south of Tunnel Hill. All units advanced without serious opposition, except at Tunnel Hill, where a rebel cavalry force put up stiff resistance but was finally driven off. During the afternoon the Union troops moved into position in front of the mountain gap through which ran the Western & Atlantic tracks, the Union line roughly paralleling Rocky Face Ridge, which ran along the west side of Dalton. There the bluecoats halted for the night.

"Until that day," Johnston related, "I had regarded a battle in the broad valley in which Dalton stands as inevitable. The greatly superior strength of the Federal army made the chances of battle altogether in its favor. It had also places of refuge in case of defeat, in the intrenched pass of Ringgold and in the fortress of Chattanooga; while we, if beaten, had none nearer than Atlanta, 100 miles off, with three rivers intervening. General Sherman's course indicating no intention of giving battle east of Rocky-face, we prepared to fight on either side of the ridge."[22]

While Johnston's main force was occupied with Thomas's army outside Dalton, McPherson took the two corps of the Army of the Tennessee to Snake Creek Gap. McPherson's Sixteenth Corps, commanded by Major General Grenville Dodge, led the way, his first brigade slipping through the gap around midnight on May 8. Around daylight on the morning of the 9th Dodge moved two divisions forward to a winding, north-south road that connected Dalton to Calhoun, a community on the East Tennessee & Georgia rail line about five miles below Resaca. The road passed Resaca about a mile to the west. From there the further advance on the town and railroad was planned.

General Cox, then with Schofield's Army of the Ohio outside Dalton, described the situation at Resaca:

> Resaca itself stands in the elbow at the junction of the Connasauga [river] with the Oostanaula [river], and on the north bank of the latter stream. Camp Creek, another small stream, flows into the river just west of the village, and the high plateau bordering it and the more rugged hills between it and the Connasauga a little further north, made it a very strong place for the intrenched camp which the Confederate commander had prepared there. It was held by two brigades under General Canty [sic], and such a force could easily defend it against a very strong column.[23]

Seeing the rebels' fortifications, McPherson decided they were too strong to be taken by storm, or that the cost in expected casualties did not justify a frontal assault, or that positioning his troops for an assault could result in their being cut off from the rest of

Sherman's army. Late in the afternoon of the 9th, after scattered fighting throughout the day, he withdrew his troops back to Snake Creek Gap, halting at the gap's southern end.

Sherman, who had great expectations for the success of McPherson's mission, took the news of the withdrawal hard. "Sherman was disappointed in this," General Cox related in his chronicle of the campaign, "and when they met, told McPherson that he [McPherson] had lost a great opportunity; but he carefully spared the feelings of his subordinate, with whom his friendship was most intimate, and he applied his energies at once to making the most of the actual situation."[24] Another officer, Captain Henry Stone, serving on General Thomas's staff, was on the scene when Sherman received the news. He gave a different account of Sherman's reaction of "disappointment"— the word Sherman used in recounting the events. "Disappointment is a mild word to apply to the feeling he showed when he learned of the failure of his cherished scheme. If he had said, 'I was extremely angry, and almost determined to relieve McPherson of his command,' his statement would have been nearer the truth."[25]

In Johnston's mind, at least, McPherson's withdrawal was the smart and right move to make. When Johnston learned that the Army of the Tennessee had arrived at Snake Creek Gap on May 8, he sent a brigade from Dalton to reinforce Brigadier General James Cantey's brigade that was already manning the fortifications at Resaca and he later ordered General Hood to take three divisions and hurry to Resaca to join Cantey. Also on the way were ten thousand infantry and four thousand cavalry commanded by Lieutenant General Leonidas Polk, coming to Johnston's aid from Mississippi. "General Sherman ... blames McPherson for not seizing the place," Johnston observed. "That officer [McPherson] tried the works and found them too strong to be seized. General Sherman says that if McPherson had placed his whole force astride the railroad, he could have there easily withstood the attack of all Johnston's army. Had he done so, 'all Johnston's army' would have been upon him at the dawn of the next day, the cannon giving General Sherman intelligence of the movement of that army. About twice his force in front and three thousand men in his immediate rear [Cantey's two brigades] would have overwhelmed him, making a most auspicious beginning of the campaign for the Confederates."[26]

Sherman let two days pass without taking any significant action, then on Thursday, May 12 he started shifting his troops around the west side of Dalton, moving toward Snake Creek Gap and leaving Johnston wondering. Johnston was still holding onto the idea that the main assault would come from Crow Valley, north of Dalton. Was the movement toward Snake Creek Gap a feint for a Crow Valley attack? Or was it a signal that Resaca now was the point of Sherman's big assault? He wrestled with the answers.

General Polk had arrived at Resaca in the afternoon of May 11, some of his troops having preceded him, but most of them en route from Rome, Georgia on hastily commandeered railway cars. That evening Polk, along with Hood, whose troops had been halted at Tilton when McPherson withdrew back to Snake Creek Gap, took a train to Dalton to confer with Johnston. After discussions that lasted almost till midnight, Johnston decided, for the sake of prudence, to leave Hood and two of his divisions where they were in Tilton, about halfway between Dalton and Resaca, near enough to respond to an attack from Crow Valley or at Resaca. He was hedging. At the same time, Hood was doing some personal hedging. He had already had two brushes with death, having suffered a wound at Gettysburg that crippled his left arm and another at Chickamauga that cost him his right leg. After the meeting with Johnston, Hood had Polk, the former Episcopal bishop, baptize him, using water drawn from a horse trough. That act of ministry done, Polk then took the train back to Resaca.

Anxious to divine Sherman's intentions, Johnston wired Polk the next day, May 12, to ask him for intelligence on the Union troop movement. Polk wired back to tell Johnston three Union corps were now opposite Resaca and, most significantly, that "Sherman is at Snake Creek Gap." That bit of information gave Johnston the answer he had been seeking. The major attack would be at Resaca, for wherever Sherman was, Johnston concluded, there also would be the main event. Quickly shelved were whatever plans Johnston had for turning back a Union attack at Crow Valley and then driving a broken Union army back into Tennessee. Sherman now and first had to be met at Resaca.

During the evening of May 12, with one last thought of a Crow Valley attack, Johnston ordered Brigadier General Joseph Wheeler to take his cavalry on a sweeping reconnaissance of the valley to make sure Sherman had indeed moved his troops from the north side of Dalton. Johnston then boarded a train for Resaca. Hood went with him as far as Tilton.

About 10 o'clock in the morning of Friday, May 13 Johnston's Army of Tennessee left Dalton to move into position at Resaca. As the men marched down the road, as if on parade, Johnston, astride his bay horse, sat watching them troop by him. "We passed old Joe and his staff," one of the marchers, Sam Watkins of the First Tennessee Regiment, recounted. "He has on a light or mole colored hat, with a black feather in it. He is listening to the firing going on at the front. One little cheer, and the very ground seems to shake with cheers. Old Joe smiles as blandly as a modest maid, raises his hat in acknowledgement, makes a polite bow, and rides toward the firing."[27]

The rebel army reached Resaca just as Sherman's troops, approaching from Snake Creek Gap, came up against Major General William W. Loring's division, of Polk's corps, about a mile outside the town. "Their approach," Johnston related, "was delayed long enough by Loring's opposition to give me time to select the ground to be occupied by our troops. And while they were taking this ground the Federal army was forming in front of them. The left of Polk's corps occupied the west face of the intrenchment of Resaca. Hardee's corps, also facing to the west, formed the center. Hood's, its left division facing to the west and the two others to the north-west, was on the right, and, crossing the railroad, reached the Connasauga. The enemy skirmished briskly with the left half of our line all the afternoon."[28]

"Briskly" may have understated the nearly continuous exchange of fire, which was at times intense, the Union troops persistently attacking all along the Confederate line, as if probing to find a weak spot. As darkness deepened at day's end, the firing tapered off and died. In the light of the new day, Saturday, May 14, the firing resumed on both sides, the Union troops seeming to concentrate their heaviest assault at the spot on the rebel line where Hood's and Hardee's corps connected. Between 10 A.M. and 2 P.M. Johnston's forces turned back three Union attempts to break through the rebel line. Late in the day the Confederates reciprocated with an assault on Sherman's left flank, Johnston ordering Hood to attack with two reinforced divisions (Major General Alexander P. Stewart's and Major General Carter L. Stevenson's), signaling to the troops with his sword as he sat mounted on his horse atop a hillock near the center of the line. "He [Hood] was instructed to ... drive the enemy from the railroad, the object of the operation being to prevent them from using it," Johnston related. "The attack was extremely well conducted and executed, and before dark (it was begun at 6 P.M.) the enemy was driven from his ground. This encouraged me to hope for a more important success; so General Hood was directed to renew the fight next morning. His troops were greatly elated by this announcement, made to them that evening."[29]

That night, riding from the right side of his line, where the success had been gained, to the left side, Johnston discovered the success there had been won by Sherman's troops.

Forward units of Polk's command had been driven from a hill that commanded the Confederates' bridges over the Oostanaula River, and Union troops were reported crossing the Oostanaula on pontoon bridges they had laid near Calhoun, Georgia, about five miles below Resaca. Two divisions were said to have already crossed. Johnston instantly changed his plans. He called off the advance he had earlier ordered Hood to make the next day. He ordered a division of Hardee's corps to march immediately to the spot where the Union troops had crossed the Oostanaula. He further ordered his army's chief engineer, Lieutenant Colonel Stephen Prestman, to carve out a road during the night and lay a pontoon bridge across the Oostanaula about a mile above the bridges now commanded by Union artillery.

The morning of the 15th — Sunday — began with heavy skirmishing against the entire rebel front, which continued throughout the day. Repeated assaults against the line of rebel entrenchments were repulsed. Then came some confusion. Sometime after noon, intelligence was received saying that the report of the Union's crossing of the Oostanaula was incorrect. Johnston again reversed his orders to Hood and now instructed him to renew his advance on the Union left as had been planned, telling him to move out as soon as he was joined by three brigades from Polk's and Hardee's corps. Just as Hood was about to move forward, a new message was received at Johnston's command post stating that the original intelligence about the Union crossing was accurate after all and that the right of Sherman's army was pouring across the Oostanaula near Calhoun, to the rear of Johnston's position at Resaca. "Upon this," Johnston related, "the idea of fighting north of the Oostanaula was abandoned at once, and the orders to Lieutenant-General Hood were countermanded. Stewart's division did not receive the countermand from corps headquarters in time to prevent its execution of the previous order, and engaging the enemy, and of course it suffered before being recalled."[30]

A stand at Resaca, Johnston decided, was no longer feasible. He had not enough troops, he explained to his commanders, to repel the Union force at his rear and at the same time hold his existing position. "The danger that threatened our line of communications made me regard the continued occupation of Resaca as too hazardous," he related. "The army was therefore ordered to cross the river about midnight; Polk's and Hardee's corps by the railroad-bridge and one on the trestles near it; and Hood's by the pontoon-bridge laid by Colonel Prestman the night before."[31] Confederate pickets kept up a steady musket fire to distract the Union forces in front of them while their wagons and artillery pieces took to the roads heading south. Once across the Oostanaula, Johnston's troops burned the railroad bridge, and his engineers took up the pontoon bridge and loaded it aboard wagons to take with them. The withdrawal from Resaca was complete. The fight for Resaca had cost the Confederates an estimated 2,800 casualties. Union losses were estimated at 2,747. Sherman put his losses, at Dalton and Resaca, at 600 killed and 3,375 wounded.

Sherman's troops entered Resaca at daylight on May 16. They spent little time there, however. Sherman ordered a rapid pursuit of the retreating rebels, McPherson's army moving by Lay's Ferry, on the right, Thomas's by the railroad and Schofield's on the left, by the road that crossed the Oostanaula above Echota.

Hardee's corps was ordered to take a position at Calhoun that would allow him to check Sherman's leading units, advancing from the northwest. The other rebel corps halted south of Calhoun, where Johnston and his staff arrived in the late afternoon of May 16 and set up a command post that would prove very temporary. Johnston had hoped to find a good defensive position near Calhoun, covering the several roads leading southward from Snake Creek Gap and the area of Resaca, but, as he reported, "No such were there." Eagerly searching his map, he spied a spot about a mile north of Adairsville, about fifteen miles south of Calhoun, where, according to the map drawn by his engineers, the valley of Oothcaloga Creek was so narrow that his army could form a line of battle across it, with his flanks holding the heights on the right and left, and there present a stout barrier to the Union advance. On the morning of May 17, as Sherman's troops drew ever closer, the Confederates marched southward toward Adairsville.

New disappointment awaited Johnston at the site. Upon reaching it he could see that the valley was much wider than the map indicated and that the heights were not so high and commanding. Johnston quickly determined there was no defensive advantage to be had there, and so after giving his troops a rest, he ordered them to Cassville, about ten miles farther to the southeast and that much closer to Atlanta. Before setting out with his army, which had been recently reinforced by the arrival from Mississippi of the 3,700-man cavalry division of Polk's command, Johnston agreed to a request from his wife. She had written to Polk to tell him Johnston had never been baptized and to ask that he rectify that neglect. In a candlelight ceremony witnessed by Hood and Hardee, Polk baptized the commanding general.

Once more studying his maps, Johnston saw there were two roads leading southward out of Adairsville. One followed the railroad southwestward to Kingston, west of Cassville, and then turned sharply eastward to Cassville. The other went directly to Cassville, passed through the town and on the south side of town was joined by the road from Kingston. "The probability that the Federal army would divide — a column following each road — gave me a hope of engaging and defeating one of them before it could receive aid from the other," Johnston recalled. He asked the engineer officer who was familiar with the area to describe it to him. "He described the country on the direct road as open, and unusually favorable for attack. It was evident, from the map, that the distance between the two Federal columns would be greatest when that following the railroad should be near Kingston. Lieutenant Buchanan [the engineer officer] thought that the communications between the columns at this part of their march would be eight or nine miles, by narrow and crooked country roads."[32]

Johnston's plan was for Hood and Polk to take the direct road to Cassville and Hardee to take the road that followed the railroad to Kingston. At an appropriate spot on the direct road, Hardee would form a line of battle in front of the pursuing Union column, and Hood would strike the column's left flank from a country road that paralleled the direct road about a mile to the east.

In the morning of May 18 Hardee's corps marched to Kingston, and Polk's and Hood's corps took the direct road to Cassville, halting about a mile north of the town. Polk's troops deployed in two lines, crossing the road and facing Adairsville. Hood's troops halted near the country road from which he would hit the Union column's flank. During the day, Jackson's cavalry had observed a Union column on the Kingston road, and Wheeler's cavalry had spied another column of bluecoats headed toward Cassville on the direct road. Sherman had taken the bait, and Johnston was ready for him.

Johnston narrated the initial action that followed:

Next morning [Thursday, May 19], when Brig.-General Jackson's reports showed that the head of the Federal column following the railroad was near Kingston, Lieutenant-General Hood was directed to move with his corps to a country road about a mile to the east of that from Adairsville, and parallel to it, and to march northward on that road, right in front. Polk's corps, as then formed, was to advance to meet and engage the enemy approaching from Adairsville;

and it was expected that Hood's would be in position to fall upon the left flank of those troops as soon as Polk attacked them in front. An order was read to each regiment, announcing that we were about to give battle to the enemy. It was received with exultation.[33]

Then came the surprise, described by Johnston:

When General Hood's column had moved two or three miles, that officer received a report from a member of his staff, to the effect that the enemy was approaching on the Canton road, in rear of the right of the position from which he [Hood] had just marched. Instead of transmitting this report to me, and moving on in obedience to his orders, he fell back to that road and formed his corps across it, facing to our right and rear, toward Canton, without informing me of this strange departure from the instructions he had received. I heard of this erratic movement after it had caused such loss of time as to make the attack impracticable; for its success depended on accuracy in timing it. The intention was therefore abandoned.[34]

Hood had barely got started on his northward march when he received a report that a Union column of unknown strength was on a road to his right and fearing that if he continued northward, the enemy force would be at his rear, he ordered his troops to fall back and take a defensive position. It turned out that the Union column that had been spotted was a unit of Major General Daniel Butterfield's division. It had become lost and was trying to find its way back to the main body of Butterfield's troops. The accidental presence of an unthreatening, inferior enemy force had spooked Hood, the reputed fighter.

Johnston then turned to a Plan B, which was to take a stand on a ridge southeast of Cassville and entice Sherman to attack him there. Retiring to his tent not long after dark, with his troops in place, Johnston found Polk's aide, Colonel William Gale, waiting for him with an invitation to come to Polk's headquarters for a meeting with Hood and Polk. After he had eaten his supper, Johnston, accompanied by Major General Samuel French, went to hear what Hood and Polk had to say.

"The two officers, General Hood taking the lead," Johnston related, "expressed the opinion very positively that neither of their corps would be able to hold its position next day; because, they said, a part of each was enfiladed by Federal artillery.... On that account they urged me to abandon the ground immediately, and cross the Etowah. A discussion of more than an hour followed, in which they very earnestly and decidedly expressed the opinion, or conviction rather, that when the Federal artillery opened upon them next day it would render their positions untenable in an hour or two.

"Although the position was the best we had occupied, I yielded at last, in the belief that the confidence of the commanders of two of the three corps of the army, of their inability to resist the enemy, would inevitably be communicated to their troops, and produce that inability. Lieutenant-General Hardee, who arrived after this decision, remonstrated against it strongly, and was confident that his corps could hold its ground, although less favorably posted. The error was adhered to, however, and the position abandoned before daybreak."[35]

The Army of Tennessee, many of its troops disheartened by the hasty, unexpected withdrawal, straggled through the sultry Georgia night, passing through Cartersville, following the railroad, crossing the Etowah River about noon, burning the bridges behind them, and finally going into bivouac around the community of Allatoona, below the Allatoona Mountains, during daylight on Saturday, May 21.

On May 23 Johnston received intelligence from his cavalry that Sherman was attempting another flanking maneuver, crossing the Etowah ten miles west of Cartersville, near Stilesboro, then moving southward in three columns. Johnston promptly issued orders to meet the threat. He ordered Hardee that afternoon to march by way of New Hope Church, a Methodist meetinghouse about twelve miles southwest of Allatoona, to the intersection of the New Hope Church road with the road that led from Stilesboro to Dallas and Atlanta. Polk was ordered to take a road to the left of Hardee's route and move to that same Stilesboro-Dallas road. Hood was ordered to follow Hardee the next day, May 24.

"Hardee's corps reached the point designated to him that afternoon," Johnston related. "Polk's was within four miles of it to the east, and Hood's within four miles of New Hope Church, on the road to it from Alatoona [sic]. On the 25th the latter reached New Hope Church, early in the day. Intelligence was received from General Jackson's [cavalry] troops soon after, that the Federal army was near — its right at Dallas, and its line extending toward Alatoona."[36] General Sherman explained the Union army's movement: "Dallas, the point [the army was] aimed at, was a small town on the other or east side of this [Pumpkin Vine] creek, and was the point of concentration of a great many roads that led in every direction. Its possession would be a threat to Marietta and Atlanta, but I could not then venture to attempt either, till I had regained the use of the railroad, at least as far down as its *debouche* from the Allatoona range of mountains. Therefore, the movement was chiefly designed to compel Johnston to give up Allatoona."[37]

With haste the Confederates felled trees and stacked logs to build breastworks behind which they would attempt to hold off the advancing bluecoats. About an hour and a half before sunset the Union artillery opened "a brisk cannonade," as Johnston called it, against the rebel line opposite New Hope Church, giving its announcement of the coming assault. The brunt of the Union assault, made by an estimated twenty thousand infantrymen of General Hooker's corps during a furious thunderstorm, was borne by Major General Alexander Stewart's division of Hood's corps. Seeing the point of the attack, Johnston dispatched a courier to Stewart to ask if he needed reinforcements. Stewart's confident answer: "My own troops will hold the position."[38] Holding it inflicted, by Hooker's count, 1,665 casualties on the attackers. Rebel losses were estimated at 350.

The next morning, Thursday, May 26, after a night of rain, Johnston discovered that Sherman's line had moved, now extending much farther to the rebel right than it had on Wednesday. Johnston shifted Polk's corps to the right to cover the new Union position, although there was no significant action that day. Late in the afternoon on the 27th a Union force emerged from the woods near Pickett's Mill to strike the rebel line's right flank, but was crushed by the Confederates' heavy fire, suffering some 1,450 casualties. Rebel casualties numbered about 450.

Johnston planned a counterattack on the Union left for the 28th, at Hood's suggestion and with Hood's corps playing the key role. The attack never came off, though, Hood aborting the operation, reporting to Johnston that Union troops had strengthened their line and that an attack on it would be, as he said, "inexpedient." Hood had punted once again.

Skirmishing continued each day, but generally a lull in the fighting prevailed. On June 4 Johnston decided to take a new position. "It was evident ," he reported, "that the great body of the Federal army was moving to its left rear, toward the railroad, the movement being covered by its long line of intrenchment. The Confederate army then marched to a position selected beforehand, and carefully marked out by Colonel Prestman, the chief-engineer. Its left was on Lost Mountain, and its right, composed of cavalry, beyond the railroad and behind Noonday Creek."[39]

By now Johnston had given up any idea of launching a major offensive against Sherman's army. There was too much evidence of the unbearably high cost of attacking entrenched troops, and he was convinced it should not be attempted. Instead, he would exact the high cost from the Union army. His intention was to fight and fall back. Repeatedly. That tactic, however, drove President Davis into frenzies. While Lee was doing in Virginia the same thing Johnston was doing in Georgia, fighting and falling back, Davis condemned Johnston and praised Lee. Johnston nevertheless remained steadfast, declaring that, "We held every position occupied until our communications were strongly threatened; then fell back only far enough to secure them, watching for opportunities to attack, keeping near enough to the Federal army to assure the Confederate Administration that Sherman could not send reenforcements to Grant, and hoping to reduce the odds against us by partial engagements."[40]

Union skirmishers and probing attacks along the rebel line were all turned back from behind the Confederate entrenchments. On the evening of June 13, however, General Hardee told Johnston that he was afraid the outpost on Pine Mountain, the tallest peak between Lost Mountain and Kennesaw Mountain, might be at risk, being too far, he thought, from the line manned by his corps. Hardee suggested that he and Johnston visit the outpost the next day and decide whether it should be maintained. The next morning the two of them, accompanied by Polk, who wanted to get a high-level view of the ground in front of his corps, rode up the height. Johnston described the tragic event that followed:

> Just when we had concluded our examination, and the abandonment of the hill had been decided upon, a party of soldiers, that had gathered behind us from mere curiosity, apparently tempted an artillery officer whose battery was in front, six or seven hundred yards from us, to open his fire upon them; at first firing shot very slowly. Lieutenant-General Polk, unconsciously exposed by his characteristic insensibility to danger, fell by the third shot, which passed from left to right through the middle of his chest. The death of this eminent Christian and soldier, who had been distinguished in every battle in which the Army of Tennessee had been engaged, produced deep sorrow in our troops.[41]

For the next two days Union skirmishers probed the rebel line, looking for a weakness and at last finding one on the Confederates' left near Lost Mountain. Johnston adjusted his line to correct it, but fearing another sweeping flanking movement by Sherman, he decided to pick up and move again, this time to the western slopes of Kennesaw Mountain. His army moved into its new position there during the night of June 18 and began digging new defensive works.

On the morning of June 27, the third successive day with clear skies and no rain, Sherman's artillery opened on the Confederates' Kennesaw Mountain emplacements with fire from fifty guns, and his infantry began a laborious ascent of Kennesaw's slopes, at first in waves of skirmishers and then massed in a thick column, Sherman intending to drive his column like a human spear through the thin rebel line. The failure was disastrous, Sherman's losses exceeding three thousand, while Johnston lost 552.

On the 1st and 2nd of July rebel outposts reported Union troops shifting to the Union's right, heading toward the Chattahoochee River, the last natural barrier on the way to Atlanta. Johnston countered with another movement of his army, abandoning his position on Kennesaw Mountain and marching six miles southward to form a new line of defense near Smyrna. On July 4 Sherman again shifted to gain the rebels' flank, and Johnston retreated to a new position that straddled the Chattahoochee, with part of his army just north (or west) of the Chattahoochee and the rest on the south (or east side).

Sherman responded with a further advance, a new line of entrenchments and a new flanking movement that carried General Schofield's troops across the Chattahoochee upriver of Johnston's position. At that, Johnston withdrew all his troops to the south bank of the river and prepared to establish new defensive lines at the very gates of Atlanta.

When news of that move reached Richmond, President Davis, frustrated and angry, decided it was time to have the axe fall. On the evening of Sunday, July 17, at his headquarters three miles north of Atlanta, Johnston got the word. It came in a telegram from the Confederate army's adjutant general, Samuel Cooper:

> I am directed by the Secretary of War to inform you that as you have failed to arrest the advance of the enemy to the vicinity of Atlanta, far in the interior of Georgia, and express no confidence that you can defeat or repel him, you are hereby relieved from command of the Army and Department of Tennessee....[42]

Two hours after Johnston received that message Hood also received a message from Richmond. It informed him that he had been promoted to the rank of full general and had been placed in command of the Army of Tennessee. The job of saving Atlanta was now his. He had repeatedly violated army regulations and backstabbed Johnston to get it, and now he had it.

General Sigel and the Battle of New Market, May 15, 1864

Major General Franz Sigel was the man to whom General Grant assigned the vital task of sweeping the Shenandoah valley clear of rebel forces. He got the job because he commanded the Army's Department of West Virginia, and Grant needed the department's nine thousand troops.

Sigel was thirty-nine years old in the spring of 1864, slim and bony-faced, with a mustache that curved down past the sides of his mouth and a dark beard that traced his jawline as if penciled on it. A German immigrant and a refugee from a failed German revolution, he was another of President Lincoln's generals appointed for political reasons. Unlike some of the others, though, Sigel had military training and experience. He had graduated from the Karlsruhe Military Academy, had been commissioned in the army of Baden (once an independent German state; now a part of Germany) and had risen to the rank of colonel before the four-thousand-man army of revolutionaries he had recruited and commanded was wiped out by Prussian and Wurttemberg forces in April 1848. Following the collapse of the revolution he had fled first to Switzerland, then to England and in 1852 he had immigrated to the United States.

At first he lived in New York City and got a job teaching in the city's public schools, then he had moved to St. Louis, where he became a professor at the German-American Institute. In 1860 he was elected director of the St. Louis public school system and by then had become influential in St. Louis's German immigrant community. When the war started in 1861 he was commissioned a colonel in command of the Third (U.S.) Missouri Infantry. Keen on keeping Missouri in the Union and in winning the support of German immigrants, Lincoln had Sigel promoted to brigadier general in August 1861. Sigel's record as a commander in combat wasn't anything to recommend him. He had been defeated in the German revolution and had been defeated in the Battle of Carthage, Missouri when he faced a Confederate-sympathizing Missouri militia force. He had served under Brigadier General Nathaniel Lyon at the Battle of Wilson's Creek near Springfield, Missouri in August 1861, and in that battle Sigel's column was routed by rebel troops, and General Lyon was killed.

His best day in the field had come at the Battle of Pea Ridge in northwest Arkansas on March 8, 1862, when he commanded two divisions — composed mostly of German immigrants — in a Union army led by Brigadier General Samuel R. Curtis. Sigel helped defeat a rebel army of superior numbers commanded by Major General Earl Van Dorn.

On March 21, 1862, Sigel was promoted to major general, then was given command of a division operating in the Shenandoah valley and was harassed and defeated by Stonewall Jackson. He was later given command of a corps in Major General John Pope's newly organized Army of Virginia and shared in another massive defeat in the Second Battle of Bull Run (Second Manassas). By then Sigel had gained a reputation for ineptness. But he

remained an influential, even inspirational figure among the nation's German immigrants, a continuing consideration in Washington.

Apparently because of that consideration President Lincoln in March 1864 instructed Secretary of War Stanton to put Sigel in command of the Army's newly formed Department of West Virginia, which then forced Grant to deal with him in the execution of Grant's plan for ending the war.

On March 29 Sigel received his first orders from Grant in a letter delivered to him at his headquarters in Cumberland, Virginia by Major General Edward Ord. The letter, as Sigel reported it, said that he "should immediately assemble 8000 infantry, 1500 cavalry ('picked men'), besides artillery, provided with ten days' rations, at Beverly [West Virginia], for the purpose of marching by Covington to Staunton; the troops to be under the command of General Ord...."[1] Sigel said he took

U.S. Maj. Gen. Franz Sigel. A German immigrant, Sigel was believed to be influential among German-American voters and was made a major general for political reasons. He proved incompetent in the field. In reporting Sigel's defeat at New Market, U.S. Army chief of staff General Halleck told Grant, "Sigel is in full retreat.... He will do nothing but run; never did anything else." (Library of Congress) "the most energetic measures" to get the troops and their supplies to Beverly, but was hampered by days of rain that made it impossible to move even empty wagons over the soggy roads. Only 6,500 men could be assembled for the intended expedition, he informed Grant. Amid the delays and the problems, which he observed while spending days in Sigel's headquarters, General Ord decided he had had enough and asked Grant to relieve him, which he did, replacing him with Brigadier General William W. Averell.

Grant's plan was for Sigel to march southwest through the Shenandoah valley from Winchester to Staunton, where he would link up with the columns of Averell and Brigadier General George Crook, both of which would also march southwestward, to the west of Sigel's column. Crook's objective was the Virginia & Tennessee Railroad and the railroad bridge over the New River near Dublin, Virginia. Averell's objectives were the lead mines and salt works at Wytheville and Saltville.

From the link-up at Staunton the three columns would proceed eastward to join General Meade and the Army of the Potomac. In the meantime, they would have ripped up and disrupted the Confederates' railway supply line, deprived the rebels of two crucial necessities — lead and salt — and cut a wide swath of devastation and destruction through an area of Virginia that was vital to keeping General Lee's rebel army fed. Grant had little confidence that Sigel himself would accomplish much, saying so when he wrote to Sherman and told him, "From the expedition from the Department of West Virginia I do not calculate on very great results; but it is the only way I can take troops from there."[2]

Sigel and his infantry reached Winchester on Sunday, May 1, while his cavalry units advanced as far as Cedar Creek and Strasburg. "From our position at Winchester and Cedar Creek," Sigel related, "we learned that there was no hostile force in the Shenandoah Valley, except General Imboden's cavalry and mounted infantry, reported to be about 3000 strong. It seemed to me, therefore, necessary to advance farther south toward Staunton, in order to induce Breckinridge to send a part of his forces against us, and thereby facilitate the operations of Crook and Averell. Before leaving Winchester, a force of 500 cavalry, under Colonel Jacob Higgins, was sent toward Wardensville to protect our right flank, and Colonel William H. Boyd, with 300 select horsemen, into the Luray Valley to cover our left flank...."[3]

Brigadier General John D. Imboden, commanding the Confederate force that Sigel had learned was alone in defending the length of the Shenandoah valley, was a forty-one-year-old lawyer, former teacher at a school for the deaf, dumb and blind, and a former member of the House of Delegates in the Virginia legislature, where he had served two terms. He was born and grew up in Staunton. In November 1859 he was given a commission as captain in the Staunton artillery unit of the Virginia State Militia, a unit he had helped organize. He commanded that unit when it participated in the capture of Harpers Ferry and commanded an artillery battery at the First Battle of Bull Run (First Manassas). Deafened in one ear by the firing of an artillery piece, he gave up the artillery in September 1862 and recruited a battalion of partisan rangers that became the 62nd Virginia Mounted Infantry and fought under Stonewall Jackson. He was appointed brigadier general in January 1863. His brigade served under Jeb Stuart in the Gettysburg campaign. On July 21, 1863 General Lee, commanding all Confederate operations in Virginia, assigned Imboden as commander of the Valley District, comprising the area west of the Blue Ridge Mountains as far south as the James River.

"By the month of April, 1864," Imboden related, "information reached us that General Sigel had established himself at Winchester, and was preparing for a forward movement with over eight thousand infantry, twenty-five hundred cavalry, and three or four field-batteries. On the 2d of May I broke camp at Mount Crawford, in Rockingham County, something over seventy miles from Winchester, and moved to meet Sigel and find out as far as possible his strength and designs and report the facts to General Lee."[4] Included in Imboden's command were the 62nd Mounted Infantry Brigade, the 23rd Virginia Cavalry, the 18th Virginia Cavalry, a cavalry battalion from Maryland, part of another Maryland cavalry battalion, a unit of partisan rangers, a horse artillery unit with six field guns, and the signal corps of the Valley District.

By this stage of the war, the Confederates, including General Imboden, desperate for manpower, were looking for help wherever it could be found, including those too young or too old for conscription. Imboden reported that he "ordered General William H. Harman at Staunton to notify the 'reserves' (militia) of Rockingham and Augusta Counties, consisting of men over forty-five and boys between sixteen and eighteen years of age, and all detailed men on duty in shops, at furnaces, etc., to be ready to move at a moment's notice. A similar notification was sent to General Francis H. Smith, Commandant of the Virginia Military Institute at Lexington, where there were about three hundred cadets under eighteen years of age at school. My veteran troops, 'effective present,' numbered but 1492 men when we left Mount Crawford on the 2d of May, to which should be added about 100 men scouting either in front of or behind Sigel. Harman's 'reserves' did not amount to one thousand men, and these were undisciplined and armed mostly with hunting-rifles and shot-guns. This was the total scattered and incongruous force in front of Sigel in the valley the first week in May."[5]

On May 5 Imboden's motley army reached Woodstock, Virginia, about twelve miles below Sigel's position at Strasburg. Intelligence from Imboden's scouts and residents of the area gave Imboden a clear idea of the force he was facing. "About eleven thousand men were reported in my front," he reported. "The Signal Corps in the mountains west of us reported a force of 7000 men at Lewisburg, only a little over 100 miles west from Staunton, apparently awaiting Sigel's movements to cooperate with him."[6] Imboden swiftly relayed that information to Lee and made, as he said, the most earnest appeals to him, asking Lee to send more troops to the valley immediately. Lee responded that he was too sorely pressed by Grant to be able to spare any men to aid the defense of the Shenandoah valley. Imboden would have to do the best he could with what he had. Although he had offered no help, Lee ordered Imboden to retard Sigel's advance in every way he could and to be careful to avoid being surrounded and captured.

Imboden set out to do his best. From atop Massanutten Mountain, overlooking Strasburg, his signalmen on May 8 spotted the two cavalry reconnaissance parties that Sigel had sent out, one moving westward on the road to Moorefield, West Virginia and one moving eastward through Front Royal, Virginia. "These facts," Imboden related, "convinced me that Sigel, before venturing to advance, meant to ascertain whether he had enemies in dangerous force within striking distance on either flank, an investigation that would consume several days. As there were no troops, except my little band, nearer than General Lee's army, it was manifestly important to attack these detachments as far from Strasburg as possible and delay their return as long as possible."[7]

Imboden turned first to Sigel's reconnaissance detail moving on Imboden's left. Leaving Colonel George H. Smith in charge at his Woodstock headquarters, Imboden himself led the attack force, composed of the 18th Virginia Cavalry Regiment — commanded by Colonel George Imboden, the general's brother — the partisan rangers commanded by Captain John

N. McNeill, and two field pieces from the battery commanded by Captain J.H. McClanahan. "It was given out that I was about to move camp some five or six miles back toward the North Mountain in search of better grazing for our horses," General Imboden related. "This ruse was practiced to prevent any Union man (and there were plenty around us) from taking the information of the movement to Sigel that night."[8] The plan was to take the attack force that night through a mountain pass called the Devil's Hole and intercept the reconnaissance detail on the Moorefield road some twenty miles from Strasburg. "We set out from Woodstock about 4 P.M. on Sunday [May 8] across the North Mountain, and, having accomplished the purposes of the expedition," Imboden reported vaguely, "on Monday, late in the night, reached Mount Jackson, where I found Colonel Smith, who, in the exercise of sound discretion, had fallen back from Woodstock."[9]

Sigel's account offers slightly more detail than Imboden's. "Before leaving Winchester," Sigel reported, "a force of 500 cavalry, under Colonel Jacob Higgins, was sent toward Wardensville to protect our right flank, and Colonel William H. Boyd, with 300 select horsemen, into the Luray Valley to cover our left flank, especially from Mosby; but Colonel Higgins was attacked and beaten by a detachment of Imboden's brigade between Wardensville and Moorefield on the 9th of May, and pursued north toward Romney."[10]

Imboden said he had received intelligence that Sigel's reconnaissance party moving on Imboden's right was on its way to New Market and was expecting to join Sigel's main force there by the middle of the week. "Upon this information," Imboden reported, "we laid a trap for Colonel Boyd, and on Wednesday [May 11] we captured 464 men, nearly all of this force."[11]

Sigel claimed that Boyd's force had but three hundred men in it and that "Colonel Boyd was ambuscaded on his way from the Luray Valley to New Market on the 13th and defeated, suffering a loss of 125 men and 200 horses."[12] General Sigel seems to have been confused about the date, the ambush having actually occurred on May 11, and perhaps about the casualties as well. "To gain more detailed information," he wrote, "two regiments of infantry, under Colonel August Moore, assisted by five hundred of the 1st New York (Lincoln) Cavalry, under Major Timothy Quinn, were sent forward on the 13th."[13]

"This force," Sigel continued in his account, "met a part of Imboden's troops near Mount Jackson on the 14th, forced them across the Shenandoah, took possession of the bridge, and, animated by this success, followed them as far as New Market, seven miles beyond Mount Jackson, or nineteen miles from the position of our forces at Woodstock. Having received information of this little exploit late at night of the 14th, and also that Breckinridge was on his march down the Valley, and considering that in case of an attack the position of Mount Jackson would afford many advantages as a defensive point, I ordered the troops to move at 5 A.M. on the 15th. They arrived at Mount Jackson at about 10 o'clock A.M.... Major T.F. Lang — an officer of General Averill's staff, and temporarily attached to my headquarters — whom I had ordered to the front, sent me a note, saying that our troops were in a good position and 'eager for the fight.'"[14]

Major General John Breckinridge, commanding a rebel force numbering more than 2,500 veteran troops, was on his way from southwestern Virginia to reinforce Imboden at New Market. On Thursday, May 12, Breckinridge wired Imboden to tell him he had arrived in Staunton and was on his way to reinforce Imboden. Thursday and Friday, Imboden reported, were spent "in perfect quiet at New Market, awaiting Sigel from the north-east and Breckinridge from the south-west, being well-informed of the movements of each."[15]

Imboden described the area of the impending clash with Sigel's army:

In 1864 the village of New Market had a population of about one thousand. Its site is one of the most beautiful in the far-famed Shenandoah Valley. The north fork of the Shenandoah River flows behind a range of hills that rise gently to a height of perhaps four hundred feet north-west of the town. These hills were cleared and in cultivation on their slope facing the town, and at their foot runs the valley turnpike, the main street of New Market and the great highway of the valley during the war.

About a mile east and south of the turnpike flows Smith's Creek, a mill-stream.... Five miles north-east of New Market the valley turnpike crosses the north fork of the Shenandoah, on the boundary of the celebrated 'Meem Plantation.' Rude's Hill, one mile nearer New Market than the river at the bridge, overlooks the whole of the Meem bottom from an elevation of perhaps seventy-five or one hundred feet.... From this hill to New Market, four miles, the country is undulating, and was cleared and in a high state of cultivation.

Between New Market and Smith's Creek, where the road to Luray crosses it, there was in 1864 a body of perhaps one hundred acres or more of woodland, and the town and its outskirts were ornamented with many orchards. From about the center of the town a deep little valley, or rather ravine, leads to the north fork of the Shenandoah River....[16]

Imboden received reports that Sigel's advance was so slow and cautious that he would not be able to proceed past Rude's Hill, about four miles north of New Market, by the end of the day on Saturday, May 14. Imboden then took time to ride to Lacey Springs, ten miles south of New Market, where he met up with Breckinridge and had dinner with him. During dinner a courier came to Imboden with a message from Colonel Smith, commanding during Imboden's absence, saying that Sigel's cavalry, 2,500 strong, had reached Rude's Hill, and that the Confederate 18th Cavalry, vigorously pressed, was falling back and that Smith had formed a line of battle just west of the town to cover the retreat. Imboden immediately started to leave to join his troops and as he did, Breckinridge, taking charge, ordered Imboden to hold New Market "at all hazards" until dark and then fall back four miles to a previously prepared position.

When he arrived back in New Market, Imboden saw that his line of battle extended from halfway up the hillside west of the town, across the valley turnpike toward Smith's Creek to a spot concealed by woodlands. McClanahan's artillery was posted on the extreme left of the line, up the hillside, giving it the advantage of plunging fire across the town and down on Sigel's guns. "From what I saw," Imboden wrote, "I felt no apprehension of any attempt to dislodge us that evening."[17]

At daylight Breckinridge's troops arrived, and Breckinridge looked over the ground and established his line of battle. "He had brought with him," Imboden recounted, "two small infantry brigades, commanded respectively by Brigadier-Generals John Echols and Gabriel C. Wharton.... He also had Major William McLaughlin's artillery — six guns — and a section of the cadet battery from the Virginia Military Institute, temporarily attached to McLaughlin. He had also ordered out the full corps of cadets — boys from 16 to 18 years old — and they were present to the number of 225, under command of Colonel Ship[p], one of their professors, and an excellent soldier in every sense. The 'reserves' from Augusta and Rockingham Counties had also been ordered out, but had not had time to assemble from their scattered homes, and were not up. The entire force, above enumerated and present, of all arms, did not exceed three thousand men. My whole effective force, then present, did not exceed 1600 additional men."[18] The total Confederate force facing Sigel, then, did not exceed 4,600 men, according to Imboden. Breckinridge, though, was satisfied. Having studied the ground and the rebel formation, he told Imboden, "We can attack and whip them here, and I'll do it."[19]

Breckinridge issued orders at once for all the troops to advance as rapidly as possible, and for Major McLaughlin not to wait for the infantry, but to bring up his guns immediately. "I was ordered," Imboden related, "as soon as the artillery and infantry came up, to concentrate all my cavalry and with McClanahan's battery take position on our extreme right next to Smith's Creek, to cover that flank. Within little more than an hour these dispositions were all made and McLaughlin 'opened the ball.'"[20]

Colonel George D. Wells of the 34th Massachusetts Infantry described the ensuing action from his troops' perspective, recording also the battle's outcome:

> The rebels advanced in three lines of battle, each, I think, as heavy as ours, with masses on the right and left. The ground was perfectly open, not a tree or shrub to obstruct the view. Nothing could be finer than their advance. Their yelling grew steadily nearer: our skirmishers and infantry in front came back on the double-quick, some of them running through and over my lines.
>
> The air was filled with bullets and bursting shells, and my men began to fall. I was ordered to deploy one company across my front as skirmishers, and Captain Leach, with Company G, went forward, and his groups halted and deployed in the tumult about 200 yards in advance, each man taking his exact interval and dressing to the right as steadily as on drill. The officers in the line were giving their orders in low tones, and every man stood, his gun at the ready, his finger on the trigger waiting to see the face of his foe. It was a marvel to me then and is now how men who almost never before had heard the rebel yell and the terrible din of the battlefield could be so entirely calm and self-possessed.
>
> Soon our men in front were, by the confusion, cleared away, the rebel lines were plainly seen, and the battle began. Our front fire was heavy, and the artillery had an enfilading fire, under which their first line went down. They staggered, went back, and their whole advance halted. Their fire ceased to be effective. A cheer ran along our line, and the first success was ours. I gave the order to "cease firing." Just then Colonel Thoburn, brigade commander, rode along the lines telling the men to "prepare to charge." He rode by me shouting some order I could not catch, and went to the regiment on my left, which immediately charged. I supposed this to be his order to me, and I commanded to fix bayonets and charge. The men fairly sprang forward. As we neared the crest of the hill we met the entire rebel force advancing and firing. The regiment on my left, which first met the fire, turned and went back, leaving the Thirty-fourth rushing alone into the enemy's line. I shouted to them to halt but could not make a single man hear or heed me, and it was not until they had climbed an intervening fence, and were rushing ahead on the other side, that I was able to run along the lines, and, seizing the color bearer by the shoulder, hold him fast as the only way of stopping the regiment.
>
> The wings surged ahead, but, losing sight of the colors, halted. The alignment rectified, we faced about and marched back to our position in common time. I could hear the officers saying to the men, and the men to each other, "Don't run!" "Keep your line!" "Common time!" &c. On reaching our position the regiment was halted, faced about, and resumed its fire. The path of the regiment between our line and the fence was sadly strewn with our fallen. Just as we halted Lieutenant-Colonel Lincoln fell....
>
> I was able to look about the field, and saw, to my surprise, that the artillery had limbered up and was moving off the field, and that the infantry had gone, save one regiment, which was gallantly holding its ground far to the left. The rebel line advanced until I could see, above the smoke, two battle-flags on the hill in front of the position where the artillery had been posted. I ordered a retreat, but they could not hear or would not heed the order. I was finally obliged to take hold of the color bearer, face him about, and tell him to follow me, in order to get the regiment off the field. They fell back slowly, firing in retreat, and encouraging each other not to run. But the rebels were coming on at the double-quick and concentrating their whole fire upon us. I told the men to run and get out of fire as quickly as possible, and rally behind the first cavalry line found to the rear. The colors were halted several times by different officers in positions where it was impossible to make a stand, and would only start again at my direct

order. I felt much relieved on receiving an order from General Sullivan, who was conspicuous on the field, that the line would be formed on the ridge and no stand made before it was reached.

I directed the color bearer to march directly there without halting, and, after getting out of fire, rode to the rear and went round into the pike and toward the front looking for stragglers. I saw none, and, meeting the colors, found most of the regiment with them. The new line was formed under the personal supervision of Generals Sigel, Stahel, and Sullivan. The pursuit of the enemy was checked and the command was gallantly withdrawn along the single road and across the narrow bridge into Mount Jackson in the most admirable order and without a single casualty.

That night we stood in line until along about 9 o'clock; marched behind the wagon train till 6 o'clock the next morning, and reached Strasburg about 5 P.M. of Monday, having been fifty-five hours almost continuously marching under arms in a constant and pouring storm. The march in that time was fifty-two miles....

The casualties foot up over 200 killed and wounded. Five out of every six who went in have the marks of bullets somewhere.... I have to regret the loss of some of the most noble and gallant spirits of my command.[21]

From the Confederate side a description of the battle was provided by the commander of the Virginia Military Institute's cadets, Lieutenant Colonel Scott Shipp:

At 12 o'clock on the night of the 14th received orders to prepare to march immediately, without beat of drum and as noiselessly as possible. We moved from camp at 1.30 o'clock, taking position in the general column in rear of Echols' brigade, being followed by the column of artillery under the command of Major McLaughlin. Having accomplished a distance of six miles and approached the position of the enemy, as indicated by occasional skirmishing with his pickets in front, a halt was called, and we remained on the side of the road two or three hours in the midst of a heavy fall of rain.

The general having determined to receive the attack of the enemy, made his dispositions for battle, posting the corps [of cadets] in reserve. He informed me that he did not wish to put the Cadets in if he could avoid it, but that should occasion require it, he would use them freely....

[I] was instructed ... to take position, after the deployments should have been made, 250 or 300 yards in rear of the front line of battle, and to maintain that distance. Having begun a flank movement to the left, about two miles south of New Market, the nature of the ground was such as to render it impossible that the [cadet] artillery should continue with the infantry column. I ordered Lieutenant Minge to join the general artillery column in the main road and to report to Major McLaughlin. After that I did not see the section of artillery until near the close of the engagement....

Continuing the advance on the ground to the left of the main road and south of New Market, at 12:30 P.M. we came under fire of the enemy's batteries. Having advanced a quarter of a mile under the fire we were halted and the column was deployed, the march up to this time having been by flank in column. The ground in front was open, with skirts of woods on the left. Here General Breckinridge sent for me and gave me in person my instructions. The general's plans seem to have undergone some modification. Instead of one line, with a reserve, he formed his infantry in two, artillery in the rear and to the right, the cavalry deployed and, guarding the right flank, left flank resting on a stream. Wharton's brigade of infantry constituted the first line; Echols' brigade the second. The battalion of Cadets, brigaded with Echols, was the last battalion but one from the left of the second line.... Wharton's line advanced; Echols' followed at 250 paces in rear. As Wharton's line ascended a knoll it came in full view of the enemy's batteries, which opened a heavy fire, but not having gotten the range, did but little damage. By the time the second line reached the same ground the Yankee gunners had the exact range, and their fire began to tell on our line with fearful accuracy. It was here that Captain Hill and others fell. Great gaps were made through the ranks, but the cadet, true to his discipline, would close in to the center to fill the interval and push steadily forward. The alignment of the battalion under this terrible fire, which strewed the ground with killed and wounded for more than a mile on open ground, would have been creditable even on a field day.

The advance was thus continued until having passed Bushong's house, a mile or more beyond New Market, and still to the left of the main road, the enemy's batteries, at 250 or 300 yards, opened on us with canister and case-shot, and their long lines of infantry were put into action at the same time. The fire was withering. It seemed impossible that any living creature could escape; and here we sustained our heaviest loss, a great many being wounded and numbers knocked down, stunned, and temporarily disabled. I was here disabled for a time, and the command devolved upon Captain H.A. Wise, Company A. He gallantly pressed onward.

We had before this gotten into the front line. Our line took a position behind a line of fence. A brisk fusillade ensued; a shout, a rush, and the day was won. The enemy fled in confusion, leaving killed, wounded, artillery, and prisoners in our hands. Our men pursued in hot haste until it became necessary to halt, draw ammunition, and re-establish the lines for the purpose of driving them from their last position on Rude's Hill, which they held with cavalry and artillery to cover the passage of the river, about a mile in their rear. Our troops charged and took the position without loss. The enemy withdrew, crossed the river, and burnt the bridge.

The engagement closed at 6.30 P.M. The Cadets did their duty, as the long list of casualties will attest....[22]

The cadets' casualties numbered eight killed and forty-eight wounded. Their greatest loss occurred at the storming of a Union artillery position, which they overran and captured. "A wild yell went up," Imboden related, "when a cadet mounted a caisson and waved the Institute flag in triumph over it."[23]

At 8 P.M. on the day of the battle General Sigel from his headquarters near Strasburg sent the U.S. Army's adjutant general a terse telegram reporting the disastrous engagement:

A severe battle was fought to-day at New Market between our forces and those of Echols and Imboden, under Breckinridge. Our troops were overpowered by superior numbers. I, therefore, withdrew them gradually from the battle-field, and recrossed the Shenandoah at about 7 P.M. Under the circumstances prevailing I find it necessary to retire to Cedar Creek. The battle was fought on our side by 5,500 in all against 8,000 to 9,000 of the enemy. We lost about 600 killed and wounded, and 50 prisoners.

The next day, May 16, he wired the adjutant general a second report:

After the battle of yesterday I retired gradually to Strasburg and Cedar Creek, bringing all my trains and all the wounded that could be transported from the battle-field with me. In consequence of the long line and the trains which had to be guarded I could not bring more than six regiments into the fight, besides the artillery and cavalry. The enemy have about 7,000 infantry, besides the other arms. Our losses are about 600 killed and wounded, and 50 prisoners. Five pieces of artillery had to be left on the field after being disabled or the horses shot. The retrograde movement to Strasburg was effected in perfect order, without any loss of material or men. The troops are in very good spirits, and will fight another battle if the enemy should advance against us. I will forward the full report, with list of casualties, by letter.

General Grant, hoping to hear good news from the campaign in the Shenandoah valley, instead got the bad news in a wire from General Halleck: "Sigel is in full retreat on Strasburg. He will do nothing but run; never did anything else."[24]

On Saturday, May 21 Sigel was told he had been relieved. Major General David Hunter would be the new commander of the Department of West Virginia, and the fight would go on.

The End of the CSS *Alabama*,
June 11 to June 19, 1864

A wearied and worn ship after two years of roving the world's high seas, attacking United States commercial shipping wherever it could be found and making itself the scourge of the American maritime industry, the Confederate cruiser *Alabama* on Saturday, June 11, 1864, steamed into the harbor at Cherbourg, France, on the English Channel, for rest and desperately needed repairs. It had been at sea for 534 of the previous 657 days.

The *Alabama*'s commander was Confederate navy Captain Raphael Semmes, fifty-four years old, a prideful veteran naval commander with a handlebar mustache waxed and twirled at both ends. A native of Maryland, Semmes had made his home in Mobile in 1849. He had served in the U.S. Navy from the time he was appointed a midshipman at age sixteen until the state of Alabama seceded from the Union on January 11, 1861, whereupon he resigned his U.S. commission and became a commander in the Confederate navy. Since then he had captained two Confederate raiders, the *Sumter*, which during six months in 1861 and early

Raphael Semmes, captain of the Confederate raider *Alabama*. Attempting to prove his ship was more than a privateer waging war on unarmed merchant vessels, Semmes boldly challenged the USS *Kearsarge* to a death duel in the English Channel. (LIBRARY OF CONGRESS)

1862 had captured seventeen U.S. merchant ships before it was abandoned, and the *Alabama*, which in its twenty-two months of service had captured 447 vessels, most of which had been released, some freed on payment of ransom, some burned and at least one of them sunk, the U.S. warship *Hatteras*, which the *Alabama* sank after a fight of less than fifteen minutes off the Texas coast near Galveston. The *Alabama* had also taken two thousand prisoners, including sailors and passengers, who later had been freed. The ship's actions, strangely, had never caused any loss of life.

The *Alabama* was specially made for its job of harassing Union shipping. It was, as described by its first officer, John McIntosh Kell, built for speed rather than battle. "Her lines," he wrote, "were symmetrical and fine; her material the best. In fifteen minutes her propeller could be hoisted, and she could go through every evolution under sail without any impediment. In less time her propeller could be lowered; with sails furled, and yards braced within two points of a head-wind, she was a perfect steamer. Her speed, independent, was from ten to twelve knots; combined, and under favorable circumstances, she could make fifteen knots. When ready for sea she drew fifteen feet of water."[1]

Despite having been built for speed, not battle, the *Alabama* was indeed a ship of war. It carried eight guns: one Blakely 100-pounder rifled gun, mounted forward; one eight-inch solid-shot gun, mounted aft of the mainmast; and six 32-pounders, three mounted on each broadside. One hundred and twenty men and twenty-four officers comprised the ship's crew. Most of the officers were former officers in the U.S. Navy, but nearly all the crewmen were either English, Irish or Welsh. Some were said to belong to the Royal Navy Reserve.

The *Alabama* could maintain its lengthy voyages by using steam power only when necessary and otherwise sailing under wind power. To keep its crew fed it seized provisions from the vessels it captured, and it was supplied with water from the condensing apparatus of its two 300-horsepower steam engines that drove its two-bladed screw propeller. The only need it had to seek port occasionally was to replenish its supply of coal.

To acquire a ship such as the *Alabama* the Confederacy's secretary of the navy, Stephen Mallory, had to go to England, or at least send his representative, Captain James D. Bulloch, who supervised the construction of the ship by the John Laird Sons and Company, of Birkenhead, England. The vessel was initially identified simply as hull No. 290 and when it was launched on July 29, 1862, it was named the *Enrica*, the identity of its owner and its purpose kept secret. A civilian crew, with Bulloch aboard, took it to Terceira Island in the Azores, where Semmes took over the task of refitting it and arming it for warfare, its guns having been manufactured in England and shipped to Terceira. In international waters on August 24, 1862 it was renamed and commissioned the CSS *Alabama* during a ceremony in which a navy band played *Dixie* and Captain Semmes read his orders from Jefferson Davis directing him to take command of the ship. Eighty-three sailors, responding to Semmes's offer of a signing bonus, prize money and triple wages paid in gold, signed on, joining twenty-four officers to comprise the ship's first crew. From the Azores the *Alabama* sailed to the northeast U.S. coast to begin its mission of harassing and hampering American commercial shipping, a mission it successfully fulfilled for twenty-two months before putting in to Cherbourg on June 11.

"Our little ship was now showing signs of the active work she had been doing," Kell, the executive officer, related. "Her boilers were burned out, and her machinery was sadly in want of repairs. She was loose at every joint, her seams were open, and the copper on her bottom was in rolls."[2] There was other critical impairment to its fighting ability, soon to become evident.

After being granted permission to enter the Cherbourg harbor and dock, Captain Semmes on the next day, Sunday, June 12, according to his account, called on the port admiral to see about having the needed repairs done. "My arrival," Semmes reported, "had, of course, been telegraphed to Paris, and indeed, by this time, had been spread all over Europe. The Admiral regretted that I had not gone into Havre, or some other commercial port, where I would have found private docks. Cherbourg being exclusively a naval station, the docks all belonged to the [French] Government, and the Government would have preferred not to dock and repair a belligerent ship. No positive objection was made, however, and the matter was laid over, until the Emperor could be communicated with. The Emperor was then at Biarritz, a small watering-place on the south coast, and would not be back in Paris for several days."[3]

Semmes had planned to put the ship in drydock immediately and give his crew a two-month leave while it was being overhauled. "They would have been discharged, and dispersed, in the first twenty-four hours after my arrival," he said, "but for this temporary absence of the Emperor."

While Captain Semmes and his officers and crew waited for the emperor to return to Paris, they learned on the third day of their wait that the U.S. Navy's sloop-of-war *Kearsarge* was steaming toward Cherbourg.

The *Kearsarge*'s commander, Captain John A. Winslow, had been notified by a telegram from the U.S. minister to France that the *Alabama* had arrived in Cherbourg. At the time, Sunday, June 12, the *Kearsarge* was lying at anchor in the Scheldt, off Flushing, Holland, and its crew was quickly summoned from shore by a signal gun, steam was raised, and the *Kearsarge* promptly put to sea. When Captain Winslow announced to his crew that they were going after the *Alabama,* the crew responded with cheers.

The *Kearsarge*, named for Mount Kearsarge in New Hampshire, had been launched on September 11, 1861 at the Portsmouth Navy Yard in Kittery, Maine and was commissioned as a U.S. warship on January 24, 1862, under the command of Captain Charles Pickering, who had since been succeeded by Captain Winslow. Within two weeks of its commissioning it was off on the mission for which it had been built — hunting down and destroying or capturing Confederate raiders such as the *Alabama*. It was 201 feet in length, thirty-three feet eight inches in the beam and drew fourteen feet three inches of water. Like the *Alabama*, it had both steam engines and sails and could make thirteen knots. It was armed with two 11-inch smoothbore Dahlgren guns, four 32-pounder guns and one 30-pounder Parrott rifle. Most of its officers were former merchant-marine officers, and, unlike *Alabama*'s crew, only eleven of its crewmen were foreign-born.

Its first voyage was to the coast of Spain and then to Gibraltar, where it joined the several U.S. Navy vessels that after months of hunting the *Sumter* in the Mediterranean had finally bottled it up in the harbor at Gibraltar, ending its raiding career. In the meantime, Semmes, having abandoned the *Sumter,* had taken command of the *Alabama* in August 1862, beginning its raiding cruises. The *Kearsarge* then took on the task of finding the *Alabama* and ending its depredations. From Cadiz the *Kearsarge* steamed to the Canary Islands, off the northwest coast of Africa, to Madeira on Portugal's coast, to the Outer Hebrides, off the west coast of Scotland, then to the English Channel, searching for the rebel raider. The search concluded with the report that the *Alabama* was at Cherbourg.

On Tuesday, June 14, as the *Kearsarge* approached Cherbourg, the *Alabama*'s Confederate flag could be seen from a distance as the raider lay inside the harbor's breakwater. Because of France's neutrality restrictions, the *Kearsarge* would not be allowed to remain in the Cherbourg harbor longer than twenty-four hours, and so Captain Winslow chose not to enter the harbor but instead anchored outside the harbor to keep a constant watch on the harbor entrances.

On Wednesday Winslow paid an official visit to the French admiral commanding the maritime district and to the U.S. commercial agent, who turned over to Winslow a surprising note from Captain Semmes. The policy of the *Alabama* had been understood to be opposed to a conflict, to use its speed to escape rather than to be exposed to injury or even destruction, the Confederacy having so few such ships that it could not afford to lose one. But Captain Semmes made clear that he was challenging the *Kearsarge* to a fight. His note, addressed to the Confederacy's commercial agent in Cherbourg, read as follows:

C.S.S. "Alabama," Cherbourg, June 14th 1864

To A. Bonfils, Esq., Cherbourg.

Sir: I heard that you were informed by the U.S. Consul that the *Kearsarge* was to come to this port solely for the prisoners landed by me, and that she was to depart in twenty-four hours. I desire you to say to the U.S. Consul that my intention is to fight the *Kearsarge* as soon as I can make the necessary arrangements. I hope these will not detain me more than until tomorrow evening, or after the morrow morning at furthest. I beg she will not depart before I am ready to go out.

I have the honor to be, very respectfully,

Your obedient servant,

R. Semmes, Captain

Bonfils, the Confederacy's agent, had forwarded the note to the U.S. commercial agent, a man named Liais, and asked Liais to give a copy of it to Captain Winslow, which Liais did. The note was needless. Winslow had no intention of departing before the *Alabama* came out into international waters. The *Kearsarge*'s whole purpose was to rid the oceans of the *Alabama*'s menace, and now it stood with a golden opportunity to fulfill its mission.

Winslow assembled his officers to discuss the expected battle. He guessed that the *Alabama* would seek neutral waters in event of defeat and he wanted the fight to occur several miles out in neutral waters, to avoid the possibility the *Alabama* could limp back to safety in the harbor. *Kearsarge*'s officers were determined not to surrender, but to fight to the last, and, if they lost, to go down with colors flying.

What puzzled Winslow, for a while, was why Semmes wanted to fight, why he would risk his vessel to a needless disaster. The *Kearsarge*, if taken or destroyed, could be replaced, but not the *Alabama*. After some discussion among *Kearsarge*'s officers, they concluded that Semmes would fight because he thought he would be the victor and for one other compelling reason: He wanted to prove that his ship was not a privateer, intended only for attack upon merchant vessels, but a true ship of war. *Kearsarge*'s surgeon, John M. Browne, believed Semmes had been stung by criticism, that he had been goaded into battle by newspaper editorials that had challenged him to take advantage of the opportunity to meet the U.S. warship and show that the *Alabama* was not a corsair preying on defenseless merchantmen, but a ship-of-war, able and willing to fight the enemy waiting outside the harbor.

During their days of waiting, the officers of the *Alabama* were eying the *Kearsarge* from afar. "We examined her closely with our glasses," Kell reported, "but she was keeping on the opposite side of the harbor, out of the reach of a very close scrutiny." When Semmes decided to fight, he had informed Kell of his decision and asked, "What do you think of it?" The question set off a comparison of the two vessels. "We discussed the battery," Kell reported, "and especially the advantage the *Kearsarge* had over us in her 11-inch guns. She was built for a vessel of war ... and though she carried one gun less, her battery was more effective at point-blank range. While the *Alabama* carried one more gun, the *Kearsarge* threw more metal at a broad-side; and while our heavy guns were thus more effective at long range, her 11-inch guns gave her greatly the advantage at close range. She also had a slight advantage in her crew, she carrying 163, all told, while we carried 149."[4] Having considered well the *Kearsarge*'s advantages, Kell wrote, Semmes nevertheless planned to fight.

"My crew," Semmes reported, "seemed not only willing, but anxious for the combat; and I had every confidence in their steadiness and drill; but they labored under one serious disadvantage. They had had but very limited opportunities of actual practice at target-firing, with shot and shell. The reason is obvious. I had no means of replenishing either shot or shell, and was obliged, therefore, to husband the store I had on hand for actual conflict." As for the *Kearsarge*'s advantages, Semmes believed "the disparity was not so great, but that I might hope to beat my enemy in a fair fight."[5]

Sunday, June 19 dawned fair and bright, with a light breeze blowing, and between nine and ten o'clock that morning, the *Alabama* weighed anchor and steamed out of the western entrance of the Cherbourg harbor, followed by the French ironclad frigate *Couronne*, which in turn was followed by the privately owned steam-and-sail yacht *Deerhound*, flying the flag of the English Royal Mersey Yacht Club. "Our men were neatly dressed and our officers in full uniform," Kell related. "The report of our going out to fight the *Kearsarge* had been circulated, and many persons from Paris and the surrounding country had come down to witness the engagement. With a large number of inhabitants of Cherbourg they collected on every prominent point on the shore that would afford a view seaward. As we rounded the breakwater we discovered the *Kearsarge* about seven miles to the northward and eastward. We immediately shaped our course for her, called all hands to quarters, and cast loose the starboard battery."[6]

As the Confederate raider steamed ahead, Captain Semmes ordered all hands aft and, climbing upon a gun carriage, he addressed his crew: "Officers and seamen of the 'Alabama'! You have, at length, another opportunity of meeting the enemy—the first that has been presented to you since you sank the *Hatteras*! In the meantime, you have been all over the world, and it is not too much to say, that you have destroyed, and driven for protection under neutral flags, one half of the enemy's commerce, which, at the beginning of the war, covered every sea. This is an achievement of which you may well be proud; and a grateful country will not be unmindful of it. The name of your ship has become a household word wherever civilization extends. Shall that name be tarnished by defeat? The thing is impossible! Remember that you are in the English Channel, the theater of so much of the naval glory of our race, and that the eyes of all Europe are at this moment upon you. The flag that floats over you is that of a young Republic, who bids defiance to her enemies, whenever, and wherever found. Show the world that you know how to uphold it! Go to your quarters!"[7]

Surgeon Browne described the scene aboard the *Kearsarge* that Sunday morning:

> At 10 o'clock the *Kearsarge* was near the buoy marking the line of shoals to the eastward of Cherbourg, at a distance of about three miles from the entrance. The decks had been holy-stoned, the bright work cleaned, the guns polished, and the crew dressed in Sunday suits. They were inspected at quarters and dismissed to attend divine service. Seemingly no one thought of the enemy; so long awaited and not appearing, speculation as to her coming had nearly ceased. At 10:20 the officer of the deck reported a steamer approaching from Cherbourg—a frequent occurrence, and consequently it created no surprise. The bell was tolling for service when some one shouted, "She's coming, and heading straight for us!" Soon, by the aid of a glass, the officer

of the deck made out the enemy and shouted, "The *Alabama*!" The drum beat to general quarters; Captain Winslow put aside the prayer-book, seized the trumpet, ordered the ship about, and headed seaward. The ship was cleared for action, with the battery pivoted to starboard.[8]

Kell recounted the action of the *Alabama*:

In about forty-five minutes we were somewhat over a mile from the *Kearsarge*, when she headed for us, presenting her starboard bow. At a distance of a mile we commenced the action with our 100-pounder pivot-gun from our starboard bow. Both ships were now approaching each other at high speed, and soon the action became general with broadside batteries at a distance of about five hundred yards. To prevent passing, each ship used a strong port helm. Thus the action was fought around a common center, gradually drawing in the circle. At this range we used shell upon the enemy. Captain Semmes, standing on the horse-block abreast the mizzen-mast with his glass in hand, observed the effect of our shell. He called to me and said, "Mr. Kell, use solid shot; our shell strike the enemy's side and fall into the water."[9]

Semmes guessed that the ineffectiveness of the *Alabama*'s shells was owing to defective ammunition. He would later discover, in outrage, that his guess was in error. Kell continued his description of the fight:

After using solid shot for some time, we alternated shell and shot. The enemy's 11-inch shells were now doing severe execution upon our quarter-deck section. Three of them successively entered our 8-inch pivot-gun port; the first swept off the forward part of the gun's crew; the second killed one man and wounded several others; and the third struck the breast of the gun-carriage, and spun around on the deck till one of the men picked it up and threw it overboard. Our decks were now covered with the dead and the wounded, and the ship was careening heavily to starboard from the effects of the shot holes on her water-line....

The port side of the quarter-deck was so encumbered with the mangled trunks of the dead that I had to have them thrown overboard, in order to fight the after pivot-gun.... At this moment the chief engineer came on deck and reported the fires put out, and that he could no longer work the engines....[10]

Captain Semmes recounted the conclusion of the battle in his official report of the engagement:

After the lapse of about one hour and ten minutes, our ship was ascertained to be in a sinking condition, the enemy's shell having exploded in our side, and between decks, opening large apertures through which the water rushed with great rapidity. For some few minutes I had hopes of being able to reach the French coast, for which purpose I gave the ship all steam, and set such of the fore-and-aft sails as were available. The ship filled so rapidly, however, that before we had made much progress, the fires were extinguished in the furnaces, and we were evidently on the point of sinking. I now hauled down my colors, to prevent the further destruction.[11]

From the *Kearsarge*'s perspective Surgeon Browne described the battle's closing minutes:

The *Kearsarge* gunners had been cautioned against firing without direct aim, and had been advised to point the heavy guns below rather than above the water-line, and to clear the deck of the enemy with the lighter ones. Though subjected to an incessant storm of shot and shell, they kept their stations and obeyed instructions.

The effect upon the enemy was readily perceived, and nothing could restrain the enthusiasm of our men. Cheer succeeded cheer; caps were thrown in the air or overboard; jackets were discarded; sanguine of victory, the men were shouting, as each projectile took effect: "That is a good one!" "Down, boys!" "Give her another like the last!" "Now we have her!" and so on, cheering and shouting to the end.

After the *Kearsarge* had been exposed to an uninterrupted cannonade for eighteen minutes, a 68-pounder Blakely shell passed through the starboard bulwarks below the main rigging, exploded upon the quarter-deck, and wounded three of the crew of the after pivot-gun. With these exceptions, not an officer or man received serious injury....

We had completed the seventh rotation on the circular track and had begun the eighth, when the *Alabama*, now settling, sought to escape by setting all available sail (fore-trysail and two jibs), left the circle amid a shower of shot and shell, and headed for the French waters; but to no purpose.... The *Kearsarge* pursued, keeping a line nearer the shore, and with a few well-directed shots hastened the sinking. Then the *Alabama* was at our mercy. Her colors were struck, and the *Kearsarge* ceased firing. I was told by our prisoners [later taken from the sinking ship] that two of the junior officers swore they would never surrender, and in a mutinous spirit rushed to the two port guns and opened fire upon the *Kearsarge*. Captain Winslow, amazed at this extraordinary conduct of an enemy who had hauled down his flag in token of surrender, exclaimed, "He is playing us a trick; give him another broadside." Again the shot and shell went crashing into her sides, and the *Alabama* continued to settle by the stern. The *Kearsarge* was laid across her bows for raking, and in position to use grape and canister.

A white flag was then shown over the stern of the *Alabama* and her ensign was half-masted, union down. Captain Winslow for the second time gave orders to cease firing. Thus ended the fight, after a duration of one hour and two minutes....[12]

First Officer Kell's complaint that "the *Kearsarge* deliberately fired into us five shot" after the *Alabama* had hauled down its colors neglected to include the fact that the *Alabama*

***Kearsarge* vs. *Alabama*.** After a fierce battle that lasted an hour and two minutes, the rebel ship, mortally wounded and sinking, surrendered. Despite having surrendered, Semmes and eleven of his officers and twenty-six men of his crew escaped capture by boarding a British ship that plucked them from the water and sped away to safety in England. (LIBRARY OF CONGRESS)

had fired on the *Kearsarge* after the colors were struck. Captain Semmes, who was especially incensed by the *Kearsarge's* retaliatory fire, also neglected to mention the *Alabama* had fired despite its colors having been lowered. "Although we were now but 400 yards from each other, the enemy fired upon me five times after my colors had been struck," Semmes wrote in his official report. "It is charitable to suppose that a ship of war of a Christian nation could not have done this intentionally."[13]

To Semmes' remark Browne in his account replied, "He is silent as to the renewal by the *Alabama* of the fight after his surrender — an act which, in Christian warfare, would have justified the *Kearsarge* in continuing the fire until the *Alabama* had sunk beneath the waters."[14] Browne went on with his account of the battle's conclusion:

Boats were now lowered from the *Alabama*. Her master's-mate, Fullam, an Englishman, came alongside the *Kearsarge* with a few of the wounded, reported the disabled and sinking condition of his ship, and asked for assistance. Captain Winslow inquired, "Does Captain Semmes surrender his ship?" "Yes," was the reply. Fullam then solicited permission to return with his boat and crew to assist in rescuing the drowning, pledging his word of honor that when this was done he would come on board and surrender. Captain Winslow granted the request. With less generosity he could have detained the officer and men, supplied their places in the boat from the ship's company, secured more prisoners, and afforded equal aid to the distressed. The generosity was abused, as the sequel shows. Fullam pulled to the midst of the drowning, rescued several officers, went to the yacht *Deerhound*, and cast his boat adrift, leaving a number of men struggling in the water.

It was now seen that the *Alabama* was settling fast. The wounded, and the boys who could not swim, were sent away in the quarter-boats, the waist-boats having been destroyed. Captain Semmes dropped his sword into the sea and jumped overboard with the remaining officers and men.

Coming under the stern of the *Kearsarge* from the windward, the *Deerhound* was hailed, and her commander requested by Captain Winslow to run down and assist in picking up the men of the sinking ship. Or, as her owner, Mr. John Lancaster, reported: "The fact is, that when we passed the *Kearsarge*, the captain cried out, 'For God's sake, do what you can to save them'; and that was my warrant for interfering in any way for the aid and succor of his enemies..".. The *Alabama* sank in forty-five fathoms of water, at a distance of about four and a half miles from the breakwater, off the west entrance [to Cherbourg harbor]....[15]

Semmes and Kell swam out far enough from the sinking ship to avoid being sucked down into the vortex of the ship as it sank. "We then turned to get a last look at her," Semmes recounted, "and see her go down. Just before she disappeared, her main top-mast, which had been wounded, went by the board; and, like a living thing in agony, she threw her bow high out of the water, and then descended rapidly, stern foremost, to her last resting-place. A noble Roman once stabbed his daughter, rather than she should be polluted by the foul embrace of a tyrant. It was with a similar feeling that Kell and I saw the *Alabama* go down. We had buried her as we had christened her, and she was safe from the polluting touch of the hated Yankee!"[16]

As his ship slipped beneath the waves, Semmes, wounded in the hand by broken iron rigging, was plucked from the sea by the *Deerhound*, which had lowered its two boats to aid in the rescue effort, and he and Fullam, as well as Kell, eleven other officers and twenty-six men of *Alabama's* crew, sailed away to safety in England aboard the *Deerhound*, despite having surrendered. The *Alabama's* remaining survivors — some seventy individuals, including officers and men — were picked up by two boats from the *Kearsarge* and by the French pilot boats that had followed the *Alabama* out of the harbor. Those taken aboard the *Kearsarge*, Browne reported, fraternized with the *Kearsarge's* crewmen, who shared their clothes, supper and grog with their prisoners. In the battle the *Alabama* had lost nine killed, twenty-one wounded and ten drowned.

According to Kell, when he and Semmes and the others came aboard the *Deerhound*, the yacht's owner, John Lancaster, came to Semmes and said, "I think every man has been picked up. Where shall I land you?"

"I am now under English colors," Semmes replied, "and the sooner you put me with my officers and men on English soil, the better." The speedy *Deerhound* then hastened off to Southampton. "That evening," Kell reported, "we landed in Southampton, and were kindly received by the people with every demonstration of sympathy and kindly feeling. Thrown upon their shores by the chances of war, we were taken to their hearts and homes with that generous hospitality which brought to mind with tenderest feeling our own dear Southern homes, in *ante-bellum* times."[17]

Semmes, who had gained his fame as an armed marauder amassing victories over unarmed merchant vessels, now having lost to an equal, turned out to be a sore loser. When he learned that the *Kearsarge*'s hull was protected by chain armor, he yelled, "Foul!" The protective armor was iron anchor chain secured to the mid-section of the sides of the vessel, from the rail down to the waterline. The chains were covered by boards painted the same black as the ship's hull, making them hard to detect from a distance, and Semmes had not known of their existence going into the battle. Admiral David Farragut had used the same sort of anchor-chain armor on his vessels when he ran past Fort Jackson and Fort St. Philip on the Mississippi River below New Orleans in April 1862, and the *Kearsarge*'s executive officer, Lieutenant Commander James S. Thornton, had served with Farragut then. Putting chain armor on the *Kearsarge* was his idea.

The *Kearsarge*'s armor had been installed in early 1863 while the ship was in port in the Azores, and there was no secret about it. "In our visit to European ports," Browne related, "the use of sheet-chains [extra anchor chain] for protective purposes had attracted notice and caused comment. It is strange that Captain Semmes did not know of the chain armor; supposed spies had been on board and had been shown through the ship, as there was no attempt at concealment; the same pilot had been employed by both ships, and had visited each during the preparation for battle."[18]

Nevertheless, Semmes fumed that Captain Winslow "did not show me a fair fight, for, as it afterward turned out, his ship was iron-clad. It was the same thing, as if two men were to go out to fight a duel, and one of them, unknown to the other, were to put on shirt of mail under his outer garment. The days of chivalry being past, perhaps it would be unfair to charge Captain Winslow with deceit in withholding from me the fact that he meant to wear armor in the fight. He may have reasoned that it was my duty to find it out for myself. Besides, if he had disclosed this fact to me, and so prevented the engagement, the Federal Secretary of the Navy would have cut off his head to a certainty...." Winslow had cheated, Semmes insisted, and his fellow Yankees had approved his cheating. "So far from having any condemnation to offer," Semmes wrote, "the press, that chivalrous exponent of the opinions of a chivalrous people, was rather pleased at the 'Yankee trick.' It was characteristic, 'cute,' 'smart.'"[19]

In the final analysis, however, it was not the *Kearsarge*'s iron chains that made the difference in the fight. According to Browne, the shots that struck the *Kearsarge* would not have been significantly more effective without the chains. The actual crucial factor was the *Alabama*'s defective ammunition, which Semmes himself blamed for his defeat. "I should have beaten him in the first thirty minutes of the engagement," he declared, "but for the defect of my ammunition, which had been two years on board, and become much deteri-orated by cruising in a variety of climates.... I lodged a rifled percussion shell near her [*Kearsarge's*] stern post — *where there were no chains*— which failed to explode because of the defect of the cap. If the cap had performed its duty, and exploded the shell, I should have been called upon to save Captain Winslow's crew from drowning, instead of his being called upon to save mine."[20]

Browne tended to agree: "A 100-pounder rifle shell entered at the starboard quarter and lodged in the stern-post. The blow shook the ship from stem to stern. Luckily the shell did not explode, otherwise the result would have been serious, if not fatal."[21]

"On so slight an incident," Semmes concluded, "the defect of a percussion cap, did the battle hinge."[22]

General Hunter's War,
May 21 to June 30, 1864

Major General David Hunter probably felt no awkwardness in meeting with General Sigel to assume command of the Department of West Virginia and its troops. It was something that had to be done, and Hunter had enough self-assurance to believe he could do a lot better than the hapless Sigel, whose ineptness had reduced him to an object of scorn and ridicule. Hunter's cousin, Colonel David Hunter Strother, had served under Sigel and told Hunter, "We can afford to lose such a battle as New Market to get rid of such a mistake as ... Sigel."[1]

But there were still the political ramifications to be considered, and so Hunter, reportedly at Lincoln's request, did what could be done to let Sigel down easy. The two men held a friendly conversation at Sigel's — now Hunter's — headquarters at Cedar Creek on May 21, and Hunter said he hoped Sigel would remain in the department and accept command of either the department's infantry division or the reserve division, which was composed of the troops posted at Harpers Ferry and along the line of the Baltimore & Ohio railroad. Sigel waited until the next day to accept the offer. He was given command of the reserve division. On that same day, Sunday, May 22, he left for the division's headquarters at Martinsburg, West Virginia.

It wasn't the first time Hunter had taken over from a commander who had been relieved because he failed to do what was expected of him. In orders issued on October 28, 1861 Lincoln had fired Major General John Fremont from his post as commander of the U.S. Army's Department of

U.S. Maj. Gen. David Hunter. He was keen on burning houses and other buildings and wreaking havoc on civilians in the Shenandoah valley, but ran from a fight with Jubal Early's tough Confederate troops. He was, one historian declared, "a criminal in uniform, an arsonist on a binge." (NATIONAL ARCHIVES AND RECORDS ADMINISTRATION)

the West and replaced him with Hunter. Lincoln had earlier sent a team of officers to St. Louis to investigate Fremont, and the investigator who wrote the report on him declared that Fremont — another of Lincoln's hand-picked generals — lacked "the intelligence, the experience, and the sagacity necessary to his command."[2] The command that General Hunter assumed in that case had lasted only briefly, until the Department of the West was divided into two departments, and Hunter was moved to other assignments. In June 1862, when Hunter commanded the Army's Department of the South, he himself had been relieved from duty by a temporary suspension following the defeat of his army in its attempt to take Charleston.

The son of a Presbyterian army chaplain, Hunter was born in Princeton, New Jersey and raised in Washington, D.C. He was about seven weeks shy of his sixty-second birthday when he relieved Sigel. He had graduated from West Point, class of 1822, and had been in the Army, out of the Army and then in it again. He had served during the Second Seminole War and during the Mexican War, rising to the rank of major. In 1860, while posted at Fort Leavenworth, Kansas, he captured Lincoln's attention by writing letters to him denouncing slavery, having become an ardent abolitionist. Lincoln was impressed with him enough that Hunter received an invitation to ride to Washington on the train carrying Lincoln to the capital for his inauguration in February 1861. In May 1861, five weeks after the Confederates assaulted Fort Sumter, Hunter, capitalizing on his association with the president, was appointed brigadier general. He participated in the first Battle of Bull Run in July 1861 and was named a major general in August.

In March 1862 he had been given command of the Department of the South, including Florida, Georgia and South Carolina, which placed him in command of the Army's Tenth Corps. He soon proved himself to be something of a loose cannon. On his own authority he recruited blacks in the occupied sections of South Carolina to form the Army's first black regiment, the First South Carolina Volunteers, which he was ordered to disband but which was later approved by Congress. In May 1862 he issued a general order intended to free all slaves in the states of his jurisdiction. The order stated that "Slavery and martial law in a free country are altogether incompatible; the persons in these three states — Georgia, Florida, and South Carolina — heretofore held slaves, are therefore declared forever free."[3] Alarmed about possible effects that the edict might have on the border states, Lincoln quickly countermanded Hunter's order and summoned Hunter to Washington, where he was forced to cool his heels if not his head.

Grant knew Hunter. In November 1863 at his headquarters near Chattanooga Grant even shared his bedroom with him for three weeks. Hunter had been sent by Secretary Stanton ostensibly to inspect Grant's command, but perhaps more than that to check up on Grant's drinking habits, about which rumors abounded. Grant received him with cordiality. General Baldy Smith, commenting on the visit, called Hunter "a great Puritan" and said he complained about the soldiers playing cards — as innocent an amusement, Grant remarked, as the men could have. In his official report to Stanton, Hunter said that he had been with Grant day and night and assured the secretary that Grant was conscientious, hard-working and satisfactorily temperate. "He only took two drinks during the three weeks I was with him," Hunter reported.[4]

So unbridled was Hunter in the display of his abolitionist and anti-secession passions that he had his own cousin, Andrew Hunter, a prominent lawyer, arrested for suspected Confederate sympathies and had Andrew's mansion near Harpers Ferry burned to the ground, along with all its contents. One of Hunter's observers, Henry duPont, a young captain of artillery and a West Point graduate (as well as a member of the aristocratic duPont family of Delaware), called Hunter a man "dominated by prejudices and antipathies so intense and so violent as to render him at times quite incapable of taking a fair and unbiased view."[5]

Shortly after assuming command at Cedar Creek, he also displayed his spirit of vengefulness, as evidenced in this order that he issued:

> For every train fired on or soldier assassinated, the house or other property of every secession sympathizer residing within a circuit of five miles shall be destroyed by fire; and for all public property taken or destroyed, an assessment of five times the value of such property will be made upon the secession sympathizers residing within a circuit of ten miles around the point at which the offense was committed.[6]

The judgment contained in the order was implemented even before the order was issued. On May 23 Hunter's adjutant ordered the commander of the First New York Cavalry to send out a two-hundred-man detail "to proceed to Newtown to-morrow morning at three o'clock for the purpose of burning every house, store, and outbuilding in that place.... You will also burn the houses, etc., of all rebels between Newtown and Middletown."[7] Incensed by the order, Confederate Colonel Harry Gilmor warned Hunter that if Hunter's troops burned Newtown, he — Gilmor — would hang every one of the forty Union enlisted men and six officers who were Gilmor's prisoners and send their bodies to Hunter. At the time, Gilmor's battalion of cavalry was harassing the rear of Hunter's column and was confronting the Union detail sent to burn Newtown. The commander of Hunter's detail, having received Gilmor's warning note addressed to Hunter, on his own initiative decided to spare the town, but wrung from its terrified citizens their oath of allegiance to the United States.

Even knowing Hunter, Grant approved of his replacing Sigel, having high hopes that Hunter would do what Sigel had failed to do. Giving instructions to Hunter through Halleck, Grant wrote that Hunter should occupy Staunton and then move east of the Blue Ridge Mountains. When joined, as planned, by General Crook's cavalry, which was moving southwestward on the west side of the Blue Ridge, Hunter would have a force of some 17,000 men, Grant estimated. With them Hunter should advance, Grant said, to Charlottesville and then to Lynchburg, "living on the country" and destroying the railroads and canals "beyond possibility of repair for weeks."[8]

Hunter's army — the seven to eight thousand troops that had been beaten at New Market — moved out from its bivouac at Cedar Creek and Strasburg on the morning of Thursday, May 26, trudging down a rain-sodden, muddy road under gloomy skies. When it reached New Market on June 1, it quickly drove back Imboden's shrunken force of about one thousand cavalrymen and six field pieces, most of the rest of the rebel army that had repulsed Sigel having been shifted to Lee's hard-pressed Army of Northern Virginia. Imboden telegraphed Lee to inform him of Hunter's advance, and Lee promptly responded by telling him to call out all the reserves he could find and to wire Brigadier General William E. "Grumble" Jones in southwest Virginia to hurry to his aid with all available troops. When Imboden did, Jones wired back that he was coming with about three thousand men, moving up through Lynchburg and Staunton. He said he would reach Imboden by Saturday, June 4.

Shortly after dawn on June 4 Jones and his staff arrived at Mount Crawford, about ten miles below Harrisonburg on the Shenandoah valley road. His force was combined with Imboden's, and Jones assumed command. He positioned his troops northeast of the community of Piedmont, about a mile north of New Hope. Colonel Strother, General Hunter's cousin and also his chief of staff, described the ground that was to become the battlefield:

The enemy's position was strong and well chosen. It was on a conclave of wooded hills commanding an open valley between and open, gentle slopes in front. On our [U.S.] right in advance of the village of Piedmont was a line of log and rail defenses very advantageously located in the edge of a forest and just behind the rise of a smooth, open hill so that troops moving over this hill could be mowed down by musketry from the works at short range and to prevent artillery from being used against them. The left flank of this palisade rested on a steep and impracticable bluff sixty feet high and washed at its base by the Shenandoah.[9]

On the morning of June 5 Hunter launched his attack. His cavalry drove back Imboden's Virginia cavalrymen, and Imboden barely escaped capture. Under a ferocious artillery bombardment from the guns commanded by Captain duPont, the Confederate artillery was silenced, and the infantry took over the fight. The outnumbered rebels twice repelled Hunter's assaults before their left wing was flanked and their line attacked from both front and rear. In the attack General Jones was shot in the head and killed. The Confederates suffered 1,488 casualties in the day's fighting. Union losses amounted to 863, including killed and wounded.

Taking over from the fallen General Jones was Brigadier General John C. Vaughn, commander of a Tennessee cavalry brigade, and he and Imboden led the fleeing survivors of the Battle of Piedmont southeastward toward Waynesboro. Instead of pursuing them, though, Hunter pressed on toward Staunton, and when they reached it, the Union troops entered the town as if in a parade, with two bands blaring "Yankee Doodle." True to his reputation, Hunter ordered the town's jail emptied, releasing an assortment of criminals into the community, and had his troops begin the fiery destruction of railroad buildings, storehouses, wagon shops, stables and a woolen mill while a mob plundered the stores of the town's merchants.

On Wednesday, June 8 Hunter's army in Staunton was joined, as planned, by the forces of generals Crook and Averell, which had been moving parallel to Hunter's column, on its right. The addition of their twelve thousand men brought Hunter's army to a total of some twenty thousand troops. Hunter called a council of war with Crook and Averell to get their advice on how best to proceed from Staunton, Grant having issued confusing instructions to Hunter on June 6, leaving much to Hunter's discretion:

> ... According to the instructions I sent to General Halleck for your guidance, you were to proceed to Lynchburg and commence there [the destruction of the Virginia Central Railroad and the James River canal]. It would be of great value to us to get possession of Lynchburg for a single day. But that point is of so much importance to the enemy, that in attempting to get it [,] such resistance may be met as to defeat your getting onto the [rail] road or canal at all. I see, in looking over the letter to General Halleck on the subject of your instructions, that it rather indicates that your route should be from Staunton [to Lynchburg] via Charlottesville. If you have so understood it, you will be doing just what I want. The direction I now give is, that if this letter reaches you in the valley between Staunton and Lynchburg, you immediately turn east by the most practicable road until you strike the Lynchburg branch of the Va. Central road. From thence move eastward along the line of the road, destroying it completely and thoroughly, until you join General Sheridan. After the work laid out for General Sheridan and yourself is thoroughly done, proceed to join the Army of the Potomac by the route laid out in General Sheridan's instructions.
>
> If any portion of your force, especially your cavalry, is needed back in your Department, you are authorized to send it back.
>
> If on receipt of this you should be near to Lynchburg and deem it practicable to reach that point, you will exercise your judgment about going there.

If you should be on the railroad between Charlottesville and Lynchburg, it may be practicable to detach a cavalry force to destroy the canal. Lose no opportunity to destroy the canal.[10]

Considering all of Grant's "ifs," Hunter asked, what should he do? Colonel Strother recommended continuing the march southward on the valley road, taking Lexington and Buchanan, crossing the Blue Ridge Mountains at Peaks of Otter and approaching Lynchburg from the west. Crook advised caution, apparently thinking that going first to Charlottesville, due east of Staunton, and linking up with Sheridan's force there was a better idea. Like Grant, he realized that Lee would attempt to hold Lynchburg at all costs, heavily reinforcing it as soon as he could, and that taking Lynchburg would be an extremely tough assignment. Crook said that unless Hunter's army moved on Lynchburg quickly, Strother's plan would fail. A speedy assault, he argued, made before Lee could reinforce Lynchburg's defenders, was essential to success. Hunter decided to go to Lynchburg by way of Lexington.

Lexington was the home of the Virginia Military Institute, whose cadets had helped gain the rebel victory over Sigel at New Market. The first Union troops to enter the town were the troops of Crook and Averell, who reached Lexington about noon on Saturday, June 11. They met musket fire and a few artillery rounds from the troops of Brigadier General John McCausland, but the fire proved only a token resistance before the rebel troops withdrew in the face of the overwhelming Union force. Also beating a hasty retreat were the V.M.I. cadets who had fought at New Market and who had returned to school just days before Hunter's army arrived. Lexington was left to the mercy of Hunter and his troops.

Among the first targets of unrestrained troops were the buildings of V.M.I., where the trunks containing the belongings of the cadets were looted along with other contents of the buildings. The school's library and the science building, which housed laboratories and scientific instruments and specimens, were also ransacked. Finally, after having made a temporary headquarters in the V.M.I. superintendent's house and quartered his officers in the houses of the school's faculty, Hunter the next morning ordered V.M.I.'s buildings burned. His justification was that the school was, as he said, "a most dangerous establishment where treason was systematically taught.... I believed the States Rights conspirators had with subtlety and forethought established and encouraged the school for the express purpose of educating the youth of the country into such opinions as would render them ready and efficient tools wherewith to overthrow the government of the country when the hour and opportunity arrived."[11]

While much of V.M.I. was aflame, Hunter turned his attention to the home of John Letcher, who had been Virginia's governor at the time of its secession and during the early days of the war. Letcher was a native of Lexington and made his home there. Although he was not in Lexington at the moment, his family was. Hunter ordered the Letcher house burned, on the grounds that Letcher had earlier, Hunter said, issued "a violent and inflammatory proclamation ... inciting the population of the country to rise and wage guerrilla warfare on my troops."[12] Having set the Letcher house ablaze, Hunter's troops moved on to plunder the library of Washington College and a number of private residences. Henrietta Lee, one of General Lee's relatives, no doubt expressed the wrathful feelings of those civilians whose homes were looted and/or burned, as hers was, by Hunter's troops. She wrote a letter to Hunter to tell him the "curses of thousands, the scorn of the manly and upright and the hatred of the true and honorable, will follow you and yours through all time, and brand your name *infamy*."[13]

Some of Hunter's subordinates had the same opinion as Henrietta Lee. Rutherford Hayes, who was later to become the nation's nineteenth president and who was at the time a colonel commanding a brigade in Crook's division, recorded his sentiments in his diary. "General Hunter burns the Virginia Military Institute. This does not suit many of us. General Crook, I know, disapproves. It is surely bad." And in a letter he wrote to his family Hayes predicted that "General Hunter will be as odious as Butler and Pope to the Rebels and not gain our good opinion either."[14] As the cadets' barracks were consumed in flames, Hunter stood on a nearby hill and watched the conflagration. His aide, Colonel Charles Halpine, reported that Hunter "rubbed his hands and chuckled with delight [saying], 'Doesn't that burn beautifully?'"[15] Halpine also commented on the burning of the Letcher residence, writing in his diary, "My God! How I felt on seeing Gov. Letcher's family sitting out on the lawn on their trunks and furniture, while their house was on fire beside them. The old fool [Letcher] deserves it all; but it is hard on the women."[16] (The United States Congress in later years, agreeing that Hunter had gone too far in burning V.M.I., compensated the school for "the damage and destruction of its library, scientific apparatus, and the quarters of the professors."[17] The school was not compensated for the destruction of the cadets' barracks, however, it being deemed a legitimate military target that had come under fire from duPont's artillery and was later burned.)

The speedy assault on Lynchburg that Crook had urged was forced to wait until Hunter had finished his burnings. It was also delayed by his decision to wait in Lexington for the arrival of a wagon-trainload of ammunition, rather than starting for Lynchburg and having the wagon train catch up with him en route. Finally, on the morning of Tuesday, June 14, after three days in Lexington, Hunter put his army on the move toward Lynchburg. On the way, his troops stopped to burn at least one residence and several ironworks, including one large enough to employ some five hundred people. By the evening of June 15 Hunter's army had reached Bedford (formerly Liberty), about ten miles west of Lynchburg, and halted there. Hunter made himself comfortable in a brick house he seized as his headquarters and mulled over the intelligence he had received regarding the strength of the Confederates protecting Lynchburg.

"Negro refugees just from the town represented that it was occupied only by a few thousand armed invalids and militia, and that its inhabitants in the greatest panic were fleeing with their movable property by every available route," Hunter related. "At the same time, from other sources worthy of respect, we were assured that all the rebel forces of West Virginia were concentrated there under Breckinridge, and that Ewell's corps of veteran troops, 20,000 strong, had already reinforced them. To determine the truth I determined to advance on Lynchburg immediately."[18]

"Immediately" was the next morning, Thursday, June 16. Hunter ordered his commanders to feel out Lynchburg's defenses, and by late that day his army had moved about seven miles closer to the town. General Averell reported that his division, advancing along the Big Otter River, had met some stiff resistance as it felt out the rebel positions, but at day's end, Hunter still had no clear idea of the strength of the enemy he was facing. He knew, though, that he would not be reinforced by the two divisions of Sheridan's cavalrymen, which Grant's plan had called for. On June 11 Sheridan had run into two Confederate cavalry divisions that Lee had sent to block his advance on Charlottesville, and after an inconclusive battle at Trevilian Station, Sheridan learned that Hunter was already moving on Lynchburg and that there would be no rendezvous with him in Charlottesville even if Sheridan could get past the rebel cavalry. He then decided to abort the mission.

Meanwhile Lee had ordered Lieutenant General Jubal Early to pull from the line near Cold Harbor a force of some eight thousand infantry, plus artillery, and hurry to Lynchburg.

Early's troops marched as far as Charlottesville and reached there on June 16. Dissatisfied with the slow pace, Early wired Breckinridge, commanding the rebel defenders at Lynchburg, and asked him to send railroad cars to Charlottesville to move the troops the last seventy-five miles to Lynchburg. Then he waited till the next day for the rail trains to arrive. Along with Major General Stephen Ramseur's division, Early finally reached Lynchburg about one o'clock in the afternoon on Friday, June 17 while the Confederate rail service struggled to move the rest of his troops to catch up with their commander.

Hunter, too, was hampered by delays. He had planned to launch his attack on Lynchburg's defenders early in the morning on the 17th, but he found that the bridge over Big Otter Creek wasn't ready to take his artillery across it and he had to wait for his engineers to complete their repairs on it. While Hunter anxiously waited he was told by one of his staff members about a civilian resident of the area, a man named Leftwich, who was bragging about Confederate victories. Hunter became so enraged by Leftwich's reported remarks that he ordered Leftwich's house burned — which it promptly was — and ordered Leftwich to be held as a prisoner.

When at last Hunter was able to launch the Union assault later on the 17th, it met with initial success, pushing back the outnumbered rebel defenders to within five miles of the town. The Confederate resistance stiffened, though, as Early's troops began arriving, and the Union drive was stopped around 4 P.M. Hunter ordered an artillery bombardment of the rebel positions, but then decided it was too late in the day for a new attack and he called off the bombardment. He ordered the troops to make camp, intending to resume the fight the next day, Saturday, June 18.

During the night, the noise of railroad traffic and of the movement of troops could be heard in the distance, leading Hunter and his officers to conclude that Breckinridge's troops were being reinforced. Estimating Breckinridge's troops already numbered between ten and fifteen thousand, Hunter concluded that his fifteen thousand men would be outnumbered by Lynchburg's defenders once they were reinforced. Actually, Breckinridge's troops probably numbered no more than five thousand, including the cadets of V.M.I., and even after all of Early's troops arrived, Hunter would still command a superior force.

On Saturday morning Hunter ordered skirmishers to probe the center of the rebel line, and after doing so, the infantrymen of Brigadier General Jeremiah Sullivan's division reported that the rebel line seemed stronger than it had the day before. Sullivan, believing an assault on the rebel line would prove disastrous, advised against an attack. The morning then passed with exchanges of fire from the two sides but without any movement of troops. Around 1 P.M. the Confederates broke from their position and struck the center of the Union line, forcing Sullivan's men back until Hunter himself, mounted and brandishing his sword, rallied the fleeing bluecoats and stabilized the Union line. By three o'clock the fighting had stopped.

During their assault, a number of Confederates had been captured, and when they were interrogated, they were found to be from Early's corps. They told their Union interrogators that the reinforcements amounted to between twenty thousand and thirty thousand fresh troops. Meanwhile, reports were coming to Hunter's headquarters from the two flanks of the Union line, where Averell and Crook were meeting stronger resistance. Early's troops were evidently making a difference all along the rebel line.

Facing what he believed to be a force double the strength of his own, Hunter decided to give up the fight and withdraw. Averell and Crook concurred in the decision. To defend his decision, Hunter blamed a shortage of ammunition. His supply line had been repeatedly disrupted by rebel guerrillas—who had quickly moved into Lexington and Staunton to repossess those towns once Hunter's army had cleared out. (In his account of the battle, General Early, with some persuasiveness, cast doubt on Hunter's claim of an ammunition shortage. "...it appears that this expedition [Hunter's] had been long contemplated and was one of the prominent features of the campaign of 1864.... Can it be believed that Hunter set out on so important an expedition with an insufficient supply of ammunition? ... Had Hunter moved on Lynchburg with energy, that place would have fallen before it was possible for me to get there."[19])

Hunter's skirmishers continued to engage the Confederate line while the main body of the Union force began reforming so that it would be ready to move westward once the sun went down and darkness covered the withdrawal. When night came, Hunter and his staff returned to the supposedly haunted house they had occupied two days earlier, and Hunter's entire army slipped silently away from the field of battle at the outskirts of Lynchburg. Their absence was not discovered by Early until around midnight, when darkness prevented an attempt to overtake them. Pursuit would have to wait until daylight.

On Sunday morning the pursuit began. The main body of Hunter's army moved through Bedford [Liberty], where it continued northwestward on its way to the Buford Gap pass through the Blue Ridge Mountains. Averell's troopers were assigned the task of guarding the column's rear as it marched, attracting hundreds of slaves who joined the column in a flight to freedom. Early's pursuing rebels ran up against Averell's rear guard west of Bedford near dark on Sunday evening, and a brisk engagement followed, Hunter's artillery helping to bring Early's pursuit to a temporary halt. Hunter's army rested in place until midnight, when, by the light of a full moon, its march was resumed. It reached Buford Gap at dawn on Monday, June 20.

From Buford Gap Hunter took his troops to Bonsack's Station, a stop on the Virginia & Tennessee Railroad, destroying bridges, stations and equipment as it went, but avoiding a confrontation with Early's force. The rear guard clashed with Early's troops in two minor battles, one around two o'clock Monday afternoon as Hunter's column moved southwestward toward Salem, and another about nine o'clock in the morning on Tuesday, June 21. Hunter fled from the latter engagement, hurrying westward toward New Castle. At that point, as Hunter kept moving his army westward, farther away from the crucial battlefields, Early gave up the chase.

Hunter reached New Castle on June 22. He passed over Barbour and Warm Spring mountains and continued on to White Sulphur Springs, reaching there late on the 24th. He marched through Lewisburg on the 26th and finally arrived at Charleston on the 30th, his army worn, starving and demoralized—and far removed from the war.

Behind General Hunter was the trail he left, blazed by smoldering ruins and wanton destruction. General Early described it:

> The scenes on Hunter's route from Lynchburg had been truly heart-rending. Houses had been burned, and helpless women and children left without shelter. The country had been stripped of provisions and many families left without a morsel to eat. Furniture and bedding had been cut to pieces, and old men and women robbed of all the clothing they had except that on their backs. Ladies trunks had been rifled and their dresses torn to pieces in mere wantonness. Even the negro girls had lost their little finery.[20]

Hunter seemed to have a penchant for burning. According to General Crook, during the retreat, women would often ask him to protect their property and when they did, "his inevitable answer would be, 'Go away! Go away, or I will burn your house!'" A Union soldier from Connecticut who wrote about the march from Lynchburg conceded that "Gen. Hunter is a great one for burning property." But, he wrote, "everything he destroyed is rebel property, and should have been destroyed." Another soldier wrote, "General Hunter, for reasons best known to himself, has ordered the burning of many fine old Virginia mansions with all their contents. Many fine appearing ladies weep while their homes are burning." A Confederate officer described his view of Hunter's trail: "It was a scene of desolation. Ransacked houses, crying women, clothes from the bed chambers and wardrobes of ladies, carried on bayonets, and dragged on the road, the garments of little children, and here and there a burning house marked the track of Hunter's retreat."[21]

Major General John Brown Gordon, commander of the Second Corps of the Confederates' Army of Northern Virginia, theorized that there was a psychological reason for Hunter's behavior in refusing to do battle at the edge of Lynchburg or confront the outnumbered rebel army that pursued him: "It was then and still is incomprehensible to me that the small force under Early seemed to have filled Hunter with sudden panic. His hurried exit from Lynchburg was in marked contrast with his confident advance.... He ran away without any fight at all ... precipitately, and did not stop until he had found a safe retreat beyond the mountains toward the Ohio. If I were asked an opinion as to this utterly causeless fright and flight, I should be tempted to say that conscience, the inward monitor which 'makes cowards of us all,' was harrowing General Hunter, and causing him to see an avenger wrapped in every gray jacket before him."[22]

Historian Joseph Judge delivered an even harsher verdict: General Hunter — Black Dave, as he came to be known and as Judge called him — had "proved himself a criminal in uniform, an arsonist on a binge, and, like all bullies, he had run when confronted."[23]

And the Confederates still held their grip on the Shenandoah valley.

Petersburg,
June 12 to June 18, 1864

Several miles out on the road from Cold Harbor, while the Army of the Potomac was moving southward under the cover of darkness on the evening of June 12, General Grant, on Cincinnati, was joined by a senior officer as he rode in the column of march. The officer had devised a plan to build a new line of trenches that could cover the army's withdrawal in the event Grant decided to move toward the James River from its position at Cold Harbor. Smoking a cigar, Grant calmly listened while the officer explained the details and usefulness of his plan. After a few minutes, Grant broke in and, letting him know the needlessness of the plan, told the officer, "The army has already pulled out from the enemy's front and is now on its march to the James."[1]

The officer was astonished. So secretive had Grant been about his intentions that this senior officer had no idea what the army was doing or where it was now going. Grant had delivered his orders to his corps commanders in strict confidence. Only those who needed to know knew that the Army of the Potomac was on its way to the south side of the James, where it would join forces with General Butler's army and attempt to capture Petersburg.

Secretiveness had become habitual for Grant since he had assumed the awesome responsibilities that were now his. He had learned, his aide, Lieutenant Colonel Horace Porter, explained, that in the field there were always visitors eager for information about the army's movements, eager to grasp the least intimations of the general's intentions and ready to circulate them without regard for the possibility that such information could reach the ears of the enemy. Grant had come to accept the maxim, Porter said, that "the unspoken word is a sword in the scabbard, while the spoken word is a sword in the hand of one's enemy."[2]

The secrecy, as intended, beclouded the Confederate camp. General Lee didn't learn about the movement of the Army of the Potomac until the next morning, June 13. And even then he drew the wrong conclusion, the one Grant had hoped for. Grant had sent General Warren's corps toward Richmond not only to guard the Long Bridge road until the bulk of the army had crossed the Chickahominy but as a feint designed to have Lee believe Grant was attempting another flanking movement.[3] Lee took the bait. Supposing that Grant's entire army was on the march toward the capital, Lee at 10 P.M. on the 13th wired Richmond: "At daybreak this morning it was discovered that the army of General Grant had left our

115

front. Our skirmishers were advanced between one and two miles, but failing to discover the enemy, were withdrawn, and the army was moved to conform to the route taken by him."[4] That route, on the Long Bridge road, was the one traveled only by Warren's corps.

A detachment of Grant's cavalry troopers had been sent to dismount and wade across the Chickahominy and chase the Confederate pickets from the site near Long Bridge, some fifteen miles below Cold Harbor, where Union engineers would throw a pontoon bridge across the Chickahominy, all the stationary bridges in the area having been destroyed. The rebel pickets were run off, the pontoon bridge was swiftly constructed, and Warren's corps marched across it on the morning of the 13th, then proceeded westward along the Long Bridge road. Warren's orders were to move some distance along that road and make demonstrations to draw the attention of the rebels.

Grant's other corps were also on the march. General Baldy Smith's corps was on its way to Bermuda Hundred by way of White House. General Hancock's corps had crossed the Chickahominy behind Warren's corps, headed for the James. General Burnside's corps and General Wright's corps had followed Hancock's corps, all headed for the James. Grant, after leaving his camp on the night of the 12th, had stopped temporarily at Long Bridge, where he was in a position to communicate with Warren. He later resumed his ride and reached Wilcox's Landing, on the bank of the James, on the evening of the 13th and camped there. It was at Wilcox's Landing that the crossing of the James would occur. On the night of the 13th Warren's corps withdrew from its position on the Long Bridge road and reached the James on the afternoon of June 14, ready to resume its position in the column.

During the day on the 14th, Grant took a steamer up the James to Bermuda Hundred, where he met with Butler and went over plans for the attack on Petersburg. Grant was guessing that Lee had not had time to reinforce the Petersburg garrison and that the city was still lightly defended. "His instructions [to Butler]," Colonel Porter recorded, "were that as soon as Smith's troops reached their destination they should be reinforced by as many men as could be spared from Butler's troops — about 6000,— and move at once against Petersburg."[5] When the briefing ended, Grant returned to Wilcox's Landing, arriving about 1 P.M.

Construction of the pontoon bridge across the James began later that afternoon. By eleven o'clock that night, the bridge was completed. Laid atop one hundred and one pontoons, the bridge was twenty-one hundred feet long and was held in place, against the river's swift current, by cables fastened to ships that were anchored in the river for just that purpose. Once the bridge was finished, Grant's troops began streaming across. A flotilla of ferryboats aided in the crossing, carrying men, wagons and artillery. By dawn on the morning of June 15 all of Hancock's infantry and four artillery batteries were safely on the south bank of the James while the rest of the army continued to pour across.

Later that morning Grant stood atop a bluff on the north side of the river, observing the crossing. "His cigar had been thrown aside, his hands were clasped behind him, and he seemed lost in the contemplation of the spectacle," Porter related. "The great bridge was the scene of a continuous movement of infantry columns, batteries of artillery, and wagon-trains. The approaches to the river on both banks were covered with masses of troops moving briskly to their positions or waiting patiently their turn to cross.... Drums were beating the march, bands were playing stirring quicksteps.... It was a matchless pageant that could not fail to inspire all beholders with the grandeur of achievement and the majesty of military power."[6]

The crossing continued throughout the day on the 15th and 16th. By midnight on the

16th Grant's entire army—which Grant estimated at 115,000 men—along with its supply wagons and its artillery, was on the south side of the James River. The entire operation was accomplished without a serious mishap or the loss of a wagon or animal. The only casualties were those suffered by Warren's troops and the cavalry during minor clashes with Confederates along the Long Bridge road. The crossing had not been achieved without risk, though. Adam Badeau, Grant's aide-de-camp and semi-official chronicler, described the dangers:

> Lee would be easily able to interpose, if Grant attempted to cross the former stream [the James River] at any point near the rebel lines. It was necessary, therefore, to make a wide detour to avoid interruption, and no good point for crossing the James could be found, nearer than Wilcox's landing, twelve miles east of City Point by the river, and thirty-five from Grant's position at Cold Harbor. Windmill Point, on the southern bank, immediately opposite Wilcox's landing, is twenty miles by road from Petersburg. The James river here is twenty-one hundred feet in width, and over eighty feet in depth. Thus, in order to reach Petersburg, Grant would be obliged to march more than fifty miles, and to cross both the Chickahominy and the James, the latter at an extremely difficult point; while Lee was not more than six miles from Richmond, nor twenty-five from Petersburg; he could cross the James where it was only a few hundred feet in width, he had a railroad to facilitate the movement of his army, and no interruption to fear from an enemy while on the way.
>
> The army of the James [Butler's command] would be particularly exposed during the execution of the manoeuvre, for if Lee should detect the withdrawal of Grant, and divine its object, he would be able to throw his whole command on the southern side [of the James], and fall upon Butler in force, before the army of the Potomac could arrive.[7]

There was also the possibility that Confederate gunboats would descend the James from Richmond and attempt to thwart or delay the crossing. Federal gunboats were stationed in the river below Richmond, but there was no assurance they would prevent every rebel vessel from attacking the troops before and during the crossing. Grant foresaw and took care of that possibility: "I had previously ordered General Butler to have two vessels loaded with stone and carried up the river to a point above that occupied by our gunboats, where the channel was narrow, and sunk there so as to obstruct the passage and prevent Confederate gunboats from coming down the river.... I ordered this done."[8]

Grant also had ordered Baldy Smith to make a forced march to White House and immediately board transport steamers that would hurriedly carry them to City Point, where they would be joined by Butler's Army of the James. Grant figured that if Lee decided to attack Butler, the reinforcing troops of Smith's corps would allow Butler to hold off the rebels until the main body of the Army of the Potomac could join the battle.

Grant had little reason to believe that Butler could handle an important engagement on his own. Butler's original orders from Grant had instructed him to move out from his base at Fort Monroe and elsewhere on May 4, in coordination with the other armies in Grant's grand plan, and advance on Richmond along the south side of the James River. Butler and his troops had landed from steamers at Bermuda Hundred, the neck of land above the confluence of the James and Appomattox rivers. He was then fifteen miles below Richmond. His plodding advance had been halted on May 16 at Fort Darling at Drewry's Bluff, eight miles from Richmond, when Beauregard came out from Petersburg to challenge him. Beaten back, Butler retreated to his base at Bermuda Hundred. Beauregard then had established a defensive line between the two rivers, above Butler's position, to hold him check. The clash at Battle of Drewry's Bluff had cost Butler's force 422 killed, 2,380 wounded, and 210 missing or captured. Confederate losses were estimated at 400 killed, 2,000 wounded, and 100 missing or captured.[9]

In Badeau's opinion, Butler since then had botched an attack on Petersburg, making only a half-hearted attempt at it with troops of Smith's corps and in so doing had lost a golden opportunity to seize the city. Badeau described that failure:

> On the 9th [of June], Butler sent [Major General Quincy Adams] Gillmore with two thousand infantry, and [Brigadier General August] Kautz at the head of fifteen hundred cavalry, in the direction of Petersburg; they were to destroy the bridges across the Appomattox river, and, if possible, capture the town. Gillmore returned, reporting the works in his front too strong to assault, but Kautz carried the fortifications on the southern side, and entered Petersburg, driving before him about fourteen hundred rebels, mostly militia; being, however, unsupported, he also was obliged to retire. The bridges were not destroyed, and Gillmore was at once relieved by Butler from command…. Had a sufficient force been sent against the isolated and almost defenceless town, it could not only have been taken, but held, and months of weary toil and thousands of precious lives would have been saved. But a force of only thirty-five hundred men was sent, and these returned, after having absolutely been in possession of the prize.[10]

Not only had the attack failed but it had alerted the Confederates to Petersburg's vulnerability. General Beauregard, commanding Confederate armies between the James and the Cape Fear rivers, fired off a series of wires to Confederate headquarters in Richmond, urging that reinforcements be sent to Petersburg.

A city of about 18,000 population, Petersburg was protected by a line of entrenchments that started on the south bank of the Appomattox River, about a mile beyond the east side of the city, and extended in a semicircle to a point on the river about a mile beyond the west side of the city. The fortifications were manned by a force described by the former commandant at Petersburg, Confederate Brigadier General R.E. Colston:

> On the 9th of June the lines were entirely stripped of regular troops, with the exception of Wise's brigade on our extreme left, and of Sturdivant's battery of four guns. Every other regiment had been ordered across the James to aid General Lee on the north side. A few skeleton companies of home guards (less than 150 men) occupied the redoubts half a mile from the river on the left, which were armed with heavy artillery. Then came a gap of a mile and a half to lunette 16, occupied by 30 home guards with 4 pieces of stationary artillery. One mile farther to the right were two howitzers of Sturdivant's battery; one mile farther still were lunettes 26, 27, and 28, at the intersection of the lines with the Jerusalem road; but neither there nor for four miles more to the river on our right was there a man or gun.[11]

It was by that force that Butler's assault had been repelled on June 9. General Beauregard, though, held no hope that that same garrison could withstand the larger mass of Union troops that he knew was gathering on the south bank of the James. But his pleas for help were being ignored by the Confederate brass in Richmond. "From Swift Creek, early on June 14th," he related, "I telegraphed to General Bragg: 'Movement of Grant's across Chickahominy and increase of Butler's force render my position here critical. With my present forces I cannot answer for consequences. Cannot my troops sent to General Lee be returned at once? …' No answer came. Late in the evening of the same day, having further reason to believe that one corps at least of General Grant's army was already within Butler's lines, I telegraphed to General Lee: 'A deserter from the enemy reports that Butler has been reenforced by the Eighteenth and a part of the Tenth Army Corps.' To this dispatch, likewise, there came no response."[12]

Richmond seemed gripped by confusion and indecision. According to one report, "The departments and shops were closed. The influx of citizens from all parts of the state, north of the James, was great and continuous; the stock of provisions had failed when the Petersburg and Danville roads were cut.... [U]ncertainty as to Grant's intentions was painful. Troops were hurried now to the north, now to the south side of the James. Orders were given, and countermanded...."[13]

Despairing of getting help from Richmond and growing more and more desperate, Beauregard dispatched an emissary to General Lee to plead face to face. "I sent one of my aides, Colonel Samuel B. Paul, to General Lee with instructions to explain to him the exact situation," Beauregard recounted. "General Lee's answer to Colonel Paul was not encouraging. He said that I must be in error in believing the enemy had thrown a large force on the south side of the James; that the troops referred to by me could be but a few of Smith's corps going back to Butler's lines. Strange to say, at the very time General Lee was thus expressing himself to Colonel Paul, the whole of Smith's corps was actually assaulting the Petersburg lines. But General Lee finally said that he had already issued orders for the return of Hoke's division; that he would do all he could to aid me, and even come himself should the necessity arise."[14]

General Baldy Smith's corps, on Grant's orders, had indeed crossed the Appomattox River at daybreak on Wednesday, June 15, with Kautz's cavalry spearheading the advance, and after moving past a strong rebel position on the northeast side of Petersburg, had forced the Confederates back along a three-and-a-half-mile front. "The Confederates were now driven back at all points," Porter reported, "four guns were taken and turned upon the retreating troops, the line of intrenchments was carried, and three hundred prisoners and sixteen pieces of artillery captured." Then Smith, known for a high degree of caution, inexplicably halted his advance. "Instead of following up this advantage with his whole force in an attempt to seize the city," Porter related, "Smith made no further advance. Staff-officers from Grant had reached Smith at four o'clock, saying that Hancock was marching toward him. Hancock's troops reached a point a mile in the rear of Hinks's division of Smith's command about half-past six, and two divisions of Hancock's corps were ordered to push on and cooperate in the pending movement. Night soon after set in, and Smith contented himself with having two divisions of Hancock's corps occupy the works which had been captured."[15]

Meanwhile, as the night deepened, rebel reinforcements began arriving and taking positions in Smith's front. Beauregard now had about ten thousand troops manning the fortifications. On his own initiative, he had shifted two divisions, those of Major General Robert Hoke and Major General Bushrod Johnson, from the rebel line that was keeping Butler in check at Bermuda Hundred. Although still hugely outnumbered by the fifty thousand Union troops that faced them, the rebels were strongly entrenched and fiercely determined.

In temporary command until General Meade could arrive, Hancock prepared a massive assault. He formed a broad line of advance, placing Burnside's corps on the left, Hancock's corps on the right and his own corps in the center. At 5:30 P.M. on the 16th he put all three corps in motion, slowly advancing on the rebel line. The Confederates stubbornly resisted, falling back to new breastworks as their first line was pierced, halting the Union advance. When Meade arrived on the field, he ordered a new assault. That one forced the Confederates back temporarily, until they launched a sweeping counterattack that drove the Union troops back from the ground they had gained and cost them many prisoners. The day ended with the Union troops digging in not far from the rebel works.

At dawn on the 17th two brigades of Burnside's corps under Brigadier General Robert B. Potter crept up to the rebel line and burst upon it in a surprise attack. At first successful, the swift attack captured almost a mile of the rebel fortifications and some six hundred prisoners, but was eventually stopped. Two more thrusts were made on the Confederate position on the 17th, one by Brigadier General John Hartranft's brigade and one by Brigadier General James Ledlie's division, both of Burnside's corps. Both were repulsed, the firing lasting until after eleven o'clock that night.

About half past midnight Beauregard began to stealthily move his line back about a mile, tightening the wall of defense by reducing its circumference. "The digging of trenches was begun by the men as soon as they reached their new position," Beauregard reported. "Axes, as well as spades; bayonets and knives, as well as axes — in fact, every utensil that could be found — were used. And when all was over, or nearly so, with much anxiety still, but with comparative relief, nevertheless, I hurried off this telegram to General Lee [at 12:40 A.M. on the 18th]: 'All quiet at present. I expect renewal of attack in morning. My troops are becoming much exhausted. Without immediate and strong reenforcements, results may be unfavorable. Prisoners report Grant on the field with his whole army.'"[16]

Lee, despite all reports, doggedly held onto his belief that Grant was not moving his army on Petersburg. He wired Beauregard on the 18th: "Am not yet satisfied as to General Grant's movements; but upon your representations will move at once to Petersburg."[17] Beauregard took heart from that message. "Late as had been the credence given by General Lee to

Union troops at Petersburg. Repeated assaults on the Confederate works were repulsed by the rebels with heavy Union casualties, including 1,688 killed and 8,513 wounded. General Meade told his commanders, "I suppose you cannot make any more attacks, and I feel satisfied all has been done that can be done." (NATIONAL ARCHIVES AND RECORDS ADMINISTRATION)

my representations of Grant's movements," Beauregard reported, "it was, fortunately, not yet too late, by prompt and energetic action, to save Petersburg — and, therefore, Richmond."[18]

Major General Joseph Kershaw's division, numbering some five thousand men, was the first to reach Petersburg, arriving early Saturday morning, June 18. Beauregard ordered it into place on the new line of entrenchments. Major General Charles Field's division, also numbering about five thousand, arrived about two hours later, bringing Beauregard's total force to twenty thousand men. General Lee himself arrived about eleven-thirty that same morning.

The Union force had also been strengthened. Warren's corps had arrived and had increased the attacking army to some sixty-seven thousand troops. General Meade was now commanding that army, Grant having decided to stay at his City Point headquarters. Meade ordered an attack at daybreak, and the blue-coated troops moved out as ordered, only to find that the Confederates had abandoned their earthworks and moved closer to Petersburg. "Our lines were advancing," Meade's aide-de-camp, Lieutenant Colonel Theodore Lyman, reported, "and there was an inexplicable silence along the skirmish line."[19] The explanation was soon discovered to be the absence of rebel troops from where they were thought to be. The mission now became a probing search for the new Confederate position.

"At 6.50 [A.M.] came an order for all the line to advance and to attack the enemy if

Union siege mortar. After General Meade conceded that assaults on the Confederate line were futile, Union troops settled down to a prolonged siege and brought up artillery to hammer the rebel position. This heavy mortar was nicknamed The General. (LIBRARY OF CONGRESS)

found," Lyman related. "A little later, after seven, Major Roebling came in and reported he had discovered the enemy's new line of works, that ran along a high ground beyond the railroad, and that they were all there, with batteries in position. Soon after [,] General Warren mounted, and we all rode to the front, over a wide oat-field past the works captured last evening, from which we were afterwards driven."[20] Lyman's account described the action that followed:

> After much difficulty in advancing the different divisions, we at last drove the enemy from the railroad cut and a gully beyond, and got in, to about 200 yards of their works. At 3.30 in the afternoon the first assault took place. We rode out on an open field to watch it. In front was a broad expanse, quite flat; then the railroad cut with a fringe of bushes, and then a gradual rise crowned by the Rebel rifle-pits and batteries, which were distant perhaps half a mile. Close to us, on each side, were our batteries, firing as fast as they could, and the rebels were sending back shot, shell, and shrapnel as hard as possible....
>
> It was as I expected — forty-five days of constant marching, assaulting and trenching are a poor preparation for a rush! The men went in, but not with spirit; received by a withering fire, they sullenly fell back a few paces to a slight crest and lay down, as much as to say, "We can't assault but we won't run." The slopes covered with dead and wounded bore testimony that they were willing to give proof of courage even in circumstances that they deemed desperate.
>
> Another attack at six resulted no better, save that the lines were at all points pressed in on those of the enemy.... I returned after dark, feeling pretty sad.... The whole thing resulted just as I expected. You cannot strike a full blow with a wounded hand.[21]

General Meade, ordinarily impatient and quick-tempered, accepted his weary troops' failure, knowing they had done their best. "Sorry to hear you cannot carry the works," he told the generals he had earlier scolded. "Get the best line you can, and be prepared to hold it. I suppose you cannot make any more attacks, and I feel satisfied all has been done that can be done." In so saying, he signaled the end of Grant's attempts to take Petersburg by direct assault.

Grant confirmed Meade's conclusion. In the presence of his staff officers late that evening he remarked, "I am perfectly satisfied that all has been done that could be done, and that the assaults to-day were called for by all the appearance and information that could be obtained. Now, we will rest the men, and use the spade for their protection, till a new vein can be struck."[22]

Beauregard was pleased. "The truth is that, despite the overwhelming odds against us, every Federal assault, on the 18th, was met with most signal defeat, 'attended,' says Mr. Swinton, the Federal historian, 'with another mournful loss of life.' This was, in fact, very heavy, and exceeded ours in the proportion of nine to one."[23] Indeed, Union casualties were estimated at 1,688 killed, 8,513 wounded, and 1,185 missing or captured. Confederate losses were estimated at 200 killed, 2,900 wounded, and 900 missing or captured.[24] Some U.S. units suffered unusually severe casualties. The First Maine Heavy Artillery Regiment suffered the heaviest loss of all — 632 of its 900 men. "No event of our war," Beauregard observed with satisfaction, "was more remarkable than the almost incredible resistance of the men who served under me at Petersburg, on the 15th, 16th, 17th, and 18th of June, before the arrival of Lee."[25]

"There was no further attempt on the part of General Meade to assault our lines," Beauregard reported. "The spade took the place of the musket, and the regular siege was begun."[26]

The March to Washington,
June 23 to July 12, 1864

General Early was satisfied that Hunter and his army were gone beyond his reach. "As the enemy had got into the mountains, where nothing useful could be accomplished by pursuit," he remarked, "I did not deem it proper to continue it farther."[1]

He had other reasons to call off the chase. "A great part of my command had had nothing to eat for the last two days, except a little bacon which was obtained at Liberty," he recounted. "The cooking utensils were in the trains, and the effort to have bread baked at Lynchburg had failed. Neither the waggon [*sic*] trains, nor the artillery of the 2nd Corps, were up, and I knew that the country, through which Hunter's route led for forty or fifty miles, was, for the most part, a desolate mountain region; and his troops were taking everything in the way of provisions and forage which they could lay their hands on.... My command had marched sixty miles, in the three days pursuit, over very rough roads, and that part of it from the Army of Northern Virginia had had no rest since leaving Gaines' Mill. I determined, therefore, to rest on the 22nd, so as to enable the waggons and artillery to get up, and prepare the men for the long march before them."[2]

The wait for the wagons and artillery would also allow time, Early hoped, for the arrival of the shoes he had requested from Richmond. Of his ten thousand infantrymen and dismounted cavalry troopers, he reported, almost half were barefooted or nearly so.[3]

On Thursday, June 23 Early ordered his troops, still waiting for their shoes, to begin the long march that he said lay before them. Early's original orders, delivered orally to him by General Lee on June 12, instructed him to prepare the Army of Northern Virginia's Second Corps, Stonewall Jackson's former command, for a march from its position near Gaines' Mill westward into the Shenandoah valley, taking with it two battalions of artillery. That evening he received Lee's written orders telling him to move out at three o'clock the following morning. He was to head for the Shenandoah by way of Charlottesville, pass through the Blue Ridge by Brown's Gap or Swift Run Gap and strike Hunter's column in the rear as it moved up the valley toward Lynchburg. He was to destroy Hunter's army if possible. That was his *first* objective. After that, he was to march northward down the valley, cross the Potomac River around Leesburg or around Harpers Ferry and then march on Washington City, as the U.S. capital was then called. The idea was not to capture Washington, but merely to threaten it and force General Grant to shift troops to defend it, easing Grant's pressure on the rebels' beleaguered army at Petersburg.

Having reached Lynchburg, Early received more instructions. "I had received a telegram from General Lee," Early wrote in his memoir, "directing me, after disposing of Hunter, either to return to his [Lee's] army or carry out the original plan, as I might deem most expedient under the circumstances in which I found myself." After Hunter had fled and Early had given up the chase, Lee repeated that he was leaving it to Early to decide whether the condition of his troops would permit the expedition across the Potomac to be carried out. Early quickly decided it would.

He resumed the march on the 23rd and reached Buchanan that night, where his column took the route over which Hunter had advanced. It was then that Early and his troops were able to observe the destruction that Hunter and his army had wreaked. Early dispatched his cavalry, under the command of Major General Robert Ransom, to move down the west side of the valley, paralleling the main column, in case Hunter should decide to re-enter the valley.

On the morning of Saturday, June 25, Early's main column reached Lexington. The route of march was up Main Street and past the cemetery where the remains of General Stonewall Jackson lay buried. Two eyewitnesses recorded the troops' passing the flower-bedecked grave of their beloved commander, restored by townspeople following its desecration by Hunter's troops. "Not a man spoke," one of the witnesses wrote. "Not a sound was uttered. Only the tramp, tramp of passing feet told that his surviving veterans were passing in review, while the drooping and tattered flags saluted his sacred dust." The other

witness wrote, "Many a tear was seen trickling down the cheeks of his veterans. How many ... had crossed the river and were then resting beneath the shade of the trees with him." Confederate Brigadier General William Lewis, also in the line of march, later wrote to his sister and told her she could have "no idea what feelings passed over me" as the somber, gray-coated column marched past the cemetery.[4]

Early himself was one of Jackson's veterans. He had been a division commander in Jackson's corps at the time Jackson was shot. Now forty-seven years old, he had graduated from West Point in 1837, finishing eighteenth in a class of fifty cadets. He was a veteran of the Seminole War and of the Mexican War, in which he had served as a U.S. officer. A lawyer and a former member of the Virginia legislature, he had opposed secession, but once Virginia had voted to secede, he volunteered and was appointed a brigadier general in the

Confederate Lt. Gen. Jubal Early. He was known to his men as "Ol' Jube" and had a reputation for harshness toward subordinates, irascibility, a short temper, an unbridled use of profanity and a poor sense of direction, but was aggressive, courageous and eager to take the initiative. (LIBRARY OF CONGRESS)

Virginia militia. He later became a colonel in the Confederate army and was promoted to brigadier general after the First Battle of Bull Run (First Manassas) in July 1861. He became a division commander to succeed the wounded previous commander and became commander of the Army of Northern Virginia's Second Corps when its former commander, General Ewell, Jackson's successor, became too ill to continue to serve. He was promoted to lieutenant general in May 1864.

Known to his men as "Old Jube," Early, who never married, had a reputation for harshness toward subordinates, irascibility, a short temper and an unbridled use of profanity—and for a poor sense of direction—but he was the kind of commander that Lee liked, a Stonewall Jackson type, aggressive, self-reliant, courageous and bold, eager to take the initiative, needing no detailed instructions. He was also known for his dislike of cavalry. He blamed cavalry commanders Imboden and McCausland for Hunter's escape. He was about six feet tall, of solid build, with a slight stoop, a receding hairline and a ragged, gray-streaked beard. As a Richmond newspaper writer reported, he was "a person who would be singled out in a crowd. A large white felt hat, ornamented by a dark feather, and an immense white, fulled cloth overcoat, extending to the heels, give him a striking and unique appearance. His face is remarkable, and none could be more expressive of pertinacity and resolution."[5]

On Sunday June 26 Early reached Staunton, a day ahead of his column, and there he took stock of his expeditionary force and decided on some adjustments. The day was spent, he related, "in reducing transportation and getting provisions from Waynesboro, to which point they had been sent over the railroad. Some of the guns and a number of the horses belonging to the artillery were now unfit for service, and the best were selected, and about a battalion taken from Breckenridge's [sic] artillery, under Lt. Col. King, to accompany us, in addition to the two battalions brought with the 2nd Corps. The rest were left behind with a portion of the officers and men in charge of them. The dismounted cavalry had been permitted to send for their horses ... and Col. Bradley T. Johnson, who had joined me at this place with a battalion of Maryland Cavalry, was assigned to the command of Jones' brigade, with the temporary rank of Brigadier-General....

"General Breckenridge had accompanied us from Lynchburg, and, to give him a command commensurate with his proper one, and at the same time enable me to control the cavalry more readily, [Major General John B.] Gordon's division of infantry was assigned to his command in addition to the one under Elzey, and Ransom, in charge of the cavalry, was ordered to report to me directly....

"The official reports at this place [Staunton] showed about two thousand mounted men for duty in the cavalry, which was composed of four small brigades, to wit: Imboden's, McCausland's, Jackson's and Jones' (now Johnson's).... The official reports of the infantry showed 10,000 muskets for duty, including Vaughn's dismounted cavalry...."[6]

At Staunton Early received another telegraph message from Lee, once more telling him it was up to him to decide whether to pursue the original plan of marching on Washington. He promptly telegraphed Lee that he would continue the march. "I determined," he wrote in his memoir, "to carry out the original design at all hazards."[7] At 3 A.M. on June 28, with two days of rations in their haversacks and a five-day supply carried in wagons, Early's troops resumed their march. Left behind were empty wagons to bring their expected new shoes to them. In the long column of marchers were some fourteen thousand infantrymen and four thousand cavalry troopers, plus artillery.

The first day's march took them less than ten miles, much of the day being consumed by the slow crossing of the south fork of the Shenandoah River. The next day they made twenty-four miles, pushing past Harrisonburg before stopping for the night. At Winchester, which they reached on July 2, Early got new instructions. Lee told him to hold up. He was to stop long enough to destroy as much of the Baltimore & Ohio Railroad and the Chesapeake & Ohio Canal as was possible. "Unless the Baltimore and Ohio railroad was torn up," Early explained, "the enemy would have been able to move troops from the West over that road to Washington."[8] Lee wanted Union troops moved not from the West, but from the environs of Richmond and Petersburg.

Early detailed the opening action in the lower Shenandoah valley:

> On the night of the 2nd, McCausland was sent across North Mountain, to move down Back Creek, and burn the railroad bridge at its mouth, and then to move by North Mountain depot to Hainesville, on the road from Martinsburg to Williamsport; and early on the morning of the 3rd, Bradley Johnson was sent by Smithfield and Leetown, to cross the railroad at Kearneysville, east of Martinsburg, and unite with McCausland at Hainesville, so as to cut off the retreat of Sigel, who was at Martinsburg with a considerable force.
>
> Breckenridge [sic] moved, on the same morning, direct for Martinsburg, with his command preceded by Gilmor's battalion of cavalry, while I moved, with Rodes' and Ramseur's divisions, over the route taken by Johnson, to Leetown. On the approach of Breckenridge, Sigel, after very slight skirmishing, evacuated Martinsburg, leaving behind considerable stores, which fell into our hands. McCausland burned the bridge over Back Creek, captured the guard at North Mountain depot, and succeeded in reaching Hainesville; but Johnson encountered a force at Leetown, under Mulligan, which, after hard fighting, he drove across the railroad....[9]

Sigel fell back to Maryland Heights, opposite Harpers Ferry. On July 4 the rebel divisions of General Rodes and General Ramseur attacked the Union garrison at Harpers Ferry and drove it back to a defensive position on Maryland Heights, where it was joined by Sigel's troops. At first, Early had planned to use Harpers Ferry as a base of operations, but he gave up that idea when he saw how thoroughly the Union forces' position on Maryland Heights commanded Harpers Ferry. He decided to cross the Potomac at Shepherdstown, east of Martinsburg, and drive eastward on Frederick. "On the 7th [of July], the greater portion of the cavalry was sent across the mountain in the direction of Frederick," Early related, "and, that night, the expected shoes having arrived and been distributed, orders were given for a general move next morning."[10]

In early morning on Saturday, July 9 Bradley Johnson's cavalry brigade reached the north side of Frederick with orders to wreak havoc on the rail lines that went from Baltimore to Harrisburg and Philadelphia. He was to burn the bridges over the Gunpowder River and cut the rail line that ran between Baltimore and Washington. He was also to threaten Baltimore and then move toward Point Lookout, at the tip of the peninsula formed by the Potomac River and Chesapeake Bay, where there was a Union prisoner-of-war camp that held as many as fifty thousand Confederates. The cavalry's objective would be to free the rebel prisoners if Early's army could get through Washington.[11]

Driving Union skirmishers before it, Early's main column moved into Frederick and took over the town on the 9th. Early issued orders forbidding looting and abuse of the town's residents, warning of swift punishment for violators, but he demanded from the town government a tribute of $200,000 under threat of an artillery shelling. The town had been used by Union troops as a supply depot, making it a military target. The mayor protested, but to no avail. Earlier, General Early had extorted $20,000 from the town government of Hagerstown, the difference in the two sums being caused by a cavalry officer's misreading of Early's order, which had actually demanded $200,000 from Hagerstown also.

The Frederick city council borrowed the money from the town's five banks, eventually paying more than $600,000 in principal and interest before the town's notes were retired on October 1, 1951.[12]

Early's movements soon set off an alarm in Washington — and in Grant's headquarters. General Halleck on July 3 wired Grant, then encamped at City Point, that Early was moving toward the Potomac. Halleck let Grant know the danger, telling him, "The three principal officers on the line are Sigel, Stahel, and Max Weber. You can, therefore, judge what probability there is of a good defense if the enemy should attack the line in force."[13] Until July 3 Grant had thought Early was at Petersburg. Now, though, made aware of Early's threat to Washington, he replied to Halleck, saying that if the Confederates crossed the Potomac, "I can send an army corps from here to meet them or cut off their return south."[14]

With the army of Black Dave Hunter unavailable to help, responsibility for defending the lower Shenandoah valley fell to Major General Lew Wallace, who had his headquarters in Baltimore. Grant, in his memoir, reported Wallace's response to Early's threat: "His [Wallace's] surplus of troops with which to move against the enemy was small in number. Most of these were raw and, consequently, very much inferior to our veterans and to the veterans which Early had with him; but the situation of Washington was precarious, and Wallace moved with commendable promptitude to meet the enemy at the Monocacy."[15]

Monocacy, also known as Monocacy Junction and Frederick Junction, was a community three miles southeast of Frederick, and beside it the Monocacy River flows southwestward to the Potomac, forming a natural barrier that lay across the southeastward path of Early's army as it advanced on Washington. The river was spanned by three bridges near Monocacy, one carrying the Baltimore & Ohio rail line, one the turnpike to Washington and one the road to Baltimore. Monocacy, General Wallace decided, was the place to confront Early's army. Wallace's force numbered about 5,800 men, and he positioned them at the bridges and fords, presenting a six-mile front to the advancing rebels. With little hope of turning back Early's superior numbers, Wallace intended only to delay Early and allow time for reinforcements from Grant to arrive to defend Washington. The confrontation would also allow Wallace to gain an accurate estimate of the strength of the Confederate force.

General Early described the engagement that ensued:

> The enemy in considerable force under General Lew Wallace, was found strongly posted on the eastern bank of the Monocacy near the Junction, with an earthwork and two block houses commanding both the railroad bridge and the bridge on the Georgetown pike [the road to Washington]. Ramseur's division was deployed in front of the enemy, after driving his skirmishers across the river, and several batteries were put in position, when a sharp artillery fire opened from both sides. Rodes' division had come up from Jefferson [southwest of Frederick] and was placed on Ramseur's left, covering the roads from Baltimore and the crossings of the Monocacy above the Junction. Breckenridge's [sic] command, with the trains, was in the rear between Frederick and the Junction, while the residue of the cavalry was watching a force of the enemy's cavalry which had followed from Maryland Heights.
>
> The enemy's position was too strong, and the difficulties of crossing the Monocacy under fire too great, to attack in front without greater loss than I was willing to incur. I therefore made an examination in person to find a point at which the river could be crossed, so as to take the enemy in flank.[16]

Two attempts by McCausland's cavalry to turn Wallace's left flank were turned back. Then Early ordered General Gordon's division to support McCausland, a move that turned the battle. Early's account continues:

This division crossed at the same place [the ford where McCausland had crossed], and Gordon was ordered to move forward and strike the enemy on his left flank, and drive him from the positions commanding the crossings in Ramseur's front, so as to enable the latter to cross. This movement was executed under the personal superintendence of General Breckenridge, and, while Ramseur skirmished with the enemy in front, the attack was made by Gordon in gallant style, and, with the aid of several pieces of King's artillery which had been crossed over, and Nelson's artillery from the opposite side, he threw the enemy into great confusion and forced him from his position. Ramseur immediately crossed on the railroad bridge and pursued the enemy's flying forces, and Rodes crossed on the left and joined in the pursuit....

The pursuit was soon discontinued, as Wallace's entire force had taken the road towards Baltimore, and I did not want prisoners.... All the troops and trains were crossed over the Monocacy that night, so as to resume the march early next day.[17]

By Early's count, Confederate losses in the battle at Monocacy totaled about seven hundred, dead and wounded. Union losses were put at 1,294, counting dead, wounded and captured.[18] Early estimated the number of unwounded Union troops captured at between six hundred and seven hundred.[19]

The rebels' march to Washington resumed at daybreak on Sunday, July 10. Traveling the Georgetown pike, the Confederates covered some twenty miles and at the end of the day bivouacked about four miles west of Rockville after McCausland's cavalrymen drove off a detachment of Union cavalry. At dawn on the 11th the rebel column was again on the move. For the second day the weather was hot and dry, the road "exceedingly dusty," as Early put it. "The heat during the night had been very oppressive, and but little rest had been obtained. This day [Monday] was an exceedingly hot one.... While marching, the men were enveloped in a suffocating cloud of dust, and many of them fell by the way from exhaustion. Our progress was therefore very much impeded, but I pushed on as rapidly as possible, hoping to get into the fortifications around Washington before they could be manned."[20]

As the Confederates neared the ring of fortifications around Washington, Early and his troops could see a cloud of dust behind the defenders' works and then watched as a column of Union troops filed into the fortification, turning to the left and right, and then sending out a line of skirmishers. Within minutes the defenders' artillery opened on the Confederates. "This defeated our hopes of getting possession of the works by surprise," Early reported, "and it became necessary to reconnoitre."[21]

What the reconnaissance revealed was the extent of the Union fortifications, which were described by Major General John G. Barnard, chief engineer of the Army of the Potomac:

Every prominent point, at intervals of eight hundred to one thousand yards, was occupied by an inclosed field-fort; every important approach or depression of ground, unseen from the forts, swept by a battery for field-guns; and the whole connected by rifle-trenches which were in fact lines of infantry parapets, furnishing emplacement for two ranks of men, and affording covered communication along the line, while roads were opened wherever necessary, so that troops and artillery could be moved rapidly from one point of the immense periphery to another, or, under cover, from point to point along the line.

The counterscarps were surrounded by abatis; bomb-proofs were provided in nearly all the forts; all guns not solely intended for distant fire placed in embrasures and well traversed. All commanding points on which an enemy would be likely to concentrate artillery to overpower that of one or two of our forts or batteries were subjected not only to the fire, direct and cross, of many points along the line, but also from heavy rifled guns from distant points unattainable by the enemy's field guns.

With all these developments, the lines certainly approximated to the maximum degree of strength which can be attained from unrevetted earth-works. Inadequately manned as they were, the fortifications compelled at least a concentration and an arraying of force on the part of the assailants, and thus gave time for the arrival of succor.[22]

General Barnard also reported the strength of the Union defenders manning the Washington fortifications as Early's column came within sight of them: "The effective forces were 1819 infantry, 1834 artillery, and 63 cavalry north of the Potomac, and 4064 infantry, 1772 artillery, and 51 cavalry south thereof. There were besides in Washington and Alexandria, about 3900 effectives and about 4000 (six regiments) of Veteran Reserves. The foregoing constitute a total of about 20,400 men. Of that number, however, but 9600, mostly perfectly raw troops, constituted the garrison of the defenses. Of the other troops, a considerable portion were unavailable, and the whole would form but an inefficient force for service on the lines."[23]

General Early reported the strength of his force: "The rapid marching which had broken down a number of the men who were barefooted or weakened by previous exposure, and had been left in the Valley and directed to be collected at Winchester, and the losses in killed and wounded at Harper's Ferry, Maryland Heights, and Monocacy, had reduced my infantry to about 8,000 muskets. Of those remaining, a very large number were greatly exhausted by the last two days marching, some having fallen by sunstroke, and I was satisfied, when we arrived in front of the fortifications, that not more than one-third of my force could have been carried into action."[24]

The rebel reconnaissance consumed the day and when it was done, Early gained a clear idea of the strength of the Union position. "On the right was Rock Creek," he reported, "running through a deep ravine which had been rendered impassable by the felling of the timber on each side, and beyond were the works on the Georgetown pike which had been reported to be the strongest of all. On the left, as far as the eye could reach, the works appeared to be of the same impregnable character. The position was naturally strong for defence, and the examination showed, what might have been expected, that every appliance of science and unlimited means had been used to render the fortifications around Washington as strong as possible."[25]

Knowing he had to make a decision and had to make it soon, Early called a council of war. "After dark on the 11th, I held a consultation with Major-Generals Breckenridge, Rodes, Gordon and Ramseur, in which I stated to them the danger of remaining where we were, and the necessity of doing something immediately, as the probability was that the passes of the South Mountain and the fords of the upper Potomac would soon be closed against us."[26] After hearing what his generals had to say, the specifics of which he left unreported, Early decided to make a try at the Union defenses. "Being very reluctant to abandon the project of capturing Washington, I determined to make an assault on the enemy's works at daylight next morning, unless some information should be received before that time showing its impracticability, and so informed those officers."[27]

During the night, Early received that information. General Johnson, operating near Baltimore, had learned that two corps of Grant's army had arrived in Washington, and Johnson promptly passed that information to Early. "This caused us to delay the attack until I could examine the works again," Early related, "and as soon as it was light enough to see, I rode to the front and found the parapets lined with troops. I had, therefore, reluctantly, to give up all hopes of capturing Washington, after I had arrived in sight of the dome of the Capitol, and given the Federal authorities a terrible fright."[28]

During the afternoon of the 12th a reconnaissance force was sent out from Washington, but was driven back by Rodes's division, allowing Early's army to wait till dark to withdraw from their position at the edge of Washington. "About dark we commenced retiring," Early related, "and did so without molestation. Passing through Rockville and Poolsville, we crossed the Potomac at White's Ford, above Leesburg in Loudon County, on the morning of the 14th, bringing off the prisoners captured at Monocacy and everything else in safety."[29]

Early rested his troops near Leesburg on the 14th and 15th, and on the morning of the 16th the rebel column continued its march back to the Shenandoah valley, pausing long enough, however, to inflict more terror on frightened Northerners. On July 28, having learned of General Hunter's burning of Virginia Military Institute and other buildings in Lexington, Early ordered Brigadier General John McCausland — a V.M.I. alumnus and former faculty member — to take his cavalry into Chambersburg, Pennsylvania, a town of about six thousand residents, twenty miles north of Hagerstown, Maryland, and demand from its citizens $100,000 in gold or $500,000 in U.S. currency or else have their town put to the torch. When the town was unable to pay, McCausland, on July 30, following Early's orders, set fires that burned most of Chambersburg, including residences, public and commercial buildings, churches and schools.

15

The Mining Disaster,
June 21 to July 30, 1864

As the passing June days led deeper into summer, the weather around Petersburg grew ever warmer, so much so that Grant's besieging army had switched to summer uniforms. Thin, dark-blue flannel blouses replaced the heavy coats the troops had been wearing. Like those of his staff officers, Grant's summer blouse was single-breasted, with four brass buttons down the front. "It was substantially the coat of a private soldier," his aide, Colonel Porter, observed, "with nothing to indicate the rank of an officer except the three gold stars of a lieutenant-general on the shoulder straps....

"The general, when he put on the blouse, did not take the pains to see whether it fitted him or to notice how it looked, but thought only of the comfort it afforded, and said, 'Well, this is a relief,' and then added: 'I like to put on a suit of clothes when I get up in the morning, and wear it until I go to bed, unless I have to make a change in my dress to meet company.'"[1]

Grant had made his headquarters at City Point (now Hopewell), at the junction of the James and Appomattox rivers, which gave him easy communication by water with Fort Monroe, with Butler's command post and with Washington, D.C. as well. Rail service to and through the town was restored, and a branch line of the City Point Railroad was built to reach points immediately behind the Union line, south of Petersburg.

City Point was humming with activity. The wharves were crowded with materiel, equipment and supplies for the besieging army and with the docked ships that had brought it all. An immense supply depot was being established. Hospitals were being erected. On level ground atop a high bluff that rose from the river a commodious house and large yard accommodated Grant and his staff. Grant assigned the house to his chief quartermaster and chose tents for his own quarters, one for his office, one for his sleeping quarters. Other tents provided quarters for the members of his staff. A mess tent was also erected. They were pitched on the house's lawn, from which a wooden stairway led down to the boat landing below the bluff.

To that modest headquarters President Lincoln came for a visit on June 21. He arrived by steamer, having traveled down the Potomac and through Chesapeake Bay, then up the James. Grant and a group of his officers stood at the wharf waiting to welcome him. When the boat docked, Grant and his officers stepped aboard it as the president descended from the upper deck. Lincoln immediately grasped Grant's hand and while vigorously shaking it congratulated him on his successes. The entire group then retired to a cabin to sit and talk.

"I hope you are very well, Mister President," Grant offered.

"Yes, I am in very good health," Lincoln responded. "But I don't feel very comfortable after my trip last night on the bay. It was rough, and I was considerably shaken up. My stomach has not yet entirely recovered from the effects."[2] When Grant suggested a glass of champagne to settle his stomach, Lincoln refused the suggestion with a laugh, saying he had seen too many men as sick from champagne as from seasickness.

Grant then invited the president to tour the Union lines. "Why, yes," Lincoln replied. "I had fully intended to go out and take a look at the brave fellows who have fought their way down to Petersburg in this wonderful campaign. And I am ready to start at any time."[3]

Grant lent Lincoln his own handsome bay, Cincinnati, to ride, a mount apparently befitting a president. Grant mounted a horse curiously named Jeff Davis, and off they went, along with three officers from Grant's staff. Colonel Porter described the sight of the tall, gangling president on horseback: "Mr. Lincoln wore a very high black silk hat and black trousers and frock-coat.... [B]y the time he had reached the troops he was completely covered with dust, and the black color of his clothes had changed to Confederate gray. As he had no straps, his trousers gradually worked up above his ankles, and gave him the appearance of a country farmer riding into town wearing his Sunday clothes. A citizen on horseback is always an odd sight in the midst of a uniformed army, and the picture presented by the President bordered upon the grotesque."[4]

The troops were unconcerned about the president's odd looks. His presence alone impressed them, and they broke out in cheers and shouts of greeting as he rode along their lines. When he reached the position held by emancipated black troops, the men of the black units broke out into cheers, tears and song. "They crowded about him and fondled his horse," Porter related. "Some of them kissed his hands, while others ran off crying in triumph to their comrades that they had touched his clothes. The President rode with bared head; the tears had started to his eyes, and his voice was so broken by emotion that he could scarcely articulate the words of thanks and congratulation which he tried to speak to the humble and devoted men through whose ranks he rode. The scene was affecting in the extreme, and no one could have witnessed it unmoved."[5]

Lincoln spent the night aboard the steamer and the next morning took it up the James to meet with Butler at Bermuda Hundred, then, farther up the river, with Admiral Samuel P. Lee, commander of the U.S. gunboats on the James. After ascending the river as far as it was considered safe to do, observing as much of the Union army's position as could be seen from the river, Lincoln had the steamer turn around and head back to City Point to end the visit, then steamed away to Washington, apparently satisfied.

The Army of the Potomac was deployed in a ring around Petersburg, with Burnside's corps on the right flank, Warren's corps next to it, then Hancock's corps (temporarily commanded by Major General David Birney while Hancock recovered from the recurring effects of a wound), and, on the left flank, Wright's corps. Butler's troops had been returned to Butler. Having decided it would be unwise to try further to storm the rebel defenses, Grant determined he would hold enough troops along the Union line to defend his position and would at the same time wreak as much damage as possible on the Confederate transportation system. Union troop movements, however, were repeatedly contested by the Confederates.

On the morning of June 22 rebels forced back advancing units of Wright's and Birney's corps. On the 23rd, while units of Wright's corps were tearing up the tracks of the Weldon Railroad, a Confederate force attacked and drove off Wright's troops. The problems along Wright's section of the line drew Grant's attention, and he ordered the siege guns that were then arriving from Washington to be placed in commanding positions to deter rebel movements. He also ordered more artillery batteries be sent to him.

Meanwhile, an unusual scheme was being developed to break through a section of the rebel line. By the assaults made on June 17 and 18, troops of General Burnside's corps were able to establish a position within 130 yards of the Confederate line, atop the far edge of a deep ravine. Posted at that section of the Union line was the 48th Pennsylvania Volunteer Infantry Regiment, composed mostly of coal miners from the upper Schuylkill area of Pennsylvania and commanded by a thirty-one-year-old mining engineer, Lieutenant Colonel Henry Pleasants. Noticing the topography at that spot on the line, Pleasants — or some of his men — came up with the idea of digging a tunnel into the side of the ravine, unobservable to the Confederates, and extending the tunnel beneath the Confederate strongpoint called Elliott's Salient, which was fortified with a battery of four field pieces and manned by two South Carolina infantry regiments. According to Pleasants' plan, the tunnel, or gallery, would be 511 feet long, four and a half feet wide and four a half to five feet high and would branch out beneath the rebel strongpoint. Into the two branches, which would be dug perpendicular to the main gallery, would be placed seven tons of gunpowder that would be set off by a fuse and would blow up the Confederate strongpoint, disintegrating the rebel troops there, collapsing the ground beneath them and creating a wide gap in the rebel line, through which Union troops would pour.

Pleasants took the idea to General Burnside, who discussed it with General Meade, who passed it on to General Grant, who approved it and devised an elaborate plan of attack in conjunction with the execution of it. Work on the tunnel began on June 25. Despite the scheme's approval, Colonel Pleasants had no easy time getting the job done. He described the difficulties:

> My regiment was only about four hundred strong. At first I employed but a few men at a time, but the number was increased as the work progressed, until at last I had to use the whole regiment — non-commissioned officers and all. The great difficulty I had was to dispose of the material got out of the mine. I found it impossible to get any assistance from anybody; I had to do all the work myself. I had to remove all the earth in old cracker-boxes; I got pieces of hickory and nailed on the boxes in which we received our crackers, and then iron-clad them with hoops of iron taken from old pork and beef barrels.... Whenever I made application I could not get anything, although General Burnside was very favorable to it.
>
> The most important thing was to ascertain how far I had to mine, because if I fell short of or went beyond the proper place, the explosion would have no practical effect. Therefore I wanted an accurate instrument with which to make the necessary triangulations. I had to make them on the farthest front line, where the enemy's sharp-shooters could reach me. I could not get the instrument I wanted, although there was one at army headquarters, and General Burnside had to send to Washington and get an old-fashioned theodolite, which was given to me.... General Burnside told me that General Meade and Major Duane, chief engineer of the Army of the Potomac, said the thing could not be done — that it was all clap-trap and nonsense; that such a length of mine had never been excavated in military operations, and could not be; that I would either get the men smothered, for want of air, or crushed by the falling of the earth; or the enemy would find it out and it would amount to nothing. I could get no boards or lumber supplied to me for my operations. I had to get a pass and send two companies of my own regiment, with wagons, outside of our lines to rebel saw-mills, and get lumber in that way, after

having previously got what lumber I could by tearing down an old bridge. I had no mining picks furnished me, but had to take common army picks and have them straightened for my mining picks....[6]

Disposing of the excavated dirt proved one of the most time-consuming parts of the operation. The dirt had to be carried out through the entire length of the tunnel, which became three tunnels when the two branches were being dug. Every night Colonel Pleasants' men had to cut down bushes to cover the fresh dirt at the entrance to the tunnel lest it be noticed by rebel observers and snipers posted in trees within the rebel lines. Finally, on July 23 the tunnels were completed and were ready to have the gunpowder placed in them. Instead of the seven tons expected, only four tons were received, the amount having been reduced on orders from General Meade. The powder was carried in in twenty-five-pound kegs and placed in the two lateral tunnels that ran parallel to the Confederate line, half the powder in one and half in the other.

As the powder was about to be placed, Meade asked Burnside to prepare a plan of attack and submit it to him. Burnside responded in a letter dated July 26:

... It is altogether possible that the enemy are cognizant of the fact that we are mining, because it is mentioned in their papers, and they have been heard at work on what are supposed to be shafts in close proximity to our galleries. But the rain of the night before last had, no doubt, much retarded their work. We have heard no sound of workmen in them either yesterday or to-day; and nothing is heard by us in the mine but the ordinary sounds of work on the surface above. This morning we had some apprehension that the left lateral gallery was in danger of caving in from the weight of the batteries above it and the shock of their firing. But all possible precautions have been taken to strengthen it, and we hope to preserve it intact.... It is ... highly important, in my opinion, that the mine should be exploded at the earliest possible moment consistent with the general interest of the campaign.... But it may not be improper for me to say that the advantages reaped from the work would be but small if it were exploded without any cooperative movement.

My plan would be to explode the mine just before daylight in the morning or at about 5 o'clock in the afternoon; mass the two brigades of the colored division in rear of my first line, in columns of division, — "double-columns closed in mass," — the head of each brigade resting on the front line, and, as soon as the explosion has taken place, move them forward, with instructions for the divisions to take half distance, and as soon as the leading regiments of the two brigades pass through the gap in the enemy's line, the leading regiment of the right brigade to come into line perpendicular to the enemy's line by the 'right companies on the right into line, wheel,' the left companies on the right into line, and proceed at once down the line of enemy's works as rapidly as possible; and the leading regiment of the left brigade to execute the reverse movement to the left, moving up the enemy's line. The remainder of the columns to move directly toward the crest in front as rapidly as possible, diverging in such a way as to enable them to deploy into columns of regiments, the right column making as nearly as possible for Cemetery Hill; these columns to be followed by the other divisions of the corps as soon as they can be thrown in.... It would, in my opinion, be advisable, if we succeed in gaining the crest, to throw the colored division right into the town. There is a necessity for the coopera-tion, at least in the way of artillery, by the troops on our right and left. Of the extent of this you will necessarily be the judge. I think our chances of success, in a plan of this kind, are more than even....[7]

Assuming his plan would be approved, Burnside had the four-thousand-man division composed of black troops begin drilling for the operation weeks in advance. He considered the black troops in better condition to lead the assault than any of the three all-white divi-sions of his corps. Meade, however, objected to using the black division, saying that it had

The mining explosion. A 31-year-old mining engineer from Pennsylvania, Lt. Col. Henry Pleasants, conceived the idea of digging a tunnel into and under the Confederate line at Petersburg and exploding a massive amount of gunpowder to open a breach in the works. The plan was carried out, but failed to yield the expected results, merely producing an enormous crater that became a death trap for Union troops. (JOHN CLARK RIDPATH)

not had experience under fire and that this mission required the very best troops. Burnside insisted on the black troops, and Meade passed the matter, and his arguments, to Grant for his decision. Grant agreed with Meade and later revealed his and Meade's real reason for doing so: "General Burnside wanted to put his colored division in front, and I believe if he had done so it would have been a success. Still I agreed with General Meade as to his objections to that plan. General Meade said that if we put the colored troops in front (we had only one division) and it should prove a failure, it would then be said, and very properly, that we were shoving these people ahead to get killed because we did not care anything about them. But that could not be said if we put white troops in front."[8]

Grant and Meade decided against using the black division, the only troops trained for the operation, but Burnside was not notified of the decision until the day before the operation was to be executed. One of the white divisions would have to be pressed into the lead position at the last minute. To choose which of the white divisions it would be, Burnside had the division commanders draw straws. Major General James F. Ledlie, commander of the First Division, won — or lost — the draw. Other changes were made to Burnside's attack plan. Instead of the charging troops moving to the right and left to drive the rebels from their entrenchment and protecting against flank attacks by the rebels, Meade ordered that Burnside's troops immediately head for the crest of Cemetery Hill, commanding the Confederate position.

Sandbags were placed around the kegs of black powder to direct its explosive force upward, and then two fuses were spliced together to form a ninety-eight-foot-long fuse that was attached to the kegs. During the night of July 29 all was put in readiness. The troops of Burnside's corps, white and black, were positioned in the ravine, and men of the other corps were positioned to reinforce them in the breakthrough. Batteries totaling 110 field pieces and fifty-four mortars were standing by to commence firing on the rebel line. A feint had been made near Richmond to draw part of Petersburg's garrison away.

At 3:15 A.M. on Saturday, July 30 Colonel Pleasants lighted the fuse, then climbed up on the Union parapet to witness the spectacle. The troops in the ravine waited for the explosion. Minutes passed. At 3:30 there was only silence. At 4:15 there was still only silence. Something had gone wrong. Two members of Pleasants' regiment — Sergeant Henry Rees and Lieutenant Jacob Douty — volunteered to enter the tunnel to find out what was wrong. They discovered that the fuse had sputtered out at the splice. They bravely relighted it and quickly scrambled back out of the tunnel.

About 4:45 A.M. the four tons of black powder exploded with hellish effect. An eyewitness, Major William H. Powell, described the scene and the action:

> It was a magnificent spectacle, and as the mass of earth went up into the air, carrying with it men, guns, carriages, and timbers, and spread out like an immense cloud as it reached its altitude, so close were the Union lines that the mass appeared as if it would descend immediately upon the troops waiting to make the charge. This caused them to break and scatter to the rear, and about ten minutes were consumed in re-forming for the attack. Not much was lost by this delay, however, as it took nearly that time for the cloud of dust to pass off. The order was then given for the advance. As no part of the Union line of breastworks had been removed ... the troops clambered over them as best they could. This in itself broke the ranks, and they did not stop to re-form, but pushed ahead toward the crater, about 130 yards distant, the debris from the explosion having covered up the abatis and *chevaux-de-frise* in front of the enemy's works.
>
> Little did these men anticipate what they would see upon arriving there: an enormous hole in the ground about 30 feet deep, 60 feet wide, and 170 feet long, filled with dust, great blocks of clay, guns, broken carriages, projecting timbers, and men buried in various ways — some up to their necks, others to their waists, and some with only their feet and legs protruding from the earth....
>
> The whole scene of the explosion struck every one dumb with astonishment as we arrived at the crest of the debris. It was impossible for the troops of the Second Brigade to move forward in line, as they had advanced; and, owing to the broken state they were in, every man crowding up to look into the hole, and being pressed by the First Brigade, which was immediately in

rear, it was equally impossible to move by the flank, by any command, around the crater. Before the brigade commanders could realize the situation, the two brigades became inextricably mixed, in the desire to look into the hole.

However, Colonel Marshall yelled to the Second Brigade to move forward, and the men did so, jumping, sliding, and tumbling into the hole, over the debris of material, and dead and dying men, and huge blocks of solid clay. They were followed by General Bartlett's brigade. Up on the other side of the crater they climbed, and while a detachment stopped to place two of the dismounted guns of the battery in position on the enemy's side of the crest of the crater.... In doing so members of these regiments were killed by musket-shots from the rear, fired by the Confederates who were still occupying the traverses and intrenchments to right and left of the crater.... When the Union troops attempted to re-form on the enemy's side of the crater, they [the Confederates] had faced about and delivered a fire into the backs of our men. This coming so unexpectedly caused the forming line to fall back into the crater.

Had General Burnside's original plan, providing that two regiments should sweep down inside the enemy's line to the right and left of the crater, been sanctioned, the brigades of Colonel Marshall and General Bartlett could and would have re-formed and moved on to Cemetery Hill before the enemy realized fully what was intended; but the occupation of the trenches to the right and left by the enemy prevented re-formation, and there being no division, corps, or army commander present to give orders to other troops to clear the trenches, a formation under fire from the rear was something no troops could accomplish....[9]

The operation, the Battle of the Crater, ended shortly after one o'clock that afternoon. It had proved a total failure, a costly disaster. Burnside's four divisions lost fifty-two officers and 376 men killed, 105 officers and 1,556 men wounded, and eighty-seven officers and 1,652 men captured — a total of 3,828 casualties[10], with nothing gained for their loss. Confederate casualties, killed and wounded, totaled about 1,500.

General Grant gave his assessment of the operation: "Ledlie's division marched into the crater immediately on the explosion, but most of the men stopped there in the absence of any one to give directions; their commander having found some safe retreat to get into before they started.... The effort was a stupendous failure. It cost us about four thousand men, mostly, however, captured; and all due to inefficiency on the part of the corps commander and the incompetency of the division commander who was sent to lead the assault."[11]

Damn the Torpedoes,
August 4 to August 5, 1864

Aboard the USS *Hartford* on the evening of August 4, as the ship rested at anchor off the entrance to Mobile Bay, its officers sat around the long wardroom table writing letters. What they wrote, they realized, might be their last words to their loved ones. Some wrote the sort of things one would say if indeed they were last words, for they all knew this night might be the final opportunity to say what was in their thoughts, to express feelings deep in their hearts. Beyond tomorrow's sunrise, they knew, life was highly uncertain.

The plans for them were completed. At daybreak the next morning the *Hartford*, flagship of Admiral David Glasgow Farragut's fleet, was to take its place in the line of U.S. warships attempting to storm past the guns of Fort Morgan and Fort Gaines, the forbidding fortresses that guarded the narrow entrance to Mobile Bay, one on the right side of the channel, the other on the left. If the ships — and those aboard them — managed to make it past the forts, they then would have to evade the ship-killing torpedoes lurking beneath the surface of the water. That good fortune gained, they then would face three Confederate gunboats and, worst of all, the fearsome monster ironclad ram CSS *Tennessee* that lay in wait for the survivors.

The *Tennessee* was 209 feet long and at the widest part of her deck was forty-eight feet in the beam. It was built on a wood frame and sheathed in five- and six-inch-thick iron plates. Its outside deck was covered with two-inch-thick plates. It had ten gun ports, two on each side, three forward and three aft, and was armed with six guns — a seven-and-a-half-inch Brooke rifled gun forward and aft, and four Brooke six-inch rifled guns, two on each broadside. It carried a crew of 110. It was a ship killer.

The officers and sailors of the Union fleet had great confidence in their commander, Admiral Farragut. He could get them safely through if anybody could. He had run past daunting rebel forts before, past the guns of Fort St. Philip and Fort Jackson on the Mississippi below New Orleans, something that few Navy men had thought wooden vessels could do. A year later he had blasted past the guns of Port Hudson, Louisiana and then, even more hazardously, had run past the Confederates' imposing river defenses at Vicksburg. Now he needed to get his ships, and the crews that manned them, past Fort Morgan.

When the letters had been written, a lighter spirit — feigned or true — took over the

Hartford's wardroom. Army First Lieutenant John Coddington Kinney was there to witness it. He was one of the signal officers who had arrived at the fleet's anchorage just that morning, carried there by tugboat from New Orleans and assigned to vessels of the fleet so they could communicate with the U.S. troops that would later be landed. "Unrestrained jollity" broke out in the wardroom, Kinney reported, and for an hour or so "old officers forgot, for the moment, their customary dignity, and it was evident that all were exhilarated and stimulated by the knowledge of the coming struggle.... Finally, after a half-hour's smoke under the forecastle, all hands turned in. The scene on the flag-ship was representative of the night before the battle throughout the fleet."[1]

The fleet's mission was to capture Mobile Bay, a major artery through which supplies for the Confederate army flowed. Farragut, commanding the Union vessels that were blockading gulf ports, had made the capture of Mobile Bay his prime objective once the Mississippi River had been opened in the summer of 1863. Admiral David Dixon Porter, Farragut's adoptive brother and author of *The Naval History of the Civil War*, explained the importance of Mobile Bay and the silencing of its protective forts:

> In January, 1864, Admiral Farragut began to turn his attention to the forts in Mobile Bay, which up to that time had been a complete protection to the blockade-runners, which passed in and out almost with impunity in spite of the greatest watchfulness on the part of the blockading fleet. There were several channels in the Bay with wide shoal grounds in and about their approaches, over which the Confederate light-draft vessels could pass, but where the Federal ships-of-war could not follow them.
>
> The city of Mobile, in consequence, became one of the most important rendezvous for blockade-runners, as it was situated some miles up the bay, and could only be reached through tortuous channels, with which only experienced pilots were familiar. The people of Mobile felt quite secure against any attempt on the part of the Union gun-boats to pass their defences, and the blockade-runners laid as safely at their wharves as if they had been in the docks of Liverpool.
>
> While the forts at the entrance of Mobile Bay remained intact, the Confederates could continue to supply their armies through Mobile City and the numerous railroads running from it to all parts of the South.[2]

Fort Morgan stood on the right side of the entrance channel, a strong, old brick fort built on the western tip of Mobile Point, which juts out into the gulf on the east side of the bay. It occupied the site where Fort Bowyer had once stood to refuse passage to a British fleet attempting to invade the bay during the War of 1812. Fort Morgan bristled with a total of thirty-eight guns of various sizes and bores, arranged in three tiers within the fort, and twenty-nine other heavy guns mounted in the batteries just outside the fort. All the guns were in point-blank range of whatever vessels dared to enter the channel. The fort was protected by a wall of sandbags that covered the expanse of its exposed front. The Confederates considered it impregnable. Some 640 officers and men comprised its garrison, commanded by Brigadier General Richard L. Page, a former career U.S. naval officer.

Three miles northwest of Fort Morgan, on the left side of the channel, stood Fort Gaines, another brick fortress, built on the eastern tip of Dauphin Island. A lesser threat than Fort Morgan, Fort Gaines mounted twenty-seven guns. Farther to the northwest, at the bay's western entrance called Grant's Pass, a third protective fort, Fort Powell, was under construction on Tower Island. It mounted six heavy guns.

Admiral Farragut planned to get past the most formidable and forbidding of those fortifications — Fort Morgan — the same way he had passed forts St. Philip and Jackson. In his fleet were fourteen wooden ships and four ironclad monitors. The wooden vessels would be paired, two ships tied together side by side with huge cables, or ropes, the larger and more heavily armed vessels to starboard, closest to the guns of Fort Morgan. If the starboard ship were to become disabled by the fort's cannonades, its port-side partner, like a towboat, would keep it moving past the fort. Blankets of linked chains, like enormous bullet-proof vests, were fastened to the sides of the vessels, extending down to two feet below the water line. Protective sandbags were piled up around exposed parts of the ships' machinery. Coal in the ships' bunkers was shifted to provide a barrier to shot coming in toward the ships' boilers. Farragut issued detailed instructions to his ship commanders to have it all done:

GENERAL ORDER, NO. 10

Strip your vessels and prepare for the conflict. Send down all your superfluous spars and rigging. Trice up or remove the whiskers. Put up the splinter nets on the starboard side and barricade the steersman with sails and hammocks. Lay chains or sand-bags on the deck over the machinery to resist a plunging fire. Hang the sheet chains over the side, or make any other arrangement for security that your ingenuity may suggest. Land your starboard boats or lower them and tow them on the port side, and lower the port boats down to the water's edge....[3]

The battle plan called for the ironclad monitor gunboats — *Tecumseh, Manhattan, Winnebago* and *Chickasaw*— to precede the wooden ships, taking their position to the starboard side of the wooden vessels, between them and Fort Morgan, to keep the fort and its water batteries (those outside the fort) under fire and to draw rebel fire away from the wooden ships — and to be the first to take on the dread *Tennessee.*

The wooden ships were paired as follows and were placed in line in this order: *Brooklyn* (2,070 tons displacement, 24 guns) and *Octorara* (829 tons, six guns); *Hartford* (1,900 tons, 21 guns) and *Metacomet* (974 tons, six guns); *Richmond* (1,929 tons, 20 guns) and *Port Royal* (805 tons, six guns); *Lackawanna* (1,533 tons, eight guns) and *Seminole* (801 tons, eight guns); *Monongahela* (1,378 tons, eight guns) and *Kennebec* (507 tons, five guns); *Ossipee* (1,240 tons, 11 guns) and *Itasca* (507 tons, six guns); and *Oneida* (1,032 tons, nine guns) and *Galena* (738 tons, ten guns).

Farragut had intended to lead the line of ships with the *Hartford*, but his officers prevailed upon him to allow the *Brooklyn* take the lead. "This vessel," Admiral Porter explained, "had four chase-guns and an ingenious apparatus for picking up torpedoes," and besides, "in their [the officers'] judgment, the flag-ship should not lead and be too much exposed. The proper place for the flag-ship was, in fact, the middle of the line, but Farragut would only yield so far as to have one ship in advance of him. He did not believe in the principle that a flag-officer should not lead. He considered it one of the privileges of high rank in the Navy, and that it was an honor to be sought by every one who desired to set a proper example to those under his command."[4]

Included in Farragut's General Order No. 10 were instructions for opening and continuing fire on Fort Morgan, which would be on the vessels' starboard side:

It will be the object ... to get as close to the fort as possible before opening fire. The ships, however, will open fire the moment the enemy opens upon us, with their chase and other guns, as fast as they can be brought to bear. Use short fuzes for the shell and shrapnel, and as soon as within three or four hundred yards, give the grape. It is understood that heretofore we have fired too high; but with grape-shot it is necessary to elevate a little above the object, as grape will dribble from the muzzle of the gun. If one or more of the vessels be disabled, their partners must carry them through, if possible; but if they cannot, then the next astern must render the required assistance; but as the Admiral contemplates moving with the flood-tide it will only require sufficient power to keep the crippled vessels in the channel.

Vessels that can, must place guns upon the poop and topgallant forecastle, and in the tops on the starboard side. Should the enemy fire grape, they will remove the men from the topgallant forecastle and poop to the guns below, until out of grape range.

The howitzers must keep up a constant fire from the time they can reach with shrapnel until out of range.

D.G. Farragut,
Rear-Admiral, Commanding
West Gulf Blockading Squadron[5]

In an additional order, leaving no stone unturned or detail overlooked, Farragut instructed his commanders on what to do once they had passed the fort:

So soon as the vessels have passed the fort and kept away northwest, they can cast off the gun-boats at the discretion of the senior officer of the two vessels, and allow them to proceed up the bay to cut off the enemy's gun-boats that may be attempting to escape up to Mobile. There are certain black buoys placed by the enemy from the piles [which the Confederates had driven into the water to form obstructions] on the west side of the channel, across it towards Fort Morgan. It being understood that there are torpedoes and other obstructions between the buoys, the vessels will take care to pass eastward of the easternmost buoy, which is clear of all obstructions.

So soon as the vessels arrive opposite the end of the piles, it will be best to stop the propeller of the ship, and let her drift the distance past by her head-way and the tide; and those having side-wheel gun-boats will continue on by the aid of their paddle-wheels, which are not likely to foul with the enemy's drag-ropes.[6]

Farragut had planned to have his fleet under way by dawn on Friday, August 5, but a thick fog rolled in after midnight and caused a delay in the ships' forming up their battle line, and the line did not start to move until 5:45 A.M., as a light breeze began to scatter much of the fog, clearing the skies for a sunny August morning. Onward the ships came, "like phantoms in the fog," Lieutenant Kinney observed. An hour after the fleet was in motion, the opening gun sounded, a fifteen-inch shell that was fired from the *Tecumseh* and burst over Fort Morgan. Thirty minutes later the fleet came within range of the fort, and commenced a general artillery assault, the fort and the Confederate fleet up ahead of the Union vessels swiftly returning the fire.

Lieutenant Kinney described the action:

The [Confederate] fleet took position across the entrance to the bay and raked the advance [U.S.] vessels fore and aft, doing great damage, to which it was for a time impossible to make effective reply. Gradually the fleet came into close quarters with Fort Morgan, and the firing on both sides became terrific. The wooden vessels moved more rapidly than the monitors, and as the *Brooklyn* came opposite the fort, and approached the torpedo line, she nearly came alongside the rear monitor. To have kept on would have been to take the lead, with the ram *Tennessee* approaching and with the unknown danger of the torpedoes underneath.

At this critical moment the *Brooklyn* halted and began backing and signaling with the army signals. The *Hartford* was immediately behind and the following vessels were in close proximity, and the sudden stopping of the *Brooklyn* threatened to bring the whole fleet into collision, while the strong inflowing tide was likely to carry some of the vessels to the shore under the guns of the fort....

In the intense excitement of the occasion it seemed that hours had passed, but it was just twenty minutes from the time we went below [to aid the ship's surgeons], when an officer shouted down the hatchway: "Send up an army signal officer immediately; the *Brooklyn* is signaling." In a moment the writer [Kinney] was on deck, where he found the situation as already described. Running on to the forecastle, he hastily took the *Brooklyn*'s message, which imparted the unnecessary information, "The monitors are right ahead; we cannot go on without passing them."

The reply was sent at once from the admiral, "Order the monitors ahead and go on." But still the *Brooklyn* halted, while, to add to the horror of the situation, the monitor *Tecumseh*, a few hundred yards in the advance, suddenly careened to one side and almost instantly sank to the bottom, carrying with her Captain Tunis A.M. Craven and the greater part of his crew, numbering 114 officers and men. The pilot, John Collins, and a few men who were in the turret jumped into the water and were rescued by a boat from the *Metacomet*, which, under charge of Acting Ensign Henry C. Nields, rowed up under the guns of the fort and through a deadly storm of shot and shell and picked them up.

Meantime, the *Brooklyn* failed to go ahead, and the whole fleet became a stationary point-blank target for the guns of Fort Morgan and of the rebel vessels. It was during these few perilous moments that the most fatal work of the day was done to the fleet.[7]

The *Tecumseh*, according to one report, had taken aim for the *Tennessee*, which had moved just west of the buoy marking the end of the line of torpedoes. Captain Craven, the monitor's commander, had ordered his helmsman to dash straight at the *Tennessee*, ignoring or forgetting Farragut's instructions to keep east of that last buoy. When the two vessels were about a hundred yards apart, the *Tecumseh* hit one of the torpedoes, which exploded under the turret, blasting a gaping hole in the bottom of the vessel. The order was given for the crew to leave quarters, but the water had rushed in so fast that the vessel keeled over and went down before all but a few could escape.

While the *Hartford*, along with the ships behind it, was stalled by the recalcitrant *Brooklyn*, its crewmen were being subjected to an horrific slaughter, which Lieutenant Kinney reported:

> The sight on deck was sickening beyond the power of words to portray. Shot after shot came through the side, mowing down the men, deluging the decks with blood, and scattering mangled fragments of humanity so thickly that it was difficult to stand on the deck, so slippery was it.... The bodies of the dead were placed in a long row on the port side, while the wounded were sent below until the surgeons' quarters would hold no more. A solid shot coming through the bow struck a gunner on the neck, completely severing head from body. One poor fellow ... lost both legs by a cannon-ball; as he fell he threw up both arms, just in time to have them also carried away by another shot. At one gun, all the crew on one side were swept down by a shot which came crashing through the bulwarks. A shell burst between the two forward guns in charge of Lieutenant Tyson, killing and wounding fifteen men. The mast upon which the writer [Kinney] was perched was twice struck....[8]

Farragut again ordered the *Brooklyn* to go on, but again the order was ignored. Farragut had taken a perch in the rigging of the *Hartford*'s mainmast, secured by a rope that the *Hartford*'s commander, Fleet-Captain Percival Drayton, a South Carolinian, had insisted be placed around Farragut lest he be wounded and fall to his death on the deck. Farragut was near enough to the ship's pilot, in the maintop, just above Farragut's head, to communicate with him. He asked the pilot, Martin Freeman, if the water was deep enough for the *Hartford* to pass to the left of the *Brooklyn*. When Freeman replied that it was, Farragut responded, "I will take the lead," and immediately ordered the *Hartford* ahead at full speed.

"As he passed the *Brooklyn*," Kinney related, "a voice warned him of the torpedoes, to which he returned the contemptuous answer, 'Damn the torpedoes.' This is the current story, and may have some basis of truth. But as a matter of fact, there was never a moment when the din of the battle would not have drowned any attempt at conversation between

U.S. Adm. David G. Farragut. He climbed into the rigging of his flagship and was tied in to prevent his falling to the deck. From that perch he directed the action of his fleet as it blasted its way past the fort that guarded the entrance to Mobile Bay. It was then that he was reported to have shouted to the USS *Brooklyn*, stalled in front of the line of warships, "Damn the torpedoes!" and ordered the *Brooklyn* to move ahead. (LIBRARY OF CONGRESS)

the two ships, and while it is quite probable that the admiral made the remark it is doubtful if he shouted it to the *Brooklyn*."[9]

The *Hartford* then veered to port with the *Metacomet* still beside it and rushed far ahead of the rest of the fleet. Kinney recounted the action:

> Taking advantage of the situation, the Confederate gun-boat *Selma* kept directly in front of the flag-ship and raked her fore and aft, doing more damage in reality than all the rest of the enemy's fleet. The other [Confederate] gun-boats, the *Gaines* and the *Morgan*, were in shallow water on our starboard bow, but they received more damage from the *Hartford*'s broadsides than they were able to inflict. Meanwhile, the ram *Tennessee*, which up to this time had contented herself with simply firing at the approaching fleet, started for the *Hartford*, apparently with the intention of striking her amidships. She came on perhaps for half a mile, never approaching nearer than a hundred yards, and then suddenly turned and made for the fleet, which, still in front of the fort, was gradually getting straightened out and following the *Hartford*. This change of course on the part of the ram has always been a mystery....[10]

The rebel gunboat *Gaines* was crippled by fire from the *Hartford*'s guns and run aground, where its crew set the boat ablaze and escaped from it. The rebel gunboat *Morgan* retreated to shallow water near the fort and later escaped to Mobile. The *Selma*, which had been the most effective of the Confederate gunboats, sped away after the *Metacomet* cut loose from the *Hartford* and started after the rebel vessel. It was overtaken by the *Metacomet*, and when a shot had wounded its captain and killed its first lieutenant, the *Selma* surrendered.

"When the ram *Tennessee* turned away from the *Hartford*," Kinney reported, "she made for the fleet, and in their crowded and confused condition it seemed to be a matter of no difficulty to pick out whatever victims the Confederate [fleet] commander (Admiral Franklin Buchanan) might desire, as he had done in 1861 when commanding the *Merrimac* in Hampton Roads. Before he could reach them the line had become straightened, and the leading vessels had passed the fort."[11]

Captain (later Rear Admiral) Thornton Jenkins, commander of the USS *Richmond*, described the *Tennessee*'s engagement with the U.S. fleet:

> As she approached, every one on board the *Richmond* supposed that she would ram the *Brooklyn*; that, we thought, would be our opportunity, for if she struck the *Brooklyn* the concussion would throw her port side across our path, and being so near to us, she would not have time to "straighten up," and we would strike her fairly and squarely, and most likely sink her.
>
> The guns were loaded with solid shot and heaviest powder charge; the forecastle gun's crew were ordered to get their small-arms and fire into her gun-ports; and as previously determined, if we came in collision at any time, the orders were to throw gun charges of powder in bags from the fore and main yard-arms down her smoke-stack (or at least try to do so). To our great surprise, she sheered off from the *Brooklyn*, and at about one hundred yards put two shot or shells through and through the *Brooklyn*'s sides ... doing much damage.
>
> Approaching, passing, and getting away from the *Richmond*, the ram received from us three full broadsides of 9-inch solid shot, each broadside being eleven guns. They were well aimed and all struck, but when she was examined ... no other indications were seen than scratches. The musketry fire into the two ports prevented the leveling of her guns, and therefore two of her shot or shell passed harmlessly over the *Richmond*....
>
> The *Tennessee* passed toward the *Lackawanna*, the next vessel astern, and avoided her — wishing either to ram Captain Strong's vessel (*Monongahela*), or cross his bow and attack McCann's vessel (the *Kennebec*, Strong's consort). Strong was ready for her, and, anticipating her object, made at her, but the blow (by the quick manoeuvring of the *Tennessee*) was a glancing one, doing very little damage to either Strong's or McCann's vessel. Thence the *Tennessee*, after firing

two broadsides into the *Oneida*, proceeded toward the fort, and for a time entirely disappeared from our sight....[12]

"Whatever damage was done by the *Tennessee* to the fleet in passing the fort," Kinney stated, "was by the occasional discharge of her guns. She failed to strike a single one of the Union vessels, but was herself run into by the *Monongahela*, Captain Strong, at full speed."[13]

Suffering the worst of the Union ships passing the fort was the *Oneida*, at the end of the line. A shell exploded in its boiler, and two other shots cut the wheel ropes and disabled the forward pivot gun. Among the vessel's casualties — eight killed and thirty wounded — was its captain, Commander J.R.M. Mullany, who was wounded. Crippled by its loss of steering, the *Oneida* was propelled on by its partner, the *Galena*.

Once the fleet had passed Fort Morgan and while the *Tennessee* rested under the fort's guns, all vessels except the *Metacomet*, *Port Royal*, *Kennebec* and *Itasca*, which were chasing the fleeing rebel gunboats, made their way to where the *Hartford* had anchored in deep water inside the bay and they anchored, too.

Lieutenant Kinney pictured the respite and its abrupt conclusion:

The thunder of heavy artillery now ceased. The crews of the various vessels had begun to efface the marks of the terrible contest by washing the decks and clearing up splinters. The cooks were preparing breakfast, the surgeons were busily engaged in making amputations and binding arteries, and under canvas, on the port side of each vessel, lay the ghastly line of dead waiting the sailor's burial. As if by mutual understanding, officers who were relieved from immediate duty gathered in the ward-rooms to ascertain who of their mates were missing, and the reaction from such a season of tense nerves and excitement was just setting in when the hurried call to quarters came and the word passed around, "The ram is coming."[14]

Confederate navy Commander James D. Johnston, a Kentuckian and former career officer in the U.S. Navy, captained the *Tennessee*. He described the action:

The heavier ships of the fleet, together with the monitors, steamed up the bay to a point about four miles above Fort Morgan, where they were in the act of anchoring when it was discovered that the ram was approaching with hostile intent. Upon this apparently unexpected challenge the fleet was immediately put in motion, and the heavier vessels seemed to contend with each other for the glory of sinking the daring rebel ram, by running themselves up on her decks, which extended some thirty feet at each end of the shield, and were only about eighteen inches above the surface of the water. So great was their eagerness to accomplish this feat that the *Lackawanna*, one of the heaviest steamers, ran bows on into the *Hartford*, by which both vessels sustained greater damage than their united efforts in this direction could have inflicted upon their antagonist....

The monitors kept up a constant firing at short range. The two double-turreted monitors (*Chickasaw* and *Winnebago*) were stationed under the stern of the *Tennessee*, and struck the after end of her shield so repeatedly with 11-inch solid shot that it was found at the close of the action to be in a rather shaky condition. One of these missiles had struck the iron cover of the stern port and jammed it against the shield so that it became impossible to run the gun out for firing, and Admiral Buchanan, who superintended the battery during the entire engagement, sent to the engine room for a machinist to back out the pin of the bolt upon which the port cover revolved.

While this was being done a shot from one of the monitors struck the edge of the port cover, immediately over the spot where the machinist was sitting, and his remains had to be taken up with a shovel, placed in a bucket and thrown overboard. The same shot caused several iron splinters to fly inside of the shield, one of which killed a seaman, while another broke the admiral's leg below the knee. The admiral sent for me, and as I approached he quietly remarked, "Well, Johnston, they've got me. You'll have to look out for her now. This is your fight, you know."

I replied, "All right, sir. I'll do the best I know how." While returning to the pilot-house I felt the vessel careen so suddenly as nearly to throw me off my feet. I discovered that the *Hartford* [actually the *Lackawanna*] had run into the ram amidships, and that while thus in contact with her the Federal crew were using their small-arms by firing through the open ports. However, only one man was wounded in this way, the cause of all our other wounds being iron splinters from the washers on the inner ends of the bolts that secured the plating. I continued on my way to the pilot-house, and upon looking through the narrow peep-holes in its sides to ascertain the position of the enemy's ships, I discovered that the wooden vessels had mostly withdrawn from the action, leaving it to the monitors to effect the destruction of the ram at their leisure.[15]

Aboard the *Hartford* Lieutenant Kinney was observing the action from his perspective. He later recorded it:

The ram from the first headed for the *Hartford*, and paid no attention to her assailants, except with her guns. The *Monongahela,* going at full speed, struck the *Tennessee* amidships — a blow that would have sunk almost any vessel of the Union navy, but which inflicted not the slightest damage on the solid iron hull of the ram.... Her own iron prow and cutwater were carried away, and she was otherwise badly damaged about the stern by the collision. The *Lackawanna* was close behind and delivered a similar blow with her wooden bow, simply causing the ram to lurch slightly to one side. As the vessels separated [,] the *Lackawanna* swung alongside the ram, which sent two shots through her and kept on her course for the *Hartford*, which was now the next vessel in the attack. The two flag-ships approached each other, bow to bow, iron against oak....

It was a thrilling moment for the fleet, for it was evident that if the ram could strike the *Hartford* the latter must sink. But for the two vessels to strike fairly, bows on, would probably have involved the destruction of both, for the ram must have penetrated so far into the wooden ship that as the *Hartford* filled and sank she would have carried the ram under water. Whether for this reason or some other, as the two vessels came together the *Tennessee* slightly changed her course, the port bow of the *Hartford* met the port bow of the ram, and the ships grated against each other as they passed. The *Hartford* poured her whole port broadside against the ram, but the solid shot merely dented the side and bounded into the air....

The *Tennessee* now became the target for the whole fleet, all the vessels of which were making toward her, pounding her with shot, and trying to run her down. As the *Hartford* turned to make for her again, we ran in front of the *Lackawanna*, which had already turned and was moving under full headway with the same object. She struck us on our starboard side, amidships, crushing halfway through.... For a time it was thought that we must sink, and the cry rang out over the deck: "Save the admiral! Save the admiral!" ... But the admiral sprang into the starboard mizzen-rigging, looked over the side of the ship, and, finding there were still a few inches to spare above the water's edge, instantly ordered the ship ahead again at full speed, after the ram.

The unfortunate *Lackawanna*, which had struck the ram a second blow, was making for her once more, and, singularly enough, again came up on our starboard side, and another collision seemed imminent. And now the admiral became a trifle excited. He had no idea of whipping the rebels to be himself sunk by a friend, nor did he realize at the moment that the *Hartford* was as much to blame as the *Lackawanna*. Turning to the writer [Kinney] he inquired, "Can you say 'For God's sake' by signal?"

"Yes, sir," was the reply.

"Then say to the *Lackawanna*, 'For God's sake get out of our way and anchor!'...."

It was a hasty message, for the fault was equally divided, each ship being too eager to reach the enemy, and it turned out all right, by a fortunate accident, that Captain Marchand [of the *Lackawanna*] never received it.... [The signal officer positioned on a mast on the *Lackawanna* had his view blocked when the ship's U.S. flag wafted across his face and he saw only the first part of the signaled message — "For God's sake get out —."]

The remainder of the story is soon told. As the *Tennessee* left the *Hartford* she became the target of the entire fleet, and at last the concentration of solid shot from so many guns began to tell.... Finally, one of the *Chickasaw*'s shots cut the rudder-chain of the ram and she would no longer mind her helm.... [J]ust as the *Ossipee* (Captain [William E.] LeRoy) was about to strike her the *Tennessee* displayed a white flag, hoisted on an improvised staff through the grating over her deck.... Suddenly the terrific cannonading ceased, and from every ship rang out cheer after cheer, as the weary men realized that at last the ram was conquered and the day won....[16]

The *Tennessee*'s captain, Commander Johnston, provided his account of the end of the battle:

Realizing the impossibility of directing the firing of the guns without the use of the rudder, and that the ship had been rendered utterly helpless, I went to the lower deck and informed the admiral of her condition, and that I had not been able to bring a gun to bear upon any of our antagonists for nearly half an hour, to which he replied: "Well, Johnston, if you cannot do them any further damage, you had better surrender." With this sanction of my own views I returned to the gun-deck, and after another glance about the bay to see if there was any chance of getting another shot, and seeing none of the enemy's ships within range of our broadside guns, I went to the top of the shield and took down the boat-hook to which the flag had been lashed after having been shot away several times during the fight.... [A]s soon as I returned to the gun-deck and had a flag of truce attached to the boat-hook the firing ceased.

Having returned to the top of the shield, I saw one of the heaviest ships of the fleet approaching rapidly, apparently for the purpose of making another attempt to sink the ram. Seeing the flag of truce, the commander stopped his ship, but her momentum was too great to be overcome in the short intervening space, and she struck the ram on the starboard quarter, but without injuring it. As she did so her commander hailed, saying: "This is the United States steamer *Ossipee*. Hello, Johnston, how are you? Le Roy — don't you know me? I'll send a boat alongside for you."

The boat came and conveyed me on board the *Ossipee*, at whose gangway I was met by her genial commander, between whom and myself a life-long friendship had existed. When I reached the deck of his ship, he remarked, "I'm glad to see you, Johnston. Here's some ice-water for you — I know you're dry; but I've something better than that for you down below." I thanked him cordially, but was in no humor for receiving hospitalities graciously, and quietly followed him to his cabin, where he placed a bottle of "navy sherry" and a pitcher of ice-water before me and urged me to help myself. Calling his steward, he ordered him to attend to my wishes as he would his own. I remained on board six days, during which time I was visited by nearly all the commanding officers of the fleet.

Within an hour after I was taken on board the *Ossipee* Admiral Farragut sent for me to be brought on board his flag-ship, and when I reached her deck he expressed regret at meeting me under such circumstances, to which I replied that he was not half as sorry to see me as I was to see him.[17]

It was about 10 A.M. when the guns went silent. Johnston made the formal surrender of the *Tennessee* to LeRoy, and Lieutenant Giraud of the *Ossipee* was sent aboard the *Tennessee* to take command. Admiral Buchanan surrendered his sword to him. Also going aboard the captured ram was U.S. Marine Captain Heywood and a contingent of Marines. When he met Buchanan, Heywood let him know that they had met before, Heywood having been on the U.S. frigate *Cumberland* when it was sunk by Buchanan in the *Merrimac* at Hampton Roads.

The *Chickasaw* towed the crippled *Tennessee* to the *Hartford* and had it anchor there. The dead and wounded were removed, and the remainder of the crew was taken prisoner.[18] Late that afternoon the wounded of both sides, including Admiral Buchanan, who lost a leg, were placed aboard the *Metacomet* and taken to the U.S. naval hospital in Pensacola for treatment, passing Fort Morgan under a truce arranged with the fort's commander, General Page. Nine of the *Tennessee*'s crew had been wounded and two killed.

Total Confederate casualties from the four vessels engaged in the battle amounted to twelve killed and twenty wounded, plus, according to Farragut's report, 190 prisoners taken from the *Tennessee* and 90 from the *Selma*. Union losses totaled 52 killed and 170 wounded, plus the 93 crewmen of the *Tecumseh* who drowned when the ship went down, and four of the crew who were captured. Other than the crew of the *Tecumseh*, the crew of the *Hartford* had suffered the most severely, losing 25 killed and 28 wounded. The *Brooklyn* lost 11 killed and 43 wounded; the *Lackawanna*, four killed and 35 wounded; the *Oneida*, eight killed and 30 wounded; the *Monongahela*, none killed and six wounded; the *Metacomet*, one killed and two wounded; the *Ossipee*, one killed and one wounded; the *Richmond*, none killed and two wounded; the *Galena*, none killed and one wounded; the *Octorara*, one killed and ten wounded; and the *Kennebec*, one killed and six wounded.

The fearsome CSS *Tennessee* was taken into the U.S. Navy, repaired and renamed the USS *Tennessee*.

On the afternoon of August 5, following the surrender of the *Tennessee*, the U.S. monitor *Chickasaw* shelled Fort Powell, driving off its garrison, which abandoned the works about ten o'clock that night and escaped to the mainland. The next day, Saturday, August 6, the *Chickasaw* turned its guns on Fort Gaines, which on August 4 had been invested by U.S. troops landed on Dauphin Island in preparation for the fleet's assault on Mobile Bay's defenses. Seeing the hopelessness of his situation, the commander of Fort Gaines surrendered to the U.S. Army and Navy on the morning of August 7. The Union troops, a 5,500-man force under the command of Major General Gordon Granger, then laid siege to Fort Morgan, which after two weeks of intense bombardment by Farragut's fleet at last capitulated on Tuesday, August 23.

Mobile Bay was then completely in the hands of Union forces. The city of Mobile was closed to blockade-runners and the flow of Confederate supplies. Gratified, General Grant observed that "we have all of Mobile Bay that is valuable."[19]

Stalemate at Atlanta,
July 17 to August 23, 1864

On the same day — Sunday, July 17 — that General Joe Johnston learned he had been relieved of command of the Confederate army defending against the Union advance through Georgia, General Sherman set his troops in motion on the final leg of the drive to capture Atlanta. That morning the last two corps of Sherman's army, Major General John Palmer's and Major General Joseph Hooker's, crossed to the east side of the Chattahoochee River, on the northwestern outskirts of the city, and there Sherman organized his forces for a decisive assault on Atlanta's defenses.

Sherman's three Union armies, now comprising 112,000 men, were facing a Confederate force of about 51,000, now commanded by General Hood, dug in around Atlanta. Sherman directed the Army of the Tennessee, his former command, now commanded by General McPherson, to move eastward across the northern edge of Atlanta, toward Stone Mountain, turning the right flank of the rebel defenders and at the same time tear up the rail line by which Hood could be reinforced by Lee's troops, a possibility about which Grant the day before had warned Sherman. While the Army of the Tennessee moved eastward, the Army of the Cumberland and the Army of the Ohio were to advance straight ahead into Atlanta from the northwest.

The Army of the Tennessee was the first to move, beginning its march on the 17th and making eight miles before it halted for the night near Nancy Creek, having encountered little opposition except by cavalry.

"On the 18th," Sherman reported, "all the armies moved on a general right wheel, Thomas [commanding the Army of the Cumberland] to Buckhead, forming line of battle facing Peach-Tree Creek; Schofield [commanding the Army of the Ohio] was on his left, and McPherson well over toward the railroad between Stone Mountain and Decatur, which he reached at 2 P.M. of the day, about four miles from Stone Mountain, and seven miles east of Decatur, and there he turned toward Atlanta, breaking up the railroad as he progressed, his advance-guard reaching Decatur about night, where he came into communication with Schofield's troops...."[1]

Sherman was making his moves based on his familiarity with Johnston's style of opposition, repeatedly parrying while Sherman thrust, but the morning of the 18th brought news that Sherman was now facing a new adversary, about whom he had little knowledge. He explained:

> About 10 A.M. of that day (July 18th), when the armies were all in motion, one of General Thomas's staff-officers brought me a citizen, one of our spies, who had just come out of Atlanta, and had brought a newspaper of the same day, or of the day before, containing Johnston's order relinquishing the command of the Confederate forces in Atlanta, and Hood's order assuming the command. I immediately inquired of General Schofield, who was his class-mate at West Point, about Hood, as to his general character, etc., and learned that he was bold even to rashness, and courageous in the extreme; I inferred that the change of commanders meant "fight."
>
> Notice of this important change was at once sent to all parts of the army, and every division commander was cautioned to be always prepared for battle in any shape. This was just what we wanted, viz., to fight in open ground, on any thing like equal terms, instead of being forced to run up against prepared intrenchments; but, at the same time, the enemy having Atlanta behind him, could choose the time and place of attack, and could at pleasure mass a superior force on our weakest points. Therefore, we had to be constantly ready for sallies.[2]

The inference that Sherman drew about Hood was correct, as he soon discovered. In his memoir he recounted the action that followed the crossing of the Chattahoochee, the Battle of Peachtree Creek:

> On the 19th the three armies were converging toward Atlanta, meeting such feeble resistance that I really thought the enemy intended to evacuate the place. McPherson was moving astride of the railroad, near Decatur; Schofield along a road leading toward Atlanta, by Colonel Howard's house and the distillery; and Thomas was crossing "Peach-Tree" [Creek] in line of battle, building bridges for nearly every division as deployed. There was quite a gap between Thomas and Schofield, which I endeavored to close by drawing two of [corps commander Major General Oliver] Howard's divisions nearer Schofield.
>
> On the 20th I was with General Schofield near the centre, and soon after noon heard heavy fighting in front of Thomas's right, which lasted an hour or so, and then ceased. I soon learned that the enemy had made a furious sally, the blow falling on Hooker's corps (the Twentieth), and partially on Johnson's division of the Fourteenth, and Newton's of the Fourth. The troops had crossed Peach-Tree Creek, were deployed, but at the time were resting for noon, when, without notice, the enemy came pouring out of their trenches down upon them, they became commingled, and fought in may places hand to hand.
>
> General Thomas happened to be near the rear of Newton's division, and got some field-batteries in a good position, on the north side of Peach-Tree Creek, from which he directed a furious fire on a mass of the enemy, which was passing around Newton's left and exposed flank. After a couple of hours of hard and close conflict, the enemy retired slowly within his trenches, leaving his dead and many wounded on the field. Johnson's and Newton's losses were light, for they had partially covered their fronts with light parapet; but Hooker's whole corps fought in open ground, and lost about fifteen hundred men. He reported four hundred rebel dead left on the ground, and that the rebel wounded would number four thousand; but this was conjectural, for most of them got back within their own lines.
>
> We had, however, met successfully a bold sally, had repelled it handsomely, and were also put on our guard; and the event illustrated the future tactics of our enemy....[3]

On the 21st, however, Sherman still had something to learn about Hood's tactics. On that day, Union troops got some temporary relief from the heat when a thunderstorm moved into the area during the afternoon. When it cleared away, troops of U.S. Brigadier General Manning Force's brigade, from atop a recently captured bald hill, spotted Confederate columns on the move, marching southward toward the left of the Union line. That information was passed up the chain of command to McPherson and Sherman. Apparently still thinking of Johnston, Sherman decided that the southward march meant the rebels were evacuating Atlanta after having taken a beating on the 20th, and by the night of the 21st rumors that the Confederates were pulling out of Atlanta were floating among the Union troops.

McPherson, who was another of Hood's classmates at West Point and who knew a good deal about him, wasn't so sure. He thought that the southward movement might be aimed at the Army of the Tennessee's left side, which was the left flank of the Union line and which was dangerously exposed. To strengthen his left, McPherson at eight o'clock on the morning of the 22nd ordered Major General Grenville Dodge, commander of the Sixteenth Corps, to shift one of his divisions—Major General Thomas Sweeny's—to the extreme left side of the line. When McPherson notified Sherman of the move, Sherman responded with a note directing him instead to put Dodge's entire corps to work tearing up the railroad between Decatur and Atlanta.

McPherson couldn't accept that order. He was convinced that Hood would launch another attack that day and taking several of his staff officers with him, he rode over to Sherman's headquarters to discuss the matter. Believing that if Hood attacked, the attack would come by one o'clock that afternoon, McPherson urged Sherman to wait till afternoon to have the troops start tearing up the railroad instead of taking a position on the line. Sherman recounted the meeting with McPherson:

> We went back to the Howard House [Sherman's headquarters], a double frame-building with a porch, and sat on the steps, discussing the chances of battle, and of Hood's general character. McPherson had also been of the same class at West Point with Hood, Schofield, and Sheridan. We agreed that we ought to be unusually cautious and prepared at all times for sallies and for hard fighting, because Hood, though not deemed much of a scholar, or of great mental capacity, was undoubtedly a brave, determined, and rash man; and the change of commanders at that particular crisis argued the displeasure of the Confederate Government with the cautious but prudent conduct of General Joe Johnston.[4]

In other words, Sherman realized the Confederate brass in Richmond wanted aggressive action and Hood was the general just rash enough to supply it. Sherman went along with McPherson's idea of putting Dodge's troops on the left of the line, the likeliest point of a rebel attack, and holding off using them to tear up the rail line until later that day, Friday, July 22.

Having had the situation explained, Sherman, as he said, "assented at once." He and McPherson then walked down the road a short distance and sat beneath a tree, where Sherman took out a map and informed McPherson of his next planned moves. "While we sat there," Sherman related, "we could hear lively skirmishing going on near us (down about the distillery), and occasionally round-shot from twelve or twenty-four pound guns came through the trees in reply to those of Schofield, and we could hear similar sounds all along down the lines of Thomas to our right, and his [McPherson's] own to the left; but presently the firing appeared a little more brisk.... We took my pocket-compass (which I always carried), and by noting the direction of the sound, we became satisfied that the firing was too far to our left rear to be explained by known facts, and he hastily called for his horse, his staff, and his orderlies."[5]

McPherson mounted and galloped off toward the sounds of battle. On the way he met Major General John Logan and Major General Frank Blair near the railroad tracks, conferred briefly, and each of the three then hurried off to the battle line. McPherson went first to General Dodge and saw that things were going well there. He sent off several aides and orderlies with dispatches and then galloped onward to pass to the left of Blair's position, riding a trail that cut through thick woods. Accounts vary, but he was apparently alone. The time was about eleven o'clock in the morning.

Suddenly a group of Confederate infantrymen, along with their commanding officer, Captain Richard Beard, emerged from the woods on the left side of the trail. "Not a word was spoken," Beard later reported. "I threw up my sword to him as a signal to surrender. He checked his horse slightly, raised his hat as if he were saluting a lady, wheeled his horse's head to the right, and dashed off to the rear in a full gallop." A shot fired by Private Robert F. Coleman struck him, and he pitched off his horse and fell to the ground.[6]

Still clinging to life, McPherson was found minutes later by a Union soldier, George Reynolds, who had been wounded and was making his way to a field hospital. McPherson was barely alive and unable to speak. Reynolds recognized him and gave the general water from his canteen and stayed with him till he died, nearly an hour later. When a group of Confederate officers later came up, they wanted to know who the dead man was, and when Reynolds told them, they removed from McPherson's coat pocket some papers and took his watch (some reports say they also took his field glasses, his wallet and his sword belt, on which he wore no sword). Reynolds asked them to let him stay with McPherson's body, to guard it until he could get help, and the rebel officers agreed and left him there with the dead general. Once they had gone, Reynolds left to report the news and to get help.

Meanwhile, McPherson's horse returned to the Union lines, "bleeding, wounded and riderless," as Sherman reported it. "McPherson was then in his prime (about thirty-four years old), over six feet high, and a very handsome man in every way, was universally liked, and had many noble qualities."[7] He was actually thirty-five. He had finished first in his class at West Point, the class of 1853. He was engaged to be married to Emily Hoffman of Baltimore, who in June had agreed to postpone their wedding after Sherman wrote to her to tell her how much he needed McPherson. She was inconsolable after his death, becoming reclusive and remaining unmarried.

In his memoir Sherman recounted the disposition of McPherson's remains:

> Within an hour [of learning of McPherson's death] an ambulance came in (attended by Colonels Clark

U.S. Maj. Gen. James McPherson. Riding alone in a contested area, he was suddenly confronted by a Confederate infantry detail and ordered to stop and surrender. Instead, he spurred his horse and was shot and killed as he sped off. He was one of Sherman's most effective and most promising generals. (JOHN CLARK RIDPATH)

and Strong, and Captains Steele and Gile), bearing McPherson's body. I had it carried inside of the Howard House, and laid on a door wrenched from its hinges. Dr. Hewitt, of the army, was there, and I asked him to examine the wound. He opened the coat and shirt, saw where the ball had entered and where it came out, or rather lodged under the skin, and he reported that McPherson must have died in a few seconds after being hit; that the ball had ranged upward across his body and passed near the heart. He was dressed just as he left me, with gauntlets and boots on, but his pocket-book was gone. On further inquiry I learned that his body must have been in possession of the enemy some minutes, during which time it was rifled of the pocket-book, and I was much concerned lest the letter I had written him that morning should have fallen into the hands of some one who could read and understand its meaning. Fortunately the spot in the woods where McPherson was shot was regained by our troops in a few minutes, and the pocket-book found in the haversack of a prisoner of war captured at the time, and it and its contents were secured by one of McPherson's staff....

I ordered Captains Steele and Gile to carry the body to Marietta. They reached that place the same night, and, on application, I ordered his personal staff to go on and escort the body to his home, in Clyde, Ohio, where it was received with great honor, and ... buried in a small cemetery, close by his mother's house ... [and beside] the family orchard, in which he used to play when a boy .[8]

Sherman soon turned his attention back to the battle, which was becoming more intense. One of the first things he had to do was appoint a replacement for McPherson. For the time being he chose thirty-eight-year-old Major General John A. "Black Jack" Logan, the senior corps commander in the Army of the Tennessee and a popular choice among the troops. Logan was not a West Pointer, but had served as a lieutenant during the Mexican War and had later become a lawyer and politician. "I ordered the staff officer who brought this message [of McPherson's death] to return at once," Sherman reported, "to find General Logan, ... to report the same facts to him, and to instruct him to drive back this supposed small force, which had evidently got around the Seventeenth Corps through the blind woods in rear of our left flank."[9]

True to McPherson's suspicions, Hood had not been withdrawing from the city, but intended to strike back by assaulting the weak left side of the Union line. The withdrawal from the rebel line of entrenchments outside Atlanta had only been to concentrate his troops in a tighter circle of entrenchments closer to the city—and to entice Sherman to follow. Hood had ordered Lieutenant General William Hardee to march his corps around the Union left flank and Major General Benjamin Cheatham to attack the Union front with his corps while Major General Joseph Wheeler's cavalry threatened Sherman's supply line.

Major General Oliver O. Howard, then commander of the Army of the Cumberland's Fourth Corps, summarized the conflict:

As soon as Hood, from a prominent point in front of Atlanta, beheld Hardee's lines emerging from the thickets of Bald Hill, and knew by the smoke and sound that the battle was fully joined, he hurried forward Cheatham's division to attack Logan all along the east front of Atlanta. At the time, I sat beside Schofield and Sherman near the Howard house, and we looked upon such parts of the battle as our glasses could compass. Before long we saw the line of Logan broken, with parts of two batteries in the enemy's hands. Sherman put in a cross-fire of cannon, a dozen or more, and Logan organized an attacking force that swept away the bold Confederates by a charge in double-time. Blair's soldiers repulsed the front attack of Cheatham's and Maney's divisions, and then, springing over their parapets, fought Bate's and Maney's men from the other side [of the rebel parapet]. The battle continued till night, when Hood again yielded the field to Sherman and withdrew.[10]

The day's fighting had cost Sherman's armies 3,722 casualties. Hood had lost around 7,500,[11] a huge loss to a rebel force already badly outnumbered.

Now Sherman faced a new crisis — the appointment of a permanent commander for the Army of the Tennessee. Logan wanted to keep the job. Hooker thought *he* should have it. Sherman ended up picking neither, but gave the command to General Howard instead. With remarkable candor, Sherman explained his selection: "General Logan had taken command of the Army of the Tennessee by virtue of his seniority, and had done well; but I did not consider him equal to the command of three corps. Between him and General Blair there existed a natural rivalry. Both were men of great courage and talent, but were politicians by nature and experience, and it may be that for this reason they were mistrusted by regular officers like Generals Schofield, Thomas, and myself.... I regarded both Generals Logan and Blair as 'volunteers,' that looked to personal fame and glory as auxiliary and secondary to their political ambition, and not as professional soldiers."[12]

In a conference with General Thomas and Major General Thomas J. Wood, a division commander in the Army of the Cumberland, Sherman settled on Howard. "We discussed fully the merits and qualities of every officer of high rank in the army, and finally settled on Major-General O.O. Howard as the best officer who was present and available for the purpose."[13]

Knowing Logan would be disappointed, as he was, Sherman wrote him a conciliatory note on July 27, telling him, "No one could have a higher appreciation of the responsibility that devolved on you so unexpectedly and the noble manner in which you met it.... I will not fail to give you every credit for having done so well. You have command of a good corps, a command that I would prefer to the more complicated one of a Dept., and if you will be patient it will come to you soon enough. Be assured of my entire confidence."[14] He signed the note, "Your friend."

Hooker was another case entirely. "General Hooker was offended because he was not chosen to succeed McPherson," Sherman recalled in his memoir, "but his chances were not even considered; indeed, I had ... been more than once disposed to relieve him of his corps, because of his repeated attempts to interfere with Generals McPherson and Schofield...."[15]

According to one story that was told at the time, President Lincoln wired Sherman urging him to give Hooker command of the Army of the Tennessee, and Sherman told him his choice was Howard. When Lincoln persisted, Sherman offered to resign, and Lincoln decided to let the matter drop.[16]

"As soon as it became known that General Howard had been chosen to command the Army of the Tennessee," Sherman reported, "General Hooker applied to General Thomas to be relieved of the command of the Twentieth Corps, and General Thomas forwarded his application to me approved and *heartily* [the italics were Sherman's] recommended. I at once telegraphed to General Halleck, recommending [Major] General [Henry] Slocum (then at Vicksburg) to be his successor."[17] Hooker departed as an embittered enemy of Sherman, believing Sherman had rejected him out of envy. "He knew," Hooker told Sherman's biographer, Samuel Bowman, "that whenever I rode by there the soldiers' hats went up, and he knew they despised him."[18]

General Howard was from Leeds, Maine, had graduated from Bowdoin College when he was nineteen and had then gone to West Point, graduating fourth in the class of 1854. He was married, the father of six children, and while serving during the Seminole Wars in Florida had been converted to evangelical Christianity and for a time had considered becoming a minister, but after the attack on Fort Sumter, he decided to stay in the Army. He was twice wounded in his right arm at the Battle of Fair Oaks in June 1862, and his arm had been amputated. Promoted to major general in November 1862, he was a corps commander at the Battle of Chancellorsville and suffered an embarrassing defeat by Stonewall Jackson. His corps was again routed at Gettysburg on July 1, 1863, but later held off attacks by General Early on July 2 and helped repulse Pickett's charge on July 3. Despite that lackluster record, Howard was well respected by his fellow officers, and despite the fact he was an Easterner among Midwesterners, he was quickly accepted by the troops of the Army of the Tennessee.

By July 26 Sherman had decided to test Hood's defenses on the Confederates' far left, on the west side of Atlanta, the Union attempts on the east and north having proved futile. On the morning of the 27th the Army of the Tennessee pulled out of its position on the left side of the Union line and marched to the rear of the line around to the right side, placing Howard's troops beyond the left flank of Hood's line and in position to cut the rail line that was supplying Hood's army. Howard arrived to take over his new command as the troops were beginning to move shortly after dawn. They moved by divisions, one at a time, marching past the rear of Schofield's and Thomas's armies, heading for the southwest side of the city, to a position near a Methodist meeting house called Ezra Church. The corps of generals Dodge and Blair had taken their positions by day's end on the 27th, but Logan's corps, moving into position on the far right, was not quite up to the ridge that he was supposed to occupy and had to wait till daylight on the 28th to complete his movement. Howard recounted the action that ensued that morning:

> About 8 o'clock Sherman was riding with me through the wooded region in rear of Logan's forces, when the skirmishing [which had begun the day before] began to increase, and an occasional shower of grape cut through the tree-tops and struck the ground beyond us. I said: "General, Hood will attack me here."
>
> "I guess not — he will hardly try it again," Sherman replied. I said that I had known Hood at West Point, and that he was indomitable. As the signs increased, Sherman went back to Thomas, where he could best help me should I need reenforcement. Logan halted his line, and the regiments hurriedly and partially covered their front with logs and rails, having only a small protection while kneeling or lying down. It was too late for intrenching. With a terrifying yell, Hood's men charged through the forest. They were met steadily and repulsed. But in the impulse a few Confederate regiments passed beyond Logan's extreme right. To withstand them four regiments came from Dodge; Inspector-General Strong led thither two from Blair, armed with repeating-rifles; and my chief-of-artillery placed several batteries so as to sweep that exposed flank. These were brought in at the exact moment, and after a few rapid discharges, the repeating-rifles being remarkable in their execution, all the groups of flankers were either cut down or had sought safety in flight.
>
> This battle was prolonged for hours. We expected help from Morgan's division of Palmer's corps, coming back from Turner's Ferry; but the Confederate cavalry kept it in check. Our troops have exhibited nerve and persistency; Logan was cheerful and hearty and full of enthusiasm. He stopped stragglers and sent them back, and gave every needed order. Blair was watchful and helpful, and so was Dodge. After the last charge had been repelled I went along my lines, and felt proud and happy to be intrusted with such brave and efficient soldiers. Hood, having again lost three times as many as we, withdrew within his fortified lines. Our skirmishers cleared the field, and the battle of Ezra Church was won; and with this result I contented myself.[19]

The fighting ended as darkness covered the field. Its ferocity moved Howard to tell troops of the Fifty-fifth Illinois regiment as he rode along the battle line, "I thought I had seen fighting before, but I never saw anything like this." It had cost the U.S. forces 632 casualties. The Confederates had lost about three thousand.[20] The cries and moanings of the wounded and dying rose from the field throughout the night. Sunrise brought dreadful sights to add to the sounds. "Acre upon acre of the open field lay before us at daylight strewn with dead men, guns, accoutrements and clothing," an officer of the Fifty-fifth Illinois wrote. Along one fence line, he reported, "the rebels lay in a windrow, in some places two or three piled across each other." Along the bank of a small stream, bodies lay thickly together where the wounded, desperate for water, had crawled to drink from the stream and had died there.[21]

Sherman took satisfaction from the way his troops had fought under their new commander, General Howard. "This was, of course, the first fight in which General Howard had commanded the Army of the Tennessee," Sherman wrote, "and he evidently aimed to reconcile General Logan in his disappointment, and to gain the heart of the army, to which he was a stranger. He very properly left General Logan to fight his own corps, but exposed himself freely; and after the firing had ceased, in the afternoon he walked the lines; the men, as reported to me, gathered about him in the most affectionate way, and he at once gained their respect and confidence. To this fact I at the time attached much importance, for it put me at ease as to the future conduct of that most important army."[22]

Sherman's armies had won the battle, but his main objectives had not been achieved. No breakthrough had occurred, and neither had a disruption of the rebels' vital rail line between East Point and Atlanta. An expedition comprising three Union cavalry divisions that was aimed at cutting the line to East Point, south of Atlanta, had been defeated and the commander of one of the divisions — Major General George Stoneman — had been taken prisoner in the disastrously failed attempt. Also defeated in the same operation was a scheme conceived by Stoneman to capture the Confederates' prisoner-of-war camp at Andersonville, Georgia, and free the 23,000 Union soldiers that were being held captive there in deplorable conditions. The cavalry units that were to combine for the assault on Andersonville were stymied by the rebel resistance to their advance and were unable to join forces to capture the notorious prison camp.

July passed into August, and still the combatants remained stalemated in the struggle to take or hold Atlanta. "Like a long storm," Howard commented, "the siege operations set in."[23]

Sherman gave a status report on his forces: "The month of August opened hot and sultry, but our position before Atlanta was healthy, with ample supply of wood, water, and provisions. The troops had become habituated to the slow and steady progress of the siege. The skirmish lines were held close up to the enemy, were covered by rifle-trenches or logs, and kept up a continuous clatter of musketry. The main lines were held farther back, adapted to the shape of the ground, with muskets loaded and stacked for instant use. The field batteries were in select positions, covered by handsome parapets, and occasional shots from them gave life and animation to the scene. The men loitered about the trenches carelessly, or busied themselves in constructing ingenious huts out of the abundant timber, and seemed as snug, comfortable, and happy, as though they were at home.

"General Schofield was still on the extreme left, Thomas in the centre, and Howard on the right. Two divisions of the Fourteenth Corps (Baird's and Jeff. C. Davis's) were detached to right rear, and held in reserve."[24]

Despairing of his cavalry's ability to accomplish his goal of breaking the rail line to Atlanta from the south, Sherman determined to have his infantry do the job, but when he assigned the mission, he ran into opposition not of the rebels' making. He ordered General Schofield, commanding the Army of the Ohio's Twenty-third Corps, positioned on the right side of the Union line, to cross Utoy Creek and hit the East Point-Atlanta rail line.

To strengthen Schofield's twelve-thousand-man force, Sherman ordered the Fourteenth Corps to join in the operation. The Fourteenth, comprising some 18,000 men, was commanded by Major General John M. Palmer, an Illinois lawyer, politician, reputed friend of Lincoln and special guardian of his own self-importance. Sherman called him "a man of ability, but not enterprising." Sherman put Schofield in command of the operation and placed Palmer under his orders. "But General Palmer," Sherman related, "claimed to rank General Schofield in the date of his commission as major-general, and denied the latter's right to exercise command over him."[25] Sherman described the situation:

> On the 4th of August I ordered General Schofield to make a bold attack on the railroad, anywhere about East Point, and ordered General Palmer to report to him for duty. He at once denied General Schofield's right to command him; but, after examining the dates of their respective commissions, and hearing their arguments, I wrote to General Palmer.

> *August 4th—10.45 P.M.*
> From the statements made by yourself and General Schofield to-day, my decision is, that he ranks you as a major-general, being of the same date of present commission, by reason of his previous superior rank as brigadier-general. The movements of to-morrow are so important that the orders of the superior on that flank must be regarded as military orders, and not in the nature of cooperation. I did hope that there would be no necessity for my making this decision; but it is better for all parties interested that no question of rank should occur in actual battle. The Sandtown road, and the railroad, if possible, must be gained to-morrow, if it costs half your command. I regard the loss of time this afternoon as equal to the loss of two thousand men.

> I also communicated the substance of this to General Thomas, to whose army Palmer's corps belonged, who replied on the 5th:

> I regret to hear that Palmer has taken the course he has, and I know that he intends to offer his resignation as soon as he can properly do so. I recommend that his application be granted.[26]

In the meantime, the operation, which became known as the Battle of Utoy Creek, was going awry. "I am compelled to acknowledge," Schofield wrote to Sherman on the night of the 5th, "that I have totally failed to make any aggressive movement with the Fourteenth [Palmer's] Corps.... I propose to-morrow to take my own troops (Twenty-third Corps) to the right, and try to recover what has been lost by two days' delay. The force may likely be too small."[27]

Sherman then summoned Palmer to report to him in person. "He came on the 6th to my headquarters," Sherman wrote, "and insisted on his resignation being accepted, for which formal act I referred him to General Thomas. He then rode to General Thomas's camp, where he made a written resignation of his office as commander of the Fourteenth Corps, and was granted the usual leave of absence to go to his home in Illinois, there to await further orders."[28] Thomas recommended that Brigadier General Jefferson C. Davis be promoted to major general and succeed Palmer as commander of the Fourteenth Corps. "These changes," Sherman remarked, "had to be referred to the President, in Washington, and were, in due time, approved and executed; and thenceforward I had no reason to complain of the slowness or inactivity of that splendid corps."[29]

The Battle of Utoy Creek, however, had proved a disaster, the diminished Union force being repulsed with a loss of some five hundred men.

At the same time, President Davis, who had been so insistent that General Johnston face the Union army and fight, now cautioned Hood about doing what Johnston had been relieved for not doing. On August 5 Davis, having noticed the losses Hood was suffering in defense of Atlanta, wrote to Hood and told him, "The loss consequent upon attacking him [Sherman] in his intrenchments requires you to avoid that, if practicable."[30] Davis's words had unwittingly validated Johnston's generalship.

Sherman, meanwhile, was growing ever more frustrated by the stubbornness of the Confederates' defenses and the amount of punishment the city of Atlanta was showing itself capable of enduring. Daily bombardment of the city by his artillery was unavailing. Atlanta was not going to be hammered into submission. The rebel line of entrenchments was too forbidding for a direct assault, and Sherman was unwilling to attempt one — unless, as he said, "some accident or positive neglect on the part of our antagonist should reveal an opening."[31]

Now, if not before, Sherman realized that overcoming Hood's defenses required a massive effort by the Union's armies. He resolved to make that massive effort. On August 10 he telegraphed General Grant, in Washington at the time, and informed him of his new plan: "Since July 28th Hood has not attempted to meet us outside his parapets. In order to possess and destroy effectually his communications, I may have to leave a corps at the railroad-bridge [over the Chattahoochee River, northwest of Atlanta], well entrenched, and cut loose with the balance to make a circle of desolation around Atlanta. I do not propose to assault the works, which are too strong, nor to proceed by regular approaches...."[32]

In his memoir Sherman revealed his thinking. "[W]e were held in check by the stubborn defense of the place, and a conviction was forced on my mind that our enemy would hold fast, even though every house in town should be battered down by our artillery. It was evident that we must decoy him out to fight us on something like equal terms, or else, with the whole army, raise the siege and attack his communications."[33]

On Saturday, August 13 he issued orders to implement the plan he had sketched out in his message to Grant: "I gave general orders for the Twentieth Corps to draw back to the railroad-bridge at the Chattahoochee, to protect our [supply] trains, hospitals, spare artillery, and the railroad-depot, while the rest of the army should move boldly to some point on the Macon Railroad below East Point."[34]

Sherman further decided he should try to get more and better results from his cavalry. He would, as he expressed it, "recompose" the cavalry divisions in hopes of making them more effective, both for offense and defense. Before implementing his new plan, he placed Major General Judson Kilpatrick's cavalry division on the Union line's right rear, in support of Schofield's exposed right flank. He put Major General Kenner Garrard's cavalry division on the left side of the line and placed Major General Edward McCook's cavalry division a distance behind the line, near Marietta and the Union-held railroad. He soon got an opportunity to evaluate his cavalry commanders. Rebel cavalry raids had cut the telegraph lines as well as the rail line, and Sherman ordered Garrard and Kilpatrick to lead their troopers out to make reconnaissances on both flanks of the Union line, Garrard on the left and Kilpatrick on the right. "The former moved with so much caution that I was displeased," Sherman reported, "but Kilpatrick, on the contrary, displayed so much zeal and activity that I was attracted to him at once.... I summoned him to me, and was so pleased with his spirit and confidence, that I concluded to suspend the general movement of the main army, and to send him with his small division of cavalry to break up the Macon road [south of Atlanta] about Jonesboro...."[35]

Kilpatrick and his troopers rode off on their critical assignment — what Sherman hoped would be a quick fix — during the night of August 18. Sherman reported the results: "[He] returned to us on the 22d, having made the complete circuit of Atlanta. He reported that he had destroyed three miles of the railroad about Jonesboro, which he reckoned would take ten days to repair; that he had encountered a division of infantry and a brigade of cavalry (Ross's); that he had captured a battery and destroyed three of its guns, bringing one in as a trophy, and he also brought in three battle-flags and seventy prisoners. On the 23d, however, we saw [railroad] trains coming into Atlanta from the south, when I became more than ever convinced that cavalry could not or would not work hard enough to disable a railroad properly...."[36]

Kilpatrick had shown himself to be, as one Union officer put it, "a frothy braggart, without brains and not overstocked with desire to die on the field."[37] Sherman had judged him to be "a hell of a damned fool," but had mistakenly thought such a fool was what his cavalry needed then. Kilpatrick had proved somewhat less than what was needed.

Sherman had hoped Kilpatrick and his cavalry would make quick work of the demolition of Hood's railroad supply lines, but with that failure, Sherman reverted to the plan as ordered on August 13. He was now more than ever determined to break the stalemate.

Atlanta Is Burning,
August 24 to November 16, 1864

General Sherman wanted to make sure the first phase of his plan was workable. On Wednesday, August 24 he mounted his horse and rode from his headquarters back to the Chattahoochee River railroad bridge that his army had crossed to assail Atlanta a month earlier. He wanted to see for himself and satisfy himself that just one of his seven corps could defend the bridge, securing it for continued communication. Beside and around the bridge were the works that had formed a defensive line established by General Johnston to hold off Sherman's advancing army. Those works were still in good condition, Sherman decided after inspecting them, good enough to be used now to defend against Confederate troops. Satisfied, Sherman returned to his headquarters and later that evening wired General Halleck to apprise him of his plans:

> I will be all ready, and will commence the movement around Atlanta by the south, to-morrow night, and for some time you will hear little of us. I will keep open a courier line back to the Chattahoochee bridge, by way of Sandtown. The Twentieth Corps will hold the railroad-bridge, and I will move with the balance of the army, provisioned for twenty days.[1]

Leaving the Twentieth Corps at the bridge, Sherman intended to move his six other corps—some 60,000 troops—on a massive sweep around the west and south sides of Atlanta, determined to destroy once and for all the railroads south of the city and thereby interdict the flow of supplies and provisions that were keeping Hood's army and the city of Atlanta alive and resistant. All previous efforts had failed. The partial siege and the horrific daily shelling of the city were seen to be futile and had shown the citizens of Atlanta to be too resilient. "It was painful, yet strange, to mark how expert grew the old men, women, and children in building their little underground forts, in which to fly for safety during the storm of shell and shot," Hood later wrote. "Often 'mid the darkness of night were they constrained to seek refuge in these dungeons beneath the earth; albeit, I cannot recall one word from their lips expressive of dissatisfaction or willingness to surrender."[2]

Remaining convinced that the rebel fortifications were too strong to storm, Sherman had resolved to shut off Atlanta's lifeline. "After the [Union army's] destruction of the Augusta [rail] road," General Hood wrote, "the holding of Atlanta—unless some favorable opportunity offered itself to defeat the Federals in battle—depended upon our ability to hold intact the [rail] road to Macon."[3] The destruction of that rail line became Sherman's major objective.

On the night of Thursday, August 25, the night Sherman's big guns fell silent, Sherman made his first move. The Twentieth Corps, commanded by Major General Henry W. Slocum, pulled back from its position on the Union line and took up its new position at the bridge. The Fourth Corps, commanded by Major General David S. Stanley, shifted to fill the gap where the Twentieth had been. Sherman described the next moves:

> The next night (26th) the Fifteenth and Seventeenth Corps, composing the Army of the Tennessee, ... drew out of their trenches, made a wide circuit, and came up on the extreme right of the Fourth and Fourteenth Corps of the Army of the Cumberland ... along Utoy Creek, facing south. The enemy seemed to suspect something that night, using his artillery pretty freely; but I think he supposed we were going to retreat altogether. An artillery-shot, fired at random, killed one man and wounded another, and the next morning some of his [Hood's] infantry came out of Atlanta and found our camps abandoned. It was afterward related that there was great rejoicing in Atlanta "that the Yankees were gone;" the fact was telegraphed all over the South, and several trains of cars (with ladies) came up from Macon to assist in the celebration of their grand victory.[4]

On Sunday, the 28th, Sherman's three armies executed a huge left wheel, turning eastward to extend across the southern approaches to Atlanta, capturing a length of the West Point Railroad, which led to Atlanta from the southwest, and advancing toward the Macon Railroad, which formed a junction with the West Point tracks at East Point, ten miles southwest of Atlanta. Schofield's Army of the Ohio was aiming for the Rough and Ready station of the Macon line, four miles below East Point. Howard's Army of the Tennessee was headed for Jonesboro, on the Macon line about ten miles below Rough and Ready [now Mountain View]. Thomas's Army of the Cumberland was headed for a point on the Macon Railroad midway between Rough and Ready and Jonesboro.

The troops reached the West Point tracks on the 28th and spent the next day demolishing them. "The track was heaved up in sections the length of a regiment, then separated rail by rail; bonfires were made of the ties and of fence-rails on which the rails were heated, carried to trees or telegraph-poles, wrapped around and left to cool," Sherman reported. "Such rails could not be used again; and, to be still more certain, we filled up many deep cuts with trees, brush, and earth, and commingled with them loaded shells, so arranged that they would explode on an attempt to haul out the bushes."[5]

By now Hood had discovered that the sudden silence of Union artillery and the newly emptied trenches of Union infantry did not signal a withdrawal, but instead presaged a new assault on the Macon railroad. Early on the morning of the 28th, Hood related, "the enemy were reported by [Brigadier General Frank C.] Armstrong in large force at Fairburn, on the West Point [rail] road. It became at once evident that Sherman was moving with his main body to destroy the Macon road, and that the fate of Atlanta depended upon our ability to defeat this movement.... In fact, every precaution was taken not only to hold our sole line of communication unto the last extremity, but also, in case of failure, to avoid loss or destruction of stores and material."[6]

Hood went on to describe the final fight to hold the Macon rail line, the decisive Battle of Jonesboro:

> The morning of the 30th found our general line extended farther to the left — Hardee being in the vicinity of Rough and Ready with [Lieutenant General Stephen D.] Lee's corps on his right, near East Point. Information from our cavalry clearly indicated that the enemy would

strike our road at Jonesboro. After consultation with the corps commanders, I determined upon the following operations as the last hope of holding on to Atlanta.

A Federal corps crossed Flint River, at about 6 P.M., near Jonesboro, and made an attack upon [Brigadier General Joseph H.] Lewis's brigade, which was gallantly repulsed. This action became the signal for battle. General Hardee was instructed to move rapidly with his troops to Jonesboro, whither Lieutenant-General Lee, with his corps, was ordered to follow during the night. Hardee was to attack with the entire force early on the morning of the 31st, and drive the enemy, at all hazards, into the river in their rear.

In the event of success, Lee and his command were to be withdrawn that night back to Rough and Ready; [Lieutenant General Alexander P.] Stewart's corps, together with Major-General G.W. Smith's State troops, were to form line of battle on Lee's right, near East Point, and the whole force move forward the following morning, attack the enemy in flank, and drive him down the Flint River and the West Point railroad. In the meantime the cavalry was to hold in check the corps of the enemy, stationed at the railroad bridge across the Chattahoochee, near the mouth of Peach Tree Creek, whilst Hardee advanced from his position near Jonesboro or directly on Lee's left....

The attack was not made till about 2 P.M., and then resulted in our inability to dislodge the enemy. The Federals had been allowed time, by the delay, to strongly intrench; whereas had the assault been made at an early hour in the morning the enemy would have been found but partially protected by works....

This failure gave to the Federal army the control of the Macon road, and thus necessitated the evacuation of Atlanta at the earliest hour possible....

[T]he battle of Jonesboro' was fought, and on the following day, September 1st, at 2 A.M., Lieutenant-General Lee, with his corps, marched from Jonesboro' to the vicinity of Rough and Ready, and so posted his troops as to protect our flank, whilst we marched out of Atlanta at 5 P.M. the same day....[7]

Sherman's account of the operation, published in the September 24, 1864 issue of *Harper's Weekly*, provided a model of succinctness:

ATLANTA, SEPTEMBER 7.

On the 25th of August, pursuant to a plan of which the War Department had been fully advised, I left the Twentieth Corps at the Chattahoochee Bridge, and with the balance of the army I drew off from the siege....

I moved rapidly south, reached the West Point Railroad near Fairborn [*sic*] on the 27th and broke up twelve miles of it. When moving east my right approached the Macon Railroad near Jonesborough, and my left near Rough and Ready. The enemy attacked the right wing of the Army of the Tennessee, and were completely beaten.

On the 31st, and during the combat, I pushed the left of the centre rapidly to the railroad above, between Rough and Ready and Jonesborough.

On the 1st of September we broke up about eight miles of the Macon Road, and turned on the enemy at Jonesborough, assaulted him and his lines, and carried them, capturing Brigadier-General Gorman [Govan] and about 2000 prisoners, with eight guns and much plunder. Night alone prevented our capturing all of Hardee's corps, which escaped south that night.

That same night, Hood, in Atlanta, finding all his railroads broken and in our possession, blew up his ammunition, seven locomotives and eighty cars, and evacuated Atlanta, which, on the next day, September 2, was occupied by the corps left for that purpose, Major-General Slocum commanding, we following the retreating rebel army to near Lovejoy's station, thirty miles south of Atlanta, where, finding him strongly intrenched, I concluded it would not pay to assault as we already had the great object of the campaign, viz., Atlanta. Accordingly the army gradually and leisurely returned to Atlanta; and it is now encamped eight miles south of the city, and tomorrow will move to the camps appointed. I am now writing in Atlanta, so I could not be uneasy in regard to our situation.

We have as the result of this quick, and, as I think, well executed movement, 27 guns, over

3000 prisoners, and have buried over 400 rebel dead, and left as many wounded; they could not be removed.

The rebels have lost, besides the important city of Atlanta and stores, at least 500 dead, 2500 wounded, and 3000 prisoners, whereas our aggregate loss will not foot 1500.

If that is not success, I don't know what is.

SHERMAN, Major-General

The first Union troops to enter evacuated Atlanta were those of General Slocum's Twentieth Corps, which had stood watch over the Chattahoochee River bridge on the northwest side of the city. After the first day of the Battle of Jonesboro, Sherman had instructed Slocum to make a reconnaissance of the road leading into Atlanta, and doing so, Slocum had discovered the rebels still holding their line of entrenchments. Late the following night, September 1, Slocum and his men could hear the thunderous explosions in the city, and at daybreak on Friday, September 2 Slocum put his three divisions on the road to Atlanta to find out what the explosions meant. They found the Confederates' trenches empty now, save for scattered personal belongings left behind in haste. Daylight also brought a view of a sky clouded by black smoke rising from the city in the distance.

About mid-morning, on the outskirts of the city, a cavalry detail encountered a group of civilians riding out to meet them, bearing a white flag. The group included Atlanta's mayor — James Calhoun — a member of the city council and several prominent citizens. Captain Henry Scott, leading the cavalry detail, received the group and was asked by the mayor if he was in command of the advancing troops. Scott answered that he wasn't, but if the Atlanta delegation would wait, he would go get the commander. Minutes later he returned with Colonel John Coburn, commander of the 70th Indiana Regiment, and introduced him to the mayor and the others. Mayor Calhoun told Coburn that the last of the Confederate troops had left the city and that Coburn could enter the city and take possession of it, assuring him that there would be no resistance. In that exchange between the two men, Atlanta was surrendered. "The fortune of war has placed Atlanta in your hands," the mayor declared.

As Slocum's troops entered the city, they saw scenes of destruction that mutely explained the explosions heard the night before. The railroad cars that had been loaded with supplies, equipment and munitions — twenty-eight of them crammed with three million cartridges, five thousand rifles, thousands of explosive shells, kegs of gunpowder and thirteen artillery pieces — had been parked on tracks beside a row of factories, foundries, mills and other industrial buildings and had been set ablaze by Hood's retreating army to keep them out of Union hands. The fires had set off monstrous explosions and a hellish conflagration that razed every structure, homes and commercial buildings alike, for several hundred yards on either side of the tracks. Massive pieces of debris, torn and twisted metal, shattered masonry and broken lumber lay everywhere within reach of the explosions' force. Smoky fires still smoldered.

Sherman was still with his troops in the vicinity of Jonesboro and hadn't yet learned of the surrender, but General Slocum had already wired the news to Washington: "Sherman has taken Atlanta." Sherman finally got word from Slocum later in the day, receiving a handwritten note from Slocum. "Of course, the glad tidings flew on the wings of electricity to all parts of the North," Sherman later wrote, "where the people had patiently awaited news of their husbands, sons, and brothers, away down in 'Dixie Land'; and congratulations came pouring back full of good-will and patriotism. This victory was most opportune; Mr. Lincoln himself told me afterward that even he had previously felt in doubt, for the summer was fast passing away; that General Grant seemed to be checkmated about Richmond and Petersburg, and my army seemed to have run up against an impassable barrier, when, suddenly and unexpectedly, came the news that 'Atlanta was ours, and fairly won....'"[8]

Now Lincoln was doubtless thinking that his re-election, highly uncertain before the capture of Atlanta, might, like Atlanta, be fairly won as well. To General Sherman the president wrote a note of congratulation:

> The national thanks are rendered by the President to Major-General W.T. Sherman and the gallant officers and soldiers of his command before Atlanta, for the distinguished ability and perseverance displayed in the campaign in Georgia, which, under Divine favor, has resulted in the capture of Atlanta. The marches, battles, sieges, and other military operations, that have signalized the campaign, must render it famous in the annals of war, and have entitled those who have participated therein to the applause and thanks of the nation.
>
> ABRAHAM LINCOLN,
> *President of the United States.*[9]

After "due reflection," as he said, Sherman abandoned the idea of pursuing Hood's army and instead decided to move into Atlanta and occupy it. He would, he said, "enjoy a short period of rest and ... think well over the next step required in the progress of events." He issued orders for each of his three armies to take up new positions. The Army of the Cumberland would be posted in and around Atlanta; the Army of the Tennessee would be posted at East Point; and the Army of the Ohio would be posted at Decatur. "I rode back to Jonesboro' on the 6th, and there inspected the rebel hospital, full of wounded officers and men left by Hardee in his retreat," Sherman recounted. From Jonesboro he moved to Rough and Ready and then on September 8 rode into Atlanta and established his headquarters in a house across the street from the courthouse square.

"[I] at once set about a measure already ordered," he reported, "of which I had thought much and long, viz., to remove the entire civil population.... I peremptorily required that all the citizens and families resident in Atlanta should go away, giving to each the option to go south or north, as their interests or feelings dictated. I was resolved to make Atlanta a pure military garrison or depot, with no civil population to influence military measures. I had seen Memphis, Vicksburg, Natchez and New Orleans, all captured from the enemy, and each at once was garrisoned by a full division of troops, if not more; so that success was actually crippling our armies in the field by detachments to guard and protect the interests of a hostile population. I gave notice of this purpose, as early as the 4th of September, to General Halleck, in a letter concluding with these words: 'If the people raise a howl against my barbarity and cruelty, I will answer that war is war, and not popularity-seeking. If they want peace, they and their relatives must stop the war.'"[10]

After making his intentions known to Halleck, Sherman informed Hood about them, explaining the plan to him in a letter dated September 7:

> GENERAL: I have deemed it to the interest of the United States that the citizens now residing in Atlanta should remove, those who prefer it to go south, and the rest north. For the latter I can provide food and transportation to points of their election in Tennessee, Kentucky, or farther north. For the former I can provide transportation by [rail] cars as far as Rough and Ready, and also wagons; but, that their removal may be made with as little discomfort as possible, it will be necessary for you to help the families from Rough and Ready to the cars at Lovejoy's. If you consent, I will undertake to remove all the families in Atlanta who prefer to go south to Rough and Ready, with all their movable effects, viz., clothing, trunks, reasonable furniture, bedding, etc., with their servants, white and black, with the proviso that no force shall be used toward the blacks, one way or the other. If they want to go with their masters or mistresses, they may

do so; otherwise they will be sent away, unless they be men, when they may be employed by our quartermaster. Atlanta is no place for families or non-combatants, and I have no desire to send them north if you will assist in conveying them south. If this proposition meets your views, I will consent to a truce in the neighborhood of Rough and Ready, stipulating that any wagons, horses, animals, or persons sent there for the purposes herein stated, shall in no manner be harmed or molested; you in your turn agreeing that any cars, wagons, or carriages, persons or animals sent to the same point shall not be interfered with. Each of us might send a guard of, say, one hundred men, to maintain order, and limit the truce to, say, two days after a certain time appointed.

I have authorized the mayor to choose two citizens to convey to you this letter, with such documents as the mayor may forward in explanation, and shall await your reply. I have the honor to be your obedient servant,

W.T. SHERMAN, Major-General Commanding[11]

Two days later Hood wrote back agreeing with the procedure for aiding in the evacuation of Atlanta residents seeking to go south, but protesting the entire plan: "...permit me to say," Hood wrote, "that the unprecedented measure you propose transcends, in studied and ingenious cruelty, all acts ever before brought to my attention in the dark history of war. In the name of God and humanity, I protest, believing that you will find that you are expelling from their homes and firesides the wives and children of a brave people."[12]

Sherman the next day fired back an answer brimming with indignation and no lack of eloquence:

... You style the measures proposed "unprecedented," and appeal to the dark history of war for a parallel, as an act of "studied and ingenious cruelty." It is not unprecedented; for General Johnston himself very wisely and properly removed the families all the way from Dalton down, and I see no reason why Atlanta should be excepted. Nor is it necessary to appeal to the dark history of war, when recent and modern examples are so handy. You yourself burned dwelling-houses along your parapet, and I have seen to-day fifty houses that you have rendered uninhabitable because they stood in the way of your forts and men....

In the name of common-sense, I ask you not to appeal to a just God in such a sacrilegious manner. You who, in the midst of peace and prosperity, have plunged a nation into war — dark and cruel war — who dared and badgered us to battle, insulted our flag, seized our arsenals and forts that were left in the honorable custody of peaceful ordnance-sergeants, seized and made "prisoners of war" the very garrisons sent to protect your people against negroes and Indians, long before any overt act was committed by the (to you) hated Lincoln Government; tried to force Kentucky and Missouri into rebellion, spite of themselves; falsified the vote of Louisiana; turned loose your privateers to plunder unarmed ships; expelled Union families by the thousands, burned their houses, and declared, by an act of your Congress, the confiscation of all debts due Northern men for goods had and received! Talk thus to the marines, but not to me, who have seen these things, and who will this day make as much sacrifice for the peace and honor of the South as the best-born Southerner among you! If we must be enemies, let us be men, and fight it out as we propose to do, and not deal in such hypocritical appeals to God and humanity. God will judge us in due time, and he will pronounce whether it be more humane to fight with a town full of women and the families of a brave people at our back, or to remove them in time to places of safety among their own friends and people.[13]

In answer to the appeal issued by Atlanta's mayor, Sherman wrote words of refusal and explanation. His letter, dated September 12, was addressed to Mayor Calhoun and city council members E.E. Rawson and S.C. Wells:

GENTLEMEN: I have your letter of the 11th, in the nature of a petition to revoke my orders removing all the inhabitants of Atlanta. I have read it carefully, and give full credit to your statements of the distress that will be occasioned, and yet shall not revoke my orders, because they were not designed to meet the humanities of the case, but to prepare for the future struggles in which millions of good people outside of Atlanta have a deep interest. We must have peace, not only at Atlanta, but in all America. To secure this, we must stop the war that now desolates our once happy and favored country. To stop war, we must defeat the rebel armies which are arrayed against the laws and Constitution that all must respect and obey. To defeat those armies, we must prepare the way to reach them in their recesses, provided with the arms and instruments which enable us to accomplish our purposes. Now, I know the vindictive nature of our enemy, that we may have many years of military operations from this quarter; and, therefore, deem it wise and prudent to prepare in time. The use of Atlanta for warlike purpose is inconsistent with its character as a home for families. There will be no manufactures, commerce, or agriculture here, for the maintenance of families, and sooner or later want will compel the inhabitants to go. Why not go now, when all the arrangements are completed for the transfer, instead of waiting till the plunging shot of contending armies will renew the scenes of the past month? Of course, I do not apprehend any such thing at this moment, but you do not suppose this army will be here until the war is over. I cannot discuss this subject with you fairly, because I cannot impart to you what we propose to do, but I assert that our military plans make it necessary for the inhabitants to go away, and I can only renew my offer of services to the make their exodus in any direction as easy and comfortable as possible.

You cannot qualify war in harsher terms than I will. War is cruelty, and you cannot refine it; and those who brought war into our country deserve all the curses and maledictions a people can pour out. I know I had no hand in making this war, and I know I will make more sacrifices to-day than any of you to secure peace. But you cannot have peace and a division of our country. If the United States submits to a division now, it will not stop, but will go on until we reap the fate of Mexico, which is eternal war. The United States does and must assert its authority, wherever it once had power; for, if it relaxes one bit to pressure, it is gone, and I believe that such is the national feeling. This feeling assumes various shapes, but always comes back to that of Union. Once admit the Union, once more acknowledge the authority of the national Government, and, instead of devoting your houses and streets and roads to the dread uses of war, I and this army become at once your protectors and supporters, shielding you from danger, let it come from what quarter it may. I know that a few individuals cannot resist a torrent of error and passion, such as swept the South into rebellion, but you can point out, so that we may know those who desire a government, and those who insist on war and its desolation.

You might as well appeal against the thunder-storm as against these terrible hardships of war. They are inevitable, and the only way the people of Atlanta can hope once more to live in peace and quiet at home, is to stop the war, which can only be done by admitting that it began in error and is perpetuated in pride.

We don't want your negroes, or your horses, or your houses, or your lands, or any thing you have, but we do want and will have a just obedience to the laws of the United States. That we will have, and, if it involves the destruction of your improvements, we cannot help it.

You have heretofore read public sentiment in your newspapers, that live by falsehood and excitement; and the quicker you seek for truth in other quarters, the better. I repeat then that, by the original compact of Government, the United States had certain rights in Georgia, which have never been relinquished and never will be; that the South began war by seizing forts, arsenals, mints, custom-houses, etc., etc., long before Mr. Lincoln was installed, and before the South had one jot or tittle of provocation. I myself have seen in Missouri, Kentucky, Tennessee, and Mississippi, hundreds and thousands of women and children fleeing from your armies and desperadoes, hungry and with bleeding feet. In Memphis, Vicksburg, and Mississippi, we fed thousands upon thousands of the families of rebel soldiers left on our hands, and whom we could not see starve. Now that war comes home to you, you feel very different. You deprecate its horrors, but did not feel them when you sent car-loads of soldiers and ammunition, and moulded shells and shot, to carry war into Kentucky and Tennessee, to desolate the homes of hundreds and thousands of good people who only asked to live peace at their old homes, and under the Government of their inheritance. But these comparisons are idle. I want peace, and believe it can only be reached through union and war, and I will ever conduct war with a view to perfect and early success.

But, my dear sirs, when peace does come, you may call on me for any thing. Then will I share with you the last cracker, and watch with you to shield your homes and families against danger from every quarter.

Now you must go, and take with you the old and feeble, feed and nurse them, and build for them, in more quiet places, proper habitations to shield them against the weather until the mad passions of men cool down, and allow the Union and peace once more to settle over your old homes at Atlanta. Yours in haste,

W.T. SHERMAN, *Major-General commanding*[14]

In the end, Sherman did as he said he was going to do. "By the middle of September," he wrote in his memoir, "all these matters were in progress, the reports of the past campaign were written up and dispatched to Washington, and our thoughts began to turn toward the future."[15]

The near future would be occupied with defensive moves that had him moving forces to combat the actions of Hood's escaped army, which included the cavalry of Lieutenant General Joseph E. Wheeler, who, along with General Forrest and his considerable cavalry force, continued to harass Sherman's line of communications above Atlanta. Sherman quickly wearied of continually playing defense, hustling off here and there to meet the moment's emergency, the initiative gone from his hands. He urged Grant to let him regain the initiative by marching southeastward across Georgia, weakening the state's war-making ability and assaulting the people's morale.

He ordered General Thomas's corps to deal with Hood's threats and sought another task for himself. Promising Grant that Thomas could handle Hood, Sherman urged approval of his proposed march through Georgia. "General Thomas will have a force strong enough to prevent his [Hood's] reaching any country in which we have an interest; and he has orders, if Hood turns to follow me, to push for Selma, Alabama," Sherman told Grant. "No single army can catch Hood, and I am convinced the best results will follow from our defeating Jeff. Davis's cherished plan of making me leave Georgia by manoeuvring. Thus far I have confined my efforts to thwart this plan ... but I regard the pursuit of Hood as useless...."[16]

By October 19, although still lacking Grant's approval, Sherman had become determined to make his proposed march. He telegraphed the chief commissary and acting chief quartermaster in Atlanta, Brigadier General Amos Beckwith, and told him, "I want to prepare for my big raid. On the lst of November I want nothing in Atlanta but what is necessary for war.... I propose to abandon Atlanta, and the railroad back to Chattanooga, to sally forth to ruin Georgia and bring up on the seashore. Make all dispositions accordingly...."[17]

By November 2 Grant had finally come around to Sherman's thinking. "With the force ... that you have left with General Thomas," Grant wrote, "he must be able to take care of Hood and destroy him.... I say, then, go on as you propose."[18] On November 6 Sherman wired Grant and laid out his plan in detail and set November 10 as the date he would start his march. On November 8 Sherman received a clear go-ahead from Grant: "I see no present reason for changing your plan. Should any arise, you will see it, or if I do I will inform you. I think every thing here is favorable now. Great good fortune attend you! I believe you will be eminently successful, and, at worst, can only make a march less fruitful of results than hoped for."[19]

On November 8 Sherman let his troops know what lay ahead for them and what would be expected from them:

Ruins of Atlanta. An Illinois soldier writing home told of seeing "factories, warehouses, machine shops, foundries, arsenals, the railroad depot" all in flames as Union troops pulled out of Atlanta. A newspaper reporter traveling with Sherman's army reported, "The Tyre of the South [Atlanta] was laid in ashes, and the Gate City was a thing of the past." (LIBRARY OF CONGRESS)

HEADQUARTERS MILITARY DIVISION OF THE MISSISSIPPI,
IN THE FIELD, KINGSTON, GEORGIA, *November 8, 1864.*

The general commanding deems it proper at this time to inform the officers and men of the Fourteenth, Fifteenth, Seventeenth, and Twentieth Corps, that he has organized them into an army for a special purpose, well known to the War Department and to General Grant. It is sufficient for you to know that it involves a departure from our present base, and a long and difficult march to a new one. All the chances of war have been considered and provided for, as far as human sagacity can. All he asks of you is to maintain that discipline, patience, and courage, which have characterized you in the past; and he hopes, through you, to strike a blow at our enemy that will have a material effect in producing what we all so much desire, his complete overthrow. Of all things, the most important is, that the men, during marches and in camp, keep their places and do not scatter about as stragglers or foragers, to be picked up by a hostile people in detail. It is also of the utmost importance that our wagons should not be loaded with any thing but provisions and ammunition. All surplus servants, non-combatants and refugees, should move to the rear, and none should be encouraged to encumber us on the march. At some future time we will be able to provide for the poor whites and blacks who seek to escape the bondage under which they are now suffering. With these few simple cautions, he hopes to lead you to achievements equal in importance to those of the past.
By order of Major-General W.T. Sherman,
L.M. Dayton, *Aide-de-Camp.*[20]

On November 10 Sherman began calling to Atlanta all his troops that were posted outside Atlanta and that would join the march. He issued orders for Brigadier General John Corse to withdraw from garrisoning Rome after burning "all the mills, factories, etc., etc." in Rome. He issued similar orders for the burning of Marietta. Other towns in north Georgia were also put to the torch — Cassville, Cartersville, Kingston, Acworth, Big Shanty.

On the night of November 11 the first new fires in Atlanta were noticed. Eight buildings on Decatur Street went up in flames. Other fires then broke out elsewhere in the city, many of them set by individual soldiers bent on arson, burning houses not intended to be burned.

By November 12 the last railway trains loaded with wounded and with surplus supplies and equipment had pulled out, heading north, and on the 12th Sherman ordered the northbound rail line torn up and the telegraph lines cut, severing the last lines of communication with the North. On the evening of November 13 units of the Army of the Tennessee crossed the Chattahoochee, reporting to Atlanta from their previous posts, and bivouacked on the southwest side of Atlanta. From their camp they could see dark smoke rising from the first of Atlanta's doomed buildings, staining the sky. "Factories, warehouses, machine shops, foundries, arsenals, the railroad depot, and other public buildings were in flames," a soldier from Illinois reported. "Coming through Atlanta the smoke almost blinded us."[21]

By November 15 much of the city had become engulfed in fire, a blazing, smoking, enormous mass of destruction. News correspondent David P. Conyngham, an eyewitness, reported, "The streets were now in one fierce sheet of flame; houses were falling on all sides, and fiery flakes of cinders were whirled about. Occasionally shells exploded, and excited men rushed from the choking atmosphere, and hurried away from the city of ruins. At a distance the city seemed overshadowed by a cloud of black smoke, through which, now and then, darted a gushing flame of fire, or projectiles hurled from the burning ruin. The sun looked, through the hazy cloud, like a blood-red ball of fire; and the air, for miles around, felt impressive and intolerable. The Tyre of the South was laid in ashes, and the 'Gate City' was a thing of the past."[22]

Others gave witness to the awful destruction. Major James A. Connolly of the 123rd Illinois Infantry Regiment wrote in his diary on the 15th, "All the pictures and verbal descriptions of hell I have ever seen never gave me half so vivid an idea of it, as did this flame-wrapped city to-night. Gate City of the South, farewell!"[23] Lieutenant Colonel Charles F. Morse, a Massachusetts infantry commander in the Twentieth Corps, also watched the city burn on the night of the 15th. "We sat on top of our house for hours watching it," he wrote. "For miles around, the country was light as day. The business portion of Atlanta, embracing perhaps twenty acres, covered with large storehouses and public buildings, situated in the highest part of the city, was all on fire at one time, the flames shooting up for hundreds of feet into the air.... On the morning of the 16th nothing was left of Atlanta except its churches, the City Hall and private dwellings. You could hardly find a vestige of the splendid railroad depots, warehouses, etc. It was melancholy, but it was war prosecuted in deadly earnest."[24] Sherman's engineers estimated that by seven o'clock on the morning of the 16th 37 percent of the city had been destroyed.[25]

By 7 A.M. on November 16 Sherman was on his way out of the smoking, ruined city. "We rode out of Atlanta by the Decatur road, filled by the marching troops and wagons of the Fourteenth Corps;" he wrote in his memoir, "and reaching the hill, just outside of the old rebel works, we naturally paused to look back upon the scenes of our past battles.... Behind us lay Atlanta, smouldering and in ruins, the black smoke rising high in air, and hanging like a pall over the ruined city.... Some band, by accident, struck up the anthem of 'John Brown's soul goes marching on'; the men caught up the strain, and never before or since have I heard the chorus of 'Glory, glory, hallelujah!' done with more spirit, or in better harmony of time and place. Then we turned our horses' heads to the east; Atlanta was soon lost behind the screen of trees, and became a thing of the past.... I have never seen the place since."[26]

And so Sherman turned his back on the wasted city, leaving it behind so that he might bear the war not to the South's army alone, but to its people.

19

Sheridan in the Valley,
July 31, 1864, to March 2, 1865

Grant was ready to shake up Dave Hunter's command. Its troops had been summoned from safety in West Virginia to ward off Jubal Early's advance on Washington and now they were idling between the Potomac River and Emmitsburg, Maryland, near the Pennsylvania line, ostensibly defending the nation's capital. A major problem with the command was its commander, Hunter, a brave warrior against civilians but not so much against tough rebel forces, from which he had consistently fled in the struggle to possess the strategic Shenandoah River valley. There were other problems, too.

The officer that Grant had in mind to replace Hunter was the Army of the Potomac's little (five foot five), oddly built (short legs, long arms), pugnacious, hard-swearing cavalry commander, thirty-three-year-old Philip Henry Sheridan, who had already proved his merit as an able fighter and leader of men. Preparatory to installing Sheridan in the new job, Grant ordered Sheridan to report to him at City Point and when he promptly arrived there on July 31, Grant briefed him on the situation in the Shenandoah valley.

"The Shenandoah Valley was very important to the Confederates," Grant later explained, "because it was the principal storehouse they now had for feeding their armies about Richmond.... It had been the source of a great deal of trouble to us heretofore to guard that outlet to the north, partly because of the incompetency of some of the commanders, but chiefly because of interference from Washington. It seemed to be the policy of General Halleck and Secretary Stanton to keep any force sent there, in pursuit of the invading army, moving right and left so as to keep between the enemy and our capital; and, generally speaking, they pursued this policy until all knowledge of the whereabouts of the enemy was lost. They [the Confederates] were left, therefore, free to supply themselves with horses, beef cattle, and such provisions as they could carry away from Western Maryland and Pennsylvania. I determined to put a stop to this."[1]

Grant's initial attempt to place Sheridan in command of the U.S. forces operating in the Shenandoah valley, designated the Middle Military Department, had been thwarted by Stanton, who objected to Sheridan on the ground that he was too young for such an important command. Now Grant was trying again, this time with increased determination. He proposed to keep Hunter in nominal command, having him retain administrative duties, but put Sheridan in charge of operations in the field.

At their July 31 meeting Grant informed Sheridan of the new assignment and gave him specific instructions. "He went on to say," Sheridan related, "that he wanted me to push the enemy ... and if Early retired up the Shenandoah Valley, I was to pursue, but if he crossed the Potomac [moving northward] I was to put myself south of him and try to compass his destruction."[2]

He sent Sheridan off to Monocacy, where Hunter's command then had its headquarters, with instructions to take command of the troops. The next morning, August 1, Grant wired Halleck and told him, "I am sending General Sheridan for temporary duty whilst the enemy is being expelled from the border. Unless General Hunter is in the field in person, I want Sheridan put in command of all the troops in the field, with instructions to put himself south of the enemy and follow him to the death. Wherever the enemy goes let our troops go also. Once started up the valley they ought to be followed until we get possession of the Virginia Central Railroad."

Then, to make sure Sheridan got an army to command, whether or not Lincoln and Stanton went along with the new plan, Grant ordered: "If General Hunter is in the field, give Sheridan direct command of the 6th corps and cavalry division. All the cavalry, I presume, will reach Washington in the course of to-morrow."[3] That final sentence referred to the additional cavalry units Grant was sending to strengthen the force Sheridan would command.

Following his meeting with Grant, Sheridan returned to his headquarters at Hancock Station and made arrangements for handing off his current duties to take on the new ones.

He then set out for Washington, en route to Monocacy, arriving in the capital on Thursday, August 4 and making an obligatory call on Halleck and Stanton. Accompanied by Stanton, he went to see President Lincoln at the White House. In their brief conversation Lincoln told Sheridan that he had at first agreed with Stanton that Sheridan was too young for the job, but that he had changed his mind after Grant had separated the paper-shuffling part of the job from the fighting part. Lincoln said he thought Grant had "plowed round" the difficulties and he, Lincoln, was now satisfied with the arrangement.[4]

Stanton, though, seemed unconvinced, which bothered Sheridan. "Mr. Stanton," Sheridan related, "remained silent during these remarks, never once indicating whether he, too, had become reconciled to my selection or not; and

U.S. Maj. Gen. Philip H. Sheridan. At age 33, Sheridan was considered by Secretary of War Stanton and President Lincoln too young to command the U.S. forces operating in the Shenandoah valley, but Grant insisted, and Sheridan got the job of driving Early and the Confederates out of the strategically important valley. (JOHN CLARK RIDPATH)

although, after we left the White House, he conversed with me freely in regard to the campaign I was expected to make, seeking to impress on me the necessity for success from the political as well as from the military point of view, yet he utterly ignored the fact that he had taken any part in disapproving the recommendation of the general-in-chief."[5]

The political point of view was dominant, and Stanton wanted to be sure Sheridan knew it. The public perception in the North was that the war was going poorly. Grant's momentum had stalled at Petersburg; Sherman had not yet had significant success in his pursuit of Joe Johnston's army into Georgia; and Early had just shown how close the war could come to the nation's capital. With the presidential election a mere three months away, Lincoln and the members of his administration were seriously worried about losing it, and if the election were lost, they knew, the costly, critical effort to preserve the Union would be lost as well. Military success was essential—because political success depended on it. "I deemed it necessary to be very cautious," Sheridan later wrote, "...the authorities at Washington having impressed upon me that the defeat of my army might be followed by the overthrow of the party in power."[6] Sheridan had got the message.

From Washington Sheridan took a special train to Monocacy, and there he again met with Grant. Lincoln, it turned out, had seen the dispatch that Grant had sent to Halleck on August 1, stating that Grant wanted Sheridan to "follow the enemy to the death." Lincoln liked that idea, but having seen the failures of past commanders, he was pessimistic. He wired Grant at City Point on August 3 and told him, "I repeat to you it will neither be done nor attempted unless you watch it every day, and hour, and force it."[7] And so, to force it and satisfy the president, Grant immediately hurried to Monocacy, without stopping at Washington on his way.

When Grant got to Monocacy, Lincoln's attitude and remark became more understandable. "I found General Hunter's army encamped there," Grant reported, "scattered over the fields along the banks of the Monocacy [River], with many hundreds of cars and locomotives, belonging to the Baltimore and Ohio Railroad, which he had taken the precaution to bring back and collect at that point. I asked the general where the enemy was. He replied that he did not know. He said the fact was, that he was so embarrassed with orders from Washington moving him first to the right and then to the left that he had lost all trace of the enemy."[8]

Grant quickly set out to find whatever Confederate force there was. He ordered the trains prepared to move and ordered the troops to board them. He also ordered the cavalry and wagon trains to move out. He issued instructions for the entire force to push toward Halltown, about four miles above Harpers Ferry, in the Shenandoah River valley. "I knew," Grant said, "that the valley was of such importance to the enemy that, no matter how much he was scattered at that time, he would in a very short time be found in front of our troops moving south."[9]

Grant then wrote instructions for Hunter, and he told him in person that Sheridan was in Washington and that another division was on its way. He suggested that Hunter set up a new headquarters in Baltimore or elsewhere and give Sheridan command of the troops in the field. At that request, Hunter said he preferred to be relieved entirely of the command, that Halleck distrusted him and that he didn't want to hamper the war effort. Grant responded by saying simply, "Very well then."

When Sheridan arrived at Monocacy, on Saturday, August 6, he found Grant and a couple of Grant's staff members waiting for him at the station. Grant quickly and briefly informed him of the current status of Hunter and the troops and handed over to him the orders he written to Hunter:

General: Concentrate all your available force without delay in the vicinity of Harper's Ferry, leaving only such railroad guards and garrisons for public property as may be necessary.

Use in this concentration the railroad, if by so doing time can be saved. From Harper's Ferry, if it is found that the enemy has moved north of the Potomac in large force, push north, following and attacking him wherever found; following him, if driven south of the Potomac, as long as it is safe to do so. If it is ascertained that the enemy has but a small force north of the Potomac, then push south the main force, detaching, under a competent commander, a sufficient force to look after the raiders and drive them to their homes....

There are now on the way to join you three other brigades of the best of cavalry, numbering at least five thousand men and horses. These will be instructed, in the absence of further orders, to join you by the south side of the Potomac. One brigade will probably start to-morrow.

In pushing up the Shenandoah Valley, as it is expected you will have to go first or last, it is desirable that nothing should be left to invite the enemy to return. Take all provisions, forage, and stock wanted for the use of your command. Such as cannot be consumed, destroy. It is not desirable that the buildings should be destroyed — they should, rather, be protected; but the people should be informed that so long as an army can subsist among them recurrences of these raids must be expected, and we are determined to stop them at all hazards.

Bear in mind, the object is to drive the enemy south; and to do this you want to keep him always in sight. Be guided in your course by the course he takes.

Make your own arrangements for supplies of all kinds, giving regular vouchers for such as may be taken from loyal citizens in the country through which you march.[10]

With the troops having already moved out to find Early's army and with nothing further to do in Monocacy, Sheridan reboarded his special train after an hour or two and left for Harpers Ferry. He set up his headquarters there in what he described as "a small and very dilapidated hotel" and as soon as that was done, he called in the command's chief engineering officer, Lieutenant John R. Meigs, to help him learn the topographical features of the area in which he would be operating.

Meigs was the twenty-three-year-old son of the U.S. Army's chief quartermaster, Montgomery Meigs. He had finished first in his class at West Point and was, Sheridan stated, "most intelligent in his profession." Together they went over the maps of the region, with Meigs elaborating on the maps. "Meigs was familiar with every important road and stream," Sheridan reported, "and with points worthy of note west of the Blue Ridge, and was particularly well equipped with knowledge regarding the Shenandoah Valley, even down to farmhouses. He imparted with great readiness what he knew of this, clearly pointing out its configuration and indicating the strongest points for Confederate defense...."[11]

Early and his Confederate army were already well acquainted with the area. Early's troops were mostly men who had served under Stonewall Jackson, who had had great success operating in the Shenandoah valley, winning practically every battle against Union forces. The rebel army under Early was about twenty thousand strong.[12] It comprised a corps of three divisions, commanded by generals Robert Rodes, Stephen D. Ramseur and John B. Gordon; the infantry of General Breckinridge that had come up from southwestern Virginia to aid in the defense of Lynchburg; three artillery battalions; and four cavalry brigades that were organized into a division commanded by Major General Lunsford Lomax.

Sheridan would face that Confederate force with an army totaling more than thirty-five thousand men, including some eight thousand cavalry troopers. His infantry included the Sixth Corps, commanded by Major General Horatio Wright, which was composed of three divisions, commanded by brigadier generals David A. Russell, George W. Getty and James B. Ricketts; a division from the Ninth Corps commanded by Brigadier General

William Dwight; and the two divisions of the undersize Army of West Virginia, commanded by Brigadier General George Crook. His cavalry, which he organized into a corps, comprised three divisions, two that had been shifted from the Army of the Potomac. The cavalry corps was commanded by Brigadier General Wesley Merritt.

"The difference of strength between the two armies at this date was considerably in my favor," Sheridan conceded, "but the conditions attending my situation in a hostile region necessitates so much detached service to protect trains, and to secure Maryland and Pennsylvania from raids, that my excess in numbers was almost canceled by these incidental demands that could not be avoided."[13]

Union scouts soon discovered that Early had fallen back to a strong defensive position around Bunker Hill, about twelve miles south of Martinsburg, West Virginia. Sheridan took time to form up his army in preparation for assaulting Early's right flank and rear, and while he did so, Early began withdrawing up the valley, moving southward toward Winchester, Virginia. Sheridan then planned to bring Early to battle at Winchester. Early, however, quickly withdrew farther up the valley turnpike, to Fisher's Hill, near Strasburg.

Sheridan soon learned that Early's troops were not the only rebel force with whom he had to contend. The hit-and-run, mounted Confederate raiders of Lieutenant Colonel John Mosby attacked Sheridan's train of supply wagons, burning most of the wagons, taking some two hundred prisoners and riding off with some six hundred Union horses. Then a new threat arose. On Sunday, August 14 Sheridan received a warning from Grant, in a message dated August 12 and sent via Halleck, that General Lee was rushing reinforcements to Early: "Inform General Sheridan that it is now certain two (2) divisions of infantry have gone to Early, and some cavalry and twenty (20) pieces of artillery. This movement commenced last Saturday night. He must be cautious, and act now on the defensive until movements here [at Petersburg] force them to detach to send this way...."[14]

Those reinforcements, Sheridan figured, would give Early the numerical advantage and he promptly consulted his map of the valley and decided the best defensive position could be had at Halltown, southeast of Martinsburg. Back he marched to Halltown, whence he had begun his campaign a week earlier. On the way, he wreaked as much destruction as he could, issuing orders for his troops to destroy all wheat and hay in a wide swath and seize all horses, mules and cattle that could be useful to his army.

Now Early was the pursuer instead of the pursued and for a while he was believed to be planning another foray into Maryland. General Early chronicled the movements:

> On the morning of the 17th [of August], it was discovered that the enemy was falling back, and I immediately moved forward in pursuit....
> On the 18th we took position to cover Winchester....
> On the 19th· my main force moved to Bunker Hill....
> On the 20th our cavalry had some skirmishing with the enemy's on the Opequon [Creek], and on the 21st, by concert, there was a general movement towards Harper's Ferry — my command moving through Smithfield towards Charlestown....
> I demonstrated on the enemy's front on the 22nd, 23rd, and 24th, and there was some skirmishing....[15]

And so it went for the next four weeks, neither commander believing he had enough strength to take on the other. Restless and eager to discover just how much rebel strength he was facing, Sheridan sent out what he called "an efficient body of scouts,"[16] some fifty of his troopers who had volunteered to put on Confederate uniforms and go behind the rebel lines to gather intelligence. The "scouts" operated under the command of one of

Sheridan's staff officers, Major H.K. Young, and would be paid from a special Secret Service Fund for the information they gathered, the amount of the payment depending on the usefulness of the information.

"In a few days," Sheridan recounted, "two of my scouts put me in the way of getting news conveyed from Winchester. They had learned that just outside of my lines, near Millwood, there was living an old colored man, who had a permit from the Confederate commander to go into Winchester and return three times a week, for the purpose of selling vegetables to the inhabitants. The scouts had sounded this man, and, finding him both loyal and shrewd, suggested that he might be made useful to us within the enemy's lines; and the proposal struck me as feasible, provided there could be found in Winchester some reliable person who would be willing to co-operate and correspond with me."[17]

General Crook had learned of some of the loyalist residents of Winchester while his troops occupied the town earlier, and Sheridan asked him if he knew someone who might be willing to gather and pass information to them. Crook suggested a young Quaker schoolteacher named Rebecca Wright. Sheridan thought about it and decided he would try to contact her. He sent two of his scouts to the cabin of the vegetable peddler, Tom Laws, and had them bring Laws to him at his headquarters late at night. Laws came and when Sheridan asked him if he knew Miss Wright, he replied that he knew her well. "I told him what I wished to do," Sheridan related, "and after a little persuasion he agreed to carry a letter to her on his next marketing trip. My message was prepared by writing it on tissue paper, which was then compressed into a small pellet, and protected by wrapping it in tin-foil so that it could be safely carried in the man's mouth. The probability of his being searched when he came to the Confederate picketline was not remote, and in such event he was to swallow the pellet."[18]

The message to Miss Wright, dated September 15, read:

> I learn from Major-General Crook that you are a loyal lady, and still love the old flag. Can you inform me of the position of Early's forces, the number of divisions in his army, and the strength of any or all of them, and his probable or reported intentions? Have any more troops arrived from Richmond, or are any more coming, or reported to be coming?
> You can trust the bearer.
> I am, very respectfully, your most obedient servant,
>   P.H. Sheridan, Major-General, Commanding.[19]

Miss Wright replied the next day, September 16:

> I have not communication whatever with the rebels, but will tell you what I know. The division of General Kershaw, and Cutshaw's artillery, twelve guns and men, General Anderson commanding, have been sent away, and no more are expected, as they cannot be spared from Richmond. I do not know how the troops are situated, but the force is much smaller than represented. I will take pleasure hereafter in learning all I can of their strength and position, and the bearer may call again.
> Very respectfully yours,
>   ********[20]

Delighted and emboldened by Miss Wright's information, Sheridan immediately began planning an assault on Early's lines at Newtown, southeast of Winchester. At the same time, Grant, despite having warned Sheridan to be cautious and assume a defensive position, had grown impatient over his inactivity and ordered Sheridan to meet him at Charles Town, northeast of Winchester, for a conference, which was held on September 16, a Friday. "When Sheridan arrived," Grant related, "I asked him if he had a map showing the positions of his army and that of the enemy. He at once drew one out of his side pocket, showing all roads and streams, and the camps of the two armies. He said that if he had permission he would move so and so (pointing out how) against the Confederates, and that he could 'whip them.' Before starting I had drawn up a plan of campaign for Sheridan, which I had brought with me; but, seeing that he was so clear and so positive in his views and so confident of success, I said nothing about this and did not take it out of my pocket."[21]

Grant asked Sheridan if he could launch the attack by the following Tuesday, four days away. "Oh, yes," Sheridan replied. "[I can] be off before daylight on Monday."[22] Grant gave him the go-ahead for the attack as Sheridan had planned it, commencing Monday morning.

Sheridan's forces moved out at three o'clock Monday morning, September 19. The attack did not go according to Sheridan's plan. Unavoidable delays and confusion caused it to go awry. "My idea was to attack Ramseur and Wharton, successively, at a very early hour and before they could get succor," Sheridan related, "but I was not in condition to do it till nearly noon, by which time Gordon and Rodes had been enabled to get upon the ground at a point from which, as I advanced, they enfiladed my right flank, and gave it such a repulse that to re-form this part of my line I was obliged to recall the left from some of the ground it had gained. It was during this reorganization of my lines that I changed my plan as to Crook, and moved him from my left to my right.[23]

Crook's troops struck the right of Breckinridge's division and the left of Gordon's, forcing them both to give way. As they fell back, Wright broke up Rodes's section of the rebel line and pushed Ramseur's division back into old trenches just outside of Winchester. Torbert's cavalry, though, dashed around the rebels' drawn-in left flank, and the troops of Crook, Emory and Wright slammed into the front of the new rebel position, forcing the Confederates to turn and flee in disorder.

On the right side of the rebel line Merritt's U.S. cavalry brigades, led by Brigadier General George A. Custer, Brigadier General Charles R. Lowell and Colonel Thomas C. Devin, the troopers brandishing sabers or pistols, charged Breckinridge's infantry and Fitzhugh Lee's cavalry and rode them down, capturing a battery of five guns and about 1,200 prisoners. Suddenly panic seized the rebels, and they fled into and through Winchester to escape.

"Just after entering the town," Sheridan wrote, "Crook and I met, in the main street, three young girls, who gave us the most hearty reception.... During the day they had been watching the battle from the roof of the Meredith residence [the home of two of the girls], with tears and lamentations, they said, in the morning when misfortune appeared to have overtaken the Union troops, but with unbounded exultation when, later, the tide set in against the Confederates.... When cautioned by Crook, who knew them well, and reminded that the valley had hitherto been a race-course, one day in the possession of friends, and the next of enemies — and warned of the dangers they were incurring [by their enthusiastic welcome] ... they assured him that they had no further fears of that kind now, adding that Early's army was so demoralized by the defeat it had just sustained that it would never be in condition to enter Winchester again."[24]

While they were in the town, Sheridan had Crook take him to the home of Rebecca Wright so he could meet her and thank her for her considerable contribution to the Union victory. After thanking her, he took a seat at one of her schoolroom desks to write a dispatch "announcing that we had sent Early's army whirling up the valley."[25]

General Early gave his opinion of the engagement:

This battle, beginning with the skirmishing in Ramseur's front, had lasted from daylight until dark, and, at the close of it, we had been forced back two miles, after having repulsed the enemy's first attack with great slaughter to him, and subsequently contested every inch of ground with unsurpassed obstinacy. We deserved the victory, and would have had it, but for the enemy's immense superiority in cavalry, which alone gave it to him....

I had lost a few pieces of artillery and some very valuable officers and men, but the main part of my force and all my trains had been saved, and the enemy's loss in killed and wounded was far greater than mine. When I look back to this battle, I can but attribute my escape from utter annihilation to the incapacity of my opponent.[26]

Sheridan had entered the fight, which came to be known as the Battle of Opequon and also as the Third Battle of Winchester, with about forty thousand troops, Early with about twelve thousand. Union losses totaled an estimated 5,020, including killed and wounded. Confederate losses were put at 3,610, including killed and wounded. One of the Confederate casualties was the mortally wounded commander of the Twenty-second Virginia Infantry Regiment, Colonel George S. Patton, whose grandson and namesake later became a famed U.S. general in World War Two.

President Lincoln promptly responded to Sheridan's good news, the best he had had in awhile. On the day after the battle, September 20, he wired Sheridan: "Have just heard of your great victory. God bless you all, officers and men. Strongly inclined to come see you." More tangible thanks came in the form of a promotion for Sheridan, on Grant's recommendation. He was made a brigadier general in the regular Army and given permanent command of the Middle Military Department. Congratulations also came from Secretary Stanton as well as from generals Grant, Sherman and Meade.

Sheridan let his weary army find rest in the cool of the September 19 evening, believing they would be better for it the next day, when more might be expected of them. Early's beaten troops meanwhile pressed on in their retreat, hastening up the valley turnpike as darkness enveloped them. "Drearily and silently," rebel General Gordon related, "with burdened brains and aching hearts, leaving our dead and many of the wounded behind us, we rode hour after hour, with our sore-footed, suffering men doing their best to keep up; anxiously inquiring for their commands and eagerly listening for orders to halt and sleep.... The only lamps to guide us were the benignant stars, dimly lighting the gray surface of the broad limestone turnpike. It was, however, a merciful darkness. It came too slowly for our comfort; but it came at last, and screened our weary and confused infantry from further annoyance by Sheridan's horsemen."[27]

The Confederates didn't stop that night until they had reached Fisher's Hill, a mile south of Strasburg, some twenty miles south of Winchester, and had moved into the defense line they had occupied more than a month earlier. The "hill" is a steep ridge that stretches across the floor of the Shenandoah valley, providing a strong, natural defensive barrier to an advancing army. By the time Sheridan's troops reached it the next morning, September 20, the rebels were firmly dug in atop it, their right flank anchored on the forbiddingly impassable Massanutten mountain range, their left flank about four miles to the west, at the foot of North Mountain. Tracing the base of Fisher's Hill was a shallow stream called Tumbling Run. To guard against the possibility of a Union cavalry move that might flank the Massanuttens and come up behind the rebel line, Early positioned Fitzhugh Lee's cavalry brigade on his right. Lee himself would not be with his troopers, having been knocked out of action by a wound suffered during the Winchester (Opequon) battle.

Impressed by the apparent strength of Early's front, Sheridan, in consultation with his generals, decided on another sweeping flanking attack, led by Crook's corps, as at Winchester. "I resolved to move Crook, unperceived if possible," Sheridan related, "over to the eastern face of Little North Mountain, whence he could strike the left and rear of the Confederate line, and as he broke it up, I could support him by a left half-wheel of my whole line of battle. The execution of this plan would require perfect secrecy, for the enemy from his signal-station on Three Top [hill] could plainly see every movement of our troops in daylight."[28]

During the night of September 21 Crook's troops stealthily moved into woods where they would remain till daylight on the 22nd, while the rest of Sheridan's army got into position. General Ricketts' division struck the front of Early's line, and Crook's corps made its way through the timber on the east face of Little North Mountain, then emerged into the clearing at the base of the mountain and dashed for the left flank of the rebel line. By the time the Confederates saw the mass of blue-coated infantry rushing toward them, it was too late. "Loudly cheering, Crook's men quickly crossed the broken stretch in rear of the enemy's left, producing confusion and consternation at every step," Sheridan recounted. "About a mile from the mountain's base Crook's left was joined by Ricketts, who in proper time had begun to swing his division into the action, and the two commands moved along in rear of the works so rapidly that, with but slight resistance, the Confederates abandoned the guns massed near the centre."[29]

The swinging movement of Ricketts' division was followed successively, from right to left, by the other units along Sheridan's front. In a matter of minutes, Early's line broke up, his troops routed. "The stampede was complete," Sheridan wrote, "the enemy leaving the field without semblance of organization, abandoning nearly all his artillery and such other property as was in the works, and the rout extending through the fields and over the roads toward Woodstock, Wright and Emory in hot pursuit."[30]

As his troops chased the fleeing Confederates, Sheridan, on his black gelding, Rienzi (named for the town in Mississippi where he had won a skirmish), raced along with them in pursuit, shouting, "Run, boys, run! Don't wait to form! Don't let 'em stop!"[31] The dogged pursuit lasted through the night, until Sheridan finally called a halt at Woodstock, about ten miles south of Fisher's Hill, to let his troops rest and re-form their units.

At Woodstock on the morning of the 23rd he received unwelcome news. Neither of his cavalry commanders had done as he had instructed them. Both had failed to accomplish their parts of Sheridan's plan to finally destroy Early's army. Torbert, ordinarily dependable, was supposed to have moved around the south end of the Massanuttens to head off the retreating Confederates and bag them. He had run up against Fitzhugh Lee's cavalry and, failing to use his superior numbers, had fallen back to Front Royal. Averell, often a disappointment, had made no effort to pursue the routed rebels, and no one at Woodstock seemed to know where he was. He finally showed up with his troopers around noon on the 23rd. They had taken time out for a good night's rest and had ridden into Woodstock at their leisure. After angrily chewing him out, Sheridan relieved Averell of command and ordered him to Wheeling to wait there for further orders. Colonel William H. Powell then was placed in command of Sheridan's First Cavalry Division.

And so despite his two big victories, Sheridan had been foiled in his attempt to crush or capture Early's army, which, with no Union cavalry to pursue them, fled to refuges in the fastnesses of the Blue Ridge Mountains. Even so, Grant was pleased with the results of the Battle of Fisher's Hill and, as he had done after receiving news of the victory at Winchester, he ordered his artillery to fire a one-hundred-gun salute — using live ammunition — into the beleaguered city of Petersburg.

Of the estimated 9,500 Confederate troops that had faced Sheridan in the Battle of Fisher's Hill, Early had lost 1,234, most of them taken prisoner. Sheridan had lost 528, including killed and wounded. Early had been less than diligent in protecting his left flank, which proved highly vulnerable to Crook's flanking attack and provided the key to Sheridan's success at Fisher's Hill; but ignoring any failing that was his own, Early managed to find a way to again insult his chief adversary, stating in his memoir: "...the movement on my left flank was again made by Crook. If Sheridan had not had subordinates of more ability and energy than himself, I should probably have had to write a different history of my Valley campaign."[32]

Sheridan now was ready to call off the campaign against Early's army. He worried that his transportation system would be unable to supply him beyond Harrisonburg. He was, he wired Grant, "94 miles from Martinsburg and 104 miles from Harpers Ferry." A long way from both of his supply depots, he was constantly under threat from hit-and-run rebel raiders, including not only guerrillas but the particularly worrisome Forty-third Virginia Cavalry Battalion, commanded by Lieutenant Colonel John Mosby, which preyed on Union supply trains. Clashes between Mosby's troopers and U.S. cavalry degenerated into a series of vengeful lynchings and murders of prisoners by both sides.

Believing he had accomplished his mission of reducing the threat from Early's army and devastating the countryside, Sheridan proposed that his valley campaign be terminated north of Staunton and that he "be permitted to return, carrying out on the way my original instructions for desolating the Shenandoah country so as to make it untenable for permanent occupation by the Confederates."[33] His plan was to continue to wreak havoc on the land and then send the bulk of his army to reinforce Grant at Petersburg. Grant at first resisted, suggesting Sheridan move eastward instead, but finally relented, and let Sheridan decide his own course of action.

Sheridan's decision was to withdraw down the valley at least as far as Strasburg, and he began moving his troops northward from Harrisonburg on October 6. By then his troops had already laid waste the farms scattered throughout some four hundred square miles, burning barns, factories, mills and anything else that could serve the Confederate war effort. A soldier in the Sixty-first Georgia Regiment, Private G.W. Nichols, described what he saw of the Union assault on the valley countryside: "We had an elevated position and could see Yankees out in the valley driving off all the horses, cattle, sheep and killing the hogs and burning all the barns and shocks of corn and wheat in the fields, and destroying everything that could feed or shelter man or beast. They burnt nearly all the dwelling houses, the valley was soon filled with smoke."[34]

For three days after Sheridan turned northward, rebel cavalry under the command of twenty-eight-year-old Major General Thomas Rosser (one of Custer's friends at West Point) followed the retreating blue column, harassing the rear units, until Sheridan ordered his cavalry chief, General Torbert, who had ducked the fight at Fisher's Hill, to "give Rosser a drubbing next morning or get whipped himself."[35] The infantry would be halted, Sheridan told Torbert, until the cavalry engagement was over — and, moreover, Sheridan would be watching from atop Round Top Mountain, which offered a panoramic view of the action. Sheridan described the fight, the Battle of Tom's Brook:

> The engagement soon became general across the valley, both sides fighting mainly mounted. For about two hours the contending lines struggled with each other along Tom's Brook, the charges and counter charges at many points being plainly visible from the summit of Round Top, where I had my headquarters for the time.

The open country permitting a sabre fight, both sides seemed bent on using that arm. In the centre the Confederates maintained their position with much stubbornness, and for a time seemed to have recovered their former spirit, but at last they began to give way on both flanks, and as these receded, Merritt and Custer went at the wavering ranks in a charge along the whole front. The result was a general smash-up of the entire Confederate line, the retreat quickly degenerating into a rout the like of which was never before seen. For twenty-six miles this wild stampede kept up, with our troopers close at the enemy's heels.... In the fight and pursuit Torbert took eleven pieces of artillery, with their caissons, all the wagons and ambulances the enemy had on the ground, and three hundred prisoners.... [C]itizens of the valley, intensely disgusted with the boasting and swaggering that had characterized [Rosser's brigade] ... baptized the action ... the "Woodstock Races," and never tired of poking fun at General Rosser about his precipitous and inglorious flight....[36]

Far from inflicting the whipping that Rosser had promised before the fight, the Confederates suffered losses that included twenty killed and fifty wounded, besides the estimated 280 taken prisoner. Union losses amounted to ten killed and forty-seven wounded.

General Early was then at New Market, his army reinforced by Major General Joseph Kershaw's division of South Carolinians as well as Rosser's cavalry brigade. His combative spirit was undiminished by his two recent defeats, and he was spoiling for another fight with Sheridan. General Lee spurred him to new action, telling him, "You must not be discouraged, but continue to try. I rely upon your judgment and ability, and the hearty cooperation of your officers and men to secure it [victory]. With your united force it can be accomplished."[37]

Mindful that he was outnumbered, but relying on what he believed was the fighting superiority of Confederate troops and on the element of surprise, Early was eager to accept Lee's challenge and he soon started moving his army northward, in the wake of the long blue column. On October 12 he received more reason for boldness. Intelligence came to him that Sheridan had reduced his force by sending troops—Wright's corps—to Grant at Petersburg. On Thursday, October 13 Early moved his troops into their familiar entrenchments on Fisher's Hill.

(On that same day, Colonel Mosby's rebel troopers west of Harpers Ferry held up a train carrying Union paymasters. They tore up a section of track, burned the train and dashed away with $173,000 in payroll cash.)

Early wanted to scout out the area for himself and so he took a reconnaissance detail in force with him to discover what he could. On Hupp's Hill, between Strasburg and Cedar Creek , he could see Sheridan's army positioned on high ground north of the creek. While he was there observing, a Union division moved out into the open, and an artillery battery in Early's reconnaissance force opened on the Union troops, drawing a quick response from Sheridan's artillery. Early and his detail withdrew to the rebel entrenchments, there to wait and ponder a plan to assault Sheridan's position.

The artillery exchange had sounded the alarm for Sheridan. It had confirmed for him the belief that Early was planning an attack. He quickly ordered General Wright, who was already on the road to Petersburg, to return immediately with his corps, which would be positioned on the right and rear of the line Sheridan was forming on the north side of Cedar Creek. Crook's corps was placed on the left flank, and Emory's next do it. The cavalry units of Merritt and Custer would be positioned to the right of Wright's troops. The Union left flank was believed to be protected by rough terrain that discouraged an approach from that end of the line.

As fate would have it, on the same day that Sheridan saw a fight brewing, he received a wire from Secretary Stanton, who was preparing to visit Grant at City Point. Stanton wanted to talk with Sheridan before that visit with Grant and he asked Sheridan to meet with him in Washington. A request was the same as a summons, Sheridan knew, and he promptly made arrangements to leave his headquarters at Cedar Creek the next morning.

Before boarding his train at Rectortown, Sheridan received a note from General Wright, whom Sheridan had left in command, saying that his signalmen had intercepted and deciphered a coded message transmitted by signal flags from the rebel signal station on Three Top Mountain. The message read, "To Lieutenant General Early. Be ready to move as soon as my forces join you and we will crush Sheridan." It was signed, "Longstreet, Lieutenant General." Longstreet was in fact still out of action, recovering from the wound he received in the Battle of the Wilderness, and whether Sheridan knew that or not, he was suspicious of the message's genuineness. He decided it was a ruse, but nevertheless became more wary of a possible impending attack by Early. Taking no chances, he called off a planned cavalry raid on Charlottesville and cautioned Wright to "look well to your ground and be well prepared" for a rebel assault.

With a coterie of his staff officers Sheridan arrived in Washington on the morning of October 17 and went to the War Department to confer with Stanton and Halleck. He managed to persuade them that rather than having his army cross the Blue Ridge and operate east of the Shenandoah valley, a strong defensive line should be established astride the valley, strong enough for a reduced force to hold it against any assault that could be made by a northward-moving Confederate army. Once that line was established, the bulk of his army could join forces with Grant. Having won Stanton and Halleck over, Sheridan was ready — eager — to return to Cedar Creek. Four hours later he and his party, augmented by two engineer officers who would design the defensive line Sheridan had in mind, boarded a special train that sped them from Washington to Martinsburg, which they reached after dark and where they spent the night.

On the morning of Tuesday, October 18 Sheridan and his party, escorted by a detail of some three hundred cavalrymen, set off on horseback for Winchester. Slowed by the two engineers, who were unaccustomed to long rides by horseback, the party didn't reach Winchester, twenty-eight miles distant, until the middle of the afternoon. Sheridan dispatched a messenger to Wright to discover the situation along the Union line at Cedar Creek, took the engineers out to get the lay of the land, returned to the residence where he would spend the night and when the messenger came back with Wright's report that all was quiet there, he went to bed, reassured and expecting to ride the rest of the way to his headquarters the next day.

Around six o'clock in the morning on the 19th, Sheridan was awakened by the officer on picket duty in Winchester and was told that sounds of artillery fire were coming from the direction of Cedar Creek. Sheridan asked him if the firing was continuous, and the officer replied that it was irregular. "It's all right," Sheridan told him. "Grover has gone out this morning to make a reconnaissance and he is merely feeling the enemy."[38]

Unable to get back to sleep, Sheridan got up and got dressed. Soon the picket officer was back to report that the artillery firing was continuing and could be heard clearly from his position on the outskirts of Winchester. He said, though, when Sheridan asked him, that it didn't sound like a battle. Nevertheless, Sheridan went downstairs, requested that breakfast be hurried up and ordered the horses to be saddled. Around nine o'clock he and his party reached the edge of town, where he paused, listening to the sounds of cannonading.

As he continued to ride toward Cedar Creek the sounds of firing indicated his forces were falling back.

"At Mill Creek my [cavalry] escort fell in behind," Sheridan related, "and we were going ahead at a regular pace, when, just as we made the crest of the rise beyond the stream, there burst upon our view the appalling spectacle of a panic-stricken army — hundreds of slightly wounded men, throngs of others unhurt but utterly demoralized, and baggage-wagons by the score, all pressing to the rear in hopeless confusion, telling only too plainly that a disaster had occurred at the front. On accosting some of the fugitives, they assured me that the army was broken up, in full retreat, and that all was lost; all this with a manner true to that peculiar indifference that takes possession of panic-stricken men."[39] Now suddenly the intercepted message came back to his mind: "Be ready when I join you and we will crush Sheridan."

Having discovered a narrow trail around the base of Massanutten Mountain on the Union left flank and having seen that the left was only lightly guarded, Early had moved against the Union line in three columns, Gordon's division fording the north fork of the Shenandoah River and advancing on Crook's left flank, and Kershaw's and Brigadier General Gabriel Wharton's divisions fording Cedar Creek and striking Crook's and Emory's front. Crook's troops were taken by complete surprise. They offered brief and slight resistance, then broke and ran, hundreds falling prisoner. Others, including Colonel Joseph Thoburn and Colonel Howard Kitching, were felled by gunshot and killed. Like a mighty wave, the rebels rolled forward and struck Emory's troops on their left front, routing them. On the right side of the Union line, Wright's corps, now enlivened by the noise of battle, fought to hold the Confederates back, withdrawing, but slowly.

Sheridan sent word to Colonel Oliver Edwards, commander of the brigade in Winchester, telling him to stretch his men across the valley, near Mill Creek, and stop the fleeing troops. He then thought about forming a new line of defense at the edge of Winchester, but quickly decided to try to rally the troops where they were. "About this time Colonel Wood, my chief commissary, arrived from the front and gave me fuller intelligence, reporting that everything was gone, my headquarters captured, and the troops dispersed. When I heard this I took two of my aides-de-camp, Major George A. Forsyth and Captain Joseph O'Keefe, and with twenty men from the escort started for the front, at the same time directing Colonel James W. Forsyth and Colonels Alexander and Thom to remain behind and do what they could to stop the runaways."[40] Sheridan's headquarters were at a residence called Belle Grove House, between Crook's and Emory's corps, and had he been there when the rebel troops burst into the house at about five o'clock that morning, he likely would have been taken prisoner, which is what Early had intended.

Hurrying on with his escort, Sheridan was forced to ride through the adjoining fields to get past the throngs of wounded men and wagons that blocked the road. When he was able to return to the roadway, he found it lined with troops who, though unhurt, had fled from the front and now at what they considered a safe distance, had stopped to make coffee. When they saw him, they threw their hats into the air, picked up their muskets and fell into a line behind him, following him and cheering as they marched back to the scene of battle. Officers on horseback who saw him coming galloped off to the sides of the road to tell their men that Sheridan had returned.

"In this way the news was spread to the stragglers off the road, when they, too, turned their faces to the front and marched toward the enemy, changing in a moment from the depths of depression, to the extreme of enthusiasm," Sheridan related. "I already knew that

Sheridan rides to the rescue at Cedar Creek. While Sheridan was in Washington, D.C., called there inopportunely by Secretary Stanton, General Early launched a surprise attack on Sheridan's position near Cedar Creek in Virginia. Sheridan returned just in time to rally his routed troops and drive Early's rebel army back in a stunning Union victory. (JOHN CLARK RIDPATH)

even in the ordinary condition of mind, enthusiasm is a potent element with soldiers, but what I saw that day convinced me that if it can be excited from a state of despondency, its power is almost irresistible."[41]

"We must face the other way!" Sheridan shouted to the men as he met them. "We will go back and recover our camp!"[42]

Outside Newtown, which he had to circumvent to avoid the mass of men and wagons clogging the streets, Sheridan happened on Major William McKinley (the future U.S. president), a member of Crook's staff, who rode into Newtown to spread the news of Sheridan's return. Hurrying forward, riding parallel to the valley turnpike, to the west of it, he came up to the rear of General Getty's division of Wright's Corps. That division and the cavalry were the only troops still facing the rebels and resisting them, apparently acting as a rear guard for the rest of the retreating Union army. Their position was about three miles north of the line that Sheridan's troops had held before the Confederate assault.

The cavalry chief, General Torbert, was the first officer to spot Sheridan. He rode up to his commander and announced to him, "My God! I am glad you've come!"[43] Sheridan jumped Rienzi over the rail barricade and continued his ride to the front, waving his hat and urging the troops to follow him. "Men," he shouted, "by God, we'll whip 'em yet!" The troops were suddenly electrified by his rallying calls. "Instantly a mighty revulsion of feeling took place," Major Hazard Stevens of Getty's staff reported. "Hope and confidence returned at a bound…. Now we all burned to attack the enemy, to drive him back, to retrieve our honor and sleep in our old camps that night. And every man knew that Sheridan would do it."[44]

Sheridan met with Wright and told him they would make a stand at the line that Getty and the cavalry were holding. He told Wright to get his staff and have them bring up the troops of his corps and Emory's corps and from the right rear of Getty's troops. Sheridan then rode off to shift Custer's division to the right side of the line, meeting Ricketts' division and Brigadier General Frank Wheaton's division as they marched to the front. The troops cheered when they saw him and rushed to the fray on the double.

"Between half-past and 4 o'clock, I was ready to assail," Sheridan recounted, "and decided to do so by advancing my infantry line in a swinging movement, so as to gain the Valley pike with my right between Middletown and the Belle Grove House; and when the order was passed along, the men pushed steadily forward with enthusiasm and confidence.... My whole line as far as the eye could see was now driving everything before it, from behind trees, stone walls, and all such sheltering obstacles.... Beyond Cedar Creek, at Strasburg, the pike makes a sharp turn to the west toward Fisher's Hill, and here Merritt uniting with Custer, they together fell on the flank of the retreating [rebel] columns, taking many prisoners, wagons, and guns, among the prisoners being Major-General Ramseur, who, mortally wounded, died the next day."[45]

The remarkable turnaround of the fortunes of war concluded in a resounding triumph for Sheridan and his men. Early's broken army, which could not be rallied by its officers, withdrew south to New Market.

The victory had come partly as a gratuity from Early, who had failed to press the attack after the quick success that morning, and from those of Early's troops who had quit the fight so they could loot the Union camps. Early blamed his troops. In his report to General Lee dated October 20 he wrote: "But for their bad conduct I should have defeated Sheridan's whole force." In a second report he wrote: "We had within our grasp a glorious victory, and lost it by the uncontrollable propensity to plunder, in the first place, and the subsequent panic ... which was without sufficient cause."[46] In his memoir, Early wrote, "This was the case of a glorious victory given up by my own troops after they had won it, and it is to be accounted for, on the ground of the partial demoralization caused by the plunder of the enemy's camps, and from the fact that the men undertook to judge for themselves when it was proper to retire.... There was an individuality about the Confederate soldier which caused him to act often in battle according to his own opinions, and thereby impair his own efficiency; and the tempting bait offered by the rich plunder of the camps of the enemy's well-fed and well-clothed troops, was frequently too great for our destitute soldiers, and caused them to pause in the career of victory."[47]

General Gordon, however, offered a different reason for Early's loss of what had promised to be a "glorious" rebel victory. In his memoir he summarized the situation as it had existed at mid-morning:

At little after sunrise we had captured nearly all of the Union artillery; we had scattered in veriest rout two thirds of the Union army.... Only the Sixth [Wright's] Corps of Sheridan's entire force held its ground. It was on the right rear and had been held in reserve. It stood like a granite breakwater, built to beat back the oncoming flood; but it was also doomed unless some marvellous intervention should check the Confederate concentration which was forming against it. That intervention did occur....

General Early came upon the field, and said: "Well, Gordon, this is glory enough for one day. This is the 19th. Precisely one month ago to-day we were going in the opposite direction."

His allusion was to our flight from Winchester on the 19th of September. I replied: "It is very well so far, general; but we have one more blow to strike, and then there will not be left an organized company of infantry in Sheridan's army."

I pointed to the Sixth Corps and explained the movements I had ordered, which I felt sure would compass the capture of that corps — certainly its destruction. When I had finished, he said: "No use in that; they will all go directly."

"That is the Sixth Corps, general. It will not go unless we drive it from the field."

"Yes, it will go too, directly."

My heart went into my boots.... And so it came to pass that the fatal halting, the hesitation, the spasmodic firing, and the isolated movements in the face of the sullen, slow, and orderly retreat of this superb Federal corps, lost us the great opportunity, and converted the brilliant victory of the morning into disastrous defeat in the evening.[48]

When General Grant received the news of the Cedar Creek victory, he ordered another hundred-gun salute, again fired with live ammunition into the streets of Petersburg. And to Washington he fired a telegram urging Sheridan's promotion to major general in the regular Army. Sheridan was notified of the promotion in a congratulatory message from Secretary Stanton: "...for the personal gallantry, military skill, and just confidence in the courage and patriotism of your troops, displayed by you on the 19th day of October at Cedar Run, whereby, under the blessing of Providence, your routed army was reorganized, a great National disaster averted, and a brilliant victory achieved over the rebels for the third time in pitched battle within thirty days, Philip H. Sheridan is appointed a major-general in the United States Army."[49]

Union losses in the battle were put at 5,665, including 644 killed, 3,430 wounded and 1,591 captured or missing. Confederate losses were estimated at 2,910, including 1,860 killed or wounded and 1,050 captured.

By November 10 Early had reassembled enough of his army and received enough reinforcements to make him want to have another go at Sheridan. He again had received intelligence that Sheridan was sending troops to Grant and he decided to move against a reduced Union force. "On the 11th," Early related, "on our approach to Cedar Creek, it was found that the enemy had fallen back towards Winchester, after having fortified and occupied a position on Hupp's Hill subsequently to the battle of Cedar Creek." Some skirmishing followed the reappearance of the rebel force, but Early soon decided against an all-out attack. "Discovering that the enemy continued to fortify his position, and showed no disposition to come out of his lines with his infantry, and not being willing to attack him in his intrenchments, after the reverses I had met with, I determined to retire, as we were beyond the reach of supplies. After dark on the 12th, we moved to Fisher's Hill, and next day returned in the direction of New-Market, where we arrived on the 14th, no effort at pursuit being made."[50]

For Early, the action in the valley was over until winter was past, and he went into winter quarters at Staunton. He began dismantling his army, sending his cavalry off to find feed and forage elsewhere, since there was none available in the valley. His artillery, dependent on horsepower to move its field pieces, was sent off to Lee, the guns that were without horses being hauled away by railroad. "This was a deplorable state of things," Early admitted, "but it could not be avoided, as the horses of the cavalry and artillery would have perished had they been kept in the Valley."[51] A brigade from General Wharton's division was sent away on special assignment. A company of partisan rangers was also detached, as was the infantry battalion commanded by Major Harry Gilmor.

Sheridan was taking advantage of the lull in action against Early by attempting to stop Mosby's continuing depredations. On November 28 he ordered Merritt to destroy Mosby's operations base in northwest Virginia. Merritt's troopers were instructed to "clear the country of forage and subsistence, so as to prevent the guerrillas from being harbored there in the future[,] their destruction or capture being well-nigh impossible, on account of their intimate knowledge of the mountain region." Merritt, Sheridan reported, "carried out his instructions with his usual sagacity and thoroughness, sweeping widely over each side of his general line of march with flankers, who burned the grain and brought in large herds of cattle, hogs and sheep, which were issued to the troops."[52] Mosby and his men remained at large, but on Mosby's initiative in early November, the two sides reached agreement that men captured by either side would be treated humanely as prisoners of war, which ended the executions both sides had been committing.

Sheridan's actions in the Shenandoah River valley finally concluded at Waynesboro, east of Staunton, on the west side of the Blue Ridge, on the road to Charlottesville. Sheridan had been ordered by Grant to destroy the Virginia Central Railroad and the James River canal, capture Lynchburg if practicable, and then either join Sherman or return to Winchester. He had reached Staunton on his southward march on the valley turnpike, at the head of a column of some ten thousand cavalry troopers and artillerymen, plus wagons bearing supplies and equipment, plodding through a cold rain. On March 2 he turned eastward at Staunton after learning that Early had gathered a force and was positioned at Waynesboro. Unwilling to leave such a rebel force at his rear, Sheridan determined to eliminate it. As the head of his column neared Waynesboro, it came upon a line of rebel breastworks on a ridge west of the town. The line was manned by two brigades of infantry that were supported by eleven pieces of artillery and several hundred cavalrymen under the command of General Rosser. It was to be Early's last stand. Custer, heading the lead elements of the Union column, discovered Early's left flank was exposed and sent a dismounted force around it while at the same time hitting the line in a frontal assault. The Union force in front burst through as the flanking troops rolled up the rebel line, scattering the defenders. More than fifteen hundred Confederates, practically the entire rebel force, were taken prisoner, although Early and his generals were not among them, having managed to slip away and flee. From Waynesboro Sheridan continued to move eastward, crossing the Blue Ridge and leaving the valley behind. "This decisive victory," he declared, "closed hostilities in the Shenandoah Valley."[53]

Sheridan had accomplished his mission and a vital part of Grant's strategic plan. The Shenandoah valley would no longer harbor a rebel army or sustain the rebellion.

The Presidential Election,
June 8 to November 8, 1864

The Soldiers' Home in Washington, D.C., was a federal facility established to care for as many two hundred Army veterans, the needy, the infirm, the disabled. Its residents in 1864 included some who had served in the War of 1812 and many who had fought in the Mexican War or the Indian wars. Its buildings stood on a 270-acre tract of wooded land, about three miles northwest of the White House, and one of them was a spacious two-story, stuccoed brick house that was available for use by the president. For Lincoln it became a summer residence, a retreat from the city's swelter and the pressures of life in the executive mansion. He and Mary would move out there in June and stay till November. Around eight-thirty each morning he would ride to the White House, either on horseback or in a barouche, escorted by two dozen or so cavalry troopers with drawn sabers. Some evenings he would work at the White House deep into the night, particularly when Mary was out of town, and on those nights he often would dismiss the troopers and simply mount his horse and ride back to the Soldiers' Home alone, through the dark.

About eleven o'clock on an August evening in 1864 the soldier standing guard at the gate to the grounds of the Soldiers' Home, Private John W. Nichols of the 150th Pennsylvania Infantry Regiment, heard a gunshot in the darkness. Within seconds President Lincoln came riding hard up the curving lane from the main road, hatless. Nichols asked him what had happened, and Lincoln told him that someone had fired a gun, spooking the horse, which sped off so suddenly that Lincoln's tall black hat was jolted from his head. After admitting the president through the gate, Nichols and another guard made their way down the lane to investigate. At the main road they found Lincoln's hat. There were two holes in it, one on either side of the crown, inches above the brim. Bullet holes. The president of the United States had just missed being assassinated.

Private Nichols gave the hat back to Lincoln the next day, whereupon the president told him that he should keep quiet about the incident. At the White House, though, Lincoln mentioned it to Ward Hill Lamon, his former law partner and long-time crony. Lamon was also the U.S. marshal for the District of Columbia and Lincoln's sometime bodyguard. He was one of those who had urged Lincoln to make better use of the security services available to him. Relating the incident to Lamon, the president concluded with the strangely naive comment, "I can't bring myself to believe that anyone has shot at me or will deliberately shoot at me with the deliberate purpose of killing me."[1]

With the war dragging on, its cost in lives and resources mounting — more than 90,000 casualties so far in 1864 — hostility toward Lincoln had spread like a malignancy. He became the personification of the war. Whatever a person felt about the war, he felt something similar about Lincoln. If he was impatient with the progress of the war, he was likely to be disgruntled with Lincoln. If he opposed further war, he was likely to resent Lincoln for not negotiating with the rebels for peace. Of course Lincoln was eager for peace, too, but not so eager as to forgo his two conditions for gaining it — restoration of the Union and abolition of slavery. Among many in the nation, though, Lincoln's conditions were not so important as was a termination of the awful, never ending conflict.

Much of the press reflected the public's dark mood toward Lincoln and its feelings about reelecting him in November. "As President of the United States," the *New York Herald* editorialized, "he must have enough sense to see and acknowledge he has been an egregious failure." The *New York World*, failing to marshal enough caustic words of its own, reprinted some from the Richmond, Virginia *Examiner*: "The fact begins to shine out clear ... that Abraham Lincoln is lost; that he will never be president again ... the obscene ape of Illinois is about to be deposed from the Washington purple, and the White House will echo to his little jokes no more." A Wisconsin newspaper went the farthest, declaring that if Lincoln were re-elected, "We hope that a bold hand will be found to plunge the dagger into the Tyrant's heart for the public welfare."[2]

With such corrosive thoughts lodged in the minds of many, it should have been no surprise to Lincoln that eventually somebody would take a shot at him. His loss of popularity owing to the fortunes of war was aggravated by his new sentiments regarding slavery. In his inaugural address delivered on March 4, 1861 he declared, "I have no purpose, directly or indirectly, to interfere with the institution of slavery in the states where it exists. I believe I have no lawful right to do so, and I have no inclination to do so." He later had vowed that if he could save the Union without freeing any slave or by freeing all slaves, he would do either. The Emancipation Proclamation, which he had issued in January 1863, granting freedom to slaves in certain areas of the South, had reversed his policy and ignited anger in Southerners and their Northern sympathizers alike. When he insisted the South renounce slavery before peace talks could begin, more criticism followed. When he began to maneuver for peace by suggesting terms favorable to the rebels, he brought on more condemnation. When he made known his preference for a soft peace, one without vengeance, Northerners who felt the rebels should pay a harsher price for their rebellion found more fault. Meanwhile, the war went on and on while the public waxed wearier and more frustrated with the passing of each dismal day.

Many political leaders and much of the press bemoaned the public's disapproval and the hopelessness of Lincoln's reelection chances. A previously strong Lincoln supporter, Joseph Medill, editor of the Chicago *Tribune*, forecast that, "Thanks to Mr. Lincoln's blunders & follies we will be kicked out of the White House." Leonard Swett, a Lincoln advisor and aide, after trying to rally support for him among Republican leaders in New York, reported, "Unless material changes can be wrought, Lincoln's election is beyond any possible hope." Henry Raymond, editor of *The New York Times* and chairman of the National Union party, told him in a cheerless, candid letter in late August:

> I am in active correspondence with your staunchest friends in every state and from them all I
> hear but one report. The Tide is setting strongly against us. Hon. E.B. Washburne writes that

"were an election to be held now in Illinois we should be beaten." Mr. Cameron writes that Pennsylvania is against us. Gov. Morton writes that nothing but the most strenuous efforts can carry Indiana. This state [New York], according to the best information I can get, would go 50,000 against us to-morrow. And so of the rest....

Two special causes are assigned for this great reaction in public sentiment — the want of military successes, and the impression in some minds, the fear and suspicion in others, that we are not to have peace in any event under this administration until Slavery is abandoned. In some way or other the suspicion is widely diffused that we can have peace with Union if we would.[3]

When he asked one prominent Republican for his support and was refused, Lincoln told him, "You think I don't know I am going to be beaten, but I do and unless some great change takes place, badly beaten."[4]

His reelection drive had been troubled from the start. A band of severely disgruntled radicals, convinced that Lincoln was so incompetent that he could not be reelected, had pulled away from the Republican party and formed a party of their own, calling it the Radical Democracy party, and on May 31, in Cleveland, they had opened a convention that chose John C. Fremont as their nominee for president and John Cochrane for vice president. Fremont was the embittered general whom Lincoln had fired after he issued an emancipation proclamation of his own as military commander in Missouri, which Lincoln ordered him to rescind lest it stampede Missouri into secession. At the time — August 1861 — Fremont dispatched his wife, Jessie, the daughter of Missouri Senator Thomas Hart Benton, to Washington to protest his dismissal to Lincoln in person. In a fit of huffiness on being rebuffed, Jessie warned Lincoln that her husband was no ordinary soldier, that in a test of political strength, Lincoln would find him a worthy adversary.

The platform that the disaffected radical Republicans came up with included demands for continued prosecution of the war, a constitutional amendment that abolished slavery, authorization for the U.S. Congress to govern the seceded states once the war was won, and the seizure of rebel property for distribution to Union veterans of the war.

Lincoln supporters were facing a Republican defection as well as the public's disenchantment, but the news was not all bad. Democrats, whose nominee would be Lincoln's major opponent, were likewise suffering a schism. Their party was sharply divided between War Democrats on the one hand and Peace Democrats on the other. The War Democrats, the larger of the two factions, didn't like Lincoln, but they did like his stand on continuing the war till it was clearly won and the Union was restored. They were not interested in freeing slaves, however, believing abolition to be an extraneous issue. The object of the war, they argued, was to destroy the rebel armies and restore the Union, while leaving Southerners' rights and property unaffected.

The Peace Democrats advocated an immediate end to the war, at any price. If immediate peace meant a permanent Confederate States of America and permanent slavery, so be it. Let the Union be forever sundered. Peace Democrats and War Democrats alike considered the policies of Lincoln and his administration, particularly the military draft, to be unconstitutional, autocratic and a usurpation of power. Their slogan was "the Constitution as it is, the Union as it was, and the Negroes where they are." Peace Democrats had come to be known as Copperheads, an epithet originated by the Cincinnati *Daily Commercial*, whose editorialist had cast these Southern sympathizers as deadly snakes in the grass, saying they were "like copperheads and rattlesnakes in winter, cold in their stiff and silent coils ... venomous enemies of our government found in our midst."[5]

The Democrats had already settled on the man they would run against Lincoln, even though their convention would not be held until late August. He was another general whom

Lincoln had fired — thirty-seven-year-old George Brinton McClellan. He was the man who had formed a disciplined fighting force from a beaten Union army but had failed to have it fight, causing his removal. He was also the man who was too busy to see fellow West Pointer Ulysses Grant when Grant, as a civilian at the start of the war, came to see him about a job on McClellan's staff. McClellan was then the newly appointed commander of the Army's Department of Ohio, a dapper, power-seeking little man who, some thought, had had his eye on the presidency for a long time and had seen his Army career as a stepping stone to it. Now he would get his chance — and with it, a golden opportunity to get even with the president who had fired him.

Lincoln's first task was to win renomination by his party, which had renamed itself the National Union party, hoping to widen its appeal and attract defecting War Democrats, of whom there were a considerable number, including Major General Benjamin Butler and Senator Andrew Johnson of Tennessee, the only U.S. senator from a seceded state to remain loyal to the Union. Republicans had taken over a pro-Union coalition movement begun by Missouri politico Frank Blair in 1861. Believing Republicans needed to move toward the middle of the range of political feeling, Lincoln had co-opted the movement, and the Republican party had become, after the Union coalition's successes in the 1862 elections, the National Union party. When the loyal Republicans held their convention in June, it did so as the National Union party, with moderate Republicans dominating it.

A corps of politicians was at work rounding up convention delegates for Lincoln, and its work was paying off. Pennsylvania's fifty-two votes were all going for Lincoln. New York's delegation was voting unanimously for Lincoln. Iowa's delegation was unanimous for him, as were Missouri's and Louisiana's. With the nomination beginning to look assured, Lincoln turned his attention to the matter of a vice presidential candidate. Hannibal Hamlin, a senator from Maine, had been his running mate in the 1860 election, giving the ticket an East-West balance. Now he was thinking of a Republican-Democrat balance, and after keeping his confidants guessing for weeks — and sounding out General Butler as a possibility — he settled on someone who would give the ticket not only a Democrat but a Southerner: Andrew Johnson of Tennessee.

Like Lincoln, Johnson had come up the hard way. Born in Raleigh, North Carolina in 1808, he had spent his childhood in poverty following the death of his father when he was three years old. His mother later remarried and apprenticed him to a tailor. With no formal education, he taught himself to read and write. As a young teenager he worked as a tailor in Laurens, South Carolina, but when he was about seventeen, he quit his apprenticeship and moved to Greeneville, Tennessee, where he got a job as a tailor and at age eighteen married sixteen-year-old Eliza McCardle, with whom he eventually had five children.

In Greeneville he discovered his public-speaking skill and entered politics, serving successively as alderman, mayor, state representative, state senator, U.S. representative, governor of Tennessee (from 1853 to 1857) and U.S. senator. In March 1862 Lincoln appointed him military governor of Tennessee and gave him the rank of brigadier general. Johnson believed the Constitution supported the right to own slaves, but he was unwilling to abandon the Union to defend slavery. His sentiments were those of a populist, Jacksonian Democrat, and to explain his anti-secession stand, he asserted, "Damn the negroes! I am fighting those traitorous aristocrats, their masters!"[6]

Johnson was Lincoln's choice, but it would be up to the convention delegates to make him the party's choice. The convention, officially the National Union party convention, was scheduled to open on Tuesday, June 7 at the Front Street Theater in Baltimore. The theater was the best venue the Republican organizers of the convention could find in Baltimore, the more suitable building, the city's convention hall, being unavailable, though unused and vacant, because Lincoln's bitter radical Republican foe, Representative Henry Winter Davis of Maryland, had previously rented the convention hall to deny its use by the delegates preparing to renominate Lincoln.

On the first roll-call vote of the state delegations, held on the second day of the convention, Lincoln received the votes of every delegation except Missouri's. Missouri cast its twenty-two votes for Ulysses Grant (who had already assured Lincoln that he had no interest in running for president). At the end of the roll call, however, Missouri switched its votes to Lincoln, making him the unanimous choice of the convention.

While professing that he had no preference for vice president, Lincoln, who remained in Washington during the convention's proceedings, dispatched his operatives to Baltimore to promote the candidacy of Andrew Johnson. When the time for nominations came, the Indiana delegation nominated Johnson. Pennsylvania's delegation nominated Hamlin, and a part of the New York delegation nominated Daniel S. Dickinson, a New York politician and engaging speaker whose fondness for Biblical allusions and quotations had won him the nickname of "Scripture Dick." The first roll call gave Johnson 200 votes, Hamlin 150 and Dickinson 108. Seven other candidates, who included Benjamin Butler, together received a total of 61 votes. When the delegations then began switching their votes, it became obvious that Johnson was the winner, and a motion was made that his nomination be unanimous, and that motion passed with an explosion of cheering.

The other significant business of the convention was the drafting and approval of the National Union party's platform, on which Lincoln and Johnson would run. A committee headed by Henry Raymond hammered together a platform of eleven planks: (1) To quell the rebellion and punish the rebels; (2) to insist on the rebels' unconditional surrender, without compromise; (3) a Constitutional amendment to end and forever prohibit slavery in the United States; (4) to express the nation's gratitude to the soldiers and sailors of the U.S. armed forces; (5) to approve the measures taken by President Lincoln to preserve the Union; (6) to call for harmony among government officials and their endorsement of the platform; (7) to guarantee the rights and just treatment of Union soldiers, regardless of race, and to prosecute rebel offenses against them; (8) to establish a liberal immigration policy that would encourage foreign immigration; (9) the speedy construction of a transcontinental railroad; (10) a stable economy and responsibility in government spending; (11) enforcement of the Monroe Doctrine, barring new footholds in America by foreign governments.

Committees were appointed to notify Lincoln and Johnson of the convention's decisions, and when that was done, the convention's business was finished, and the delegates adjourned their convention at four-thirty in the afternoon on Wednesday, June 8. The next day, in a turbid formal response to the convention's action, Lincoln concluded by saying, "I have not permitted myself, gentlemen, to conclude that I am the best man in the country, but I am reminded, in this connection, of a story of an old Dutch farmer, who remarked to a companion once that it was not best to swap horses when crossing streams."

Eleven weeks later, on the morning of Monday, August 29, some twelve thousand delegates to the Democrats' national convention began streaming into the Wigwam, the mammoth, two-story wood building beside Lake Michigan in Chicago that had been built four years earlier to house the 1860 Republican convention that nominated Lincoln the first time. Calling the Democrats' convention to order was the party's national chairman, financier and multimillionaire August Belmont of New York, who told the delegates, "The [Lincoln] administration cannot save the Union. We can. Mister Lincoln views many things above the Union. We put the Union first of all. He thinks a proclamation [is] worth more than peace. We think the blood of our people more precious than edicts of the president."[7]

Belmont was sounding the theme of the Democrats' campaign — peace without insistence on the abolition of slavery. When the convention's chairman, New York Governor Horatio Seymour, took over the gavel and the podium, he repeated the theme, telling the massed delegates, "We demand no conditions for the restoration of our Union. We are shackled with no hates, no prejudices, no passions."[8]

On the second day of the convention the committees that had been at work the previous afternoon and evening brought their reports to the floor. At four o'clock that afternoon the resolutions committee presented the platform it had crafted and intended for the convention to adopt. There were only six planks in the platform, all but the second one too agreeable or too vague to cause controversy. Plank No. 1 affirmed the Constitution; No. 3 deplored military interference in recent elections in the border states; No. 4 reaffirmed the Constitution; No. 5 deplored "the shameful disregard" of the Lincoln administration for Union soldiers being held as prisoners of war; and No. 6 pledged sympathy and support to Union soldiers and sailors.

The language of plank No. 2 was not as strong as the Peace Democrats wanted it to be, but it was the best they could get the resolutions committee to agree to. Its author was Clement Vallandigham, the radical Copperhead flag-bearer who as a member of the Ohio delegation had managed to get appointed to the committee. "This convention," the resolution stated, "does explicitly declare ... that after four years of failure to restore the Union by the experiment of war, during which, under the pretence of military necessity ... the Constitution itself has been disregarded in every part ... justice, humanity, liberty, and the public welfare demand that immediate efforts be made for a cessation of hostilities ... that at the earliest practicable moment peace may be restored on the basis of the federal Union of the States."

When the platform was read aloud to the convention delegates, wild cheering erupted from the crowd as the words of the second plank sounded across the vast assembly hall. Peace Democrats were in demonstrable approval while the War Democrats, believing their choice of a nominee to be a hugely more important battle to be fought and won, acceded to the quick-peace plank without a fight.

The platform was adopted by the convention, which then moved on to the business of choosing a presidential candidate. First to be nominated was McClellan, John P. Stockton of New Jersey, McClellan's home state, rising to make the nomination. Others stood to nominate their favorites, among whom were former Connecticut Governor Thomas H. Seymour, a Copperhead, and New York Governor Horatio Seymour, the convention's chairman. McClellan was the overwhelming choice, the first ballot giving him 174 votes to 38 for Thomas Seymour and 12 for Horatio Seymour. By the time the delegations, catching the drift, had switched their votes, and Horatio Seymour had withdrawn his name, McClellan had 202.5 votes to Thomas Seymour's 23.5. The delegates then picked their vice presidential candidate, George H. Pendleton of Ohio, a Peace Democrat. That done, the delegates on August 31 closed their convention.

At his home in Orange, New Jersey, McClellan was promptly notified of the convention's decisions, but he was in no hurry to respond. No doubt totally satisfied with his selection, he was less so with the platform's second plank, the "peace plank." For a week following his notification he stewed about how he should respond. While he stewed, fellow Democrats volunteered advice about what he should do. Many said he should disavow the platform's injunction to immediately initiate negotiations for a ceasefire that would lead to peace. The *New York Evening Post*, agreeing with the sentiments of many War Democrats, in an editorial said, "It is impossible to vote for General McClellan, or any other candidate ... on that Chicago platform."[9] On the other hand, Copperhead leader Vallandigham, author of the contentious plank, wrote to McClellan to tell him that he should accept the platform as it was adopted and should not "insinuate even a little war" into his letter accepting the party's nomination. Vallandigham warned that, "If anything implying war is presented, two hundred thousand men in the West will withdraw their support & may go further still."[10]

McClellan's dilemma was how to seem to repudiate the peace plank, satisfying the War Democrats, while at the same time holding the support of Peace Democrats and Copperheads. The challenge was tough enough for a professional politician and many times more so for a professional soldier. The Democrats waited, along with the rest of the nation, for McClellan's reply, so long in coming that President Lincoln, remembering McClellan's procrastinations on the battlefield, wryly observed to a White House visitor, "Oh, he's entrenching."

Finally, eight days after the Democrats in convention had named him their presidential candidate, and after six drafts to get down just the right wording, McClellan responded in a letter addressed to the committee that had notified him. He released it to the press at midnight on September 8:

> GENTLEMEN: I have the honor to acknowledge receipt of your letter, informing me of my nomination by the Democratic National Convention, recently assembled at Chicago, as their candidate at the next election for President of the United States.
>
> It is unnecessary for me to say to you that this nomination comes to me unsought.
>
> ... The effect of long and varied service in the army, during war and peace, has been to strengthen and make indelible in my mind and heart, the love and reverence for the Union, Constitution, laws and flag of our country, impressed upon me in early youth.... These feelings have thus far guided the course of my life, and must continue to do so to its end.
>
> The existence of more than one Government over the region which once owned our flag is incompatible with the peace, the power and the happiness of the people.
>
> The preservation of our Union was the sole avowed object for which the war was commenced. It should have been conducted for that object only, and in accordance with those principles which I took occasion to declare when in active service.
>
> Thus conducted, the work of reconciliation would have been easy, and we might have reaped the benefits of our many victories on land and sea.
>
> ... The reestablishment of the Union in all its integrity, is, and must continue to be, the indispensable condition in any settlement. So soon as it is clear or even probable, that our present adversaries are ready for peace, upon the basis of the Union, we should exhaust all the resources of statesmanship practised by civilized nations, and taught by the traditions of the American people, consistent with the honor and interests of the country to secure such peace, reestablish the Union and guarantee for the future the constitutional rights of every State. The Union is the one condition of peace — we ask no more.
>
> ... I could not look in the face my gallant comrades of the army and navy, who have survived so many bloody battles, and tell them that their labors and the sacrifices of so many of our slain and wounded brethren had been in vain; that we had abandoned that Union for which we have so often periled our lives.... No peace can be permanent without Union.
>
> As to the other subjects presented in the resolutions of the convention, I need only say that I should seek, in the Constitution of the United States and the laws framed in accordance therewith, the rule of my duty, and the limitations of executive power; endeavor to restore economy in public expenditure, reestablish the supremacy of law, and by the operation of a more vigorous nationality, resume our commanding position among the nations of the earth.

… Believing that the views here expressed are those of the convention and the people you represent, I accept the nomination.

He concluded his letter with an obligatory statement of humility, affirming that he was "conscious of my own weakness" and that he would "seek fervently the guidance of the Ruler of the universe." Such a statement may have come hard to the man who, after being called to Washington by Lincoln and appointed commander of U.S. armies in the summer of 1861, had said to his wife in a letter, "I find myself in a new & Strange position here — Presdt, Cabinet, Genl Winfield Scott & all deferring to me — by some strange operation of magic. I seem to have become the power of the land. I almost think that were I to win some small success now I could become Dictator or anything else that might please me — but nothing of that kind would please me — I won't be Dictator. Admirable self denial."[11]

So now the line was drawn. McClellan and the Democrats would have the U.S. Army and Navy fight to restore the Union, but not to abolish slavery and free four million black Americans from enslavement. Lincoln and the Republicans — the National Union party — would have the U.S. Army and Navy fight not only to restore the Union but to abolish slavery. In neither case, though, would there be peace without the condition of reunion — a mighty blow laid on the peace-now-and-at-any-price Copperheads and Southern sympathizers everywhere.

When Copperhead Clement Vallandigham learned of McClellan's stand, he called off his plans for a speaking tour to campaign for the Democratic ticket and he refused to provide any other support. The Confederacy's ambassador to France, John Slidell, summed up the significance of McClellan's stand: "It effectually destroys the hopes that we had begun to entertain of an early termination of the war and renders the success or failure of his [McClellan's] candidature a matter of comparative indifference."[12] Some Peace Democrats proposed calling the party back into convention either to rewrite their platform or replace their candidate. Nothing came of their objections, though.

The Republicans — the National Union party — had been having their own fits of misgiving, some calling for a new convention, where they could replace Lincoln with someone they thought more electable. Those Republican calls, like those from Peace Democrats, went for nought.

Once McClellan had been nominated, Republican opinion began to shift in Lincoln's favor. Republicans who had wanted to see Lincoln defeated decided now that they didn't want him defeated by McClellan. And by the end of September, there was no other option. On September 22 John Fremont issued a statement saying he was no longer a candidate, possibly the result of a deal arranged by Radical Republicans. On September 23, the day after Fremont withdrew, Lincoln removed from his cabinet Montgomery Blair, the U.S. postmaster general, a long-time foe of Radical Republicans, who hated him for his opposition to abolition and for other offenses. Lincoln immediately chose the former Republican governor of Ohio, William Dennison, to replace Blair.

More than any other event, though, Sherman's capture of Atlanta on September 2 had produced a change in the public's and the press's attitude toward Lincoln. Sherman's victory had returned hope to the nation. In mid–September, after months of despair, there was renewed hope that the awful conflict could be won and ended — and that Lincoln could lead the nation back to peace and union. "Let it be understood how near we are to the end of the Rebellion," Horace Greeley, ordinarily no supporter of Lincoln, editorialized in his *New York Daily Tribune*, "and that no choice is left us now but the instrument put into our hands, and that with that we can and must finish it…. Mr. Lincoln has done seven-eighths of the work after his fashion; there must be vigor and virtue enough left in him to do the other fraction.... We MUST re-elect him, and, God helping us, we WILL."[13]

While feelings were still high from the capture of Atlanta, word came of Sheridan's victory over Jubal Early at Winchester on September 19. A little more than a month before Winchester, on August 5, Farragut had won the Battle of Mobile Bay. Exactly a month *after* Winchester, on October 19, Sheridan at Cedar Creek smashed and sent packing that rebel army that had crossed the Potomac and threatened the U.S. capital. Buoyed by successive victories on land and sea, Lincoln's reelection prospects rose dramatically.

The fight for votes, meanwhile, grew as fierce as the conflicts on the battlefield. Condemning the Democrats' peace plank as traitorous and brushing aside McClellan's repudiation of it, Republican orators and the Republican press kept up a continuous fire against the Democrats' nominee. "We want the builders of that platform to come squarely before the people," *The New York Times* urged. "We want the men who accept it, and who thereby declare that peace should be sought through an immediate cessation of hostilities, instead of through a steady and unwavering and more determined prosecution of the war, to come before the people of this country for their votes." When they did, the *Times* asserted, the Democrats' platform and its makers would be sunk "as speedily as Capt. Winslow sunk the *Alabama*."[14]

A French journalist observing the campaign, Edouard Laboulaye, gave his summary of the significance of the voters' decision. A vote for Lincoln, he said, was a vote for restoring the Union and abolishing slavery. A vote for McClellan was a vote to restore the Union and retain slavery. If McClellan were elected, Laboulaye wrote, "The South will have insanely violated the Constitution, ruined thousands of homes, after which it will come back into the Union, more invulnerable, more arrogant, and more insolent than ever. For the negroes, no hope; for the poor whites, eternal dependence, perpetual debasement; for the rich planters, the intoxication of power and success."[15]

Lincoln's Republican adversaries around the country, ever more aware that it must be Lincoln or McClellan, took the stump not to laud Lincoln but to blast McClellan and the Peace Democrats. Professional politicians of both parties put their organizations in operation, raising money, enlisting voters, manning the stump. Republican efforts — and the turn of the tide of public opinion about Lincoln — were being manifested in state elections, giving more hope to Lincoln and his supporters. In Vermont on September 6 the Union party's candidate for governor and all its candidates for Congress were elected. Voters in Maine a week later reelected their Republican governor. On October 11 Ohio elected as governor Republican Rutherford B. Hayes and swamped the Democratic candidates for Congress. In Indiana the Republican governor, Oliver P. Morton, was reelected, and Republicans gained four congressional seats. Pennsylvania also elected a Republican congressional delegation.

While others were out on the hustings stumping for him, Lincoln kept a low profile, as did McClellan, declining invitations to speak, refusing to campaign, believing, as he said, "it is not customary for one holding the office and being a candidate for reelection, to do so."[16] He figured the voters already knew what his policies were, where he stood on the issues, and there was no need for him to go over them again and again. He further felt there was no need for *ad hominem* attacks on his opponent. His criticism of McClellan's candidacy was only that if McClellan were elected, he would be unable to resist the pressures from Peace Democrats to come to terms with the seceded states and that he would ultimately preside over the dissolution of the Union.

But Lincoln was active behind the scenes, wheeling and dealing with Republican political leaders and office holders, rewarding supporters, punishing those who failed to support him, taking privileges and patronage from them, shutting them out of government access and influence. He also picked the speakers that the Republican speakers' bureau was asked to provide.

Democrats protested that the National Republican Committee had commandeered space in the Capitol. "Committee rooms of the Senate and House of Representatives are filled with clerks," they claimed, "busy in mailing Lincoln documents all over the loyal states."[17] Republican campaign workers were busy in other ways, too, requiring campaign donations from federal employees and from federal contractors, particularly suppliers of war equipment, and requiring editorial support from newspapers that hoped to have campaign ads placed on their pages.

Finally, Election Day arrived — Tuesday, November 8. In the White House, around noon, Lincoln expressed his doubts to his journalist friend Noah Brooks, the Washington correspondent of the *Sacramento Daily Union*, saying that before the Republican convention he had been confident that he would be renominated, but about the election he was "very far from being certain." Early that evening results began trickling in. At six-thirty Lincoln was 1,500 votes ahead in Indianapolis. In Springfield, Illinois, his old hometown, he was ahead by 20 votes. About seven o'clock Lincoln and his secretary John Hay walked through the rain to the War Department to get the news as it came over the War Department's telegraphs. When they arrived, Lincoln was handed a telegram reporting that he had a 10,000-vote lead in Philadelphia. Other news had him 15,000 votes ahead in Baltimore and 5,000 ahead throughout Maryland. Another report had him winning Boston by 5,000 votes. When another telegram came saying he was taking Pennsylvania, Lincoln's happy response was, "As Pennsylvania goes, so goes the Union, they say."

Indeed. Lincoln would go on to win all but three of the twenty-five states that participated in the election, McClellan winning Delaware, Kentucky and New Jersey. The three new states, Kansas, Nevada and West Virginia, participating for the first time, all went for Lincoln. The popular vote totaled 2,218,388, or 55 percent, for Lincoln, and 1,812, 807, or 45 percent, for McClellan. Lincoln's Electoral College vote totaled 212, McClellan's, 21.

Abraham Lincoln, then, would remain president of the United States of America. The nation had spoken. Lincoln was its choice. The widely circulated and widely read *Harper's Weekly* proclaimed the significance of that choice:

> Abraham Lincoln and Andrew Johnson have been elected, by enormous and universal majorities in almost all the States, President and Vice-President of the United States for the next four years. This result is the proclamation of the American people that they are not conquered; that the rebellion is not successful; and that, deeply as they deplore war and its inevitable suffering and loss, yet they have no choice between war and national ruin, and must therefore fight on. In an unfortunate moment for himself General McClellan permitted his name to be used as the symbol of the cowardice and subjugation of his fellow citizens, and from that moment his defeat was a foregone conclusion.
>
> The moral effect of the election both at home and abroad will be of the most impressive character. It shows our foreign enemies that they have nothing to hope from the divisions of this country, while the rebels will see in it the withering and invincible purpose of their loyal fellow citizens, who ask of them nothing but obedience to the Constitution of the United States, and the laws and acts made in pursuance of it. Whenever they shall choose to overthrow the military despotism that holds them fast — whenever they shall see that no great section of this country can, under equal and respected laws, have any permanent and profound interest from all the rest — then they will find that the loyal men of the country are longing to throw down their arms and cement a Union that shall be eternal.

But the lesson of the election is, that every constitutional act and law must be absolutely respected. There must be no threats, no revolts, and no hope of extorting terms by arms. The Constitution is the sole condition of the Government; and if citizens differ as to what is constitutional, that difference must be peacefully and constitutionally settled. This is what the people have declared by four years of war, and this is what they confirm by the re-election of Mr. Lincoln. In himself, notwithstanding his unwearied patience, perfect fidelity, and remarkable sagacity, he is unimportant; but as the representative of the feeling and purpose of the American people he is the most important fact in the world....[18]

For Lincoln, reading the election results as they came into the War Department, the realization that he had won came as a huge relief. "He took it very calmly," Noah Brooks reported. "[He] said that he was free to confess that he felt relieved of suspense and was glad that the verdict of the people was so likely to be clear, full and unmistakable."

He had thought about possible defeat, though, and had imagined what it would be like, how he would feel if defeated. "Being only mortal after all," he told Brooks, "I should have been a little mortified if I had been beaten in a canvass before the people.... [But] that sting would have been more than compensated by the thought that all my official responsibilities were soon to be lifted off my back."[19]

Across the Mississippi,
May to December 1864

Major General Edward Richard Sprigg Canby, the officer who superseded General Banks as U.S. Army commander in Louisiana, was, according to a federal official in New Orleans who knew him, thoroughly a soldier who did his job quietly and without ostentation, in contrast to Banks, "the dancing master." He was described as tall, with a face that made him seem both thoughtful and kind, and a manner that was modest and unassuming.[1] He was forty-six years old and a native of Kentucky.

The army that Canby took over from Banks on May 18, except for General A.J. Smith's troops, who were returned to General Sherman, moved from Simmesport to Morganza, Louisiana, on the west side of the Mississippi, about forty miles above Baton Rouge, and for weeks they idled there in their bivouac on the *batture*, the strip of land between the river's edge and the levee. They drilled and did calisthenics in the relatively cool hours of early morning and in the evening and spent most of the day beneath shade trees or in their tents, trying to escape the heat of Louisiana summer, or else fished or swam in the river to relieve the monotony of camp life. Epidemics of one malady or another periodically swept through the camp — scurvy, dysentery, smallpox — and many succumbed to them, the victims being buried beside the river near the camp.

In late June Canby began a reorganization of his army, taking several regiments from his Thirteenth Corps to form a new division in the Nineteenth Corps, and at the end of June, following orders, he started moving some of his troops to New Orleans, where they boarded transports bound for Virginia to reinforce Grant. Left in Louisiana were the newly formed division, some other infantry, Canby's artillery and his cavalry. In late July Canby shipped two thousand of his troops to Mobile Bay to join the expeditionary force commanded by Major General Gordon Granger in its effort to capture Fort Gaines and Fort Morgan, which it succeeded in doing in August.

In Louisiana, on both sides of the Mississippi, the actions of Union troops were now limited mostly to scattered engagements with guerrillas and with minor Confederate raiding parties. The Red River Expedition had sapped the strength of the rebels as well as that of the Union force, and a period of relative quiet ensued.

In Alexandria, thirty-eight-year-old Lieutenant General Richard Taylor, who had led the Confederate troops that defeated Banks's army at Mansfield, saving Louisiana from Union occupation, stressed over his failure to capture Banks's army, blaming his superior, General Edmund Kirby Smith, for the failure. He contended that Smith, commander of the Confederate army's Trans-Mississippi Department, had abruptly detached from him his best troops, Major General John G. Walker's Texas Division, to meet the Union threat in Arkansas, depriving Taylor of a substantial, perhaps critical, part of his force. Smith grew so aggravated with Taylor's continuing criticism that on June 10 he relieved him as commander of the military District of West Louisiana, which Taylor in disgust had requested. Smith ordered Taylor to Natchitoches, Louisiana to await further orders.

An aristocratic, once wealthy owner of a large Louisiana sugar-cane plantation, which he had inherited from his father, former U.S. President Zachary Taylor, Taylor had good political connections. He was active in Louisiana politics and had been a delegate to the Democratic national convention in 1860. His sister was Jefferson Davis's first wife. After a six-week wait in Natchitoches, Taylor was appointed by Davis as commander of the Confederate army's Department of Alabama, Mississippi and East Louisiana. To report for his new assignment, he had to get across the Mississippi River, no easy feat, since the river was under the constant watch of Union gunboats. "On a dark night," Taylor related, "in a small canoe, with horses swimming alongside, I got over without attracting the attention of a gunboat anchored a short distance below."[2] Awaiting him was additional notable service in the rebel army on the east side of the Mississippi, but the rebel cause on the west side of the river had lost him.

Kirby Smith turned his attention toward Arkansas and Missouri while Canby, following instructions from President Lincoln, turned *his* attention from military matters to policing the scandalous cotton trade in Louisiana. Trying to make a contribution to the rebels' war effort, Smith decided to marshal the forces available to him, attack Major General Frederick Steele's weak Union army that was occupying Arkansas, destroy it and then push into Missouri, hoping to capture Missouri and turn it into a Confederate state, even at this late stage of the war. Missouri's Confederate governor-in-exile, Thomas C. Reynolds, eager to return to the Union-occupied Missouri capital, Jefferson City, and reinstate himself, was urging Smith to get such a campaign started.

Earlier, on May 19, Smith had ordered Major General Sterling Price to stockpile supplies and gather intelligence about the Union forces in preparation for an invasion of Missouri. Price was the Mexican War veteran, former Missouri militia commander and onetime Missouri governor who now commanded the Confederate forces in Arkansas from his headquarters in Camden. Smith had no intention of having Price lead the invasion, though, having no confidence in Price's abilities. In a letter to President Davis, Smith had said that Price was not capable of "organizing, disciplining, nor operating an army," but that his "name and popularity would be a strong element of success in an advance on Missouri."[3] Until he became exasperated with Richard Taylor, Smith had wanted Taylor to lead the Missouri offensive. Now Taylor was unavailable.

Smith's plan was to launch the campaign in mid–August, when he was sure that the troops would be in condition and wagons and horses would be available and Missouri's corn crop was ripe enough to provide the invaders with food and forage. Price, however, wanted to move right away. Nevertheless, Smith held up, even while Missouri Governor Reynolds was growing impatient for action.

On July 18 Reynolds wrote to Price proposing a cavalry raid as a possible alternative to the major offensive that Smith had in mind. Reynolds asked Price what he thought of the idea and would he be willing to take command of a cavalry raid. Price wrote back to Reynolds saying, "If it is not General Smith's purpose to concentrate the troops and take possession of the Arkansas [River] Valley I would like to take command of the expedition.... My opinion is that the people of Missouri are ready for a general uprising and that the time was never more propitious for an advance of our forces into Missouri."[4]

Smith, too, received a letter from Reynolds, as well as one from Price, both urging a meeting to discuss the desirability of a cavalry raid into Missouri. The three men met at Smith's headquarters in Shreveport in early August, and having reached agreement, Smith on August 4 ordered Price to "make immediate arrangements for a movement into Missouri, with the entire cavalry force of your district."[5]

The selection of a commander for the raid was left up in the air. Like Smith, Reynolds was highly doubtful of Price's ability to bring off a successful raid, but with no good alternative, he settled on Price to lead the expedition, asking Smith to be sure to send with Price the best available division and brigade commanders and an efficient staff. Smith reluctantly agreed to put Price in command. When he briefed Price on the assignment, Smith told him that the enlistment of new men into the Confederate army was to be his main task. He was to make the capture of St. Louis his first objective in accomplishing that task. Possession of St. Louis, Smith said, "will do more toward rallying Missourians to your standard than the possession of any other point."[6]

In the event he was forced to retreat from Missouri, Smith stated, Price was to withdraw through Kansas and Indian Territory [Oklahoma], seizing all the horses, mules, cattle and everything else of military value that his troops could find as they returned to Arkansas. And he was to bring back as many recruits as could be found. Smith furthermore instructed Price that he was to see to it that his men committed no "wanton acts of destruction and devastation."[7]

Smith told Price to organize his army into three divisions, to be commanded by Major General James F. Fagan, Major General John S. Marmaduke and Major General Joseph O. Shelby, the officers on whom Smith apparently intended the expedition's success to depend.

Price left his Camden headquarters in southwest Arkansas on August 28 and the next day reached Princeton, thirty miles north of Camden, where he took command of two of the divisions of his army, Fagan's and Marmaduke's. On August 30 he and his troops began their northward trek, all the while kept under Union surveillance. Price sent detachments to make demonstrations against Fort Smith and Little Rock, keeping General Steele guessing about his intentions, and then crossed the Arkansas River at Dardanelle, about half-way between Little Rock and Fort Smith. From there Price's column marched eastward and reached Pocahontas, in northeast Arkansas, fifteen miles from the Missouri line, on September 15, having passed through Steele's Union lines without interference.

At Pocahontas the divisions of Fagan and Marmaduke were joined by Shelby's troops, bringing Price's strength up to about twelve thousand men. Price then organized his force, which he called the Army of Missouri, into three cavalry divisions, as instructed by Smith. Many of Shelby's men were recent conscripts and other raw recruits enlisted by Shelby during the summer. About four thousand of them had no weapons, and many who did had only long-barreled muskets, instead of carbines, that were impractical for use by mounted troops. About a thousand of the new recruits had no horses. Many were poorly clothed and ill shod. Regardless, Price took them all into his army, intending to arm the weaponless, mount the horseless and clothe and shod the uniformless with whatever he could capture from Union forces. Shelby's new enlistees, already organized into regiments, would be distributed throughout the three divisions.

After four days spent organizing, equipping and otherwise preparing, the Army of Missouri set out from Pocahontas on the morning of September 19, marching in three parallel columns, their plodding pace set by the trains of slow-moving supply wagons and the foot speed of unmounted men. Price, a hulking three hundred pounds, was making the march in an ambulance drawn by four mules. Before the day was done, the motley rebel army crossed into Missouri.

At St. Louis Major General William Rosecrans commanded the U.S. Army's Department of the Missouri, comprising about ten thousand troops, mostly militiamen, scattered around the state, at Jefferson City, Rolla, Springfield and other points as well as St. Louis. In early September he received intelligence on Price's army and asked Washington for reinforcements. Washington promptly responded by sending him 4,500 veteran troops from Major General A.J. Smith's division, men of Sherman's army who earlier had been lent to Banks for his Red River expedition. While headed down the Mississippi to rejoin Sherman they were redirected up to St. Louis. Not long after Price's columns crossed into Missouri, units of Rosecrans' militiamen confronted Price's lead elements and took several prisoners. From them Rosecrans learned the size of the rebel army — larger than he had thought — and that it was marching straight to St. Louis. He immediately began to mass a force, including A.J. Smith's troops, to meet the imminent threat. On September 24 Rosecrans received a report that rebel units had been spotted just below Pilot Knob, about eighty-five miles south of St. Louis.

Also on the 24th, at Fredericktown, about twenty miles east of Pilot Knob, Price got a report from spies that there was a fifteen-hundred-man garrison posted at Pilot Knob. He was also told that there were eight thousand troops under A.J. Smith posted south of St. Louis. Those two items of news gave him pause. To press on toward St. Louis, ignoring the garrison at Pilot Knob, would leave a considerable enemy force in his rear. What was more, he could see that taking St. Louis was going to be more than he had bargained for. He called a war council with his three division commanders and asked their advice. Fagan and Marmaduke advised taking care of the Pilot Knob garrison first. Shelby advised bypassing Pilot Knob and continuing on to St. Louis. Price decided to move against Pilot Knob. His decision was probably based not only on his reluctance to leave a substantial Union force at his rear but also on his new doubt that he could take St. Louis and an assumption that he could more easily seize arms, horses and supplies at Pilot Knob than at St. Louis.

In early morning on the 26th he sent Shelby's troopers northward to tear up the tracks and burn the bridges of the Iron Mountain Railroad above Pilot Knob to stall reinforcements from St. Louis, and he set Fagan's and Marmaduke's divisions into motion, headed for Arcadia, about two miles south of Pilot Knob. As leading elements of Fagan's division neared Arcadia late that afternoon they first ran into skirmishers and then heavy resistance from reinforced Union pickets, who drove Fagan's troopers back, inflicting heavy casualties as they did so. Darkness and rain halted the fight, and Price made plans to renew the attack the next day, Tuesday, September 27.

Wiley Britton, a trooper serving in the U.S. Sixth Kansas Cavalry Regiment and a contemporary historian, recorded the engagement from the Union perspective:

> Rosecrans [upon learning of the Confederates' presence near Pilot Knob] at once commenced collecting his forces to meet and check the enemy. General Thomas Ewing, Jr., was in command of the District of South-east Missouri. Pilot Knob, near Iron Mountain, was a port of

importance, with fortifications of considerable strength, and was on Price's direct line of march to St. Louis, which was only eighty-six miles distant....

Ewing had 1051 men at that post, which were only enough to man the works. Having got his troops and artillery all up, Price opened the attack on the fort at daylight on the 27th, and kept it up all day with great resolution. But Ewing's well-served artillery of eleven pieces and his thousand small-arms repulsed every assault made by the Confederates. When night came, however, Ewing was satisfied that he could not hold out another day against the superior attacking force, and he determined to evacuate the fort. Shortly after midnight his troops marched out, and a few moments later his magazine was blown up, and the ammunition which could not be taken along was destroyed [by Ewing]. Ewing then marched with his force and joined the troops engaged in the defense of St. Louis and of Jefferson City.[8]

Fagan reportedly had told Price the Union works at Pilot Knob could be taken by his division alone in twenty minutes. Marmaduke had bettered that boast by saying that with the support of a couple of artillery pieces he could take the fort in less than twenty minutes. Fagan had about four thousand men; Marmaduke had about three thousand. They faced one thousand defenders.

The two artillery pieces that Marmaduke had asked for were quickly silenced by the return fire of Ewing's artillery when the attack began. The guns of the fort swept the field as the rebels, Marmaduke's and Fagan's, advanced on foot. The dead and the wounded virtually covered the ground. The new men whom Shelby had recruited quickly sought to escape the hail of shot and shell by lying in a creek bed, refusing to be rallied and to resume the advance despite shouts and curses from their officers. Most of Marmaduke's men stayed in the creek bed until night came and let them withdraw in darkness. Fagan and Price together managed to rally Fagan's troopers, and when the units had been re formed, Fagan urged Price to let him make another attack. Price shook his head and refused, having decided to wait till the next day to try again.

When they heard it, the explosion of the Union ammunition dump was interpreted by Price's troops as an accident, and it was not until eight o'clock the next morning, September 28, that Price learned what the explosion had actually meant and that Ewing had slipped away during the night. The Battle of Pilot Knob, the first test of the Army of Missouri's prowess, was over. It had cost Price's army more than a thousand casualties. Ewing and his little garrison of defenders had lost seventy-three men. Price had won a tactical victory and held the field, but he had gained little or nothing to compensate for his losses.

Although he ordered Marmaduke to begin an immediate pursuit of the fleeing bluecoats, it was nearly noon by the time Marmaduke could get his men remounted and ready to begin the chase. About ten miles north of Pilot Knob Ewing's troops ran headlong into advance units of Shelby's division, which was on its way south to rejoin Price's army after destroying sections of the Iron Mountain Railroad tracks. The rebel advance unit was quickly routed, and Ewing captured a number of its men. From a prisoner Ewing learned that Potosi, about ten miles north of his present position, the town where he had hoped to find refuge, had been occupied by Shelby's troops and that A.J. Smith's Union force had pulled back from its position at Mineral Point, just east of Potosi. Needing a new escape route to safety, Ewing turned his troops westward from Caledonia, heading toward Rolla, some seventy-five miles distant.

Marmaduke's division continued the chase and at Caledonia, after Ewing had turned westward, Marmaduke was joined by Shelby's division in the pursuit. Although Marmaduke's and Shelby's troops were on horseback and Ewing's men were on foot, the Confederates struggled to catch up and when they finally did, about thirty-five miles from Rolla, they found Ewing waiting for them behind hastily erected fortifications. Marmaduke and Shelby thought about attacking, but at last decided against it since Ewing's force would no longer be a threat to Price's army. They turned and rode off to rejoin Price.

By now Price had concluded that if his Army of Missouri couldn't overcome the garrison at Pilot Knob, there wasn't much chance it would succeed against the much stouter defenses at St. Louis, and so he abandoned his plans to attack St. Louis. On September 29 he moved out from Pilot Knob and headed toward Jefferson City.

The rebels encountered only slight resistance as they trooped some one hundred and thirty miles across the rolling hills of central Missouri, living off the land as they advanced, raiding and pillaging in areas largely sympathetic to the South. Missouri's Confederate governor, Thomas Reynolds, who was riding with Price's army, bent on returning to Jefferson City, described the conduct of Price's men as they marched through Missouri:

> It would take a volume to describe the acts of outrage; neither station, age, nor sex was any protection. Southern men and women were as little spared as Unionists; the elegant mansion of General Robert E. Lee's accomplished niece and the cabin of the negro were alike ransacked; John Deane, the first civilian ever made a State prisoner by Mr. Lincoln's [Missouri] Government, had his watch and money robbed from him in broad day, as unceremoniously as the German merchant at Frederickstown [*sic*] was forced, a pistol at his ear, to surrender his concealed greenback ... the clothes of a poor man's infant were as attractive spoil as the merchant's silk and calico or the curtain from the rich man's parlor ... jeweled rings forced from the fingers of delicate maidens whose brothers were fighting in Georgia in Cockrell's Confederate Missouri brigade.[9]

Price's column was moving at a rate of fifteen miles a day, a sluggish pace for cavalry. In its train were more than five hundred slow-moving wagons—many of them suspected of being loaded with officers' plunder—as well as a horde of camp followers described in one account as a "rabble of deadheads, stragglers and stolen negroes on stolen horses."[10] On October 6 the column ran into serious opposition and had to fight its way across a branch of the Osage River about six miles from Jefferson City. In the exchange of fire, rebel Colonel David Shanks, a brigade commander in Shelby's division, was mortally wounded, and Brigadier General M. Jeff Thompson, who had recently been released from U.S. custody in a prisoner exchange, took over Shanks' command.

The next day, October 7, Price and his troops occupied the hills that overlook Jefferson City from the south side. What he saw discouraged him. The Union forces had built five forts with connecting rifle pits between them, and they were fully manned behind forbidding *chevaux-de-frise*. Again remembering Pilot Knob, Price decided against an assault. He deployed and made a feint with a brief artillery bombardment, but soon withdrew back to his position in the hills. In the early morning of October 8 he put his troops on the road again, headed now for Boonville, about fifty miles northwest of Jefferson City.

As Price left Jefferson City, Major General Alfred Pleasonton was arriving to take command of U.S. troops there. Pleasonton was the swaggering little forty-year-old dandy, an unmarried ladies' man, who had commanded the Army of the Potomac's cavalry and had gained such a reputation for creating fanciful reports of action that he became known as the Knight of Romance. Grant had replaced him with Phil Sheridan and had sent Pleasonton to Missouri. Learning that Price had set out toward Boonville, Pleasonton ordered Brigadier General John Sanborn to take off after him with a force of four thousand cavalry troopers, but with instructions not to engage Price in battle without first being reinforced from St. Louis and Springfield. Pleasonton himself stayed behind in Jefferson City to take care of administrative duties.

Price's column, to which now was attached a motley throng of camp followers that included looters, vandals and assorted ruffians, reached Boonville on October 10 and was at first warmly welcomed by the town's pro-Confederate populace. The residents soon discovered, though, as their visitors resorted to their wanton ways, what sort of guests they had welcomed. General Thompson ruefully commented on the army's mob behavior: "What was done and not done there I do not propose to relate [,] as I had only to try to control my own Brigade, to save their reputation from the demoralization which was seizing the army. The plunder of Boonville nearly completed this demoralization [,] for many officers and men loaded themselves, their horses and wagons with 'their rights' and now wanted to turn Southward and save what they had."[11] Price, although having forbidden looting and having at times punished offenders, seemed callous now and, according to Governor Reynolds, connived at the riotous behavior of his troops. "The hotel occupied as General Price's own headquarters," Reynolds claimed, "was the scene of public drunken revelry by night."[12]

While at Boonville Price worked on increasing the size of his army, recruiting and conscripting new men and boys (all white males between ages 17 and 50 were subject to Confederate conscription) and taking on the services of the notorious guerrilla bands of William Quantrill and William T. "Bloody Bill" Anderson.

On October 13, after Sanborn's Union cavalrymen had approached to within several miles of Boonville, Price moved on, continuing westward. Easy conquests followed at Glasgow, where the rebels captured the 550-man Union garrison and a large quantity of weapons, and Sedalia, where a Union militia unit surrendered to Jeff Thompson. The rebel army moved on to Marshall. On the 18th it reached Waverly, General Shelby's hometown, where Price's army linked up with Quantrill's guerrillas. Price gave them scouting duties and assigned them to Shelby's division. On the 19th the army marched from Waverly to Lexington, encountered Union scouts and drove them back through the town, but by their presence he had received a warning that Union troops were in front of him. He was to learn that Major General Samuel Ryan Curtis, commander of the U.S. Army's Department of Kansas, was entering the fight. Curtis had fifteen thousand troops, militia and volunteers, poised just across the Missouri-Kansas line, outside Kansas City.

Speeding up his march, Price pushed on toward Independence, on the eastern outskirts of Kansas City. On the 21st, about five miles east of Independence, he ran up against the troops of Major General James G. Blunt, some two thousand men from Curtis's command. They had formed a defensive line behind stone walls on the west side of the Little Blue River, opposing Price's passage across the river. The outnumbered Union force, armed with repeating rifles, put up a stubborn defense against Marmaduke's troops, but at last had to give ground when Price ordered Shelby's division into the battle. Threatened with encirclement, Blunt withdrew to Independence.

Blunt formed a new defensive line just west of Independence on the west bank of the Big Blue River. Determined to hold up Price's march until help from Rosecrans could arrive, Curtis put all the troops he had into that new line, including most of the Kansas militia, who had at first balked at crossing into Missouri but now realized Price's army was threatening Kansans on its westward march. Help for Curtis and Blunt's forces was indeed on the way. Pleasonton's cavalry was hurrying from Jefferson City to catch up with Price's army, and A.J. Smith's infantry was on the march from Lexington.

The Confederates, led by Price in person, dismounted and stormed across the Big Blue, climbed the west bank and drove off the defenders. Shelby's troopers then poured across the river, routing several Kansas militia regiments. Then Pleasanton's cavalry arrived. Trooper Wiley Britton summarized the action:

> On the 22d, just as Curtis's troops were being driven from the Big Blue back upon the State line and Kansas City, Pleasonton's cavalry came up and attacked the rear of Price's army, east of Independence, and routed it and drove it in great disorder through the town.... The night of the 22d Price's army encamped on the west side of the Big Blue, just south of Westport. Pleasonton's cavalry encamped that night around and in the neighborhood of Independence, east of the Big Blue. Curtis's forces were encamped from Kansas City to Westport and along the State line west of Westport.
>
> At daylight on the 23d the columns of Pleasonton began to move west, and those of Curtis to move south, and in a short time afterward they became warmly engaged with the Confederates, who were drawn up in the line of battle two and a half miles south of Westport. The opposing armies fought over an area of five or six square miles, and at some points the fighting was furious. At times there were as many as forty or fifty guns throwing shot and shell and grape and canister. About the middle of the afternoon Price's lines began to give way, and by sundown the entire Confederate army was in full retreat southward along the State line, closely pursued by the victorious Federal forces.[13]

To cover their retreat the rebel troops set the broad expanse of prairie grass on fire, creating a huge screen of smoke that obscured them. The Battle of Westport was over, concluded by the Army of Missouri's southward flight. More than thirty thousand troops, of both sides, had been involved in the battle, making it one of the war's largest engagements west of the Mississippi. Each side had suffered approximately fifteen hundred casualties.

From Westport the rebel army moved toward Fort Scott as swiftly as its wagon train would allow, discarding impedimenta as it proceeded down the extreme eastern side of Kansas, leaving beside the road broken-down wagons, caissons, harnesses, muskets, debris of many kinds and sick and wounded and others too starved, too weary to go any farther, content to lie on the ground and wait to be captured by the pursuing Union troopers. As the Confederates struggled southward, many of them took time to exact revenge on the Kansans whose country they were passing through, burning barns, houses, crops, haystacks, farm implements, sending clouds of smoke into the sky, making their path unmistakable to their pursuers.

Reaching the Marais des Cygnes River late on October 24, Price halted his army and made camp on a high ridge on the north side of the river, near the Trading Post settlement, his troops having to pitch tents in a pouring rain. At dawn on the 25th the Union cavalry struck, opening with an artillery bombardment of the rebel position and following with a cavalry attack. Price quickly ordered his men to hurry across the rain-swollen river, their withdrawal, with wagons, being covered by Fagan's troopers. Held off by the rebels' rear guard, the Union cavalrymen were unable to prevent the escape of Price's army, although about one hundred Confederates were taken prisoner and two artillery pieces were captured. The chase then resumed.

About six miles farther down the road, at Mine Creek, the dogged pursuers caught up with the rear of the rebel column again. The brigades of Colonel John F. Phillips and Lieutenant Colonel Frederick Benteen (later to gain fame with George Custer's Seventh Cavalry at Little Bighorn), faced the Confederates' mounted rear guard as Price's precious wagons forded the creek. The troopers of Marmaduke's and Fagan's divisions formed up in a line three ranks deep and eight hundred yards long, extending across the open prairie, Fagan's men on the west side of the road, Marmaduke's on the east, with eight artillery pieces supporting, four in the center and two on each flank. Phillips' and Benteen's combined force comprised about twenty-five hundred men, less than half of the massed rebel force they were facing.

Benteen ordered the charge, and with bugles sounding, the blue-coated troopers galloped forward, through a volley of rifle fire that dropped some from their saddles but failed to slow the charge. Benteen's brigade hit Marmaduke's center, and Phillips' brigade struck Fagan's left flank. The Confederates' long-barreled muzzle-loaders proved completely inadequate for the close-quarter fight, no match for the Union troopers' breech-loading carbines, revolvers and sabers. Marmaduke's men bolted and fled in a rout. Hundreds of rebels, unable to get across the creek fast enough, raised their hands in surrender. Marmaduke was one of those taken prisoner. Brigadier General William Cabell was another.

Fagan was trying desperately to hold his men together on his side of the line, but they hurriedly withdrew to a hillock behind them, to the south, and attempted to make a stand. Benteen's cavalrymen, supported by artillery, charged up at them and scattered them, sending them dashing for the Fort Scott road. Price, who had been with the forward elements of the column, arrived on the scene late — too late to stanch the massive flight of rebel troopers escaping the onslaught. Soon the battlefield was emptied of Confederate survivors of the attacks.

"The scene after the battle was terrifying," a resident of the area remarked later. "Fully 300 horses horribly mangled were running and snorting and trampling the dead and wounded. Their blood had drenched them and added to the ghastliness of it all."[14]

The Army of Missouri's casualties were estimated at twelve hundred, counting dead and wounded. Union casualties were put at one hundred.

The third engagement of the day, October 25, lay ahead. Shelby's troopers tried valiantly to impede the Union pursuit, stopping periodically to turn and fire on the pursuers, then galloping off again to close up on the rebel column as it hastened southward. Late that afternoon the column approached the Marmiton River, and again the wagon train struggled to make a crossing, forcing another stand to stave off a Union assault and prevent capture of the wagons. Price, ever protective of the wagons, rallied about a thousand of his dispirited troops and with them on a hastily assembled defensive line behind a stone fence he placed a mass of his unarmed recruits. Two brigades of Pleasonton's cavalrymen, under the command of Brigadier General John H. McNeil, came pounding up to the rebel position. McNeil, who had been put off once before by the appearance of large numbers of the unarmed recruits, not knowing they had no weapons, now again was deterred by their mere appearance and failed to launch an all-out assault (which would have probably smashed Price's army once and for all). Instead, his men spent the next two hours skirmishing and fending off a gallant but vain charge by the rebels of Colonel Charles H. Tyler's brigade. By then it was night, and Price withdrew the remains of his army into the darkness. McNeil, his own men and horses exhausted, made no attempt to follow further. The Union troopers rode off to Fort Scott to rest and recover.

Once he had crossed the Marmiton, apparently deciding it was time to speed up his flight to safety, Price ordered the destruction of all wagons that were not absolutely necessary and those drawn by ailing teams, together comprising about a third of the train. They were all set ablaze, the night sky suddenly illumined by the flames. At about two o'clock in the morning on October 26, his starving, woebegone army and its caravan hit the road again. The soldiers trudged through the bitter cold of an early winter, through rain and sleet and snow. Ill clothed to meet such conditions, many of the marchers developed pneumonia and fell by the wayside unattended. Desertions multiplied.

Confederate Maj. Gen. Sterling Price. In the autumn of 1864 he commanded the rebel forces in northern Arkansas and was assigned the task of leading a raid into Missouri. Its failure concluded organized Confederate resistance west of the Mississippi. (LIBRARY OF CONGRESS)

On November 1 the column reached Canehill, in northwest Arkansas, and Price ordered a halt to rest the men. While there, whole regiments of Arkansans deserted, and Price was powerless to stop or retrieve them. The march resumed on November 4, now headed westward into Indian Territory, pursued at a day's distance by Curtis's U.S. troopers, who on November 8 finally gave up the grueling chase. Price's men plodded on. Major John N. Edwards of Shelby's division chronicled the trek and detailed the conditions:

After crossing the Arkansas the worst stage of misery came upon the army, and the sufferings were intense. Horses died by thousands; the few wagons were abandoned almost without exception; the sick had no medicines and the healthy ate no food; the army had no organization and the subordinate officers no hope. Bitter freezing weather added terrors to the route and weakness to the emaciated, staggering column. Small-pox came at last, as the natural consequence, and hundreds fell out by the wayside to perish without help and be devoured by coyotes without a burial.[15]

On November 10 Price furloughed the Arkansas brigades, essentially dismissing them from his army. On November 11 he gave Shelby permission to drop out of the column and encamp for a rest on the Canadian River. Price and the few troops that remained with him continued their escape into Texas and later into Mexico.

The Army of Missouri, once the symbol of hope for the Confederate cause in Missouri and beyond, was now a useless, broken derelict. Battle losses, desertions, sickness and starvation had reduced it to a fraction of its original strength. On December 15 Price had but thirty-five hundred men, only a third of whom were armed, and fewer than half were mounted. Most, if not all, were, as one account put it, so ill, exhausted and demoralized that they were "not in a fit condition to fight any body of men."[16] On the west side of the Mississippi the Confederacy's fighters were now no longer a force, no more a threat.

22

Hood's Last Campaign, October 15, 1864, to January 23, 1865

General Hood mostly kept to his command post while his Confederate army bivouacked in the picturesque valley at Cross Roads, Georgia, about nine miles south of LaFayette, in the extreme northwest corner of the state. He was pondering what to do next with the forty thousand troops of his Army of Tennessee. Since withdrawing from Atlanta in early September, Hood had been harassing Sherman's communications line that extended down from Chattanooga, hoping, as Hood said, "by manoeuvers to draw Sherman back into the mountains, then beat him in battle, and at least regain our lost territory."[1]

Sherman, though, had no intention of being drawn into the mountains of Tennessee, believing Georgia was where he could most injure the Confederate cause and do the most to help end the war. Although he was turning his back on Hood's annoying raids, he was not ignoring him altogether. He was sending General Thomas and the 35,000-man Army of the Cumberland to Nashville in case Hood launched a campaign that threatened the Union hold on Tennessee.

After "serious thought and perplexity," as he said, Hood decided what *he* would do. "I conceived the plan of marching into Tennessee with the hope to establish our line eventually in Kentucky...," he wrote. "I decided to make provision for twenty days' supply of rations in the haversacks and wagons; to order a heavy reserve of artillery to accompany the army, in order to overcome any serious opposition by the Federal gun-boats; to cross the Tennessee at or near Guntersville, and again destroy Sherman's communications at Stevenson and Bridgeport; to move upon Thomas and Schofield, and to attempt to rout and capture their army before it could reach Nashville. I intended then to march upon that city, where I would supply the army and re-enforce it, if possible, by accessions from Tennessee."[2]

Hood's scheme swelled with bigger ambitions once, as he hoped, Nashville had been captured. He detailed his plan: "I was imbued with the belief that I could accomplish this feat, afterward march north-east, pass the Cumberland River at some crossing where the gun-boats, if too formidable at other points, were unable to interfere, then move into Kentucky....

"In this position I could threaten Cincinnati, and recruit the army from Kentucky and

209

Tennessee…. If Sherman should cut loose and move south — as I then believed he would do after I left his front without previously worsting him in battle — I would occupy at Richmond, Kentucky, a position of superior advantage, as Sherman, upon his arrival at the seacoast, would be forced to go on board ship, and, after a long detour by water and land, repair to the defense of Kentucky and Ohio or march direct to the support of Grant.

"If he should return to confront my forces, or follow me directly from Georgia into Tennessee and Kentucky, I hoped then to be in condition to offer battle; and, if blessed with victory, to send reenforcements to General Lee, in Virginia, or to march through the gaps in the Cumberland Mountains and attack Grant in rear…. If, on the other hand, he [Sherman] should march to join Grant, I could pass through the Cumberland gaps to Petersburg, and attack Grant in rear at least two weeks before he, Sherman, could render him assistance.

"This move, I believed, would defeat Grant, and allow General Lee, in command of our combined armies, to march upon Washington or turn upon and annihilate Sherman. Such is the plan," Hood declared, "which during the 15th and 16th [of October], as we lay in bivouac near Lafayette [sic], I maturely considered, and determined to carry out."[3]

Hood's army broke camp and moved out toward Guntersville, Alabama on October 17. Stopping at Gadsden, Alabama on the way, Hood met with General Beauregard, commander of the Confederate army's Division of the West, Hood's nominal commanding officer. He went over his plans with Beauregard, who then conferred with Hood's corps commanders, Lieutenant General Stephen D. Lee, Lieutenant General Alexander P. Stewart and Major General Benjamin F. Cheatham, and after deliberations that consumed two days, Beauregard gave his approval to Hood's plan.

On October 22, with twenty days' rations in their haversacks and on wagons, as planned, Hood's troops began their northwestward march from Gadsden, using all the roads that led to Guntersville, on the Tennessee River. Instead of crossing the river at Guntersville, however, Hood decided to march farther downriver, where his intended rendezvous with the cavalry of Major General Nathan Bedford Forrest could be more easily accomplished. Forrest was in Jackson, Tennessee, after raids in west Tennessee, and was being delayed by high water in the Tennessee River, which prevented his crossing it.

By October 31 the bulk of Hood's army had reached Tuscumbia, Alabama, and there beside the banks of the Tennessee Hood encamped his troops for three weeks while they waited for repairs to the railroad that was needed to bring up their supplies. On November 14 Forrest, with some ten thousand cavalrymen, at last arrived, and on the 15th Hood's army began crossing the river to Florence, Alabama. On November 19 Forrest's cavalry began moving northward toward Nashville, and on the 21st Hood's infantry moved out behind them, marching in three parallel columns, Cheatham's corps on the left, Lee's in the center, and Stewart's on the right, all screened by Forrest's cavalrymen.

Noticing Hood's movements and his growing menace to middle Tennessee, Sherman had ordered General Schofield to take the Army of the Ohio's Twenty-third Corps and hurry to reinforce Thomas. Schofield's orders were to watch Hood's movements, but to avoid a battle if possible. He was to fall back toward Nashville and fight the Confederates as he fell back, so as to slow Hood's advance until reinforcements from Thomas in Nashville could reach him.

On November 14 the first of Schofield's divisions reached Pulaski, Tennessee, about twenty miles above the Alabama line, where it joined forces with the U.S. Fourth Corps, commanded by Major General David S. Stanley, which Sherman had also sent to reinforce

Thomas. The combined Union force, of which Schofield assumed command, totaled something less than eighteen thousand men.[4]

Southwest of Pulaski, Hood's army, which, augmented by Forrest's cavalry, now amounted to more than fifty thousand troops, was marching northeastward on a course that would take them past the right flank of Schofield's south-facing position at Pulaski and put them in Schofield's rear. Hood's progress was being slowed by miserable weather — rain, snow, hail, freezing temperatures — and the sodden dirt roads that turned into clammy quagmires during thaws, but by November 20 the advancing rebel army had made enough progress to set off alarms at Thomas's Nashville headquarters, and Thomas on that date ordered Schofield to prepare to fall back to Columbia, Tennessee, on the Duck River, thirty miles above Pulaski.

On November 22 the van of Hood's column reached Lawrenceburg, sixteen miles due west of Pulaski, on a road that ran direct to Columbia. That same day, Schofield ordered two divisions — those of Major General Jacob D. Cox and Brigadier General George D. Wagner — to march to Lynnville, about halfway between Pulaski and Columbia. The next day, November 23, Schofield ordered his two other divisions, under the command of General Stanley, to move out with the wagon trains and follow Cox's and Wagner's divisions.

The moves were made just in time. When Cox was within nine miles of Columbia, early in the morning on the 24th, he was roused by sounds of gunfire to the west. Quickly marching his troops on a road that led south of Columbia, he reached the road from Lawrenceburg just in time for his infantry to confront Forrest's cavalry as it attacked Colonel Horace Caprin's brigade. In another hour Forrest would have been in possession of the crossings of Duck River, and the only line of communication with Nashville would have been in the hands of the rebels.[5]

Cox's troops checked the advance of Forrest's cavalrymen and by seven o'clock that morning they had formed a defensive line behind a creek. With the arrival of Stanley's corps three hours later a strong position was established, covering the south side of Columbia. Schofield then decided Hood would probably attempt to flank the Union position and he began preparing a fall-back line. Schofield ordered Cox to shift two brigades of his division to the north side of Duck River during the night of the 25th to cover the pontoon bridge that had just been laid across the river, and in daylight on the 26th Cox's troops threw up breastworks and dug rifle pits to entrench skirmishers along the river bank.

Hood delayed an all-out assault on the Union position until all of his troops were in place. Once his infantry had been massed, he began crossing the river above Columbia.

Schofield responded by moving his entire army to the north side of the river during the night of the 27th, destroying the pontoon bridge and partly destroying the railway bridge as he withdrew. He wired Thomas to assure him that he was holding on as long as he could. Early in the morning of the 28th Thomas wired back and instructed Schofield to withdraw to Franklin and there make a stand above the Harpeth River.

Hood laid a pontoon bridge across Duck River during the night of the 28th, and Cheatham and Stewart started moving their corps across the river at dawn on the 29th. The rest of Hood's troops followed them.

When reports of the Confederates' crossing reached Schofield, he ordered General Stanley to move the divisions of General Wagner and Major General Nathan Kimball to the town of Spring Hill, about ten miles northeast of Columbia on the road to Nashville, taking the wagon trains and the reserve artillery with them. In less than thirty minutes they were on the way.

From Spring Hill roads radiated out in all directions. If Hood were able to possess Spring Hill, he would not only block the road to Nashville but roads to everywhere else. Schofield would be trapped. Before the sun rose to reveal a bright autumn morning on November 29 Confederate Major General Patrick Cleburne's division, Cheatham's lead division, was making its way across Duck River at Davis's Ford, about five miles east of Columbia, moving toward Spring Hill in hot pursuit, the rest of Hood's force following.

Just before noon, as General Stanley's troops neared Spring Hill, Stanley received a report that a division of Forrest's cavalry was approaching from the east. Stanley ordered his troops to move into the town on the double and occupy it. The lead brigade deployed as it advanced, and as the other brigades came up, all were deployed to form a semicircle stretching from the railroad station north of the town to a point east of it, including a knoll that commanded all the approaches from the east. Most of the artillery was placed on a rise south of the town. The trains were parked within the semicircle. The three brigades of Major General Luther P. Bradley's division, numbering fewer than four thousand men, took their position on the knoll on the east side of the line, virtually isolated from the rest of Schofield's force. By then it was about 4 P.M.

No sooner were Bradley's men in place than they were struck by Cleburne's division. Two attacks were repulsed, with heavy casualties, but a third assault drove Bradley's troops back and inflicted a disabling wound on Bradley. As Bradley's men fell back in the fading light of the short November day, the rebels started across a broad cornfield in pursuit, and when they did, eight Union guns emplaced on the knoll opened on them with case shot, dropping the Confederates in their tracks, scattering them and stopping their advance as night enveloped the field. Confederate reinforcements, men of the division of Major General John C. Brown, took a position to the right of Cleburne's division and were to join Cleburne's troops in a new assault, but Brown never launched his attack, deterred by reports of a Union threat on his right and the failure of Forrest's cavalry to show up to protect his flank. It was 6:15 P.M. by the time Brown and his corps commander, General Cheatham, were able to confer, and by then the battlefield was in total darkness.

Schofield arrived at Spring Hill about 7 P.M., in the company of Major General Thomas Ruger's division and a brigade commanded by Major General Walter C. Whitaker. About 11 P.M. Cox arrived with his division. Soon after that, Schofield discovered that the road to Franklin was open, that despite his expectations, he had found no rebel troops blocking their way. By one o'clock on the morning of November 30 Schofield's army was on the move again, marching toward Franklin, Cox's division leading the way, a train of wagons five miles long trailing behind him, while Major General Thomas J. Wood's division marched to his right to fend off possible rebel attacks from the east. In the fight at Spring Hill Schofield had suffered an estimated 350 casualties; Hood's casualties were put at 500.

Hood's plan had been to move Cheatham's and Stewart's corps around the eastern flank of Schofield's force to block its escape. Through failures to communicate his intentions, however, the Confederate attack amounted to not much more than the assaults on the knoll. He was outraged upon later learning that Schofield was escaping. He wailed over what he believed to be Cheatham's failure: "It was reported to me about this hour [around midnight on November 29] that the enemy was marching along the road [to Franklin], almost under the light of the camp-fires of the main body of the army…. The Federals, with immense wagon-trains, were permitted to march by us the remainder of the night, within gunshot of our lines…. Had I dreamed for one moment that Cheatham would have failed to give battle, or at least to take position across the pike and force the enemy to assault him, I would myself have ridden to the front and led the troops into action...."[6]

Instead of riding to the front and leading the troops into action, however, Hood, according to one account, had had a big dinner at the house where he had set up his headquarters, had gone through several rounds of drinks with fellow officers and had gone to bed at nine o'clock on the night of the 29th. It turned out that Cheatham, who received most of the blame for not attacking and thus allowing Schofield's force to escape, had never received orders to launch an attack during the night.

The town of Franklin is about eighteen miles above Spring Hill on the road to Nashville, situated in a bend of the Harpeth River, which bordered the town on the north and east. The road from Columbia and, about five hundred yards to the east of it, the Nashville & Decatur Railroad, running parallel, entered Franklin from the south side and bent slightly to the northeast as they passed through the town and crossed the river, the train tracks traversing a deep cut before reaching the railroad bridge, which was intact. The pike bridge had been partly destroyed. On a hill on the north side of the river, commanding the pike, the railroad, the pike bridge and the railroad bridge, was an earthworks fortification called Fort Granger, which had been built a year earlier. Entering the town from the southwest and merging with the Nashville pike at the center of town was the Carter's Creek pike.

Schofield's column made it to Franklin without serious interference, being only slightly harassed by Forrest's cavalry, which made several attacks on the wagon train without much effect. Cox's division, at the head of the column, reached the south side of town before dawn on November 30 and, following orders, Cox moved his troops to either side of the roadway and halted to allow the wagons to pass into the town.

While the wagons passed, Cox and his staff took advantage of the break and entered the house of a family named Carter, on a rise west of the pike, to sleep on the floor for a few minutes' rest. Schofield later arrived at the Carter house, complaining that the pontoons he had requested from Nashville had not arrived. He needed them to cross the Harpeth River, the pike bridge having been burned. If Hood attacked before a bridge could be improvised, Schofield would have to defend against an attack with the river at his back. He ordered Cox to assume command of both divisions of the Twenty-third Corps and told him to have his men begin entrenching as daylight came, forming a line extending left and right from the hillock on which the Carter house stood.

The line of entrenchments, with its center in front of the Carter house on the Columbia pike, stretched from the railroad cut at the river, southeast of the town, around the south and west sides of the town, and back to the river on the northwest side of Franklin. "The Twenty-third Corps immediately began the building of breastworks," General Cox related in his account of the action, "and by noon [of the 30th] a strong intrenchment had been completed.... An old cotton gin ... furnished timber for head-logs, and upon the knoll near the railway, at the Carter house, and in one or two other places, where the slope was sufficient, strong epaulements for artillery were constructed inside of and somewhat higher than the infantry parapet. At the Columbia turnpike the full width of the road was left open, for it was all needed to enable the doubled lines of wagons and artillery to pass, and a retrenchment crossing the road a few rods in rear was built to command the opening and its approach."[7]

Siding and other lumber were torn from nearby buildings to provide planking for the railroad bridge across the Harpeth so that the bridge could be used by wagons. The piles that had supported the burned pike bridge were found to be sound enough to rebuild upon. They were sawn off just above the surface of the river, and crossbeams and planking were hammered into place to provide a second bridge over the river. By noon both bridges had been made usable for Schofield's column.

The Twenty-third Corps' artillery had not waited for the bridge repairs, but had forded the river near the pike bridge. Its batteries were positioned in the earthworks fort on the north bank, where they would soon be joined by batteries of the Fourth Corps. As the remainder of Schofield's army arrived at Franklin, the units were directed into place along the curving line of entrenchments that girdled the south and west sides of town.

The Union line faced an open plain on the south, which was bounded by a range of high hills, through which ran the road from Spring Hill and Columbia. The only obstructions to the view from the entrenchments were a grove of locust trees between the Columbia pike and the Carter's Creek pike, some farm buildings and some fruit orchards.

In front of the line of entrenchments on the south a four-foot-wide, two-foot-deep ditch was dug, and the Union infantrymen were posted behind a four-foot-high parapet of dirt and fence rails that rose behind the ditch. The riflemen stood in a trench four feet deep and they would fire on the approaching enemy through gaps between the rails of the parapet. In front of the southeast section of the line thick Osage-orange bushes provided a natural abatis, which was thinned out just enough to allow riflemen to fire on advancing troops. Forward of the line, about a half a mile, were posted two infantry brigades of Wagner's division, those of Colonel John Q. Lane and Colonel Joseph Conrad.[8] General Wood's division of the Fourth Corps and Schofield's entire cavalry, commanded by Major General James Harrison Wilson, were positioned north of the Harpeth to guard against a possible flanking attempt. Schofield's plan was to hold his position at Franklin until the rebuilt bridges were ready for his troops and wagon train to cross the river. By 3 P.M. on the 30th the wagons were across, and Schofield intended to have the troops across by six if the Confederates had not attacked by then.

Hood had reached the field below Franklin around one o'clock that afternoon. Standing on Winstead Hill, two miles south of the bristling Union line, he gazed out on the ground before him, considering his next move. Forrest, who had arrived before Hood and had already scouted out the Union position, advised against a frontal assault, saying the Union line was so strong that it couldn't be overcome without heavy losses. Hood disagreed. "I do not think the Federals will stand strong pressure from the front," he told Forrest, apparently thinking Schofield was merely making a rear-guard attempt to delay the Confederates while the rest of his army continued on to Nashville. "The show of force they are making is a feint ... to hold me back from a more vigorous pursuit."[9]

Cheatham, already in Hood's doghouse for his inactivity at Spring Hill, also advised against a frontal assault. "I do not like the looks of this fight," he told Hood. "The enemy has an excellent position and is well fortified." Hood brushed aside the objections, saying he would rather fight here where Union forces had had only a few hours to dig in than fight them in Nashville where, he said, they've been strengthening themselves for three years.[10]

Forrest told Hood, "If you will give me one strong division of infantry with my cavalry, I will ... flank the Federals from their works within two hours' time."[11] Hood refused, later explaining that "the nature of the [Union] position was such as to render it inexpedient to attempt any further flanking movements."[12]

Hood had made up his mind. "I ... decided, before the enemy would be able to reach his stronghold at Nashville, to make that same afternoon another and final effort to overtake and rout him, and drive him into the Big Harpeth River at Franklin."[13] He described the battle's opening moves:

It was about 3 P.M. when Lieutenant-General Stewart moved to the right of the pike and began to establish his position in front of the enemy. Major-General Cheatham's corps as it arrived in turn, filed off to the left of the road, and was also disposed in line of battle…. General Forrest was ordered to post cavalry on both flanks, and, if the assault proved successful, to complete the ruin of the enemy by capturing those who attempted to escape in the direction of Nashville. Lee's corps, as it arrived, was held in reserve, owing to the lateness of the hour and my inability, consequently, to post it on the extreme left….

Shortly afterward Cheatham and Stewart reported all in readiness for action, and received orders to drive the enemy from his position into the river at all hazards. About that time Cleburne returned, and, expressing himself with an enthusiasm which he had never before betrayed in our intercourse, said, "General, I am ready, and have more hope in the final success of our cause than I have had at any time since the first gun was fired." I replied, "God grant it!" He turned and moved at once toward the head of his division; a few moments thereafter he was lost to my sight in the tumult of battle…. [W]ithin forty minutes … he lay lifeless upon or near the breastworks of the foe.[14]

Patrick Cleburne, killed by a shot in the chest, was a handsome, gallant, thirty-six-year-old Irish immigrant, the son of a physician, who had once served in the British army and had come to America to escape the Irish famine in 1849. He had made a new life for himself in Helena, Arkansas, working in a pharmacy and joining a militia company that elected him its captain, becoming a colonel and regimental commander after the war broke out, and eventually rising to division commander and the rank of major general. Waiting for him and for the end of the conflict that separated them was his fiancée, Susan Tarleton of Mobile, who now, like so many other civilian victims of the war, would never see her loved one again.

The Union troops in the fortified line south of Franklin had got their first warning of the rebel assault around two o'clock, when across the expanse of field they noticed movement on the distant hills, the waving of signal flags and troops deploying in line of battle.

General Cox, an eyewitness to the battle, described the action:

It was now four o'clock, and to the amazement of the thousands who were watching them, Wagner's infantry [the two brigades that had been posted forward of the fortified line] opened fire. There was a rattling fusillade for a few moments, Cleburne and Brown were checked for an instant, but the Confederate forces passed the flanks of Lane and Conrad [the two forward brigades], to right and left, a rush and a yell followed, and the two hapless brigades came streaming to the rear in a disorganized crowd, running rapidly to reach the parapets behind them…. A few moments later, the head of the flying [Confederate] mass was seen swarming over the works at the turnpike, and orders were sent for all reserves to charge…. Neither Colonel White … nor Colonel Opdycke waited for the word to charge, but were in motion before the order could reach them…. Opdycke made part of his brigade oblique to the left till clear of obstacles, and they then charged headlong upon the enemy … and Strickland's brigade rallying with them, the Confederates were driven back here also; but that the gap was open longer here than on the left, was proven by the enemy's dead who were found fifty yards within the lines.

Stanley [though sick], forgetting his illness, had mounted his horse at the first sound of the cannonade, and the commandants of the two corps met on the turnpike just as Opdycke and his men were rushing to the front. Four guns, which had been placed a few yards to the left of the road, were in the enemy's hands, and were loaded with canister. These were turned upon the flank of Reilly's line, but the frightened horses had run off with the ammunition chests which contained the primers, and while the captors were unsuccessfully trying to fire the pieces, the reserve was upon them…. There was a few minutes' fierce melee, but … all of the men in gray who were inside the parapet were dead or prisoners. Yet the successive lines of assailants charging the works allowed no respite…. Our men, who had been driven back from the line, rallied by officers of all grades, returned to their posts, mingling with those who were there, making a wall three or four deep, those in rear loading the muskets for those who were firing. While rallying these men Stanley was wounded, his horse was shot under him, and he was reluctantly persuaded to return to his quarters for surgical help.

Farther to the right ... the Confederates of Brown's division held the outside of the parapet, so that when their comrades were driven back they were able to prevent our men from reaching it again. These, seizing upon fences and such material as came to hand, made a new barricade within about twenty-five yards of the first, and across the narrow interval the battle raged with most persistent fierceness.... Officers and men had been conscious that with the centre broken, nothing but superhuman exertions could keep one wing, at least, of the little army from being driven into the river. They were equal to the occasion and they saved the day.[15]

A much briefer account of the battle was provided by General Hood:

The two corps [Cheatham's and Stewart's] advanced in battle array at about 4 P.M., and soon swept away the first line of the Federals, who were driven back upon the main line. At this moment resounded a concentrated roar of musketry ... which now proclaimed that the possession of Nashville was once more dependent upon the fortunes of war. The conflict continued to rage with intense fury; our troops succeeded in breaking the main line at one or more points, capturing and turning some of the guns on their opponents.

Just as this critical moment of the battle, a brigade of the enemy, reported to have been Stanley's [Opdycke's brigade, of Stanley's corps] gallantly charged, and restored the Federal line, capturing at the same time about one thousand of our troops within the intrenchments. Still the ground was obstinately contested, and at several points upon the immediate sides of the breastworks the combatants endeavored to use the musket upon one another, by inverting and raising it perpendicularly, in order to fire; neither antagonist, at this juncture, was able to retreat without almost a certainty of death. It was reported that soldiers were even dragged from one side of the breastworks to the other by men reaching over hurriedly and seizing their enemy by the hair or the collar.

Just before dark Edward Johnson's division of Lee's corps moved gallantly to the support of Cheatham; although it made a desperate charge and succeeded in capturing three stand of colors, it did not effect a permanent breach in the line of the enemy. Unfortunately, the two remaining divisions could not become engaged owing to the obscurity of night. The struggle continued with more or less violence until 9 P.M., when skirmishing and much desultory firing followed until about 3 A.M. the ensuing morning. The enemy then withdrew, leaving his dead and wounded upon the field. Thus terminated one of the fiercest conflicts of the war.[16]

The battle had cost Hood 6,252 casualties, including 1,750 killed and 3,800 wounded, plus those captured or reported missing. Among the dead were six generals — Cleburne, John C. Carter, John Adams, States Rights Gist, Hiram Granbury, and Otho Strahl. Wounded were generals John C. Brown, Francis Cockrell, Zachariah Deas, Arthur Manigault, Thomas M. Scott and Jacob H. Sharp. Captured was Brigadier General George W. Gordon. The Confederate casualties also included fifty-five regimental commanders.

Union losses totaled 2,326, including 189 killed, 1,033 wounded and 1,104 missing or captured. General Cox noted in his account of the battle that more than one thousand of the Union losses were from the two brigades of Wagner's division that had been mistakenly and disastrously posted in front of the fortified line.

While Schofield's stubborn fighters slipped away and resumed their march toward Nashville, Hood was left wondering what to do with his diminished force, which the Battle of Franklin had reduced by nearly a quarter. "After the failure of my cherished plan to crush Schofield's army before it reached its strongly fortified position around Nashville," Hood wrote later, "I remained with an effective force of only 23,053." That force, he said, comprised 18,342 infantry, 2,405 artillery and 2,306 cavalry. "I was therefore well aware of our inability to attack the Federals in their new stronghold with any hope of success.... I knew equally well that in the absence of the prestige of complete victory I could not venture with my small force to cross the Cumberland River into Kentucky, without first receiving reenforcements from the Trans-Mississippi Department."[17] He was still clinging to the futile hope that he would receive troops from Texas — an unlikely event, not only because of the unavailability of additional rebel troops but because the Union Navy controlled the Mississippi River with its gunboats, barring any large-scale Confederate crossing.

"I could not afford to turn southward," Hood explained, "unless for the special purpose of forming a junction with the expected reenforcements from Texas, and with the avowed intention to march back again upon Nashville. In truth, our army was in that condition which rendered it more judicious the men should face a decisive issue rather than renounce the honor of their cause, without having made a last and manful effort to lift up the sinking fortunes of the Confederacy.

"I therefore determined to move upon Nashville, to intrench, to accept the chances of reenforcements from Texas, and, even at the risk of an attack in the meantime by overwhelming numbers, to adopt the only feasible means of defeating the enemy with my own reduced numbers., viz., to await his attack, and, if favored by success, to follow him into his works.... In accordance with these convictions I ordered the army to move forward on the 1st of December in the direction of Nashville...."[18]

Meanwhile, General Thomas, at his Nashville headquarters, was pondering the task of destroying Hood's army. Schofield's troops arrived at Nashville on the morning of Thursday, December 1, and Thomas merged them into the force he was patiently gathering there, including General A.J. Smith's three divisions, nearly twelve thousand men, which had arrived from Missouri in the past two days, and 5,200 troops under Major General James B. Steedman, mostly men who had been on their way to join or rejoin Sherman in Georgia but were too late to do so before he left Atlanta. They were brought to Nashville from Chattanooga by rail. Thomas had as well the approximately six thousand infantry and artillery and three thousand cavalry already posted at Nashville. In addition, there was the makeshift division composed of men, including civilian employees, assigned to the chief quartermaster, Brigadier General J.L. Donaldson, some ten thousand men. Thomas further had about eight thousand troops, under the command of Major General Lovell Rousseau, in a heavily fortified position at Murfreesboro, about thirty miles southeast of Nashville. Thomas was assembling as many reinforcements as could be had.

Hood reached the outskirts of Nashville on December 2 and, while Thomas's troops merely watched, the Confederates promptly formed a line of battle, taking up positions on a line of hills in front of the Union defenses. They then began digging in, building a four-mile-long line of earthworks. Hood placed Stephen Lee's corps in the center of the line, which stretched across the Franklin pike; Stewart's corps was posted on Lee's left, and Cheatham's corps occupied the right. Forrest's cavalrymen were posted on the flanks, between the line of works and the Cumberland River, which flows past the north side of the city.

The Union position was a seven-mile-long, semicircular line of entrenchments that extended around the city on the east, south and west, the north side being protected by the river and the Union gunboats stationed there. Clockwise around the semicircle, from the left side of the line, were Steedman's division, Schofield's corps, Wood's corps and Smith's corps, which had been redesignated as the Detachment Army of the Tennessee. Wilson's cavalry was posted on the north side of the Cumberland. All waited, mysteriously, while Hood's troops got into place.

In City Point, Virginia, keeping up with the situation in Tennessee, the Union Army's general in chief was growing ever more impatient. Since Thomas's force outnumbered Hood's army three to one, Grant couldn't understand why Thomas didn't show more aggressiveness and swiftly attack and overpower Hood. "He [Thomas] had troops enough even to annihilate him in the open field," Grant complained. "To me his delay was unaccountable — sitting there and permitting himself to be invested, so that, in the end, to raise the siege he would have to fight the enemy strongly posted behind fortifications."[19]

Grant allowed that the weather at Nashville was terrible, with freezing rain that coated the ground with slippery ice, but he insisted that the situation was urgent and demanded immediate action. "I was afraid," he explained, "that the enemy would find means of moving, elude Thomas and manage to get north of the Cumberland River. If he did this, I apprehended most serious results from the campaign in the North, and was afraid we might even have to send troops from the East to head him off if he got there, General Thomas's movements being always so deliberate and so slow, though effective in defence."[20]

Grant began bombarding Thomas with telegraph messages, prodding him to take action. "If Hood is permitted to remain quietly about Nashville, you will lose all the road back to Chattanooga and possibly have to abandon the line of the Tennessee," he wrote to Thomas on December 2. In a second message that same day he told Thomas, "You will now suffer incalculable injury upon your railroads if Hood is not speedily disposed of. Put forth therefore every possible exertion to attain this end. Should you get him to retreating give him no peace." On December 5 he told him, "Is there not danger [of] Forrest moving down the Cumberland to where he can cross it? It seems to me whilst you should be getting up your cavalry as rapidly as possible to look after Forrest, Hood should be attacked where he is." On December 6 he issued Thomas a direct order: "Attack Hood at once and wait no longer for a remnant of your cavalry. There is great danger of delay resulting in a campaign back to the Ohio River."[21]

Even so, Thomas still delayed. On December 8 Grant told him, "It looks to me evident the enemy are trying to cross the Cumberland River, and are scattered. Why not attack at once? ... Now is one of the finest opportunities ever presented of destroying one of the three armies of the enemy. If destroyed he never can replace it. Use the means at your command, and you can do this and cause a rejoicing that will resound from one end of the land to the other."[22]

Nevertheless, the delay continued. On December 11 Grant again wired Thomas, telling him, "If you delay attack longer the mortifying spectacle will be witnessed of a rebel army moving for the Ohio River, and you will be forced to act, accepting such weather as you find. Let there be no further delay.... I am in hopes of receiving a dispatch from you to-day announcing that you have moved. Delay no longer for weather or reinforcements."[23]

Finally Grant ran out of tolerance. He warned Thomas that unless he acted promptly, he would be relieved of command. "He replied that he was very sorry," Grant related, "but he would move as soon as he could." Grant now had had enough. He ordered Major General John "Black Jack" Logan to go to Nashville and relieve Thomas. He told Logan not to reveal the order relieving Thomas until he reached Nashville and if Thomas by then had launched the attack, Logan should not deliver the order but notify Grant by telegraph. After Logan had left Grant's headquarters and was on his way, Grant decided he should go himself to relieve Thomas and he soon departed to do so.

He got as far as Washington, D.C. He ended his journey there after hearing the latest news from Thomas. After two weeks of delay, the maddeningly cautious general was at last moving against Hood.

About 8 A.M. on December 15, warm air having thawed the ground's icy covering, Steedman's infantry — including two black brigades — and artillery struck the right side of Hood's line, between the Franklin pike and the railroad just east of it, in a vigorous feint that kept Cheatham's corps occupied throughout the day while the corps of Smith and Wood, plus a dismounted cavalry brigade commanded by Brigadier General Edward Hatch, hit the rebels' left flank, Stewart's section of the rebel line, with the main attack. The Union force wheeled to the left to line up parallel with the Hillsboro pike, which paralleled the Granny White pike and the Franklin pike, east of the Hillsboro pike. They then pressed forward.

By noon the Union troops had reached the Hillsboro pike, and Hood responded to the growing threat by quickly shifting Lee's units from the center to reinforce Stewart. By one-thirty Stewart's position along Hillsboro pike could no longer be held against the Union attackers, and Stewart's troops broke and fell back toward the Granny White pike, where darkness overtook them and their attackers and where they spent much of the night regrouping and digging in for a new assault Hood knew would be coming the next day. To prepare for a new assault, Hood established a new, two-mile-long line in the Brentwood hills, from Shy's Hill on his left to Overton's Hill at his center, covering his two main escape routes to the south — the Granny White pike and the Franklin pike. He further reinforced his left by moving units of Cheatham's corps from the right side of his line.

The next day, Friday, December 16, Thomas's army spent most of the morning adjusting to the new Confederate position. Thomas's plan this time was again to attack Hood's right, using Schofield's corps to drive back Cheatham, and to strike a mighty blow on Hood's left again while Wilson took his cavalry around to the rear of the rebel line to block a retreat. The assault was launched at noon, and Wood and Steedman made little progress against Lee on Overton's Hill, but around 4 P.M. Cheatham's corps, on Shy's Hill, was routed and driven to the rear. Wood then struck Lee again and drove him from Overton's Hill as darkness crept across the field, accompanied by a heavy rain. "In those few minutes," Colonel Henry Stone, a

Confederate Gen. John Bell Hood. His grandiose plan to recapture central Tennessee and invade Kentucky and Ohio ended at the Battle of Nashville. (LIBRARY OF CONGRESS)

member of Thomas's staff, reported, "an army was changed into a mob, and the whole structure of the rebellion in the South-west, with all its possibilities, was utterly overthrown."[24]

Hood described the battle's conclusion: "The enemy ... massed a body of men — apparently one division — at the base of this mound [Overton's Hill], and, under the fire of artillery, which prevented our men from raising their heads above the breastworks, made a sudden and gallant charge up to and over our intrenchments. Our line, thus pierced, gave way; soon thereafter it broke at all points, and I beheld for the first and only time a Confederate army abandon the field in confusion. I was seated upon my horse not far in rear when the breach was effected, and soon discovered that all hope to rally the troops was vain."[25]

Hood hastily herded his shattered army through the darkness and pouring rain and retreated toward Franklin, streaming down the Franklin pike, continuing his flight and eventually recrossing the Tennessee River at Bainbridge, Alabama, near Florence. With them they took the tatters of Hood's grandiose scheme to sweep through Tennessee and Kentucky and threaten Ohio, then attack Grant from the rear, allowing Lee a victory and rescuing the Confederacy.

The Battle of Nashville proved to be the high-water mark of rebel action in the West and the last of major Confederate offensive campaigns anywhere. It had cost the rebel army an estimated six thousand men —1,500 killed or wounded and 4,500 missing or captured — while Union losses amounted to 387 killed, 2,558 wounded and 112 missing or captured. When the remnant of Hood's army — the Army of Tennessee that Joe Johnston had so judiciously shepherded — reached the end of its retreat at Tupelo, Mississippi in early January, its survivors barely totaled ten thousand men, about a quarter of what its strength had been when Hood took command of it. General Grant could strike it from his list of foes. It would not be a major threat again.

Neither would John Bell Hood. On January 13, a week after reaching Tupelo, he wired the Confederate secretary of war, asking to be relieved of command. President Davis granted his request. "I bade farewell to the Army of Tennessee on the 23d of January, 1865," Hood recounted, "after having served with it somewhat in excess of eleven months, and having performed my duties to the utmost of my ability."[26] He was given no other command.

The March to the Sea,
November 16 to December 21, 1864

On a beautiful, clear, sunny day, with a nip in the north Georgia November air, Sherman's army started out on its monumental march. To the practiced observer, though, the assembled troops didn't seem soldiers marching as to war. They seemed more a mighty army on its way to a good time. Their commander, the mercurial General Sherman, noticed in them, in the officers as well as in the men, an unusual feeling of exhilaration, a devil-may-care attitude. It was, Sherman perceived, "a feeling of something to come, vague and undefined, still [,] full of venture and intense interest."[1]

That's the way they might have been expected to feel. They were beginning a history-making, controversy-causing, unprecedented, three-hundred-mile march from the Appalachian foothills, through Georgia's rich farmlands, through its piney woods, all the way to the marshlands of its low country and then at last to the glistening shore of the Atlantic. It was, as history has recorded it, Sherman's March to the Sea.

From its very conception it was intended to inflict havoc and hardship on the people of Georgia. "Until we can repopulate Georgia," Sherman told Grant, seeking his approval for the proposed march, "it is useless to occupy it, but the utter destruction of its roads, houses and people will cripple their military resources.... I can make this march, and make Georgia howl!"[2]

To those who had known him well and for a long time, Sherman had shown little or no evidence of a hateful or vengeful spirit that would drive him to the wantonness that lay ahead. As a youngster, according to his brother John, who was a U.S. senator from Ohio, Sherman was "quiet in his manner and easily moved by sympathy or affection."[3] As a cadet at West Point he had a reputation as a high-spirited mischief maker, a fun guy to be around. William Rosecrans, a fellow cadet who, like Sherman, later became a major general, described him as "one of the most popular and brightest fellows in the academy." Rosecrans remembered him as "a bright-eyed, red-headed fellow, who was always prepared for a lark of any kind.... He was ... one of those fellows who used to go down to Benny Havens's [tavern] of the dark of night at the risk of expulsion to eat oysters and have a good time."[4] Dennis Mahan, one of the academy's most distinguished professors, remembered him well. "If he wasn't at work he was in mischief," Mahan recalled. "If, while explaining something to his class at the black-board, I heard any slight disturbance, denoting some fun, I was seldom wrong, in turning round, in holding up my finger to Mr. Sherman. But one was more than repaid for any slight annoyance of this kind, by his irrepressible good nature...."[5]

As a new lieutenant posted in South Carolina Sherman had exhibited a charming manner that had won him many friends among the elite of sedate Charleston, friends who were later mystified by his conduct during the war and who wrote to him to express chagrin and wonder. To one such old acquaintance Sherman responded movingly: "If I know my own heart, it beats as warmly as ever toward those kind and generous families that greeted us with such warm hospitality in days past, but still present in memory; and today were ... any and all of our cherished circle, their children or even their children's children, to come to me as of old, the stern feelings of duty would melt as snow before the genial sun, and I believe I would strip my own children that they might be sheltered...."[6]

When the states of the South began seceding, Sherman, who had served with the Army in Louisiana and as a civilian had been the first superintendent of the newly founded Louisiana Seminary of Learning (later to become Louisiana State University), decided that war was on its way and that his place was, as it had been, in the U.S. Army. David Boyd, his friend and colleague at the Louisiana school, claimed that Sherman "turned his back on his best & truest friends, because he thought we were wrong! Still, his great living heart never ceased to beat warmly for us of the South."[7]

The destructive march that Sherman planned for those of the South was intended to terminate ultimately at Richmond, but he meant to take a circuitous route that had Savannah as its first major destination, or possibly Port Royal, South Carolina. He had also considered cutting across the Florida panhandle and marching to Pensacola. The route through Georgia that he finally chose was carefully thought out. He had mapped it out after studying census figures that showed which counties were the biggest agricultural producers. His troops would be living off the land, and Sherman wanted to know exactly where the richest land was. "Georgia has a million inhabitants," he remarked before starting out. "If they can live, we should not starve."[8] Even so, Sherman's troops were taking with them in their wagon trains 1.2 million individual rations, enough to feed them for about twenty days. They were also taking a huge herd of beef cattle, driving them along as part of the marching column. The oats and corn being carried in wagons for the horses and mules would last only about five days, Sherman estimated, but the column by then would be in country well stocked with corn, already gathered into barns, ready for the taking.

In the column's wagons was also enough small-arms ammunition to provide two hundred rounds per man. In addition, each man carried with him forty rounds of ammunition, the authorized amount. Some carried more. The only organized opposition they would be facing, though, was Joe Wheeler's Confederate cavalry corps and about three thousand Georgia militiamen commanded by General Gustavus W. Smith. No major battles were expected.

Sherman gave the details of the rolling elements of his army. "The greatest possible attention had been given to the artillery and wagon trains," he recalled. "The number of guns [artillery pieces] had been reduced to sixty-five, or about one gun to each thousand men, and these were generally in batteries of four guns each.

"Each gun, caisson, and forge, was drawn by four teams of horses. We had in all about twenty-five hundred wagons, with teams of six mules to each, and six hundred ambulances, with two horses each.... The wagon-trains were divided equally between the four corps, so that each had about eight hundred wagons, and these usually on the march occupied five

Sherman's march to the sea. On the morning of November 16, 1864 General Sherman put his army of 65,000 men on the move through Georgia, marching southeastward from Atlanta, intending to wreak havoc and, as he said, "make Georgia howl." (JOHN CLARK RIDPATH)

miles or more of road. Each corps commander managed his own train; and habitually the artillery and wagons had the road, while the men, with the exception of the advance and rear guards, pursued paths improvised by the side of the wagons, unless they were forced to use a bridge or causeway in common."[9]

Sherman divided his army into two wings, as he called them, which would move more or less parallel to each other. The right wing, commanded by Major General Oliver O. Howard, was composed of the Fifteenth Corps, commanded by Major General Peter J. Osterhaus, and the Seventeenth Corps, commanded by Major General Frank P. Blair. The left wing, commanded by Major General Henry W. Slocum, was composed of the Fourteenth Corps, commanded by Major General Jefferson Columbus Davis, and the Twentieth Corps, commanded by Brigadier General Alpheus S. Williams. The cavalry was a separate division, not part of either corps, and was commanded by Brigadier General H. Judson Kilpatrick, known to his troopers as Kill-cavalry for his sometimes reckless disregard for the lives of his men and also known for his bouts of drunkenness and for consorting with prostitutes.

After purging from the marchers all noncombatants and all who were sick, Sherman had ready for the march 62,209 officers and men, including 55,329 infantry, 5,068 cavalry and 1,812 artillery. All, he reported, "may be assumed to have been able-bodied, experienced

Ripping up the railroad. As they moved through Georgia, Sherman's troops tore up railroad tracks as well as inflicting other damage. "I attached much importance to this destruction of the railroad," he said, **"[and] gave it my own personal attention."** (JOHN CLARK RIDPATH)

soldiers, well armed, well equipped and provided, as far as human foresight could, with all the essentials of life, strength, and vigorous action."[10] "The army was reduced, one might say," said Captain Daniel Oakey of the Second Massachusetts Volunteers, one of the marchers, "to its fighting weight, no man being retained who was not capable of a long march."[11]

On the morning of November 16 the enormous procession was under way, the right wing and cavalry moving southeast toward Jonesboro, along the rail line, and the left wing moving eastward through Decatur toward Madison. The idea, Sherman explained, was to threaten Macon and Augusta at the same time and prevent a concentration of Confederate forces at his actual objective, which was Milledgeville, the Georgia capital, about one hundred miles to the southeast, between the apparent routes of the two wings. Sherman planned to be there in seven days. He hoped to average fifteen miles a day over the entire march to the sea.

The first day got the leading elements of the left wing almost to Lithonia, and the men camped by the roadside in sight of Stone Mountain. Some rear elements halted at Decatur, just outside of Atlanta. From there and all along the road the flames of Atlanta could be seen, and not of Atlanta only. According to the accounts of Decatur residents, Sherman's troops immediately began destroying the outbuildings of farms and homes along their way. "I could stand out on the verandah and for two or three miles watch them as they came on," Martha Amanda Quillen wrote in a letter to her cousin. "I could mark when they reached the residence of each and every friend on the road."[12] That night two men of the

129th Illinois infantry regiment were shot by unknown and unapprehended assailants in Decatur.

As they proceeded, the troops ripped up the train tracks that ran beside the road, building bonfires with the piled-up ties and heating the rails in the fire until they could be wrapped like giant pretzels around nearby trees or telegraph poles. "I attached much importance to this destruction of the railroad," Sherman confessed, "gave it my own personal attention, and made reiterated orders to others on the subject."[13]

From the outset the column of marchers drew crowds of onlookers, and the troops reacted as if staging a martial parade. On the 17th the procession reached Covington, which Sherman called a "handsome town," and the troops dressed up their ranks, their color bearers unfurled the units' flags, and the regimental bands struck up "patriotic airs," as Sherman called them. "The white people came out of their houses to behold the sight, spite of their deep hatred of the invaders," Sherman reported, "and the negroes were simply frantic with joy."[14] At Covington Sherman received an invitation to dine with the sister of one of his fellow cadets at West Point, Sam Anderson. The invitation, sent by a messenger, reached him too late for him to accept, though, and he continued on with the troops and camped with them that evening on the banks of the Ulcofauhachee River, about four miles east of Covington.

It was there that Sherman strode up to a nearby plantation house and spoke with a crowd of slaves who were gathered there, among them a fine-looking, gray-haired old man whom Sherman singled out for conversation. "I asked him if he understood about the war and its progress," Sherman related. "He said he did; that he had been looking for 'the angel of the Lord' ever since he was knee-high, and, though we professed to be fighting for the Union, he supposed that slavery was the cause, and that our success was to be his freedom. I asked him if all the negro slaves comprehended this fact, and he said they surely did."[15]

Sherman took the opportunity of his conversation with the old man to explain his position on having freed blacks join the line of march. He told the man that he wanted the slaves to remain where they were and not tag along with the soldiers, making it necessary for the army to feed them. He said he could accept "a few of their young, hearty men as pioneers [laborers]; but that, if they followed us in swarms of old and young, feeble and helpless, it would simply load us down and cripple us in our great task." His army's success, Sherman said, meant the slaves' freedom. "I believe that old man spread this message to the slaves, which was carried from mouth to mouth, to the very end of our journey."[16]

It was also at that plantation outside Covington that Sherman saw that not all of his troops were going to follow his rules. A soldier walked by carrying a ham, a jug of molasses and a big piece of honeycomb. When he noticed that Sherman was watching him, he said to a comrade beside him, quoting Sherman's general orders, "Forage liberally on the country." Sherman didn't mention whether he found humor in the remark, but he stopped the soldier and reproved him, telling him that foraging was to be done only by designated details and that all foraged goods were to be turned over to the commissaries for fair distribution to the men who remained in their ranks.

In accounts sympathetic to the aggrieved Georgians, the troops of several of Sherman's regiments were reported to have plundered Covington on their way through, not excluding slave cabins and whatever property was found in them. Other reports claimed that at Covington robust, young male slaves were forced at bayonet point to join the march to work as laborers.[17]

Madison, through which the Twentieth Corps passed, fared no better than Covington, perhaps worse. David Conyngham, a New York *Herald* reporter traveling with Sherman's army, described the damage:

> Our troops entered the town next morning [November 17], and a brigade was detailed to destroy all the works around the depot and railroad track, also to burn a pile of nearly two hundred bales of cotton in a hut near. While this work was being executed, the stragglers, who manage to get to the front when there is plunder in view, and vagabonds of the army, crowded into the town, and the work of pillage went on with a vengeance. Stores were ripped open; goods, valuables, and plate, all suddenly and mysteriously disappeared.... All the stores were gutted, and the contents scattered and broken around....[18]

Sherman was traveling with the Fourteenth Corps, in the left wing, and turned with it to the south after leaving Covington, headed for Shady Dale on a route to Milledgeville. Slocum was traveling with the Twentieth Corps, which tore up the railroad tracks as far east as Madison, then turned southward to approach Milledgeville by way of Eatonton. The marchers had now entered into Georgia's land of plenty. "We found abundance of corn, molasses, meal, bacon, and sweet-potatoes," Sherman recounted. "We also took a good many cows and oxen, and a large number of mules. In all these the country was quite rich, never before having been visited by a hostile army."[19]

Sherman explained how the foragers worked:

> Each brigade commander had authority to detail a company of foragers, usually about fifty men, with one or two commissioned officers selected for their boldness and enterprise. This party would be dispatched before daylight with a knowledge of the intended day's march and camp; would proceed on foot five or six miles from the route traveled by their brigade, and then visit every plantation and farm within range. They would usually procure a wagon or family carriage, load it with bacon, corn-meal, turkeys, chickens, ducks, and every thing that could be used as food or forage, and would then regain the main road, usually in advance of their train. When this came up, they would deliver to the brigade commissary the supplies thus gathered by the way. Often would I pass these foraging-parties at the road-side, waiting for their wagons to come up, and was amused at their strange collections — mules, horses, even cattle, packed with old saddles and loaded with hams, bacon, bags of corn-meal, and poultry of every character and description.[20]

After just two days of looting, Sherman's troops had accumulated more food than it could consume, and tons of it were abandoned, left to rot, on the roadside.

The New York *Herald* reporter, David Conyngham, provided his observations of the way the foraging parties operated:

> Every brigade and regiment had its organized, foraging party, which were joined by every officer's servant and idler about the camps.
>
> These, scattered over the country, without any order or discipline, pounced like harpies on the unfortunate inhabitants, stripping them of all provisions, jewelry, and valuables they could discover.
>
> In most instances they burned down houses to cover their depredations, and in some cases took the lives of their victims, as they would not reveal concealed treasures. These gangs spread like locusts over the country. In all cases where the foraging parties were under the command of a respectable officer, they acted with propriety, simply taking what provisions and necessaries they needed. They might as well have stripped the place, though, for soon came the bummers,* and commenced a scene of ruin and pillage.[21]

---

*Conyngham used the term "bummers" to mean the stragglers who looted the countryside, not the army's authorized foragers.

Sherman's view of the foragers differed from Conyngham's, to the point of naïveté. "Although this foraging was attended with great danger and hard work," he wrote, "there seemed to be a charm about it that attracted the soldiers, and it was a privilege to be detailed on such a party."[22] He often turned a blind eye to the excesses, and when he couldn't ignore them, he steeled himself against the things he saw. He told his secretary, Major Henry Hitchcock, a St. Louis lawyer who handled Sherman's correspondence, "I'll have to harden my heart to these things." Other times he shifted blame, saying, "Jeff Davis is responsible for all this." In his memoirs he conceded some abuses. "No doubt," he wrote, "many acts of pillage, robbery, and violence, were committed by these parties of foragers, usually called 'bummers'; for I have since heard of jewelry taken from women, and the plunder of articles that never reached the commissary; but these acts were exceptional and incidental. I never heard of any cases of murder or rape...."[23]

Major Hitchcock found fault with Sherman's attitude concerning the foragers. He confided in his journal, "I am bound to say I think Sherman lacking in enforcing discipline. Brilliant and daring, fertile, rapid and terrible, he does not seem to me to carry out things in this respect...." Hitchcock thought that effective discipline could be gained by having provost marshals establish "a rigid system of roll calls in every company required at every halt — severe punishment inflicted not only on men who straggle but also on officers who fail to prevent it." Dismayed by the cruelty, Hitchcock declared, "It is a terrible thing to consume and destroy the sustenance of thousands of people, and most distressing to see and hear the terror and grief and want of these women and children." Yet, like Sherman, he deemed cruelty justified. "But if that terror and grief and want shall help to paralyze their husbands and fathers who are fighting us...," he wrote, "it is a mercy in the end."[24]

As for cases of rape, Sherman later admitted there were some, at least two that he had learned about.[25] The actual number was apparently greater by far, of both white women and black, though few cases were reported, the victims unwilling to endure the shame, and only the most heinous cases were discovered, such as that of twenty-seven-year-old Mrs. Kate Latimer Nichols of Milledgeville, who was raped by two Union soldiers as she lay sick in bed and later died in a mental institution.

Other victims of the violence included dogs found along the routes of march. "[F]ew bloodhounds were allowed to live," Conyngham reported, "except some peculiar one that took the fancy of an officer. As for the general run of these animals, they were relentlessly shot down," ostensibly to prevent their tracking down Union soldiers or ever again tracking down runaway slaves.[26]

Within a matter of days the pattern of arson, foraging, pillage and destruction was established as the left wing moved toward Milledgeville. Major Nicholas Grumbach, commander of the 149th New York Volunteer Regiment, in his official report summarized his division's progress:

November 19, marched at 5 A.M. [from Madison]. Regiment, brigade, and division left the corps and went on an expedition by themselves. Our brigade was second in line and halted at 2 P.M. until the Second Brigade, which was in the advance, destroyed a large section of the Augusta railroad. Bivouacked at 3:30 P.M. on a large plantation at Blue Spring. Destroyed about 80 rods of the railroad.

November 20, marched at 8 A.M., One hundred and forty-ninth in advance of division. Reached Oconee River at 9 A.M.; halted for the night at Denham's Mills, and regiment went on picket. The regimental headquarters were at the house of Mr. Denham, owner of the mills and plantation. He had previously left with his family for Secessia.

November 21, marched at 9 A.M.; regiment rear guard. As we passed the mills of Mr. Denham they were burning splendidly. Bivouacked at dark till November 22. Marched at 7 A.M. and rejoined the corps at 12 M; sighted Milledgeville at 4 P.M. and passed through the capital city at 8 P.M., and crossed the Oconee River and bivouacked one mile east of the river at 11 P.M.....[27]

As the troops neared Milledgeville, they "revelled in the splendid homes and palatial residences of some of the wealthy planters here," Conyngham reported. "The men, with that free and easy, devil-may-care sort of way, so characteristic of soldiers, made themselves quite as much at home in the fine house of the planter as in the shanty of the poor white trash or the negro. They helped themselves, freely and liberally, to everything they wanted, or did not want. It mattered little which."[28]

By the 22nd Milledgeville had become practically emptied of state officials. Members of the legislature had appropriated themselves three thousand dollars to charter a train to whisk them out of town before Sherman's army arrived. Among the absent officials was Governor Joseph E. Brown, who had fled to safety after exhorting inmates of the state penitentiary in Milledgeville to join the militia to defend their state, offering them pardons for joining, which most of them accepted. Instead of trying to defend the capital, though, the militia in Milledgeville — including the newly recruited convicts, prison guards and young cadets of the Georgia Military Institute as well as two companies of infantry and an artillery battery, some 460 men and boys altogether — had hurried out of town on a southbound train during the night of the 19th. Left behind were civilians who scrambled to move the state's archives from the government buildings to the nearby insane asylum for protection and others who frantically sought to bury or otherwise hide their silver and jewelry and other valuables. Hundreds of other civilians had loaded up wagons with furniture, clothing and household effects and had taken to the road as refugees.

Sherman, riding with the Fourteenth Corps in the left wing, reached Milledgeville during the morning of Wednesday, November 23, a day behind the Twentieth Corps's arrival. By then the weather had turned cold and blustery, so cold that water in the soldiers' canteens had frozen overnight, but the troops of the Twentieth Corps had ignored the cold and formed up into a parade formation to march through the town, their flags unfurled and bands playing. Two regiments encamped on the capitol grounds, and men of the 107th New York regiment raised a flag on the capitol dome while the bands struck up *The Star-Spangled Banner* and the troops cheered.

Sherman found temporary shelter in the vacated governor's mansion, made bleak by the removal of the mansion's furniture, carpets and draperies as well as the food from the kitchen and cellar. He recalled the brief stay in the town:

> Some of the officers (in the spirit of mischief) gathered together in the vacant hall of Representatives, elected a Speaker, and constituted themselves the Legislature of the State of Georgia! A proposition was made to repeal the ordinance of secession, which was well debated, and resulted in its repeal by a fair vote! I was not present at these frolics, but heard of them at the time, and enjoyed the joke.
>
> Meantime orders were made for the total destruction of the arsenal and its contents, and of such public buildings as could be easily converted to hostile uses. But little or no damage was done to private property, and General Slocum, with my approval, spared several mills, and many thousands of bales of cotton, taking what he knew to be worthless bonds, that the cotton should not be used for the Confederacy....[29]

From Atlanta the right wing had advanced on two roads leading to Macon, the Fifteenth Corps marching through Jonesboro, McDonough and Indian Springs to the crossing of the

Ocmulgee River at Planters Factory, and the Seventeenth Corps marching farther east on a parallel route but arriving at the same crossing of the Ocmulgee.

Kilpatrick's cavalrymen were assigned the duty of guarding the right flank of the marching infantrymen. Not far out of Atlanta they had encountered skirmishers of General Smith's Georgia militia and had driven them back to Lovejoy's Station, west of McDonough. From Lovejoy's Smith's infantry had quickly begun to withdraw toward Macon, but two brigades of militia cavalry, supported by two artillery pieces, remained in the rebels' defensive lines at Lovejoy's. Kilpatrick dismounted his troopers and had them charge the militiamen on foot, promptly carrying the rebel works and capturing the two guns. They then remounted and chased off after the militiamen retreating to Macon, following them for several miles before breaking off the pursuit and joining General Howard's infantry at the crossing of the Ocmulgee.

On two canvas-pontoon bridges Howard's two corps and Kilpatrick's cavalry crossed to the east side of the Ocmulgee on November 18, 19 and 20. Howard then led the Seventeenth Corps eastward toward Monticello, where he turned to the southeast, toward Gordon, Kilpatrick's cavalrymen riding on his right flank. To ward off a possible strike by rebel cavalry on the marching column, Kilpatrick, supported by the Fifteenth Corps, made a feint toward Macon, attacking the rail line east of Macon, destroying a train of rail cars and tearing up a mile of track. About four miles from Macon on November 22 Kilpatrick's troopers ran up against rebel cavalry and drove the troopers back toward Macon, but then was stopped and overpowered by a division of militia infantry and had to be rescued by a brigade of the Fifteenth Corps. "This brigade," Sherman later noted, "was in part armed with Spencer repeating-rifles [a lever-action rifle that could fire seven rounds without reloading] and its fire was so rapid that General Smith insists to this day that he encountered a whole division.... [He] made no further effort to molest our operations from that direction."[30] In the engagement the Union brigade suffered ninety-four casualties, the Confederates an estimated six hundred or more. Major General Charles Walcutt, the Union brigade commander, was wounded in the leg and had to make the rest of the trip to Savannah in a carriage. The Fifteenth Corps moved on to Griswoldville, and the Seventeenth Corps to Gordon.

At Gordon General Howard received a visit from Sherman, who rode over from Milledgeville to see him. Sherman briefed Howard on the progress of the left wing and included in the conversation tales of the troops' adventures and misadventures. "The stories of the mock Legislature at the State capital," Howard later remarked, "of the luxurious supplies enjoyed all along, and of the constant fun and pranks of 'Sherman's bummers,' rather belonged to that route than ours. Possibly we had more of the throngs of escaping slaves, from the baby in arms to the old negro hobbling painfully along the line of march — negroes of all sizes, in all sorts of patched costumes, with carts and broken-down horses and mules to match."[31]

Howard, a West Pointer from Maine known for his piety and nicknamed "the Christian general," summarized his two corps' experiences during the remainder of the march: "We brought along our wounded (over 200, I believe) in ambulances, and though they were jolted over corduroy roads and were much exposed to hardship, and participated in the excitements of the march, they all reached Savannah without the loss of a life. Our system of foraging was sufficiently good for the army, but the few citizens, women and children, who remained at home, suffered greatly."[32]

On November 24, Thanksgiving, the left wing resumed its march, Sherman now traveling with the Twentieth Corps, which started off to the southeast, down the road to Sandersville. According to one report, before he left, Sherman summoned the head of Milledgeville's hospital, Dr. R.J. Massey, and told him that he was leaving behind the twenty-eight Union soldiers who were too sick to travel. When Doctor Massey asked what he should do with them, Sherman is reported to have replied, "If they die, give them a decent burial. If they live, send them to Andersonville, of course. They are prisoners of war. What else can you do? If I had your men, I would send them to prison."[33]

At Sandersville Sherman halted the left wing until he received word on the 26th that the right wing was abreast of the left, having reached Tenille, a railroad station about six miles south of Sandersville. The Seventeenth Corps was moving eastward, tearing up the railroad as it went, and the Fifteenth Corps was marching eastward on a road south of the rail line. Kilpatrick took his cavalrymen rapidly toward Waynesboro, feinting an attack on Augusta. Sherman ordered him to attempt to capture Millen, on the rail line south of Waynesboro, and free the Union soldiers held in the Confederate prison there. Kilpatrick ran into Wheeler's rebel cavalry on the way and after skirmishing with it and learning that the Union POWs had been moved from Millen, Kilpatrick turned back to Louisville, about twenty-five miles east of Sandersville., reaching it on the 29th and finding the left wing there.

He remained at Louisville a couple of days to rest his horses and was then ordered, as Sherman put it, "to engage Wheeler and give him all the fighting he wanted."[34] Supported by the infantry division of Major General Absolom Baird of the Fourteenth Corps, he moved back toward Waynesboro on December 2 and encountered Wheeler's troopers on the way. With repeated charges Kilpatrick drove Wheeler back through Waynesboro and up the road toward Augusta. The rebel opposition having been removed, the Seventeenth Corps advanced into Millen on December 3, Sherman now riding with it. The direct rail line between Augusta and Savannah was torn up as three of Sherman's four corps — all but the Fifteenth — proceeded southeastward through the narrowing space between the southeastward-flowing Ogeechee and Savannah rivers. The Fifteenth advanced along the south side of the Ogeechee.

"[F]rom Millen onward the march of the whole army was a methodic progress with no noticeable opposition," Major General Jacob Cox reported in his account of the march, "for even Wheeler's horsemen kept a respectful distance, and soon crossed to the left [north] bank of the Savannah."[35]

General Beauregard, commander of the Confederates' Division of the West, without any available troops to order to Georgia's defense, could send only words of exhortation and from his headquarters in Corinth, Mississippi he issued this rallying cry to the people of Georgia: "Arise for the defense of your native soil! ... Obstruct and destroy all the roads in Sherman's front, flank, and rear, and his army will soon starve in your midst. Be confident. Be resolute. Trust in an overruling Providence, and success will soon crown your efforts...."[36] Sherman had already let his officers know what they should do if the actions that Beauregard urged were actually done — "army commanders should order and enforce a devastation more or less relentless, according to the measure of such hostility."[37] When he saw rebel cavalry burn stacks of fodder in fields near Sandersville, Sherman ordered nearby unoccupied houses burned, and when he entered the town, he issued a stern public warning: "I told certain citizens (who would be sure to spread the report) that, if the enemy attempted to carry out their threat to burn their food, corn, and fodder, in our route, I would most undoubtedly execute to the letter of the general orders of devastation made at the outset of the campaign. With this exception, and one or two minor cases near Savannah, the people did not destroy food, for they saw clearly that it would be ruin to themselves."[38]

One tactic that the rebels tried set off outrage in Sherman. He described it:

On the 8th [of December], as I rode along, I found the column turned out of the main road, marching through fields. Close by, in the corner of a fence, was a group of men standing around a handsome young officer, whose foot had been blown to pieces by a torpedo planted in the road. He was waiting for a surgeon to amputate his leg, and told me that he was riding along with the rest of brigade-staff of the Seventeenth Corps, when a torpedo trodden on by his horse had exploded, killing the horse and literally blowing off all the flesh from one of his legs. I saw the terrible wound, and made full inquiry into the facts. There had been no resistance at that point, nothing to give warning of danger, and the rebels had planted eight-inch shells in the road, with friction-matches to explode them by being trodden on. This was not war, but murder, and it made me very angry.

I immediately ordered a lot of rebel prisoners to be brought from the provost-guard, armed with picks and spades, and made them march in close order along the road, so as to explode their own torpedoes, or to discover and dig them up. They begged hard, but I reiterated the order ... they found no other torpedoes till near Fort McAllister.[39]

Relief from the toils of the march came in a variety of diversions. "[I]f we got into camp in good time," Conyngham related, "dog and cock fighting enlivened the evening. Groups of officers were collected with two roosters in the centre, with erect feathers and defiant heads, sparring and fencing, until at length one of them lay quivering on the daisy, to the no small satisfaction of all parties present, except the defunct warrior and his backers."[40] Dog fights were staged between mastiffs or bloodhounds that had been exempted from execution and brought along on the march for later entertainment.

Horse racing was another diversion reported by Conyngham: "As we picked up some of the first-blooded horses of the south ... we could not help trying their mettle. Therefore, if we only halted a day, we were sure to get up a race, which was generally well attended. One of these came off in Georgia, near a stream, with the enemy at one side and we racing at the other. It was a very exciting race, and bets were freely laid and taken; but as the enemy became spiteful, and did not seem to relish the thing, we had to deploy a heavy line of skirmishers along the stream to keep them amused, and prevent them from spoiling our fun."[41]

Dancing and singing around campfires in the evening, with music supplied by the black camp followers, provided entertainment for the troops as well as the officers. Some managed entertainment of a more personal nature. "The good-looking [young mulatto women] led luxurious lives, stowed away in baggage-wagons during the day, and feasted at the servants' mess at night," Conyngham wrote. "It would be vexatious to the Grand Turk or Brigham Young, if they could only see how many of these dark houries were in the employment of officers' servants and teamsters. I have seen officers themselves very attentive to the wants of pretty octoroon girls, and provide them with horses to ride."[42]

Sherman's army pressed on toward Savannah, passing through pine forests and across troublesome streams and swamps. In Screven County, at Horse Creek, the Twentieth Corps had to wade through water four feet deep for a distance of some thirty yards. On swampy ground miles of logs had to be laid to corduroy the roads. To get across streams pontoon bridges often had to be hastily assembled and then disassembled once the troops and wagon train had crossed. The commander of the Fourteenth Corps was thirty-six-year-old Major General Jefferson Davis, who had enlisted in the Army at age eighteen, had received a battlefield commission during the Mexican War and had been in the garrison at Fort Sumter when it was surrendered. He saw stream crossings as opportunities to shake off the hordes of newly freed slaves who were dogging the heels of his troops. On three occasions — at Buckhead, Ebenezer and Lockner creeks[43] — Davis ordered the bridges removed before the blacks could cross them, even though Wheeler's Confederate cavalrymen were threatening the rear of Davis's column and were likely to make prisoners of the blacks. Many of the blacks plunged into the water to escape the rebel troopers and rejoin Davis's column. Many of them drowned, swept away in the current. Others were shot or captured by Wheeler's troopers and returned to their owners. Relating the incident at Ebenezer Creek, an eyewitness, Colonel Charles Kerr of the Sixteenth Illinois Cavalry Regiment, years later told a group of Civil War veterans, "It was unjustifiable and perfidious, and across the stretch of twenty years my soul burns with indignation … as I recall it."[44]

By December 10 all four of Sherman's corps had reached the Confederates' defensive perimeter at the edges of Savannah, and Sherman placed the corps so that they completely invested the rebel positions and the city, with the Fourteenth Corps on the left, the Savannah River on its left flank, the Twentieth Corps next, then the Seventeenth and then the Fifteenth, on the extreme right. "At Savannah," Sherman observed, "we had again run up against the old familiar parapet, with its deep ditches, canals, and bayous, full of water; and it looked as though another siege was inevitable. I accordingly made a camp or bivouac near the Louisville road, about five miles from Savannah, and proceeded to invest the place closely."[45]

He also determined to make contact with the U.S. fleet, which, loaded with supplies, was, according to the plan, waiting for him and his army in Ossabaw Sound, where the Ogeechee River debouches into the sea, just below Savannah. Guarding the mouth of the Ogeechee, to prevent enemy vessels from steaming up it to the south side of the city, was the Confederates' Fort McAllister, the southernmost of the string of fortifications that protected the city from naval attacks. Sherman would have to take Fort McAllister if the fleet was to be able to reach his army, and if the fort were captured, the south side of Savannah would be exposed, the left flank of the rebels' defensive line turned. Sherman decided to take Fort McAllister.

First he would have to rebuild King's Bridge, the one-thousand-foot-long bridge that spanned the Ogeechee about fourteen miles southwest of Savannah. It had been mostly destroyed by the city's defenders, who set it ablaze. The pilings, though, were still standing, and Sherman instructed General Howard to bring up a division and all his engineers to rebuild the bridge's roadway atop those pilings. They immediately went to work.

"On the evening of the 12th," Sherman related, "I rode over myself, and spent the night at Mr. King's house, where I found General Howard, with [Brigadier] General [William] Hazen's division of the Fifteenth Corps. His engineers were hard at work on the bridge, which they finished that night [after three days' work], and at sunrise Hazen's division passed over. I gave General Hazen, in person, his orders to march rapidly down the right [south] bank of the Ogeechee, and without hesitation to assault and carry Fort McAllister by storm. I knew it to be strong in heavy artillery, as against an approach from the sea, but believed it open and weak to the rear.

"I explained to General Hazen, fully, that on his action depended the safety of the whole army, and the success of the campaign."[46] Hazen's division was the same one that Sherman had commanded at Shiloh and Vicksburg. In it, he said, he felt "a special pride and confidence."[47]

After seeing Hazen off on his mission, Sherman rode about ten miles down the north side of the Ogeechee to the Cheeves rice plantation, where General Howard had set up a signal station on a platform atop the plantation's rice mill, from which Fort McAllister, about three miles away, could be clearly seen. "Leaving our horses behind the stacks of rice-straw," Sherman related, "we all got on the roof of a shed attached to the mill, wherefrom I could communicate with the signal-officer above, and at the same time look out toward Ossabaw Sound, and across the Ogeechee River at Fort McAllister." The fort occasionally fired an artillery shot across the marsh toward the rice mill, where Union artillerymen had emplaced a couple of twenty-pounder Parrott guns, but otherwise, Sherman remarked, everything at the fort "looked as peaceable and quiet as on the Sabbath."[48]

The fort was an earthworks fortification with seven heavy guns permanently mounted and eight light field guns mounted in barbette. The sides that faced the land were protected by a parapet, a ditch, a palisade, fraise, abatis and chevaux-de-frise. In addition, torpedoes had been planted in the ground around it. Its garrison numbered about two hundred and thirty officers and men. Hazen decided to attack it from the three land sides, three brigades advancing simultaneously.

Sherman described the action as seen from the roof of the shed:

About 2 P.M. we observed signs of commotion in the fort, and noticed one or two guns fired inland, and some musket-skirmishing in the woods close by.

This betokened the approach of Hazen's division, which had been anxiously expected, and soon thereafter the signal-officer discovered about three miles above the fort a signal-flag, with which he conversed, and found it to belong to General Hazen, who was preparing to assault the fort, and wanted to know if I were there. On being assured of this fact, and that I expected the fort to be carried before night, I received by signal the assurance of General Hazen that he was making preparations, and would soon attempt the assault. The sun was rapidly declining, and I was dreadfully impatient....

When the sun was about an hour high, another signal-message came from General Hazen that he was all ready, and I replied to go ahead.... Almost at that instant of time, we saw Hazen's troops come out of the dark fringe of woods that encompassed the fort, the lines dressed as on parade, with colors flying, and moving forward with a quick, steady pace. Fort McAllister was then all alive, its big guns belching forth dense clouds of smoke, which soon enveloped our assaulting lines. One color went down, but was up in a moment. On the lines advanced, faintly seen in the white, sulphurous smoke; there was a pause, a cessation of fire; the smoke cleared away, and the parapets were blue with our men, who fired their muskets in the air, and shouted so that we actually heard them, or felt that we did. Fort McAllister was taken....[49]

The battle had lasted only fifteen minutes. Union casualties, most of them caused by the torpedoes, amounted to twenty-four killed and one hundred and ten wounded. The garrison's losses totaled forty-eight, including killed and wounded.[50] That evening, Sherman dined with Hazen at Hazen's headquarters. Confederate Major G.W. Anderson, who had commanded Fort McAllister's garrison, was their dinner guest.

The 18,000 rebel troops guarding Savannah were commanded by Lieutenant General William J. Hardee, who was observing the virtual encirclement of the city by Sherman's army and was calculating how many days there were before he had to make his move. Once Fort McAllister had been captured, Hardee realized, Sherman could be easily supplied from the Ogeechee, sea-going ships being able to unload their cargo onto shallow-draft vessels that could come up the river to the rear of the right side of Sherman's line. Meanwhile, Sherman's engineers had gone to work to drain the flooded rice fields that stood in front of Savannah as a natural barrier. When those fields were drained, Union troops would have a broad field on which to advance against the city, instead of merely the narrow causeways that allowed the defenders to concentrate their fire on advancing columns. The water covering the rice fields was subsiding day by day, and Sherman's commanders had already moved batteries of siege guns into position. Portable bridges had been gathered to be carried across the fields to span ditches for advancing attackers. Hardee could see a Union assault was in the making. He determined to avoid being trapped in the city, his front to his enemy, his back to the sea.

Hoping that Hardee could see futility in further resistance and that lives that would be lost in an assault could be spared, Sherman sent Hardee this note, containing some exaggeration, on December 17:

> Headquarters Military Division of the Mississippi,
> in the field, Savannah, Georgia, December 17, 1864
>   General William J. Hardee, commanding Confederate Forces in Savannah.
>   General: You have doubtless observed, from your station at Rosedew, that sea-going vessels now come through Ossabaw Sound and up the Ogeechee to the rear of my army, giving me abundant supplies of all kinds, and more especially heavy ordnance necessary for the reduction of Savannah. I have already received guns that can cast heavy and destructive shot as far as the heart of your city; also I have for some days held and controlled every avenue by which the people and garrison of Savannah can be supplied, and I am therefore justified in demanding the surrender of the city of Savannah, and its dependent forts, and shall wait a reasonable time for your answer, before opening with heavy ordnance. Should you entertain the proposition, I am prepared to grant liberal terms to the inhabitants and garrison; but should I be forced to resort to assault, or the slower and surer process of starvation, I shall then feel justified in resorting to the harshest measures, and shall make little effort to restrain my army—burning to avenge the national wrong which they attach to Savannah and other large cities which have been so prominent in dragging our country into civil war. I inclose you a copy of General Hood's demand for the surrender of the town of Resaca, to be used by you for what it is worth.
>   I have the honor to be your obedient servant,
>   W.T. Sherman, *Major-General*[51]

On that same day, December 17, Hardee replied, rebutting several of Sherman's statements and boldly telling him, "Your demand for the surrender of Savannah and its dependent forts is refused."[52]

On the night of the 19th, realizing the time had come, Hardee began evacuating his troops from Savannah. He sent them across the pontoon bridge that had been thrown over the Savannah River, marching them onto the South Carolina side. On the night of the 20th he completed the evacuation. Seeing the rebel line abandoned, Major General John Geary of the U.S. Twentieth Corps, commanding the division closest to the line, promptly marched his troops into Savannah shortly after daybreak on December 21.

Sherman moved his headquarters into the city on the morning of the 22nd and on the 23rd he sent a dispatch to the president, which Lincoln received on Christmas Eve: "I beg to present to you, as a Christmas gift, the city of Savannah...."[53]

24

The Fight for Fort Fisher, December 24, 1864, to January 15, 1865

The proposal came from the U.S. secretary of the Navy, Gideon Welles. Off and on he had been advocating a joint Army-Navy assault on Fort Fisher since the winter of 1862, but Secretary of War Edwin Stanton had kept putting him off, on the grounds that the Army was needed more elsewhere and troops couldn't be spared for a Fort Fisher mission.

Fort Fisher, at the mouth of the Cape Fear River, protected the access of blockade runners to Wilmington, North Carolina, the Confederates' last remaining major seaport, through which passed annually an estimated sixty to seventy million dollars worth of arms and supplies to keep the rebels' fight going. Those goods were being shipped from European ports, particularly British ports, to Bermuda and to Nassau in the Bahamas and then placed aboard blockade runners for the trip to Wilmington. Although the U.S. Navy's blockading vessels were stopping many of the blockade runners, many others were getting through, taking advantage of moonless nights and bad weather. "The blockade runners," Rear Admiral David D. Porter, commander of the Navy's North Atlantic Blockading Squadron, remarked, "were very fast steamers, well-manned, and with experienced pilots, and so regular were their trips to Wilmington, that their arrival was counted on almost as confidently as if they had been mail-steamers."[1] Even when they were caught, the blockade runners often would beach their vessels, and under protection of rebel artillery on shore, their crews would unload their cargo and slip away, burning their vessels behind them.

In September 1864 Secretary Welles at last got results on his proposal. When again requesting Army troops for a joint operation, he received a promise of cooperation from General Grant, who had grasped the importance of Fort Fisher. "It was ... important to us to get possession of it," Grant explained, "not only because it was desirable to cut off their [Confederate] supplies so as to insure a speedy termination of the war, but also because foreign governments, particularly the British Government, were constantly threatening that unless ours could maintain the blockade of that coast they should cease to recognize any blockade. For these reasons I determined, with the concurrence of the Navy Department, in December, to send an expedition against Fort Fisher for the purpose of capturing it."[2]

Admiral Porter thought it was about time. He contended that if the fortification had been attacked earlier in the war, capturing it would have been a simple matter. "Early in

235

Interior of Fort Fisher. Built to protect the mouth of the Cape Fear River and provide blockade runners with access to Wilmington, North Carolina, the fort was described by U.S. Navy Adm. David D. Porter as "the most formidable series of works in the Confederacy." (LIBRARY OF CONGRESS)

the contest," he wrote, "a squadron of light-draft gun-boats could have made their way past the small batteries and taken possession of Cape Fear River, closing that channel of blockade-runners, and paving the way for the troops to hold the point on which Fort Fisher was finally built. But this was not attempted until the fortifications were so far advanced as to become the most formidable series of works in the Confederacy."[3]

Fort Fisher was built on the southern tip of a long, narrow, sandy strip of land called Federal Point, which forms a peninsula between the Atlantic Ocean and the Cape Fear River. Below the southern tip of Federal Point the river turns eastward a short distance and empties into the ocean through two inlets. The fort commanded not only the channel through which every vessel entering the river from the ocean must pass, but Federal Point was so narrow that the fort also commanded the lower end of the river. Shaped like a figure 7, the fort consisted of sand parapets as high as twenty feet with a ditch and a loopholed palisade in front of them, one parapet facing north and running across the peninsula from ocean to river, five hundred yards long, and another parapet facing the sea and running thirteen hundred yards along the ocean down to the tip of the peninsula. Where the two parapets met at the northeast angle there was a heavily armed bastion, and another bastion stood at the river end of the north-facing parapet. At the southern tip of the sea-facing parapet there was another heavily armed work called the mound battery. A rifle trench extended from the mound battery westward to the river, terminating at a citadel called Battery Buchanan, with four guns commanding the upper inlet and covering the land approach as well. Battery Buchanan was garrisoned by a detachment from the Confederate navy and was built as a fortification to which the Fort Fisher garrison, if overpowered, might retreat and escape by boat at night, and to which reinforcements for Fort Fisher might be landed under cover of darkness. The river side of Fort Fisher was left open.

U.S. Major General Jacob Cox described the fort's armament: "Two field-pieces ... [at the entrance in the north-facing parapet] gave a flanking fire upon the ditch and assisted the guns in the bastions in sweeping the front.... This front was armed with twenty-one heavy guns and three mortars. A formidable system of torpedoes had been planted beyond the palisade, to be discharged by electricity from within the fort. To protect the guns from enfilading naval fire, very heavy traverses had been built, about a dozen in number, at right angles to the parapet and rising ten feet above the gunners' heads. These were strongly built, as hollow bomb-proofs, and served both as magazines and as shelter for the garrison when driven from the guns by a cannonade from the fleet.... The sea-front was built in the same way, but was not so continuously heavy as the other, the guns being grouped in batteries connected by a lighter parapet for infantry. Twenty-four guns were on this face.... The armament was mostly of eight- and ten-inch columbiads, interspersed with heavy rifled cannon."[4]

Manning those guns and protecting the works was Fort Fisher's garrison, which numbered fewer than fifteen hundred officers and men in December 1864. It was commanded by Colonel William Lamb, a twenty-nine-year-old former newspaper editor from Norfolk, Virginia who had assumed command on July 4, 1862 and had been building and strengthening the fort ever since.

To command the U.S. naval force that would execute the assault on Fort Fisher Secretary Welles appointed Rear Admiral David D. Porter. In his job as head of the Navy's North Atlantic Blockading Squadron, Porter succeeded Rear Admiral David Farragut, who was first to be offered command of the Fort Fisher mission but declined it because of poor health.

In command of the troops that would participate in the mission was Major General Benjamin F. Butler, whom Grant was obliged to appoint because Butler commanded the Army department that embraced Fort Fisher as well as other points along the Atlantic coast held by U.S. forces. Both Grant and Porter knew that Butler was not the man who should be in charge. Porter even went so far as to suggest that Butler *not* be placed in command. Agreeing, Grant picked Major General Godfrey Weitzel of the Army of the James to be the actual leader of the mission's troops. Grant thought Army protocol would be satisfied by having Weitzel receive his orders through Butler, who, Grant intended, would serve merely as the nominal commander.

Butler, however, had a different idea of what his role would be. Inspired by reports of a massive, devastating accidental explosion of gunpowder at Erith, England on October 1, 1864, he proposed an unusual element as a key part of the assault. "I believed," he wrote in his memoir, "that possibly, by bringing within four or five hundred yards of Fort Fisher a large mass of explosives, and firing the whole in every part at the same moment — for it was the essence of the experiment to have the powder all exploded at the same instant — the garrison would at least be so far paralyzed as to enable, by a prompt landing of men, a seizure of the fort." He managed to present his idea to President Lincoln and others in Washington. "I found that the idea had received so much favor at Washington," he related, "that it was determined it should be tried."[5]

Butler was hopeful for bigger things than the destruction of Fort Fisher, imagining that "if it should prove a success the whole system of offensive warfare by naval procedure would be changed, for no forts near harbors would be safe if a small vessel loaded with gunpowder and run ashore under a fort and exploded would destroy the people in it, and no garrison would ever remain in a fort when such a vessel was seen approaching."[6]

In early December a fleet of warships, nearly 60 vessels, was assembled in Hampton Roads, including an obsolete gunboat, the *Louisiana*, which would be freighted with two hundred and thirty-five tons of gunpowder and would become the bomb boat.

By now Butler had decided that he must go along on the mission and take charge himself. "I was to go in its command for a reason which was agreed upon between us [Butler and Grant] in the consultation. The reason was this, that General Weitzel, while a very able general, was quite a young man, and I was very anxious to see this powder expedition go on and succeed, for it was a very grave one."[7] Weitzel was in fact twenty-nine years old, the same age as Fort Fisher's commander. He was a professional soldier, a graduate of West Point, ranked second in his class, and in two and a half years had risen from lieutenant to the rank of major general and had become a corps commander. Butler, forty-six years old, was a New Hampshire politician and lawyer who had no military training or experience except as leader of the peacetime New Hampshire militia, a largely political position. He had been appointed a major general at the start of the war, when President Lincoln was making generals of fellow politicians almost willy-nilly.

Grant was highly doubtful about Butler's big-bang idea. "I had no confidence in the success of the scheme," he confessed, "and so expressed myself; but as no serious harm could come of the experiment, and the authorities in Washington seemed desirous to have it tried, I permitted it."[8] Grant described what happened:

> The steamer [*Louisiana*] was sent to Beaufort, North Carolina, and was there loaded with powder and prepared for the part she was to play in the reduction of Fort Fisher.
>
> General Butler chose to go in command of the expedition himself, and was all ready to sail by the 9th of December (1864). Very heavy storms prevailed, however, at that time along that part of the sea-coast, and prevented him from getting off until the 13th or 14th. His advance arrived off Fort Fisher on the 15th. The naval force had been already assembled, or was assembling, but they were obliged to run into Beaufort for munitions, coal , etc.; then, too the powder-boat was not yet fully prepared. The fleet was ready to proceed on the 18th; but Butler, who had remained outside from the 15th up to that time, now found himself out of coal, fresh water, etc., and had to put into Beaufort to replenish. Another storm overtook him, and several days more were lost before the army and navy were both ready at the same time to co-operate.
>
> On the night of the 23d the powder-boat was towed in by a gunboat as near to the fort as it was safe to run. She was then propelled by her own machinery to within about five hundred yards of the shore. There the clockwork, which was to explode her within a certain length of time, was set and she was abandoned. Everybody left, and even the vessels put out to sea to prevent the effect of the explosion upon them.
>
> At two o'clock in the morning the explosion took place — and produced no more effect on the fort, or anything else on land, than the bursting of a boiler anywhere on the Atlantic Ocean would have done. Indeed when the troops in Fort Fisher heard the explosion they supposed it was the bursting of a boiler in one of the Yankee gunboats.[9]

So much for General Butler's plan to take Fort Fisher without a fight and change the nature of coastal warfare in the process. What was more, Butler wasn't even there to witness the explosive spectacle, having been delayed at Beaufort. In his memoir he made no further mention of his big idea.

Attention now focused on Butler's attacking army, brought to the scene on transports. Following an horrific bombardment of the fort on December 24, during which Porter's fleet fired one hundred and fifteen shells per minute onto and into the fortification, the troops landed north of Fort Fisher, out of range of its guns, on Christmas day, their landing covered by protective gunboats. Grant detailed the action:

> They [the U.S. troops] formed a line across the peninsula and advanced, part going north, and part toward the fort, covering themselves as they did so. [Brigadier General Newton Martin] Curtis pushed forward and came near to Fort Fisher, capturing the small garrison at what was called the Flag Pond Battery. Weitzel accompanied him to within a half a mile of the works. Here he saw that the fort had not been injured [by the naval bombardment], and so reported to Butler, advising against an assault. [Major General Adelbert] Ames, who had gone north in his advance, captured 228 of the reserves. These prisoners reported to Butler that sixteen hundred of [Confederate Major General Robert F.] Hoke's division of six thousand from Richmond had already arrived and the rest would soon be in his rear.
>
> Upon these reports Butler determined to withdraw his troops from the peninsula and return to the fleet. At that time there had not been a man on our side injured except by one of the shells from the fleet. Curtis had got within a few yards of the works.... At night Butler informed Porter of his withdrawal, giving the reasons above stated, and announced his purpose as soon as his men could embark to start for Hampton Roads. Porter represented to him that he had sent to Beaufort for more ammunition. He could fire much faster than he had been doing, and would keep the enemy from showing himself until our men were within twenty yards of the fort....
>
> Butler was unchangeable. He got all his troops aboard, except Curtis's brigade, and started back.[10]

Grant was unequivocal in his denunciation of Butler's actions. "My instructions to him, or to the officer who went in command of the expedition," Grant wrote, "were explicit in the statement that to effect a landing would be of itself a great victory, and if one should be effected, the foothold must not be relinquished; on the contrary, a regular siege of the fort must be commenced.... But General Butler seems to have lost sight of this part of his instructions, and was back at Fort Monroe [Butler's headquarters] on the 28th."[11]

Ever careful about criticizing Lincoln's political generals, Grant wired a non-accusatory telegram to the president to report the mission's failure: "The Wilmington expedition has proven a gross and culpable failure. Many of the troops are back here [in Virginia]. Delays and free talk of the object of the expedition enabled the enemy to move troops to Wilmington to defeat it. After the expedition sailed from Fort Monroe, three days of fine weather were squandered, during which the enemy was without a force to protect himself. Who is to blame will, I hope, be known."[12]

A congressional investigation to determine culpability was soon held after the Fort Fisher affair became a national scandal and the bomb boat — which became "Butler's powder boat" in the press — became a national joke. Butler, the lawyer and politician, made an eloquent defense of himself, shifting blame to Porter for not being at the rendezvous point when he should have been. There was no getting around Butler's failure to follow Grant's orders, though. Grant testified that "General Butler came away from Fort Fisher in violation of the instructions which I gave him."[13] The instructions were to entrench if the fort did not quickly fall and stay in place and cooperate with the Navy until the fort did fall. Butler obviously knew the orders for he included them in his memoir: "The object of the expedition will be gained on effecting a landing on the mainland between Cape Fear River and the Atlantic, north of the north entrance to the river. Should such landing be effected, whether the enemy hold Fort Fisher or the batteries guarding the river there, the troops should intrench themselves, and by co-operation with the navy effect the reduction and capture of those places...."[14]

In the end, Grant requested permission to remove Butler from command. On January 4, 1865 Grant wrote to Secretary of War Stanton: "I am constrained to request the removal of General Butler from the command of the Department of Virginia and North Carolina. I do this with reluctance, but the good of the service requires it. In my absence General Butler necessarily commands, and there is a lack of confidence felt in his military ability, making him an unsafe commander for a large army. His administration of his department is also objectionable."[15] When he found that Stanton had gone to see Sherman in Savannah, Grant then wired President Lincoln on January 6, asking for prompt action. Grant got the okay the next day, and on January 8 he sent two of his aides, Lieutenant Colonel O.E. Babcock and Lieutenant Colonel Horace Porter, to Butler's headquarters to deliver the written order relieving him of his duties and his command. In a final public rationalization of his conduct Butler stood before his massed troops in review and told them, "I have refused to order the useless sacrifice of the lives of such soldiers and I am relieved of your command. The wasted blood of my men does not stain my garments. For my action I am responsible to God and my country."[16] He then bade the troops farewell and was escorted to the steamer that would take him home. His military career was ended, as were his chances to succeed Lincoln in the White House, believed to have been his longtime, motivating ambition.

Admiral Porter wasted no time in calling for a second assault on Fort Fisher. "The moment Butler's troops re-embarked, the Admiral," he recounted, referring to himself, "sent a swift steamer to General Grant and told him the situation of affairs, urging him to send 'other troops and another General.'"[17] Grant was quick to respond. His choice for a new general was thirty-seven-year-old Brigadier General Alfred Howe Terry, a New Haven, Connecticut lawyer who had become a colonel of volunteers, which he led with distinction in the first Battle of Bull Run (First Manassas). For the Fort Fisher mission Terry was given command of a division and a brigade from the Twenty-fourth Corps, plus a division of the Twenty-fifth Corps and two light artillery batteries, more than eight thousand men altogether. They sailed off on transports to rendezvous with Porter at Beaufort, North Carolina, which they reached on January 8, 1865.

Porter had not met Terry before, and his first impression of him was not favorable. "Terry was rather cold and formal in his manner," Porter related, "and did not meet the Admiral [Porter] at once with the frankness of a true soldier. He had, however, been a long time under the command of General Butler, who, for a wonder, had treated him very well, because he saw he was a good soldier, and a man of talent besides.... Of course, Terry had heard *his* side of the story, and was cautious in his first approaches; but all this wore off like snow before a summer's sun when Terry found that the Admiral had but one object in view — the capture of Fort Fisher, and did not care how it was done or who got the credit of it. On his second visit Terry was quite a different man, and they soon understood each other."[18]

Porter was further encouraged about Terry when he saw that, unlike Butler, who, Porter claimed, was "fond of display, and whose staff was exceptionally large," Terry "had no staff, wore no spurs, and we do not think he owned a sword. He had a well-formed head, full of sense, which served him in lieu of feathers, sword, boots, spurs and staff — of which a general can have too many."[19]

Grant had briefed Terry about Porter and in his instructions he told Terry "to defer to Admiral Porter's opinions in all that related to nautical matters, and to confide in his judgment, as he was an officer who had the nerve to carry out anything he might propose."[20]

The plan that Terry and Porter settled on called for Porter to send a force of Marines and sailors against Fort Fisher's sea-facing parapet while Terry's infantry and artillery assailed the north-facing parapet. Another force would dig in and establish a defensive line across Federal Point to guard against a rebel attack from the rear, Hoke's six thousand Confederate troops known to be somewhere north of the fort.

Stormy weather once again delayed the landing of the Union troops, but at eight o'clock on the morning of January 13 the troops started going ashore about five miles above the fort while Porter's ironclad gunboats, from within twelve hundred yards of the fort, poured shells into it to keep its garrison occupied. Launches and other small boats of the fleet carried the troops from their transports to the beach in heavy surf, the oared boats going in close enough for the men to climb over the gunwales and jump into the knee-deep, or deeper, water, many of them falling and disappearing temporarily beneath the waves. None were lost as they splashed, waded and stormed their way onto the sandy beach, unopposed. By two o'clock that afternoon they and their supplies were all ashore. Admiral Porter described the landing operation:

> The most important matter to the Confederates was to prevent a landing by the Federal troops, or to dislodge them as soon as they got on shore, and drive them into the sea; but this had been anticipated by having a line of sixteen or seventeen gun-boats anchored inside of the transports within one hundred yards of the beach, the "Brooklyn" with her heavy battery lying in the centre of the line; and, before a single boat was allowed to leave a transport, there was opened all along the line such a tremendous fire from the vessels reaching as far as Cape Fear River, about a thousand yards distant, that no troops could withstand it five minutes.
>
> General Terry landed his troops as rapidly as one hundred and twenty boats could put them on shore. With their intrenching tools, within an hour after landing, they had thrown up heavy intrenchments right across the land to the river, and manned them so that at the very first step the fort was comparatively cut off from all support. By two o'clock, 8,000 troops had been landed, and the artillery posted behind the breastworks....
>
> General Hoke had the immediate command of the Confederate troops, and it was his purpose to attack the Federals as they landed from the boats. His cavalry was thrown out on the right flank to observe the Federal movements, and report the first step towards establishing a line across the neck of land to the river; but it was found in the morning [January 14] that, owing to the want of vigilance on the part of the Confederates, the Federals had laid out a second line of defence during the night; General Terry's troops, passing between Hoke's cavalry and threading their way through the thick undergrowth of the marsh, made their advance to the river, and the next morning held an intrenched line on Hoke's right flank, extending nearly across the peninsula.[21]

Colonel Lamb and his garrison braced for a Union assault. "The night of the 12th of January," Lamb recorded in his account of the battle, "from the ramparts of Fort Fisher, I saw the great armada returning. My mounted pickets had informed me of its coming. I began at once to put my works in order for action. I had but 800 men,—the 36th North Carolina,—at least 100 of whom were not fit for duty. Sunrise the next morning revealed to us the most formidable armada the world had ever known,[22] supplemented by transports carrying about 8500 troops.... I had telegraphed for reenforcements, and during the day and night following about 700 arrived ... giving me 1500, all told, up to the morning of January 15th, including the sick and slightly wounded."[23] Later reinforcements would increase his strength to more than two thousand.

Most of Hoke's six thousand troops, it turned out, were unavailable to oppose the Union landing because General Braxton Bragg, appointed commander of the Confederate army's Department of North Carolina by President Davis six weeks earlier and charged with the defense of Wilmington, had called the troops to Wilmington for a parade, and by the time they returned to Federal Point, the Union troops were ashore. Without any orders to mount an attack, Hoke merely had his men deploy in a skirmish line across the peninsula in hopes of blocking a Union advance on Wilmington.

Terry, meanwhile, had his men build campfires at the landing site to make it appear they were bivouacking on the beach, and as darkness fell, his main force began advancing southward along the river, toward the fort. About two miles above the fort the troops started digging the second set of breastworks mentioned in Porter's account. Colonel Joseph C. Abbott's brigade and Brigadier General Charles J. Paine's division, composed of black troops, were posted on that line of breastworks.

All the while, Porter's fleet continued to hammer the fort. "All day and night on the 13th and 14th of January," Colonel Lamb recounted, "the navy continued its ceaseless torment; it was impossible to repair damages at night on the land-face. The *Ironsides* and monitors bowled their eleven and fifteen-inch shells along the parapet, scattering shrapnel in the darkness. We could scarcely gather up and bury our dead without fresh casualties. At least two hundred had been killed and wounded in the two days since the fight began. Only three or four of my land guns were of any service."[24] It was Porter's intention to diminish Fort Fisher's defenses as much as possible before an effort was made to storm the fort.

While the bombardment raged during the 13th, a Friday, Major General W.H.C. Whiting, the Confederate district commander in Wilmington, Lamb's commanding officer, suddenly and unexpectedly arrived at the fort with his staff, having walked up from Battery Buchanan. "Lamb, my boy," he said, taking Lamb by surprise as he stood on the works, "I have come to share your fate. You and your garrison are to be sacrificed."[25]

"Don't say so, general," Lamb replied. "We shall certainly whip the enemy again." Whiting then gave Lamb a picture of hopelessness, telling him he had just come from Wilmington, where General Bragg, Whiting's commander, was hurriedly removing his supplies and ammunition and was looking for a position to which he could fall back in the face of the impending Union assault on Fort Fisher. "I offered him [Whiting] the command," Lamb related, "although he came unarmed and without orders; but he refused, saying he would counsel with me, but would leave me to conduct the defense."[26]

The telegraph line between Fort Fisher and Bragg's headquarters at Sugar Loaf, seven miles above the north end of Federal Point, was still up, and Lamb asked Whiting to wire Bragg and urge him to order an attack on the Union force that night, when darkness would prevent the U.S. fleet from supporting Terry's troops with their armament, and saying that the fort's garrison would launch an attack on the Union force simultaneous with an attack on it from the north. The call for help went out, but no reply was received from Bragg's headquarters.

On the evening of the 14th, after a second day of bombardment, General Terry climbed into a small boat at the ocean's edge and had himself rowed out to Porter's flagship, the *Malvern*, for a meeting with the admiral, arriving on board the vessel at 9 P.M. Terry sought assurance that the fleet's artillery could take out the fort's remaining guns on the north parapet before he sent his troops against the fort; and further, he wanted the fleet's guns to blast apart the wooden palisade in front of the parapet so that his troops could swiftly rush through the gap made by the Navy's shells. Porter promised him it would be done, seeming somewhat wounded that Terry would question the Navy's ability to meet the challenge. The two officers went over the details of their battle plan. The fleet's warships would be signaled at nine o'clock the following morning, January 15, to assume their arranged battle positions and would open fire as soon as they anchored. Terry's infantry and the Navy's force of seamen and Marines would launch their separate assaults at 3 P.M., the soldiers attacking Fort Fisher's north face and the naval force attacking the sea face on the east. "The Admiral and General," Porter remarked, "had a perfect understanding and established a system of signals by the Army Code, by which they could converse at pleasure, even amid the din of battle, when they were nearly a mile apart."[27]

Promptly at 9 A.M. the next morning, a Sunday, the warships began moving into position and about two hours later opened a heavy fire on the beleaguered rebel fortress. The upper batteries of the fort returned the fire as best they could, but inflicted no serious damage on the fleet. The Confederates working the heavy guns of the Mound Battery, after stubbornly directing a galling fire on the fleet, were at last driven from their positions by the fleet's artillery, and their big guns fell silent. The steady and well-aimed bombardment eventually disabled most of the guns on the fort's north face, and they, too, were rendered silent.

Inside the fort, Colonel Lamb observed the damage and the increasing threat. "The sea was calm, the naval gunners had become accurate by practice, and before noon but one heavy gun, protected by the angle of the north-east bastion, remained serviceable on that [the north] face. The harvest of wounded and dead was increased, and at noon I had not 1200 men to defend the long line of works. The enemy were now preparing to assault; we saw their skirmish-line on the left digging rifle-pits close to our torpedo lines and their columns along the river-shore massing for the attack, while their sharp-shooters were firing upon every head that showed itself upon our [north] front."[28]

Lieutenant Commander Thomas O. Selfridge, commander of the U.S. gunboat *Huron*, a participant in the assault, detailed the actions of the Union forces:

> Before noon the signal was made for the assaulting column of sailors and marines to land. From thirty-five of the sixty ships of the fleet boats shoved off, making, with their flags flying as they pulled toward the beach in line abreast, a most spirited scene. The general order of Admiral Porter required that the assaulting column of sailors should be armed with cutlasses and pistols. It was also intended that trenches or covered ways should be dug for the marines close to the fort and that our assault should be made under the cover of their fire; but it was impossible to dig such shelter trenches near enough to do much good under fire in broad daylight.
>
> The sailors as they landed from their boats were a heterogeneous assembly, companies of two hundred or more from each of the larger ships, down to small parties of twenty each from the gun-boats. They had been for months confined on shipboard, had never drilled together, and their arms, the old-fashioned cutlass and pistol, were hardly the weapons to cope with the rifles and bayonets of the enemy. Sailor-like, however, they looked upon the landing in the light of a lark, and few thought the sun would set with a loss of one-fifth of their number....
>
> The whole force marched up the beach and lay down under the cover just outside rifle range, awaiting the movements of the army.... At a preconcerted signal the sailors sprang forward to the assault, closely following the water's edge, where the inclined beach gave them a slight cover. We were opened upon in front by the great mound battery, and by the fire of a thousand rifles. Though many dropped rapidly under this fire, the column never faltered, and when the angle where the two faces of the fort unite was reached the head halted to allow the rear to come up. This halt was fatal, for as the others came up they followed suit and lay down till the space between the parapet and the edge of the water was filled....
>
> The rush of the sailors was over; they were packed like sheep in a pen, while the enemy were crowding the ramparts not forty yards away, and shooting into them as fast as they could fire. There was nothing to reply with but *pistols*.... Flesh and blood could not long endure being

killed in this slaughter-pen, and the rear of the sailors broke, followed by the whole body, in spite of all efforts to rally them....

A loss of some three hundred in killed and wounded attests the gallant nature of the assault....[29]

The advance of the Army on the fort's north parapet was led by the brigade of Brigadier General Newton Martin Curtis, which had also led the attack in December. Curtis's troops moved out of their entrenchment about 2:30 P.M. and advanced by stages to a point near the bastion at the river end of the parapet. The two other brigades of General Ames's division, Colonel Galusha Pennypacker's brigade and Colonel Louis Bell's brigade, moved up also, one behind the other. On a signal, the fleet's fire was shifted away from the westernmost part of the parapet, and Curtis's men charged the half-bastion next to the river, hurrying across the marshy ground. A detail of axe-wielding infantrymen rushed up to the palisade and began hacking away at the parts of it still standing, hindering the troops' way to the parapet. So swiftly did they clear away the shattered palisade that Curtis's troops immediately swarmed over the parapet and began fighting their way to the first traverse.

When Lamb turned from the fort's sea face after the repulse of the sailors' and Marines' assault, he saw, with astonishment, three Union battle flags flying atop the north parapet. Whiting noticed them, too, at the same time, and ordered a group of defenders to pull down the flags and drive the attackers from the parapet, rushing toward the flags as he did so. "They ... recovered the gun-chamber with great slaughter," Lamb related, "and on the parapet and on the long traverse of the next gun-chamber the contestants were savagely firing into each other's faces, and in some cases clubbing their guns, being too close to load and fire.

"Whiting had quickly been wounded by two shots and had been carried to the hospital bomb-proof. I saw that the Confederates were exposed not only to the fire in front, but to a galling infantry fire from the captured salient. I saw also a fresh force pouring into the left of the work, now offering no resistance."[30]

The fresh force was Pennypacker's brigade, which stormed into the melee. While taking the third traverse, Colonel Pennypacker was severely wounded. Next in the unrelenting Union assault came the troops of Bell's brigade, which took positions along the river inside the fort.

"We had now to contend with a column advancing around the rear of the left bastion into the interior plane of the fort," Lamb related in his account. "It moved slowly and cautiously.... I met it with an effective infantry fire, my men using the remains of an old work as a breastwork and taking advantage of every object that would afford cover, for we were now greatly outnumbered.... As my men would fall others would take their places. It was a soldier's fight at that point, for there could be no organization; the officers of both forces were loading and firing with their men. If there has ever been a longer or more stubborn hand-to-hand encounter, I have failed to meet with it in history."[31]

By 6 P.M. the Union force had taken nine of the north parapet's seventeen traverses, and Terry then ordered Colonel Abbott's brigade, of the Twenty-fourth Corps' First Division, and the Twenty-seventh Regiment, the black regiment of General Paine's division of the Twenty-fifth Corps, to move up from the entrenchment line and reinforce Ames's men inside the fort. Abbott continued the attack on the north face, sweeping the Confederates from their positions there, and Ames's troops threw their weight against the defenders on the sea face.

While attempting to rally his men and have them charge Ames's troops with bayonets, waving his sword and urging the defenders forward, Lamb was shot in the left hip. His bayonet charge failed when the Union troops let loose a volley of musket fire. Lamb was carried off to the fort's hospital, realizing on the way that his wound would not allow him to rejoin the fight. "In the hospital," he related, "I found General Whiting suffering uncomplainingly from his two wounds. He told me Bragg had ignored his presence in the fort and had not noticed his messages [urging Bragg to order an attack].... I again sent a message to Bragg begging him to come to the rescue.... About 8 o'clock at night my aide came to me and said the ammunition was giving out...; that the enemy had possession of nearly all of the land-face; that it was impossible to hold out much longer, and suggested that it would be wise to surrender the fort, as a further struggle might be a useless sacrifice of life.

"I replied that so long as I lived I would not surrender the fort; that Bragg must soon come to the rescue, and it would save us. General Whiting remarked, 'Lamb, when you die I will assume command, and I will not surrender the fort.'"[32]

Less than an hour later Lamb received word that Abbott's and Paine's troops had emptied the north face of defenders. Confederate Major James Reilly, upon whom command of the fort and garrison had devolved following the wounding of Colonel Lamb, then had both Whiting and Lamb carried on stretchers to Battery Buchanan, at the southwest extremity of the fort.

"When we reached Battery Buchanan there was a mile of level beach between us and our pursuers, swept by two 11-inch guns and a 24-pounder, and in close proximity to the battery, a commodious wharf where transports could have come to carry the men off," Lamb related. "We expected to cover with this battery the retreat of the remnant of the garrison, but we found the guns spiked, and every means of transportation, even the barge and crew

Battle of Fort Fisher. After a failed attempt against it on Christmas 1864, the fort was captured in a fiercely fought joint Army-Navy operation on January 15, 1865. (LIBRARY OF CONGRESS)

of the colonel commanding [Lamb], taken by Captain R.F. Chapman, of our navy, who, following the example of General Bragg, had abandoned us to our fate."[33]

Also abandoning Lamb and his garrison to their fate was General Hoke. He had made some demonstrations against the line of entrenchments occupied by Paine's troops, and the survivors of the Navy's assault on the sea face were quickly moved to reinforce Paine. A light skirmish followed, and Hoke and his six thousand rebel troops withdrew.

The fate of Lamb and his men was soon learned. About 10 P.M. Abbott's brigade advanced to Battery Buchanan and forced the surrender. Lamb records the surrender as having been received from Major James Hill and Lieutenant George Parker. Lamb came away a wounded prisoner and a sore loser, believing that the U.S. Army had violated the rules. "[Even] after the land armament, with palisades and torpedoes, had been destroyed [by the U.S. Navy's artillery fire], no assault would have been practicable in the presence of Bragg's force," Lamb maintained, "had it been under a competent officer.... Had there been no fleet to assist the army at Fort Fisher the Federal infantry could not have dared assault it until its land defenses had been destroyed by gradual approaches. For the first time in the history of sieges the land defenses of the works were destroyed, not by any act of the besieging army, but by the concentrated fire, direct and enfilading, of an immense fleet poured upon them without intermission, until torpedo wires were cut, palisades breached ... and the slopes of the work were rendered practicable for assault."[34]

Admiral Porter tended to agree with Lamb on the point of his fleet's contribution to the fight for Fort Fisher. "We visited Fort Fisher and the adjoining works," he wrote in his account of the battle, "and found their strength greatly beyond what had been conceived. An engineer might be excused for saying they could not be captured except by regular siege.... [Y]et it was captured by a handful of men under the fire of the guns of the fleet, and in seven hours after the attack began in earnest. We cannot say too much in praise of the conduct of the fleet during the time it had been engaged in these operations."[35]

Porter took great satisfaction from the victory, won by the combined efforts of the U.S. Army and Navy. "Thus ended one of the most remarkable battles on record," he remarked, "and one which did more damage to the Confederate cause than any that took place during the war. Twenty-five hundred Confederates manned Fort Fisher: eighteen hundred were taken prisoner; the rest were killed or wounded."[36] General Whiting was among those who later died of their wounds.

The Union forces had paid a heavy cost in lives as well. Casualty reports varied, but the estimates were that as many as 955 soldiers were killed, wounded or missing in the January assault. When the casualties in the December attack were added to those, the Army's estimated losses totaled as many as 1,234 killed, wounded or missing. The Navy's losses totaled 393 sailors and Marines killed or wounded in the January assault, and eighty-three casualties in the December assault. Total Union losses for both battles were estimated at between 1,290 to 1,710.[37] Among some fifty Army officers killed or wounded was Colonel Bell, killed, and Colonel Pennypacker and General Curtis, wounded.

The dead of both sides were buried temporarily on the beach beside the fort and would later be reinterred in cemeteries in Wilmington, the Union dead in one, the Confederates in another.

Five weeks after Fort Fisher fell, on February 22, Wilmington was surrendered to Union forces that, supported by Navy vessels, had marched and fought their way up both banks of the Cape Fear River and confronted a then defenseless city, which they promptly occupied.

Sherman in the Carolinas,
January 21 to March 24, 1865

Sherman was feeling, as he said, "great uneasiness" after reading Grant's two recent letters. Both of them reached him after Fort McAllister had been taken, the fort's capture having opened the Ogeechee River to Union steamers carrying mail to him and his men. In the first letter, written on December 3, Grant told Sherman, "I do not intend to give you any thing like directions for future action, but will state a general idea I have, and will get your views." In the second, written December 6, Grant was more disappointingly definite. "I have concluded," Grant wrote, "that the most important operation toward closing out the rebellion will be to close out Lee and his army…. My idea now is that you establish a base on the sea-coast, fortify and leave in it all your artillery and cavalry, and enough infantry to protect them…. With the balance of your command come here by water with all dispatch…."[1]

Sherman was very much concerned. Immediately embarking for Virginia represented a total and bothersome change in his plans. In a long reply to Grant, written on December 16, before the capture of Savannah, Sherman tactfully let the general in chief know what he had intended to do, perhaps hinting at his disappointment: "[W]ith my present command, I had expected, after reducing Savannah, instantly to march to Columbia, South Carolina; thence to Raleigh, and thence to report to you. But this would consume, it may be, six weeks' time after the fall of Savannah…."[2] Dutifully, Sherman swallowed hard and accepted his commander's orders, promising Grant he would "not delay my execution of your order of the 6th, which will depend alone upon the time it will require to obtain transportation by sea."[3] It turned out that, according to General Halleck's estimate, obtaining sufficient transport ships and moving Sherman's troops to Virginia by sea would take two months or so, which Halleck pointed out to Grant. Having already been advised that Sherman could reach him in six weeks after the capture of Savannah and knowing Sherman's desire to continue his wrathful march, Grant changed his mind about having Sherman's troops come to him by sea. On December 16 Halleck wrote to Sherman to tell him so: "General Grant's wishes … are that this whole matter of your future actions should be entirely left to your discretion."[4] Two days later, on December 18, Grant himself wrote Sherman a similar message and congratulated him on the success of his campaign thus far.

Sherman replied to Grant on the same day he received that letter. "I am pleased that you have modified your former orders," he wrote, "for I feared that the transportation by sea would very much disturb the unity and morale of my army, now so perfect."[5] In that same letter Sherman sketched out his plan for the continued march, as Grant had requested him to do:

> I feel no doubt whatever as to our future plans. I have thought them over so long and well that they appear as clear as daylight. I left Augusta untouched on purpose, because the enemy will be in doubt as to my objective point, after we cross the Savannah River, whether it be Augusta or Charleston, and will naturally divide his forces. I will then move either on Branchville or Columbia, by any curved line that gives us the best supplies, breaking up in our course as much railroad as possible; then, ignoring Charleston and Augusta both, I would occupy Columbia and Camden, pausing there long enough to observe the effect. I would then strike for the Charleston & Wilmington Railroad, somewhere between the Santee and Cape Fear Rivers, and, if possible, communicate with the fleet under Admiral Dahlgren (whom I find a most agreeable gentleman, accommodating himself to our wishes and plans). Then I would favor an attack on Wilmington.... Charleston is now a mere desolated wreck, and is hardly worth the time it would take to starve it out.... But, on the hypothesis of ignoring Charleston and taking Wilmington, I would then favor a movement direct on Raleigh. The game is then up with Lee, unless he comes out of Richmond, avoids you and fights me; in which case I should reckon on your being on his heels. Now that Hood is used up by Thomas, I feel disposed to bring the matter to an issue as quick as possible. I feel confident that I can break up the whole railroad system of South Carolina and North Carolina, and be on the Roanoke, either at Raleigh or Weldon, by the time spring fairly opens; and, if you feel confident that you can whip Lee outside of his intrenchments, I feel equally confident that I can handle him in the open country.[6]

In an earlier letter to Grant, written on December 18, Sherman had revealed an additional purpose in continuing the march: "With Savannah in our possession, at some future time if not now, we can punish South Carolina as she deserves, and as thousands of the people in Georgia hoped we would do. I do sincerely believe that the whole United States, North and South, would rejoice to have this army turned loose on South Carolina, to devastate that State in the manner we have done in Georgia, and it would have a direct and immediate bearing on your campaign in Virginia."[7]

Sherman was keenly aware that his troops held hard feelings toward South Carolina and were eager to punish its people. "Somehow, our men had got the idea that South Carolina was the cause of all our troubles," Sherman wrote in his memoir. "[H]er people were the first to fire on Fort Sumter, had been in a great hurry to precipitate the country into civil war; and therefore on them should fall the scourge of war in its worst form. Taunting messages had also come to us, when in Georgia, to the effect that, when we should reach South Carolina, we would find a people less passive, who would fight us to the bitter end, daring us to come over, etc.; so that I saw and felt that we would not be able longer to restrain our men as we had done in Georgia."[8]

Sherman now had the freedom to do as he thought best, which was to storm through South Carolina and wreak havoc. "My aim then was, to whip the rebels, to humble their pride, to follow them to their inmost recesses, and make them fear and dread us."[9] At the same time he sought to strike fear in the hearts of Southerners, however, he seemed to resent their feeling it. Among Savannah's twenty-five thousand residents were the wife of Confederate General Gustavus Smith and a brother of Confederate General Hardee. Smith's wife and Hardee's brother, a cotton merchant, both came to Sherman at his Savannah headquarters, on separate occasions, with notes from the generals addressed to Sherman, asking protection for Mrs. Smith and Hardee's brother. Sherman found it strange that the two generals, having heard reports of the horrors committed by Sherman's troops, should, as he said, "commit their families to our custody." He protested that "These officers knew well that these reports [of atrocities] were exaggerated in the extreme, and yet tacitly assented to these false publications, to arouse the drooping energies of the people of the South."[10]

Before taking to the road again, Sherman took steps to stabilize the situation in Savannah. He had no intention of treating Savannah, a seaport useful to the Union, the same way he had treated Atlanta. He appointed General Geary, whose division had been the first to enter Savannah, as the city's commandant, to act, Sherman said, as "a sort of governor." Geary, an able administrator, had been governor of the Kansas Territory and had earlier served as the first mayor of San Francisco.

"He very soon established a good police, maintained admirable order, and I doubt if Savannah, either before or since, has had a better government than during our stay," Sherman boasted. "Schools were opened, and the churches every Sunday were well filled with most devout and respectful congregations; stores were reopened, and markets for provisions, meat, wood, etc. were established, so that each family, regardless of race, color, or opinion, could procure all the necessaries and even luxuries of life, provided they had the money. Of course, many families were actually destitute of this, and to these were issued stores from our own stock of supplies."[11]

Preparations for the defense of the city were also made, just in case. Colonel Poe, Sherman's chief engineer, laid out a new, tighter line for a defensive parapet that would allow Savannah to be held by a relatively small garrison, and a large detail of soldiers was promptly put to work to construct it. Supplies, which were arriving almost daily aboard river steamers, were being stockpiled in a large depot.

Heavy rains also delayed the resumption of Sherman's march, which he had hoped to start around the middle of January. The roads were rendered virtually impassable. The Savannah River was so swollen it overflowed its banks and flooded vast areas around the city. At Sister's Ferry, forty miles upstream from Savannah, where the left wing of Sherman's army was to cross, the river had swelled to a width of three miles, and the accelerated current, carrying all manner of debris, had swept away the pontoon bridge that General Slocum's engineers had thrown across it.

Sherman's plan was to have the troops of General Howard's right wing shipped on transports north to Beaufort, South Carolina, via Hilton Head, feinting on Charleston, while Slocum's left wing marched westward, as if to attack Augusta, thereby continuing to divide the Confederate forces, which were now under the overall command of Beauregard. Those forces included eighteen thousand troops commanded by Hardee, 6,700 cavalrymen commanded by Wheeler, 1,450 men of the Georgia militia under Gustavus Smith's command and eleven thousand troops, infantry and artillery, that had been part of Hood's army in Tennessee, only about half of whom had so far made it to South Carolina. Of that aggregate, an estimated 33,450 men were available to try to block the new phase of Sherman's march.[12]

On January 19 Sherman issued orders to commence the movement of his whole army: "These were to group the right wing of the army at Pocotaligo [South Carolina], already held by the Seventeenth Corps, and the left wing and cavalry at or near Robertsville, in South Carolina."[13] Two days later, on January 21, Sherman, with his headquarters staff, plus horses and wagons, boarded a steamer for Hilton Head, there to confer with Major General John G. Foster, commander of the U.S. Army's Department of the South, whose headquarters were at Hilton Head. Foster was to take command of the garrison at Savannah. From

Hilton Head Sherman proceeded to Beaufort, which he reached on January 23. On the 24th he rode to a plantation near Pocotaligo, where he stopped for the night and slept on the floor of an abandoned house. To keep warm during the bitter-cold night he burned a mantel clock and a wooden bed frame in the fireplace, which was, he claimed, "the only act of vandalism that I recall done by myself personally during the war."[14] The next morning he rode to Pocotaligo, situated on a north-south road and from which another road led northeastward through pine forests to Charleston.[15]

Sherman felt that his presence at Pocotaligo, where the right wing was assembling, would further deceive Hardee and the Confederate command into thinking Charleston was Sherman's objective. General Howard and his right-wing troops reached Pocotaligo with little opposition. Hardee had apparently decided he would make a stand only on the east side of the line of the Salkehatchie and Combahee rivers, east of Pocotaligo. One of Howard's divisions was sent to make a demonstration near the Combahee as if to cross it, and then on February 1 the right wing began its march northward along the west side of the Salke-hatchie with orders to cross the river at Rivers Bridge, about thirty-five miles above Poco-taligo. Sherman rode with Logan's Fifteenth Corps. Kilpatrick's cavalry rode to Barnwell to make a crossing some twenty miles farther up the Salkehatchie. About eight miles north of Barnwell, on the South Carolina Railroad, was Blackville, where Sherman intended the two wings of his army to come together. He was keeping in contact with General Slocum as both wings advanced.

Until the right wing approached Rivers Bridge, on February 3, the only impediment to their progress was the trees that Wheeler's rebel cavalrymen had felled into the roadway to hinder the Union advance. They were quickly cleared away. On the east bank of the Salkehatchie at Rivers Bridge, though, a Confederate infantry brigade attempted to prevent the Seventeenth Corps from crossing the still-swollen river. Men of General Giles Smith's division and General Mower's division waded across the river through shoulder-high water above the crossing, entered the swamp on the east side of the river and flanked the defending Confederates, driving them from the crossing. "It was in this attack that General Wager Swayne lost his leg, and he had to be conveyed back to Pocotaligo," Sherman related. "Still, the loss of life was very small, in proportion to the advantages gained, for the enemy at once abandoned the whole line of the Salkehatchie."[16]

The crossing of the Salkehatchie and the forbidding swamps that bordered it, even without an enemy to contest their advance, was a monumentally difficult undertaking for Sherman's army, which, as it moved, built bridges spanning dozens of streams, corduroyed miles of marshy roads and passed through a virtually impassible terrain with their horses, artillery and supply wagons. Confederate General Hardee, familiar with the area, confessed, "I wouldn't have believed it if I hadn't seen it happen."

On February 5, with Kilpatrick's cavalry at Barnwell and elements of the Twentieth Corps having reached Bufort's Bridge, just above Rivers Bridge, Sherman issued orders to march to Midway to strike the vital South Carolina Railroad there. Riding with the Fifteenth Corps through a rainstorm, Sherman reached Midway on the 7th, by which time the Seventeenth Corps had already occupied Midway, the town having been taken first by foragers who, looking for plunder, had stumbled into it and seized the railroad. The troops that followed them in then set about the task of tearing up the tracks, burning the ties and twisting the rails. General Slocum, commander of Sherman's left wing, in his account of the march, described the technique of railroad destruction:

A detail of men to do the work should be made on the evening before operations are to com-mence. The number to be detailed being, of course, dependent upon the amount of work to be done, I estimate that one thousand men can easily destroy about five miles of track per day, and do it thoroughly.... Your detail should be divided into three sections of about equal numbers. I will suppose the detail to consist of three thousand men. The first thing to be done is to reverse the relative positions of the ties and iron rails, placing the ties up and the rails under them. To do this, Section No. 1, consisting of one thousand men, is distributed along one side of the track, one man at the end of each tie. At a given signal each man seizes a tie, lifts it gently till it assumes a vertical position, and then at another signal pushes it forward so that when it falls the ties will be over the rails. Then each man loosens his tie from the rail. This done, Section No. 1 moves forward to another portion of the road, and Section No. 2 advances and is distrib-uted along the road recently occupied by Section No. 1. The duty of the second section is to collect the ties, place them in piles of about thirty ties each — place the rails on the top of these piles, the center of each rail being over the center of the pile, and then set fire to the ties. Sec-tion No. 2 then follows No. 1. As soon as the rails are sufficiently heated Section No. 3 takes the place of No. 2; and upon this devolves the most important duty, viz., the effectual destruc-tion of the rail.... Unless closely watched, soldiers will content themselves with simply bending the rails around trees.... No rail should be regarded as properly treated till it has assumed the shape of a doughnut; it must not only be bent but twisted ... which precludes all hope of restoring it to its former shape except by re-rolling.[17]

Slocum's left wing had been delayed several days while waiting for a pontoon bridge to be built across the flood-widened Savannah River and had been further delayed after crossing into South Carolina, impeded by torpedoes planted in the roadway, which killed or wounded a number of his men. "This was unfortunate for that section of the state," Slocum wrote, hinting at the retaliatory destruction his troops inflicted there. "Planting torpedoes for the defense of a position is legitimate warfare, but our soldiers regarded the act of placing them in a highway where no contest was anticipated as something akin to poisoning a stream of water; it is not recognized as fair or legitimate warfare. If that section of South Carolina suffered more severely than any other, it was due in part to the blundering of people who were more zealous than wise."[18]

On February 9 Slocum reached Blackville, and the next day Sherman rode to Blackville to confer with him and Kilpatrick. Satisfied that all was going well, Sherman issued orders for the march to continue toward Columbia, the right wing striking Orangeburg on its way, the left wing moving northward by a parallel route, and Kilpatrick feinting toward Aiken to keep the rebels worried about an assault on Augusta, then covering the army's left flank to ward off possible attacks by Wheeler's rebel cavalry.

The march resumed on February 11. Sherman's orders were for all corps, after crossing the South Edisto River, to halt on the road that led from Orangeburg to Augusta, called the Edgefield Road, and wait until it was certain that the Seventeenth Corps had taken pos-session of Orangeburg, an objective Sherman considered important. "Its occupation," he explained, "would sever the communication between Charleston and Columbia."[19] The leading elements of all of Sherman's columns reached the Edgefield road on the 12th, and there the Seventeenth Corps turned right, toward Orangeburg.

As the lead division, General Giles Smith's division, neared the Edisto River, just outside the town, it ran up against rebel defenders on the opposite side of the river and was forced to unlimber a battery of artillery to attempt to force passage across the river. Sherman then ordered Mower's division to drop below the town about five miles and cross there to flank the Confederates. "He laid his pontoon bridge," Sherman related, "but the bottom on the other side was overflowed, and the men had to wade through it, in places as deep as their waists. I was with this division at the time, on foot, trying to pick my way across the overflowed bottom."[20] When the rebel defenders realized the Union troops had effected a crossing below their position, Sherman figured, they would quickly abandon the position and withdraw, which was what they in fact did. Giles Smith's men then repaired the broken bridge across the Edisto at the point the Confederates had been defending, and the blue-coated troops streamed across. Sherman was among the first to cross the bridge and enter Orangeburg.

Even before he and his troops entered the town, Sherman could see there were buildings on fire. A store had apparently been set ablaze by its owner, and the flames had spread to other buildings. The Union troops soon extinguished those fires, but started new ones to destroy the railroad depot and bales of stored cotton. That done, a stretch of the railroad was torn up and a large hospital sheltering orphaned children was supplied with food, and then the troops pulled out of Orangeburg and headed for the South Carolina capital, Columbia.

On the morning of February 16 the Fifteenth Corps, with whom Sherman was riding, reached the outskirts of Columbia, its lead units arriving in time to see the bridge spanning the Broad River, west of the city, engulfed in flames. Sherman then instructed Slocum to move his two corps across the Broad at Alston, fifteen miles above Columbia. From his vantage point, Sherman could see the handsome, granite state house, its construction unfinished, and also the ruins of the train station, still smoldering from the fire set by Confederates before withdrawing. That night, Sherman camped near an abandoned prisoner-of-war camp known as Camp Sorghum, opposite Columbia. There he saw, as he said, "the mud-hovels and holes in the ground which our prisoners had made to shelter themselves from the winter's cold and the summer's heat."[21]

During the night of the 16th and early morning of the 17th General Howard had had Colonel George Stone's brigade ferry itself across the river on rafts made from pontoons, and by daybreak that brigade had established a defensive position on the Columbia side of the river to cover the construction of a pontoon bridge. About mid-morning on the 17th, while Sherman sat on a log with Howard, watching the men assemble the bridge, he received a message carried from the far side of the river, sent by Colonel Stone. The mayor of Columbia, Stone reported, had come to Stone carrying a white flag and handed him a message of surrender addressed to Sherman. "The Confederate forces having evacuated Columbia," the mayor, Dr. Thomas L. Goodwyn, wrote, "I deem it my duty ... to ask for its citizens the treatment accorded by the usages of civilized warfare. I therefore respectfully request that you will send a sufficient guard in advance of the army, to maintain order...."[22]

Sherman told Howard to let Colonel Stone go into the city and that the rest of the troops would enter Columbia as soon as the pontoon·bridge was ready.

The messenger who brought Mayor Goodwyn's note also brought a note from the mother superior of a convent school in Columbia, Sister Baptista Lynch. "She claimed to have been a teacher in a convent in Brown County, Ohio," Sherman related, "at the time my daughter Minnie was a pupil there, ... therefore asking special protection.... I gave the note to my brother-in-law, Colonel [Charles] Ewing, then inspector-general on my staff, with instructions to see this lady, and assure her that we contemplated no destruction of any private property in Columbia at all."[23]

Things did not go as Sherman contemplated. During the evening of the 17th he was awakened by the brilliance of flames that lighted up the room where he was sleeping. Arising, he discovered that Columbia was on fire, its residences and other buildings alike, the blaze being spread by a high wind. "The whole air," Sherman related, "was full of sparks and of flying masses of cotton, shingles, etc., some of which were carried four or five blocks, and started new fires." By the time the wind calmed and the fires were brought under control, which was around four o'clock in the morning of the 18th, the flames, as Sherman reported, "had burned out the very heart of the city, embracing several churches, the old State-House, and the school or asylum of that very Sister of Charity who had appealed for my personal protection.[24]

Sherman denied responsibility for the massive blaze. He blamed Wade Hampton's rebel troopers, who had set fires before evacuating the city. General Slocum in his account described the effects of the catastrophe and gave a different explanation of its cause:

> The lurid flames could easily be seen from my camp, many miles distant. Nearly all the public buildings, several churches, an orphan asylum, and many of the residences were destroyed. The city was filled with helpless women and children and invalids, many of whom were rendered houseless and homeless in a single night. No sadder scene was presented during the war. The suffering of so many helpless and innocent persons could not but move the hardest heart. The question as to who was immediately responsible for this disaster has given rise to some controversy. I do not believe that General Sherman countenanced or was in any degree responsible for it. I believe the immediate cause of the disaster was a free use of whisky (which was supplied to the soldiers by citizens with great liberality). A drunken soldier with a musket in one hand and a match in the other is not a pleasant visitor to have about the house on a dark, windy night, particularly when for a series of years you have urged him to come, so that you might have an opportunity of performing a surgical operation on him.[25]

Sherman claimed that he did all he could to take care of those who had lost their homes. "General Howard, in concert with the mayor did all that was possible to provide other houses for them; and by my authority he turned over to the Sisters of Charity the Methodist College, and to the mayor five hundred beef-cattle, to help feed the people; I also gave the mayor ... one hundred muskets, with which to arm a guard to maintain order after we should leave the neighborhood.[26]

Even so, arson had been and continued to be the major form of punishment inflicted by Sherman's army as it burned and marauded its way deeper into South Carolina. From Hardeeville to Orangeburg the path of Slocum's wing was marked by ruined communities — Purysburgh, Robertville, Lawtonville, McPhersonville. The New York *Herald* reporter traveling with Slocum's columns wrote that "Houses were burned as they were found. Whenever a view could be had from high ground, black columns of smoke were seen rising here and there within a circuit of twenty or thirty miles."[27] Kilpatrick's cavalrymen set fire to houses and other buildings in Barnwell, and his officers threw themselves a party at the town's hotel to celebrate the destruction. Kilpatrick sent a boastful message to Sherman saying, "We have changed the name of Barnwell to Burnwell."[28]

The atrocities of Sherman's army in the Carolinas, as in Georgia, included incidents of rape. Near Aiken an elderly Baptist minister was found by Confederate cavalrymen crying outside a house beside the road on which a squad of Wheeler's troopers was following the Union column at a distance. The minister told the rebel cavalrymen that Yankee soldiers had just left there after raping his daughter. The Confederates sped off and caught up with a group of Union bummers. They killed all but one of the bummers and left the lone survivor, who pleaded innocence, lying in the road, severely wounded, lying among the corpses of his comrades. More raping, of both white and black women and girls, was to come. Two days after Sherman's troops pulled out of Columbia seven Union soldiers were reported to have tied up a teenage white girl and taken turns raping her. When rebel soldiers came upon her family's house later the same day, they found the house ransacked, the girl's mother raving hysterically and the girl dead.

From that atrocity more murders followed. The rebel soldiers tracked the Union rapists, caught them and slashed their throats, leaving them dead beside the road, with a sign that read, "These are the seven." Other Union soldiers were picked off by Confederates and killed. The bodies of twenty-one of Slocum's soldiers were discovered thrown into a ravine. Eighteen of Kilpatrick's troopers were similarly slain and left with a sign saying, "Death to all foragers." To retaliate, Sherman reportedly ordered his commanders to kill a Confederate prisoner for each Union soldier found murdered. He instructed his generals: "If our foragers commit excesses, punish them yourself, but never let an enemy judge between our men and the law."[29]

While denying responsibility for burning Columbia, Sherman, curiously, also claimed credit for its destruction. Recounting his troops' departure from the city, he wrote, "Having utterly ruined Columbia, the right wing began its march northward, toward Winnsboro, on the 20th."[30] The army reached Winnsboro on February 21, pillaged a number of its residences and left it by the end of the day.

At Winnsboro the two wings again separated, Howard's right wing turning eastward toward Camden, on its way to Cheraw, and Slocum's left wing continuing northward, as if bound for Charlotte, keeping Beauregard guessing, requiring him to keep his forces divided. Kilpatrick was ordered to take his cavalry northward to Chester, South Carolina and then turn northeastward. The entire army was now marching through days of ceaseless rain.

Riding with the Twentieth Corps, Sherman reached Rock Hill, South Carolina on the 22nd and crossed the Catawba River there on the 23rd, after a pontoon bridge had been laid across it. The heavy rain so swelled the river that the bridge was washed away shortly after Sherman and the troops of the Twentieth Corps had crossed it, leaving the Fourteenth Corps on the west side of the river. Sherman and the Twentieth Corps then waited four days till the Fourteenth Corps could cross. While they waited, Sherman heard that Hardee had evacuated Charleston and that Wilmington, North Carolina had been captured. On hearing those items of news, Sherman, as he said, "had every reason to be satisfied that our march was fully reaping all the fruits we could possibly ask for."[31]

Once General Jeff Davis got his Fourteenth Corps across the Catawba, Sherman and the left wing continued their march on February 27, with Kilpatrick and his cavalrymen following Davis's column at its left rear, the entire mass of blue-coated troops moving toward Cheraw, to which Hardee and his Confederate army had fled by rail after leaving Charleston.

Hardee had quickly moved through Cheraw and constructed a strong defensive works on the far side of the Pee Dee River, which flows past the east side of the town. Slocum's troops crossed the river on a bridge at Sneedsboro, upstream of Cheraw, flanking Hardee's position, and Howard's troops crossed on a pontoon bridge downstream of Cheraw. Hardee was compelled to withdraw. Slocum playfully described his troops' reward for occupying the town:

> On the 3d of March we arrived at Cheraw, where we found a large supply of stores sent from Charleston for safe-keeping. Among the stores was a large quantity of very old wine of the best quality, which had been kept in the cellars of Charleston many years, with no thought on the part of the owners that in its old age it would be drunk from tin cups by Yankee soldiers. Fortunately for the whole army the wine was discovered by the Seventeenth Corps and fell into the

hands of the generous and chivalrous commander of that corps,—General Frank P. Blair,—who distributed it with the spirit of liberality and fairness characteristic of him.[32]

Besides the wine, which included what Sherman called "the finest madeira I ever tasted," the troops also captured 24 artillery pieces, two thousand muskets and thirty-six hundred barrels of gunpowder. After three days in Cheraw, Sherman's army crossed the Pee Dee River on a pontoon bridge and moved on, headed for Fayetteville, North Carolina. "Having secured the passage of the Pedee [sic]," Sherman stated, "I felt no uneasiness about the future, because there remained no further great impediment between us and Cape Fear River, which I felt assured was by that time in possession of our friends."[33]

On March 8 Sherman, traveling with the Fifteenth Corps, in the right wing, reached Laurel Hill, North Carolina, just across the state line, and eager to make contact with the Union force he assumed was in Wilmington, he asked a Corporal Pike to disguise himself, make his way to the Cape Fear River, some thirty miles distant, find a small boat and float it down to Wilmington to deliver a letter, in cipher, to the Union army commander who, Sherman supposed, would be there to receive it. He gave another volunteer, a young sergeant, the same assignment, instructing him to carry a copy of the same letter to the Union commander in Wilmington, and he then sent the two couriers off that night, each on a separate route. The letter read:

HEADQUARTERS MILITARY DIVISION OF THE MISSISSIPPI,
IN THE FIELD, LAUREL HILL, *Wednesday, March 8, 1865.*
Commanding Officer, Wilmington, North Carolina:
We are marching for Fayetteville, will be there Saturday, Sunday, and Monday, and will then march for Goldsboro.
If possible, send a boat up Cape Fear River, and have word conveyed to General Schofield that I expect to meet him about Goldsboro.' We are all well and have done finely. The rains make our roads difficult, and may delay us about Fayetteville, in which case I would like to have some bread, sugar, and coffee. We have abundance of all else. I expect to reach Goldsboro' by the 20th instant.
W.T. SHERMAN, *Major-General*[34]

"Both messengers arrived safely at Wilmington," General Slocum reported, "and on Sunday [March 12], the day after our arrival at Fayetteville, the shrill whistle of a steamboat floating the Stars and Stripes announced that we were once more in communication with our own friends. As she came up, the banks of the river were lined by our soldiers, who made the welkin ring with their cheers."[35]

The effect of the steamboat's arrival on the men was, Sherman said, "electric." "No one can realize the feeling," he remarked, "unless, like us, he has been for months cut off from all communication with friends, and compelled to listen to the croakings and prognostications of open enemies."[36] With the steamboat came mail from home and supplies of clothing. And when the boat left to return to Wilmington, it took away many of the contrabands—freed slaves—that had attached themselves to the columns of soldiers during the march from Columbia. On other return trips down the Cape Fear, many more contrabands were removed to Wilmington. "I must rid our army of from twenty to thirty thousand useless mouths," Sherman told Major General Alfred Terry, now the U.S. commander in Wilmington, in a letter to him carried by the steamboat.[37] Sherman also told Terry, and General Schofield as well, to move with their effective forces straight to Goldsboro, an important railroad junction, with rail lines leading from Wilmington and connecting with Charlotte. At Goldsboro Schofield's and Terry's forces were to rendezvous with Sherman's army. Schofield was then at New Bern, on the North Carolina coast.

Sherman's troops had taken Fayetteville after a brush with Hampton's Confederate troopers in which Hampton killed or captured a number of Union foragers, but in the face of a large force advancing on him, he withdrew and burned the bridge across the Cape Fear River as he retreated. Sherman's men replaced it with two pontoon bridges. After destroying the huge Confederate arsenal, machine shops and foundries in Fayetteville, the Union forces crossed the Cape Fear River and pulled out of Fayetteville on March 13 and 14, now bound for Goldsboro, some fifty miles to the northeast. "We were now entering upon the last stage of the great march," Slocum later wrote, "which was to unite the Army of the West with that of the East in front of Richmond. If this march could be successfully accomplished [,] the Confederacy was doomed. General Sherman did not hope or expect to accomplish it without a struggle. He anticipated an attack and made provision for it."[38]

"[T]he Seventeenth Corps [was] still on the right," Sherman recounted, "the Fifteenth next in order, then the Fourteenth and Twentieth on the extreme left; the cavalry acting in close concert with the left flank. With almost certainty of being attacked on this flank, I had instructed General Slocum to send his corps-trains under strong escort by an interior road, holding four divisions ready for immediate battle. General Howard was in like manner ordered to keep his trains well to his right, and to have four divisions unencumbered, about six miles ahead of Slocum, within easy support."[39]

Sherman now rode with Slocum, moving with the army's left flank up the road to Raleigh, roughly paralleling the Cape Fear River. During the night of March 15, thirteen miles from Fayetteville, Slocum's column ran into strong resistance from Hardee's forces, which included infantry, artillery and cavalry. With the Cape Fear River on one side of him and the North River on the other side, Sherman was forced to attack Hardee from the front. From a prisoner, Colonel Albert Rhett, who that night had been captured by Slocum's skirmishers, Sherman learned that Hardee was actually in the process of falling back, the resistance to Slocum's advance being but a rear-guard action.

The next day, the 16th, in a heavy rain, Slocum's column, continuing to advance toward Raleigh, encountered a new strong position that Hardee had set up near Averysboro. A brigade's flanking movement to the left, made while a division struck Hardee's front and Kilpatrick's cavalry threatened on the right, swept away Hardee's first line, resulting in the loss of 217 rebels taken prisoner, 108 killed and sixty-eight wounded, plus the capture of three field pieces. Union losses were twelve officers and sixty-five men killed and 477 men wounded. Later, as the day was ending, the Union column encountered a new line of rebel entrenchments and encamped in front of it for the night. When the sun rose the next morning, March 17, Sherman could see that Hardee had withdrawn from that position during the night and was retreating toward Smithfield, southeast of Raleigh.

From Averysboro Sherman's left wing turned eastward, toward Goldsboro, the Fourteenth Corps leading the advance. Sherman stayed with Slocum until early in the morning of March 19, when the column was about five miles from Bentonville, with Goldsboro less than thirty miles away. "Supposing that all danger was over," Sherman related, "I crossed over to join Howard's column, [several miles] to the right, so as to be nearer to Generals Schofield and Terry, known to be approaching Goldsboro.'"[40]

Since March 3 Sherman had known that General Joseph Johnston had been called out of forced retirement by General Robert E. Lee, now general in chief of all Confederate armies, and had been ordered by Lee to command the Confederate forces in the Carolinas. Johnston's military abilities were highly respected among Union forces, and Sherman knew he was in for a more stubborn and well conceived defense against his advance than he had seen so far. He estimated Johnston's potential strength at about forty-five thousand, including infantry, artillery and cavalry, a figure that would have been accurate except for recent Confederate losses, in battle, through desertion and through the provisions of their terms of enlistment, the militias of Georgia and South Carolina having gone home. Johnston's actual numbers, unknown to Sherman, were about twenty-six thousand infantry and artillery and about six thousand cavalry.[41]

After moving over to Howard's column on the 17th, Sherman heard artillery fire that sounded as if it were coming from the head of Slocum's column and at first he thought it was Slocum encountering Hardee's infantry or Hampton's cavalry, as usual, and there was little to be concerned about. Later in the day, though, a courier reached him with the message that Slocum had run up against Johnston's entire army as he was approaching Bentonville. Sherman quickly sent orders to Slocum to hold his ground, informing him that reinforcements from Howard's wing would soon be on the way to him. "I hoped General Slocum would hold Johnston's army facing west, while I would come on his rear from the east," Sherman recounted. "The Fifteenth Corps, less one division (Hazen's), still well to the rear, was turned at once toward Bentonsville [sic]; Hazen's division was ordered to Slocum's flank, and orders were also sent for General Blair, with the Seventeenth Corps, to come to the same destination."[42] While those movements were being made, the sounds of artillery fire continued.

Slocum gave his account of the initial action:

> A line for defense was at once selected, and as the troops came up they were placed in position and ordered to collect fence-rails and everything else available for barricades. The men used their tin cups and hands as shovels, and needed no urging to induce them to work....
>
> General Carlin's division of the Fourteenth Corps had the advance, and as the enemy exhibited more than usual strength, he had deployed his division and advanced to develop the position of the enemy. Morgan's division of the same corps had been deployed on Carlin's right. Colonel H.G. Litchfield, inspector-general of the corps ... rode up, and in reply to my inquiry as to what he had found in the front he said, "Well, General, I have found something more than Dibrell's cavalry — I find infantry intrenched along our whole front, and enough of them to give us all the amusement we shall want for the rest of the day."[43]

The Confederates advanced in force, and Major General William Carlin's division was compelled to fall back, but did so in good order and reformed. Slocum quickly ordered the Twentieth Corps to connect with the Fourteenth, and a gap between the two corps was filled by a brigade of the Twentieth just in time to meet the rebel attack. "The enemy fought bravely," Slocum recounted, "but their line had become somewhat broken in advancing through the woods, and when they came up to our line, posted behind slight intrenchments, they received a fire which compelled them to fall back. The assaults were repeated over and over again until a late hour, each assault finding us better prepared for resistance."[44]

During the night, General Hazen's division of the Fifteenth Corps arrived, and Slocum placed it on the right of the Fourteenth Corps. Early the next morning, March 20, four more brigades of Slocum's wing arrived on the field, and the entire day was spent positioning Slocum's men. On the morning of the 21st Howard's wing arrived, after marching twenty miles over bad roads and skirmishing with rebel forces most of the way. Johnston now was facing Sherman's entire army, nearly ninety thousand men, arrayed against his estimated twenty-two thousand infantry and five thousand cavalry.[45] The Confederate formation was roughly V-shaped, with the village of Bentonville between the two sides of the V. Slocum's wing faced one side of the V, and Howard's wing faced the other. At the Confederates' flanks was Mill Creek, spanned by a bridge on the north side of Bentonville.

Sherman missed a chance to destroy Johnston's army when about noon on the 21st the troops of General Mower, commanding the First Division of the Seventeenth Corps, charged through the rain and burst the rebel line, then swiftly pushed toward the bridge over Mill Creek. Sherman promptly ordered him back to reconnect with his corps. "I think I made a mistake there," Sherman later conceded, "and should rapidly have followed Mower's lead with the whole of the right wing, which would have brought on a general battle, and it could not have resulted otherwise than successfully to us, by reason of our vastly superior numbers."[46] But Sherman was still unsure of the strength of Johnston's army, and he preferred to wait until the troops of Schofield and Terry arrived to reinforce him, forming an overwhelming force.

During the night of the 21st Johnston crossed Mill Creek and withdrew, retreating toward Raleigh and concluding the Battle of Bentonville. "The plans of the enemy to surprise us and destroy our army in detail were well formed and well executed," Slocum commented, "and would have been more successful had not the men of the Fourteenth and Twentieth corps been veterans, and the equals in courage and endurance of any soldiers of this or any other country."[47]

During the three days of fighting Sherman's losses totaled eleven officers and 180 men killed, twelve officers and 1,105 men wounded, and 296 men missing. Johnston reported his losses as 223 killed, 1,467 wounded and 653 missing, numbers that Sherman disputed as being low. "General Slocum accounts for three hundred and thirty-eight prisoners captured, and General Howard for twelve hundred and eighty-seven, making sixteen hundred and twenty-five in all, to Johnston's six hundred and fifty-three — a difference of eight hundred and seventy-two."[48]

Sherman didn't pursue the retreating Confederates, being content, as he remarked, to let them go. Instead of pursuing, he rode to Cox's Bridge on March 22 and met General Terry, leading two divisions of the Tenth Corps coming from Wilmington. The next day, March 23, he and Terry rode into Goldsboro, where General Schofield was waiting for him with the Twenty-third Corps. During the 23rd and 24th the entire Union force assembled at Goldsboro and went into bivouac, there to rest for several days before returning to war.

"Thus was concluded," Sherman wrote in his memoir, "one of the longest and most important marches ever made by an organized army in a civilized country.... In our route we had captured Columbia, Cheraw, and Fayetteville, important cities and depots of supplies, had compelled the evacuation of Charleston City and Harbor, had utterly broken up all the railroads of South Carolina, and had consumed a vast amount of food and forage, essential to the enemy for the support of his own armies. We had in mid-winter accomplished the whole journey of four hundred and twenty-five miles in fifty days, averaging ten miles per day, allowing ten lay-days, and had reached Goldsboro' with the army in superb order, and the trains almost as fresh as when we had started from Atlanta."[49]

The Fall of Petersburg and the Capture of Richmond, March 25 to April 3, 1865

General Grant was worried. In late March, in the rough, two-room cabin that was his quarters at City Point, as he pondered what his next move must be, his big concern was that General Lee would somehow find a way to slip out of the stranglehold Grant had imposed on the Confederates around Richmond and Petersburg. "I felt that the situation of the Confederate army was such that they would try to make an escape at the earliest practicable moment," Grant wrote in his memoir, "and I was afraid, every morning, that I would awake from my sleep to hear that Lee had gone, and that nothing was left but a picket line."[1]

If that should happen, catching Lee and his fleeing army would be no easy matter. The railroad south to Danville, Virginia and beyond was still in rebel hands, and Lee could put his troops and necessary stores on rail cars and be off and quickly gone. "I knew he could move much more lightly and more rapidly than I," Grant remarked, "and that, if he got the start, he would leave me behind so that we would have the same army to fight again farther south — and the war might be prolonged another year."[2]

Grant's fear was well founded. Lee was indeed thinking the way Grant imagined. Lee knew his numbers and could estimate Grant's. As of March 1, 1865 Lee had at best about seventy-five thousand available fighting men,[3] perhaps fewer.[4] That number was shrinking every day, through sickness and desertions, his men despairing of victory, hungry, cold and ill clothed, tortured by thoughts of their families back home struggling to care for themselves. Grant had one hundred and eleven thousand men under his immediate command, troops well fed, well clothed and well equipped.[5] What was more, that number would soon be growing by as much as one hundred thousand troops with the arrival of the armies of Sherman, Sheridan and Thomas. Lee could hope for no such reinforcement, the South's manpower sources having been exhausted and there being little chance that Johnston, facing Sherman in North Carolina, would be able to come to Lee's aid.

Seeking counsel, Lee in early March had called to his headquarters outside Richmond Lieutenant General John B. Gordon, whose military wisdom he had come to respect. Lee had had Gordon study the reports of over-all troop strength, spread out for him on a table top, and then had asked Gordon what he thought it would be best to do.

"General, it seems to me there are but three courses," Gordon had answered, "and I name them in the order in which I think they should be tried. First, make terms with the enemy, the best we can get. Second, if that is not practicable, the best thing to do is to retreat — abandon Richmond and Petersburg, unite by rapid marches with General Johnston in North Carolina, and strike Sherman before Grant can join him. Or, lastly, we must fight and without delay."

"I agree with you fully," Lee had responded.[6]

Foreseeing the inevitable, Lee at that time, apparently with President Davis's concurrence, had already contacted Grant about the possibility of a surrender with terms. On March 2 Lee had a written a letter to Grant, telling him, "Sincerely desiring to leave nothing untried which may put an end to the calamities of war, I propose to meet you at such convenient time and place as you may designate, with the hope that, upon an interchange of views, it may be found practicable to submit the subjects of controversy between the belligerents to a convention of the kind mentioned. In such event I am authorized to do whatever the result of the proposed interview may render necessary or advisable...."[7]

Grant had immediately sent a copy of the letter to Secretary of War Stanton and had asked for instructions. Stanton received the letter at the Capitol, where he and President Lincoln and the rest of the cabinet were then meeting. Stanton passed it over to Lincoln, who read it, considered it for several seconds and penned a reply for Stanton to forward to Grant. "The President directs me to say," the reply read, "that he wishes you to have no conference with General Lee unless it be for the capitulation of General Lee's army, or on some minor or purely military matter. He instructs me to say that you are not to decide, discuss, or confer upon any political questions. Such questions the President holds in his own hands, and will submit them to no military conferences or conventions. Meanwhile, you are to press to the utmost your military advantages."[8] Lincoln had made it clear there would be no deal.

Having received Lincoln's instructions, Grant replied to Lee: "In regard to meeting you on the 6th instant, I would state that I have no authority to accede to your propositions for a conference on the subject proposed. Such authority is vested in the President of the United States alone...."[9] Lee then informed Davis of the rejection. Tenacious in his insistence that the United States must accept the Confederacy as an independent nation, Davis now saw there could be no peace without the total defeat of either the U.S. or the Confederate forces and he had not given up hope that the Confederates could finally prevail. Blind to reality, Davis possessed, as Lee confided to an associate, a "remarkable faith in the possibility of still winning our independence."[10]

With time running out until Sheridan's army would join Grant at Petersburg and present a force against which he could not defend, Lee decided to act. His plan was to wait until the roads, which had been made muddy morasses by frequent rain, dried out enough for horses and mules to haul his army's wagons and artillery. Then he planned to burst through the Union line with half of his force. He would take that half swiftly to North Carolina to join forces with Johnston and with that combined force he would attack and crush Sherman, then turn and attack Grant. It was a long shot, but his only chance.

The target for the breakthrough attack would be Fort Stedman, a small fortification point of the Union line on the northeast side of Petersburg, near the Southside Railroad tracks and about a half mile from the Appomattox River. The opposing lines there were about 150 yards apart, with pickets facing each other only fifty yards apart. Lee intended to strike Fort Stedman and overrun it, then split his attacking force in two, one half turning left to assault the artillery batteries on the left, and one half turning right to assault the batteries on the right. He hoped to so sever the Union line that Grant would be forced to abandon the south and southwest portions of it, shortening it and allowing Lee to defend against the shortened line with half his force while he marched the other half to join Johnston for an attack on Sherman.

The assault on Fort Stedman was described by Grant's aide-de-camp and secretary, Brigadier General Adam Badeau:

> At half-past four on the morning of March 25th, long before dawn, the rebels moved against [Brigadier General John] Parke's line east of Fort Steadman [sic], with [Confederate General] Gordon's corps reinforced by [Major General] Bushrod Johnson's division. Taking advantage of Grant's order allowing deserters to bring their arms with them across the lines, they sent forward squads of pretended deserters, who by this ruse gained possession of several of the picket posts. These were closely followed by a strong storming party of picked men, and this again by three heavy columns. Parke's pickets were overwhelmed after one discharge of their pieces; the trench guard, though resisting stoutly, was unable to withstand the rush of numbers, and the main line was broken.
>
> The rebels turned at once to the right and left, and their right-hand column soon gained a small battery, open in the rear, from which they assaulted Fort Steadman [sic]. The garrison, consisting of a battery of heavy artillery, made a vigorous resistance, but being attacked in front, flank, and rear, was overpowered; most of the men were captured, and the guns were turned at once on the national troops on either side. The enemy then pushed gradually westward, driving the garrisons from several unenclosed batteries. It was still quite dark, and almost impossible to distinguish friend from foe; this, of course, augmented the difficulty of forming the troops to check the progress of the enemy, and rendered the use of artillery from a distance at first altogether impracticable.[11]

Within minutes three Union batteries had been overrun and captured, and a three-hundred-yard gap in the line had been opened. Grant narrated the continuation of the battle, which took a dramatic turn once daylight came:

> Parke, commanding the 9th corps when this breach took place, telegraphed the facts to Meade's headquarters, and learning that the general was away, assumed command himself and with commendable promptitude made all preparations to drive the enemy back. [Major] General [John] Tidball gathered a large number of pieces of artillery and planted them in rear of the captured works so as to sweep the narrow space of ground between the lines very thoroughly. [Major General John] Hartranft was soon out with his division, as also was [Major General Orlando] Willcox.
>
> Hartranft to the right of the breach headed the rebels off in that direction and rapidly drove them back into Fort Stedman. On the other side they were driven back into the intrenchments which they had captured, and batteries eleven and twelve were retaken by Willcox early in the morning.
>
> Parke then threw a line around outside of the captured fort and batteries, and communication was once more established. The artillery fire was kept up so continuously that it was impossible for the Confederates to retreat, and equally impossible for reinforcements to join them. They all, therefore, fell captives into our hands. This effort of Lee's cost him about four thousand men, and resulted in their killing, wounding and capturing about two thousand of ours.[12]

Other sources put Union losses at 72 killed, 450 wounded and 522 captured or missing. Confederate losses were estimated at 600 killed, 2,400 wounded and 1,000 captured or missing.

Parke's troops not only drove back the rebels from the Union line but swept into the trenches of the rebel picket line, taking more than eight hundred prisoners and shortening the distance between the Union line and that of the rebels. Repeated rebel attempts to retake the trenches were repulsed, with considerable rebel losses.

While Lee was plotting a breakthrough at Fort Stedman, Grant had been forming an attack plan of his own. On March 24, the day before the Fort Stedman assault, Grant issued orders for a movement against the Confederate positions to commence on March 29. Major General Edward Ord, with three divisions of infantry and Brigadier General Ranald Mackenzie's cavalry, was to move in advance from the north side of the James River and take a position on the extreme left of the line outside Petersburg on the night of the 27th. Major General Andrew Humphreys, commanding the Second Corps, and Major General Gouverneur Warren, commanding the Fifth Corps, were to move out of their position on the left of the line and advance toward the community of Five Forks, from which the Union forces could strike the Southside Railroad and the Danville Railroad, two supply links absolutely vital to Lee and his defending army at Petersburg and Richmond.

On March 26 Sheridan arrived at City Point, coming from the Shenandoah valley with about nine thousand troopers, and received Grant's instructions for the cavalry's part in the westward push of the Union line.

"Finally the 29th of March came," Grant related, "and fortunately there having been a few days free from rain, the surface of the ground was dry, giving indications that the time had come when we could move. On that date I moved out with all the army available after leaving sufficient force to hold the line about Petersburg.... This movement was made for the purpose of extending our lines to the west as far as practicable towards the enemy's extreme right, or Five Forks.... My hope was that Sheridan would be able to carry Five Forks, get on the enemy's right flank and rear, and force them to weaken their centre to protect their right so that an assault in the centre might be successfully made. [Major] General [Horatio] Wright's corps had been designated to make this assault, which I intended to order as soon as information reached me of Sheridan's success."[13]

Grant assumed that Lee would make a strong effort to defend the railroads that were so important to him, and the assumption proved correct. "Lee had been as prompt as Grant to recognize that Five Forks was a strategic point of great importance," Grant's aide, Lieutenant Colonel, later brigadier general, Horace Porter, related, "and, to protect his right, had sent [Major General George] Pickett there with a large force of infantry and nearly all the cavalry."[14]

The heavy rains that had made quagmires of roads and fields returned on the 30th, moving some of Grant's officers to suggest postponing the operation, but he decided to press the attack nevertheless. On the morning of the 31st, the beginning of a cloudy, dismal day, Sheridan, having already moved out toward Five Forks, reported that the Confederates were entrenched there to a distance of a mile west of Five Forks.

"General Grant had expected that Warren [whose infantry corps was expected to support Sheridan's cavalry] would be attacked that morning," Porter reported, "and had warned him to be on the alert. Warren advanced his corps to ascertain with what force the enemy held the White Oak road [the east-west road that passed through Five Forks] and to try to drive him from it; but before he had gone far he met with a vigorous assault."[15] By the time Porter reached the scene to discover Warren's situation, all three divisions of Warren's corps had been stopped and were falling back. Reinforcements were quickly ordered up from General Humphreys' corps, and by noon the rebel advance had been halted and after Major General Nelson Miles's division struck the rebels' flank, they soon fell back.

"The general [Grant] was becoming apprehensive lest the infantry force that had moved against Warren might turn upon Sheridan, who had only cavalry with which to resist, as the weather had rendered it impracticable thus far to send him a corps of infantry as intended, and the general-in-chief was urgent that a strong forward movement should be made by the Fifth Corps [Warren's] for the purpose of deterring the enemy from detaching infantry from that portion of his line. This advance was made later in the afternoon [of the 31st], and with decided success."[16]

Sheridan's troopers, hurrying toward Five Forks, ran into a combined force of rebel cavalry and infantry and was pushed back to Dinwiddie Court House, southeast of Five Forks. When Porter found Sheridan a little north of Dinwiddie Court House, his confidence was undisturbed by the setback. "He said he had had one of the liveliest days in his experience," Porter recounted, "fighting infantry and cavalry with cavalry only, but that he was concentrating his command on the high ground just north of Dinwiddie, and would hold that position at all hazards."[17] He told Porter that with the corps of infantry he was expecting to join his cavalry force, he could take the initiative the next morning and cut off the entire force that Lee had detached.

"This force is in more danger than I am," Sheridan told Porter. "If I am cut off from the Army of the Potomac, it is cut off from Lee's army, and not a man in it should ever be allowed to get back to Lee. We at last have drawn the enemy's infantry out of its fortifications, and this is our chance to attack it."[18]

When Sheridan asked for infantry reinforcement, Grant that evening ordered Warren to hurry to support him with the Fifth Corps. Sheridan didn't want the Fifth Corps. He didn't want to have to deal with its overcautious, plodding, argumentative commander, General Warren. But Warren's corps was the closest to Sheridan's position and could reach him quickest. On the evening of March 31 Grant ordered Warren to hurry to Sheridan's aid. "It was expected," Porter reported, "that the infantry would reach its destination in ample time to take the offensive at break of day."[19]

Warren was slow getting started, however. Two of his divisions did not even leave their positions on White Oak Road until five o'clock in the morning on April 1. The third division, that of Major General Romeyne Ayres, took time to rebuild a burned bridge before crossing Gravelly Run, which earlier had been forded by Sheridan's cavalrymen without need of a bridge and without a problem. The bridge repair wasn't completed until 2 A.M. on the 1st. Warren himself didn't report to Sheridan until about eleven o'clock that morning. Before the day was over, Sheridan, aggressive and impatient, fed up with Warren's dilatoriness and lack of a sense of urgency, relieved him of command and appointed Major General Charles Griffin to command the Fifth Corps.

About one o'clock that afternoon Sheridan learned that the rebels he had encountered earlier, General Pickett's force, were falling back to their entrenched position at Five Forks. He prepared to assault those rebel works with dismounted cavalry and Fifth Corps infantrymen. "This battle must be fought and won before the sun goes down," he told his officers. "All the conditions may be changed in the morning; we have but a few hours of daylight left us. My cavalry are rapidly exhausting their ammunition, and if the attack is delayed much longer they may have none left."[20]

At four o'clock, with all of Sheridan's force in position, the order was issued for the assault to commence. General Porter narrated the fight:

The Confederate infantry brigades were posted from right to left as follows: Terry, Corse, Steuart, Ransom, and Wallace. General Fitzhugh Lee, commanding the cavalry, had placed

W.H.F. Lee's two brigades on the right of the line, Munford's division on the left, and Rosser's in rear of Hatcher's Run to guard the trains.... Ayres threw out a skirmish-line and advanced across an open field, which sloped down gradually toward the dense woods, just north of the White Oak road. He soon met with a fire from the edge of this woods, a number of men fell, and the skirmish-line halted and seemed to waver. Sheridan now began to exhibit those traits that always made him such a tower of strength in the presence of an enemy. He put spurs to his horse and dashed along in front of the line of battle from left to right, shouting words of encouragement.... "Come on, men," he cried. "Go at 'em with a will." ... Just then a man on the skirmish-line was struck in the neck; the blood spurted as if the jugular vein had been cut. "I'm killed!" he cried, and dropped on the ground. "You're not hurt a bit," cried Sheridan; "Pick up your gun, man, and move right on to the front." Such was the electric effect of his words that the poor fellow snatched up his musket and rushed forward a dozen paces before he fell never to rise again.[21]

General Ayres's troops moved down the slope, advancing steadily toward the woods from which the rebel fire was coming. Then they caught heavy fire on their left flank and had to change direction, facing more to the west. The rebel fire intensified as the Union troops moved into the woods, struggling through dense undergrowth. Soon they started to fall back, breaking their formation. Porter continued his description of the battle:

Sheridan now rushed into the midst of the broken lines, and cried out: "Where is my battle-flag?" As the sergeant who carried it rode up, Sheridan seized the crimson and white standard, waved it above his head, cheered on the men, and made heroic efforts to close up the ranks. Bullets were humming like a swarm of bees. One pierced the battle-flag, another killed the sergeant who had carried it.... Ayres and his officers were equally exposing themselves at all points in rallying the men, and soon the line was steadied.... Ayres, with drawn saber, rushed forward once more with his veterans, who now behaved as if they fallen back to get a "good-ready," and with fixed bayonets and a rousing cheer dashed over the earth-works, sweeping everything before them, and killing or capturing every man in their immediate front whose legs had not saved him....

The dismounted cavalry had assaulted as soon as they heard the infantry fire open. The natty cavalrymen, with tight-fitting uniforms, short jackets, and small carbines, swarmed through the pine thickets and dense undergrowth, looking as if they had been especially equipped for crawling through knot-holes. Those who had magazine guns created a racket in those pine woods that sounded as if a couple of army corps had opened fire.

The cavalry commanded by the gallant [Major General Wesley] Merritt made a final dash, went over the earth-works with a hurrah, captured a battery of artillery, and scattered everything in front of them. Here Custer, Devin, Fitzhugh, and the other cavalry leaders were in their element, and vied with each other in deeds of valor.[22]

The blue-coated soldiers had carried the Confederates' earthworks fortification that was just north of White Oak Road and ran parallel to·it, from a point about three-fourths of a mile east of Five Forks to a point about a mile west of Five Forks, with an angle, or traverse, one hundred yards long running perpendicular to it at the rebel left flank. Sheridan had spurred his horse, Rienzi, up the angle, and the horse had bounded over the angle and landed among a line of prisoners. Nearly 1,500 rebel soldiers were captured at the angle alone. Altogether, some five thousand of Pickett's force were taken prisoner. By seven-thirty that evening, the Battle of Five Forks was over.

Hearing the news, Grant became eager to launch an attack against the entire Petersburg defensive line. As he came out of his quarters to join some of his staff officers around a campfire about nine-thirty that night, he calmly announced to them, "I have ordered an immediate assault along the lines."[23] His corps commanders talked him out of an *immediate* attack, and instead an attack was ordered to commence at four o'clock the next morning, Sunday, April 2.

It, too, was postponed. It was still dark at that early hour, and the troops needed daylight to clear away and work their way through or over the abatis and chevaux-de-frise the rebels had erected in front of their entrenchment. At four-forty-five, though, there was light enough to make out clearly the rebel line and the gray-clad soldiers manning it. The Union artillery then opened on the Confederate position, the first of two parallel lines of fortifications the Union forces must carry to reach Petersburg. "The thunder of hundreds of guns shook the ground like an earthquake," Porter related, "and soon the troops were engaged all along the lines."[24] At five-fifteen General Wright wired that he had carried the rebel works in his front. Soon after, Parke reported he had captured the works in his front and had taken 800 prisoners. At six-forty Grant notified President Lincoln that Wright and Parke had pierced the Confederate line and that Sheridan, with his cavalry, the Fifth Corps and Miles's division of the Second Corps, was sweeping down on the rebel line from the west. No report from Ord had been received, but Grant told Lincoln, "All now looks highly favorable."

Soon Ord's report came in. He had broken through also. General Humphreys reported he had captured the line in front of him at seven-thirty. Around eight-thirty Ord reported that he had captured the Confederate works south of Hatcher's Run, on the east side of the line. "By noon," Porter related, "nearly all the outer line of works was in our possession, except two strong redoubts which occupied a commanding position, named respectively Fort Gregg and Fort Whitworth. The general [Grant] decided that these should be stormed, and about 1 o'clock three of Ord's brigades swept down upon Fort Gregg.... For half an hour after our men had gained the parapet a bloody hand-to-hand struggle continued, but nothing could stand against the onslaught of Ord's troops.... By half-past two 57 of the brave garrison lay dead, and about 250 had surrendered. Fort Whitworth was at once abandoned, but the guns of Fort Gregg were opened [by Ord's men] upon the garrison as they marched out, and the commander ... and sixty men were surrendered."[25]

Several of his commanders now urged Grant to order an assault on the rebels' inner line and capture Petersburg that afternoon. He refused, saying he didn't want to sacrifice the lives of his men to achieve a result that was going to occur anyway. He predicted that Lee's troops would evacuate the city during the night.

He was more prescient than his generals knew. Lee began moving his troops out of Petersburg about ten o'clock that evening, and by three o'clock in the morning on April 3 they were gone. Grant was up at daylight on the 3rd, and the first report brought to him that morning was that Parke's men had gone through the lines at 4 A.M., capturing a few skirmishers, and that the city had surrendered about four-thirty to Colonel Ralph Ely of the Eighth Michigan Regiment.

Grant immediately instructed General Meade, commanding the Army of the Potomac, to push westward with all possible speed in an effort to overtake Lee's retreating army.

"About 9 A.M. the general [Grant] rode into Petersburg," Porter recounted. "Many of the citizens, panic-stricken, had escaped with the army. Most of the whites who remained staid [sic] indoors, a few groups of negroes gave cheers, but the scene generally was one of complete desertion. Grant rode along quietly with his staff until he came to a comfortable-looking brick house, with a yard in front, situated on one of the principal streets, and here he and the officers accompanying him dismounted and took seats on the piazza. A number of the citizens soon gathered on the sidewalk and gazed with eager curiosity upon the commander of the Yankee armies."[26]

In response to Grant's invitation, President Lincoln, who had been waiting aboard a steamer at City Point, came to see what Grant's troops had achieved, arriving at Petersburg later that day with his twelve-year-old son, Tad. Though eager to join the pursuit of Lee's army, Grant delayed his departure so that he could be present when Lincoln arrived. The president, with Tad, was directed to Grant at the brick house. When he found it, Lincoln "came in through the front gate with long and rapid strides, his face beaming with delight," Porter reported. "He seized General Grant's hand as the general stepped forward to greet him, and stood shaking it for some time and pouring out his thanks and congratulations."[27]

After about an hour and a half, Grant decided he must be on his way, having given up on receiving news of the situation at Richmond so that he could pass it on to the president. Grant told Lincoln he had to ride on to the front and join Ord's column, and the two men parted, Lincoln shaking Grant's hand again and wishing him every success.

Grant and his staff had ridden about nine miles when a rider carrying a message from Major General Godfrey Weitzel, the Twenty-fifth Corps commander, overtook him. The message read: "We took Richmond at 8:15 this morning. I captured many guns. Enemy left in great haste. The city is on fire in two places. Am making every effort to put it out."[28] The long-sought prize had been won. Impassive as usual, Grant responded by merely saying, "I am sorry I did not get this before we left the president. However, I suppose he has heard the news by this time." Then, as a second thought, he said, "Let the news be circulated among the troops as rapidly as possible."[29]

A more detailed report of the capture of Richmond came later from Weitzel's aide-de-camp, Thomas T. Graves:

> About 2 o'clock on the morning of April 3d bright fires were seen in the direction of Richmond. Shortly after, while we were looking at these fires, we heard explosions, and soon a prisoner was sent in by General Kautz. The prisoner was a colored teamster, and he informed us that immediately after dark the enemy had begun making preparations to leave, and that they were sending all of the teams to the rear. A forward movement of our entire picket-line corroborated this report. As soon as it was light General Weitzel ordered Colonel E.E. Graves, senior aide-de-camp, and Major Atherton H. Stevens, Jr., provost-marshal, to take a detachment of forty men from the two companies (E and H) of the 4th Massachusetts Cavalry, and make a reconnaissance. Slowly this little band of scouts picket their way in. Soon after we moved up the New Market road at a slow pace.
>
> As we approached the inner line of defenses we saw in the distance divisions of our troops, many of them upon the double-quick, aiming to be the first in the city.... As we neared the city the fires seemed to increase in number and size, and at intervals loud explosions were heard.
>
> On entering we found Capitol Square covered with people who had fled there to escape the fire and were utterly worn out with fatigue and fright. Details were at once made to scour the city and press into service every able-bodied man, white or black, and make them assist in extinguishing the flames.... In this manner the fire was extinguished and perfect order restored in an incredibly short time after we occupied the city. There was absolutely no plundering upon the part of our soldiers; orders were issued forbidding anything to be taken without remuneration, and no complaints were made of infringement of these orders.[30]

As one of Weitzel's aides was riding through the streets, rounding up men to help extinguish the fires, "he was hailed by a servant in front of a house, toward which the fire seemed to be moving," Graves reported. "The servant told him that his mistress wished to speak to him. He dismounted and entered the house, and was met by a lady, who stated that her mother was an invalid, confined to her bed, and as the fire seemed to be approaching she asked for assistance. The subsequent conversation developed the fact that the invalid was no other than the wife of General R.E. Lee, and the lady who addressed the aide was her daughter, Miss Lee. An ambulance was furnished by Colonel E.H. Ripley, of the 9th Vermont, and a corporal and two men guarded them until all danger was past."[31]

From Confederate Captain Clement Sulivane came a final report of the abandonment of the Confederate capital as the defending garrison escaped to the south of the city:

> Shortly before day [on April 3] General [Richard] Ewell [commander of the Richmond garrison] rode in person to my headquarters and informed me that General G.W.C. Lee was then crossing the pontoon [bridge] at Drewry's; that he would destroy it and press on to join the main army; that all the bridges over the [James] river had been destroyed, except Mayo's, between Richmond and Manchester, and that the wagon bridge over the canal in front of Mayo's had already been burned by Union emissaries. My command was to hasten to Mayo's bridge and protect it, and the one remaining foot-bridge over the canal leading to it, until General [M.W.] Gary, of South Carolina, should arrive.
>
> I hurried to my command, and fifteen minutes later occupied Mayo's bridge, at the foot of 14th street, and made military dispositions to protect it to the last extremity. This done, I had nothing to do but listen for sounds and gaze on the terrible splendor of the scene. And such a scene probably the world has seldom witnessed. Either incendiaries, or (more probably) fragments of bombs from the arsenals, had fired various buildings, and the two cities, Richmond and Manchester, were like a blaze of day amid the surrounding darkness....
>
> By daylight, on the 3d, a mob of men, women, and children, to the number of several

Ruins of a bridge over the James River at Richmond. The fleeing rebel garrison burned Richmond's bridges behind it as it hurriedly evacuated the Confederate capital after the fall of Petersburg. (Library of Congress)

thousands, had gathered at the corner of 14th and Cary streets and other outlets, in front of the bridge, attracted by the vast commissary depot at that point.... The depot doors were forced open and a demoniacal struggle for the countless barrels of hams, bacon, whisky, flour, sugar, coffee, etc., etc., raged about the buildings among the hungry mob. The gutters ran whisky, and it was lapped as it flowed down the streets, while all fought for a share of the plunder. The flames came nearer and nearer, and at last caught in the commissariat itself.

At daylight the approach of the Union forces could be plainly discerned. After a little [while] came the clatter of horses' hoofs galloping up Main street. My infantry guard stood to arms, the picket across the canal was withdrawn, and the engineer officer lighted a torch of fat pine.... Presently a single company of [Confederate] cavalry appeared in sight, and rode at headlong speed to the bridge. "My rear-guard," explained Gary. Touching his hat to me he called out, "All over, good-bye; blow her to h-ll," and trotted over the bridge....

The engineer officer, Dr. Lyons and I walked leisurely to the island [about halfway across the bridge], setting fire to the provided combustible matter as we passed along, and leaving the north section of Mayo's bridge wrapped in flame and smoke. At the island we stopped to take a view of the situation north of the river, and saw a line of blue-coated horsemen galloping in furious haste up Main street. Across 14th street they stopped, and they dashed down 14th street to the flaming bridge. They fired a few random shots at us three on the island, and we retreated to Manchester. I ordered my command forward, the lieutenant of engineers saluted and went about his business, and myself and my companion sat on our horses for nearly a half-hour, watching the occupation of Richmond.

We saw another string of horsemen in blue pass up Main street, then we saw a dense column of infantry march by, seemingly without end; we heard the very welkin ring with cheers as the United States forces reached Capitol Square, and then we turned and slowly rode on our way.[32]

The next day, Tuesday, April 4, as if to confirm Richmond's return to the Union, the president of the United States, Abraham Lincoln, strode through the city's streets, taking in what was left of the once proud and defiant symbol of the Confederacy. Richmond had been captured.

The Meeting at the
McLean House, April 9, 1865

General Lee had warned President Davis in March about the imminent necessity of abandoning Richmond. Davis recognized the possibility of losing the city, but he still clung to a hope for the cause's survival. If Richmond had to be abandoned, he decided, the Confederacy's capital should be moved to Danville, Virginia, near the North Carolina line, and the fight would be carried on. By the end of March virtually all the Confederacy's officials had fled Richmond. Davis and his cabinet members were the only Confederate government authorities who remained.

On March 31, the Confederate army's situation having become desperate, Davis put his wife, Varina, and their four children aboard a special two-car train to Charlotte and tearfully bade them goodbye. So rattled was he that he forgot to withdraw from the bank the twelve thousand dollars he had received from the sale of his horses and carriage, money he meant for Varina to use to support herself and the children.

Two days later, on Sunday, April 2, he was attending the morning worship service at St. Paul's Episcopal Church in Richmond, sitting alone in his regular pew, listening to the choir, when the bad news was brought to him by the church's sexton. It came in the form of a copy of a telegram sent by General Lee to the Confederates' new secretary of war, John Breckinridge, at ten-forty Sunday morning. Lee's line at Petersburg had been broken, and to save his army he was evacuating his position. "I see no prospect of doing more than holding our position here till night," the telegram read. "I am not certain I can do that.... I advise that all preparations be made for leaving Richmond to-night...."[1] Davis studied the telegram, rose from his seat, put on his overcoat and walked up the aisle and out of the church.

From St. Paul's he walked to his offices, between Franklin and Main streets, and there summoned his cabinet members. He read them Lee's message, told them to pack up the records of their departments and get ready to leave Richmond. Some ten hours later, shortly after 11 P.M., the train bearing him and his associates, except Breckinridge, the old soldier, who remained at his post, pulled out of the Richmond depot, headed for Danville, a hundred and fifty miles to the southwest.

Lee was plotting a similar course. He planned to cross to the north side of the Appomattox River, avoiding Grant's position, and head westward toward Amelia Court House, then turn southwestward and follow the tracks of the Richmond & Danville Railroad, his shattered army to be supplied by rail during its long march to Danville. In Lee's column would be some thirty thousand infantry, some two hundred pieces of horse-drawn artillery and more than a thousand wagons that when moving would fill thirty miles of roadway. With that bulky procession he hoped to stay ahead of what he knew would be Grant's pursuing army. He was also hoping that his dwindling force would be reinforced by Joe Johnston's army, moving up from North Carolina, at a point somewhere around the Roanoke River, below Lynchburg.

At the end of their frantic first day of flight, on the evening of Sunday, April 2, Lee's weary soldiers rested by the roadside and early the next morning, seeming refreshed, once more took to the muddy road. Lee, too, seemed to have his spirits revived, relieved that he was in open country again.

The starting point for Grant's pursuing army was between Petersburg and Sutherland's Station, just west of Petersburg. The first part of Grant's route would parallel Lee's as both armies hurried toward the Danville rail line, the two armies marching on roads about fifteen miles apart. Grant ordered Sheridan to move his cavalry out in the advance of the long blue column. Following the cavalry were General Griffin's corps and the rest of the Army of the Potomac, under the command of General Meade. General Ord and the Army of the James would follow the tracks of the South Side Railroad, on a more southwesterly route toward Burkeville. They would attempt to get in front of Lee's column and as they moved southwestward they were to adapt the tracks of the five-foot-gauge South Side rail line to accommodate the Union rolling stock, which was built for the standard four-foot-eight-and-a-half-inch gauge. The repair would be effected simply by moving one rail closer to the other.

By the evening of April 3 the troops of the Army of the Potomac had got as far as Sutherland's Station, nine miles west of Petersburg, and after getting as much sleep as they could beside the road, they resumed the march at 3 A.M. on April 4.

"The 4th was another active day," General Porter, Grant's aide, a lieutenant colonel at the time, reported. "The troops found that this campaign was to be won by legs, that the great walking-match had begun, and success would attend the army that should make the best distance record. Grant marched this day with Ord's troops. Meade was sick, and had to take at times to an ambulance."[2]

Major General Wesley Merritt took a force of the Army of the Potomac's cavalry toward the Appomattox, and Major General George Crook led another cavalry force toward the Danville road between Jetersville and Burkeville. He was then to move up to Jetersville, which would place him directly in front of Lee's column, which now had reached Amelia Court House, about fifteen miles above Jetersville. Grant's purpose was not merely to follow Lee's army but to head it off and destroy or capture it. The going was at times slow, the roads bad, the infantry giving way, as ordered, to the cavalry units.

Shortly after noon Grant received a dispatch from Sheridan saying: "Merritt reports that the force in his front have all crossed to the north side of the Appomattox river.... Crook has, no doubt, reached the Danville road before this, and I am moving with the Fifth Corps from Deep creek as rapidly as possible in the direction of Amelia court-house."[3]

Later in the day Grant received intelligence that two railroad trains loaded with supplies for Lee were on the way from Danville to Farmville. Grant made a quick deduction and sent a message to Sheridan: "It was understood that Lee was accompanying his troops, and that he was bound for Danville by way of Farmville. Unless you have information more positive of the movements of the enemy, push on with all dispatch to Farmville, and try to intercept the enemy there."[4]

Sheridan in the meantime had learned that Lee was at Amelia Court House. He ordered General Griffin to have the Fifth Corps entrench across the Danville road and man their position until he could be reinforced. Sheridan then notified Grant and Meade that he had intercepted Lee. Rousing himself, the still ill Meade promptly issued orders to his commanders, the orders including the exhortation that, "The troops will be put in motion regardless of every consideration but the one of ending the war."[5] He sent another message to Grant: "I have ordered Humphreys to move out at all hazards at three A.M.; but if the rations can be issued to them prior to that, to march as soon as issued.... You may rest assured that every exertion will be made by myself and subordinate commanders to reach the point with the men in such condition that they may be available for instant action. From all I gather, Humphreys has nine or ten miles to march, and Wright from twenty-one to twenty-two."[6]

By 3 A.M. on April 5 the corps of both Humphreys and Wright were on the move toward Lee's army, Humphreys running into a traffic jam with the cavalry units of Merritt and Major General Ranald Mackenzie, which were also moving and taking precedence over the infantry as all crowded along the road in the darkness. It was not till about 8 A.M. that Humphreys was able to put his troops in motion again.

During the night, Grant had camped at Wilson's Station, on the South Side Railroad, twenty-seven miles west of Petersburg, and before daylight on the morning of the 5th he was up and writing orders, including instructions for Sherman, telling him: "All indications now are that Lee will attempt to reach Danville with the remnant of his force.... I will push on to Burksville [sic], and, if a stand is made at Danville, will in a few days go there. If you can possibly do so, push on from where you are, and let us see if we cannot finish the job with Lee and Johnston's armies. Whether it will be better for you to strike for Goldsboro, or nearer to Danville, you will be better able to judge when you receive this. Rebel armies are now the only strategic points to strike at."[7]

Around noon on the 5th Grant, riding with Ord's column, reached Nottoway Court House, about ten miles east of Burkeville, where he halted for several hours, finding the front porch of a tavern to use as a temporary headquarters. While there, he received a dispatch from Sheridan reporting that he had intercepted a column of Lee's troops on the road from Amelia Court House to Burkeville and had captured six pieces of artillery and some wagons. The noose was beginning to tighten around the fleeing Confederate army.

Rejoining the march, Grant continued on the road that ran along the South Side Railroad tracks until he reached a spot about halfway between Nottoway and Burkeville. It was then nearly dark. Suddenly a rider in a Confederate uniform emerged from the dense woods on the north side of the road and was seized by the troopers of Grant's headquarters escort. He turned out to be one of Sheridan's scouts, carrying a message from Sheridan to Grant. "He took from his mouth a piece of tobacco," General Badeau, Grant's secretary, reported, "in which was wrapped a small pellet of tinfoil. This, when opened, was found to contain a dispatch from Sheridan."[8] On tissue paper rolled up inside the tinfoil was a note Sheridan had written at Jetersville, halfway between Burkeville and Amelia Court House, at three o'clock that afternoon, reporting the capture of two hundred of Lee's wagons, some artillery and a number of prisoners at Paine's Crossroads. "I wish you were here yourself," Sheridan told Grant. "I feel confident of capturing the army of Northern Virginia, if we exert ourselves. I see no escape for Lee...."[9]

Grant exerted himself and rode with an escort through the shadowy woods, following the scout, to get to Sheridan that evening. He found him with his troopers, encamped along the road that ran northeast to Amelia Court House. After a supper of coffee and cold chicken, Sheridan briefed Grant, who soon decided his army's next moves and issued orders to Sheridan and to Meade, encamped nearby.

At daybreak on the 6th the Army of the Potomac started toward Amelia Court House, the Fifth Corps moving up along the Danville railroad line, the Second Corps half a mile west of the railroad, the Sixth Corps east of it, both the Second and the Sixth corps treading across fields through open country. Sheridan and his cavalry now headed toward Deatonsville, about five miles west of the railroad, and Ord marched westward toward Farmville to destroy the bridge over the Appomattox River, Grant believing that Lee might attempt to retreat across the river there where the Appomattox makes a big, bowl-shaped curve. Grant himself moved out on the road that ran from Burkeville to Farmville.

Lee, meanwhile, was beset with problems. Desertions, especially among the Virginia troops, whose homes were not far away, were continuing to weaken his army. Hunger was fast becoming starvation, for troops and animals alike. Horses and mules were dying for want of forage. Expecting to find rations waiting for them at Amelia Court House, many of the rebel troops became demoralized when they found none. Until provisions could reach them by rail from Danville, the only food would have to come from foraging in a countryside that was nearly exhausted of food. Lee realized that the spirits of his men — those who remained with him — would soon be broken if they could not be fed. He knew, too, that Union troops were threatening the Danville rail line and that whatever provisions were shipped from Danville might never reach him.

Now he discovered that U.S. troops were barring his way southward. Early in the afternoon on April 5 he had ridden with General Longstreet about seven miles from Amelia Court House and had found Sheridan's cavalry, with infantry close by, entrenching in a strong position across his army's intended path. He was left with but one option — turn westward, pass through open country that made him vulnerable to cavalry attacks on his flank, and march to Lynchburg, without food. During the night of the 5th he began the march toward Lynchburg, dividing his army to use all available roads for all possible speed.

On the morning of the 6th Confederate Lieutenant General Richard H. Anderson's corps and General Ewell's corps ran into trouble on the east-west stage road that ran from Petersburg to Lynchburg. Ewell's official report details the action:

> On crossing a little stream known as Sailor's [or Sayler's] Creek, I met General Fitzhugh Lee, who informed me that a large force of cavalry held the road just in front of General Anderson, and was so strongly posted that he had halted a short distance ahead. The trains were turned into the road nearer the [Appomattox] river, while I hurried to General Anderson's aid.... General Anderson informed me that at least two divisions of cavalry were in his front, and suggested two modes of escape — either to unite our forces and break through, or to move to the right through the woods and try to strike a road which ran toward Farmville. I recommended the latter alternative ... but I left the disposition to him. Before any were made the enemy appeared in rear of my column in large force preparing to attack. General Anderson informed me that he would make the attack in front, if I would hold in check those in the rear, which I did until his troops were broken and dispersed. I had no artillery, all being with the train [which had turned off the Lynchburg-Petersburg road, heading toward Farmville].
>
> My line ran across a little ravine which leads nearly at right angles toward Sailor's Creek.... [T]he enemy's artillery took a commanding position, and, finding we had none to reply, soon approached within 800 yards and opened a terrible fire. After nearly half an hour of this their

infantry advanced, crossing the creek above and below us at the same time. Just as it attacked, General Anderson made his assault, which was repulsed in five minutes. I had ridden up near his lines with him to see the result, when a staff officer ... brought him word of its failure. General Anderson rode rapidly toward his command. I returned to mine to see if it were yet too late to try the other plan of escape. On riding past my left I came suddenly upon a strong line of the enemy's skirmishers advancing upon my left rear. This closed the only avenue of escape; as shells and even bullets were crossing each other from front and rear over my troops, and my right was completely enveloped, I surrendered myself and staff to a cavalry officer who came in by the same road General Anderson had gone out on.... General [G.W.C.] Lee had been captured, as had General Kershaw, and the whole of my command.[10]

Another account of the fight came from General Badeau, who was with Grant:

These [Confederate] troops were really surrounded; two divisions of the Sixth corps were on their flanks, a fresh division and Wright's artillery in front, and Merritt's cavalry in their rear. Wright looked upon the entire command as prisoners, and had ordered the artillery to cease firing, out of humanity; when this little force charged against the Sixth corps front and drove it across the creek. There was a moment of desperate hand-to-hand fighting, but the national troops moved up on every side; a tremendous storm of artillery from eighteen guns opened on the command, and there was nothing to do but yield. Some of the men floundered wildly back through the creek, and gave themselves up to the very brigades they had just driven across.
A moment later the two sections of Sixth corps closed like gates upon the entire rebel force, while from the hillsides in the rear Merritt and Crook suddenly swept through the pine-trees like a whirlwind. There was one bewildering moment in which the rebels fought on every hand, and then they threw down their arms and surrendered. Ewell, in command of the force, Kershaw, Custis Lee, Semmes, Corse, DeFoe, Barton — all generals, hundreds of inferior officers, and seven thousand men, were prisoners.... [T]he entire rear-guard of Lee's army was destroyed.
A few officers escaped on the backs of artillery horses, and some of the men broke their muskets before submitting. A part of the wagon train had gone on during the battle, but Ewell's command surrendered on the open field.[11]

Also on the morning of the 6th, a small Union force was waging a desperate fight at Farmville. To cut off one of Lee's possible escape routes, General Ord ordered Colonel Francis Washburn of the Fourth Massachusetts Cavalry Regiment to take two infantry regiments to destroy the so-called High Bridge, a twenty-five-hundred-foot-long railroad bridge that spanned the Appomattox River and its flood plain, and a wagon bridge nearby, about four miles east of Farmville. Not long after Washburn had left from Burkeville, Ord heard that the lead units of a rebel column were approaching the Burkeville-Farmville road from the northeast and were threatening to get between the main body of Ord's corps and Washburn's detachment. Ord then sent Colonel Theodore Read, one of his staff officers, with a detachment of eighty cavalrymen to catch up with Washburn and have him return to Burkeville. Read got through to Washburn before the Confederates reached the Farmville-Burkeville road, but when he and Washburn turned around to return to Burkeville, they found their way blocked by a force of some twelve hundred rebel cavalrymen commanded by Major General Thomas Rosser.

"Read drew his men up into line of battle," Grant related, "his force now consisting of less than six hundred men, infantry and cavalry, and rode along their front, making a speech to his men to inspire them.... He then gave the order to charge. This little band made several charges, of course unsuccessful ones, but inflicted a loss upon the enemy more than equal to their entire number. Colonel Read fell mortally wounded, and then Washburn;

and at the close of the conflict nearly every officer of the command and most of the rank and file had been either killed or wounded. The remainder then surrendered.

"The Confederates took this to be only the advance of a larger column which had headed them off, and so stopped to intrench; so that this gallant band of six hundred had checked the progress of a strong detachment of the Confederate army."[12] In Farmville were the wagonloads of provisions — 80,000 rations of meal and about 40,000 rations of bread — but threatened by approaching U.S. troops, the rebel teamsters had pulled out of Farmville before the troops could be fed.

The next day, April 7, Lee's troops crossed to the north side of the Appomattox at High Bridge in an effort to continue their westward movement. They set fire to the bridges once across. General Humphreys' U.S. Second Corps, however, quickly came up to the south end of the bridges, drove off the rebel rear guard, extinguished the flames and marched across to continue the pursuit of Lee's diminished army. Humphreys, Grant reported, "followed Lee to the intersection of the road crossing at Farmville with the one from Petersburg. Here Lee held a position which was very strong, naturally, besides being intrenched. Humphreys was alone, confronting him all through the day, and in a very hazardous position. He put on a bold face, however, and assaulted with some loss, but was not assaulted in return."[13]

Grant had come to Farmville from Burkeville early in the morning of the 7th, riding through a steady rain and over roads crowded with his troops, carrying with him thoughts of a conversation he had had in Burkeville with a Doctor Smith, who had been an officer in the U.S. regular Army and who was a relative of General Ewell, who had commanded the Richmond garrison and was now a U.S. prisoner. Smith told Grant that Ewell had remarked to him that when the Union force had managed to cross the James River, he, Ewell, knew the Confederate cause was lost and that it was the duty of the Confederate authorities to negotiate the best terms they could while they still had a right to claim concessions. The authorities had thought otherwise, though. Now the cause was clearly lost, and Confederate leaders had no right to claim anything, Ewell had said. Ewell had told Smith, Smith said, that someone was responsible for every man killed now and that every death would be little better than murder. Ewell said he was not sure that Lee would consent to surrender his army without first consulting Davis, but he hoped he would.

"I rode in to Farmville on the 7th," Grant recounted, "arriving there early in the day. Sheridan and Ord were pushing through, away to the south. Meade was back towards the High Bridge, and Humphreys confronting Lee [across the river from Farmville].... After having gone into bivouac at Prince Edward's Court House [west of Farmville], Sheridan learned that seven [railroad] trains of provisions and forage were at Appomattox, and determined to start at once and capture them; and a forced march was necessary in order to get there before Lee's army could secure them. He wrote me a note telling me this.

"This fact, together with the incident related the night before by Dr. Smith, gave me the idea of opening correspondence with General Lee on the subject of the surrender of his army. I therefore wrote to him on this day...."[14] Grant's note to Lee read:

HEADQUARTERS ARMIES OF THE U.S.,
5 P.M., *April 7, 1865.*

GENERAL R.E. LEE,
          Commanding C.S.A

The results of the last week must convince you of the hopelessness of further resistance on the part of the Army of Northern Virginia in this struggle. I feel that it is so, and regard it as my duty to shift from myself the responsibility of any further effusion of blood, by asking of you the surrender of that portion of the Confederate States army known as the Army of Northern Virginia.

U.S. GRANT,
Lieut.-General[15]

Grant then gave the note to his adjutant general, Major General Seth Williams, and instructed him to take it to Humphreys' front and have it sent into Lee's lines. Grant decided to spend the night in Farmville, awaiting an answer from General Lee. He took a room in the hotel there and was told it was the same room that Lee had occupied the night before.

Lee replied to Grant's note within an hour after receiving it, but the reply didn't reach Grant till after midnight. It read:

April 7, 1865

GENERAL:— I have received your note of this day. Though not entertaining the opinion you express on the hopelessness of further resistance on the part of the Army of Northern Virginia, I reciprocate your desire to avoid useless effusion of blood, and therefore before considering your proposition, ask the terms you will offer on condition of surrender.

R.E. LEE,
General.

LIEUT.-GENERAL U.S. GRANT,
    Commanding Armies of the U.S.

Grant found that response less than satisfactory, but believed it deserved another note, which he wrote the next morning:

April 8, 1865

GENERAL R.E. LEE,
    Commanding C.S.A.

Your note of last evening in reply to mine of same date, asking the condition on which I will accept the surrender of the Army of Northern Virginia is just received. In reply I would say that, peace being my great desire, there is but one condition I would insist upon, namely: that the men and officers surrendered shall be disqualified for taking up arms again against the Government of the United States until properly exchanged. I will meet you, or will designate officers to meet any officers you may name for the same purpose, at any point agreeable to you, for the purpose of arranging definitely the terms upon which the surrender of the Army of Northern Virginia will be received.

U.S. GRANT,
Lieut.-General[16]

Not yet ready for a surrender, Lee answered with a note written in his own hand:

8h Ap' '65

Genl

I recd at a late hour your note of today. In mine of yesterday I did not intend to propose the surrender of the Army of N. Va.— but to ask the terms of your proposition. To be frank, I do not think the emergency has arisen to call for the surrender of this Army, but as the restoration of peace should be the sole object of all, I desired to know whether your proposals would lead to that and I cannot therefore meet you with a view to surrender the Army of N. Va.— but as far as your proposal may affect the C.S. forces under my command & tend to the restoration of peace, I shall be pleased to meet you at 10 A.M. tomorrow on the old stage road to Richmond between the picket lines of the two armies.

Very respy your Obt Sevt
R.E. Lee,
Genl.

Lt. Genl U.S. Grant
Commng Armies of the U.S.[17]

When Lee and his party rode out to meet Grant on the stage road at 10 A.M. the next day, Sunday, April 9, they met instead Lieutenant Colonel Charles Whittier, who informed Lee that he had no instructions to conduct Lee and his party to a meeting place, but had merely been instructed to deliver a note to General Lee. Lee took it and read it:

Headquarters Armies of the United States
April 9, 1865

General R.E. Lee,
Commanding C.S. Armies

General: Your note of yesterday is received. As I have no authority to treat on the subject of peace the meeting proposed for 10 A.M. today could lead to no good. I will state, however, General, that I am equally anxious for peace with yourself, and the whole North entertain the same feeling. The terms upon which peace can be had are well understood. By the South laying down their arms they will hasten that most desirable event, save thousands of human lives, and hundreds of millions of property not yet destroyed. Sincerely hoping that all our difficulties may be settled without the loss of another life, I subscribe myself, etc.,

Very respectfully, your obedient servant,
U.S. GRANT
Lieutenant-General[18]

Grant had written that note early in the morning of the 9th and after some breakfast coffee with several officers at General Meade's headquarters, he left to find Sheridan. He was suffering from a severe headache that had kept him awake during the night, but when Colonel Porter suggested he ride in a covered ambulance to avoid the sun's intense heat, he refused, calling for his favorite mount, Cincinnati.

While the exchange of notes was going on between Grant and Lee, Sheridan's troopers were busy. Sheridan had directed Custer to take his cavalry division south of Appomattox Station, about five miles south of the town of Appomattox Court House, to get west of the rebel supply trains, seize them and destroy the railroad line. Custer arrived there on the night of the 8th. On his approach, three trains filled with rebel supplies steamed off and escaped, but four others were captured by Custer.

Around 6 A.M. on the 9th the troops of the Army of the James and Griffin's corps, all racing to head off Lee, arrived at Sheridan's cavalry position as Lee's army was approaching. After conferring with Sheridan, General Ord, commanding the Army of the James and senior officer on the field, took command of the infantry and positioned his two corps across the valley where Lee's army must pass, concealing them in the woods. Sheridan moved to the front of the oncoming rebels, and the Army of the Potomac moved into a position to place them at the rebels' rear. Sheridan dismounted his cavalrymen and instructed them to fall back gradually, to give Ord time to form his lines and strike the Confederate column in the flank while the troopers moved off to the right and remounted.

Crook's cavalry division was soon heavily engaged, but made a stubborn resistance. Lee's infantry greatly outnumbered Sheridan's hard-pressed cavalrymen, and Sheridan sent word to Ord to hurry his attack. "It looked as if Sheridan was deserting the field," Badeau reported, "and meant to allow the rebel army to pass. Lee's men gave once more the battle-yell, and quickened their pace, and doubled their fire, when suddenly, the cavalry having all retired, the infantry line emerged from the woods.... The rebels neglected to fire, and their line rolled back, wavering and staggering, with the certainty that they were doomed. The three [Union] commands of infantry all advanced at the double-quick step, covering the valley and all the adjacent hillsides, while Sheridan moved briskly around to the enemy's left, and was about to charge on the confused mass, when Lee sent forward a white flag with a request for a cessation of hostilities."[19]

Lee dashed off another note to Grant, saying, "I now ask an interview, in accordance with the offer contained in your letter of yesterday."[20]

Grant was riding on the road from Farmville to Appomattox Court House when a lieutenant from Meade's staff delivered Lee's note. He promptly replied: "Your note of this date [April 9] is but this moment (11.50 A.M.) received, in consequence of my having passed from the Richmond and Lynchburg road to the Farmville and Lynchburg road. I am at this writing about four miles west of Walker's Church and will push forward to the front for the purpose of meeting you. Notice sent to me on this road where you wish the interview to take place will meet me."[21] Grant handed the note to Colonel Orville Babcock, a member of his staff, and instructed him to take it to Lee by the most direct route. Babcock delivered the note to Lee about a quarter past noon on the 9th.

During the halt in the fighting Sheridan rode to Appomattox Court House and met with two of the Confederates' generals, Cadmus Wilcox and John B. Gordon, apparently in an effort to find out what the rebels had in mind. They told him that negotiations for a surrender were pending between Lee and Grant. If that was so, Sheridan said, the attack on his lines in an attempt to escape capture should not have been made. He told the rebel generals that he needed some assurance that a surrender was intended. Gordon gave him his personal assurance, later telling Sheridan that the surrender was only awaiting the arrival of Grant.

When Grant came within about five miles of Appomattox Court House, Sheridan's adjutant general rode up to meet him, coming from the direction of Appomattox Court House and bearing a note for Grant from Lee, which turned out to be a duplicate of the note Grant had received earlier. "Lee was so closely pressed," Colonel Porter explained, "that he was anxious to communicate with Grant by the most direct means, and as he could not tell with which column Grant was moving he sent in one copy of his letter on Meade's front and one on Sheridan's."[22]

During their ride to Appomattox Court House, Porter asked Grant about his headache and how he felt. Grant's new reply was, "The pain in my head seemed to leave me the moment I got Lee's letter."[23]

Appomattox Court House was a community with a single street and about half a dozen houses. Lee had ridden to it with, among others, his military secretary, Colonel Charles Marshall, Grant's aide, Colonel Babcock, and Babcock's orderly. When the group reached the village, they were met by one of its residents, Wilmer McLean. They told him that General Lee was looking for a place he could meet with General Grant. McLean took Lee to one of the first houses they had come to, but Lee decided its sitting room was too small. McLean then led Lee and his party to McLean's own house, which Porter described as the best one in the village. It suited Lee. He and the other officers dismounted and entered the house to wait for Grant.

Grant and his party reached Appomattox Court House around 1 P.M. The day was April 9, Palm Sunday. His arrival was described by Colonel Porter:

> Generals Sheridan and Ord, with a group of officers around them, were seen in the road, and as our party came up General Grant said: "How are you, Sheridan?"
>
> "First-rate, thank you; how are you?" cried Sheridan, with a voice and look that seemed to indicate that on his part he was having things all his own way.
>
> "Is Lee over there?" asked General Grant, pointing up the street, having heard a rumor that Lee was in that vicinity.

"Yes, he is in that brick house," answered Sheridan.

"Well, then, we'll go over," said Grant.

The general-in-chief now rode on, accompanied by Sheridan, Ord, and some others, and soon Colonel Babcock's orderly was seen sitting on his horse in the street in front of a two-story brick house, better in appearance than the rest of the houses. He said General Lee and Colonel Babcock had gone into this house a short time before, and he was ordered to post himself in the street and keep a lookout for General Grant, so as to let him know where General Lee was....

The house had a comfortable wooden porch with seven steps leading up to it. A hall ran through the middle from front to back, and on each side was a room having two windows, one in front and one in rear. Each room had two doors, opening into the hall. The building stood a little distance back from the street, with a yard in front, and to the left was a gate for carriages and a roadway running to a stable in rear. We entered the grounds by this gate and dismounted....

General Grant mounted the steps and entered the house. As he stepped into the hall Colonel Babcock, who had seen his approach from the window, opened the door of the room on the left, in which he had been sitting with General Lee and Colonel Marshall awaiting General Grant's arrival. The general passed in, while the members of the staff, Generals Sheridan and Ord, and some general officers who had gathered in the front yard, remained outside, feeling that he would probably want his first interview with General Lee to be, in a measure, private. In a few minutes Colonel Babcock came to the front door and, making a motion with his hat toward the sitting-room, said: "The general says, come in."

It was then about half-past one.... We entered, and found General Grant sitting at a marble-topped table in the center of the room, and Lee sitting beside a small oval table near the front window, in the corner opposite to the door by which we entered, and facing General Grant. Colonel Marshall, his military secretary, was standing at his left. We walked in softly and ranged ourselves quietly about the sides of the room, very much as people enter a sick-chamber when they expect to find the patient dangerously ill. Some found seats on the sofa and the few chairs which constituted the furniture, but most of the party stood....[24]

Lee and Marshall were the only Confederates in the room. General Badeau described Lee and Grant and their conversation:

The two chiefs shook hands, and Lee at once began a conversation,[25] for he appeared more unembarrassed than his victor. He, as well as his aide-de-camp was elaborately dressed. Lee wore embroidered gauntlets and a burnished sword, the gift, it was said, of the state of Virginia, while the uniforms of Grant and those who accompanied him were soiled and worn; some had slept in their boots for days, and Grant, when he started for Farmville two days before, had been riding around in camp without a sword. He had not since visited his own head-quarters, and was therefore at this moment without side-arms....

Lee was tall, large in form, fine in person, handsome in feature, grave and dignified in bearing; if anything, a little too formal. There was a suggestion of effort in his deportment; something that showed he was determined to die gracefully; a hint of Caesar muffling himself in his mantle....

Grant as usual was simple and composed, but with none of the grand air about him. No elation was visible in his manner or appearance. His voice was as calm as ever, and his eye betrayed no emotion. He spoke and acted as plainly as if he were transacting an ordinary matter of business. No one would have suspected that he was about to receive the surrender of an army, or that one of the most terrible wars of modern times had been brought to a triumphant close by the quiet man without a sword who was conversing calmly, but rather grimly, with the elaborate gentleman in grey and gold.[26]

"What General Lee's feelings were I do not know," Grant remarked in his memoir. "As he was a man of much dignity, with an impassible face, it was impossible to say whether he felt inwardly glad that the end had finally come, or felt sad over the result, and was too manly to show it. Whatever his feelings, they were entirely concealed from my observation; but my own feelings, which had been quite jubilant on the receipt of his letter, were sad and depressed. I felt like anything rather than rejoicing at the downfall of a foe who had fought so long and valiantly, and had suffered so much for a cause, though that cause was, I believe, one of the worst for which a people ever fought, and one for which there was the least excuse."[27]

Badeau's narration of the meeting continues:

The conversation at first related to the meeting of the two soldiers in earlier years in Mexico, when Grant had been a subaltern and Lee a staff officer of [Lieutenant General Winfield] Scott. The rebel general, however, soon adverted to the object of the interview. "I asked to see you, General Grant," he said, "to ascertain upon what terms you would receive the surrender of my army."

Grant replied that the officers and men must become prisoners of war, giving up of course all munitions, weapons, and supplies, but that a parole would be accepted, binding them to go to their homes and remain there until exchanged, or released by proper authority. Lee said that he had expected some such terms as these, and made some other remark not exactly relevant. Whereupon Grant inquired: "Do I understand, General Lee, that you accept these terms?"

"Yes," said Lee; "and if you will put them into writing, I will sign them."[28]

Grant then wrote out the terms in his order notebook.

APPOMATTOX C.H., VA., Ap'l 9th, 1865.

GEN. R.E. LEE, Comd'g C.S.A.

GEN.: In accordance with the substance of my letter to you of the 8th inst., I propose to receive the surrender of the Army of N. Va. on the following terms, to wit: Rolls of all the officers and men to be made in duplicate. One copy to be given to an officer designated by me, the other to be retained by such officer or officers as you may designate. The officers to give their individual paroles not to take up arms against the Government of the United States until properly exchanged, and each company or regimental commander sign a like parole for the men of their commands. The arms, artillery and public property to be parked and stacked, and turned over to the officer appointed by me to receive them. This will not embrace the side-arms of the officers, nor their private horses or baggage. This done, each officer and man will be allowed to return to their homes, not to be disturbed by United States authority so long as they observe their paroles and the laws in force where they may reside.

Very respectfully,
U.S. GRANT,
Lt. Gen.[29]

Lee read the document, told Grant that the terms would have a happy effect on his army, and then asked for one more thing. He explained that his cavalrymen and the men of his artillery owned their horses, unlike the situation in the U.S. Army, where the Army owned the horses. Lee asked if those men were permitted to keep their horses. Grant told him the written terms would not permit that, but assuming the last battle of the war had been fought and that most of the enlisted men were small farmers who would need their horses on their farms, he said he would instruct the officers processing the paroles to let "every man of the Confederate army who claimed to own a horse or mule take the animal to his home."[30] Lee again remarked that concession would have a happy effect.

Lee then wrote out his acceptance of the surrender terms:

HEADQUARTERS ARMY OF NORTHERN VIRGINIA,
April 9, 1865

GENERAL:— I received your letter of this date containing the terms of the surrender of the

Army of Northern Virginia as proposed by you. As they are substantially the same as those expressed in your letter of the 8th inst., they are accepted. I will proceed to designate the proper officers to carry the stipulations into effect.

R.E. LEE, General.

LIEUT.-GENERAL U.S. GRANT[31]

Lee's report of the surrender, made three days later to President Davis, was nearly as reserved as his manner: "In the interview which occurred with General Grant in compliance with my request, terms having been agreed on, I surrendered that portion of the Army of Northern Virginia which was on the field, with its arms, artillery, and wagon-trains, the officers and men to be paroled, retaining their side-arms and private effects. I deemed this course the best under all circumstances by which we were surrounded."[32]

In his report Lee also explained the situation of his army: "The enemy was more than five times our numbers. If we could have forced our way one day longer it would have been at a great sacrifice of life, and at its end I did not see how a surrender could have been avoided. We had no subsistence for man or horse, and it could not be gathered in the country. The supplies ordered to Pamplin's Station from Lynchburg could not reach us, and the men, deprived of food and sleep for many days, were worn out and exhausted."[33]

While copies of the documents were being made, Grant introduced Lee to the officers who had gathered in the room. Lee was silent during all the introductions except one, merely

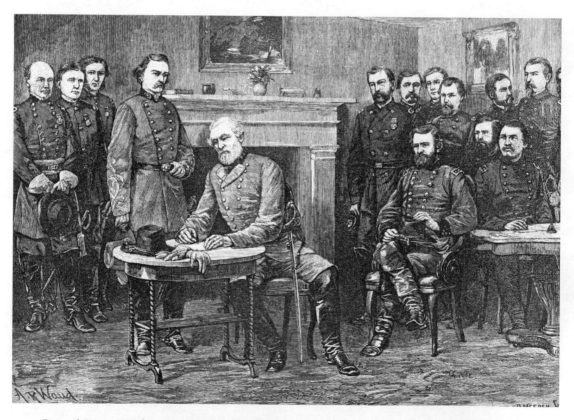

General Lee surrenders. Lee signs the document of surrender as Grant, seated, and a group of his officers looks on. Standing beside Lee is his military secretary, Col. Charles Marshall, the only Confederate besides Lee in the room. (JOHN CLARK RIDPATH)

bowing or shaking hands when one was offered. He spoke only to Major General Seth Williams, who had been his adjutant when Lee was superintendent at West Point.

That done, Lee turned to Grant again and said, "I have a thousand or more of your men as prisoners, General Grant, a number of them officers whom we have required to march along with us for several days. I shall be glad to send them into your lines as soon as it can be arranged, for I have no provisions for them. I have, indeed, nothing for my own men. They have been living for the last few days principally upon parched corn, and we are badly in need of both rations and forage. I telegraphed to Lynchburg, directing several train-loads of rations to be sent on by rail from there, and when they arrive I should be glad to have the present wants of my men supplied from them."[34]

As soon as he said that, everyone's eyes turned to Sheridan, whose cavalry had captured those trains near Appomattox Station on the night of the 8th. Grant calmly replied that he would like to have his men returned to the Union lines as soon as possible and that he would supply Lee's troops with rations.

After some sparse general conversation and the signing of the two documents, Grant's note about terms and Lee's acceptance, the meeting broke up at about four o'clock. Lee shook hands with Grant, bowed toward the others and, with Colonel Marshall, strode from the room. Grant's officers, one behind the other, followed them out onto the porch.

"Lee signaled to his orderly to bring up his horse," Porter recounted, "and while the animal was being bridled the general stood on the lowest step and gazed sadly in the direction of the valley beyond where his army lay — now an army of prisoners. He smote his hands together a number of times in an absent sort of a way; seemed not to see the group of Union officers in the yard who rose respectfully at his approach, and appeared unconscious of everything about him."[35] Then his orderly brought his horse to him, and he immediately mounted. Grant stepped down from the porch and saluted him by raising his hat. The other Union officers did the same.

Lee raised his hat in return. Then he rode off to break the solemn news to the steadfast soldiers of his defeated army.

Grant made his way to his headquarters camp, which had been relocated nearby. There at four-thirty that afternoon he telegraphed the awesome news to the United States secretary of war:

> HEADQUARTERS APPOMATTOX C.H., Va.,
> *April 9th, 1865, 4.30 P.M.*
>
> HON. E.M. STANTON, SECRETARY OF WAR,
>   WASHINGTON.
> General Lee surrendered the Army of Northern Virginia this afternoon on terms proposed by myself. The accompanying additional correspondence will show the conditions fully.
>   U.S. GRANT, Lieut.-General.[36]

It was over. Practically.

The Assassination, April 14, 1865

It would be hard to turn down President Lincoln's invitation, which was very much like a request for a command performance, but General Grant decided to do it. He had his reasons. For one, he loathed being put on display, the show business, he called it. He especially hated the forced mingling with Washington's important persons. Showing him off, though, was exactly what Lincoln had in mind. Having beaten Robert E. Lee and virtually ended the war, Grant had become the nation's most eminent hero, its biggest celebrity. Lincoln wanted the public to have a chance to see him while he was in Washington, where he arrived on Thursday, April 13. And so he invited Grant and Grant's wife, Julia, to accompany him and his wife, Mary, to Ford's Theatre to see *Our American Cousin*, which Mrs. Lincoln was keen to see and which was to have its final Washington performance the next night, the 14th.

In the process of getting seats in his favorite box at Ford's, Lincoln in a note told James Ford, the theater's business manager, that Grant would be in his party. That news was cheeringly received by Ford. With some advance publicity, the attendance by Grant would likely produce a full house.

Inviting the Grants was Mrs. Lincoln's idea. She, however, was the biggest reason Grant had for declining the invitation. Julia had had enough exposure to Mary Todd Lincoln to know she didn't want anymore. Julia had been at City Point when the president and Mary came there and Julia had seen Mrs. Lincoln pitch a fit when she noticed the wife of Major General Charles Griffin riding horseback alongside the president. Mrs. Lincoln was with Julia in a mule-drawn Army ambulance and she tried to jump out of the ambulance to get to the president and Mrs. Griffin. She had to be restrained to prevent her from doing so. The day after that incident there was another one, worse. The president was to review troops of the Twenty-fifth Corps and again he traveled by horseback while Mrs. Lincoln and Julia rode in the ambulance. When the ambulance arrived at the parade ground, where the troops were assembled in formation, Mrs. Lincoln saw the attractive wife of Major General Edward Ord on horseback, riding with the group of officers accompanying Lincoln.

Mrs. Lincoln exploded. "What does that woman mean by riding by the side of the president!" she exclaimed. When Julia tried to calm her, she turned her wrath on Julia, charging that Julia and General Grant were angling to replace the Lincolns in the White House. Seeing the ambulance bearing Julia and Mrs. Lincoln arrive, Mrs. Ord rode over to join the two women. As Mrs. Ord drew up, Mrs. Lincoln let her have it, too, calling her ugly names while the stunned officers looked on and listened. Mrs. Lincoln demanded to know how Mrs. Ord had the effrontery to ride beside the president. Mrs. Ord burst into tears at the sudden attack.

Julia now let her husband know she did not want to go to the theater with Mrs. Lincoln. The Grants' children were in school in Burlington, New Jersey, and they would provide Grant a reasonable excuse for not being able to join the Lincolns at the theater. The general and Julia were actually eager to see the children and had wanted to leave Washington as soon as possible anyway. Grant, at the War Department, sent a messenger to Julia, at Willard's Hotel, asking her to make arrangements to leave for Burlington by train on Friday.

There was another possible reason for declining the invitation. Late Thursday afternoon Grant was in the office that had been provided him in the War Department, where he could work on canceling Army contracts and reducing the size of the Army now that the war was practically over. Secretary Stanton, on his way home, stopped by Grant's office to remind him that he and Mrs. Grant were to come to the Stantons' that evening for dinner. During that brief conversation Grant mentioned to Stanton that he and Julia had been invited to go with the Lincolns to the theater the next evening.

His demeanor instantly changing, Stanton urged Grant not to go and asked him to try to persuade Lincoln not to go either. He told Grant that Washington City was full of Secessionist sympathizers and dangerous plots. He said he had made it a policy to refuse all invitations to appear in public places and that he and other cabinet members had warned the president about public appearances. Later, when the Grants arrived at the Stantons' for dinner, Grant got a dramatic indication of Stanton's concern for safety. Two soldiers were standing guard outside the house.

The next morning, April 14, Good Friday, Grant attended the cabinet meeting in the president's White House office. Lincoln wanted him to come and tell the cabinet members the details of General Lee's surrender, which Grant modestly did. When the meeting was over, and while the men lingered, Colonel Horace Porter brought the general a note from Julia, saying she hoped he would not delay their departure on the six o'clock train. Grant read it, then handed it over to Lincoln, and when Lincoln had read it, Grant told him he really couldn't stay for the play. Apparently understanding about wifely commands, Lincoln accepted Grant's decision. At a little after 2 P.M. the two men shook hands and told each other goodbye, not knowing it was for the last time.

Grant went from the White House straight to Willard's Hotel. He had barely arrived in his suite when Julia started telling him a frightening experience she'd had. "When I went to my lunch today," she said, "a man with a wild look followed me into the dining room, took a seat nearly opposite to me at the table, stared at me continually and seemed to be listening to my conversation."

Grant had become used to people staring at him and at the people who were with him and he seemed unconcerned about Julia's experience. "Oh, I suppose he did so merely from curiosity," he told Julia.

About three-thirty the wife of Major General Daniel Rucker of the Army's quartermaster department (and future mother-in-law of General Sheridan), came to the hotel with her carriage to take the Grants to the Baltimore & Ohio train station in Washington. The carriage had two seats, and Julia and Mrs. Rucker sat in the back seat, and Grant sat in front. As they drove along Pennsylvania Avenue a man on horseback who was riding in the same direction passed them and peered into the carriage as he went by. Julia noticed him and told Grant, "That is the same man who sat down at the lunch table near me. I don't like his looks."[1]

Before they reached the train station the man came riding back toward them and again stared into the carriage. This time Grant took notice of him, but passed off his behavior to the ladies so as not to alarm them.

The next odd occurrence happened while the Grants were en route on the train. They were traveling in the private car of the president of the Baltimore & Ohio Railroad, John Garrett, provided as a special courtesy to the general. The train was scheduled to arrive in Baltimore at seven-twenty-five, and sometime before the train reached Baltimore, a man suddenly appeared on the car's front platform. He tugged and pushed at the door, trying to open it, but the conductor had locked it in Washington, and the stranger was unable to open it and enter the car. Thwarted, he turned away and disappeared. The train and the Grants continued on to Baltimore and then on toward Philadelphia, which they were scheduled to reach at midnight and where they would change trains for Burlington.

Although in a good mood, Lincoln wasn't keen on going to the theater that night either, especially since the Grants wouldn't be going. But he had already made the arrangements, had told James Ford he was coming and had promised Mary they would go. So he would go. He and Mary would have company in their box even without the Grants. Mary had invited a young couple, Army Major Henry Rathbone and his fiancee, Clara Harris, daughter of New York senator Ira Harris, to come with them. The Lincolns would pick them up at the Harris house on the way.

One other person might have been with the Lincolns that evening had he not been out of town. He was Ward Hill Lamon, Lincoln's close friend and onetime law partner, now the U.S. marshal for the District of Columbia. Lamon often also served as Lincoln's bodyguard, in addition to the regular four-man staff of bodyguards provided by the Washington police department. Lamon constantly worried about the president's safety. He was one of those who, like Secretary Stanton, believed the president was in peril in public and urged him not to go out at night, especially when Lamon was not there to protect him. Lincoln had asked Lamon to go to Richmond to help with some political problems, and he had gone, but before going, Lamon had asked Lincoln to promise that he would not go out after dark while Lamon was away. Lincoln promised he would do the best he could, knowing, but not saying, he had already agreed to take Mary to Ford's Theatre Friday evening.

The eight-hour shift of William Crook, the police bodyguard who guarded the president during the day, was supposed to end at 4 P.M., but at seven, his relief, thirty-four-year-old John F. Parker, still hadn't shown up, and Crook stayed on. It was a mystery why Parker was one of the four policemen chosen to guard the president. Parker had a long record of misconduct as a police officer; he had faced numerous charges of abusive behavior to citizens and to other officers; he had been officially reprimanded; he had been found drunk and disorderly in a brothel; he had been found sleeping on the job in a streetcar, and he had generally shown himself to be irresponsible and lax in the performance of his duties, but he somehow had held onto his job.

When he finally showed up, Crook briefed him on the president's plans for the evening and told him that he was to go with the president to the theater. Crook asked him if was armed, and Parker said he was. Crook told him that because the Lincolns were taking another couple to the theater, there would be no room for him in the president's carriage and that he should leave the White House early, walk to the theater and wait there for the Lincolns' arrival and escort them inside the theater.

The play was scheduled to start at eight o'clock, but it was a little after eight before the Lincolns left the White House. Ned Burke was the carriage driver, and sitting beside him was the president's valet, Charles Forbes. The usual cavalry escort was called off, on the president's instructions. His standing order was that there be no cavalry escort when he and Mrs. Lincoln went to the theater or to church. From the front portico of the White House the carriage proceeded to the Harris house at the corner of Fifteenth and H streets, and Forbes hopped out and brought Henry Rathbone and Clara Harris to the carriage. They sat facing the Lincolns, with their backs to Burke and Forbes. At eight-twenty the carriage was on its way again. By then the night had turned damp and chilly and was threatening rain. Mary Lincoln put her arm in the president's arm and put her hand on his hand.

John Parker was standing against the wall at the theater's front entrance when the presidential carriage arrived and drove up the wooden ramp so that its occupants would not have to step into mud when they alighted from it. Forbes jumped down and helped the passengers out of the carriage and picked up the president's plaid shawl and followed the two couples. Parker then ushered the party into the theater and up to the presidential box, No. 7, at stage left in the dress circle. The play was already well into Act One as the party made its way to their seats, but the orchestra conductor interrupted the action on the stage to have the orchestra break into *Hail to the Chief* when the president was noticed. When the strains died away, the audience, a full house of 1,675 theatergoers, on their feet, erupted into loud and sustained applause.

Rathbone and Miss Harris took seats on a sofa in Box No. 8, and the Lincolns took their seats in No. 7. A partition between the two boxes had been removed to accommodate the presidential party. Mrs. Lincoln sat in an upholstered armchair, and the president sat in a large, upholstered rocking chair, placed there especially for him, on Mrs. Lincoln's left. Forbes sat in a straight-backed chair behind the Lincolns.[2] Parker took a seat in a chair at the entrance to No. 7. The stage was not visible from where he sat, though he could hear the actors, and as the play proceeded, he periodically got up to see what was happening onstage.

In their seats the president and Mrs. Lincoln soon became absorbed with the play. The president, still exulting in the good news from Appomattox Court House and perhaps feeling a bit romantic as well, took Mary's hand in his big hand and held it alongside the rocker. When she, apparently embarrassed, tried to remove her hand, he gripped it so tight that she couldn't take it away. She leaned toward him then and whispered, "What will Miss Harris think of my hanging onto you so?"

Without turning his eyes from the stage, he blandly answered, "She will think nothing of it."

There was an intermission at the end of Act One, and when the house lights came up, the audience members could look up or over at the presidential box, able to see clearly the young couple and Mrs. Lincoln, though the president, sitting in a shadow, was obscured. The low balustrade across the face of the president's box was draped with a flag that called the audience's attention to the box.

After the play resumed, police officer John Parker began thinking of something to drink. He left his seat outside the president's box, made his way downstairs, then out of the theater and into Peter Taltavul's Star Saloon, next door to the theater. Also becoming thirsty was Forbes, the valet, who later joined Parker at the bar. There they remained till after ten o'clock, leaving the president's box unguarded, the door to No. 7 unlocked.[3]

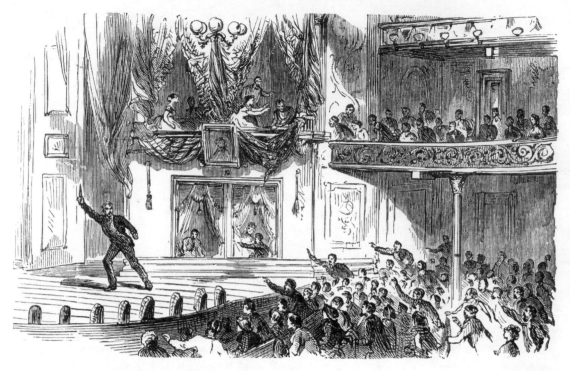

Scene of the assassination. The assassin flees across the stage at Ford's Theatre as Lincoln, mortally wounded, slumps in his rocker in the presidential box to the right of the stage. (JOHN CLARK RIDPATH)

Around ten-fifteen the play was headed toward its climax. Actor Harry Hawk, playing the character Asa Trenchard, was alone on the stage, delivering lines meant to draw guffaws from the audience: "Don't know the manners of good society, huh? Well, I guess I know enough to turn you inside out, you sockdologizing old mantrap!" As the audience burst into laughter, a loud *bang* sounded in the president's box, only partly muffled by the crowd's laughter.

A little cloud of blue smoke hung in the box, and Mrs. Lincoln quickly turned to the president. A thin young man dressed all in black suddenly was between her chair and the president's, moving hurriedly toward the balustrade. As faces in the box and in the audience turned to him, the man declared, in a voice not loud enough to be heard below, "Sic semper tyrannis!" Major Rathbone quickly jumped up from his seat and grabbed for the man, who dropped a derringer onto the floor and pulled out a large knife from his clothing. He slashed Rathbone's left arm, thrown up to ward off a thrust, the blade slicing through Rathbone's sleeve and laying open his flesh from elbow to shoulder. The man stood at the balustrade then and shouted to the audience, "Revenge for the South!" He quickly turned his back to the audience then and climbed over the balustrade, hanging by his hands till he let go and dropped fourteen feet to the floor of the stage.

Mrs. Lincoln, shocked and puzzled, glanced at her husband. He seemed to have dozed off, his body and head slumping forward. On the stage, Harry Hawk was so startled he couldn't get his lines out. He was looking up to his left, toward the president's box. The crowd also stared, not sure whether they were seeing something that was part of the play.

The man in the black suit, with black wavy hair and black mustache, had snagged the spur on his right foot in the flag draped in front of the president's box and he fell awkwardly

Ford's Theatre. The building beside the theater, on the right, housed the Star Saloon, where Lincoln's police bodyguard was having a few drinks while the president watched the play, unprotected. (LIBRARY OF CONGRESS)

on his hands and left leg, a bone in his left foot snapping on impact with the stage floor. He quickly stood and ran past Harry Hawk, hurrying to the left side of the stage, limping, seeming to be running on his left ankle. He fell, got up and ran again, disappearing into the wings. "Stop that man!" Rathbone shouted, and a tall Army major in the first row of orchestra seats climbed up on the stage and raced after the fugitive.

From the president's box now came a scream, then another one. Mrs. Lincoln could see something was wrong with the president. He wasn't sleeping. He couldn't be roused. There were calls for water to be brought to the box, and then someone shouted, "He has shot the president!" The audience began to rise from their seats and crowd the aisles, milling about, buzzing with talk, some trying to climb the steps to the dress circle. On the stage Harry Hawk stood crying. Many audience members began pouring out of the theater, spreading the evil news when they reached the street. Others jammed the doorway trying to exit the building.

Major Rathbone, his left arm bleeding profusely, managed to open the door to No. 7 after finding a prop had been placed against the inside of it to prevent its being opened from the corridor. He announced that only doctors should enter. A young man at the back of the crowd in the dress circle said he was a doctor and he squeezed forward and came into the president's box. He was Charles A. Leale, a twenty-three-year-old Army surgeon on the staff at Armory Square Hospital in Washington. He was in the audience because he had heard that the president and General Grant were going to be at the theater that night. When Doctor Leale entered the box, Rathbone asked him for help, saying, "I'm bleeding to death!" Leale looked into Rathbone's eyes, as if examining them, then brushed past Rathbone and moved to the president.

Mrs. Lincoln, crouching over the president, her head on his chest, grabbed Leale's hand. "Oh, doctor!" she cried. "Is he dead? Can he recover? Will you take charge of him? Oh, my dear husband! My dear husband!"

"I will do what I can," Leale replied, then motioned for others in the box to take her away. They urged her to the sofa in No. 8, where Miss Harris sat beside her, patting her hand and trying to comfort her.

Doctor Leale pushed the president's shoulders back, straightening his body in the rocker. He then asked for a lamp to be brought to him. "Someone hold matches until the lamp gets here," he ordered. He then began his examination. Lincoln's eyes were closed, and he made no sound of breathing. Leale could see no sign of a knife wound, which he was expecting to find, Major Rathbone having been slashed. Leale then spoke to several soldiers among the nearby bystanders. "Come here," he told them. "Get him out of the chair and put him on the floor."

When the president was laid on the floor of the box, Leale, by the light of matches, began again to look for a knife wound. He unbuttoned the president's coat and vest, removed the gold watch chain, then impatiently asked for someone to lend him a pocket knife. When he got one, he cut away Lincoln's shirt and ripped apart his undershirt. There was no wound. He bent low and put his ear to Lincoln's chest. Then he pulled up an eyelid. The president's dilated pupil showed a sign of brain injury.

Charles A. Leale, the 23-year-old Army doctor who was the first physician to reach Lincoln after the shooting. An admirer of the president, Leale was in the audience because he had heard Lincoln was going to be at Ford's Theatre that night. (LIBRARY OF CONGRESS)

By now two other physicians had entered the president's box. They were Doctor Charles Taft, who had been lifted into the box by men in the audience, and Doctor Albert F.A. King. Both stood by to assist Doctor Leale.

Leale felt the back of Lincoln's head, running his fingers through the dark hair. He discovered matted blood, and when he removed a small clot, Lincoln began a shallow breathing, and a pulse returned, although weak. Doctor Leale's finger told him the wound was a bullet hole. The president had been shot behind the left ear. The ball had not emerged from the other side of his head. Therefore, Leale quickly concluded, it was imbedded in the president's brain. Leale then made the awful pronouncement, telling the other doctors: "His wound is mortal. It is impossible for him to recover."

Even so, Leale started artificial respiration, straddling the president's supine body and pressing his mouth to Lincoln's bluish lips. For a time the president's breathing grew stronger, sounding like snoring. The lamp finally arrived. Leale now sat up straight and, directing the question to no one in particular, asked, "Can he be removed to somewhere nearby?"

Doctor King asked about taking him to the White House. Leale said he thought that, having to suffer the ride over there, the president would be dead before he reached the White House. Doctor Taft then asked an Army officer to go outside and see if he could find a nearby place to which Lincoln could be carried. While the officer was going, Leale organized a team to carry the president out of the theater. Four soldiers from Battery C of the Pennsylvania Light Artillery were recruited for the task. Two held their arms under the president's upper body, and two held his thighs. Doctor King held his left shoulder, and Doctor Leale held his head.

Together they carried him head first, Leale twisting his own head to see where they were going. Several other soldiers led the way, clearing a path for the bearers. Down the stairs they slowly descended and then eased across the lobby and then outside and onto Tenth Street, where a huge throng had gathered. Leale had the bearers stop every few steps so he could remove the clotting blood from the wound. A stout Army captain came up to Leale and said, "Surgeon, give me your commands, and I will see that they are obeyed." Leale took a look at the houses across the street and asked the captain to

John Wilkes Booth, the murderer of President Lincoln. Booth was well known to the actors and workers at Ford's Theatre and was immediately recognized as he fled across the stage. (LIBRARY OF CONGRESS)

help the bearers get across the street, through the crowd. The bearers began to inch through the mass of curious humanity that was striving for a look at the unconscious president.

The stout captain drew his sword from its scabbard and shouted, "Out of the way, you sons of bitches!" The crowd parted, and the bearers made their way to the other side of the street.

The first house considered, the one directly opposite the theater, was rejected when a soldier standing on the front stoop indicated there was no one home and the house was locked. Next door, at 453 Tenth Street, a young man holding a lighted candle was standing in the front doorway, beckoning and shouting, "Bring him in here! Bring him in here!" The house belonged to William Petersen, a tailor, a German immigrant. The young man was Henry Safford, a boarder, who had been reading in the front parlor when the commotion erupted. The bearers carried Lincoln up the front steps and into the house. Some of the crowd followed them in. The bearers followed Safford down the center hall.

On the left of the hall was a parlor and behind it a sitting room. On the right was a stairway, and behind and under it a narrow bedroom, nine by fifteen feet, with a double bed and a bureau, three straight-back chairs, a washstand with a crockery basin atop it, and a woodstove. Two windows on the outside wall looked out onto a courtyard. The head of the bed was under the stairway.

Too tall for the bed, Lincoln had to be lain diagonally on it. As Safford went through the first floor of the house turning up the gas lights, the three doctors conferred, and then Leale began removing the president's clothes so that the three physicians could make a thorough examination. When Leale noticed Mrs. Lincoln standing in the doorway, he asked that she be taken to another room to wait. The doctors found no other wound on the naked president's body. They placed him between two bedsheets and put a comforter on top of him, then recruited a soldier to bring heated blankets and hot-water bottles. Another soldier was ordered to fetch some mustard plasters, which were then placed on Lincoln, covering his body from chest to feet. Leale periodically removed the clotting blood from the wound.

Once in awhile Lincoln sighed. His breathing was raspy, like snoring. His pulse was forty-four and light. In his right eye the pupil was dilated; in the left eye the pupil had contracted. Neither was sensitive to light. A bruise was forming around his left eye.

The president had been made as comfortable as the doctors could make him, and they had done all they knew to do. Now Doctor Leale wrote some notes and called in a couple more soldiers who were standing in the hallway. He ordered them to take a note to the Lincolns' son Robert and to Lincoln's pastor, Phineas Gurley, pastor of the New York Avenue Presbyterian Church; to the Army's surgeon general, Joseph K. Barnes; to Lincoln's personal physician, Robert K. Stone; and to Leale's superior officer at Armory Square Hospital, Doctor William Bliss. The soldiers were also to summon the members of the president's cabinet. They were instructed to go first to Secretary Stanton and have him come immediately to the Petersen house.

By eleven o'clock, forty-five minutes after the shooting, the identity of the assassin was widely known. He was John Wilkes Booth, a professional actor from a family of actors. He had been recognized by Harry Hawk as he dashed across the stage in front of Hawk, who knew him, as did other actors and workers at Ford's Theatre, where Booth was well known. Those behind the curtain had recognized him as well.

It was also known within that first hour that the president was not the only one who had been attacked. Secretary of State William Seward, confined to his bed after being severely injured when his carriage had overturned earlier, had been savagely attacked by a knife-wielding stranger who had gained entrance to Seward's house by posing as a pharmacist's assistant delivering medication to Seward. The rumors were that Seward had been killed, but actually he had survived the assault. His son and daughter, trying to protect him, were also seriously wounded.

By midnight an all-out search for the assassins and possible conspirators had been launched by the Washington police and by the Army. Witnesses to the president's shooting were being questioned, especially including those who had managed to push their way into the Petersen house.

Around midnight General Grant and Julia reached the Broad Street train station in Philadelphia and were taken by Army ambulance to the Walnut Street wharf, where they would board a ferry to cross the Delaware River. On the New Jersey side of the river, in Camden, they were to board another train for the last leg of the trip to Burlington. En route to the ferry, Grant had the ambulance driver stop so he could send a telegram to Bloodgood's Hotel, near the ferry, to order dinner in advance.

Shortly after their arrival at the hotel, while they were seated in the dining room, Grant was handed a telegram, which had reached him at Bloodgood's because the telegraph operator remembered Grant had made the dinner reservation there. Grant read the telegram. His head fell, and he paused in silence. A couple more telegrams were delivered to him, and he read them, still silent.

"Ulyss," Julia said, "what do the telegrams say? Do they bring bad news?"

"I will read them to you," he replied, his voice filled with emotion. "But first prepare yourself for the most painful and startling news that could be received. And control your feelings so as not to betray the nature of the despatches to the servants." He then read to her the news of President Lincoln's assassination.[4] The telegrams reported that Seward had also been assassinated, and possibly Vice President Johnson, too. The telegrams' writer warned Grant to be on guard for his own safety and urged him to return to Washington immediately.

At the Petersen house the death watch continued through the night while in the sitting room behind the parlor Secretary of War Stanton gave orders, issued bulletins, heard witnesses' testimony, made decisions and generally served as a sort of interim president, with no authority but his forceful personality.

Mrs. Lincoln sat between two friends on the parlor sofa, accepting condolences and periodically bursting into wails of grief. "Take me inside to my husband," she pleaded to the doctors. When they did allow her into the room, she fainted at the sight of her dying husband, lying motionless on the bed, a napkin beneath his head, freshly placed there to hide blood stains in advance of her entering the room. Returned to the front parlor, she later again begged to see the president. This time she cried out to him, "Live! You must live!" Piteously she urged the doctors, "Bring Tad. He will speak to Tad. He loves him so."

Again in the parlor, she sat on the sofa, and her son Robert crouched in front of her, stroking her hand and telling her, "Mother, please put your trust in God, and all will be well."

Doctor Leale, just six weeks from having received his medical license, was superseded by his seniors, who decided that the surgeon general, Doctor Barnes, should be in charge of the president's care. Leale, though, remained at Lincoln's bedside, holding his hand. He had heard that sometimes awareness returns to such a seriously injured patient for just a fleeting moment before death. Leale wanted to be there in case that fleeting moment occurred, so that the president "would know," Leale later explained, "in his blindness, that he was in touch with humanity and had a friend."

The night crept on. Outside, a heavy rain had begun. Inside, the grim wait continued. The end was nearing. Around his right eye, behind which lay the lethal ball, Lincoln's face had turned black. His hair was disheveled. A slight ruddiness remained on his hollow cheeks. His breathing was light but rapid. His skin was cold. Moans, as if of pain, escaped from

Hanging the conspirators. Four of the convicted conspirators in Booth's assassination plot were sentenced to death and were hanged at the Arsenal Penitentiary in Washington on July 7, 1865. They were George Atzerodt, David Herold, Lewis Powell and Mary Surratt. (LIBRARY OF CONGRESS)

his lips. Around 7 A.M. Doctor Barnes asked an Army officer to bring Mrs. Lincoln back into the room.

She came in, unsteadily. Robert was already in the room, his face in his hands, sobbing. Mrs. Lincoln looked at her husband, then at her son. Then, without a word or sound from her, she was led back to the parlor.

Doctor Leale saw the president's chest heave and fall, for the last time. President Lincoln had taken his final breath. Doctor Barnes leaned over and put his head on Lincoln's chest and listened. When Barnes straightened up, he took two silver coins from his pocket and placed them over the president's dead eyes. The time was 7:22 A.M. The new day was Saturday, April 15, 1865.

Robert left the room to tell his mother it was over. Secretary Stanton, standing at the president's bedside, was the first to speak. He turned to Lincoln's pastor, the Reverend Doctor Gurley, and asked, "Doctor, will you say anything?" Gurley nodded and lowered himself to his knees beside the bed. The others also knelt, their hands on the bed. Gurley's prayer was that God would accept His servant Abraham Lincoln into His glorious kingdom. The men then stood, their eyes wet. "Now he belongs to the ages," Stanton said.

Soon the bells of Washington City began a mournful tolling. As the news leaped from telegraph lines, the tolling was taken up in Philadelphia, in New York, in Boston, in every place where Lincoln's saddened countrymen dwelt.

Giving words to the nation's grief, poet Walt Whitman penned these lines:

> O Captain! My Captain!
>   Our fearful trip is done;
> The ship has weather'd every rack,
>   the prize we sought is won;
> The port is near, the bells I hear,
>   the people all exulting,
> While follow eyes the steady keel,
>   the vessel grim and daring;
>   But O heart! Heart! Heart!
>   O the bleeding drops of red,
>   Where on the deck my Captain lies,
>   Fallen cold and dead.
> O captain! My Captain!
>   Rise up and hear the bells;
> Rise up — for you the flag is flung —
>   for you the bugle trills;
> For you bouquets and ribbon'd wreaths —
>   for you the shores a-crowding;
> For you they call, the swaying mass,
>   Their eager faces turning.
>   Here Captain! Dear Father!
>   The arm beneath your head!
>   It is some dream that on the deck
>   You've fallen cold and dead.
> My Captain does not answer,
>   his lips are pale and still;
> My Father does not feel my arm,
>   he has no pulse or will;
> The ship is anchor'd safe and sound,
>   its voyage closed and done;
> From fearful trip, the victor ship
>   comes in with object won.
>   Exult, O shores, and ring, O bells!
>   But I, with mournful tread,
>   Walk the deck my Captain lies,
>   Fallen cold and dead.

On April 26 John Wilkes Booth was discovered hiding in the barn of a tobacco farmer in northern Virginia. He was shot by Sergeant Thomas P. Corbett of the Sixteenth New York Cavalry Regiment when he refused to surrender. He died about two hours later on the farmer's front porch. Eight of Booth's co-conspirators were captured and tried by a nine-member military tribunal presided over by Major General David (Black Dave) Hunter. All defendants were found guilty. George Atzerodt, David Herold, Lewis Powell and Mary Surratt were sentenced to death by hanging. Samuel Arnold, Samuel Mudd and Michael O'Laughlen were sentenced to life in prison. Edman (Ned) Spangler was sentenced to six years in prison. The four who were condemned to death were hanged at the Arsenal Penitentiary in Washington, D.C., on July 7, 1865.

The Beginning of Peace

The last remains of the Confederate government — Jefferson Davis and his cabinet — were resting temporarily in Greensboro, North Carolina, having reached there after a flight from Danville on the news that Richmond had been captured. On April 11, at one o'clock in the morning, Lieutenant General Joseph Johnston, commanding the rebel troops that first had faced then fled from Sherman's army, was summoned to meet with Davis and his cabinet members in Greensboro. Johnston and his army were then encamped on the Neuse River, just east of Raleigh, having arrived there on the 10th.

Johnston took the first available train and arrived in Greensboro about eight o'clock on the morning of the 12th, reporting as ordered. At the meeting with him were Davis, Secretary of State Judah Benjamin, Secretary of the Navy Stephen Mallory and Postmaster General John H. Reagan. General Beauregard, the Confederate army's Division of the West commander, was also there.

Johnston thought he was going to be asked about the military situation, but as the meeting got under way, he discovered that, as he said, "the President's object seemed to be to give, not to obtain information." Davis was gripped by delusions of continuing the fight. "He said," Johnston reported, "that in two or three weeks he would have a large army in the field by bringing back into the ranks those who had abandoned them in less desperate circumstances, and by calling out the enrolled men whom the conscript bureau with its forces had been unable to bring into the army."[1] Neither opinions nor information was asked for, Johnston reported, and when Davis finished describing his fantasy, the meeting ended.

General Breckinridge, the Confederacy's secretary of war, arrived in Greensboro later that day, having come from Richmond and, as Johnston called it, "the great disaster." Johnston and Beauregard huddled with Breckinridge and, receiving his report, decided that the Confederacy was defeated. Johnston told Breckinridge he believed that "the only power of government left in the president's hands was that of terminating the war, and that this power should be exercised without more delay."[2] He also told Breckinridge that he, Johnston, was ready to repeat that opinion to Davis if given the opportunity to do so. Breckinridge promised he would get Johnston that opportunity.

The next morning, April 13, Johnston and Beauregard were called to Davis's office, there to meet with him and his cabinet. Johnston later related the remarks he made at the meeting:

Being desired by the President to do it, we [Johnston and Beauregard] compared the military forces of the two parties to the war: ours, an army of about twenty thousand infantry and artillery, and five thousand mounted troops; those of the United States, three armies that could be combined against ours, which was insignificant compared with either — Grant's, of a hundred and eighty thousand men; Sherman's, of a hundred and ten thousand, at least, and Canby's of sixty thousand — odds of seventeen or eighteen to one, which in a few weeks could be more than doubled.

I represented that under such circumstances it would be the greatest of human crimes for us to attempt to continue the war; for, having neither money nor credit, nor arms but those in the hands of our soldiers, nor ammunition but that in their cartridge-boxes, nor shops for repairing arms or fixing ammunition, the effect of our keeping the field would be, not to harm the enemy, but to complete the devastation of our country and ruin of its people. I therefore urged that the President should exercise at once the only function of government still in his possession, and open negotiations for peace.[3]

Davis asked for the opinions of his cabinet members. Breckinridge, Mallory and Reagan agreed that the fight was lost and that it was absolutely necessary to make peace. Benjamin thought otherwise. Seeming annoyed, Davis offered that it was unlikely that he or his proposals would be accepted by the U.S. government, which refused to recognize his authority. Johnston replied that it was not unusual for military commanders to initiate negotiations for peace and asked that Davis allow him to contact General Sherman to do so. Davis rejected that idea. Instead, he suggested that he would write a letter to Sherman, proposing a meeting, and that the letter be sent by Johnston. Johnston then proposed that Davis dictate a letter, that Mallory, whose penmanship was better than others, write it down and that Johnston sign it and have it delivered to Sherman. Davis agreed to that, and this message resulted:

"The results of the recent campaign in Virginia have changed the relative military conditions of the belligerents. I am therefore induced to address you, in this form, the inquiry whether, in order to stop the further effusion of blood and devastation of property, you are willing to make a temporary suspension of active operations, and to communicate to Lieutenant-General Grant, commanding the armies of the United States, the request that he will take like action in regard to other armies — the object being, to permit the civil authorities to enter into the needful arrangements to terminate the existing war."[4]

The message was dated April 13 and was received by Sherman on the 14th. He speedily replied, saying he was authorized to arrange terms for the suspension of hostilities and was willing to meet with Johnston. "I really desire to save the people of North Carolina the damage they would sustain by the march of this army through the central or western parts of the state," Sherman told him.[5]

By then Sherman was at Raleigh. The position of his troops stretched westward as far as Durham. Johnston had moved his troops from Smithfield to Raleigh and then beyond Raleigh toward Greensboro, with his rear guard positioned at Hillsborough, some twelve miles northwest of Durham.

On the 16th Sherman received Johnston's reply, proposing they meet the next day at a point halfway between Sherman's forward position and the position of Johnston's rear guard. On the morning of Monday, April 17, just as Sherman was about to leave by special train for the meeting with Johnston, the telegraph operator whose office was on the second floor of the Raleigh depot came running to Sherman and told him there was an important dispatch coming through and that Sherman needed to see it. Sherman ordered the train to wait, and after fifteen minutes the telegraph operator returned with the dispatch deciphered

**Sherman and Johnston meet. After an exchange of notes, Sherman and General Johnston, command-
ing the Confederates' last remaining large army, meet near Hillsborough, North Carolina, to arrange
Johnston's surrender.** (JOHN CLARK RIDPATH)

and written out. It was from Secretary Stanton, notifying Sherman of the president's assassination and the attempt to kill Secretary Seward. Stanton warned that attacks may also
have been planned on General Grant and other officers of the government.

Fearing that such news might set off a wave of vengeance by his outraged troops,
inflicting on Raleigh "a fate worse than that of Columbia," he said, Sherman ordered the
telegrapher not to reveal the news to anyone else until after Sherman returned from his
meeting with Johnston, which he intended to do later that day. After that, the train left
Raleigh.

It arrived at Durham about 10 A.M. on the 17th. Sherman was met by General Kilpatrick and a squadron of cavalry, and he and his staff members were provided mounts on which to ride to the meeting with Johnston. A trooper bearing a white flag rode out in front of the party at a distance. About five miles out on the road to Hillsborough the trooper was met by a Confederate rider coming his way, also bearing a flag of truce.

It turned out that Johnston was nearby, and he and Sherman, riding toward each other, soon came upon each other. "We had never met before," Sherman wrote in his memoir, "though we had been in the regular army together for thirteen years…. He was some twelve or more years my senior; but we knew enough of each other to be well acquainted at once."[6] They shook hands, and each introduced his respective staff officers. Also with Johnston was Lieutenant General Wade Hampton. The entire party rode to a house that Johnston and Hampton had just passed, a small farmhouse belonging to a couple named Bennett, who temporarily vacated it to allow their visitors to use it.

As soon as Sherman and Johnston were alone together, Sherman showed Johnston the dispatch concerning the assassination of President Lincoln. Johnston expressed chagrin. "I told General Sherman," Johnston related, "that, in my opinion, the event was the greatest possible calamity to the South."[7]

"I then told Johnston," Sherman recounted, "that he must be convinced that he could not oppose my army, and that, since Lee had surrendered, he could do the same with honor and propriety."[8]

"I replied," Johnston related, "that our relative positions were too different from those of the armies in Virginia to justify me in such a capitulation, but suggested that we might do more than he proposed: that, instead of a partial suspension of hostilities, we might, as other generals had done, arrange the terms of permanent peace…."[9]

What Johnston had in mind was gaining an armistice between all combatants, an agreement affecting his army and all other Confederate forces. Sherman asked him if he could control armies other than his own. "He said, not then," Sherman related, "but intimated that he could procure authority from Mr. Davis." During further discussion, according to Sherman, Johnston "recurred to the idea of a universal surrender, embracing his own army, that of Dick Taylor in Louisiana and Texas, and of [Major General Dabney] Maury, Forrest, and others, in Alabama and Georgia."[10]

Johnston told Sherman he thought that by the next day he could get authorization to act in the name of all the Confederate armies. The two generals then agreed to meet the next day again at noon, again at the Bennett house. They departed, Johnston heading toward Hillsborough, and Sherman toward Raleigh.

On the way back, Sherman showed the telegram about Lincoln to the officers who were with him. "I cautioned the officers to watch the soldiers closely, to prevent any violent retaliation by them, leaving that to the Government in Washington."[11] On reaching Raleigh, he issued an announcement of the president's assassination and told his men that while he believed "the great mass of the Confederate army would scorn to sanction such acts," his troops must be prepared for the war's "last and worst shape, that of assassins and guerrillas."[12]

That evening and the next morning, April 18, Sherman met with a number of his general officers, including Schofield, Slocum, Howard, Logan and Blair, and discussed with them the conversation he had had with Johnston. "Without exception," he reported, "all advised me to agree to some terms, for they all dreaded the long and harassing march in pursuit of a dissolving and fleeing army…. We discussed all the probabilities, among which was, whether, if Johnston made a point of it, I should assent to the escape from the country of Jeff. Davis and his fugitive cabinet; and some one of my general officers, either Logan or Blair, insisted that, if asked for, we should even provide a vessel to carry them to Nassau from Charleston."[13]

Meanwhile, Johnston was meeting with Confederate Secretary of War Breckinridge and Postmaster General Reagan, who had come to Hampton's quarters before dawn of the day after Johnston's meeting with Sherman. "After they had received from me as full an account of the discussion of the day before as my memory enabled me to give, and had learned the terms agreed upon, and the difficulty in the way of full agreement," Johnston related, "Mr. Reagan proposed to reduce them [the terms] to writing, to facilitate reconsideration. In doing so, he included the article for amnesty without exceptions, the only one not fully agreed to."[14]

Later on the 18th Sherman again took the train to Durham and then rode horseback to the Bennett house with his staff and several other generals. Johnston showed up two hours late, at two o'clock. Breckinridge had come with him, and Johnston asked that he be allowed to join the discussion. He wanted him to be in on the discussion so that he could help persuade Davis to accept a peace agreement that did not include amnesty for Davis and his cabinet officers. Sherman at first objected, on the grounds that Breckinridge was an official of the Confederacy, which the United States did not recognize as an entity, and that the talks should be strictly limited to the belligerents. Johnston pointed out that Breckinridge was a general in the Confederate army, and on that basis, Sherman okayed his participation in the talks. After a half hour of discussion about amnesty, Johnston showed Sherman the proposed agreement written by Reagan that morning. It included the amnesty provision. Sherman didn't accept it.

"It was in Reagan's handwriting," Sherman reported, "and began with a long preamble and terms, so general and verbose, that I said they were inadmissible. Then recalling the conversation of Mr. Lincoln, at City Point, I sat down at the table, and wrote off the terms, which I thought concisely expressed his views and wishes...."[15] This is the tentative agreement, dated April 18, that he wrote and that he and Johnston signed:

1. The contending armies now in the field to maintain the status quo until notice is given by the commanding general of any one to its opponent, and reasonable time — say forty-eight (48) hours — allowed.

2. The Confederate armies, now in existence, to be disbanded and conducted to their several State capitals, there to deposit their arms and public property in the State arsenal; and each officer and man to execute and file an agreement to cease from acts of war, and to abide the action of the State and Federal authority. The number of arms and munitions of war to be reported to the Chief of Ordnance at Washington City, subject to the future action of the Congress of the United States, and, in the mean time, to be used solely to maintain peace and order within the borders of the States respectively.

3. The recognition, by the Executive of the United States, of the several State governments, on their officers and Legislatures taking the oaths prescribed by the Constitution of the United States, and, where conflicting State governments have resulted from the war, the legitimacy of all shall be submitted to the Supreme Court of the United States.

4. The reestablishment of all the Federal courts in the several States, with powers as defined by the Constitution and laws of Congress.

5. The people and inhabitants of all the States to be guaranteed, so far as the Executive can, their political rights and franchises, as well as their rights of person and property, as defined by the Constitution of the United States and of the States respectively.

6. The Executive authority of the Government of the United States not to disturb any of the people by reason of the late war, so long as they live in peace and quiet, abstain from acts of armed hostility, and obey the laws in existence at the place of their residence.

7. In general terms — the war to cease; a general amnesty, so far as the Executive of the United States can command, on condition of the disbandment of the Confederate armies, the distribution of the arms, and the resumption of peaceful pursuits by the officers and men hitherto composing said armies.

Not being fully empowered by our respective principals to fulfill these terms, we individually and officially pledge ourselves to promptly obtain the necessary authority, and to carry out the above programme.[16]

Copies of the document were made to be sent to the generals' respective governments. Sherman sent a copy off to Washington by Major Henry Hitchcock, and it reached President Andrew Johnson on April 21. He promptly rejected it. Its flaws included language that implicitly recognized the Confederate government, that allowed the states to keep their arms, that implicitly usurped the responsibility of the U.S. president and Congress to decide reconstruction policy and that implied possible compensation for those whose slaves had been freed.

Johnson immediately called a cabinet meeting and sent for General Grant, who was then in Washington. At the cabinet meeting Grant found "the greatest consternation, lest Sherman would commit the government to terms which they were not willing to accede to and which he had no right to grant."[17] Details of the cabinet meeting were leaked to the press by Stanton, and a number of false charges were made against Sherman by Stanton, who apparently saw Sherman as a looming political threat and was eager to discredit him before the public. Grant was instructed to go to North Carolina and take charge of the situation.

"When I arrived," Grant reported, "I went to Sherman's headquarters, and we were at once closeted together. I showed him the instructions and orders under which I visited him. I told him that I wanted him to notify General Johnston that the terms which they had conditionally agreed upon had not been approved in Washington, and that he was authorized to offer the same terms I had given General Lee."[18]

On April 24 Sherman wrote to Johnston telling him, "I have replies from Washington to my communications of April 18th. I am instructed to limit my operations to your immediate command, and not to attempt civil negotiations. I therefore demand the surrender of your army on the same terms as were given to General Lee at Appomattox, April 9th instant, purely and simply."[19] In a separate dispatch sent that same day, Sherman, responding to instructions from Grant, told Johnston, "You will take notice that the truce or suspension of hostilities agreed to between us will cease in forty-eight hours after this is received at your lines, under the first of the articles of agreement."[20] The two sides were now facing a resumption of the war.

Johnston received Sherman's note in the afternoon of the 24th and that same afternoon he received by wire Davis's approval of the proposed agreement drafted by Sherman on the 18th. When Johnston notified Davis that that proposed agreement had been rejected in Washington, Davis wired new instructions to Johnston, which he received on the morning of the 25th. He was told to disband the infantry and order it to reassemble later at some specified place, and to have his cavalry and all other troops who could be mounted on horses from the train of supply wagons to escort Davis and his cabinet members on their further flight southward.

Johnston decided to ignore those instructions. Instead, he wrote to Sherman proposing another meeting at the Bennett house at noon on the 26th. Sherman again met with him, and at that meeting a document of surrender was agreed to, with terms essentially the same as those accepted by Lee:

1. All acts of war on the part of the troops under General Johnston's command, to cease from this date. 2. All arms and public property to be deposited at Greensboro, and delivered to an ordnance-officer of the United States Army. 3. Rolls of all the officers and men to be made in duplicate; one copy to be retained by the commander of the troops, and the other to be given to an officer to be designated by General Sherman. Each officer and man to give his individual obligation in writing, not to take up arms against the Government of the United States, until properly released from this obligation. 4. The side-arms of officers and their private horses and baggage to be retained by them. 5. This being done, all the officers and men will be permitted to return to their homes, not to be disturbed by the United States authorities so long as they observe their obligations, and the laws in force where they reside.[21]

A supplement was added to those terms to allow enlisted men as well as officers to keep their horses and other private property, as Grant had done, and to include in the terms of agreement "naval forces within the limits of General Johnston's command" and to promise help with water transportation for troops returning to Texas and Arkansas.

Johnston then wired the governors of the states within the area of his command, notifying them of the surrender and telling them: "The disaster in Virginia, the capture by the enemy of all our workshops for the preparation of ammunition and repairing of arms, the impossibility of recruiting our little army opposed to more than ten times its number, or of supplying it except by robbing our own citizens, destroyed all hope of successful war. I have made, therefore, a military convention with Major-General Sherman, to terminate hostilities in North and South Carolina, Georgia, and Florida. I made this convention to spare the blood of our people by the devastation and ruin inevitable from the marches of invading armies, and to avoid the crime of waging a hopeless war."[22]

On April 27 Johnston issued his general order No. 18, informing his army of the surrender and the terms agreed to.

When Johnston told Sherman that his army's supply depots in South Carolina and in Charlotte, from which he had intended to feed his men on their way home, had been plundered by civilians, Sherman provided two hundred and fifty thousand rations for the rebel soldiers, "on no other condition," Johnston related, "than my furnishing the means of transporting them by railroad from Morehead City."[23]

Thus the largest remaining Confederate army in the Southeast was dissolved, and peace moved in to replace warfare. "The United States troops that remained in the Southern States, on *military* duty," Johnston commented, "conducted themselves as if they thought that the object of the war had been the restoration of the Union. They treated the people around them as they would have done those of Ohio or New York if stationed among them, as their fellow-citizens. Those people supposed, not unnaturally, that if those who had fought against them were friendly, the great body of the Northern people, who had not fought, must be more so. This idea inspired in them a kindlier feeling to the people of the North and the Government of the United States, than that existing ten years before. It created, too, a strong expectation that the Southern States would soon resume their places in the Union."[24]

(General Johnston allowed, however, that the expectation was sorely disappointed by the "reconstruction" later imposed on the seceded states by the U.S. Congress, over President Johnson's veto. "The most despondent apprehended no such 'reconstruction' as that subsequently established by Congress," he wrote in his memoir.[25])

Following the capture of Mobile's protective forts by a Union army under the command of General Canby, Confederate forces had evacuated the city and it had been surrendered by its mayor on April 12. That same day, U.S. Major General James H. Wilson's cavalry force, which had already taken Selma, Alabama, captured Montgomery, the Alabama capital. After that, General Taylor, commander of the Confederate army's District of Alabama, Mississippi and East Louisiana, decided to combine his surviving forces in Alabama and march to North Carolina to join Johnston's army. On April 25, though, he learned that Johnston had come to tentative terms with Sherman, causing him to change the plan. He arranged to meet with General Canby on April 30 at a farmhouse beside the Gulf, Mobile & Ohio Railroad tracks about fifteen miles north of Mobile.

Taylor arrived on a railroad handcar with an aide, Colonel William M. Levy, and found Canby waiting for him. With Canby were a brigade of U.S. cavalry and an Army band. Taylor and Canby speedily worked out a ceasefire agreement that allowed either general to terminate the ceasefire on forty-eight hours' notice while they waited to hear the final outcome of the negotiations between Sherman and Johnston. When the agreement between Taylor and Canby had been concluded, the officers ate a celebratory luncheon that included champagne, and the band struck up "Hail Columbia," at the first strains of which General Canby ordered the band to play "Dixie." Taylor then asked for the resumption of "Hail Columbia," saying he hoped that Columbia would again become a happy land. The diners all drank to that worthy hope.

When Canby and Taylor learned on May 1 that Sherman and Johnston's agreement of April 18 had been disapproved in Washington and that Johnston had surrendered on April 26, Canby notified Taylor that their ceasefire would end in forty-eight hours. Taylor promptly responded, telling Canby he wanted to negotiate the surrender of all forces under his command and that the Confederate naval commander wished to surrender his forces as well. On May 4 Taylor met Canby at Citronelle, Alabama, about thirty-five miles north of Mobile, and surrendered his forces under conditions similar to those accepted by Lee and Johnston, his men to be paroled at Meridian, Mississippi, where Taylor had his headquarters.

General M. Jeff Thompson, commanding Confederate forces in northern Arkansas, consulted with his brigade commanders and then surrendered his army, 7,454 officers and men, on May 11.

On April 21 General Edmund Kirby Smith, commander of the Confederate army's Trans-Mississippi Department, informed his army that Lee and Johnston had surrendered, but urged his troops to "stand by your colors." But by May 30, after half of his troops had bailed out and gone home, he decided it was time for him to quit, too. He surrendered to Canby under the same terms granted Lee, Johnston and Taylor, thereby ending the war for some eighteen thousand rebel troops in Louisiana, Arkansas, Missouri, Texas and Indian Territory.

Encamped at Gainesville, Alabama, fifty miles northeast of Meridian, Mississippi, Lieutenant General Nathan Bedford Forrest, under Taylor's command and leading a greatly diminished force of cavalrymen, struggled with a decision on whether to go along with Taylor's surrender or lead his remaining one thousand troopers to Mexico, as many of them urged him to do. He finally decided to surrender, and his troopers signed their paroles on May 9, having reluctantly accepted the inescapable fact of defeat of their cause. In one of the great ironies of the war, it was Forrest, the vicious foe and fighter, who exhorted them to fight no more and go home in peace.

"That we are beaten is a self-evident fact," he told his men before taking leave of them, "and any further resistance on our part would be justly regarded as the very height of folly and rashness.... The government which we sought to establish and perpetuate is at an end. Reason dictates and humanity demands that no more blood be shed. Fully realizing and feeling that such is the case, it is your duty and mine to lay down our arms, submit to the 'powers that be,' and to aid in restoring peace and establishing law and order throughout the land…. You have been good soldiers, you can be good citizens. Obey the laws, preserve your honor, and the government to which you have surrendered can afford to be and will be magnanimous."[26]

For the victorious U.S. forces who had reunited the divided nation there was one more duty to be performed. Grant narrated it:

On the 18th of May orders were issued by the adjutant-general for a grand review by the President and his cabinet of Sherman's and Meade's armies. The review commenced on the 23d and lasted two days. Meade's army occupied over six hours of the first day in passing the grand stand which had been erected in front of the President's house. Sherman witnessed this review from the grand stand which was occupied by the President and his cabinet. Here he showed his resentment for the cruel and harsh treatment that had unnecessarily been inflicted upon him by the Secretary of War, by refusing to take his extended hand.

… Promptly at ten o'clock on the morning of the 24th, his troops commenced to pass in review. Sherman's army made a different appearance from that of the Army of Potomac. The latter had been operating where they received directly from the North full supplies of food and

Review grandstand. President Andrew Johnson and members of his cabinet and other dignitaries, including Grant and Sherman, watch the victorious Union armies march past this grandstand that had been built in front of the White House for the occasion. (LIBRARY OF CONGRESS)

clothing regularly: the review of this army therefore was the review of a body of 65,000 well-drilled, well-disciplined and orderly soldiers inured to hardship and fit for any duty, but without the experience of gathering their own food and supplies in an enemy's country, and being ever on the watch.

Sherman's army was not so well-dressed as the Army of Potomac, but their marching could not be excelled; they gave the appearance men who had been thoroughly drilled to endure hardships, either by long and continuous marches or through exposure to any climate, without the ordinary shelter of a camp.... In the rear of a company there would be a captured horse or mule loaded with small cooking utensils, captured chickens and other food picked up for the use of the men. Negro families who had followed the army would sometimes come along in the rear of a company, with three or four children packed upon a single mule, and the mother leading it.

The sight was varied and grand: nearly all day for two successive days, from the Capitol to the Treasury Building, could be seen a mass of orderly soldiers marching in columns of companies....[27]

And so the nation's government and the people of its capital and Washington's surrounding area hailed and saluted the men who had won the long-sought victory. Then it was all over. The marchers disbanded and dispersed and eventually went home, their job done, their trials ended.

The general who had led the victors to this grand finale believed that what lay ahead for them and their country was a new beginning. Amid the war's dark ashes, however hard to notice, Grant could see a glint of good. "I feel that we are on the eve of a new era," he wrote, "when there is to be great harmony between the Federal and the Confederate." In the agony of war, he said, "a spirit of independence and enterprise" had been born. "The war has made us a nation of great power and intelligence."[28]

The grand review. The review lasted two days, with General Meade's Army of the Potomac marching from the Capitol to the Treasury Building on May 18 and Sherman's army, the one that had marched through Georgia and the Carolinas, following it on the next day. (LIBRARY OF CONGRESS)

Chapter Notes

Chapter 1

1. Horace Porter, *Campaigning with Grant*, page 19.
2. This version of events at the White House reception is drawn from the account of Horace Porter, an eyewitness, reported in his book, *Campaigning With Grant*. Other accounts vary.
3. Bruce Catton, *Grant Takes Command*, page 121.
4. *Ibid.*, page 126.
5. Ulysses S. Grant, *The Personal Memoirs of Ulysses S. Grant*, page 403.
6. *Ibid.*, pages 403–404.
7. *Ibid.*, pages 407–408.
8. Catton, page 128.
9. Grant, pages 404–405.
10. Catton, page 129.
11. Porter, page 22.
12. *Ibid.*
13. Adam Badeau, *Military History of Ulysses S. Grant*, volume 2, page 18.
14. *Ibid.*, page 19.
15. Catton, page 133.
16. *Ibid.*, page 134.
17. Badeau, volume 2, pages 19–21.
18. *Ibid.*, page 23.
19. Catton, page 138.
20. Badeau, volume 2, page 24.

Chapter 2

1. Badeau, volume 2, pages 40–41.
2. Catton, page 140.
3. Grant, pages 408–409.
4. *Ibid.*, page 409.
5. Catton, page 141.
6. *Ibid.*, page 138.
7. Porter, page 39.
8. *Ibid.*, pages 30–31. Badeau, volume 2, page 32.
9. Grenville Dodge, *Personal Biography of Major General Grenville Dodge*, a typescript in the Iowa State Department of History and Archives, page 175. Catton, page 139.
10. William Conant Church, *Ulysses S. Grant and the Period of National Preservation and Reconstruction*, pages 248–249. Catton, page 139.
11. Grant, page 408.
12. *Ibid.*
13. Grant to Butler, April 16, 1864. Quoted in Badeau, volume 2, page 46.
14. Badeau, volume 2, page 46.

15. *Ibid.*, pages 46–47.
16. Grant, pages 412–413.
17. *Ibid.*, page 416.
18. *Ibid.*
19. Porter, page 37.
20. *Ibid.*, pages 38–39.
21. Badeau, volume 2, page 78.
22. *Ibid.*, page 79.
23. *Ibid.*, pages 84–85.
24. *Ibid.*, pages 89–90.
25. *Ibid.*, page 90.

Chapter 3

1. Memphis *Avalanche*, August 26, 1861, page 2. Jack Hurst, *Nathan Bedford Forrest: A Biography*, pages 74–75.
2. Quoted in Hurst, page 79.
3. Robert S. Henry, *"First With the Most" Forrest*, pages 536–537.
4. Robert S. Henry, *As They Saw Forrest*, page 93.
5. Memphis City Directory, 1855–1856, page 251, reproduced online at en.wikipedia.org/wiki/Nathan_Bedford _Forrest.
6. Hurst, page 54.
7. John A. Wyeth, *That Devil Forrest: Life of General Nathan Bedford Forrest*, pages 242–244.
8. *Ibid.*
9. Hurst, page 161.
10. John William Draper, *History of the American Civil War*, volume 3, page 215.
11. *Official Records*, volume 22, part 1, page 559. Quoted in Wyeth, page 315.
12. "The Capture of Fort Pillow," *Battles and Leaders of the Civil War: Retreat with Honor*, page 418.
13. Wyeth, page 319.
14. Confederate General Thomas Jordan, onetime chief of staff to General Beauregard and also to General Albert Sidney Johnston and General Bragg, wrote his account in *The Campaigns of General N.B. Forrest and of Forrest's Cavalry*, co-authored by J.P. Pryor and first published in 1868. The quote appears on page 434. It also appears in Hurst, page 170.
15. *Official Records*, serial 1, volume 22, part 1, page 354.
16. Hurst, page 171.
17. *Ibid.*
18. John Cimprich, *Fort Pillow, A Civil War Massacre, and Public Memory*, page 80.
19. *Ibid.*, page 81.
20. *Ibid.*, and Hurst, page 173.
21. Hurst, pages 172–173.
22. Brian Steel Wills, *A Battle From the Start: The Life of Nathan Bedford Forrest* (New York: HarperCollins, 1992), pages 188–189. Hurst, pages 176–177.
23. Draper, page 217.
24. *Official Records*, serial 1, volume 32, part 1, pages 610, 371. Hurst, pages 174–175.
25. Cimprich, page 129.
26. *Ibid.*, page 85.
27. *Ibid.*
28. *Official Records*, serial 1, volume 32, part 1, page 558. Hurst, page 175.
29. Wyeth, page 333.
30. *Official Records*, serial 1, volume 32, part 1, page 619. Hurst, page 178.

Chapter 4

1. Robert E. Lee Jr., *Recollections and Letters of General Robert E. Lee*, pages 122–123.
2. *Ibid.*, page 123.
3. Douglas Southall Freeman, *Lee*, page 364.
4. Douglas Southall Freeman, *R.E. Lee*, volume 3, page 255.
5. *Ibid.*, page 254. *Official Records*, serial 29, part 2, page 853.
6. Freeman, *Lee*, page 365.
7. Freeman, *R.E. Lee*, volume 3, page 264.
8. Lee, pages 105–106.
9. *Ibid.*, page 123.
10. Freeman, *R.E. Lee*, volume 3, page 268.
11. *Ibid.*

12. *Ibid.*, page 266.
13. *Ibid.*, page 268.
14. Lee, page 124.

Chapter 5

1. The eyewitness was Horace Porter, a member of Grant's staff, who authored *Campaigning With Grant*.
2. Andrew A. Humphreys, *The Virginia Campaign, 1864 and 1865*, page 20.
3. Porter, page 43.
4. *Ibid.*, pages 43–44.
5. *Ibid.*, page 47.
6. Catton, page 185.
7. Porter, page 48.
8. *Ibid.*, page 49.
9. Catton, page 186.
10. Theodore Lyman, *Meade's Headquarters, 1863–1865: Letters of Colonel Theodore Lyman from the Wilderness to Appomattox*, pages 91–92.
11. *Ibid.*, page 93.
12. Porter, page 54.
13. Lyman, page 94.
14. Freeman, *R.E. Lee*, volume 3, page 286.
15. Shelby Foote, *The Civil War: Red River to Appomattox*, page 169.
16. Catton, page 196.
17. Lyman, page 94.
18. Freeman, *R.E. Lee*, volume 3, page 290.
19. George Walsh, *"Damage Them All You Can," Robert E. Lee's Army of Northern Virginia*, pages 399–400.
20. Robert Stiles, *Four Years Under Marse Robert*, pages 246–247.
21. Southern Historical Society Papers, volume 13, page 545. Quoted in Freeman, *R.E. Lee*, volume 3, pages 294–295.

Chapter 6

1. William Riley Brooksher, *War Along the Bayous*, page 2.
2. John D. Winters, *The Civil War in Louisiana*, page 206.
3. William Tecumseh Sherman, *Memoirs of General William T. Sherman*, volume 1, page 396.
4. Brooksher, page 5.
5. *Ibid.*, page 3.
6. Sherman, op. cit., page 393.
7. *Ibid.*, page 397.
8. Grant, page 418.
9. Brooksher, page 34.
10. Richard B. Irwin in *Battles and Leaders of the Civil War: Retreat with Honor*, page 350.
11. Grant, page 412.
12. Thomas O. Selfridge in *Battles and Leaders of the Civil War: Retreat with Honor*, pages 362–363.
13. *Ibid.*
14. *Ibid.*
15. *Ibid.*, pages 363–364.
16. *Ibid.*, pages 364–365.
17. Irwin, op. cit., page 358.
18. *Ibid.*
19. Selfridge, op. cit., page 365.
20. Irwin, op. cit., page 359.
21. *Ibid.*
22. Selfridge, op. cit., page 365.
23. *Ibid.*, page 366.
24. Irwin, op. cit., pages 361–362.
25. Brooksher, page 228.

Chapter 7

1. Grant, pages 460–461.
2. *Ibid.*, page 461.

3. Humphreys, page 71.

4. Grant, page 463.

5. *Ibid.*, page 464.

6. *Ibid.*, pages 458–459.

7. Martin T. McMahon, "The Death of General John Sedgwick," *Battles and Leaders of the Civil War: Retreat with Honor*, page 175.

8. E.M. Law, "From the Wilderness to Cold Harbor," *Battles and Leaders of the Civil War: Retreat with Honor*, page 130.

9. *Ibid.*

10. *Ibid.*, page 132.

11. G. Norton Galloway, "Hand-to-Hand Fighting at Spotsylvania," *Battles and Leaders of the Civil War: Retreat with Honor*, pages 171–174.

12. Draper, volume 3, page 379.

13. Porter, page 84.

14. Grant, page 473.

Chapter 8

1. Draper, volume 3, page 381–382.

2. Frances H. Kennedy, editor, *The Civil War Battlefield Guide*, Second Edition, page 289.

3. Law, op. cit., pages 137–138.

4. Grant, pages 494–495.

5. McMahon, op. cit., pages 214–215.

6. *Ibid.*, pages 215, 217.

7. Grant, page 490.

8. Gordon C. Rhea, *Cold Harbor: Grant and Lee May 26–June 3, 1864*, page 389.

9. *Ibid.*

10. Grant, page 499.

11. *Ibid.*, page 500.

12. McMahon, op. cit., page 219.

13. *Ibid.*

14. Grant, page 501.

15. Freeman, *R.E. Lee*, volume 3, page 392.

16. *Ibid.*

17. Grant, pages 501–502.

18. *Ibid.*, page 502.

19. *Ibid.*

20. George Cary Eggleston, "Notes on Cold Harbor," *Battles and Leaders of the Civil War: Retreat with Honor*, pages 231–232.

21. Quoted in Freeman, *R.E. Lee*, volume 3, page 391.

22. Grant, page 503.

23. McMahon, op. cit., page 220.

Chapter 9

1. Craig L. Symonds, *Joseph E. Johnston: A Civil War Biography*, page 249, quoting from Sam R. Watkins, *"Co. Aytch," Maury Grays, First Tennessee Regiment, or A Side Show of the Big Show* (Wilmington, N.C.: Broadfoot Publishing Co., 1987), page 131.

2. Johnston's feelings about being called "Joe" actually befitted his dignified appearance. When a nephew wrote to say he planned to name a son after him, Johnston wrote back asking the nephew not to allow the boy to be called "Joe." That name, he protested, is "unbecoming to a gentleman."

3. Symonds, page 250.

4. Joseph E. Johnston, "Opposing Sherman's Advance to Atlanta," *Battles and Leaders of the Civil War: Retreat with Honor*, page 260.

5. *Ibid.*

6. *Ibid.*

7. Fred A. Bailey, *Class and Tennessee's Confederate Generation* (Chapel Hill: University of North Carolina Press, 1987), page 250.

8. Sam R. Watkins, op. cit., page 132. Quoted in Symonds, page 250.

9. Johnston, op. cit., page 261.

10. Editors, *Battles and Leaders of the Civil War: The Tide Shifts*, footnote on page 711.

11. Johnston, op. cit., page 261

12. Joseph E. Johnston, *Narrative of Military Operations, Directed During the Late War Between the States*, page 298.
13. *Ibid.*, page 299.
14. *Ibid.*
15. *Ibid.*, pages 301–302.
16. Figures are from Jacob D. Cox, *Sherman's Battle for Atlanta*, page 25.
17. Cox, page 31.
18. Symonds, page 208.
19. Cox, page 28.
20. *Ibid.*, page 27.
21. *Ibid.*, pages 27–28.
22. Johnston, "Opposing Sherman's Advance to Atlanta," *Battles and Leaders: Retreat with Honor*, pages 262–263.
23. Cox, page 36.
24. *Ibid.*, page 37.
25. Quoted in Hirshson, page 210.
26. Johnston, *Battles and Leaders: Retreat with Honor*, page 266.
27. Watkins, op. cit., page 148. Quoted in Symonds, pages 260–261.
28. Johnston, *Battles and Leaders: Retreat with Honor*, page 265.
29. *Ibid.*
30. Johnston, *Narrative of Military Operations*, pages 313–314.
31. *Ibid.*, page 314.
32. *Ibid.*, page 320.
33. *Ibid.*, page 321.
34. *Ibid.*, pages 321–322.
35. *Ibid.*, pages 323–324.
36. *Ibid.*, page 326.
37. Sherman, op. cit., volume 2, page 43.
38. Quoted in Symonds, page 298.
39. Johnston, *Narrative of Military Operations*, page 335.
40. *Ibid.*, page 318.
41. *Ibid.*, page 337.
42. Quoted in Symonds, page 320.

Chapter 10

1. Franz Sigel, "Sigel in the Shenandoah Valley in 1864," *Battles and Leaders of the Civil War: Retreat with Honor*, page 487.
2. Grant, pages 412–413.
3. *Ibid.*, page 488.
4. John D. Imboden, "The Battle of New Market, Va., May 15th, 1864," *Battles and Leaders of the Civil War: Retreat with Honor*, page 480.
5. *Ibid.*
6. *Ibid.*, pages 480–481.
7. *Ibid.*, page 481.
8. *Ibid.*
9. *Ibid.*
10. Sigel, op. cit., page 488.
11. Imboden, op. cit., page 481.
12. Sigel, op. cit., page 488.
13. *Ibid.*
14. *Ibid.*
15. Imboden, op. cit., page 481.
16. *Ibid.*
17. *Ibid.*, page 482.
18. *Ibid.*, page 483.
19. *Ibid.*
20. *Ibid.*
21. Colonel George D. Wells, report addressed to Massachusetts Governor John A. Andrew dated May 21, 1864. Published on the internet at civilwarhome.com/wellsnewmarket.htm.
22. S. Shipp, report to Major General F.H. Smith dated July 4, 1864. Published on the internet at civilwarhome.com/Shipp.htm.
23. Imboden, op. cit., page 484.
24. Grant, page 424.

Chapter 11

1. John McIntosh Kell, "Cruise and Combats of the 'Alabama,'" *Battles and Leaders of the Civil War: Retreat With Honor*, page 600.
2. *Ibid.*, page 607.
3. Raphael Semmes, *Memoirs of Service Afloat During the War Between the States*, page 751.
4. Kell, op. cit., page 607.
5. Semmes, pages 752–753.
6. Kell, op. cit., page 607.
7. Semmes, page 756.
8. John M. Browne, "The Duel Between the 'Alabama' and the 'Kearsarge,'" *Battles and Leaders of the Civil War: Retreat with Honor*, page 616.
9. Kell, op. cit., page 608.
10. *Ibid.*, pages 608–610.
11. Semmes, page 757.
12. Browne, op. cit., pages 618–619.
13. Semmes, pages 757–758.
14. Browne, op. cit., page 619.
15. *Ibid.*, pages 619–621.
16. Semmes, page 765.
17. Kell, op. cit., pages 613–614.
18. *Ibid.*, page 624.
19. Semmes, pages 753–754.
20. *Ibid.*, pages 761–762.
21. Browne, op. cit., page 623.
22. Semmes, page 762.

Chapter 12

1. Joseph Judge, *Season of Fire: The Confederate Strike on Washington*, page 60.
2. Shelby Foote, *The Civil War: A Narrative—Fort Sumter to Perryville*, page 98.
3. http://en.wikipedia.org/wiki/DavidHunter_Hunter, page 2.
4. Catton, page 67.
5. Judge, page 61.
6. *Ibid.*, page 62.
7. *Ibid.*, page 63.
8. Catton, pages 250–251.
9. http://en.wikipedia.org/wiki/Battleof_Piedmont, pages 2–3.
10. Grant, pages 507–508.
11. Edward A. Miller Jr., *Lincoln's Abolitionist General*, page 194.
12. Shelby Foote, *The Civil War: A Narrative—Red River to Appomattox*, page 310.
13. Gary W. Gallagher, editor, *Struggle for the Shenandoah: Essays on the 1864 Valley Campaign* (Kent, Ohio: Kent State University Press, 1991), pages 6–7.
14. Miller, page 195.
15. *Ibid.*, page 196.
16. *Ibid.*
17. *Ibid.*, page 195.
18. *Ibid.*, page 199.
19. Jubal A. Early, *A Memoir of the Last Year of the War for Independence, in the Confederate States of America*, page 48.
20. Miller, pages 210–211.
21. Judge, page 109.
22. *Ibid.*

Chapter 13

1. Porter, pages 195–196.
2. *Ibid.*, page 196.
3. *Ibid.*, page 195.
4. *Ibid.*, page 197.
5. *Ibid.*, page 198.
6. *Ibid.*, pages 199–200.
7. Badeau, volume 2, pages 341–342.

8. Grant, page 514.
9. www. mycivilwar.com/battles/640512,htm.
10. Badeau, volume 2, pages 343–345.
11. R.E. Colston, "Repelling the First Assault on Petersburg," *Battles and Leaders of the Civil War: Retreat with Honor*, pages 535–536.
12. G.T. Beauregard, "Four Days of Battle at Petersburg," *Battles and Leaders of the Civil War: Retreat with Honor*, page 540.
13. Badeau, volume 2, page 345
14. Beauregard, op. cit., page 540.
15. Porter, page 202.
16. Beauregard, op. cit., page 543.
17. *Ibid.*
18. *Ibid.*
19. Lyman, page 168.
20. *Ibid.*, pages 168–169.
21. *Ibid.*, pages 169–170.
22. Badeau, volume 2, page 374.
23. Beauregard, op. cit., page 544.
24. Edward H. Bonekemper III, *A Victor, Not a Butcher: Ulysses S. Grant's Overlooked Military Genius* (Washington, D.C.: Regnery, 2004), page 313.
25. Beauregard, op. cit., page 544.
26. *Ibid.*

Chapter 14

1. Early, pages 45–46.
2. *Ibid.*, pages 46–47.
3. *Ibid.*, page 49.
4. Judge, page 113.
5. Richmond *Whig*, October 31, 1864. Quoted in Willard K. Bushong, *Old Jube: A Biography of General Jubal A. Early*, page 187.
6. Early, page 49.
7. *Ibid.*, page 50.
8. *Ibid.*, page 51.
9. *Ibid.*
10. *Ibid.*, page 53.
11. *Ibid.*, page 54.
12. Bushong, page 197.
13. *Ibid.*, pages 197–198.
14. Catton, page 310.
15. Grant, page 521.
16. Early, page 54.
17. *Ibid.*, page 55.
18. Francis H. Kennedy, editor, *The Civil War Battlefield Guide*, second edition (Boston: Houghton Mifflin Co., 1998), page 308.
19. Early, page 55.
20. *Ibid.*, pages 56–57.
21. *Ibid.*, page 57.
22. Quoted in footnote, *Battles and Leaders of the Civil War: Retreat with Honor*, page 498.
23. *Ibid.*
24. Early, page 58.
25. *Ibid.*, pages 57–58.
26. *Ibid.*, page 59.
27. *Ibid.*
28. *Ibid.*, page 61.

Chapter 15

1. Porter, pages 203–204.
2. *Ibid.*, page 217.
3. *Ibid.*
4. *Ibid.*, page 218.
5. *Ibid.*, page 220.

6. William H. Powell, "The Battle of the Petersburg Crater," *Battles and Leaders of the Civil War: Retreat with Honor*, pages 545–546.

7. *Ibid.*, pages 546–547.

8. *Ibid.*, page 548.

9. *Ibid.*, pages 551–552.

10. *Ibid.*, page 559.

11. Grant, pages 526–527.

Chapter 16

1. John Coddington Kinney, "Farragut at Mobile Bay," *Battles and Leaders of the Civil War: Retreat with Honor*, page 386.

2. David D. Porter, *The Naval History of the Civil War*, page 565.

3. *Ibid.*, page 571.

4. *Ibid.*

5. *Ibid.*, pages 571–572.

6. *Ibid.*, page 572.

7. Kinney, op. cit., pages 387–389.

8. *Ibid.*, pages 389–390.

9. *Ibid.*, page 391.

10. *Ibid.*

11. *Ibid.*, page 392.

12. *Ibid.*, pages 393–394.

13. *Ibid.*, page 394.

14. *Ibid.*, page 395.

15. James D. Johnston, "The Ram 'Tennessee' at Mobile Bay," *Battles and Leaders of the Civil War: Retreat with Honor*, pages 403–404.

16. Kinney, op. cit., pages 395–396.

17. James D. Johnston, op. cit., page 404.

18. The prisoners included the author's great-great uncle, William Burrough Patterson, an engineer aboard the *Tennessee*.

19. Noah Andre Trudeau, *Southern Storm: Sherman's March to the Sea*, page 34.

Chapter 17

1. Sherman, op. cit., volume 2, pages 71–72.

2. *Ibid.*, page 72.

3. *Ibid.*, pages 72–73.

4. *Ibid.*, page 75.

5. *Ibid.*, page 76.

6. Accounts from *The New York Times*, July 4, 1875, and the *Confederate Veteran*, March 1903, pages 118–119, and quoted in Stanley P. Hirshson, *The White Tecumseh*, page 230.

7. Sherman, volume 2, page 76.

8. *Ibid.*, page 78.

9. *Ibid.*, page 77.

10. Oliver O. Howard, "The Struggle for Atlanta," *Battles and Leaders of the Civil War: Retreat with Honor*, pages 317–319.

11. Hirshson, op. cit., page 232.

12. Sherman, volume 2, pages 85–86.

13. *Ibid.*, page 85.

14. Note from Sherman to Logan, July 27, 1864, John A. Logan Papers, Library of Congress. Quoted in Stephen E. Woodworth, *Nothing But Victory*, page 570.

15. Sherman, volume 2, page 86.

16. Hirshson, page 233.

17. Sherman, volume 2, page 86.

18. Hirshson, page 233.

19. Howard, op. cit., page 319.

20. Hirshson, page 234.

21. Charles D. Miller, *The Struggle for the Life of the Republic* (Kent, Ohio: Kent State University Press), page 192. Quoted in Woodworth, *Nothing But Victory*, page 577.

22. Sherman, volume 2, page 91.

23. Howard, op. cit., page 320.

24. Sherman, volume 2, page 96.

25. *Ibid.*, page 99.
26. *Ibid.*, pages 99–100.
27. *Ibid.*, page 100.
28. *Ibid.*
29. *Ibid.*
30. Jacob D. Cox, *Sherman's Battle for Atlanta*, page 187.
31. Sherman, volume 2, page 102.
32. *Ibid.*
33. *Ibid.*, pages 102–103
34. *Ibid.*, page 103.
35. *Ibid.*
36. *Ibid.*, page 104.
37. Russell S. Bonds, *War Like a Thunderbolt*, page 231.

Chapter 18

1. Sherman, volume 2, page 104.
2. John B. Hood, "The Defense of Atlanta," *Battles and Leaders of the Civil War: Retreat with Honor*, pages 342–343.
3. *Ibid.*, page 341.
4. Sherman, volume 2, page 105.
5. *Ibid.*
6. Hood, op. cit., page 343.
7. *Ibid.*, pages 343–344.
8. Sherman, volume 2, page 109.
9. *Ibid.*, page 110.
10. *Ibid.*, page 111.
11. *Ibid.*, pages 118–119.
12. *Ibid.*, page 119.
13. *Ibid.*, page 120.
14. *Ibid.*, pages 125–127.
15. *Ibid.*, page 129.
16. *Ibid.*, page 165.
17. *Ibid.*, page 159.
18. *Ibid.*, page 166.
19. *Ibid.*, page 168.
20. *Ibid.*, page 174.
21. Quoted in Woodworth, *Nothing But Victory*, page 588.
22. David P. Conyngham, *Sherman's March Through the South*, page 238.
23. James A. Connolly, *Three Years in the Army of the Cumberland*, page 302.
24. Quoted in Marc Wortman, *The Bonfire: The Siege and the Burning of Atlanta*, page 336.
25. Bonds, page 358.
26. Sherman, volume 2, pages 178–179.

Chapter 19

1. Grant, page 528.
2. Philip Henry Sheridan, *Personal Memoirs of P.H. Sheridan, General United States Army*, page 180.
3. Grant, pages 528–529.
4. Sheridan, page 181.
5. *Ibid.*
6. *Ibid.*, page 197.
7. Grant, page 529.
8. *Ibid.*, pages 529–530.
9. *Ibid.*, page 530.
10. *Ibid.*
11. Sheridan, pages 182–183.
12. *Ibid.*, page 184.
13. *Ibid.*, page 197.
14. *Ibid.*, page 189.
15. Early, pages 72–74.
16. Sheridan, page 198.
17. *Ibid.*

18. *Ibid.*, page 199.
19. *Ibid.*, pages 199–200.
20. *Ibid.*, page 200.
21. Grant, page 534.
22. *Ibid.*
23. Sheridan, page 206.
24. *Ibid.*, page 205.
25. *Ibid.*
26. Early, pages 90–91.
27. Quoted in Edward J. Stackpole, *Sheridan in the Shenandoah: Jubal Early's Nemesis* pages 234–235.
28. Sheridan, pages 207–208.
29. *Ibid.*, pages 208–209.
30. *Ibid.*, page 209.
31. Quoted in Roy Morris, Sheridan, page 203.
32. Early, page 91.
33. Sheridan, page 215.
34. From G.W. Nichols, *A Soldier's Story of His Regiment* and quoted in Stackpole, pages 264–265.
35. Sheridan, page 216.
36. *Ibid.*, pages 216–217.
37. Stackpole, page 276.
38. Sheridan, page 221.
39. *Ibid.*, page 222.
40. *Ibid.*
41. *Ibid.*, page 223.
42. *Ibid.*
43. *Ibid.*
44. Hazard Stevens, "The Battle of Cedar Creek," *Papers of the Military Historical Society of Massachusetts*, volume 6, 1907, page 125. Quoted in Morris, page 215.
45. Sheridan, page 226.
46. *Official Records*, 1st Series, volume 43, part 1, page 560. Quoted in John B. Gordon, *Reminiscences of the Civil War*, page 364.
47. Early, pages 112–113.
48. Gordon, op. cit., pages 341–342.
49. Sheridan, pages 226–227.
50. Early, pages 115–116.
51. *Ibid.*, page 122.
52. Sheridan, page 230.
53. *Ibid.*, page 235.

Chapter 20

1. Charles Bracelen Flood, *1864: Lincoln at the Gates of History*, pages 266–267.
2. *Ibid.*, page 267.
3. Quoted in David E. Long, *The Jewel of Liberty: Abraham Lincoln's Re-election and the End of Slavery*, page 187.
4. Quoted in Flood, page 270.
5. *Cincinnati Daily Commercial*, September 4, 1861 and May 15, 1862. Quoted in John C. Waugh, *Reelecting Lincoln*, page 89.
6. *Encyclopedia Britannica.*
7. *Official Proceedings of the Democratic National Convention*, pages 3–4.
8. *Ibid.*
9. *New York Evening Post*, September 2, 1864. Quoted in Waugh, page 299.
10. Vallandigham letter to McClellan dated September 4, 1864, McClellan Papers. Quoted in Waugh, pages 299–300.
11. Stephen W. Sears, editor, *The Civil War Papers of George B. McClellan: Selected Correspondence, 1860–1865* (Letter from George B. McClellan to Mary Ellen McClellan, July 27, 1861), page 70.
12. Quoted in Waugh, page 301.
13. *New York Daily Tribune*, September 6, 1864. Quoted in Waugh, page 308.
14. *The New York Times*, September 18, 1864.
15. Edouard Laboulaye, *Professor Laboylaye, the Great Friend of America, on the Presidential Election*, pages 1–4.
16. Waugh, page 328.
17. Harry J. Carman and Reinhard H. Luthin, *Lincoln and the Patronage*, page 287. Quoted in Waugh, page 330.
18. *Harper's Weekly*, November 19, 1864.
19. Noah Brooks, "Personal Recollections of Abraham Lincoln," *Harper's New Monthly Magazine*, July 31, 1865, page 226.

Chapter 21

1. John D. Winters, *The Civil War in Louisiana*, page 388.
2. *Ibid.*, page 382.
3. Albert Castel, *General Sterling Price and the Civil War in the West*, pages 196–197.
4. *Ibid.*, page 200.
5. *Ibid.*
6. *Ibid.*
7. *Ibid.*
8. Wiley Britton, "Resume of Military Operations in Missouri and Arkansas, 1864–65," *Battles and Leaders of the Civil War: Retreat with Honor*, pages 375–376.
9. John N. Edwards, *Shelby and His Men: or, The War in the West* (Cincinnati, 1867, and Michigan Historical Reprint Series), page 471.
10. *Ibid.*
11. M. Jeff Thompson, "Reminiscences of M. Jeff Thompson," M. Jeff Thompson Papers, Southern Historical Collection, University of North Carolina Library, Chapel Hill, N.C. Quoted in Castel, page 227.
12. Edwards, page 471.
13. Britton, op. cit., page 377.
14. Edgar Langsdorf, "Price's Raid and the Battle of Mine Creek," *Kansas Historical Quarterly*, volume 30 (Autumn 1964), pages 281–306. Quoted in Castel, pages 241–242.
15. Edwards, pages 462–463.
16. Castel, quoting Confederate Major General John Magruder, page 252.

Chapter 22

1. J.B. Hood, "The Invasion of Tennessee," *Battles and Leaders of the Civil War: Retreat with Honor*, page 425.
2. *Ibid.*, page 426.
3. *Ibid.*, pages 426–427.
4. Colonel Henry Stone, "Repelling Hood's Invasion of Tennessee," *Battles and Leaders of the Civil War: Retreat with Honor*, page 441.
5. *Ibid.*, page 443.
6. Hood, op. cit., page 431.
7. Jacob D. Cox, *Sherman's March to the Sea, Hood's Campaigns and the Carolina Campaigns of 1865*, page 84.
8. The two brigades were apparently posted in front of the main line by mistake, General Wagner having misunderstood his orders from General Stanley. The mistake and its consequences in the subsequent battle at Franklin caused Wagner to be relieved from his command at his request.
9. Hurst, page 233.
10. Foote, *The Civil War — A Narrative: Red River to Appomattox*, page 666.
11. Hurst, page 233.
12. Foote, op. cit., page 666.
13. Hood, op. cit., page 432.
14. *Ibid.*, page 433.
15. Cox, *Sherman's March to the Sea*, pages 88–91.
16. Hood, op. cit., page 435.
17. *Ibid.*
18. *Ibid.*, page 436.
19. Grant, page 566.
20. *Ibid.*
21. *Ibid.*, pages 566–567.
22. *Ibid.*, pages 567–568.
23. *Ibid.*, page 568.
24. Stone, op. cit., page 464.
25. Hood, op. cit., page 437.
26. *Ibid.*

Chapter 23

1. Sherman, volume 2, page 179.
2. *Ibid.*, page 152.
3. John Sherman, *John Sherman's Recollections*, volume 1, pages 30–33. Quoted in Hirshson, page 8.
4. Quoted in Hirshson, pages 13–14.
5. *Ibid.*, page 14.
6. *Ibid.*, page 21.

7. *Ibid.*, page 78.
8. Burke Davis, *Sherman's March*, page 27.
9. Sherman, volume 2, pages 176–177.
10. *Ibid.*, page 172.
11. Daniel Oakley, "Marching Through Georgia and the Carolinas," *Battles and Leaders of the Civil War: Retreat with Honor*, page 672.
12. Davis, page 29.
13. Sherman, volume 2, page 180.
14. *Ibid.*
15. *Ibid.*, pages 180–181.
16. *Ibid.*, page 181.
17. Davis, page 33.
18. Conyngham, page 247.
19. Sherman, volume 2, pages 181–182.
20. *Ibid.*, page 182.
21. Conyngham, page 243.
22. Sherman, volume 2, page 182.
23. *Ibid.*, pages 182–183.
24. Davis, page 37.
25. *Ibid.*, page 43.
26. Conyngham, page 315.
27. Commander's Report: Savannah Campaign, http://149th-nysv.org/Battles/savannah_cr.htm.
28. Conyngham, pages 250–251.
29. Sherman, volume 2, page 190.
30. *Ibid.*, pages 187–188.
31. Oliver O. Howard, "Sherman's Advance from Atlanta," *Battles and Leaders of the Civil War: Retreat with Honor*, page 664.
32. *Ibid.*, pages 664–665.
33. Trudeau, page 236.
34. Sherman, volume 2, page 192.
35. Cox, *Sherman's March to the Sea*, page 34.
36. Sherman, volume 2, page 189.
37. *Ibid.*, page 175.
38. *Ibid.*, page 191.
39. *Ibid.*, page 194.
40. Conyngham, page 314.
41. *Ibid.*, pages 316–317.
42. *Ibid.*, page 277.
43. Trudeau, pages 382–383.
44. Hirshson, page 260.
45. Sherman, volume 2, page 195.
46. *Ibid.*, pages 195–196.
47. *Ibid.*, page 196.
48. *Ibid.*
49. *Ibid.*, pages 197–198.
50. Cox, *Sherman's March to the Sea*, pages 54–55.
51. Sherman, volume 2, pages 210–211.
52. *Ibid.*, page 211.
53. Howard, op. cit., page 666.

Chapter 24

1. David D. Porter, op. cit., page 683.
2. Grant, page 570.
3. David D. Porter, page 683.
4. Cox, *Sherman's March to the Sea*, page 140.
5. Benjamin F. Butler, *Butler's Book*, page 775.
6. *Ibid.*
7. *Ibid.*, page 783.
8. Grant, page 572.
9. *Ibid.*, pages 572–573.
10. *Ibid.*, pages 573–574.
11. *Ibid.*, pages 574–575.
12. *Ibid.*, page 575.

13. Rod Gragg, *Confederate Goliath*, page 104.
14. Butler, page 782.
15. Horace Porter, op. cit., page 373.
16. Gragg, page 104.
17. David D. Porter, page 711.
18. *Ibid.*
19. *Ibid.*
20. *Ibid.*, page 712.
21. *Ibid.*, pages 713–714.
22. The Spanish Armada, perhaps history's most famous armada, which King Philip II of Spain launched against England in 1588, comprised some 130 ships. The Holy League's fleet at the Battle of Lepanto in 1571, one of history's largest naval engagements, comprised 208 ships, and its enemy, the opposing Turkish fleet, comprised 251 ships. The fleet Lamb saw numbered about sixty warships, plus transports.
23. William Lamb, "The Defense of Fort Fisher," *Battles and Leaders of the Civil War: Retreat with Honor*, page 647.
24. *Ibid.*, page 648.
25. *Ibid.*, page647.
26. *Ibid.*
27. David D. Porter, pages 715–716.
28. Lamb, op. cit., page 649.
29. Thomas O. Selfridge Jr., "The Navy at Fort Fisher," *Battles and Leaders of the Civil War: Retreat with Honor*, pages 659–660.
30. Lamb, op. cit., page651.
31. *Ibid.*, page 652.
32. *Ibid.*, page 653.
33. *Ibid.*
34. *Ibid.*, page 654.
35. David D. Porter, page 717.
36. *Ibid.*, pages 716–717.
37. Gragg, page 235.

Chapter 25

1. Sherman, volume 2, pages 205–206.
2. *Ibid.*, page 209.
3. *Ibid.*, page 210.
4. *Ibid.*, page 222.
5. *Ibid.*, page 224.
6. *Ibid.*, page 225.
7. *Ibid.*, page 213.
8. *Ibid.*, page 254.
9. *Ibid.*, page 249.
10. *Ibid.*, page 236.
11. *Ibid.*
12. Cox, *Sherman's March to the Sea*, page 169.
13. Sherman, volume 2, page 253.
14. *Ibid.*, page 256.
15. Not shown on many current maps, Pocotaligo is just east of the exit where motorists today turn off Interstate 95 and head northeastward on U.S. 17 to Charleston.
16. Sherman, volume 2, page 273.
17. Henry W. Slocum, "Sherman March from Savannah to Bentonville," *Battles and Leaders of the Civil War: Retreat with Honor*, pages 685–686.
18. *Ibid.*, pages 684–685.
19. Sherman, volume 2, page 275.
20. *Ibid.*
21. *Ibid.*, page 279.
22. Davis, page 160.
23. Sherman, volume 2, pages 279–280.
24. *Ibid.*, pages 286–287.
25. Slocum, op. cit., page 686.
26. Sherman, volume 2, page 287.
27. Davis, page 146.
28. *Ibid.*, page 149.
29. *Ibid.*, page 187.

30. Sherman, volume 2, page 288.
31. *Ibid.*, page 289.
32. Slocum, op. cit., page 687.
33. Sherman, volume 2, page 291.
34. *Ibid.*, page 293.
35. Slocum, op. cit, page 688.
36. Sherman, volume 2, page 295.
37. *Ibid.*, page 298.
38. Slocum, op. cit., page 690.
39. Sherman, volume 2, page 300.
40. *Ibid.*, page 303.
41. Cox, *Sherman's March to the Sea*, pages 182–183.
42. Sherman, volume 2, page 303.
43. Slocum, op. cit., pages 693, 695.
44. *Ibid.*, page 695.
45. Cox, *Sherman's March to the Sea*, page 197.
46. Sherman, volume 2, page 304.
47. Slocum, op. cit., page 695.
48. Sherman, volume 2, page 306.
49. *Ibid.*, page 307.

Chapter 26

1. Grant, page 592.
2. *Ibid.*
3. Badeau, volume 3, page 439.
4. Some sources say Lee's force numbered no more than 50,000.
5. Badeau, volume 3, page 439.
6. Douglas Southall Freeman, *Lee*, page 452.
7. Badeau, volume 3, pages 400–401.
8. *Ibid.*, pages 401–402.
9. *Ibid.*, page 402.
10. William C. Davis, *Jefferson Davis: The Man and His Hour*, page 592.
11. Badeau, volume 3, pages 445–446.
12. Grant, page 597.
13. *Ibid.*, page 601.
14. Horace Porter, "Five Forks and the Pursuit of Lee," *Battles and Leaders of the Civil War: Retreat with Honor*, page 710.
15. *Ibid.*
16. *Ibid.*
17. *Ibid.*, page 711.
18. *Ibid.*
19. *Ibid.*
20. *Ibid.*, page 713.
21. *Ibid.*
22. *Ibid.*, pages 713–714.
23. *Ibid.*, page 715.
24. *Ibid.*, page 716.
25. *Ibid.*, page 717.
26. *Ibid.*, page 718.
27. *Ibid.*
28. *Ibid.*
29. *Ibid.*
30. Thomas Thatcher Graves, "The Occupation," *Battles and Leaders of the Civil War: Retreat with Honor*, pages 726–727.
31. *Ibid.*, page 727.
32. Clement Sulivane, "The Evacuation," *Battles and Leaders of the Civil War: Retreat with Honor*, pages 725–726.

Chapter 27

1. Badeau, volume 3, pages 528–529.
2. Horace Porter, "Five Forks and the Pursuit of Lee," *Battles and Leaders of the Civil War: Retreat with Honor*, page 719.

3. Badeau, volume 3, pages 549–550.
4. *Ibid.*, pages 550–551.
5. *Ibid.*, page 554.
6. *Ibid.*, pages 553–554.
7. *Ibid.*, pages 556–557.
8. *Ibid.*, page 561.
9. *Ibid.*
10. Horace Porter, op. cit., page 721.
11. Badeau, volume 3, pages 576–577.
12. Grant, page 621.
13. *Ibid.*, pages 621–622.
14. *Ibid.*, page 623.
15. *Ibid.*
16. *Ibid.*, page 624.
17. Badeau, volume 3, page 594.
18. *Ibid.*, pages 595–596.
19. *Ibid.*, page 597.
20. Grant, page 627.
21. *Ibid.*
22. Horace Porter, op. cit., page 733.
23. *Ibid.*
24. *Ibid.*, pages 734–737.
25. Porter states that it was Grant who started the conversation.
26. Badeau, volume 3, page 603.
27. Grant, pages 629–630.
28. Badeau, volume 3, pages 603–604.
29. Grant, pages 630–631.
30. *Ibid.*, page 632.
31. *Ibid.*
32. Robert E. Lee, "Lee's Report of the Surrender at Appomattox," *Battles and Leaders of the Civil War: Retreat with Honor*, page 724.
33. *Ibid.*
34. Horace Porter, op. cit., page 741.
35. *Ibid.*, pages 742–743.
36. Grant, page 633.

Chapter 28

1. Horace Porter, *Campaigning With Grant*, pages 498–499.
2. The accounts vary on the position of Forbes, some placing him outside the president's box, in the corridor.
3. Some accounts say Forbes remained in the corridor.
4. Horace Porter, *Campaigning With Grant*, pages 499–500.

Chapter 29

1. Joseph E. Johnston, op. cit., page 397.
2. *Ibid.*, pages 397–398.
3. *Ibid.*, pages 398–399.
4. *Ibid.*, page 400.
5. Sherman, volume 2, page 347.
6. *Ibid.*, pages 348–349.
7. Joseph E. Johnston, op. cit., page 402.
8. Sherman, volume 2, page 349.
9. Joseph E. Johnston, page 403.
10. Sherman, volume 2, page 350.
11. *Ibid.*
12. *Ibid.*, page 351.
13. *Ibid.*, pages 351–352.
14. Joseph E. Johnston, page 404.
15. Sherman, volume 2, page 353.
16. Joseph E. Johnston, pages 406–407.
17. Grant, page 645.
18. *Ibid.*

19. Sherman, volume 2, page 358.
20. *Ibid.*
21. Joseph E. Johnston, pages 412–413.
22. *Ibid.*, page 415.
23. *Ibid.*, page 418.
24. *Ibid.*, pages 419–420.
25. *Ibid.*, page 420.
26. Quoted in John Allen Wyeth, *That Devil Forrest*, page 543.
27. Grant, pages 654–655.
28. *Ibid.*, page 665.

Bibliography

Adams, George Worthington. *Doctors in Blue: The Medical History of the Union Army in the Civil War.* Baton Rouge: Louisiana State University Press, 1952.

Anderson, Bern. *By Sea and by River: The Naval History of the Civil War.* New York: Da Capo Press, 1989.

Badeau, Adam. *Military History of Ulysses S. Grant,* Volume II. Bedford, MA: Applewood Books, 2008. Originally published by D. Appleton and Company, New York, 1881.

_____. *Military History of Ulysses S. Grant,* Volume III. Whitefish, MO: Kessenger Publishing Company, 2007. Originally published by D. Appleton and Company, New York, 1882.

Bishop, Jim. *The Day Lincoln Was Shot.* New York: Harper & Brothers, 1955.

Bonds, Russell S. *War Like the Thunderbolt: The Battle and Burning of Atlanta.* Yardley, PA: Westholme Publishing, 2010.

Boritt, Gabor S., ed. *Lincoln the War President.* New York: Oxford University Press, 1992.

Brooksher, William Riley. *War Along the Bayous: The 1864 Red River Campaign in Louisiana.* Dulles, VA: Brassey's, 1998.

Bushong, Millard K. *Old Jube: A Biography of General Jubal A. Early.* Shippensburg, PA: White Mane Publishing Company, 1955.

Butler, Benjamin F. *Butler's Book: Autobiography and Personal Reminiscences of Major-General Benj. F. Butler.* Boston: A.M. Thayer & Co., 1892.

Campbell, Jacqueline Glass. *When Sherman Marched North from the Sea: Resistance on the Confederate Home Front.* Chapel Hill: University of North Carolina Press, 2003.

Campbell, R. Thomas. *Confederate Naval Forces on Western Waters.* Jefferson, NC: McFarland, 2005.

Carman, Harry J., and Reinhard H. Luthin. *Lincoln and the Patronage.* New York: Columbia University Press, 1943.

Catton, Bruce. *Grant Takes Command.* Boston: Little, Brown and Company, 1969.

_____. *A Stillness at Appomattox.* New York: Pocket Books, Inc., 1960.

_____. *Terrible Swift Sword.* New York: Pocket Books, 1967.

_____. *U.S. Grant and the American Military Tradition.* Boston: Little, Brown, 1954.

Cimprich, John. *Fort Pillow, a Civil War Massacre, and Public Memory.* Baton Rouge: Louisiana State University Press, 2005.

Coffin, Charles Carleton. *My Days and Nights on the Battle-Field.* Boston: Dana Estes and Company, 1863.

Commager, Henry Steele, ed. *The Blue and the Gray: The Story of the Civil War as Told by Participants, from the Nomination of Lincoln to the Eve of Gettysburg.* New York: Meridian, 1994.

Connolly, James A. *Three Years in the Army of the Cumberland.* Bloomington: Indiana University Press, 1959.

Conyngham, David P. *Sherman's March Through the South.* New York: Sheldon and Company, 1865.

Cox, Jacob D. *Sherman's Battle for Atlanta.* New York: Da Capo Press, 1994.

_____. *Sherman's March to the Sea: Hood's Tennessee Campaigns and the Carolina Campaigns of 1865.* New York: Da Capo Press, 1994.

Cunningham, H.H. *Doctors in Gray: The Confederate Medical Service*. Baton Rouge: Louisiana State University Press, 1958.

Davis, Burke. *The Long Surrender: A Brilliantly Realized, Panoramic History of the Collapse of the Confederacy and of the Personal Ordeal of its President, Jefferson Davis*. New York: Vintage Books, 1989.

_____. *Sherman's March*. New York: Vintage Books, 1988.

Davis, William C. *The Battle of New Market*. Baton Rouge: Louisiana State University Press, 1975.

_____. *Jefferson Davis: The Man and His Hour*. New York: HarperPerennial, 1992.

_____ and Bell I. Wiley, eds. *Photographic History of the Civil War*. New York: Black Dog and Leventhal, 1994.

Denney, Robert E. *The Civil War Years: A Day-by-Day Chronicle*. New York: Gramercy Books, 1992.

Detzer, David. *Allegiance: Fort Sumter, Charleston, and the Beginning of the Civil War*. New York: Harcourt, 2001.

Draper, John William. *History of the American Civil War*, Volume III. Boulder, CO: University Libraries, 2009. Originally published by Harper & Brothers, Publishers, New York, 1870.

Early, Jubal Anderson. *A Memoir of the Last Year of the War for Independence, in the Confederate States of America*. Lynchburg, VA: Charles W. Button, 1867. Photocopy reprint published by Nabu Press, 2010.

Eisenhower, John S.D. *Agent of Destiny: The Life and Times of General Winfield Scott*. Norman: University of Oklahoma Press, 1997.

Elliott, Charles Winslow. *Winfield Scott: The Soldier and the Man*. New York: Macmillan, 1937.

Flood, Charles Bracelen. *1864: Lincoln at the Gates of History*. New York: Simon & Schuster Paperbacks, 2009.

_____. *Lee: The Last Years*. Boston: Houghton Mifflin Company, 1998.

Foote, Shelby. *The Civil War: A Narrative, Fort Sumter to Perryville*. New York: Random House, 1958.

_____. *The Civil War: A Narrative, Red River to Appomattox*. New York: Vintage Books, 1986.

Force, M.F. *From Fort Henry to Corinth*. New York: Charles Scribner's Sons, 1903.

Freeman, Douglas Southall. *Lee*. New York: Touchstone, Simon & Schuster, 1991.

_____. *Lee's Lieutenants*. New York: Scribner, 1998.

_____. *R.E. Lee*, volume III. New York: Charles Scribner's Sons, 1935.

Funkhouser, Darlene. *Women of the Civil War: Soldiers, Spies and Nurses*. Wever, IA: Quixote Press, 2004.

Glatthaar, Joseph T. *General Lee's Army: From Victory to Collapse*. New York: Free Press, 2008.

_____. *The March to the Sea and Beyond: Sherman's Troops in the Savannah and Carolinas Campaigns*. Baton Route: Louisiana State University Press, 1985.

Gordon, John B. *Reminiscences of the Civil War*. Baton Rouge: Louisiana State University Press, 1993.

Gosnell, H. Allen. *Guns on the Western Waters*. Baton Rouge: Louisiana State University Press, 1949.

Gragg, Rod. *Confederate Goliath: The Battle of Fort Fisher*. Baton Rouge: Louisiana State University Press, 2006.

Grant, Ulysses S. *Personal Memoirs of Ulysses S. Grant*. Old Saybrook, CT: Konecky & Konecky, 1993.

Grindlesperger, James. *Fire on the Water: The USS* Kearsarge *and the CSS* Alabama. Shippensburg, PA: Burd Street Press, 2003.

Gusley, Henry O. *The Southern Journey of a Civil War Marine*. Austin: University of Texas Press, 2006.

Hansen, Harry. *The Civil War*. New York: New American Library, 2001.

Hearn, Chester G. *Admiral David Dixon Porter*. Annapolis, MD: Naval Institute Press, 1996.

_____. *When the Devil Came Down to Dixie: Ben Butler in New Orleans*. Baton Rouge: Louisiana State University Press, 1997.

Hirshson, Stanley P. *The White Tecumseh: A Biography of William T. Sherman*. New York: John Wiley & Sons, 1997.

Hoppin, James Mason. *Life of Andrew Hull Foote, Rear Admiral United States Navy*. New York: Harper & Brothers, 1874.

Horn, John. *The Petersburg Campaign, June 1864–April 1865*. Conshohocken, PA: Combined Publishing, 2000.

Humphreys, Andrew A. *The Virginia Campaign, 1864 and 1865*. New York: Da Capo Press, 1995.

Hurst, Jack. *Nathan Bedford Forrest: A Biography*. New York: Vintage Books, 1994.

Johnson, Robert Underwood, and Clarence Clough Buel, eds. *Battles and Leaders of the Civil War*, Volume I. South Brunswick, NJ: Thomas Yoseloff, 1956.

_____, eds. *Battles and Leaders of the Civil War*, Volumes II, III and IV. Secaucus, NJ: Castle, 1982.

Johnston, Joseph E. *Narrative of Military Operations, Directed, During the Late War Between the States, by Joseph E. Johnston, General, C.S.A.* New York: D. Appleton and Company, 1874. Reprinted by University Library, University of Michigan, Michigan Historical Reprint Series.

Josephy, Alvin M., Jr. *The Civil War in the American West*. New York: Vintage Civil War Library, 1993.

Judge, Joseph. *Season of Fire: The Confederate Strike on Washington*. Berryville, VA: Rockbridge, 1994.

Kennedy, Frances H., ed. *The Civil War Battlefield Guide*, 2nd edition. Boston: Houghton Mifflin Company, 1998.

Ketchum, Richard M., ed. *The American Heritage Picture History of the Civil War*, Volumes I and II. New York: American Heritage, 1960.

Konstam, Angus. *Mississippi River Gunboats of the American Civil War, 1861–65*. Oxford, UK: Osprey, 2002.

Lee, Robert E. *Recollections and Letters of General Robert E. Lee*. Old Saybrook, CT: Konecky & Konecky, 1998.

Long, David E. *The Jewel of Liberty: Abraham Lincoln's Re-election and the End of Slavery*. Mechanicsburg, PA: Stackpole Books, 1994.

Lyman, Theodore. *Meade's Headquarters, 1863–1865: Letters of Colonel Theodore Lyman from the Wilderness to Appomattox*. Boston: Massachusetts Historical Society, 1922.

Macartney, Clarence Edward. *Mr. Lincoln's Admirals*. New York: Funk & Wagnalls, 1956.

Mahan, A.T. *Admiral Farragut*. London: Sampson Low, Marston & Company, 1892.

Mahan, Dennis Hart. *Advanced-Guard, Out-Post, and Detachment Service of Troops: With the Essential Principles of Strategy and Grand Tactics (1863)*. New York: John Wiley, 1863.

Mapp, Alf J., Jr. *Frock Coats and Epaulets: The Men Who Led the Confederacy*. Lanham, MD: Madison Books, 1982.

Marvel, William. *Andersonville: The Last Depot*. Chapel Hill: University of North Carolina Press, 1994.

McFeely, William S. *Grant: A Biography*. New York: W.W. Norton & Company, 1981.

Miller, Edward A., Jr. *Lincoln's Abolitionist General: The Biography of David Hunter*. Columbia: University of South Carolina Press, 1997.

Milligan, John D., ed. *From the Fresh-Water Navy: 1861–64, Naval Letters Series*, Volume III. Annapolis, MD: United States Naval Institute, 1970.

Morgan, Sarah. *The Civil War Diary of a Southern Woman*. New York: Touchstone, 1992.

Morris, Roy, Jr. *Sheridan: The Life and Wars of General Phil Sheridan*. New York: Vintage Civil War Library, 1993.

Nicolay, John G. *The Outbreak of Rebellion*. Stamford, CT: Longmeadow Press, 1996.

Niven, John. *Gideon Welles: Lincoln's Secretary of the Navy*. New York: Oxford University Press, 1973.

Nosworthy, Brent. *The Bloody Crucible of Courage: Fighting Methods and Combat Experience of the Civil War*. New York: Carroll & Graf, 2003.

Owen, William Miller. *In Camp and Battle with the Washington Artillery of New Orleans*. Baton Rouge: Louisiana State University Press, 1999.

Page, Dave. *Ships Versus Shore: Civil War Engagements Along Southern Shores and Rivers*. Nashville, TN: Rutledge Hill Press, 1994.

Parton, James. *General Butler in New Orleans*. New York: Mason Brothers, 1864.

Patchan, Scott C. *Shenandoah Summer: The 1864 Valley Campaign*. Lincoln: University of Nebraska Press, 2007.

Porter, David D. *The Naval History of the Civil War*. Mineola, NY: Dover Publications,

Porter, Horace. *Campaigning with Grant*. New York: Mallard Press, 1991.

Pratt, Fletcher. *Civil War on Western Waters*. New York: Henry Holt, 1956.

Reynolds, Thomas C. *General Sterling Price and the Confederacy*. St. Louis: Missouri History Museum, 2009.

Rhea, Gordon C. *Cold Harbor: Grant and Lee, May 26–June 3, 1864*. Baton Rouge: Louisiana State University Press, 2002.

Scharf, J. Thomas. *History of the Confederate States Navy*. New York: Gramercy Books, 1996.

Semmes, Raphael. *Memoirs of Service Afloat During the War Between the States*. Secaucus, NJ: The Blue & Grey Press, 1987.

Sheridan, Philip Henry. *Personal Memoirs of P.H. Sheridan, General, United States Army*. Minneapolis: Filiquarian Publishing, 2011.

Sherman, William T. *Memoirs of General William T. Sherman*, Volume I. Bedford, MA: Applewood Books, 2008. Originally published by Henry S. King & Co., London, 1875.

_____. *Memoirs of General William T. Sherman*, Volume 2. Originally published by Henry S. King & Co., London, 1875. Photocopy reprint published by Nabu Press, 2010.

Simson, Jay W. *Naval Strategies of the Civil War*. Nashville: Cumberland House, 2001.

Smith, Raymond W., ed. *Out of the Wilderness: The Civil War Memoir of Cpl. Norton C. Shepard, 146th New York Volunteer Infantry*. Hamilton, New York: Edmonston Publishing, 1998.

Sorrel, G. Moxley. *At the Right Hand of Longstreet: Recollections of a Confederate Staff Officer*. Lincoln: University of Nebraska Press, 1999.

Stackpole, Edward J. *Sheridan in the Shenandoah: Jubal Early's Nemesis*. 2nd edition. Harrisburg, PA: Stackpole Books, 1992.

Steers, Edward, Jr. *Blood on the Moon: The Assassination of Abraham Lincoln*. Lexington: University Press of Kentucky, 2001.

Stiles, Robert. *Four Years Under Marse Robert*. New York: Neale Publishing Company, 1904.

Still, William N., Jr. *Iron Afloat: The Story of the Confederate Armorclads*. Columbia: University of South Carolina Press, 1985.

Swanson, James L. *Manhunt: The 12-Day Chase of Lincoln's Killer*. New York: Harper Perennial, 2006.

Sword, Wiley. *The Confederacy's Last Hurrah: Spring Hill, Franklin & Nashville*. Lawrence: University Press of Kansas.

Symonds, Craig L. *Joseph E. Johnston: A Civil War Biography*. New York: W.W. Norton & Company, 1992.

Trudeau, Noah Andre. *The Last Citadel: Petersburg, Virginia, June 1864–April 1865*. Baton Rouge: Louisiana State University Press, 1991.

_____. *Southern Storm: Sherman's March to the Sea*. New York: Harper, 2008.

United States Naval War Records Office. *Official Records of the Union and Confederate Navies in the War of the Rebellion*. Washington: Government Printing Office, 1894–1922.

United States War Department. *The War of the Rebellion: A Compilation of the Official Records of the Union and Confederate Armies*. Washington: Government Printing Office, 1880–1901.

Walsh, George. *"Damage Them All You Can": Robert E. Lee's Army of Northern Virginia*. New York: Forge, 2002.

Ward, Andrew. *River Run Red: The Fort Pillow Massacre in the American Civil War*. New York: Penguin Books, 2005.

Waugh, John C. *Reelecting Lincoln: The Battle for the 1864 Presidency*. New York: Crown Publishers, 1997.

Wert, Jeffry D. *From Winchester to Cedar Creek: The Shenandoah Campaign of 1864*. Carbondale and Edwardsville: Southern Illinois University Press, 2010.

Wheeler, Richard. *Sherman's March: An Eyewitness History of the Cruel Campaign That Helped End a Crueler War*. New York: Thomas Y. Crowell Publishers, 1978.

Wideman, John C. *Civil War Chronicles — Naval Warfare: Courage and Combat on the Water*. New York: Metro Books, 1997.

Williams, Kenneth P. *Grant Rises in the West*. Lincoln: University of Nebraska Press, 1997.

Williams, T. Harry. *P.G.T. Beauregard: Napoleon in Gray*. Baton Rouge: Louisiana State University Press, 1955.

Woodward, C. Vann, ed. *Mary Chesnut's Civil War*. New Haven, CT: Yale University Press, 1981.

Woodworth, Steven E. *Jefferson Davis and His Generals*. Lawrence: University Press of Kansas, 1990.

_____. *Nothing But Victory: The Army of the Tennessee, 1861–1865*. New York: Vintage Civil War Library, 2006.

Wortman, Marc. *The Bonfire: The Siege and Burning of Atlanta*. New York: Public Affairs, 2009.

Wright, Marcus J. *General Scott*. New York: D. Appleton, 1897.

Wyeth, John Allan. *That Devil Forrest: A Life of General Nathan Bedford Forrest*. Baton Rouge: Louisiana State University Press, 1989.

Index

Numbers in *bold italics* indicate pages with photographs.

325